KEY MATERIALS IN INTERNATIONAL ENVIRONMENTAL LAW

Key Materials in International Environmental Law

Edited by

PHILIPPE CULLET
School of Oriental and African Studies, University of London

ALIX GOWLLAND-GUALTIERI
International Environmental Law Research Centre, Geneva

Routledge
Taylor & Francis Group
LONDON AND NEW YORK

First published 2004 by Ashgate Publishing

2 Park Square, Milton Park, Abingdon, Oxfordshire OX14 4RN
711 Third Avenue, New York, NY 10017

Routledge is an imprint of the Taylor & Francis Group, an informa business

First issued in paperback 2017

British Library Cataloguing in Publication Data
Key materials in international environmental law
1.Environmental law, International 2.Treaties - Collections
I.Cullet, Philippe II.Gowlland-Gualtieri, Alix
344'.046'0261

Library of Congress Cataloging-in-Publication Data
Key materials in international environmental law / [edited] by Philippe Cullet and Alix Gowlland-Gualtieri.
p. cm.
Includes bibliographical references.
ISBN 0-7546-2416-1
1. Environmental law, International--Sources. I. Cullet, Philippe. II. Gowlland-Gualtieri, Alix.

K3583.K49 2004
344.04'6--dc22

2004015075

ISBN 13: 978-0-7546-2416-5 (hbk)
ISBN 13: 978-1-138-27785-4 (pbk)

Contents

Detailed Table of Contents

Abbreviations and Treaty Common Names

ACP	African, Caribbean and Pacific Group of States
Air Pollution Convention	Convention on Long-range Transboundary Air Pollution (Chapter 3)
AJIL	*American Journal of International Law*
Antarctic Protocol	Protocol on Environmental Protection to the Antarctic Treaty (Chapter 5)
Århus Convention	Convention on Access to Information, Public Participation in Decision-Making and Access to Justice in Environmental Matters (Chapter 2)
Basel Convention	Convention on the Control of Transboundary Movements of Hazardous Wastes and Their Disposal (Chapter 6)
Biodiversity Convention	Convention on Biological Diversity (Chapter 4)
Bonn Convention	Convention on the Conservation of Migratory Species of Wild Animals (Chapter 5)
BYIL	*British Yearbook of International Law*
Cartagena Protocol	Cartagena Protocol on Biosafety to the Convention on Biological Diversity (Chapter 4)
CBD	Convention on Biological Diversity (Chapter 4)
CCAMLR	Convention on the Conservation of Antarctic Marine Living Resources (Chapter 5)
CEC	North American Commission for Environmental Cooperation
CITES	Convention on International Trade in Endangered Species of Wild Fauna and Flora (Chapter 5)
CLC Convention	International Convention on Civil Liability for Oil Pollution Damage, 1992 (Chapter 10)
Climate Change Convention	United Nations Framework Convention on Climate Change (Chapter 3)

CMS	Convention on the Conservation of Migratory Species of Wild Animals (Chapter 5)
Convention 169	ILO Convention Concerning Indigenous and Tribal Peoples in Independent Countries (Chapter 2)
Cotonou Agreement	Partnership Agreement between the members of the ACP of the one part, and the European Community and its Member States, of the other part (Chapter 9)
CSD	UN Commission on Sustainable Development
Desertification Convention	United Nations Convention to Combat Desertification in Those Countries Experiencing Serious Drought and/or Desertification, Particularly in Africa (Chapter 5)
DSB	WTO Dispute Settlement Body (Chapter 11)
EHRR	*European Human Rights Reports*
EIA	environmental impact assessment
EJIL	*European Journal of International Law*
ENMOD	Convention on the Prohibition of Military or any Other Hostile Use of Environmental Modification Techniques (Chapter 7)
Envtl	*Environmental*
Espoo Convention	Convention on Environmental Impact Assessment in a Transboundary Context (Chapter 2)
EU	European Union
FAO	Food and Agriculture Organization
Forest Principles	Non-Legally Binding Authoritative Statement of Principles for a Global Consensus on the Management, Conservation and Sustainable Development of All Types of Forests (Chapter 5)
GATT	General Agreement on Tariffs and Trade (Chapter 9)
GEF	Global Environment Facility
IAEA	International Atomic Energy Agency
ICJ	International Court of Justice
ICLQ	*International and Comparative Law Quarterly*
ILM	*International Legal Materials*
ILO	International Labour Organisation
IMO	International Maritime Organization

International Whaling Convention	International Convention for the Regulation of Whaling (Chapter 8)
Int'l	*International*
ITLOS	International Tribunal for the Law of the Sea
ITTA	International Tropical Timber Agreement (Chapter 5)
ITTO	International Tropical Timber Organization
J.	*Journal*
JEL	*Journal of Environmental Law*
Johannesburg Declaration	Johannesburg Declaration on Sustainable Development
Joint Convention	Joint Convention on the Safety of Spent Fuel Management and on the Safety of Radioactive Waste Management (Chapter 6)
Kyoto Protocol	Kyoto Protocol to the United Nations Framework Convention on Climate Change (Chapter 3)
L.	*Law*
LMO	living modified organism
London Convention	Convention on the Prevention of Marine Pollution by Dumping of Wastes and other Matter (Chapter 8)
LOSC	United Nations Convention on the Law of the Sea (Chapters 8 and 11)
LRTAP Convention	Convention on Long-range Transboundary Air Pollution (Chapter 3)
Lugano Convention	Convention on Civil Liability for Damage Resulting from Activities Dangerous to the Environment (Chapter 10)
Madrid Protocol	Protocol on Environmental Protection to the Antarctic Treaty (Chapter 5)
MARPOL 73/78	International Convention for the Prevention of Pollution from Ships, 1973 as modified by the Protocol of 1978 relating thereto (Chapter 8)
Montreal Protocol	Protocol on Substances that Deplete the Ozone Layer (Chapter 3)
NAAEC	North American Agreement on Environmental Cooperation (Chapters 9 and 11)
NAFTA	North American Free Trade Agreement

NCP	non-compliance procedure
NGO	non-governmental organisation
Ozone Convention	Vienna Convention for the Protection of the Ozone Layer (Chapter 3)
PGRFA Treaty	International Treaty on Plant Genetic Resources for Food and Agriculture (Chapter 4)
PIC	prior informed consent
POP	persistent organic chemical
PRTR Protocol	Protocol on Pollutant Release and Transfer Registers (Chapter 2)
Ramsar Convention	Convention on Wetlands of International Importance Especially as Waterfowl Habitat (Chapter 5)
RECIEL	*Review of European Community and International Environmental Law*
Rev.	*Review*
Rio Declaration	Declaration of the UN Conference on Environment and Development (Chapter 1)
Rotterdam Convention	Convention on the Prior Informed Consent Procedure for Certain Hazardous Chemicals and Pesticides in International Trade (Chapter 6)
SEA Protocol	Protocol on Strategic Environmental Assessment to the Espoo Convention (Chapter 2)
SPS Agreement	Agreement on the Application of Sanitary and Phytosanitary Measures (Chapter 4)
Stockholm Convention	Convention on Persistent Organic Pollutants (Chapter 6)
Stockholm Declaration	Declaration of the UN Conference on the Human Environment (Chapter 1)
Straddling Stocks Convention	Agreement for the Implementation of the Provisions of the UNCLOS Relating to the Conservation and Management of Straddling Fish Stocks and Highly Migratory Fish Stocks (Chapter 8)
TRIPS Agreement	Agreement on Trade-Related Aspects of Intellectual Property Rights (Chapter 9)
UN	United Nations
UNCC	UN Compensation Commission

UNCCD	UN Convention to Combat Desertification in Those Countries Experiencing Serious Drought and/or Desertification, Particularly in Africa (Chapter 5)
UNCED	UN Conference on Environment and Development
UNCLOS	UN Convention on the Law of the Sea (Chapters 8 and 11)
UNECE	UN Economic Commission for Europe
UNEP	UN Environment Programme
UNESCO	UN Educational, Scientific and Cultural Organization
UNFCCC	UN Framework Convention on Climate Change (Chapter 3)
UNGA	UN General Assembly
UNTS	*UN Treaty Series*
UPOV Convention	International Convention for the Protection of New Varieties of Plants (Chapter 9)
World Heritage Convention	Convention for the Protection of the World Cultural and Natural Heritage (Chapter 5)
WSSD	World Summit on Sustainable Development
WTO	World Trade Organization
YbIEL	*Yearbook of International Environmental Law*
Ybk	*Yearbook*
ZaöRV	*Zeitschrift für ausländisches öffentliches Recht und Völkerrecht*

Key Websites

International institutions

CEC	http://www.cec.org
CSD	http://www.un.org/esa/sustdev/csd/csd.htm
GEF	http://www.gefweb.org
IAEA	http://www.iaea.org
ICJ	http://www.icj-cij.org
ILO	http://www.ilo.org
IMO	http://www.imo.org
ITLOS	http://www.itlos.org
ITTO	http://www.itto.or.jp
Permanent Court of Arbitration	http://www.pca-cpa.org
UN	http://www.un.org
UNECE	http://www.unece.org
UNEP	http://www.unep.org
World Bank	http://www.worldbank.org
WTO	http://www.wto.org

Treaty secretariats

Air Pollution Convention	http://www.unece.org/env/lrtap
Århus Convention	http://www.unece.org/env/pp
Basel Convention	http://www.basel.int
Biodiversity Convention	http://www.biodiv.org
Bonn Convention	http://www.wcmc.org.uk/cms
Cartagena Protocol	http://www.biodiv.org

CCAMLR	http://www.ccamlr.org
CITES	http://www.cites.org
CLC Convention	http://www.iopcfund.org
Climate Change Convention	http://unfccc.int
Convention on Nuclear Safety	http://www.iaea.org
Desertification Convention	http://www.unccd.int
Espoo Convention	http://www.unece.org/env/eia
International Whaling Convention	http://www.iwcoffice.org
Joint Convention	http://www.iaea.org
Kyoto Protocol	http://unfccc.int
London Convention	http://www.londonconvention.org
Madrid Protocol	http://www.ats.org.ar
Montreal Protocol	http://www.unep.org/ozone
Ozone Convention	http://www.unep.org/ozone
PGRFA Treaty	http://www.fao.org/ag/cgrfa
Ramsar Convention	http://www.ramsar.org
Rotterdam Convention	http://www.pic.int
Stockholm Convention	http://www.pops.int
UPOV Convention	http://www.upov.int
World Heritage Convention	http://whc.unesco.org

Selected General Readings

Birnie, P.W. and Boyle, A.E., *International Law and the Environment* (Oxford: Oxford University Press, 2002).

Brown Weiss, E. and Jacobson, H.K. (eds.), *Engaging Countries - Strengthening Compliance with International Accords* (Cambridge, Mass.: MIT Press, 1998).

Cameron, J., Werksman, J. and Roderick, P. (eds.), *Improving Compliance with International Environmental Law* (London: Earthscan, 1996)

Cullet, P., *Differential Treatment in International Environmental Law* (Aldershot: Ashgate, 2003).

de Sadeleer, N., *Environmental Principles: From Political Slogans to Legal Rules* (Oxford: Oxford University Press, 2002).

Dodds, F. (ed.), *The Way Forward - Beyond Agenda 21* (London: Earthscan, 1997).

Kiss, A. and Shelton, D., *International Environmental Law* (Ardsley, NY: Transnational Publishers, 2nd edn. 2000).

Morrison, F.L. and Wolfrum, R. (eds.), *International, Regional, and National Environmental Law* (The Hague: Kluwer Law International, 2000).

Sands, P., *Principles of International Environmental Law* (Cambridge: Cambridge University Press, 2003).

Shelton, D. (ed.), *Commitment and Compliance: The Role of Non-Binding Norms in the International Legal System* (Oxford: Oxford University Press, 2000).

Vig, N.J. and Axelrod, R.S. (eds.), *The Global Environment: Institutions, Law and Policy* (London: Earthscan, 1999).

Werksman, J. (ed.), *Greening International Institutions* (London: Earthscan, 1996).

Introduction

Basic Materials in International Environmental Law

This compilation of materials in international environmental law has been designed to serve primarily as a basic and updated reference book for students, researchers, practitioners and policy makers in international environmental law. As environmental issues are increasingly linked to those relating to human rights, development, trade and intellectual property, familiarity with key international environmental instruments is also essential for students, researchers, practitioners and policy makers in these fields.

International environmental law has developed at an increasing pace over the past few decades, and in particular since the 1992 Rio Conference on Environment and Development. Several major trends in environmental law-making on the multilateral level can be identified. A number of important instruments have been adopted in such varied fields as nuclear safety (the Convention on Nuclear Safety), chemicals and pesticides (the Rotterdam and Stockholm Conventions) and the protection of Antarctica's environment (the Madrid Protocol). States have, in some cases, favoured the adoption of framework conventions such as the Climate Change and Biodiversity Conventions which allow, in keeping with the recognition that general measures are necessary but not sufficient, for the subsequent development of protocols containing more detailed obligations. The latter include the Kyoto Protocol to the Climate Change Convention and the Cartagena Protocol to the Biodiversity Convention.

In parallel, there has been an increasing recognition of the need to adopt procedural standards to foster the implementation of existing substantive norms. This has led to the adoption of agreements on environmental impact assessment procedures and access to and disclosure of environmental information, most notably the UNECE Espoo and Århus Conventions, as well as, more generally, to a greater awareness of the need to involve non-state actors in international legal and policy processes.

Furthermore, states have become increasingly aware that there now exists a plethora of substantive standards, and that the challenge for the international community is as much to adopt new legal instruments for areas not yet covered as to ensure the implementation of existing norms. This has led to an emphasis on the development of non-compliance procedures within multilateral environment agreements such as the Montreal and Kyoto Protocols, and on the development of liability and redress regimes. The need to provide the financial means for developing states to implement their obligations under environmental agreements has been crucially highlighted, with the establishment of the GEF one of the key developments in this regard.

While there are a number of specific legal instruments that make up what is known as international environmental law, the lines between environmental law and other fields are becoming increasingly blurred. This is due to the fact that environmental protection and management has an impact on other fields of international law such as for example trade, and that consequently environmental issues cannot be approached exclusively within the realm of international environmental law. This has two important consequences for this compilation of materials. Firstly, an increasing number of treaties cannot easily be classified as belonging to only one field of international law. This is illustrated by the PGRFA Treaty which, though an 'agricultural' treaty, also includes an important environmental dimension. Secondly, there are a number of treaties in other fields of international law which have little to do with environmental management but the implementation of which has significant consequences for environmental conservation and use. The TRIPS Agreement, whose relationship with the Biodiversity Convention has been the object of much controversy in the past decade, remains a good example of this phenomenon.

This compilation does not purport to comprehensively cover all existing international environmental law materials, but rather is designed for personal use by the student and practitioner of environmental law. To this end, it comprises key texts relevant to the study and practice of international environmental law with an emphasis on the most recent developments. It primarily includes legally binding instruments, but contains also some of the basic non-binding documents. The various documents are categorized and arranged according to subject matter. While focus is put on instruments with an international scope, some regional agreements have been reproduced, especially when they deal with matters not otherwise regulated globally. Some of the instruments are reproduced in full, while in the case of others, in particular with regard to texts not exclusively relating to environmental matters, only relevant excerpts have been provided for reasons of space. In most cases, the procedural sections and technical annexes have not been reproduced.

The compilation includes at the beginning of each chapter a brief editorial introduction to the instruments reproduced. These introductions include succinct information on the scope of each instrument, thus allowing the reader to view it in its appropriate context.

Each instrument reproduced is preceded by a brief note which includes, where applicable, the date of adoption/signature and entry into force of the instrument, any amendments, its official source,[1] and the secretariat website allowing the reader to find further information. Information provided, including reference to the

---

1 While the editors have attempted to ensure that the texts reproduced are faithful to the original, readers should refer to the certified copies of the instruments for an authentic version.

number of states parties and to websites, is at 1 April 2004. The compilation supplies a brief list of selected readings relevant to the subject matter covered by each chapter as well as of more general reference texts, to provide the reader with a guide to some of the most salient and recent texts of relevance. In certain cases, references to some important international environmental cases on the subject matter are also given. Finally, the compilation contains further information useful for the reader, such as a table of the common names used for the instruments reproduced and a list of key websites.

Chapter 1 contains documents laying down foundational principles of international environmental law and sustainable development. Chapter 2 includes instruments relating to environmental rights and regulatory mechanisms. Chapter 3 is concerned with treaties that address the protection of the atmosphere. The documents relating to biodiversity, biosafety and agriculture are contained in Chapter 4. Chapter 5 addresses endangered species and habitats with specific sub-sections also devoted to desertification, forests and Antarctica. Chapter 6 deals with hazardous wastes, chemicals and pesticides, as well as environmental aspects of nuclear energy. Chapter 7 comprises documents concerning military activities and the environment. Chapter 8 includes documents relevant to the protection of the marine environment and marine resources. Chapter 9 comprises environmental aspects of documents pertaining to economics trade and finance. Instruments on liability are subsumed in Chapter 10. Finally, Chapter 11 considers instruments addressing dispute settlement and compliance in international environmental law.

This compilation would not have been possible without the support of the whole publishing team at Ashgate who should find here expression of our gratitude. Radhika Kolluru and Jawahar Raja from the International Environmental Law Research Centre (www.ielrc.org), as well as ShinWei Ng from University College London, should be thanked for their patience and dedication in collecting and proof-reading part of this volume.

Geneva/London, April 2004.

Chapter 1

General Framework

Introduction

The present chapter examines some of the most important legally non-binding international instruments adopted under the auspices of the UN that have contributed to the development and codification of fundamental principles of international environmental law and sustainable development. The first UN conference specifically addressing environmental issues took place at Stockholm in 1972. The Conference on the Human Environment adopted the Stockholm Declaration, which notably articulates the human right to a decent environment, the sovereign right of states to exploit their own resources and their responsibility to ensure that activities within their jurisdiction or control do not cause damage to the environment of other states or areas beyond the limits of national jurisdiction.

The following major UN conference on environment and development was held in Rio de Janeiro in 1992. It led to the adoption of the Rio Declaration, an instrument that has had a significant impact on the development and codification of international environmental law. The Declaration represents an endorsement by states of the relationship between environmental protection and economic development while embodying, inter alia, principles on inter- and intra-generational equity, precaution, environmental impact assessment (EIA), common but differentiated responsibility and public participation, as well as the right to development. UNCED[1] furthermore produced Agenda 21, a 300-page programme of action for achieving sustainable development, the implementation of which is monitored by the CSD. A five-year review of the progress achieved in implementing Agenda 21 was conducted by the UN General Assembly's Special Session held in 1997. A programme for the further implementation of Agenda 21 was adopted at the Special Session in the form of Resolution S-19/2.[2]

---

1 The other instruments adopted at UNCED include the Climate Change Convention (reproduced at p. 124), the CBD (reproduced at p. 169) and the Forest Principles (reproduced at p. 292).

2 Other significant General Assembly resolutions on the topic include, *e.g.*, UNGA Resolution 37/7 (Annex), World Charter for Nature (1982), 22 *ILM* 455 (1983); UNGA Resolution 47/191, Institutional arrangements to follow-up the UNCED (1992); UNGA Resolution 51/240, Agenda for Development (1997); UNGA Resolution 54/218, Implementation of and follow-up to the outcome of the UNCED and the nineteenth special session of the General Assembly (1999); UNGA Resolution

The most recent global conference on sustainable development was the WSSD convened in Johannesburg in 2002, which aimed to conduct a ten-year review of UNCED and its commitments. The Summit concluded its proceedings with the formal adoption by consensus of two political documents reproduced in this chapter, namely the Johannesburg Declaration and a 70-page Plan of Implementation that covers a broad range of issues including poverty eradication, sustainable production and consumption, water and sanitation, energy and chemicals. Both instruments contain only very general political commitments on sustainable development, and focus primarily on the implementation of existing environmental commitments rather than on the adoption of new obligations. Of note is that, in contrast to the UNCED process, the WSSD did not lead to the adoption of new international environmental treaties.

Selected readings

Beyerlin, U. and Reichard, M., 'The Johannesburg Summit: Outcome and Overall Assessment', 63 *ZaöRV* 213 (2003).

Boyle, A.E. and Freestone, D. (eds.), *International Law and Sustainable Development* (Oxford: Oxford University Press, 1999).

Freestone, D., 'The Road from Rio: International Environmental Law after the Earth Summit', 6 *JEL* 193 (1994).

Pallemaerts, M., 'International Law and Sustainable Development: Any Progress in Johannesburg?', 12 *RECIEL* 1 (2003).

Sands, P., 'International Law in the Field of Sustainable Development', 65 *BYIL* 303 (1994).

World Commission on Environment and Development, *Our Common Future* (Oxford: Oxford University Press, 1987).

Declaration of the UN Conference on the Human Environment

Adopted on 16 June 1972 at Stockholm. Source: Report of the UN Conference on the Human Environment, Doc. A/CONF.48/14/Rev.1 (1972).

The United Nations Conference on the Human Environment,

Having met at Stockholm from 5 to 16 June 1972,

55/199, Ten-year review of progress achieved in the implementation of the outcome of the United Nations Conference on Environment and Development (2000); UNGA Resolution 55/2, United Nations Millennium Declaration (2000). *See also* Final Outcome of the International Conference on Financing for Development (Monterrey Consensus), Doc. A/CONF/198/1 (2002); and WTO Doha Ministerial Declaration (reproduced at p. 502).

Having considered the need for a common outlook and for common principles to inspire and guide the peoples of the world in the preservation and enhancement of the human environment,

[Preamble and Part I not reproduced]

II. Principles

States the common conviction that:

Principle 1

Man has the fundamental right to freedom, equality and adequate conditions of life, in an environment of a quality that permits a life of dignity and well-being, and he bears a solemn responsibility to protect and improve the environment for present and future generations. In this respect, policies promoting or perpetuating apartheid, racial segregation, discrimination, colonial and other forms of oppression and foreign domination stand condemned and must be eliminated.

Principle 2

The natural resources of the earth, including the air, water, land, flora and fauna and especially representative samples of natural ecosystems must be safeguarded for the benefit of present and future generations through careful planning or management, as appropriate.

Principle 3

The capacity of the earth to produce vital renewable resources must be maintained and, wherever practicable, restored or improved.

Principle 4

Man has a special responsibility to safeguard and wisely manage the heritage of wildlife and its habitat, which are now gravely imperilled by a combination of adverse factors. Nature conservation, including wildlife, must therefore receive importance in planning for economic development.

Principle 5

The non-renewable resources of the earth must be employed in such a way as to guard against the danger of their future exhaustion and to ensure that benefits from such employment are shared by all mankind.

Principle 6

The discharge of toxic substances or of other substances and the release of heat, in such quantities or concentrations as to exceed the capacity of the environment to render them harmless, must be halted in order to ensure that serious or irreversible damage is not inflicted upon ecosystems. The just struggle of the peoples of all countries against pollution should be supported.

Principle 7

States shall take all possible steps to prevent pollution of the seas by substances that are liable to create hazards to human health, to harm living resources and marine life, to damage amenities or to interfere with other legitimate uses of the sea.

Principle 8

Economic and social development is essential for ensuring a favourable living and working environment for man and for creating conditions on earth that are necessary for the improvement of the quality of life.

Principle 9

Environmental deficiencies generated by the conditions of underdevelopment and natural disasters pose grave problems and can best be remedied by accelerated development through the transfer of substantial quantities of financial and technological assistance as a supplement to the domestic effort of the developing countries and such timely assistance as may be required.

Principle 10

For the developing countries, stability of prices and adequate earnings for primary commodities and raw materials are essential to environmental management since economic factors as well as ecological processes must be taken into account.

Principle 11

The environmental policies of all States should enhance and not adversely affect the present or future development potential of developing countries, nor should they hamper the attainment of better living conditions for all, and appropriate steps should be taken by States and international organizations with a view to reaching agreement on meeting the possible national and international economic consequences resulting from the application of environmental measures.

Principle 12

Resources should be made available to preserve and improve the environment, taking into account the circumstances and particular requirements of developing countries and any costs which may emanate from their incorporating environmental safeguards into their development planning and the need for making available to them, upon their request, additional international technical and financial assistance for this purpose.

Principle 13

In order to achieve a more rational management of resources and thus to improve the environment, States should adopt an integrated and co-ordinated approach to their development planning so as to ensure that development is compatible with the need to protect and improve environment for the benefit of their population.

Principle 14

Rational planning constitutes an essential tool for reconciling any conflict between the needs of development and the need to protect and improve the environment.

Principle 15

Planning must be applied to human settlements and urbanization with a view to avoiding adverse effects on the environment and obtaining maximum social, economic and environmental benefits for all. In this respect projects which are designed for colonialist and racist domination must be abandoned.

Principle 16

Demographic policies which are without prejudice to basic human rights and which are deemed appropriate by Governments concerned, should be applied in those regions where the rate of population growth or excessive population concentrations are likely to have adverse effects on the environment or development, or where low population density may prevent improvement of the human environment and impede development.

Principle 17

Appropriate national institutions must be entrusted with the task of planning, managing or controlling the environmental resources of States with a view to enhancing environmental quality.

Principle 18

Science and technology, as part of their contribution to economic and social development, must be applied to the identification, avoidance and control of environmental risks and the solution of environmental problems and for the common good of mankind.

Principle 19

Education in environmental matters, for the younger generation as well as adults, giving due consideration to the underprivileged, is essential in order to broaden the basis for an enlightened opinion and responsible conduct by individuals, enterprises and communities in protecting and improving the environment in its full human dimension. It is also essential that mass media of communications avoid contributing to the deterioration of the environment, but, on the contrary, disseminates information of an educational nature on the need to project and improve the environment in order to enable man to develop in every respect.

Principle 20

Scientific research and development in the context of environmental problems, both national and multinational, must be promoted in all countries, especially the developing countries. In this connection, the free flow of up-to-date scientific information and transfer of experience must be supported and assisted, to facilitate the solution of environmental problems; environmental technologies should be made available to developing countries on terms which would encourage their wide dissemination without constituting an economic burden on the developing countries.

Principle 21

States have, in accordance with the Charter of the United Nations and the principles of international law, the sovereign right to exploit their own resources pursuant to their own environmental policies, and the responsibility to ensure that activities within their jurisdiction or control do not cause damage to the environment of other States or of areas beyond the limits of national jurisdiction.

Principle 22

States shall co-operate to develop further the international law regarding liability and compensation for the victims of pollution and other environmental damage caused by activities within the jurisdiction or control of such States to areas beyond their jurisdiction.

Principle 23

Without prejudice to such criteria as may be agreed upon by the international community, or to standards which will have to be determined nationally, it will be essential in all cases to consider the systems of values prevailing in each country, and the extent of the applicability of standards which are valid for the most advanced countries but which may be inappropriate and of unwarranted social cost for the developing countries.

Principle 24

International matters concerning the protection and improvement of the environment should be handled in a co-operative spirit by all countries, big or small, on an equal footing. Co-operation through multilateral or bilateral arrangements or other appropriate means is essential to effectively control, prevent, reduce and eliminate adverse environmental effects resulting from activities conducted in all spheres, in such a way that due account is taken of the sovereignty and interests of all States.

Principle 25

States shall ensure that international organizations play a co-ordinated, efficient and dynamic role for the protection and improvement of the environment.

Principle 26

Man and his environment must be spared the effects of nuclear weapons and all other means of mass destruction. States must strive to reach prompt agreement, in the relevant international organs, on the elimination and complete destruction of such weapons.

Declaration of the UN Conference on Environment and Development

Adopted on 14 June 1992 at Rio de Janeiro. Source: Report of the UNCED, Doc. A/CONF.151/26/Rev. 1 (Vol. I), Annex II (1992). Further information: CSD, New York, USA, http://www.un.org/esa/sustdev/csd/csd.htm

The United Nations Conference on Environment and Development,

Having met at Rio de Janeiro from 3 to 14 June 1992,

Reaffirming the Declaration of the United Nations Conference on the Human Environment, adopted at Stockholm on 16 June 1972, and seeking to build upon it,

With the goal of establishing a new and equitable global partnership through the creation of new levels of cooperation among States, key sectors of societies and people,

Working towards international agreements which respect the interests of all and protect the integrity of the global environmental and developmental system,

Recognizing the integral and interdependent nature of the Earth, our home,

Proclaims that:

Principle 1

Human beings are at the centre of concerns for sustainable development. They are entitled to a healthy and productive life in harmony with nature.

Principle 2

States have, in accordance with the Charter of the United Nations and the principles of international law, the sovereign right to exploit their own resources pursuant to their own environmental and developmental policies, and the responsibility to ensure that activities within their jurisdiction or control do not cause damage to the environment of other States or of areas beyond the limits of national jurisdiction.

Principle 3

The right to development must be fulfilled so as to equitably meet developmental and environmental needs of present and future generations.

Principle 4

In order to achieve sustainable development, environmental protection shall constitute an integral part of the development process and cannot be considered in isolation from it.

Principle 5

All States and all people shall cooperate in the essential task of eradicating poverty as an indispensable requirement for sustainable development, in order to decrease the disparities in standards of living and better meet the needs of the majority of the people of the world.

Principle 6

The special situation and needs of developing countries, particularly the least developed and those most environmentally vulnerable, shall be given special priority. International actions in the field of environment and development should also address the interests and needs of all countries.

Principle 7

States shall cooperate in a spirit of global partnership to conserve, protect and restore the health and integrity of the Earth's ecosystem. In view of the different contributions to global environmental degradation, States have common but differentiated responsibilities. The developed countries acknowledge the responsibility that they bear in the international pursuit of sustainable development in view of the pressures their societies place on the global environment and of the technologies and financial resources they command.

Principle 8

To achieve sustainable development and a higher quality of life for all people, States should reduce and eliminate unsustainable patterns of production and consumption and promote appropriate demographic policies.

Principle 9

States should cooperate to strengthen endogenous capacity-building for sustainable development by improving scientific understanding through exchanges of scientific and technological knowledge, and by enhancing the development, adaptation, diffusion and transfer of technologies, including new and innovative technologies.

Principle 10

Environmental issues are best handled with participation of all concerned citizens, at the relevant level. At the national level, each individual shall have appropriate access to information concerning the environment that is held by public authorities, including information on hazardous materials and activities in their communities, and the opportunity to participate in decision-making processes. States shall facilitate and encourage public awareness and participation by making information widely available. Effective access to judicial and administrative proceedings, including redress and remedy, shall be provided.

Principle 11

States shall enact effective environmental legislation. Environmental standards, management objectives and priorities should reflect the environmental and developmental context to which they apply. Standards applied by some countries may be inappropriate and of unwarranted economic and social cost to other countries, in particular developing countries.

Principle 12

States should cooperate to promote a supportive and open international economic system that would lead to economic growth and sustainable development in all countries, to better address the problems of environmental degradation. Trade policy measures for environmental purposes should not constitute a means of arbitrary or unjustifiable discrimination or a disguised restriction on international trade. Unilateral actions to deal with environmental challenges outside the jurisdiction of the importing country should be avoided. Environmental measures addressing transboundary or global environmental problems should, as far as possible, be based on an international consensus.

Principle 13

States shall develop national law regarding liability and compensation for the victims of pollution and other environmental damage. States shall also cooperate in an expeditious and more determined manner to develop further international law regarding liability and compensation for adverse effects of environmental damage caused by activities within their jurisdiction or control to areas beyond their jurisdiction.

Principle 14

States should effectively cooperate to discourage or prevent the relocation and transfer to other States of any activities and substances that cause severe environmental degradation or are found to be harmful to human health.

Principle 15

In order to protect the environment, the precautionary approach shall be widely applied by States according to their capabilities. Where there are threats of serious or irreversible damage, lack of full scientific certainty shall not be used as a reason for postponing cost-effective measures to prevent environmental degradation.

Principle 16

National authorities should endeavour to promote the internalization of environmental costs and the use of economic instruments, taking into account the approach that the polluter should, in principle, bear the cost of pollution, with due regard to the public interest and without distorting international trade and investment.

Principle 17

Environmental impact assessment, as a national instrument, shall be undertaken for proposed activities that are likely to have a significant adverse impact on the environment and are subject to a decision of a competent national authority.

Principle 18

States shall immediately notify other States of any natural disasters or other emergencies that are likely to produce sudden harmful effects on the environment of those States. Every effort shall be made by the international community to help States so afflicted.

Principle 19

States shall provide prior and timely notification and relevant information to potentially affected States on activities that may have a significant adverse transboundary environmental effect and shall consult with those States at an early stage and in good faith.

Principle 20

Women have a vital role in environmental management and development. Their full participation is therefore essential to achieve sustainable development.

Principle 21

The creativity, ideals and courage of the youth of the world should be mobilized to forge a global partnership in order to achieve sustainable development and ensure a better future for all.

Principle 22

Indigenous people and their communities and other local communities have a vital role in environmental management and development because of their knowledge and traditional practices. States should recognize and duly support their identity, culture and interests and enable their effective participation in the achievement of sustainable development.

Principle 23

The environment and natural resources of people under oppression, domination and occupation shall be protected.

Principle 24

Warfare is inherently destructive of sustainable development. States shall therefore respect international law providing protection for the environment in times of armed conflict and cooperate in its further development, as necessary.

Principle 25

Peace, development and environmental protection are interdependent and indivisible.

Principle 26

States shall resolve all their environmental disputes peacefully and by appropriate means in accordance with the Charter of the United Nations.

Principle 27

States and people shall cooperate in good faith and in a spirit of partnership in the fulfilment of the principles embodied in this Declaration and in the further development of international law in the field of sustainable development.

Agenda 21 [excerpts]

Adopted on 13 June 1992 at Rio de Janeiro. Source: Report of the UNCED, Doc. A/CONF.151/26/Rev. 1 (Vol. 1), Annex II (1992) (the text reproduced does not incorporate the footnotes). Further information: CSD, New York, USA, http://www.un.org/esa/sustdev/csd/csd.htm

Preamble

1.1. Humanity stands at a defining moment in history. We are confronted with a perpetuation of disparities between and within nations, a worsening of poverty, hunger, ill health and illiteracy, and the continuing deterioration of the ecosystems on which we depend for our well-being. However, integration of environment and development concerns and greater attention to them will lead to the fulfilment of basic needs, improved living standards for all, better protected and managed ecosystems and a safer, more prosperous future. No nation can achieve this on its own; but together we can - in a global partnership for sustainable development.

1.2. This global partnership must build on the premises of General Assembly resolution 44/228 of 22 December 1989, which was adopted when the nations of the world called for the United Nations Conference on Environment and Development, and on the acceptance of the need to take a balanced and integrated approach to environment and development questions.

1.3. Agenda 21 addresses the pressing problems of today and also aims at preparing the world for the challenges of the next century. It reflects a global consensus and political commitment at the highest level on development and environment cooperation. Its successful implementation is first and foremost the responsibility of Governments. National strategies, plans, policies and processes are crucial in achieving this. International cooperation should support and supplement such national efforts. In this context, the United Nations system has a key role to play. Other international, regional and subregional organizations are also called upon to contribute to this effort. The broadest public participation and the active involvement of the non-governmental organizations and other groups should also be encouraged.

1.4. The developmental and environmental objectives of Agenda 21 will require a substantial flow of new and additional financial resources to developing countries, in order to cover the incremental costs for the actions they have to undertake to deal with global environmental problems and to accelerate sustainable development. Financial resources are also required for strengthening the capacity of international institutions for the implementation of Agenda 21. An indicative order-of-magnitude assessment of costs is included in each of the programme areas. This assessment will need to be examined and refined by the relevant implementing agencies and organizations.

1.5. In the implementation of the relevant programme areas identified in Agenda 21, special attention should be given to the particular circumstances facing the economies in transition. It must also be recognized that these countries are facing unprecedented challenges in transforming their economies, in some cases in the midst of considerable social and political tension.

1.6. The programme areas that constitute Agenda 21 are described in terms of the basis for action, objectives, activities and means of implementation. Agenda 21 is a dynamic programme. It will be carried out by the various actors according to the different situations, capacities and priorities of countries and regions in full respect of all the principles contained in the Rio Declaration on Environment and Development. It could evolve over time in the light of changing needs and circumstances. This process marks the beginning of a new global partnership for sustainable development.

General Assembly Resolution S-19/2, Programme for the Further Implementation of Agenda 21 [excerpts]

Adopted on 28 June 1997 at New York. Source: 19th Special Session of the UN General Assembly, 23-28 June 1997, Doc. A/RES/S-19/2 (1997). Further information: UN, New York, USA, http://www.un.org/

IV. International institutional arrangements

116. The achievement of sustainable development requires continued support from international institutions. The institutional framework outlined in chapter 38 of Agenda 21 and determined by the General Assembly in its resolution 47/191 of 22 December 1992 and other relevant resolutions, including the specific functions and roles of various organs, organizations and programmes within and outside the United Nations system, will continue to be fully relevant in the period after the nineteenth special session of the General Assembly. In the light of the ongoing discussions on reform within the United Nations, international institutional arrangements in the area of sustainable development are intended to contribute to the goal of strengthening the entire United Nations system. In this context, the strengthening of the institutions for sustainable development, as well as the achievement of the goals and objectives set out below are particularly important.

A. Greater coherence in various intergovernmental organizations and processes

117. Given the increasing number of decision-making bodies concerned with various aspects of sustainable development, including international conventions, there is an ever greater need for better policy coordination at the intergovernmental level, as well as for continued and more concerted efforts to enhance collaboration among the secretariats of those decision-making bodies. Under the guidance of the

General Assembly, the Economic and Social Council should play a strengthened role in coordinating the activities of the United Nations system in the economic, social and related fields.

118. The conferences of the parties to conventions signed at the United Nations Conference on Environment and Development or as a result of it, as well as other conventions related to sustainable development, should cooperate in exploring ways and means of collaborating in their work to advance the effective implementation of the conventions. There is also a need for environmental conventions to continue to pursue sustainable development objectives consistent with their provisions and be fully responsive to Agenda 21. To this end, inter alia, the conferences of the parties to or governing bodies of the conventions signed at the United Nations Conference on Environment and Development, or as a result of it, and of other relevant conventions and agreements should, if appropriate, give consideration to the co-location of secretariats, to improving the scheduling of meetings, to integrating national reporting requirements, to improving the balance between sessions of the conferences of the parties and sessions of their subsidiary bodies, and to encouraging and facilitating the participation of Governments in those sessions, at an appropriate level.

119. Institutional arrangements for the convention secretariats should provide effective support and efficient services, while ensuring the appropriate autonomy necessary for them to be efficient at their respective locations. At the international and national levels there is a need for, inter alia, better scientific assessment of ecological linkages between the conventions; identification of programmes that have multiple benefits; and enhanced public awareness-raising with respect to the conventions. Such tasks should be undertaken by the United Nations Environment Programme in accordance with the relevant decisions of its Governing Council and in full cooperation with the conferences of the parties to and governing bodies of relevant conventions. Efforts of convention secretariats, in response to requests from the respective conferences of the parties, to explore, where appropriate, modalities for suitable liaison arrangements in Geneva and/or New York for the purpose of enhancing linkages with delegations and organizations at those United Nations centres are welcomed and fully supported.

120. It is necessary to strengthen the Inter-Agency Committee on Sustainable Development of the Administrative Committee on Coordination and its system of task managers, with a view to further enhancing system-wide intersectoral cooperation and coordination for the implementation of Agenda 21 and for the promotion of coordinated follow-up to the major United Nations conferences in the area of sustainable development.

121. The Commission on Sustainable Development should promote increased regional implementation of Agenda 21 in cooperation with relevant regional and subregional organizations and the United Nations regional commissions, in accordance with the results of their priority-setting efforts, with a view to enhancing the role such bodies play in the achievement of sustainable development objectives

agreed at the international level. The regional commissions could provide appropriate support, consistent with their work programmes, to regional meetings of experts related to the implementation of Agenda 21.

B. Role of relevant organizations and institutions of the United Nations system

122. In order to facilitate the national implementation of Agenda 21, all organizations and programmes of the United Nations system, within their respective areas of expertise and mandates, should strengthen, individually and jointly, the support for national efforts to implement Agenda 21 and make their efforts and actions consistent with national plans, policies and priorities of member States. Coordination of United Nations activities at the field level should be further enhanced through the resident coordinator system in full consultation with national Governments.

123. The role of United Nations Environment Programme, as the principal United Nations body in the field of the environment, should be further enhanced. Taking into account its catalytic role, and in conformity with Agenda 21 and the Nairobi Declaration on the Role and Mandate of the United Nations Environment Programme, adopted on 7 February 1997, the Programme is to be the leading global environmental authority that sets the global environmental agenda, promotes the coherent implementation of the environmental dimension of sustainable development within the United Nations system, and serves as an authoritative advocate for the global environment. In this context, decision 19/32 of 4 April 1997 of the United Nations Environment Programme Governing Council on governance of the Programme and other related Governing Council decisions are relevant. The role of the United Nations Environment Programme in the further development of international environmental law should be strengthened, including the development of coherent interlinkages among relevant environmental conventions in cooperation with their respective conferences of the parties or governing bodies. In performing its functions related to the conventions signed at the United Nations Conference on Environment and Development or as a result of it, and other relevant conventions, the United Nations Environment Programme should strive to promote the effective implementation of those conventions in a manner consistent with the provisions of the conventions and the decisions of the conferences of the parties.

124. The United Nations Environment Programme, in the performance of its role, should focus on environmental issues, taking into account the development perspective. A revitalized Programme should be supported by adequate, stable and predictable funding. The Programme should continue providing effective support to the Commission on Sustainable Development, inter alia, in the form of scientific, technical and policy information and analysis of and advice on global environmental issues.

125. The United Nations Development Programme should continue to strengthen its contribution to and programmes in sustainable development and the implementation of Agenda 21 at all levels, particularly in the area of promoting

capacity-building (including through its Capacity 21 programme) in cooperation with other organizations, as well as in the field of poverty eradication.

126. The United Nations Conference on Trade and Development, in accordance with General Assembly resolution 51/167 of 16 December 1996 and relevant decisions of the Trade and Development Board on the work programme, should continue to play a key role in the implementation of Agenda 21 through the integrated examination of linkages among trade, investment, technology, finance and sustainable development.

127. The Committee on Trade and Environment of the World Trade Organization, the United Nations Conference on Trade and Development and the United Nations Environment Programme should advance their coordinated work on trade and environment, involving other appropriate international and regional organizations in their cooperation and coordination. In coordination with the World Trade Organization, the United Nations Conference on Trade and Development and the United Nations Environment Programme should continue to support efforts to promote the integration of trade, environment and development. The Commission on Sustainable Development should continue to play its important role in the deliberations on trade and environment so as to facilitate the integrated consideration of all factors relevant for achieving sustainable development.

128. Implementation of the commitment of the international financial institutions to sustainable development should continue to be strengthened. The World Bank has a significant role to play, bearing in mind its expertise and the overall volume of resources that it commands.

129. Operationalization of the global mechanism of the United Nations Convention to Combat Desertification in those Countries Experiencing Serious Drought and/or Desertification, particularly in Africa is also essential.

C. Future role and programme of work of the Commission on Sustainable Development

130. The Commission on Sustainable Development, within its mandate as specified in General Assembly resolution 47/191, will continue to provide a central forum for reviewing progress and for urging further implementation of Agenda 21 and other commitments made at the United Nations Conference on Environment and Development or as a result of it; for conducting a high-level policy debate aimed at consensus-building on sustainable development; and for catalysing action and long-term commitment to sustainable development at all levels. It should continue to undertake these tasks in complementing and providing interlinkages to the work of other United Nations organs, organizations and bodies acting in the field of sustainable development. The Commission has a role to play in assessing the challenges of globalization as they relate to sustainable development. The Commission should perform its functions in coordination with other subsidiary bodies of the Economic and Social Council and with related organizations and institutions, including making recommendations, within its mandate, to the

Economic and Social Council, bearing in mind the interrelated outcomes of recent United Nations conferences.

131. The Commission should focus on issues that are crucial to achieving the goals of sustainable development. It should promote policies that integrate economic, social and environmental dimensions of sustainability and should provide for integrated consideration of linkages, both among sectors and between sectoral and cross-sectoral aspects of Agenda 21. In this connection, the Commission should carry out its work in such a manner as to avoid unnecessary duplication and repetition of work undertaken by other relevant forums.

132. In the light of the above, it is recommended that the Commission on Sustainable Development adopt the multi-year programme of work for the period 1998-2002 contained in the appendix below.

D. Methods of work of the Commission on Sustainable Development

133. Based on the experience gained during the period 1993-1997, the Commission, under the guidance of the Economic and Social Council, should:

(a) Make concerted efforts to attract the greater involvement in its work of ministers and high-level national policy makers responsible for specific economic and social sectors, who, in particular, are encouraged to participate in the annual high-level segment of the Commission, together with the ministers and policy makers responsible for environment and development. The high-level segments of the Commission should become more interactive, and should focus on the priority issues being considered at a particular session. The Bureau of the Commission should conduct timely and open-ended consultations with the view to improving the organization of the work of the high-level segment;

(b) Continue to provide a forum for the exchange of national experience and best practices in the area of sustainable development, including through voluntary national communications or reports. Consideration should be given to the results of ongoing work aimed at streamlining requests for national information and reporting and to the results of the 'pilot phase' relating to indicators of sustainable development. In this context, the Commission should consider more effective modalities for the further implementation of the commitments made in Agenda 21, with appropriate emphasis on the means of implementation. Countries may wish to submit to the Commission, on a voluntary basis, information regarding their efforts to incorporate the relevant recommendations of other United Nations conferences in national sustainable development strategies;

(c) Take into account regional developments related to the implementation of the outcomes of the United Nations Conference on Environment and Development. It should provide a forum for the exchange of experience on regional and subregional initiatives and regional collaboration for sustainable development. This could include the promotion of the voluntary regional exchange of national experience in the implementation of Agenda 21 and, inter alia, the possible development of modalities for reviews within regions by and among those countries that voluntarily agree to do so. In this context, the Commission should encourage the availability of funding for the implementation of initiatives related to such reviews;

(d) Establish closer interaction with international financial, development and trade institutions, as well as with other relevant bodies within and outside the United Nations system, including the World Bank, the Global Environment Facility, the United Nations Development Programme, the World Trade Organization, the United Nations Conference on Trade and Development and the United Nations Environment Programme, which, in turn, are invited to take full account of the results of policy deliberations in the Commission and to integrate them in their own work programmes and activities;

(e) Strengthen its interaction with representatives of major groups, including through greater and better use of focused dialogue sessions and round tables. These groups are important resources in operationalizing, managing and promoting sustainable development and contribute to the implementation of Agenda 21. The major groups are encouraged to adopt arrangements for coordination and interaction in providing inputs to the Commission. Taking into account the Commission's programme of work, this could include inputs from:

i) The scientific community and research institutions, relating to the greater understanding of the interactions between human activity and natural ecosystems and on how to manage global systems sustainably;

ii) Women, children and youth, indigenous people and their communities, non-governmental organizations, local authorities, workers and their trade unions and farmers on the elaboration, promotion and sharing of effective strategies, policies, practices and processes to promote sustainable development;

iii) Business and industry groups on the elaboration, promotion and sharing of sustainable development practices and the promotion of corporate responsibility and accountability;

(f) Organize the implementation of its next multi-year programme of work in the most effective and productive way, including through shortening its annual meeting to two weeks. The inter-sessional ad hoc working groups should help to focus the Commission's sessions by identifying key elements to be discussed and important problems to be addressed within specific items of the Commission's programme of work. Government hosted and funded expert meetings will continue to provide inputs to the work of the Commission.

134. The Secretary-General is invited to review the functioning of the High-level Advisory Board on Sustainable Development and present proposals on ways to promote more direct interaction between the Board and the Commission, with a view to ensuring that the Board contributes to the deliberations on specific themes considered by the Commission in accordance with its programme of work.

135. The work of the Committee on New and Renewable Sources of Energy and on Energy for Development and the Committee on Natural Resources should be more

compatible with and supportive of the programme of work of the Commission. The Economic and Social Council, in carrying out its functions related to the implementation of General Assembly resolution 50/227 of 24 May 1996, should consider, at its substantive session of 1997, the most effective means of bringing this about.

136. The arrangements for the election of the Bureau should be changed in order to allow the same Bureau to provide guidance in the preparations for and to lead the work during the annual sessions of the Commission. The Commission would benefit from such a change. The Economic and Social Council should take the necessary action at its substantive session of 1997 to ensure that these new arrangements take effect.

137. The next comprehensive review of progress achieved in the implementation of Agenda 21 by the General Assembly will take place in the year 2002. The modalities of this review should be determined at a later stage.

Johannesburg Declaration on Sustainable Development

Adopted on 4 September 2002 at Johannesburg. Source: Report of the WSSD, Resolution 1 (Annex), Doc. A/CONF.199/20 and A/CONF.199/20/Corr. 1 (2002) (the text reproduced does not incorporate the footnotes). Further information: CSD, New York, USA, http://www.un.org/esa/sustdev/csd/csd.htm

From our origins to the future

1. We, the representatives of the peoples of the world, assembled at the World Summit on Sustainable Development in Johannesburg, South Africa, from 2 to 4 September 2002, reaffirm our commitment to sustainable development.

2. We commit ourselves to building a humane, equitable and caring global society, cognizant of the need for human dignity for all.

3. At the beginning of this Summit, the children of the world spoke to us in a simple yet clear voice that the future belongs to them, and accordingly challenged all of us to ensure that through our actions they will inherit a world free of the indignity and indecency occasioned by poverty, environmental degradation and patterns of unsustainable development.

4. As part of our response to these children, who represent our collective future, all of us, coming from every corner of the world, informed by different life experiences, are united and moved by a deeply felt sense that we urgently need to create a new and brighter world of hope.

5. Accordingly, we assume a collective responsibility to advance and strengthen the interdependent and mutually reinforcing pillars of sustainable development -

economic development, social development and environmental protection - at the local, national, regional and global levels.

6. From this continent, the cradle of humanity, we declare, through the Plan of Implementation of the World Summit on Sustainable Development and the present Declaration, our responsibility to one another, to the greater community of life and to our children.

7. Recognizing that humankind is at a crossroads, we have united in a common resolve to make a determined effort to respond positively to the need to produce a practical and visible plan to bring about poverty eradication and human development.

From Stockholm to Rio de Janeiro to Johannesburg

8. Thirty years ago, in Stockholm, we agreed on the urgent need to respond to the problem of environmental deterioration. Ten years ago, at the United Nations Conference on Environment and Development, held in Rio de Janeiro, we agreed that the protection of the environment and social and economic development are fundamental to sustainable development, based on the Rio Principles. To achieve such development, we adopted the global programme entitled Agenda 21 and the Rio Declaration on Environment and Development, to which we reaffirm our commitment. The Rio Conference was a significant milestone that set a new agenda for sustainable development.

9. Between Rio and Johannesburg, the world's nations have met in several major conferences under the auspices of the United Nations, including the International Conference on Financing for Development, as well as the Doha Ministerial Conference. These conferences defined for the world a comprehensive vision for the future of humanity.

10. At the Johannesburg Summit, we have achieved much in bringing together a rich tapestry of peoples and views in a constructive search for a common path towards a world that respects and implements the vision of sustainable development. The Johannesburg Summit has also confirmed that significant progress has been made towards achieving a global consensus and partnership among all the people of our planet.

The challenges we face

11. We recognize that poverty eradication, changing consumption and production patterns and protecting and managing the natural resource base for economic and social development are overarching objectives of and essential requirements for sustainable development.

12. The deep fault line that divides human society between the rich and the poor and the ever-increasing gap between the developed and developing worlds pose a major threat to global prosperity, security and stability.

13. The global environment continues to suffer. Loss of biodiversity continues, fish stocks continue to be depleted, desertification claims more and more fertile land,

the adverse effects of climate change are already evident, natural disasters are more frequent and more devastating, and developing countries more vulnerable, and air, water and marine pollution continue to rob millions of a decent life.

14. Globalization has added a new dimension to these challenges. The rapid integration of markets, mobility of capital and significant increases in investment flows around the world have opened new challenges and opportunities for the pursuit of sustainable development. But the benefits and costs of globalization are unevenly distributed, with developing countries facing special difficulties in meeting this challenge.

15. We risk the entrenchment of these global disparities and unless we act in a manner that fundamentally changes their lives the poor of the world may lose confidence in their representatives and the democratic systems to which we remain committed, seeing their representatives as nothing more than sounding brass or tinkling cymbals.

Our commitment to sustainable development

16. We are determined to ensure that our rich diversity, which is our collective strength, will be used for constructive partnership for change and for the achievement of the common goal of sustainable development.

17. Recognizing the importance of building human solidarity, we urge the promotion of dialogue and cooperation among the world's civilizations and peoples, irrespective of race, disabilities, religion, language, culture or tradition.

18. We welcome the focus of the Johannesburg Summit on the indivisibility of human dignity and are resolved, through decisions on targets, timetables and partnerships, to speedily increase access to such basic requirements as clean water, sanitation, adequate shelter, energy, health care, food security and the protection of biodiversity. At the same time, we will work together to help one another gain access to financial resources, benefit from the opening of markets, ensure capacity-building, use modern technology to bring about development and make sure that there is technology transfer, human resource development, education and training to banish underdevelopment forever.

19. We reaffirm our pledge to place particular focus on, and give priority attention to, the fight against the worldwide conditions that pose severe threats to the sustainable development of our people, which include: chronic hunger; malnutrition; foreign occupation; armed conflict; illicit drug problems; organized crime; corruption; natural disasters; illicit arms trafficking; trafficking in persons; terrorism; intolerance and incitement to racial, ethnic, religious and other hatreds; xenophobia; and endemic, communicable and chronic diseases, in particular HIV/AIDS, malaria and tuberculosis.

20. We are committed to ensuring that women's empowerment, emancipation and gender equality are integrated in all the activities encompassed within Agenda 21, the Millennium development goals and the Plan of Implementation of the Summit.

21. We recognize the reality that global society has the means and is endowed with the resources to address the challenges of poverty eradication and sustainable development confronting all humanity. Together, we will take extra steps to ensure that these available resources are used to the benefit of humanity.

22. In this regard, to contribute to the achievement of our development goals and targets, we urge developed countries that have not done so to make concrete efforts reach the internationally agreed levels of official development assistance.

23. We welcome and support the emergence of stronger regional groupings and alliances, such as the New Partnership for Africa's Development, to promote regional cooperation, improved international cooperation and sustainable development.

24. We shall continue to pay special attention to the developmental needs of small island developing States and the least developed countries.

25. We reaffirm the vital role of the indigenous peoples in sustainable development.

26. We recognize that sustainable development requires a long-term perspective and broad-based participation in policy formulation, decision-making and implementation at all levels. As social partners, we will continue to work for stable partnerships with all major groups, respecting the independent, important roles of each of them.

27. We agree that in pursuit of its legitimate activities the private sector, including both large and small companies, has a duty to contribute to the evolution of equitable and sustainable communities and societies.

28. We also agree to provide assistance to increase income-generating employment opportunities, taking into account the Declaration on Fundamental Principles and Rights at Work of the International Labour Organization.

29. We agree that there is a need for private sector corporations to enforce corporate accountability, which should take place within a transparent and stable regulatory environment.

30. We undertake to strengthen and improve governance at all levels for the effective implementation of Agenda 21, the Millennium development goals and the Plan of Implementation of the Summit.

Multilateralism is the future

31. To achieve our goals of sustainable development, we need more effective, democratic and accountable international and multilateral institutions.

32. We reaffirm our commitment to the principles and purposes of the Charter of the United Nations and international law, as well as to the strengthening of multilateralism. We support the leadership role of the United Nations as the most universal and representative organization in the world, which is best placed to promote sustainable development.

33. We further commit ourselves to monitor progress at regular intervals towards the achievement of our sustainable development goals and objectives.

Making it happen!

34. We are in agreement that this must be an inclusive process, involving all the major groups and Governments that participated in the historic Johannesburg Summit.

35. We commit ourselves to act together, united by a common determination to save our planet, promote human development and achieve universal prosperity and peace.

36. We commit ourselves to the Plan of Implementation of the World Summit on sustainable Development and to expediting the achievement of the time-bound, socio-economic and environmental targets contained therein.

37. From the African continent, the cradle of humankind, we solemnly pledge to the peoples of the world and the generations that will surely inherit this Earth that we are determined to ensure that our collective hope for sustainable development is realized.

Plan of Implementation of the World Summit on Sustainable Development [excerpts]

Adopted at Johannesburg on 4 September 2002. Source: Report of the WSSD, Resolution 2 (Annex), Doc. A/CONF.199/20 and A/CONF.199/20/Corr. 1 (2002) (the text reproduced does not incorporate the footnotes). Further information: CSD, New York, USA, http://www.un.org/esa/sustdev/csd/csd.htm

I. Introduction

1. The United Nations Conference on Environment and Development, held in Rio de Janeiro in 1992, provided the fundamental principles and the programme of action for achieving sustainable development. We strongly reaffirm our commitment to the Rio principles, the full implementation of Agenda 21 and the Programme for the Further Implementation of Agenda 21. We also commit ourselves to achieving the internationally agreed development goals, including those contained in the United Nations Millennium Declaration and in the outcomes of the major United Nations conferences and international agreements since 1992.

2. The present plan of implementation will further build on the achievements made since the United Nations Conference on Environment and Development and expedite the realization of the remaining goals. To this end, we commit ourselves to undertaking concrete actions and measures at all levels and to enhancing international cooperation, taking into account the Rio principles, including, inter alia, the principle of common but differentiated responsibilities as set out in

principle 7 of the Rio Declaration on Environment and Development. These efforts will also promote the integration of the three components of sustainable development - economic development, social development and environmental protection - as interdependent and mutually reinforcing pillars. Poverty eradication, changing unsustainable patterns of production and consumption and protecting and managing the natural resource base of economic and social development are overarching objectives of, and essential requirements for, sustainable development.

3. We recognize that the implementation of the outcomes of the Summit should benefit all, particularly women, youth, children and vulnerable groups. Furthermore, the implementation should involve all relevant actors through partnerships, especially between Governments of the North and South, on the one hand, and between Governments and major groups, on the other, to achieve the widely shared goals of sustainable development. As reflected in the Monterrey Consensus, such partnerships are key to pursuing sustainable development in a globalizing world.

4. Good governance within each country and at the international level is essential for sustainable development. At the domestic level, sound environmental, social and economic policies, democratic institutions responsive to the needs of the people, the rule of law, anti-corruption measures, gender equality and an enabling environment for investment are the basis for sustainable development. As a result of globalization, external factors have become critical in determining the success or failure of developing countries in their national efforts. The gap between developed and developing countries points to the continued need for a dynamic and enabling international economic environment supportive of international cooperation, particularly in the areas of finance, technology transfer, debt and trade and full and effective participation of developing countries in global decision-making, if the momentum for global progress towards sustainable development is to be maintained and increased.

5. Peace, security, stability and respect for human rights and fundamental freedoms, including the right to development, as well as respect for cultural diversity, are essential for achieving sustainable development and ensuring that sustainable development benefits all.

6. We acknowledge the importance of ethics for sustainable development and, therefore, emphasize the need to consider ethics in the implementation of Agenda 21.

Chapter 2

Regulatory Techniques and Environmental Rights

Introduction

This chapter includes two different types of instruments. The first section focuses on environmental impact assessment (EIA) as one specific regulatory technique used by states to foster the implementation of substantive environmental standards adopted in various treaties. It includes UNEP's 1987 non-binding Goals and Principles of Environmental Impact Assessment as well as the 1991 Espoo Convention, a regional instrument adopted in the context of the UNECE which is the only major multilateral agreement on environmental impact assessment.[1] It generally provides a framework for collaboration among states concerning proposed projects likely to pose significant adverse transboundary environmental impacts and imposes certain procedural requirements on the party proposing to undertake certain new activities. The Convention has been supplemented by the 2003 SEA Protocol which broadens the scope of the Convention by requiring an environmental assessment not only for specific projects but also for plans and programmes in chosen areas.

The second section moves on to highlight existing rights-based instruments in environmental law and relevant human rights provisions. It includes the 1998 Århus Convention which is the only environmental law treaty providing specific procedural environmental rights. This is again a regional instrument adopted in the context of the UNECE but is reproduced because it constitutes the only major multilateral agreement in this field.[2] It generally provides rights of access to information, public participation in decision-making, and access to justice in environmental matters. It has now been supplemented by the 2003 PRTR Protocol which seeks to introduce more specific commitments concerning access to information through the setting up of pollutant release and transfer registers. This chapter also includes several specific environment-related provisions found in human rights or related treaties. This comprises in particular provisions providing a

---

1 The possibility has now been open for member states of the UN from outside the UNECE region to ratify the Convention (see Article 17(3) below at p. 38).

2 Further the Convention provides that member states of the UN from outside the UNECE region can also ratify the Convention (see Article 19(3) below at p. 61).

specific recognition of a human right to a clean environment. It also incorporates environment-related provisions of the 1989 ILO Convention 169 and the 1998 Statute of the International Criminal Court. It does not, however, include treaties like the European Convention on Human Rights which does not directly mention the environment, even if some of the rights recognised therein have been applied in environment-related cases.[3]

Selected readings

Environmental impact assessment

Knox, J.H., 'The Myth and Reality of Transboundary Environmental Impact Assessment', 96 *AJIL* 291 (2002).

Okowa, P.N., 'Procedural Obligations in International Environmental Agreements', 67 *BYIL* 275 (1996).

Robinson, N.A., 'International Trends in Environmental Impact Assessment', 19 *Boston College Envtl Affairs L. Rev.* 591 (1992).

Environmental rights

Boyle, A.E. and Anderson, M.R. (eds.), *Human Rights Approaches to Environmental Protection* (Oxford: Clarendon, 1996).

Davies, P., 'Public Participation, the Aarhus Convention, and the European Community', *in* Zillman, D., Lucas, A. and Pring, G. (eds.), *Human Rights in Natural Resource Development - Public Participation in the Sustainable Development of Mining and Energy Resources* (Oxford: Oxford University Press, 2002), p. 155.

Gavouneli, M., 'Access to Environmental Information: Delimitation of a Right', 13 *Tulane Envtl L.J.* 303 (2000).

Shelton, D., 'Environmental Rights', *in* Alston, P. (ed.), *Peoples' Rights - The State of the Art* (Oxford: Oxford University Press, 2001), p. 185.

Zarsky, L. (ed.), *Human Rights and the Environment - Conflicts and Norms in a Globalizing World* (London: Earthscan, 2002).

---

[3] Convention for the Protection of Human Rights and Fundamental Freedoms, Rome, 4 November 1950, *European Treaty Series* - No. 5. For relevant cases, *see, e.g.*, López Ostra v. Spain, Judgment of 9 December 1994, 20 *EHRR* 277 (1995); and Hatton and others v. UK, Judgments of 2 October 2001 and 8 July 2003, (2002) 34 *EHRR* 1 and (2003) 37 *EHRR* 28.

Environmental impact assessment

Goals and Principles of Environmental Impact Assessment

Adopted on 17 June 1987 at Nairobi. Source: Report of the Executive Director, 14th Session of the Governing Council of UNEP, Doc. UNEP/GC.14/17 (1987) (the text reproduced does not incorporate the footnotes). Further information: UNEP, Nairobi, Kenya, www.unep.org

Environmental impact assessment (EIA)

EIA means an examination, analysis and assessment of planned activities with a view to ensuring environmentally sound and sustainable development.

The EIA goals and principles set out below are necessarily general in nature and may be further refined when fulfilling EIA tasks at the national, regional and international levels.

Goals

1. To establish that before decisions are taken by the competent authority or authorities to undertake or to authorize activities that are likely to significantly affect the environment, the environmental effects of those activities should be taken fully into account.

2. To promote the implementation of appropriate procedures in all countries consistent with national laws and decision-making processes, through which the foregoing goal may be realized.

3. To encourage the development of reciprocal procedures for information exchange, notification and consultation between States when proposed activities are likely to have significant transboundary effects on the environment of those States.

Principles

Principle 1

States (including their competent authorities) should not undertake or authorize activities without prior consideration, at an early stage, of their environmental effects. Where the extent, nature or location of a proposed activity is such that it is likely to significantly affect the environment, a comprehensive environmental impact assessment should be undertaken in accordance with the following principles.

Principle 2

The criteria and procedures for determining whether an activity is likely to significantly affect the environment and is therefore subject to an EIA, should be defined clearly by legislation, regulation, or other means, so that subject activities can be quickly and surely identified and EIA can be applied as the activity is being planned.

Principle 3

In the EIA process the relevant significant environmental issues should be identified and studied. Where appropriate, all efforts should be made to identify these issues at an early stage in the process.

Principle 4

An EIA should include, at a minimum:

(a) A description of the proposed activity;

(b) A description of the potentially affected environment, including specific information necessary for identifying and assessing the environmental effects of the proposed activity;

(c) A description of practical alternatives, as appropriate;

(d) An assessment of the likely or potential environmental impacts of the proposed activity and alternatives, including the direct, indirect, cumulative, short-term and long-term effects;

(e) An identification and description of measures available to mitigate adverse environmental impacts of the proposed activity and alternatives, and an assessment of those measures;

(f) An indication of gaps in knowledge and uncertainties which may be encountered in compiling the required information;

(g) An indication of whether the environment of any other State or areas beyond national jurisdiction is likely to be affected by the proposed activity or alternatives;

(h) A brief, nontechnical summary of the information provided under the above headings.

Principle 5

The environmental effects in an EIA should be assessed with a degree of detail commensurate with their likely environmental significance.

Principle 6

The information provided as part of EIA should be examined impartially and objectively prior to the decision.

Principle 7

Before a decision on the activity is made, government agencies, members of the public, experts in relevant disciplines and interested groups should be allowed appropriate opportunity to comment on the EIA.

Principle 8

A decision as to whether a proposed activity should be authorized or undertaken should not be taken until an appropriate period has elapsed to consider comments pursuant to principles 7 and 12.

Principle 9

The decision on any proposed activity subject to an EIA should be in writing, state the reasons therefor, and include provisions, if any, to prevent, reduce or mitigate damage to the environment.

This decision should be made available to interested persons or groups

Principle 10

Where it is justified, following a decision on an activity which has been subject to an EIA, the activity and its effects on the environment or the provisions (pursuant to Principle 9) of the decision on this activity, should be subject to appropriate supervision.

Principle 11

States should endeavour to conclude bilateral, regional or multilateral arrangements, as appropriate, so as to provide, on the basis of reciprocity, notification, exchange of information, and agreed-upon consultation on the potential environmental effect of activities under their control or jurisdiction which are likely to significantly affect other States or areas beyond national jurisdiction.

Principle 12

When information provided as part of an EIA indicates that the environment within another State is likely to be significantly affected by a proposed activity, the State in which the activity is being planned should to the extent possible:

a) notify the potentially affected State of the proposed activity;

b) transmit to the potentially affected State any relevant information from the EIA, the transmission of which is not prohibited by national laws or regulations; and

c) when it is agreed between the States concerned, enter into timely consultations.

Principle 13

Appropriate measures should be established to ensure implementation of EIA procedures.

Convention on Environmental Impact Assessment in a Transboundary Context

Adopted on 25 February 1991 at Espoo. Entered into force on 10 September 1997. Source: 1989 *UNTS* 309 (the text reproduced incorporates the amendment adopted in 2001). Number of parties to the unamended Convention: 40. Further information: Secretariat (UNECE), Geneva, Switzerland, http://www.unece.org/env/eia

The Parties to this Convention,

Aware of the interrelationship between economic activities and their environmental consequences,

Affirming the need to ensure environmentally sound and sustainable development,

Determined to enhance international co-operation in assessing environmental impact in particular in a transboundary context,

Mindful of the need and importance to develop anticipatory policies and of preventing, mitigating and monitoring significant adverse environmental impact in general and more specifically in a transboundary context,

Recalling the relevant provisions of the Charter of the United Nations, the Declaration of the Stockholm Conference on the Human Environment, the Final Act of the Conference on Security and Co-operation in Europe (CSCE) and the Concluding Documents of the Madrid and Vienna Meetings of Representatives of the Participating States of the CSCE,

Commending the ongoing activities of States to ensure that, through their national legal and administrative provisions and their national policies, environmental impact assessment is carried out,

Conscious of the need to give explicit consideration to environmental factors at an early stage in the decision-making process by applying environmental impact assessment, at all appropriate administrative levels, as a necessary tool to improve the quality of information presented to decision makers so that environmentally sound decisions can be made paying careful attention to minimizing significant adverse impact, particularly in a transboundary context,

Mindful of the efforts of international organizations to promote the use of environmental impact assessment both at the national and international levels, and taking into account work on environmental impact assessment carried out under the auspices of the United Nations Economic Commission for Europe, in particular results achieved by the Seminar on Environmental Impact Assessment (September 1987, Warsaw, Poland) as well as noting the Goals and Principles on environmental impact assessment adopted by the Governing Council of the United Nations Environment Programme, and the Ministerial Declaration on Sustainable Development (May 1990, Bergen, Norway),

Have agreed as follows:

Article 1: Definitions

For the purposes of this Convention,

i) 'Parties' means, unless the text otherwise indicates, the Contracting Parties to this Convention;

ii) 'Party of origin' means the Contracting Party or Parties to this Convention under whose jurisdiction a proposed activity is envisaged to take place;

iii) 'Affected Party' means the Contracting Party or Parties to this Convention likely to be affected by the transboundary impact of a proposed activity;

iv) 'Concerned Parties' means the Party of origin and the affected Party of an environmental impact assessment pursuant to this Convention;

v) 'Proposed activity' means any activity or any major change to an activity subject to a decision of a competent authority in accordance with an applicable national procedure;

vi) 'Environmental impact assessment' means a national procedure for evaluating the likely impact of a proposed activity on the environment;

vii) 'Impact' means any effect caused by a proposed activity on the environment including human health and safety, flora, fauna, soil, air, water, climate, landscape and historical monuments or other physical structures or the interaction among these factors; it also includes effects on cultural heritage or socio-economic conditions resulting from alterations to those factors;

viii) 'Transboundary impact' means any impact, not exclusively of a global nature, within an area under the jurisdiction of a Party caused by a proposed activity the physical origin of which is situated wholly or in part within the area under the jurisdiction of another Party;

ix) 'Competent authority' means the national authority or authorities designated by a Party as responsible for performing the tasks covered by this Convention and/or the authority or authorities entrusted by a Party with decision-making powers regarding a proposed activity;

x) 'The Public' means one or more natural or legal persons and, in accordance with national legislation or practice, their associations, organizations or groups.

Article 2: General provisions

1. The Parties shall, either individually or jointly, take all appropriate and effective measures to prevent, reduce and control significant adverse transboundary environmental impact from proposed activities.

2. Each Party shall take the necessary legal, administrative or other measures to implement the provisions of this Convention, including, with respect to proposed activities listed in Appendix I that are likely to cause significant adverse transboundary impact, the establishment of an environmental impact assessment procedure that permits public participation and preparation of the environmental impact assessment documentation described in Appendix II.

3. The Party of origin shall ensure that in accordance with the provisions of this Convention an environmental impact assessment is undertaken prior to a decision to authorize or undertake a proposed activity listed in Appendix I that is likely to cause a significant adverse transboundary impact.

4. The Party of origin shall, consistent with the provisions of this Convention, ensure that affected Parties are notified of a proposed activity listed in Appendix I that is likely to cause a significant adverse transboundary impact.

5. Concerned Parties shall, at the initiative of any such Party, enter into discussions on whether one or more proposed activities not listed in Appendix I is or are likely to cause a significant adverse transboundary impact and thus should be treated as if it or they were so listed. Where those Parties so agree, the activity or activities shall be thus treated. General guidance for identifying criteria to determine significant adverse impact is set forth in Appendix III.

6. The Party of origin shall provide, in accordance with the provisions of this Convention, an opportunity to the public in the areas likely to be affected to participate in relevant environmental impact assessment procedures regarding proposed activities and shall ensure that the opportunity provided to the public of the affected Party is equivalent to that provided to the public of the Party of origin.

7. Environmental impact assessments as required by this Convention shall, as a minimum requirement, be undertaken at the project level of the proposed activity. To the extent appropriate, the Parties shall endeavour to apply the principles of environmental impact assessment to policies, plans and programmes.

8. The provisions of this Convention shall not affect the right of Parties to implement national laws, regulations, administrative provisions or accepted legal practices protecting information the supply of which would be prejudicial to industrial and commercial secrecy or national security.

9. The provisions of this Convention shall not affect the right of particular Parties to implement, by bilateral or multilateral agreement where appropriate, more stringent measures than those of this Convention.

10. The provisions of this Convention shall not prejudice any obligations of the Parties under international law with regard to activities having or likely to have a transboundary impact.

Article 3: Notification

1. For a proposed activity listed in Appendix I that is likely to cause a significant adverse transboundary impact, the Party of origin shall, for the purposes of ensuring adequate and effective consultations under Article 5, notify any Party which it considers may be an affected Party as early as possible and no later than when informing its own public about that proposed activity.

2. This notification shall contain, inter alia:

(a) Information on the proposed activity, including any available information on its possible transboundary impact;

(b) The nature of the possible decision; and

(c) An indication of a reasonable time within which a response under paragraph 3 of this Article is required, taking into account the nature of the proposed activity;

and may include the information set out in paragraph 5 of this Article.

3. The affected Party shall respond to the Party of origin within the time specified in the notification, acknowledging receipt of the notification, and shall indicate whether it intends to participate in the environmental impact assessment procedure.

4. If the affected Party indicates that it does not intend to participate in the environmental impact assessment procedure, or if it does not respond within the time specified in the notification, the provisions in paragraphs 5, 6, 7 and 8 of this Article and in Articles 4 to 7 will not apply. In such circumstances the right of a Party of origin to determine whether to carry out an environmental impact assessment on the basis of its national law and practice is not prejudiced.

5. Upon receipt of a response from the affected Party indicating its desire to participate in the environmental impact assessment procedure, the Party of origin shall, if it has not already done so, provide to the affected Party:

(a) Relevant information regarding the environmental impact assessment procedure, including an indication of the time schedule for transmittal of comments; and

(b) Relevant information on the proposed activity and its possible significant adverse transboundary impact.

6. An affected Party shall, at the request of the Party of origin, provide the latter with reasonably obtainable information relating to the potentially affected environment under the jurisdiction of the affected Party, where such information is necessary for the preparation of the environmental impact assessment documentation. The information shall be furnished promptly and, as appropriate, through a joint body where one exists.

7. When a Party considers that it would be affected by a significant adverse transboundary impact of a proposed activity listed in Appendix I, and when no notification has taken place in accordance with paragraph 1 of this Article, the concerned Parties shall, at the request of the affected Party, exchange sufficient information for the purposes of holding discussions on whether there is likely to be a significant adverse transboundary impact. If those Parties agree that there is likely to be a significant adverse transboundary impact, the provisions of this Convention shall apply accordingly. If those Parties cannot agree whether there is likely to be a significant adverse transboundary impact, any such Party may submit that question to an inquiry commission in accordance with the provisions of Appendix IV to advise on the likelihood of significant adverse transboundary impact, unless they agree on another method of settling this question.

8. The concerned Parties shall ensure that the public of the affected Party in the areas likely to be affected be informed of, and be provided with possibilities for making comments or objections on, the proposed activity, and for the transmittal of these comments or objections to the competent authority of the Party of origin, either directly to this authority or, where appropriate, through the Party of origin.

Article 4: Preparation of the environmental impact assessment documentation

1. The environmental impact assessment documentation to be submitted to the competent authority of the Party of origin shall contain, as a minimum, the information described in Appendix II.

2. The Party of origin shall furnish the affected Party, as appropriate through a joint body where one exists, with the environmental impact assessment documentation. The concerned Parties shall arrange for distribution of the documentation to the authorities and the public of the affected Party in the areas likely to be affected and for the submission of comments to the competent authority of the Party of origin, either directly to this authority or, where appropriate, through the Party of origin within a reasonable time before the final decision is taken on the proposed activity.

Article 5: Consultations on the basis of the environmental impact assessment documentation

The Party of origin shall, after completion of the environmental impact assessment documentation, without undue delay enter into consultations with the affected Party concerning, inter alia, the potential transboundary impact of the proposed activity and measures to reduce or eliminate its impact. Consultations may relate to:

(a) Possible alternatives to the proposed activity, including the no-action alternative and possible measures to mitigate significant adverse transboundary impact and to monitor the effects of such measures at the expense of the Party of origin;

(b) Other forms of possible mutual assistance in reducing any significant adverse transboundary impact of the proposed activity; and

(c) Any other appropriate matters relating to the proposed activity.

The Parties shall agree, at the commencement of such consultations, on a reasonable time-frame for the duration of the consultation period. Any such consultations may be conducted through an appropriate joint body, where one exists.

Article 6: Final decision

1. The Parties shall ensure that, in the final decision on the proposed activity, due account is taken of the outcome of the environmental impact assessment, including the environmental impact assessment documentation, as well as the comments thereon received pursuant to Article 3, paragraph 8 and Article 4, paragraph 2, and the outcome of the consultations as referred to in Article 5.

2. The Party of origin shall provide to the affected Party the final decision on the proposed activity along with the reasons and considerations on which it was based.

3. If additional information on the significant transboundary impact of a proposed activity, which was not available at the time a decision was made with respect to that activity and which could have materially affected the decision, becomes available to a concerned Party before work on that activity commences, that Party shall immediately inform the other concerned Party or Parties. If one of the concerned Parties so requests, consultations shall be held as to whether the decision needs to be revised.

Article 7: Post-project analysis

1. The concerned Parties, at the request of any such Party, shall determine whether, and if so to what extent, a post-project analysis shall be carried out, taking into account the likely significant adverse transboundary impact of the activity for which an environmental impact assessment has been undertaken pursuant to this Convention. Any post-project analysis undertaken shall include, in particular, the surveillance of the activity and the determination of any adverse transboundary impact. Such surveillance and determination may be undertaken with a view to achieving the objectives listed in Appendix V.

2. When, as a result of post-project analysis, the Party of origin or the affected Party has reasonable grounds for concluding that there is a significant adverse transboundary impact or factors have been discovered which may result in such an impact, it shall immediately inform the other Party. The concerned Parties shall then consult on necessary measures to reduce or eliminate the impact.

Article 8: Bilateral and multilateral co-operation

The Parties may continue existing or enter into new bilateral or multilateral agreements or other arrangements in order to implement their obligations under this Convention. Such agreements or other arrangements may be based on the elements listed in Appendix VI.

Article 9: Research programmes

The Parties shall give special consideration to the setting up, or intensification of, specific research programmes aimed at:

(a) Improving existing qualitative and quantitative methods for assessing the impacts of proposed activities;

(b) Achieving a better understanding of cause-effect relationships and their role in integrated environmental management;

(c) Analysing and monitoring the efficient implementation of decisions on proposed activities with the intention of minimizing or preventing impacts;

(d) Developing methods to stimulate creative approaches in the search for environmentally sound alternatives to proposed activities, production and consumption patterns;

(e) Developing methodologies for the application of the principles of environmental impact assessment at the macro-economic level.

The results of the programmes listed above shall be exchanged by the Parties.

Article 10: Status of the Appendices

The Appendices attached to this Convention form an integral part of the Convention.

Article 11: Meeting of Parties

1. The Parties shall meet, so far as possible, in connection with the annual sessions of the Senior Advisers to ECE Governments on Environmental and Water Problems. The first meeting of the Parties shall be convened not later than one year after the date of the entry into force of this Convention. Thereafter, meetings of the Parties shall be held at such other times as may be deemed necessary by a meeting of the Parties, or at the written request of any Party, provided that, within six months of the request being communicated to them by the secretariat, it is supported by at least one third of the Parties.

2. The Parties shall keep under continuous review the implementation of this Convention, and, with this purpose in mind, shall:

(a) Review the policies and methodological approaches to environmental impact assessment by the Parties with a view to further improving environmental impact assessment procedures in a transboundary context;

(b) Exchange information regarding experience gained in concluding and implementing bilateral and multilateral agreements or other arrangements regarding the use of environmental impact assessment in a transboundary context to which one or more of the Parties are party;

(c) Seek, where appropriate, the services of competent international bodies and scientific committees in methodological and technical aspects pertinent to the achievement of the purposes of this Convention;

(d) At their first meeting, consider and by consensus adopt rules of procedure for their meetings;

(e) Consider and, where necessary, adopt proposals for amendments to this Convention;

(f) Consider and undertake any additional action that may be required for the achievement of the purposes of this Convention.

Article 12: Right to vote

1. Each Party to this Convention shall have one vote.

2. Except as provided for in paragraph 1 of this Article, regional economic integration organizations, in matters within their competence, shall exercise their right to vote with a number of votes equal to the number of their member States which are Parties to this Convention. Such organizations shall not exercise their right to vote if their member States exercise theirs, and vice versa.

Article 13: Secretariat

The Executive Secretary of the Economic Commission for Europe shall carry out the following secretariat functions:

(a) The convening and preparing of meetings of the Parties;

(b) The transmission of reports and other information received in accordance with the provisions of this Convention to the Parties; and

(c) The performance of other functions as may be provided for in this Convention or as may be determined by the Parties.

Article 14: Amendments to the Convention

1. Any Party may propose amendments to this Convention.

2. Proposed amendments shall be submitted in writing to the secretariat, which shall communicate them to all Parties. The proposed amendments shall be discussed at the next meeting of the Parties, provided these proposals have been circulated by the secretariat to the Parties at least ninety days in advance.

3. The Parties shall make every effort to reach agreement on any proposed amendment to this Convention by consensus. If all efforts at consensus have been exhausted, and no agreement reached, the amendment shall as a last resort be adopted by a three-fourths majority vote of the Parties present and voting at the meeting.

4. Amendments to this Convention adopted in accordance with paragraph 3 of this Article shall be submitted by the Depositary to all Parties for ratification, approval or acceptance. They shall enter into force for Parties having ratified, approved or accepted them on the ninetieth day after the receipt by the Depositary of notification of their ratification, approval or acceptance by at least three fourths of these Parties. Thereafter they shall enter into force for any other Party on the ninetieth day after that Party deposits its instrument of ratification, approval or acceptance of the amendments.

5. For the purpose of this Article, 'Parties present and voting' means Parties present and casting an affirmative or negative vote.

6. The voting procedure set forth in paragraph 3 of this Article is not intended to constitute a precedent for future agreements negotiated within the Economic Commission for Europe.

Article 15: Settlement of disputes

1. If a dispute arises between two or more Parties about the interpretation or application of this Convention, they shall seek a solution by negotiation or by any other method of dispute settlement acceptable to the parties to the dispute.

2. When signing, ratifying, accepting, approving or acceding to this Convention, or at any time thereafter, a Party may declare in writing to the Depositary that for a dispute not resolved in accordance with paragraph 1 of this Article, it accepts one or both of the following means of dispute settlement as compulsory in relation to any Party accepting the same obligation:

(a) Submission of the dispute to the International Court of Justice;

(b) Arbitration in accordance with the procedure set out in Appendix VII.

3. If the parties to the dispute have accepted both means of dispute settlement referred to in paragraph 2 of this Article, the dispute may be submitted only to the International Court of Justice, unless the parties agree otherwise.

Article 16: Signature

This Convention shall be open for signature at Espoo (Finland) from 25 February to 1 March 1991 and thereafter at United Nations Headquarters in New York until 2 September 1991 by States members of the Economic Commission for Europe as well as States having consultative status with the Economic Commission for Europe pursuant to paragraph 8 of the Economic and Social Council resolution 36 (IV) of 28 March 1947, and by regional economic integration organizations constituted by sovereign States members of the Economic Commission for Europe to which their member States have transferred competence in respect of matters governed by this Convention, including the competence to enter into treaties in respect of these matters.

Article 17: Ratification, acceptance, approval and accession

1. This Convention shall be subject to ratification, acceptance or approval by signatory States and regional economic integration organizations.

2. This Convention shall be open for accession as from 3 September 1991 by the States and organizations referred to in Article 16.

3. Any other State, not referred to in paragraph 2 of this Article, that is a Member of the United Nations may accede to the Convention upon approval by the Meeting of the Parties. The Meeting of the Parties shall not consider or approve any request for accession by such a State until this paragraph has entered into force for all the States and organizations that were Parties to the Convention on 27 February 2001.

4. The instruments of ratification, acceptance, approval or accession shall be deposited with the Secretary-General of the United Nations, who shall perform the functions of Depositary.

5. Any organization referred to in Article 16 which becomes a Party to this Convention without any of its member States being a Party shall be bound by all the obligations under this Convention. In the case of such organizations, one or more of whose member States is a Party to this Convention, the organization and its member States shall decide on their respective responsibilities for the performance of their obligations under this Convention. In such cases, the organization and the member States shall not be entitled to exercise rights under this Convention concurrently.

6. In their instruments of ratification, acceptance, approval or accession, the regional economic integration organizations referred to in Article 16 shall declare the extent of their competence with respect to the matters governed by this Convention. These organizations shall also inform the Depositary of any relevant modification to the extent of their competence.

7. Any State or organization that ratifies, accepts or approves this Convention shall be deemed simultaneously to ratify, accept or approve the amendment to the Convention set out in decision II/14 taken at the second meeting of the Parties.

Article 18: Entry into force

1. This Convention shall enter into force on the ninetieth day after the date of deposit of the sixteenth instrument of ratification, acceptance, approval or accession.

2. For the purposes of paragraph 1 of this Article, any instrument deposited by a regional economic integration organization shall not be counted as additional to those deposited by States members of such an organization.

3. For each State or organization referred to in Article 16 which ratifies, accepts or approves this Convention or accedes thereto after the deposit of the sixteenth instrument of ratification, acceptance, approval or accession, this Convention shall enter into force on the ninetieth day after the date of deposit by such State or organization of its instrument of ratification, acceptance, approval or accession.

Article 19: Withdrawal

At any time after four years from the date on which this Convention has come into force with respect to a Party, that Party may withdraw from this Convention by giving written notification to the Depositary. Any such withdrawal shall take effect on the ninetieth day after the date of its receipt by the Depositary. Any such withdrawal shall not affect the application of Articles 3 to 6 of this Convention to a proposed activity in respect of which a notification has been made pursuant to Article 3, paragraph 1, or a request has been made pursuant to Article 3, paragraph 7, before such withdrawal took effect.

Article 20: Authentic texts

The original of this Convention, of which the English, French and Russian texts are equally authentic, shall be deposited with the Secretary-General of the United Nations.

In witness whereof the undersigned, being duly authorized thereto, have signed this Convention.

Done at Espoo (Finland), this twenty-fifth day of February one thousand nine hundred and ninety-one.

Appendix I: List of activities; Appendix II: Content of the environmental impact assessment documentation; Appendix III: General criteria to assist in the determination of the environmental significance of activities not listed in Appendix I; Appendix IV: Inquiry procedure; Appendix V: Post-project analysis; Appendix VI: Elements for bilateral and multilateral co-operation; Appendix VII: Arbitration [not reproduced]

Protocol on Strategic Environmental Assessment to the Convention on Environmental Impact Assessment in a Transboundary Context

Adopted on 21 May 2003 at Kiev. Not in force (no ratifications). Source: Doc. ECE/MP.EIA/2003/3. Further information: Espoo Convention Secretariat (UNECE), Geneva, Switzerland, http://www.unece.org/env/eia

The Parties to this Protocol,

Recognizing the importance of integrating environmental, including health, considerations into the preparation and adoption of plans and programmes and, to the extent appropriate, policies and legislation,

Committing themselves to promoting sustainable development and therefore basing themselves on the conclusions of the United Nations Conference on Environment and Development (Rio de Janeiro, Brazil, 1992), in particular principles 4 and 10 of the Rio Declaration on Environment and Development and Agenda 21, as well as the outcome of the third Ministerial Conference on Environment and Health (London, 1999) and the World Summit on Sustainable Development (Johannesburg, South Africa, 2002),

Bearing in mind the Convention on Environmental Impact Assessment in a Transboundary Context, done at Espoo, Finland, on 25 February 1991, and decision II/9 of its Parties at Sofia on 26 and 27 February 2001, in which it was decided to prepare a legally binding protocol on strategic environmental assessment,

Recognizing that strategic environmental assessment should have an important role in the preparation and adoption of plans, programmes, and, to the extent appropriate, policies and legislation, and that the wider application of the principles of environmental impact assessment to plans, programmes, policies and legislation will further strengthen the systematic analysis of their significant environmental effects,

Acknowledging the Convention on Access to Information, Public Participation in Decision-making and Access to Justice in Environmental Matters, done at Aarhus, Denmark, on 25 June 1998, and taking note of the relevant paragraphs of the Lucca Declaration, adopted at the first meeting of its Parties,

Conscious, therefore, of the importance of providing for public participation in strategic environmental assessment,

Acknowledging the benefits to the health and wellbeing of present and future generations that will follow if the need to protect and improve people's health is taken into account as an integral part of strategic environmental assessment, and recognizing the work led by the World Health Organization in this respect,

Mindful of the need for and importance of enhancing international cooperation in assessing the transboundary environmental, including health, effects of proposed plans and programmes, and, to the extent appropriate, policies and legislation,

Have agreed as follows:

Article 1: Objective

The objective of this Protocol is to provide for a high level of protection of the environment, including health, by:

(a) Ensuring that environmental, including health, considerations are thoroughly taken into account in the development of plans and programmes;

(b) Contributing to the consideration of environmental, including health, concerns in the preparation of policies and legislation;

(c) Establishing clear, transparent and effective procedures for strategic environmental assessment;

(d) Providing for public participation in strategic environmental assessment; and

(e) Integrating by these means environmental, including health, concerns into measures and instruments designed to further sustainable development.

Article 2: Definitions

For the purposes of this Protocol,

1. 'Party' means, unless the text indicates otherwise, a State or a regional economic integration organization referred to in article 24 which has consented to be bound by this Protocol and for which the Protocol is in force;

2. 'Convention' means the Convention on Access to Information, Public Participation in Decision-making and Access to Justice in Environmental Matters, done at Aarhus, Denmark, on 25 June 1998;

3. 'The public' means one or more natural or legal persons, and, in accordance with national legislation or practice, their associations, organizations or groups;

4. 'Facility' means one or more installations on the same site, or on adjoining sites, that are owned or operated by the same natural or legal person;

5. 'Competent authority' means the national authority or authorities, or any other competent body or bodies, designated by a Party to manage a national pollutant release and transfer register system;

6. 'Strategic environmental assessment' means the evaluation of the likely environmental, including health, effects, which comprises the determination of the scope of an environmental report and its preparation, the carrying out of public participation and consultations, and the taking into account of the environmental report and the results of the public participation and consultations in a plan or programme.

7. 'Environmental, including health, effect' means any effect on the environment, including human health, flora, fauna, biodiversity, soil, climate, air, water,

landscape, natural sites, material assets, cultural heritage and the interaction among these factors.

8. 'The public' means one or more natural or legal persons and, in accordance with national legislation or practice, their associations, organizations or groups.

Article 3: General provisions

1. Each Party shall take the necessary legislative, regulatory and other appropriate measures to implement the provisions of this Protocol within a clear, transparent framework.

2. Each Party shall endeavour to ensure that officials and authorities assist and provide guidance to the public in matters covered by this Protocol.

3. Each Party shall provide for appropriate recognition of and support to associations, organizations or groups promoting environmental, including health, protection in the context of this Protocol.

4. The provisions of this Protocol shall not affect the right of a Party to maintain or introduce additional measures in relation to issues covered by this Protocol.

5. Each Party shall promote the objectives of this Protocol in relevant international decision-making processes and within the framework of relevant international organizations.

6. Each Party shall ensure that persons exercising their rights in conformity with the provisions of this Protocol shall not be penalized, persecuted or harassed in any way for their involvement. This provision shall not affect the powers of national courts to award reasonable costs in judicial proceedings.

7. Within the scope of the relevant provisions of this Protocol, the public shall be able to exercise its rights without discrimination as to citizenship, nationality or domicile and, in the case of a legal person, without discrimination as to where it has its registered seat or an effective centre of its activities.

Article 4: Field of application concerning plans and programmes

1. Each Party shall ensure that a strategic environmental assessment is carried out for plans and programmes referred to in paragraphs 2, 3 and 4 which are likely to have significant environmental, including health, effects.

2. A strategic environmental assessment shall be carried out for plans and programmes which are prepared for agriculture, forestry, fisheries, energy, industry including mining, transport, regional development, waste management, water management, telecommunications, tourism, town and country planning or land use, and which set the framework for future development consent for projects listed in annex I and any other project listed in annex II that requires an environmental impact assessment under national legislation.

3. For plans and programmes other than those subject to paragraph 2 which set the framework for future development consent of projects, a strategic environmental

assessment shall be carried out where a Party so determines according to article 5, paragraph 1.

4. For plans and programmes referred to in paragraph 2 which determine the use of small areas at local level and for minor modifications to plans and programmes referred to in paragraph 2, a strategic environmental assessment shall be carried out only where a Party so determines according to article 5, paragraph 1.

5. The following plans and programmes are not subject to this Protocol:

(a) Plans and programmes whose sole purpose is to serve national defence or civil emergencies;

(b) Financial or budget plans and programmes.

Article 5: Screening

1. Each Party shall determine whether plans and programmes referred to in article 4, paragraphs 3 and 4, are likely to have significant environmental, including health, effects either through a case-by-case examination or by specifying types of plans and programmes or by combining both approaches. For this purpose each Party shall in all cases take into account the criteria set out in annex III.

2. Each Party shall ensure that the environmental and health authorities referred to in article 9, paragraph 1, are consulted when applying the procedures referred to in paragraph 1 above.

3. To the extent appropriate, each Party shall endeavour to provide opportunities for the participation of the public concerned in the screening of plans and programmes under this article.

4. Each Party shall ensure timely public availability of the conclusions pursuant to paragraph 1, including the reasons for not requiring a strategic environmental assessment, whether by public notices or by other appropriate means, such as electronic media.

Article 6: Scoping

1. Each Party shall establish arrangements for the determination of the relevant information to be included in the environmental report in accordance with article 7, paragraph 2.

2. Each Party shall ensure that the environmental and health authorities referred to in article 9, paragraph 1, are consulted when determining the relevant information to be included in the environmental report.

3. To the extent appropriate, each Party shall endeavour to provide opportunities for the participation of the public concerned when determining the relevant information to be included in the environmental report.

Article 7: Environmental report

1. For plans and programmes subject to strategic environmental assessment, each Party shall ensure that an environmental report is prepared.

2. The environmental report shall, in accordance with the determination under article 6, identify, describe and evaluate the likely significant environmental, including health, effects of implementing the plan or programme and its reasonable alternatives. The report shall contain such information specified in annex IV as may reasonably be required, taking into account:

(a) Current knowledge and methods of assessment;
(b) The contents and the level of detail of the plan or programme and its stage in the decision-making process;
(c) The interests of the public; and
(d) The information needs of the decision-making body.

3. Each Party shall ensure that environmental reports are of sufficient quality to meet the requirements of this Protocol.

Article 8: Public participation

1. Each Party shall ensure early, timely and effective opportunities for public participation, when all options are open, in the strategic environmental assessment of plans and programmes.

2. Each Party, using electronic media or other appropriate means, shall ensure the timely public availability of the draft plan or programme and the environmental report.

3. Each Party shall ensure that the public concerned, including relevant non-governmental organizations, is identified for the purposes of paragraphs 1 and 4.

4. Each Party shall ensure that the public referred to in paragraph 3 has the opportunity to express its opinion on the draft plan or programme and the environmental report within a reasonable time frame.

5. Each Party shall ensure that the detailed arrangements for informing the public and consulting the public concerned are determined and made publicly available. For this purpose, each Party shall take into account to the extent appropriate the elements listed in annex V.

Article 9: Consultation with environmental and health authorities

1. Each Party shall designate the authorities to be consulted which, by reason of their specific environmental or health responsibilities, are likely to be concerned by the environmental, including health, effects of the implementation of the plan or programme.

2. The draft plan or programme and the environmental report shall be made available to the authorities referred to in paragraph 1.

3. Each Party shall ensure that the authorities referred to in paragraph 1 are given, in an early, timely and effective manner, the opportunity to express their opinion on the draft plan or programme and the environmental report.

4. Each Party shall determine the detailed arrangements for informing and consulting the environmental and health authorities referred to in paragraph 1.

Article 10: Transboundary consultations

1. Where a Party of origin considers that the implementation of a plan or programme is likely to have significant transboundary environmental, including health, effects or where a Party likely to be significantly affected so requests, the Party of origin shall as early as possible before the adoption of the plan or programme notify the affected Party.

2. This notification shall contain, inter alia:

(a) The draft plan or programme and the environmental report including information on its possible transboundary environmental, including health, effects; and

(b) Information regarding the decision-making procedure, including an indication of a reasonable time schedule for the transmission of comments.

3. The affected Party shall, within the time specified in the notification, indicate to the Party of origin whether it wishes to enter into consultations before the adoption of the plan or programme and, if it so indicates, the Parties concerned shall enter into consultations concerning the likely transboundary environmental, including health, effects of implementing the plan or programme and the measures envisaged to prevent, reduce or mitigate adverse effects.

4. Where such consultations take place, the Parties concerned shall agree on detailed arrangements to ensure that the public concerned and the authorities referred to in article 9, paragraph 1, in the affected Party are informed and given an opportunity to forward their opinion on the draft plan or programme and the environmental report within a reasonable time frame.

Article 11: Decision

1. Each Party shall ensure that when a plan or programme is adopted due account is taken of:

(a) The conclusions of the environmental report;

(b) The measures to prevent, reduce or mitigate the adverse effects identified in the environmental report; and

(c) The comments received in accordance with articles 8 to 10.

2. Each Party shall ensure that, when a plan or programme is adopted, the public, the authorities referred to in article 9, paragraph 1, and the Parties consulted according to article 10 are informed, and that the plan or programme is made available to them together with a statement summarizing how the environmental, including health, considerations have been integrated into it, how the comments received in accordance with articles 8 to 10 have been taken into account and the reasons for adopting it in the light of the reasonable alternatives considered.

Article 12: Monitoring

1. Each Party shall monitor the significant environmental, including health, effects of the implementation of the plans and programmes, adopted under article 11 in

order, inter alia, to identify, at an early stage, unforeseen adverse effects and to be able to undertake appropriate remedial action.

2. The results of the monitoring undertaken shall be made available, in accordance with national legislation, to the authorities referred to in article 9, paragraph 1, and to the public.

Article 13: Policies and legislation

1. Each Party shall endeavour to ensure that environmental, including health, concerns are considered and integrated to the extent appropriate in the preparation of its proposals for policies and legislation that are likely to have significant effects on the environment, including health.

2. In applying paragraph 1, each Party shall consider the appropriate principles and elements of this Protocol.

3. Each Party shall determine, where appropriate, the practical arrangements for the consideration and integration of environmental, including health, concerns in accordance with paragraph 1, taking into account the need for transparency in decision-making.

4. Each Party shall report to the Meeting of the Parties to the Convention serving as the Meeting of the Parties to this Protocol on its application of this article.

[Articles 14-26 not reproduced]

Annex I: List of projects as referred to in Article 4, Paragraph 2; Annex II: Any other projects referred to in Article 4, Paragraph 2; Annex III: Criteria for determining of the likely significant environmental, including health, effects referred to in Article 5, Paragraph 1; Annex IV: Information referred to in Article 7, Paragraph 2; Annex V: Information referred to in Article 8, Paragraph 5 [not reproduced]

Environmental rights

Convention on Access to Information, Public Participation in Decision-Making and Access to Justice in Environmental Matters[4]

Adopted on 25 June 1998 at Århus. Entered into force on 30 October 2001. Source: Doc. ECE/CEP/43. Number of parties: 27. Further information: Secretariat (UNECE), Geneva, Switzerland, http://www.unece.org/env/pp

4 The review of compliance procedure for the Århus Convention is reproduced at p. 623.

The Parties to this Convention,

Recalling principle 1 of the Stockholm Declaration on the Human Environment,

Recalling also principle 10 of the Rio Declaration on Environment and Development,

Recalling further General Assembly resolutions 37/7 of 28 October 1982 on the World Charter for Nature and 45/94 of 14 December 1990 on the need to ensure a healthy environment for the well-being of individuals,

Recalling the European Charter on Environment and Health adopted at the First European Conference on Environment and Health of the World Health Organization in Frankfurt-am-Main, Germany, on 8 December 1989,

Affirming the need to protect, preserve and improve the state of the environment and to ensure sustainable and environmentally sound development,

Recognizing that adequate protection of the environment is essential to human well-being and the enjoyment of basic human rights, including the right to life itself,

Recognizing also that every person has the right to live in an environment adequate to his or her health and well-being, and the duty, both individually and in association with others, to protect and improve the environment for the benefit of present and future generations,

Considering that, to be able to assert this right and observe this duty, citizens must have access to information, be entitled to participate in decision-making and have access to justice in environmental matters, and acknowledging in this regard that citizens may need assistance in order to exercise their rights,

Recognizing that, in the field of the environment, improved access to information and public participation in decision-making enhance the quality and the implementation of decisions, contribute to public awareness of environmental issues, give the public the opportunity to express its concerns and enable public authorities to take due account of such concerns,

Aiming thereby to further the accountability of and transparency in decision-making and to strengthen public support for decisions on the environment,

Recognizing the desirability of transparency in all branches of government and inviting legislative bodies to implement the principles of this Convention in their proceedings,

Recognizing also that the public needs to be aware of the procedures for participation in environmental decision-making, have free access to them and know how to use them,

Recognizing further the importance of the respective roles that individual citizens, non-governmental organizations and the private sector can play in environmental protection,

Desiring to promote environmental education to further the understanding of the environment and sustainable development and to encourage widespread public awareness of, and participation in, decisions affecting the environment and sustainable development,

Noting, in this context, the importance of making use of the media and of electronic or other, future forms of communication,

Recognizing the importance of fully integrating environmental considerations in governmental decision-making and the consequent need for public authorities to be in possession of accurate, comprehensive and up-to-date environmental information,

Acknowledging that public authorities hold environmental information in the public interest,

Concerned that effective judicial mechanisms should be accessible to the public, including organizations, so that its legitimate interests are protected and the law is enforced,

Noting the importance of adequate product information being provided to consumers to enable them to make informed environmental choices,

Recognizing the concern of the public about the deliberate release of genetically modified organisms into the environment and the need for increased transparency and greater public participation in decision-making in this field,

Convinced that the implementation of this Convention will contribute to strengthening democracy in the region of the United Nations Economic Commission for Europe (ECE),

Conscious of the role played in this respect by ECE and recalling, *inter alia*, the ECE Guidelines on Access to Environmental Information and Public Participation in Environmental Decision-making endorsed in the Ministerial Declaration adopted at the Third Ministerial Conference 'Environment for Europe' in Sofia, Bulgaria, on 25 October 1995,

Bearing in mind the relevant provisions in the Convention on Environmental Impact Assessment in a Transboundary Context, done at Espoo, Finland, on 25 February 1991, and the Convention on the Transboundary Effects of Industrial Accidents and the Convention on the Protection and Use of Transboundary Watercourses and International Lakes, both done at Helsinki on 17 March 1992, and other regional conventions,

Conscious that the adoption of this Convention will have contributed to the further strengthening of the 'Environment for Europe' process and to the results of the Fourth Ministerial Conference in Aarhus, Denmark, in June 1998,

Have agreed as follows:

Article 1: Objective

In order to contribute to the protection of the right of every person of present and future generations to live in an environment adequate to his or her health and well-being, each Party shall guarantee the rights of access to information, public participation in decision-making, and access to justice in environmental matters in accordance with the provisions of this Convention.

Article 2: Definitions

For the purposes of this Convention,

1. 'Party' means, unless the text otherwise indicates, a Contracting Party to this Convention;

2. 'Public authority' means:

(a) Government at national, regional and other level;

(b) Natural or legal persons performing public administrative functions under national law, including specific duties, activities or services in relation to the environment;

(c) Any other natural or legal persons having public responsibilities or functions, or providing public services, in relation to the environment, under the control of a body or person falling within subparagraphs (a) or (b) above;

(d) The institutions of any regional economic integration organization referred to in article 17 which is a Party to this Convention.

This definition does not include bodies or institutions acting in a judicial or legislative capacity;

3. 'Environmental information' means any information in written, visual, aural, electronic or any other material form on:

(a) The state of elements of the environment, such as air and atmosphere, water, soil, land, landscape and natural sites, biological diversity and its components, including genetically modified organisms, and the interaction among these elements;

(b) Factors, such as substances, energy, noise and radiation, and activities or measures, including administrative measures, environmental agreements, policies, legislation, plans and programmes, affecting or likely to affect the elements of the environment within the scope of subparagraph (a) above, and cost-benefit and other economic analyses and assumptions used in environmental decision-making;

(c) The state of human health and safety, conditions of human life, cultural sites and built structures, inasmuch as they are or may be affected by the state of the elements of the environment or, through these elements, by the factors, activities or measures referred to in subparagraph (b) above;

4. 'The public' means one or more natural or legal persons, and, in accordance with national legislation or practice, their associations, organizations or groups;

5. 'The public concerned' means the public affected or likely to be affected by, or having an interest in, the environmental decision-making; for the purposes of this definition, non-governmental organizations promoting environmental protection and meeting any requirements under national law shall be deemed to have an interest.

Article 3: General provisions

1. Each Party shall take the necessary legislative, regulatory and other measures, including measures to achieve compatibility between the provisions implementing the information, public participation and access-to-justice provisions in this Convention, as well as proper enforcement measures, to establish and maintain a clear, transparent and consistent framework to implement the provisions of this Convention.

2. Each Party shall endeavour to ensure that officials and authorities assist and provide guidance to the public in seeking access to information, in facilitating participation in decision-making and in seeking access to justice in environmental matters.

3. Each Party shall promote environmental education and environmental awareness among the public, especially on how to obtain access to information, to participate in decision-making and to obtain access to justice in environmental matters.

4. Each Party shall provide for appropriate recognition of and support to associations, organizations or groups promoting environmental protection and ensure that its national legal system is consistent with this obligation.

5. The provisions of this Convention shall not affect the right of a Party to maintain or introduce measures providing for broader access to information, more extensive public participation in decision-making and wider access to justice in environmental matters than required by this Convention.

6. This Convention shall not require any derogation from existing rights of access to information, public participation in decision-making and access to justice in environmental matters.

7. Each Party shall promote the application of the principles of this Convention in international environmental decision-making processes and within the framework of international organizations in matters relating to the environment.

8. Each Party shall ensure that persons exercising their rights in conformity with the provisions of this Convention shall not be penalized, persecuted or harassed in any way for their involvement. This provision shall not affect the powers of national courts to award reasonable costs in judicial proceedings.

9. Within the scope of the relevant provisions of this Convention, the public shall have access to information, have the possibility to participate in decision-making and have access to justice in environmental matters without discrimination as to citizenship, nationality or domicile and, in the case of a legal person, without discrimination as to where it has its registered seat or an effective centre of its activities.

Article 4: Access to environmental information

1. Each Party shall ensure that, subject to the following paragraphs of this article, public authorities, in response to a request for environmental information, make

such information available to the public, within the framework of national legislation, including, where requested and subject to subparagraph (b) below, copies of the actual documentation containing or comprising such information:

(a) Without an interest having to be stated;

(b) In the form requested unless:

 (i) It is reasonable for the public authority to make it available in another form, in which case reasons shall be given for making it available in that form; or

 (ii) The information is already publicly available in another form.

2. The environmental information referred to in paragraph 1 above shall be made available as soon as possible and at the latest within one month after the request has been submitted, unless the volume and the complexity of the information justify an extension of this period up to two months after the request. The applicant shall be informed of any extension and of the reasons justifying it.

3. A request for environmental information may be refused if:

(a) The public authority to which the request is addressed does not hold the environmental information requested;

(b) The request is manifestly unreasonable or formulated in too general a manner; or

(c) The request concerns material in the course of completion or concerns internal communications of public authorities where such an exemption is provided for in national law or customary practice, taking into account the public interest served by disclosure.

4. A request for environmental information may be refused if the disclosure would adversely affect:

(a) The confidentiality of the proceedings of public authorities, where such confidentiality is provided for under national law;

(b) International relations, national defence or public security;

(c) The course of justice, the ability of a person to receive a fair trial or the ability of a public authority to conduct an enquiry of a criminal or disciplinary nature;

(d) The confidentiality of commercial and industrial information, where such confidentiality is protected by law in order to protect a legitimate economic interest. Within this framework, information on emissions which is relevant for the protection of the environment shall be disclosed;

(e) Intellectual property rights;

(f) The confidentiality of personal data and/or files relating to a natural person where that person has not consented to the disclosure of the information to the public, where such confidentiality is provided for in national law;

(g) The interests of a third party which has supplied the information requested without that party being under or capable of being put under a legal obligation to do so, and where that party does not consent to the release of the material; or

(h) The environment to which the information relates, such as the breeding sites of rare species.

The aforementioned grounds for refusal shall be interpreted in a restrictive way, taking into account the public interest served by disclosure and taking into account whether the information requested relates to emissions into the environment.

5. Where a public authority does not hold the environmental information requested, this public authority shall, as promptly as possible, inform the applicant of the public authority to which it believes it is possible to apply for the information requested or transfer the request to that authority and inform the applicant accordingly.

6. Each Party shall ensure that, if information exempted from disclosure under paragraphs 3 (c) and 4 above can be separated out without prejudice to the confidentiality of the information exempted, public authorities make available the remainder of the environmental information that has been requested.

7. A refusal of a request shall be in writing if the request was in writing or the applicant so requests. A refusal shall state the reasons for the refusal and give information on access to the review procedure provided for in accordance with article 9. The refusal shall be made as soon as possible and at the latest within one month, unless the complexity of the information justifies an extension of this period up to two months after the request. The applicant shall be informed of any extension and of the reasons justifying it.

8. Each Party may allow its public authorities to make a charge for supplying information, but such charge shall not exceed a reasonable amount. Public authorities intending to make such a charge for supplying information shall make available to applicants a schedule of charges which may be levied, indicating the circumstances in which they may be levied or waived and when the supply of information is conditional on the advance payment of such a charge.

Article 5: Collection and dissemination of environmental information

1. Each Party shall ensure that:

(a) Public authorities possess and update environmental information which is relevant to their functions;

(b) Mandatory systems are established so that there is an adequate flow of information to public authorities about proposed and existing activities which may significantly affect the environment;

(c) In the event of any imminent threat to human health or the environment, whether caused by human activities or due to natural causes, all information which could enable the public to take measures to prevent or mitigate harm arising from the threat and is held by a public authority is disseminated immediately and without delay to members of the public who may be affected.

2. Each Party shall ensure that, within the framework of national legislation, the way in which public authorities make environmental information available to the public is transparent and that environmental information is effectively accessible, inter alia, by:

(a) Providing sufficient information to the public about the type and scope of environmental information held by the relevant public authorities, the basic terms and conditions under which such information is made available and accessible, and the process by which it can be obtained;
(b) Establishing and maintaining practical arrangements, such as:
 i) Publicly accessible lists, registers or files;
 ii) Requiring officials to support the public in seeking access to information under this Convention; and
 iii) The identification of points of contact; and
(c) Providing access to the environmental information contained in lists, registers or files as referred to in subparagraph (b) (i) above free of charge.

3. Each Party shall ensure that environmental information progressively becomes available in electronic databases which are easily accessible to the public through public telecommunications networks. Information accessible in this form should include:
(a) Reports on the state of the environment, as referred to in paragraph 4 below;
(b) Texts of legislation on or relating to the environment;
(c) As appropriate, policies, plans and programmes on or relating to the environment, and environmental agreements; and
(d) Other information, to the extent that the availability of such information in this form would facilitate the application of national law implementing this Convention,

provided that such information is already available in electronic form.

4. Each Party shall, at regular intervals not exceeding three or four years, publish and disseminate a national report on the state of the environment, including information on the quality of the environment and information on pressures on the environment.

5. Each Party shall take measures within the framework of its legislation for the purpose of disseminating, *inter alia*:
(a) Legislation and policy documents such as documents on strategies, policies, programmes and action plans relating to the environment, and progress reports on their implementation, prepared at various levels of government;
(b) International treaties, conventions and agreements on environmental issues; and
(c) Other significant international documents on environmental issues, as appropriate.

6. Each Party shall encourage operators whose activities have a significant impact on the environment to inform the public regularly of the environmental impact of their activities and products, where appropriate within the framework of voluntary eco-labelling or eco-auditing schemes or by other means.

7. Each Party shall:
(a) Publish the facts and analyses of facts which it considers relevant and important in framing major environmental policy proposals;

(b) Publish, or otherwise make accessible, available explanatory material on its dealings with the public in matters falling within the scope of this Convention; and

(c) Provide in an appropriate form information on the performance of public functions or the provision of public services relating to the environment by government at all levels.

8. Each Party shall develop mechanisms with a view to ensuring that sufficient product information is made available to the public in a manner which enables consumers to make informed environmental choices.

9. Each Party shall take steps to establish progressively, taking into account international processes where appropriate, a coherent, nationwide system of pollution inventories or registers on a structured, computerized and publicly accessible database compiled through standardized reporting. Such a system may include inputs, releases and transfers of a specified range of substances and products, including water, energy and resource use, from a specified range of activities to environmental media and to on-site and off-site treatment and disposal sites.

10. Nothing in this article may prejudice the right of Parties to refuse to disclose certain environmental information in accordance with article 4, paragraphs 3 and 4.

Article 6: Public participation in decisions on specific activities

1. Each Party:

(a) Shall apply the provisions of this article with respect to decisions on whether to permit proposed activities listed in annex I;

(b) Shall, in accordance with its national law, also apply the provisions of this article to decisions on proposed activities not listed in annex I which may have a significant effect on the environment. To this end, Parties shall determine whether such a proposed activity is subject to these provisions; and

(c) May decide, on a case-by-case basis if so provided under national law, not to apply the provisions of this article to proposed activities serving national defence purposes, if that Party deems that such application would have an adverse effect on these purposes.

2. The public concerned shall be informed, either by public notice or individually as appropriate, early in an environmental decision-making procedure, and in an adequate, timely and effective manner, *inter alia*, of:

(a) The proposed activity and the application on which a decision will be taken;

(b) The nature of possible decisions or the draft decision;

(c) The public authority responsible for making the decision;

(d) The envisaged procedure, including, as and when this information can be provided:

 i) The commencement of the procedure;

 ii) The opportunities for the public to participate;

 iii) The time and venue of any envisaged public hearing;

iv) An indication of the public authority from which relevant information can be obtained and where the relevant information has been deposited for examination by the public;

v) An indication of the relevant public authority or any other official body to which comments or questions can be submitted and of the time schedule for transmittal of comments or questions; and

vi) An indication of what environmental information relevant to the proposed activity is available; and

(e) The fact that the activity is subject to a national or transboundary environmental impact assessment procedure.

3. The public participation procedures shall include reasonable time-frames for the different phases, allowing sufficient time for informing the public in accordance with paragraph 2 above and for the public to prepare and participate effectively during the environmental decision-making.

4. Each Party shall provide for early public participation, when all options are open and effective public participation can take place.

5. Each Party should, where appropriate, encourage prospective applicants to identify the public concerned, to enter into discussions, and to provide information regarding the objectives of their application before applying for a permit.

6. Each Party shall require the competent public authorities to give the public concerned access for examination, upon request where so required under national law, free of charge and as soon as it becomes available, to all information relevant to the decision-making referred to in this article that is available at the time of the public participation procedure, without prejudice to the right of Parties to refuse to disclose certain information in accordance with article 4, paragraphs 3 and 4. The relevant information shall include at least, and without prejudice to the provisions of article 4:

(a) A description of the site and the physical and technical characteristics of the proposed activity, including an estimate of the expected residues and emissions;

(b) A description of the significant effects of the proposed activity on the environment;

(c) A description of the measures envisaged to prevent and/or reduce the effects, including emissions;

(d) A non-technical summary of the above;

(e) An outline of the main alternatives studied by the applicant; and

(f) In accordance with national legislation, the main reports and advice issued to the public authority at the time when the public concerned shall be informed in accordance with paragraph 2 above.

7. Procedures for public participation shall allow the public to submit, in writing or, as appropriate, at a public hearing or inquiry with the applicant, any comments, information, analyses or opinions that it considers relevant to the proposed activity.

8. Each Party shall ensure that in the decision due account is taken of the outcome of the public participation.

9. Each Party shall ensure that, when the decision has been taken by the public authority, the public is promptly informed of the decision in accordance with the appropriate procedures. Each Party shall make accessible to the public the text of the decision along with the reasons and considerations on which the decision is based.

10. Each Party shall ensure that, when a public authority reconsiders or updates the operating conditions for an activity referred to in paragraph 1, the provisions of paragraphs 2 to 9 of this article are applied *mutatis mutandis*, and where appropriate.

11. Each Party shall, within the framework of its national law, apply, to the extent feasible and appropriate, provisions of this article to decisions on whether to permit the deliberate release of genetically modified organisms into the environment.

Article 7: Public participation concerning plans, programmes and policies relating to the environment

Each Party shall make appropriate practical and/or other provisions for the public to participate during the preparation of plans and programmes relating to the environment, within a transparent and fair framework, having provided the necessary information to the public. Within this framework, article 6, paragraphs 3, 4 and 8, shall be applied. The public which may participate shall be identified by the relevant public authority, taking into account the objectives of this Convention. To the extent appropriate, each Party shall endeavour to provide opportunities for public participation in the preparation of policies relating to the environment.

Article 8: Public participation during the preparation of executive regulations and/or generally applicable legally binding normative instruments

Each Party shall strive to promote effective public participation at an appropriate stage, and while options are still open, during the preparation by public authorities of executive regulations and other generally applicable legally binding rules that may have a significant effect on the environment. To this end, the following steps should be taken:

(a) Time-frames sufficient for effective participation should be fixed;

(b) Draft rules should be published or otherwise made publicly available; and

(c) The public should be given the opportunity to comment, directly or through representative consultative bodies.

The result of the public participation shall be taken into account as far as possible.

Article 9: Access to justice

1. Each Party shall, within the framework of its national legislation, ensure that any person who considers that his or her request for information under article 4 has been ignored, wrongfully refused, whether in part or in full, inadequately answered,

or otherwise not dealt with in accordance with the provisions of that article, has access to a review procedure before a court of law or another independent and impartial body established by law.

In the circumstances where a Party provides for such a review by a court of law, it shall ensure that such a person also has access to an expeditious procedure established by law that is free of charge or inexpensive for reconsideration by a public authority or review by an independent and impartial body other than a court of law.

Final decisions under this paragraph 1 shall be binding on the public authority holding the information. Reasons shall be stated in writing, at least where access to information is refused under this paragraph.

2. Each Party shall, within the framework of its national legislation, ensure that members of the public concerned

(a) Having a sufficient interest or, alternatively,

(b) Maintaining impairment of a right, where the administrative procedural law of a Party requires this as a precondition, have access to a review procedure before a court of law and/or another independent and impartial body established by law, to challenge the substantive and procedural legality of any decision, act or omission subject to the provisions of article 6 and, where so provided for under national law and without prejudice to paragraph 3 below, of other relevant provisions of this Convention.

What constitutes a sufficient interest and impairment of a right shall be determined in accordance with the requirements of national law and consistently with the objective of giving the public concerned wide access to justice within the scope of this Convention. To this end, the interest of any non-governmental organization meeting the requirements referred to in article 2, paragraph 5, shall be deemed sufficient for the purpose of subparagraph (a) above. Such organizations shall also be deemed to have rights capable of being impaired for the purpose of subparagraph (b) above.

The provisions of this paragraph 2 shall not exclude the possibility of a preliminary review procedure before an administrative authority and shall not affect the requirement of exhaustion of administrative review procedures prior to recourse to judicial review procedures, where such a requirement exists under national law.

3. In addition and without prejudice to the review procedures referred to in paragraphs 1 and 2 above, each Party shall ensure that, where they meet the criteria, if any, laid down in its national law, members of the public have access to administrative or judicial procedures to challenge acts and omissions by private persons and public authorities which contravene provisions of its national law relating to the environment.

4. In addition and without prejudice to paragraph 1 above, the procedures referred to in paragraphs 1, 2 and 3 above shall provide adequate and effective remedies, including injunctive relief as appropriate, and be fair, equitable, timely and not

prohibitively expensive. Decisions under this article shall be given or recorded in writing. Decisions of courts, and whenever possible of other bodies, shall be publicly accessible.

5. In order to further the effectiveness of the provisions of this article, each Party shall ensure that information is provided to the public on access to administrative and judicial review procedures and shall consider the establishment of appropriate assistance mechanisms to remove or reduce financial and other barriers to access to justice.

Article 10: Meeting of the Parties

1. The first meeting of the Parties shall be convened no later than one year after the date of the entry into force of this Convention. Thereafter, an ordinary meeting of the Parties shall be held at least once every two years, unless otherwise decided by the Parties, or at the written request of any Party, provided that, within six months of the request being communicated to all Parties by the Executive Secretary of the Economic Commission for Europe, the said request is supported by at least one third of the Parties.

2. At their meetings, the Parties shall keep under continuous review the implementation of this Convention on the basis of regular reporting by the Parties, and, with this purpose in mind, shall:

(a) Review the policies for and legal and methodological approaches to access to information, public participation in decision-making and access to justice in environmental matters, with a view to further improving them;
(b) Exchange information regarding experience gained in concluding and implementing bilateral and multilateral agreements or other arrangements having relevance to the purposes of this Convention and to which one or more of the Parties are a party;
(c) Seek, where appropriate, the services of relevant ECE bodies and other competent international bodies and specific committees in all aspects pertinent to the achievement of the purposes of this Convention;
(d) Establish any subsidiary bodies as they deem necessary;
(e) Prepare, where appropriate, protocols to this Convention;
(f) Consider and adopt proposals for amendments to this Convention in accordance with the provisions of article 14;
(g) Consider and undertake any additional action that may be required for the achievement of the purposes of this Convention;
(h) At their first meeting, consider and by consensus adopt rules of procedure for their meetings and the meetings of subsidiary bodies;
(i) At their first meeting, review their experience in implementing the provisions of article 5, paragraph 9, and consider what steps are necessary to develop further the system referred to in that paragraph, taking into account international processes and developments, including the elaboration of an appropriate instrument concerning pollution release and transfer registers or inventories which could be annexed to this Convention.

3. The Meeting of the Parties may, as necessary, consider establishing financial arrangements on a consensus basis.

4. The United Nations, its specialized agencies and the International Atomic Energy Agency, as well as any State or regional economic integration organization entitled under article 17 to sign this Convention but which is not a Party to this Convention, and any intergovernmental organization qualified in the fields to which this Convention relates, shall be entitled to participate as observers in the meetings of the Parties.

5. Any non-governmental organization, qualified in the fields to which this Convention relates, which has informed the Executive Secretary of the Economic Commission for Europe of its wish to be represented at a meeting of the Parties shall be entitled to participate as an observer unless at least one third of the Parties present in the meeting raise objections.

6. For the purposes of paragraphs 4 and 5 above, the rules of procedure referred to in paragraph 2 (h) above shall provide for practical arrangements for the admittance procedure and other relevant terms.

Article 11: Right to vote

1. Except as provided for in paragraph 2 below, each Party to this Convention shall have one vote.

2. Regional economic integration organizations, in matters within their competence, shall exercise their right to vote with a number of votes equal to the number of their member States which are Parties to this Convention. Such organizations shall not exercise their right to vote if their member States exercise theirs, and vice versa.

Article 12: Secretariat

The Executive Secretary of the Economic Commission for Europe shall carry out the following secretariat functions:

(a) The convening and preparing of meetings of the Parties;

(b) The transmission to the Parties of reports and other information received in accordance with the provisions of this Convention; and

(c) Such other functions as may be determined by the Parties.

Article 13: Annexes

The annexes to this Convention shall constitute an integral part thereof.

Article 14: Amendments to the Convention

1. Any Party may propose amendments to this Convention.

2. The text of any proposed amendment to this Convention shall be submitted in writing to the Executive Secretary of the Economic Commission for Europe, who shall communicate it to all Parties at least ninety days before the meeting of the Parties at which it is proposed for adoption.

3. The Parties shall make every effort to reach agreement on any proposed amendment to this Convention by consensus. If all efforts at consensus have been exhausted, and no agreement reached, the amendment shall as a last resort be adopted by a three-fourths majority vote of the Parties present and voting at the meeting.

4. Amendments to this Convention adopted in accordance with paragraph 3 above shall be communicated by the Depositary to all Parties for ratification, approval or acceptance. Amendments to this Convention other than those to an annex shall enter into force for Parties having ratified, approved or accepted them on the ninetieth day after the receipt by the Depositary of notification of their ratification, approval or acceptance by at least three fourths of these Parties. Thereafter they shall enter into force for any other Party on the ninetieth day after that Party deposits its instrument of ratification, approval or acceptance of the amendments.

5. Any Party that is unable to approve an amendment to an annex to this Convention shall so notify the Depositary in writing within twelve months from the date of the communication of the adoption. The Depositary shall without delay notify all Parties of any such notification received. A Party may at any time substitute an acceptance for its previous notification and, upon deposit of an instrument of acceptance with the Depositary, the amendments to such an annex shall become effective for that Party.

6. On the expiry of twelve months from the date of its communication by the Depositary as provided for in paragraph 4 above an amendment to an annex shall become effective for those Parties which have not submitted a notification to the Depositary in accordance with the provisions of paragraph 5 above, provided that not more than one third of the Parties have submitted such a notification.

7. For the purposes of this article, 'Parties present and voting' means Parties present and casting an affirmative or negative vote.

Article 15: Review of compliance

The Meeting of the Parties shall establish, on a consensus basis, optional arrangements of a non-confrontational, non-judicial and consultative nature for reviewing compliance with the provisions of this Convention. These arrangements shall allow for appropriate public involvement and may include the option of considering communications from members of the public on matters related to this Convention.

Article 16: Settlement of disputes

1. If a dispute arises between two or more Parties about the interpretation or application of this Convention, they shall seek a solution by negotiation or by any other means of dispute settlement acceptable to the parties to the dispute.

2. When signing, ratifying, accepting, approving or acceding to this Convention, or at any time thereafter, a Party may declare in writing to the Depositary that, for a dispute not resolved in accordance with paragraph 1 above, it accepts one or both

of the following means of dispute settlement as compulsory in relation to any Party accepting the same obligation:

(a) Submission of the dispute to the International Court of Justice;

(b) Arbitration in accordance with the procedure set out in annex II.

3. If the parties to the dispute have accepted both means of dispute settlement referred to in paragraph 2 above, the dispute may be submitted only to the International Court of Justice, unless the parties agree otherwise.

Article 17: Signature

This Convention shall be open for signature at Aarhus (Denmark) on 25 June 1998, and thereafter at United Nations Headquarters in New York until 21 December 1998, by States members of the Economic Commission for Europe as well as States having consultative status with the Economic Commission for Europe pursuant to paragraphs 8 and 11 of Economic and Social Council resolution 36 (IV) of 28 March 1947, and by regional economic integration organizations constituted by sovereign States members of the Economic Commission for Europe to which their member States have transferred competence over matters governed by this Convention, including the competence to enter into treaties in respect of these matters.

Article 18: Depositary

The Secretary-General of the United Nations shall act as the Depositary of this Convention.

Article 19: Ratification, acceptance, approval and accession

1. This Convention shall be subject to ratification, acceptance or approval by signatory States and regional economic integration organizations.

2. This Convention shall be open for accession as from 22 December 1998 by the States and regional economic integration organizations referred to in article 17.

3. Any other State, not referred to in paragraph 2 above, that is a Member of the United Nations may accede to the Convention upon approval by the Meeting of the Parties.

4. Any organization referred to in article 17 which becomes a Party to this Convention without any of its member States being a Party shall be bound by all the obligations under this Convention. If one or more of such an organization's member States is a Party to this Convention, the organization and its member States shall decide on their respective responsibilities for the performance of their obligations under this Convention. In such cases, the organization and the member States shall not be entitled to exercise rights under this Convention concurrently.

5. In their instruments of ratification, acceptance, approval or accession, the regional economic integration organizations referred to in article 17 shall declare the extent of their competence with respect to the matters governed by this Convention. These organizations shall also inform the Depositary of any substantial modification to the extent of their competence.

Article 20: Entry into force

1. This Convention shall enter into force on the ninetieth day after the date of deposit of the sixteenth instrument of ratification, acceptance, approval or accession.

2. For the purposes of paragraph 1 above, any instrument deposited by a regional economic integration organization shall not be counted as additional to those deposited by States members of such an organization.

3. For each State or organization referred to in article 17 which ratifies, accepts or approves this Convention or accedes thereto after the deposit of the sixteenth instrument of ratification, acceptance, approval or accession, the Convention shall enter into force on the ninetieth day after the date of deposit by such State or organization of its instrument of ratification, acceptance, approval or accession.

Article 21: Withdrawal

At any time after three years from the date on which this Convention has come into force with respect to a Party, that Party may withdraw from the Convention by giving written notification to the Depositary. Any such withdrawal shall take effect on the ninetieth day after the date of its receipt by the Depositary.

Article 22: Authentic texts

The original of this Convention, of which the English, French and Russian texts are equally authentic, shall be deposited with the Secretary-General of the United Nations.

In witness whereof the undersigned, being duly authorized thereto, have signed this Convention.

Done at Aarhus (Denmark), this twenty-fifth day of June, one thousand nine hundred and ninety-eight.

Annex I: List of activities referred to in Article 6, Paragraph 1 (a); Annex II: Arbitration [not reproduced]

Protocol on Pollutant Release and Transfer Registers

Adopted on 21 May 2003 at Kiev. Not in force (no ratifications). Source: Doc. MP.PP/2003/1. Further information: Århus Convention Secretariat (UNECE), Geneva, Switzerland, http://www.unece.org/env/pp

The Parties to this Protocol,

Recalling article 5, paragraph 9, and article 10, paragraph 2, of the 1998 Convention on Access to Information, Public Participation in Decision-making and Access to Justice in Environmental Matters (the Aarhus Convention),

Recognizing that pollutant release and transfer registers provide an important mechanism to increase corporate accountability, reduce pollution and promote sustainable development, as stated in the Lucca Declaration adopted at the first meeting of the Parties to the Aarhus Convention,

Having regard to principle 10 of the 1992 Rio Declaration on Environment and Development,

Having regard also to the principles and commitments agreed to at the 1992 United Nations Conference on Environment and Development, in particular the provisions in chapter 19 of Agenda 21,

Taking note of the Programme for the Further Implementation of Agenda 21, adopted by the General Assembly of the United Nations at its nineteenth special session, 1997, in which it called for, inter alia, enhanced national capacities and capabilities for information collection, processing and dissemination, to facilitate public access to information on global environmental issues through appropriate means,

Having regard to the Plan of Implementation of the 2002 World Summit on Sustainable Development, which encourages the development of coherent, integrated information on chemicals, such as through national pollutant release and transfer registers,

Taking into account the work of the Intergovernmental Forum on Chemical Safety, in particular the 2000 Bahia Declaration on Chemical Safety, the Priorities for Action Beyond 2000 and the Pollutant Release and Transfer Register/Emission Inventory Action Plan,

Taking into account also the activities undertaken within the framework of the Inter-Organization Programme for the Sound Management of Chemicals,

Taking into account furthermore the work of the Organisation for Economic Co-operation and Development, in particular its Council Recommendation on Implementing Pollutant Release and Transfer Registers, in which the Council calls upon member countries to establish and make publicly available national pollutant release and transfer registers,

Wishing to provide a mechanism contributing to the ability of every person of present and future generations to live in an environment adequate to his or her health and well-being, by ensuring the development of publicly accessible environmental information systems,

Wishing also to ensure that the development of such systems takes into account principles contributing to sustainable development such as the precautionary approach set forth in principle 15 of the 1992 Rio Declaration on Environment and Development,

Recognizing the link between adequate environmental information systems and the exercise of the rights contained in the Aarhus Convention,

Noting the need for cooperation with other international initiatives concerning pollutants and waste, including the 2001 Stockholm Convention on Persistent Organic Pollutants and the 1989 Basel Convention on the Control of Transboundary Movements of Hazardous Wastes and their Disposal,

Recognising that the objectives of an integrated approach to minimizing pollution and the amount of waste resulting from the operation of industrial installations and other sources are to achieve a high level of protection for the environment as a whole, to move towards sustainable and environmentally sound development and to protect the health of present and future generations,

Convinced of the value of pollutant release and transfer registers as a cost-effective tool for encouraging improvements in environmental performance, for providing public access to information on pollutants released into and transferred in and through communities, and for use by Governments in tracking trends, demonstrating progress in pollution reduction, monitoring compliance with certain international agreements, setting priorities and evaluating progress achieved through environmental policies and programmes,

Believing that pollutant release and transfer registers can bring tangible benefits to industry through the improved management of pollutants,

Noting the opportunities for using data from pollutant release and transfer registers, combined with health, environmental, demographic, economic or other types of relevant information, for the purpose of gaining a better understanding of potential problems, identifying 'hot spots', taking preventive and mitigating measures, and setting environmental management priorities,

Recognizing the importance of protecting the privacy of identified or identifiable natural persons in the processing of information reported to pollutant release and transfer registers in accordance with applicable international standards relating to data protection,

Recognizing also the importance of developing internationally compatible national pollutant release and transfer register systems to increase the comparability of data,

Noting that many member States of the United Nations Economic Commission for Europe, the European Community and the Parties to the North American Free Trade Agreement are acting to collect data on pollutant releases and transfers from various sources and to make these data publicly accessible, and recognizing especially in this area the long and valuable experience in certain countries,

Taking into account the different approaches in existing emission registers and the need to avoid duplication, and recognizing therefore that a certain degree of flexibility is needed,

Urging the progressive development of national pollutant release and transfer registers,

Urging also the establishment of links between national pollutant release and transfer registers and information systems on other releases of public concern,

Have agreed as follows:

Article 1: Objective

The objective of this Protocol is to enhance public access to information through the establishment of coherent, integrated, nationwide pollutant release and transfer registers (PRTRs) in accordance with the provisions of this Protocol, which could facilitate public participation in environmental decision-making as well as contribute to the prevention and reduction of pollution of the environment.

Article 2: Definitions

For the purposes of this Protocol,

1. 'Party' means, unless the text indicates otherwise, a State or a regional economic integration organization referred to in article 24 which has consented to be bound by this Protocol and for which the Protocol is in force;

2. 'Convention' means the Convention on Access to Information, Public Participation in Decision-making and Access to Justice in Environmental Matters, done at Aarhus, Denmark, on 25 June 1998;

3. 'The public' means one or more natural or legal persons, and, in accordance with national legislation or practice, their associations, organizations or groups;

4. 'Facility' means one or more installations on the same site, or on adjoining sites, that are owned or operated by the same natural or legal person;

5. 'Competent authority' means the national authority or authorities, or any other competent body or bodies, designated by a Party to manage a national pollutant release and transfer register system;

6. 'Pollutant' means a substance or a group of substances that may be harmful to the environment or to human health on account of its properties and of its introduction into the environment;

7. 'Release' means any introduction of pollutants into the environment as a result of any human activity, whether deliberate or accidental, routine or non-routine, including spilling, emitting, discharging, injecting, disposing or dumping, or through sewer systems without final waste-water treatment;

8. 'Off-site transfer' means the movement beyond the boundaries of the facility of either pollutants or waste destined for disposal or recovery and of pollutants in waste water destined for waste-water treatment;

9. 'Diffuse sources' means the many smaller or scattered sources from which pollutants may be released to land, air or water, whose combined impact on those media may be significant and for which it is impractical to collect reports from each individual source;

10. The terms 'national' and 'nationwide' shall, with respect to the obligations under the Protocol on Parties that are regional economic integration organizations, be construed as applying to the region in question unless otherwise indicated;

11. 'Waste' means substances or objects which are:

(a) Disposed of or recovered;

(b) Intended to be disposed of or recovered; or

(c) Required by the provisions of national law to be disposed of or recovered;

12. 'Hazardous waste' means waste that is defined as hazardous by the provisions of national law;

13. 'Other waste' means waste that is not hazardous waste;

14. 'Waste water' means used water containing substances or objects that is subject to regulation by national law.

Article 3: General provisions

1. Each Party shall take the necessary legislative, regulatory and other measures, and appropriate enforcement measures, to implement the provisions of this Protocol.

2. The provisions of this Protocol shall not affect the right of a Party to maintain or introduce a more extensive or more publicly accessible pollutant release and transfer register than required by this Protocol.

3. Each Party shall take the necessary measures to require that employees of a facility and members of the public who report a violation by a facility of national laws implementing this Protocol to public authorities are not penalized, persecuted or harassed by that facility or public authorities for their actions in reporting the violation.

4. In the implementation of this Protocol, each Party shall be guided by the precautionary approach as set forth in principle 15 of the 1992 Rio Declaration on Environment and Development.

5. To reduce duplicative reporting, pollutant release and transfer register systems may be integrated to the degree practicable with existing information sources such as reporting mechanisms under licences or operating permits.

6. Parties shall strive to achieve convergence among national pollutant release and transfer registers.

Article 4: Core elements of a pollutant release and transfer register system

In accordance with this Protocol, each Party shall establish and maintain a publicly accessible national pollutant release and transfer register that:

(a) Is facility-specific with respect to reporting on point sources;

(b) Accommodates reporting on diffuse sources;

(c) Is pollutant-specific or waste-specific, as appropriate;

(d) Is multimedia, distinguishing among releases to air, land and water;

(e) Includes information on transfers;

(f) Is based on mandatory reporting on a periodic basis;

(g) Includes standardized and timely data, a limited number of standardized reporting thresholds and limited provisions, if any, for confidentiality;

(h) Is coherent and designed to be user-friendly and publicly accessible, including in electronic form;

(i) Allows for public participation in its development and modification; and

(j) Is a structured, computerized database or several linked databases maintained by the competent authority.

Article 5: Design and structure

1. Each Party shall ensure that the data held on the register referred to in article 4 are presented in both aggregated and non-aggregated forms, so that releases and transfers can be searched and identified according to:
(a) Facility and its geographical location;
(b) Activity;
(c) Owner or operator, and, as appropriate, company;
(d) Pollutant or waste, as appropriate;
(e) Each of the environmental media into which the pollutant is released; and
(f) As specified in article 7, paragraph 5, the destination of the transfer and, where appropriate, the disposal or recovery operation for waste.

2. Each Party shall also ensure that the data can be searched and identified according to those diffuse sources which have been included in the register.

3. Each Party shall design its register taking into account the possibility of its future expansion and ensuring that the reporting data from at least the ten previous reporting years are publicly accessible.

4. The register shall be designed for maximum ease of public access through electronic means, such as the Internet. The design shall allow that, under normal operating conditions, the information on the register is continuously and immediately available through electronic means.

5. Each Party should provide links in its register to its relevant existing, publicly accessible databases on subject matters related to environmental protection.

6. Each Party shall provide links in its register to the pollutant release and transfer registers of other Parties to the Protocol and, where feasible, to those of other countries.

Article 6: Scope of the register

1. Each Party shall ensure that its register includes the information on:
(a) Releases of pollutants required to be reported under article 7, paragraph 2;
(b) Off-site transfers required to be reported under article 7, paragraph 2; and
(c) Releases of pollutants from diffuse sources required under article 7, paragraph 4.

2. Having assessed the experience gained from the development of national pollutant release and transfer registers and the implementation of this Protocol, and taking into account relevant international processes, the Meeting of the Parties shall review the reporting requirements under this Protocol and shall consider the following issues in its further development:

(a) Revision of the activities specified in annex I;
(b) Revision of the pollutants specified in annex II;
(c) Revision of the thresholds in annexes I and II; and
(d) Inclusion of other relevant aspects such as information on on-site transfers, storage, the specification of reporting requirements for diffuse sources or the development of criteria for including pollutants under this Protocol.

Article 7: Reporting requirements

1. Each Party shall either:

(a) Require the owner or the operator of each individual facility within its jurisdiction that undertakes one or more of the activities specified in annex I above the applicable capacity threshold specified in annex I, column 1, and:
   i) Releases any pollutant specified in annex II in quantities exceeding the applicable thresholds specified in annex II, column 1;
   ii) Transfers off-site any pollutant specified in annex II in quantities exceeding the applicable threshold specified in annex II, column 2, where the Party has opted for pollutant-specific reporting of transfers pursuant to paragraph 5 (d);
   iii) Transfers off-site hazardous waste exceeding 2 tons per year or other waste exceeding 2,000 tons per year, where the Party has opted for waste-specific reporting of transfers pursuant to paragraph 5 (d); or
   iv) Transfers off-site any pollutant specified in annex II in waste water destined for waste-water treatment in quantities exceeding the applicable threshold specified in annex II, column 1b;

to undertake the obligation imposed on that owner or operator pursuant to paragraph 2; or

(b) Require the owner or the operator of each individual facility within its jurisdiction that undertakes one or more of the activities specified in annex I at or above the employee threshold specified in annex I, column 2, and manufactures, processes or uses any pollutant specified in annex II in quantities exceeding the applicable threshold specified in annex II, column 3, to undertake the obligation imposed on that owner or operator pursuant to paragraph 2.

2. Each Party shall require the owner or operator of a facility referred to in paragraph 1 to submit the information specified in paragraphs 5 and 6, and in accordance with the requirements therein, with respect to those pollutants and wastes for which thresholds were exceeded.

3. In order to achieve the objective of this Protocol, a Party may decide with respect to a particular pollutant to apply either a release threshold or a manufacture, process or use threshold, provided that this increases the relevant information on releases or transfers available in its register.

4. Each Party shall ensure that its competent authority collects, or shall designate one or more public authorities or competent bodies to collect, the information on releases of pollutants from diffuse sources specified in paragraphs 7 and 8, for inclusion in its register.

5. Each Party shall require the owners or operators of the facilities required to report under paragraph 2 to complete and submit to its competent authority, the following information on a facility-specific basis:

(a) The name, street address, geographical location and the activity or activities of the reporting facility, and the name of the owner or operator, and, as appropriate, company;
(b) The name and numerical identifier of each pollutant required to be reported pursuant to paragraph 2;
(c) The amount of each pollutant required to be reported pursuant to paragraph 2 released from the facility to the environment in the reporting year, both in aggregate and according to whether the release is to air, to water or to land, including by underground injection;
(d) Either:
    i) The amount of each pollutant required to be reported pursuant to paragraph 2 that is transferred off-site in the reporting year, distinguishing between the amounts transferred for disposal and for recovery, and the name and address of the facility receiving the transfer; or
    ii) The amount of waste required to be reported pursuant to paragraph 2 transferred off-site in the reporting year, distinguishing between hazardous waste and other waste, for any operations of recovery or disposal, indicating respectively with 'R' or 'D' whether the waste is destined for recovery or disposal pursuant to annex III and, for transboundary movements of hazardous waste, the name and address of the recoverer or disposer of the waste and the actual recovery or disposal site receiving the transfer;
(e) The amount of each pollutant in waste water required to be reported pursuant to paragraph 2 transferred off-site in the reporting year; and
(f) The type of methodology used to derive the information referred to in subparagraphs (c) to (e), according to article 9, paragraph 2, indicating whether the information is based on measurement, calculation or estimation.

6. The information referred to in paragraph 5 (c) to (e) shall include information on releases and transfers resulting from routine activities and from extraordinary events.

7. Each Party shall present on its register, in an adequate spatial disaggregation, the information on releases of pollutants from diffuse sources for which that Party determines that data are being collected by the relevant authorities and can be practicably included. Where the Party determines that no such data exist, it shall take measures to initiate reporting on releases of relevant pollutants from one or more diffuse sources in accordance with its national priorities.

8. The information referred to in paragraph 7 shall include information on the type of methodology used to derive the information.

Article 8: Reporting cycle

1. Each Party shall ensure that the information required to be incorporated in its register is publicly available, compiled and presented on the register by calendar

year. The reporting year is the calendar year to which that information relates. For each Party, the first reporting year is the calendar year after the Protocol enters into force for that Party. The reporting required under article 7 shall be annual. However, the second reporting year may be the second calendar year following the first reporting year.

2. Each Party that is not a regional economic integration organization shall ensure that the information is incorporated into its register within fifteen months from the end of each reporting year. However, the information for the first reporting year shall be incorporated into its register within two years from the end of that reporting year.

3. Each Party that is a regional economic integration organization shall ensure that the information for a particular reporting year is incorporated into its register six months after the Parties that are not regional economic integration organizations are required to do so.

Article 9: Data collection and record-keeping

1. Each Party shall require the owners or operators of the facilities subject to the reporting requirements of article 7 to collect the data needed to determine, in accordance with paragraph 2 below and with appropriate frequency, the facility's releases and off-site transfers subject to reporting under article 7 and to keep available for the competent authorities the records of the data from which the reported information was derived for a period of five years, starting from the end of the reporting year concerned. These records shall also describe the methodology used for data gathering.

2. Each Party shall require the owners or operators of the facilities subject to reporting under article 7 to use the best available information, which may include monitoring data, emission factors, mass balance equations, indirect monitoring or other calculations, engineering judgments and other methods. Where appropriate, this should be done in accordance with internationally approved methodologies.

Article 10: Quality assessment

1. Each Party shall require the owners or operators of the facilities subject to the reporting requirements of article 7, paragraph 1, to assure the quality of the information that they report.

2. Each Party shall ensure that the data contained in its register are subject to quality assessment by the competent authority, in particular as to their completeness, consistency and credibility, taking into account any guidelines that may be developed by the Meeting of the Parties.

Article 11: Public access to information

1. Each Party shall ensure public access to information contained in its pollutant release and transfer register, without an interest having to be stated, and according to the provisions of this Protocol, primarily by ensuring that its register provides for direct electronic access through public telecommunications networks.

2. Where the information contained in its register is not easily publicly accessible by direct electronic means, each Party shall ensure that its competent authority upon request provides that information by any other effective means, as soon as possible and at the latest within one month after the request has been submitted.

3. Subject to paragraph 4, each Party shall ensure that access to information contained in its register is free of charge.

4. Each Party may allow its competent authority to make a charge for reproducing and mailing the specific information referred to in paragraph 2, but such charge shall not exceed a reasonable amount.

5. Where the information contained in its register is not easily publicly accessible by direct electronic means, each Party shall facilitate electronic access to its register in publicly accessible locations, for example in public libraries, offices of local authorities or other appropriate places.

Article 12: Confidentiality

1. Each Party may authorize the competent authority to keep information held on the register confidential where public disclosure of that information would adversely affect:

(a) International relations, national defence or public security;
(b) The course of justice, the ability of a person to receive a fair trial or the ability of a public authority to conduct an enquiry of a criminal or disciplinary nature;
(c) The confidentiality of commercial and industrial information, where such confidentiality is protected by law in order to protect a legitimate economic interest;
(d) Intellectual property rights; or
(e) The confidentiality of personal data and/or files relating to a natural person if that person has not consented to the disclosure of the information to the public, where such confidentiality is provided for in national law.

The aforementioned grounds for confidentiality shall be interpreted in a restrictive way, taking into account the public interest served by disclosure and whether the information relates to releases into the environment.

2. Within the framework of paragraph 1 (c), any information on releases which is relevant for the protection of the environment shall be considered for disclosure according to national law.

3. Whenever information is kept confidential according to paragraph 1, the register shall indicate what type of information has been withheld, through, for example, providing generic chemical information if possible, and for what reason it has been withheld.

Article 13: Public participation in the development of national pollutant release and transfer registers

1. Each Party shall ensure appropriate opportunities for public participation in the development of its national pollutant release and transfer register, within the framework of its national law.

2. For the purpose of paragraph 1, each Party shall provide the opportunity for free public access to the information on the proposed measures concerning the development of its national pollutant release and transfer register and for the submission of any comments, information, analyses or opinions that are relevant to the decision-making process, and the relevant authority shall take due account of such public input.

3. Each Party shall ensure that, when a decision to establish or significantly change its register has been taken, information on the decision and the considerations on which it is based are made publicly available in a timely manner.

Article 14: Access to justice

1. Each Party shall, within the framework of its national legislation, ensure that any person who considers that his or her request for information under article 11, paragraph 2, has been ignored, wrongfully refused, whether in part or in full, inadequately answered, or otherwise not dealt with in accordance with the provisions of that paragraph has access to a review procedure before a court of law or another independent and impartial body established by law.

2. The requirements in paragraph 1 are without prejudice to the respective rights and obligations of Parties under existing treaties applicable between them dealing with the subject matter of this article.

Article 15: Capacity-building

1. Each Party shall promote public awareness of its pollutant release and transfer register, and shall ensure that assistance and guidance are provided in accessing its register and in understanding and using the information contained in it.

2. Each Party should provide adequate capacity-building for and guidance to the responsible authorities and bodies to assist them in carrying out their duties under this Protocol.

Article 16: International cooperation

1. The Parties shall, as appropriate, cooperate and assist each other:

(a) In international actions in support of the objectives of this Protocol;

(b) On the basis of mutual agreement between the Parties concerned, in implementing national systems in pursuance of this Protocol;

(c) In sharing information under this Protocol on releases and transfers within border areas; and

(d) In sharing information under this Protocol concerning transfers among Parties.

2. The Parties shall encourage cooperation among each other and with relevant international organizations, as appropriate, to promote:

(a) Public awareness at the international level;
(b) The transfer of technology; and
(c) The provision of technical assistance to Parties that are developing countries and Parties with economies in transition in matters relating to this Protocol.

Article 17: Meeting of the Parties

1. A Meeting of the Parties is hereby established. Its first session shall be convened no later than two years after the entry into force of this Protocol. Thereafter, ordinary sessions of the Meeting of the Parties shall be held sequentially with or parallel to ordinary meetings of the Parties to the Convention, unless otherwise decided by the Parties to this Protocol. The Meeting of the Parties shall hold an extraordinary session if it so decides in the course of an ordinary session or at the written request of any Party provided that, within six months of it being communicated by the Executive Secretary of the Economic Commission for Europe to all Parties, the said request is supported by at least one third of these Parties.

2. The Meeting of the Parties shall keep under continuous review the implementation and development of this Protocol on the basis of regular reporting by the Parties and, with this purpose in mind, shall:

(a) Review the development of pollutant release and transfer registers, and promote their progressive strengthening and convergence;
(b) Establish guidelines facilitating reporting by the Parties to it, bearing in mind the need to avoid duplication of effort in this regard;
(c) Establish a programme of work;
(d) Consider and, where appropriate, adopt measures to strengthen international cooperation in accordance with article 16;
(e) Establish such subsidiary bodies as it deems necessary;
(f) Consider and adopt proposals for such amendments to this Protocol and its annexes as are deemed necessary for the purposes of this Protocol, in accordance with the provisions of article 20;
(g) At its first session, consider and by consensus adopt rules of procedure for its sessions and those of its subsidiary bodies, taking into account any rules of procedure adopted by the Meeting of the Parties to the Convention;
(h) Consider establishing financial arrangements by consensus and technical assistance mechanisms to facilitate the implementation of this Protocol;
(i) Seek, where appropriate, the services of other relevant international bodies in the achievement of the objectives of this Protocol; and
(j) Consider and take any additional action that may be required to further the objectives of this Protocol, such as the adoption of guidelines and recommendations which promote its implementation.

3. The Meeting of the Parties shall facilitate the exchange of information on the experience gained in reporting transfers using the pollutant-specific and waste-

specific approaches, and shall review that experience in order to investigate the possibility of convergence between the two approaches, taking into account the public interest in information in accordance with article 1 and the overall effectiveness of national pollutant release and transfer registers.

4. The United Nations, its specialized agencies and the International Atomic Energy Agency, as well as any State or regional economic integration organization entitled under article 24 to sign this Protocol but which is not a Party to it, and any intergovernmental organization qualified in the fields to which the Protocol relates, shall be entitled to participate as observers in the sessions of the Meeting of the Parties. Their admission and participation shall be subject to the rules of procedure adopted by the Meeting of the Parties.

5. Any non-governmental organization qualified in the fields to which this Protocol relates which has informed the Executive Secretary of the Economic Commission for Europe of its wish to be represented at a session of the Meeting of the Parties shall be entitled to participate as an observer unless one third of the Parties present at the session raise objections. Their admission and participation shall be subject to the rules of procedure adopted by the Meeting of the Parties.

[Articles 18-21 not reproduced]

Article 22: Review of compliance

At its first session, the Meeting of the Parties shall by consensus establish cooperative procedures and institutional arrangements of a non-judicial, non-adversarial and consultative nature to assess and promote compliance with the provisions of this Protocol and to address cases of non-compliance. In establishing these procedures and arrangements, the Meeting of the Parties shall consider, inter alia, whether to allow for information to be received from members of the public on matters related to this Protocol.

[Articles 23-30 not reproduced]

Annex I: Activities; Annex II: Pollutants; Annex III: Disposal operations ('D') (Part A), recovery operations ('R') (Part B); Annex IV: Arbitration [not reproduced]

African Charter on Human and Peoples' Rights [excerpts]

Adopted on 27 June 1981 at Nairobi. Entered into force on 21 October 1986. Source: Organisation of African Unity Doc. CAB/LEG/67/3/Rev.5. Number of parties: 53. Further information: African Commission on Human and Peoples' Rights, Banjul, The Gambia, http://www.achpr.org/

Article 24

All peoples shall have the right to a general satisfactory environment favourable to their development.

Additional Protocol to the American Convention on Human Rights in the Area of Economic, Social and Cultural Rights [excerpts]

Adopted on 14 November 1988 at San Salvador. Entered into force on 16 November 1999. Source: Organization of American States Treaty Series, N° 69. Number of parties: 13. Further information: Inter-American Commission on Human Rights, Washington, DC, USA, http://www.cidh.oas.org/

Article 11: Right to a healthy environment

1. Everyone shall have the right to live in a healthy environment and to have access to basic public services.

2. The States Parties shall promote the protection, preservation and improvement of the environment.

ILO Convention Concerning Indigenous and Tribal Peoples in Independent Countries (Convention 169) [excerpts][5]

Adopted on 27 June 1989 at Geneva. Entered into force on 5 September 1991. Source: ILO, *International Labour Conventions and Recommendations 1977-1995* (Geneva: ILO, 1996). Number of parties: 17. Further information: International Labour Standards Department, ILO, Geneva, Switzerland, http://www.ilo.org/public/english/standards/

Article 7

1. The peoples concerned shall have the right to decide their own priorities for the process of development as it affects their lives, beliefs, institutions and spiritual well-being and the lands they occupy or otherwise use, and to exercise control, to

5 *Editors' note*: Convention 169 is the successor agreement to Convention 107 adopted in 1957. It provides much broader rights for indigenous and tribal peoples but since it has not been widely ratified Convention 107 is still the operative instrument in a number of countries. For the text of Convention 107, see Convention concerning the Protection and Integration of Indigenous and Other Tribal and Semi-Tribal Populations in Independent Countries, 26 June 1957, *in* ILO, *International Labour Conventions and Recommendations 1952-1976* (Geneva: ILO, 1996).

the extent possible, over their own economic, social and cultural development. In addition, they shall participate in the formulation, implementation and evaluation of plans and programmes for national and regional development which may affect them directly.

2. The improvement of the conditions of life and work and levels of health and education of the peoples concerned, with their participation and co-operation, shall be a matter of priority in plans for the overall economic development of areas they inhabit. Special projects for development of the areas in question shall also be so designed as to promote such improvement.

3. Governments shall ensure that, whenever appropriate, studies are carried out, in co-operation with the peoples concerned, to assess the social, spiritual, cultural and environmental impact on them of planned development activities. The results of these studies shall be considered as fundamental criteria for the implementation of these activities.

4. Governments shall take measures, in co-operation with the peoples concerned, to protect and preserve the environment of the territories they inhabit.

Article 15

1. The rights of the peoples concerned to the natural resources pertaining to their lands shall be specially safeguarded. These rights include the right of these peoples to participate in the use, management and conservation of these resources.

2. In cases in which the State retains the ownership of mineral or sub-surface resources or rights to other resources pertaining to lands, governments shall establish or maintain procedures through which they shall consult these peoples, with a view to ascertaining whether and to what degree their interests would be prejudiced, before undertaking or permitting any programmes for the exploration or exploitation of such resources pertaining to their lands. The peoples concerned shall wherever possible participate in the benefits of such activities, and shall receive fair compensation for any damages which they may sustain as a result of such activities.

Rome Statute of the International Criminal Court [excerpts]

Adopted on 17 July 1998 at Rome. Entered into force on 1 July 2002. Source: Doc. A/CONF.183/9. Number of parties: 92. Further information: International Criminal Court, The Hague, The Netherlands, http://www.icc-cpi.int

Part 1. Establishment of the Court

Article 1: The Court

An International Criminal Court ('the Court') is hereby established. It shall be a permanent institution and shall have the power to exercise its jurisdiction over persons for the most serious crimes of international concern, as referred to in this Statute, and shall be complementary to national criminal jurisdictions. The jurisdiction and functioning of the Court shall be governed by the provisions of this Statute.

Part 2. Jurisdiction, admissibility and applicable law

Article 5: Crimes within the jurisdiction of the Court

1. The jurisdiction of the Court shall be limited to the most serious crimes of concern to the international community as a whole. The Court has jurisdiction in accordance with this Statute with respect to the following crimes:
(a) The crime of genocide;
(b) Crimes against humanity;
(c) War crimes;
(d) The crime of aggression.

Article 8: War crimes

1. The Court shall have jurisdiction in respect of war crimes in particular when committed as part of a plan or policy or as part of a large-scale commission of such crimes.

2. For the purpose of this Statute, 'war crimes' means:
a) Grave breaches of the Geneva Conventions of 12 August 1949, namely, any of the following acts against persons or property protected under the provisions of the relevant Geneva Convention:
   i) Wilful killing;
   ii) Torture or inhuman treatment, including biological experiments;
   iii) Wilfully causing great suffering, or serious injury to body or health;
   iv) Extensive destruction and appropriation of property, not justified by military necessity and carried out unlawfully and wantonly;
   v) Compelling a prisoner of war or other protected person to serve in the forces of a hostile Power;
   vi) Wilfully depriving a prisoner of war or other protected person of the rights of fair and regular trial;
   vii) Unlawful deportation or transfer or unlawful confinement;
   viii) Taking of hostages.
(b) Other serious violations of the laws and customs applicable in international armed conflict, within the established framework of international law, namely, any of the following acts:
   [Paragraphs i-iii not reproduced]
   iv) Intentionally launching an attack in the knowledge that such attack will cause incidental loss of life or injury to civilians or damage to civilian objects or widespread, long-term and severe damage to the natural

environment which would be clearly excessive in relation to the concrete and direct overall military advantage anticipated;

Convention on the Protection of the Environment through Criminal Law

Adopted on 4 November 1998 at Strasbourg. Not in force (1 ratification). Source: *European Treaty Series* - No. 172. Further information: Council of Europe, Strasbourg, France, http://conventions.coe.int

Preamble

The member States of the Council of Europe and the other States signatory hereto,

Considering that the aim of the Council of Europe is to achieve a greater unity between its members;

Convinced of the need to pursue a common criminal policy aimed at the protection of the environment;

Considering that unregulated industrial development may give rise to a degree of pollution which poses risks to the environment;

Considering that the life and health of human beings, the environmental media and fauna and flora must be protected by all possible means;

Considering that the uncontrolled use of technology and the excessive exploitation of natural resources entail serious environmental hazards which must be overcome by appropriate and concerted measures;

Recognising that, whilst the prevention of the impairment of the environment must be achieved primarily through other measures, criminal law has an important part to play in protecting the environment;

Recalling that environmental violations having serious consequences must be established as criminal offences subject to appropriate sanctions;

Wishing to take effective measures to ensure that the perpetrators of such acts do not escape prosecution and punishment and desirous of fostering international co-operation to this end;

Convinced that imposing criminal or administrative sanctions on legal persons can play an effective role in the prevention of environmental violations and noting the growing international trend in this regard;

Mindful of the existing international conventions which already contain provisions aiming at the protection of the environment through criminal law;

Having regard to the conclusions of the 7th and 17th Conferences of European Ministers of Justice held in Basle in 1972 and in Istanbul in 1990, and to Recommendation 1192 (1992) of the Parliamentary Assembly,

Have agreed as follows:

Section I: Use of terms

Article 1: Definitions

For the purposes of this Convention:

a) 'unlawful' means infringing a law, an administrative regulation or a decision taken by a competent authority, aiming at the protection of the environment;

b) 'water' means all kinds of groundwater and surface water including the water of lakes, rivers, oceans and seas.

Section II: Measures to be taken at national level

Article 2: Intentional offences

1. Each Party shall adopt such appropriate measures as may be necessary to establish as criminal offences under its domestic law:

a) the discharge, emission or introduction of a quantity of substances or ionising radiation into air, soil or water which:
   i) causes death or serious injury to any person, or
   ii) creates a significant risk of causing death or serious injury to any person;
b) the unlawful discharge, emission or introduction of a quantity of substances or ionising radiation into air, soil or water which causes or is likely to cause their lasting deterioration or death or serious injury to any person or substantial damage to protected monuments, other protected objects, property, animals or plants;
c) the unlawful disposal, treatment, storage, transport, export or import of hazardous waste which causes or is likely to cause death or serious injury to any person or substantial damage to the quality of air, soil, water, animals or plants;
d) the unlawful operation of a plant in which a dangerous activity is carried out and which causes or is likely to cause death or serious injury to any person or substantial damage to the quality of air, soil, water, animals or plants;
e) the unlawful manufacture, treatment, storage, use, transport, export or import of nuclear materials or other hazardous radioactive substances which causes or is likely to cause death or serious injury to any person or substantial damage to the quality of air, soil, water, animals or plants,

when committed intentionally.

2. Each Party shall adopt such appropriate measures as may be necessary to establish as criminal offences under its domestic law aiding or abetting the commission of any of the offences established in accordance with paragraph 1 of this article.

Article 3: Negligent offences

1. Each Party shall adopt such appropriate measures as may be necessary to establish as criminal offences under its domestic law, when committed with negligence, the offences enumerated in Article 2, paragraph 1 a to e.

2. Any State may, at the time of signature or when depositing its instrument of ratification, acceptance, approval or accession, by a declaration addressed to the Secretary General of the Council of Europe, declare that paragraph 1 of this article, in part or in whole, shall only apply to offences which were committed with gross negligence.

3. Any State may, at the time of signature or when depositing its instrument of ratification, acceptance, approval or accession, by a declaration addressed to the Secretary General of the Council of Europe, declare that paragraph 1 of this article, in part or in whole, shall not apply to:

- subparagraph 1 a ii of Article 2,
- subparagraph 1 b of Article 2, insofar as the offence relates to protect monuments, to other protected objects or to property.

Article 4: Other criminal offences or administrative offences

Insofar as these are not covered by the provisions of Articles 2 and 3, each Party shall adopt such appropriate measures as may be necessary to establish as criminal offences or administrative offences, liable to sanctions or other measures under its domestic law, when committed intentionally or with negligence:

a) the unlawful discharge, emission or introduction of a quantity of substances or ionising radiation into air, soil or water;

b) the unlawful causing of noise;

c) the unlawful disposal, treatment, storage, transport, export or import of waste;

d) the unlawful operation of a plant;

e) the unlawful manufacture, treatment, use, transport, export or import of nuclear materials, other radioactive substances or hazardous chemicals;

f) the unlawful causing of changes detrimental to natural components of a national park, nature reserve, water conservation area or other protected areas;

g) the unlawful possession, taking, damaging, killing or trading of or in protected wild flora and fauna species.

Article 5: Jurisdiction

1. Each Party shall adopt such appropriate measures as may be necessary to establish jurisdiction over a criminal offence established in accordance with this Convention when the offence is committed:

a) in its territory; or
b) on board a ship or an aircraft registered in it or flying its flag; or
c) by one of its nationals if the offence is punishable under criminal law where it was committed or if the place where it was committed does not fall under any territorial jurisdiction.

2. Each Party shall adopt such appropriate measures as may be necessary to establish jurisdiction over a criminal offence established in accordance with this

Convention, in cases where an alleged offender is present in its territory and it does not extradite him to another Party after a request for extradition.

3. This Convention does not exclude any criminal jurisdiction exercised by a Party in accordance with its domestic law.

4. Each Party may, at the time of signature or when depositing its instrument of ratification, acceptance, approval or accession, by a declaration addressed to the Secretary General of the Council of Europe, declare that paragraphs 1 c and 2 of this article, in part or in whole, shall not apply.

Article 6: Sanctions for environmental offences

Each Party shall adopt, in accordance with the relevant international instruments, such appropriate measures as may be necessary to enable it to make the offences established in accordance with Articles 2 and 3 punishable by criminal sanctions which take into account the serious nature of these offences. The sanctions available shall include imprisonment and pecuniary sanctions and may include reinstatement of the environment.

Article 7: Confiscation measures

1. Each Party shall adopt such appropriate measures as may be necessary to enable it to confiscate instrumentalities and proceeds, or property the value of which corresponds to such proceeds, in respect of offences enumerated in Articles 2 and 3.

2. Each Party may, at the time of signature or when depositing its instrument of ratification, acceptance, approval or accession, by a declaration addressed to the Secretary General of the Council of Europe, declare that it will not apply paragraph 1 of this Article either in respect of offences specified in such declaration or in respect of certain categories of instrumentalities or of proceeds, or property the value of which corresponds to such proceeds.

Article 8: Reinstatement of the environment

Each Party may, at any time, in a declaration addressed to the Secretary General of the Council of Europe, declare that it will provide for reinstatement of the environment according to the following provisions of this article:

a) the competent authority may order the reinstatement of the environment in relation to an offence established in accordance with this Convention. Such an order may be made subject to certain conditions;

b) where an order for the reinstatement of the environment has not been complied with, the competent authority may, in accordance with domestic law, make it executable at the expense of the person subject to the order or that person may be liable to other criminal sanctions instead of or in addition to it.

Article 9: Corporate liability

1. Each Party shall adopt such appropriate measures as may be necessary to enable it to impose criminal or administrative sanctions or measures on legal persons on

whose behalf an offence referred to in Articles 2 or 3 has been committed by their organs or by members thereof or by another representative.

2. Corporate liability under paragraph 1 of this article shall not exclude criminal proceedings against a natural person.

3. Any State may, at the time of signature or when depositing its instrument of ratification, acceptance, approval or accession, by a declaration addressed to the Secretary General of the Council of Europe, declare that it reserves the right not to apply paragraph 1 of this article or any part thereof or that it applies only to offences specified in such declaration.

Article 10: Co-operation between authorities

1. Each Party shall adopt such appropriate measures as may be necessary to ensure that the authorities responsible for environmental protection co-operate with the authorities responsible for investigating and prosecuting criminal offences:

a) by informing the latter authorities, on their own initiative, where there are reasonable grounds to believe that an offence under Article 2 has been committed;
b) by providing, upon request, all necessary information to the latter authorities, in accordance with domestic law.

2. Any State may, at the time of signature or when depositing its instrument of ratification, acceptance, approval or accession, by a declaration addressed to the Secretary General of the Council of Europe, declare that it reserves the right not to apply paragraph 1 a of this article or that it applies only to offences specified in such declaration.

Article 11: Rights for groups to participate in proceedings

Each Party may, at any time, in a declaration addressed to the Secretary General of the Council of Europe, declare that it will, in accordance with domestic law, grant any group, foundation or association which, according to its statutes, aims at the protection of the environment, the right to participate in criminal proceedings concerning offences established in accordance with this Convention.

Section III: Measures to be taken at international level

Article 12: International co-operation

1. The Parties shall afford each other, in accordance with the provisions of relevant international instruments on international co-operation in criminal matters and with their domestic law, the widest measure of co-operation in investigations and judicial proceedings relating to criminal offences established in accordance with this Convention.

2. The Parties may afford each other assistance in investigations and proceedings relating to those acts defined in Article 4 of this Convention which are not covered by paragraph 1 of this article.

[Articles 13-21 not reproduced]

Chapter 3

The Atmosphere

Introduction

The present chapter considers three multilateral treaties that have sought to address different types of harm related to the protection of the atmosphere. They have in common that they were drafted as framework conventions allowing for the progressive development of more specific and binding commitments under subsequent protocols. The first section concerns the prevention of transboundary air pollution as regulated by the 1979 Air Pollution Convention negotiated under the auspices of the UNECE. The Convention, whilst a regional instrument, is the only international agreement addressing the regulation and control of long-range transboundary air pollution such as acid rain and other widely disseminated pollutants. It lays down general principles of international cooperation for air pollution abatement which have been furthered by eight regulatory protocols.[1]

Beyond the transboundary or regional impact of air pollution, the degradation of the global atmosphere has been the focus of more recent international regulation. The second section of this chapter reproduces the instruments that address the depletion of the ozone layer. The 1985 Ozone Convention commits governments to protect the ozone layer and to cooperate in scientific research. It is an instrument largely devoid of concrete obligations, and is for this reason only reproduced here in part. On the other hand, the Convention's 1987 Montreal Protocol has endorsed

1 These protocols are the Protocol on Long-term Financing of the Cooperative Programme for Monitoring and Evaluation of the Long-range Transmission of Air Pollutants in Europe (EMEP), Geneva, 27 September 1984, in force 28 January 1988, 27 *ILM* 701 (1988); Protocol on the Reduction of Sulphur Emissions or their Transboundary Fluxes, Helsinki, 8 July 1985, in force 2 September 1987, 27 *ILM* 707 (1988); Protocol Concerning the Control of Emissions of Nitrogen Oxides or their Transboundary Fluxes, Sofia, 31 October 1988, in force 14 February 1991, 28 *ILM* 212 (1989); Protocol on the Control of Emissions of Volatile Organic Compounds or their Transboundary Fluxes, Geneva, 18 November 1991, in force 29 September 1997, 31 *ILM* 573 (1992); Protocol on Further Reduction of Sulphur Emissions, Oslo, 14 June 1994, in force 5 August 1998, 33 *ILM* 1542 (1994); Protocol on Persistent Organic Pollutants, Århus, 24 June 1998, in force 23 October 2003, 37 *ILM* 505 (1998); Protocol on Heavy Metals, Århus, 24 June 1998, in force 29 December 2003, Doc. ECE/EB.AIR/1998/1; and Protocol to Abate Acidification, Eutrophication and Ground-Level Ozone, Gothenburg, 30 November 1999, not in force, Doc. ECE/EB.AIR/1999/1.

a much more significant role in the international control of ozone depleting substances by fixing legally binding targets for reducing and eventually eliminating the consumption and production of a range of controlled substances.

The third section focuses on the international legal framework to combat global warming.[2] The 1992 Climate Change Convention, negotiated at UNCED, has as its primary goal the stabilization of the atmospheric concentration of carbon dioxide (CO_2) and other greenhouse gases at a level that would prevent dangerous anthropogenic interference with the climate system. The Kyoto Protocol adopted in 1997 sets up a regulatory regime providing more concrete and specific obligations for states parties.[3] Significantly, it sets emission targets covering greenhouse gases for industrialized states parties, and includes novel implementation mechanisms such as joint fulfilment of commitments and implementation, the clean development mechanism (CDM) and emissions trading.

Selected readings

Transboundary air pollution

Fraenkel, A., 'The Convention on Long-Range Transboundary Pollution: Meeting the Challenge of International Cooperation', 30 *Harvard Int'l L.J.* 447 (1989).

Ishii, A., 'Merging the EU Acidification Strategy: Evaluating the 1999 Gothenburg Protocol to Abate Acidification, Eutrophication and Ground-level Ozone', 10 *RECIEL* 210 (2001).

Okowa, P.N., *State Responsibility for Transboundary Air Pollution in International Law* (Oxford: Oxford University Press, 2000).

Pallemaerts, M., 'International Legal Aspects of Long-Range Transboundary Air Pollution', 1 *Hague Ybk Int'l L.* 189 (1988).

Ozone layer depletion

Benedick, R.E., *Ozone Diplomacy* (Cambridge, Mass.: Harvard University Press, 2nd edn. 1998).

---

2 Not included here are UN General Assembly resolutions on protection of the global climate for present and future generations of mankind, in particular UNGA Resolution 43/53 (1988); UNGA Resolution 44/207 (1989); UNGA Resolution 45/212 (1990); and UNGA Resolution 46/169 (1991).

3 Real reductions in greenhouse gas emissions are however ultimately contingent upon the entry into force of the Kyoto Protocol as set forth in its Article 25 (below at p. 163). After the decision of the United States not to ratify the Protocol, its entry into force now depends on ratification by the Russian Federation.

Rowland, F.S., 'Atmospheric Changes Caused by Human Activities: From Science to Regulation', 27 *Ecology L. Quarterly* 1261 (2001).

UNEP, *Handbook for the International Treaties for the Protection of the Ozone Layer* (5th edn. 2000).

Yoshida, O., *The International Legal Régime for the Protection of the Stratospheric Ozone Layer* (The Hague: Kluwer Law International, 2001).

Climate change

Boisson de Chazournes, L., 'The United Nations Framework Convention on Climate Change: On the Road Towards Sustainable Development', *in* Wolfrum, R. (ed.), *Enforcing Environmental Standards: Economic Mechanisms as Viable Means?* (Berlin: Springer, 1996), p. 285.

Bothe, M., 'The United Nations Framework Convention on Climate Change - An Unprecedented Multilevel Regulatory Challenge', 63 *ZaöRV* 239 (2003).

Cameron, P.D. and Zillmand, D. (eds.), *Kyoto: From Principles to Practice* (The Hague: Kluwer Law International, 2001).

Nowrot, K., 'Saving the International Legal Regime on Climate Change? The 2001 Conferences of Bonn and Marrakesh', 44 *German Ybk Int'l L.* 396 (2001).

Transboundary air pollution

Convention on Long-range Transboundary Air Pollution

Adopted on 13 November 1979 at Geneva. Entered into force on 16 March 1983. Source: 1302 *UNTS* 217. Number of parties: 49. Further information: Secretariat (UNECE), Geneva, Switzerland, http://www.unece.org/env/lrtap

The Parties to the present Convention,

Determined to promote relations and cooperation in the field of environmental protection,

Aware of the significance of the activities of the United Nations Economic Commission for Europe in strengthening such relations and cooperation, particularly in the field of air pollution including long-range transport of air pollutants,

Recognizing the contribution of the Economic Commission for Europe to the multilateral implementation of the pertinent provisions of the Final Act of the Conference on Security and Cooperation in Europe,

Cognizant of the references in the chapter on environment of the Final Act of the Conference on Security and Cooperation in Europe calling for cooperation to control air pollution and its effects, including long-range transport of air pollutants, and to the development through international cooperation of an extensive programme for the monitoring and evaluation of long-range transport of air pollutants, starting with sulphur dioxide and with possible extension to other pollutants,

Considering the pertinent provisions of the Declaration of the United Nations Conference on the Human Environment, and in particular principle 21, which expresses the common conviction that States have, in accordance with the Charter of the United Nations and the principles of international law, the sovereign right to exploit their own resources pursuant to their own environmental policies, and the responsibility to ensure that activities within their jurisdiction or control do not cause damage to the environment of other States or of areas beyond the limits of national jurisdiction,

Recognizing the existence of possible adverse effects, in the short and long term, of air pollution including transboundary air pollution,

Concerned that a rise in the level of emissions of air pollutants within the region as forecast may increase such adverse effects,

Recognizing the need to study the implications of the long-range transport of air pollutants and the need to seek solutions for the problems identified,

Affirming their willingness to reinforce active international cooperation to develop appropriate national policies and by means of exchange of information, consultation, research and monitoring to coordinate national action for combating air pollution including long-range transboundary air pollution,

Have agreed as follows:

Article 1: Definitions

For the purposes of the present Convention:

(a) '*Air pollution*' means the introduction by man, directly or indirectly, of substances or energy into the air resulting in deleterious effects of such a nature as to endanger human health, harm living resources and ecosystems and material property and impair or interfere with amenities and other legitimate uses of the environment, and 'air pollutants' shall be construed accordingly;

(b) '*Long-range transboundary air pollution*' means air pollution whose physical origin is situated wholly or in part within the area under the national jurisdiction of one State and which has adverse effects in the area under the jurisdiction of another State at such a distance that it is not generally possible to distinguish the contribution of individual emission sources or groups of sources.

Article 2: Fundamental principles

The Contracting Parties, taking due account of the facts and problems involved, are determined to protect man and his environment against air pollution and shall endeavour to limit and, as far as possible, gradually reduce and prevent air pollution including long-range transboundary air pollution.

Article 3

The Contracting Parties, within the framework of the present Convention, shall by means of exchanges of information, consultation, research and monitoring, develop without undue delay policies and strategies which shall serve as a means of combating the discharge of air pollutants, taking into account efforts already made at national and international levels.

Article 4

The Contracting Parties shall exchange information on and review their policies, scientific activities and technical measures aimed at combating, as far as possible, the discharge of air pollutants which may have adverse effects, thereby contributing to the reduction of air pollution including long-range transboundary air pollution.

Article 5

Consultations shall be held, upon request, at an early stage between, on the one hand, Contracting Parties which are actually affected by or exposed to a significant risk of long-range transboundary air pollution and, on the other hand, Contracting Parties within which and subject to whose jurisdiction a significant contribution to long-range transboundary air pollution originates, or could originate, in connection with activities carried on or contemplated therein.

Article 6: Air quality management

Taking into account articles 2 to 5, the ongoing research, exchange of information and monitoring and the results thereof, the cost and effectiveness of local and other remedies and, in order to combat air pollution, in particular that originating from new or rebuilt installations, each Contracting Party undertakes to develop the best policies and strategies including air quality management systems and, as part of them, control measures compatible with balanced development, in particular by using the best available technology which is economically feasible and low- and non-waste technology.

Article 7: Research and development

The Contracting Parties, as appropriate to their needs, shall initiate and cooperate in the conduct of research into and/or development of:

(a) Existing and proposed technologies for reducing emissions of sulphur compounds and other major air pollutants, including technical and economic feasibility, and environmental consequences;

(b) Instrumentation and other techniques for monitoring and measuring emission rates and ambient concentrations of air pollutants;

(c) Improved models for a better understanding of the transmission of long-range transboundary air pollutants;

(d) The effects of sulphur compounds and other major air pollutants on human health and the environment, including agriculture, forestry, materials, aquatic and other natural ecosystems and visibility, with a view to establishing a scientific basis for dose/effect relationships designed to protect the environment;

(e) The economic, social and environmental assessment of alternative measures for attaining environmental objectives including the reduction of long-range transboundary air pollution;

(f) Education and training programmes related to the environmental aspects of pollution by sulphur compounds and other major air pollutants.

Article 8: Exchange of information

The Contracting Parties, within the framework of the Executive Body referred to in article 10 and bilaterally, shall, in their common interests, exchange available information on:

(a) Data on emissions at periods of time to be agreed upon, of agreed air pollutants, starting with sulphur dioxide, coming from grid-units of agreed size; or on the fluxes of agreed air pollutants, starting with sulphur dioxide, across national borders, at distances and at periods of time to be agreed upon;

(b) Major changes in national policies and in general industrial development, and their potential impact, which would be likely to cause significant changes in long-range transboundary air pollution;

(c) Control technologies for reducing air pollution relevant to long-range transboundary air pollution;

(d) The projected cost of the emission control of sulphur compounds and other major air pollutants on a national scale;

(e) Meteorological and physico-chemical data relating to the processes during transmission;

(f) Physico-chemical and biological data relating to the effects of long-range transboundary air pollution and the extent of the damage* which these data indicate can be attributed to long-range transboundary air pollution;

(g) National, subregional and regional policies and strategies for the control of sulphur compounds and other major air pollutants.

Article 9: Implementation and further development of the Cooperative programme for the monitoring and evaluation of the long-range transmission of air pollutants in Europe

The Contracting Parties stress the need for the implementation of the existing 'Cooperative programme for the monitoring and evaluation of the long-range transmission of air pollutants in Europe' (hereinafter referred to as 'EMEP') and, with regard to the further development of this programme, agree to emphasize:

---

* The present Convention does not contain a rule on State liability as to damage.

(a) The desirability of Contracting Parties joining in and fully implementing EMEP which, as a first step, is based on the monitoring of sulphur dioxide and related substances;

(b) The need to use comparable or standardized procedures for monitoring whenever possible;

(c) The desirability of basing the monitoring programme on the framework of both national and international programmes. The establishment of monitoring stations and the collection of data shall be carried out under the national jurisdiction of the country in which the monitoring stations are located;

(d) The desirability of establishing a framework for a cooperative environmental monitoring programme, based on and taking into account present and future national, subregional, regional and other international programmes;

(e) The need to exchange data on emissions at periods of time to be agreed upon, of agreed air pollutants, starting with sulphur dioxide, coming from grid-units of agreed size; or on the fluxes of agreed air pollutants, starting with sulphur dioxide, across national borders, at distances and at periods of time to be agreed upon. The method, including the model, used to determine the fluxes, as well as the method, including the model used to determine the transmission of air pollutants based on the emissions per grid-unit, shall be made available and periodically reviewed, in order to improve the methods and the models;

(f) Their willingness to continue the exchange and periodic updating of national data on total emissions of agreed air pollutants, starting with sulphur dioxide;

(g) The need to provide meteorological and physico-chemical data relating to processes during transmission;

(h) The need to monitor chemical components in other media such as water, soil and vegetation, as well as a similar monitoring programme to record effects on health and environment;

(i) The desirability of extending the national EMEP networks to make them operational for control and surveillance purposes.

Article 10: Executive Body

1. The representatives of the Contracting Parties shall, within the framework of the Senior Advisers to ECE Governments on Environmental Problems, constitute the Executive Body of the present Convention, and shall meet at least annually in that capacity.

2. The Executive Body shall:

(a) Review the implementation of the present Convention;

(b) Establish, as appropriate, working groups to consider matters related to the implementation and development of the present Convention and to this end to prepare appropriate studies and other documentation and to submit recommendations to be considered by the Executive Body;

(c) Fulfil such other functions as may be appropriate under the provisions of the present Convention.

3. The Executive Body shall utilize the Steering Body for the EMEP to play an integral part in the operation of the present Convention, in particular with regard to data collection and scientific cooperation.

4. The Executive Body, in discharging its functions, shall, when it deems appropriate, also make use of information from other relevant international organizations.

Article 11: Secretariat

The Executive Secretary of the Economic Commission for Europe shall carry out, for the Executive Body, the following secretariat functions:

(a) To convene and prepare the meetings of the Executive Body;

(b) To transmit to the Contracting Parties reports and other information received in accordance with the provisions of the present Convention;

(c) To discharge the functions assigned by the Executive Body.

Article 12: Amendments to the Convention

1. Any Contracting Party may propose amendments to the present Convention.

2. The text of proposed amendments shall be submitted in writing to the Executive Secretary of the Economic Commission for Europe, who shall communicate them to all Contracting Parties. The Executive Body shall discuss proposed amendments at its next annual meeting provided that such proposals have been circulated by the Executive Secretary of the Economic Commission for Europe to the Contracting Parties at least ninety days in advance.

3. An amendment to the present Convention shall be adopted by consensus of the representatives of the Contracting Parties, and shall enter into force for the Contracting Parties which have accepted it on the ninetieth day after the date on which two-thirds of the Contracting Parties have deposited their instruments of acceptance with the depositary. Thereafter, the amendment shall enter into force for any other Contracting Party on the ninetieth day after the date on which that Contracting Party deposits its instrument of acceptance of the amendment.

Article 13: Settlement of disputes

If a dispute arises between two or more Contracting Parties to the present Convention as to the interpretation or application of the Convention, they shall seek a solution by negotiation or by any other method of dispute settlement acceptable to the parties to the dispute.

Article 14: Signature

1. The present Convention shall be open for signature at the United Nations Office at Geneva from 13 to 16 November 1979 on the occasion of the High-level Meeting within the framework of the Economic Commission for Europe on the Protection of the Environment, by the member States of the Economic Commission

for Europe as well as States having consultative status with the Economic Commission for Europe, pursuant to paragraph 8 of Economic and Social Council resolution 36 (IV) of 28 March 1947, and by regional economic integration organizations, constituted by sovereign States members of the Economic Commission for Europe, which have competence in respect of the negotiation, conclusion and application of international agreements in matters covered by the present Convention.

2. In matters within their competence, such regional economic integration organizations shall, on their own behalf, exercise the rights and fulfil the responsibilities which the present Convention attributes to their member States. In such cases, the member States of these organizations shall not be entitled to exercise such rights individually.

Article 15: Ratification, acceptance, approval and accession

1. The present Convention shall be subject to ratification, acceptance or approval.

2. The present Convention shall be open for accession as from 17 November 1979 by the States and organizations referred to in article 14, paragraph 1.

3. The instruments of ratification, acceptance, approval or accession shall be deposited with the Secretary-General of the United Nations, who will perform the functions of the depositary.

[Articles 16-18 not reproduced]

Ozone layer depletion

Vienna Convention for the Protection of the Ozone Layer

Adopted on 22 March 1985 at Vienna. Entered into force on 22 September 1988. Source: 1513 *UNTS* 324. Number of parties: 187. Further information: Secretariat, Nairobi, Kenya, http://www.unep.org/ozone

Preamble

The Parties to this Convention,

Aware of the potentially harmful impact on human health and the environment through modification of the ozone layer,

Recalling the pertinent provisions of the Declaration of the United Nations Conference on the Human Environment, and in particular principle 21, which provides that 'States have, in accordance with the Charter of the United Nations and the principles of international law, the sovereign right to exploit their own resources pursuant to their own environmental policies, and the responsibility to ensure that activities within their jurisdiction or control do not cause damage to the environment of other States or of areas beyond the limits of national jurisdiction',

Taking into account the circumstances and particular requirements of developing countries,

Mindful of the work and studies proceeding within both international and national organizations and, in particular, of the World Plan of Action on the Ozone Layer of the United Nations Environment Programme,

Mindful also of the precautionary measures for the protection of the ozone layer which have already been taken at the national and international levels,

Aware that measures to protect the ozone layer from modifications due to human activities require international co-operation and action, and should be based on relevant scientific and technical considerations,

Aware also of the need for further research and systematic observations to further develop scientific knowledge of the ozone layer and possible adverse effects resulting from its modification,

Determined to protect human health and the environment against adverse effects resulting from modifications of the ozone layer,

Have agreed as follows:

Article 1: Definitions

For the purposes of this Convention:

1. 'The ozone layer' means the layer of atmospheric ozone above the planetary boundary layer.

2. 'Adverse effects' means changes in the physical environment or biota, including changes in climate, which have significant deleterious effects on human health or on the composition, resilience and productivity of natural and managed ecosystems, or on materials useful to mankind.

3. 'Alternative technologies or equipment' means technologies or equipment the use of which makes it possible to reduce or effectively eliminate emissions of substances which have or are likely to have adverse effects on the ozone layer.

4. 'Alternative substances' means substances which reduce, eliminate or avoid adverse effects on the ozone layer.

5. 'Parties' means, unless the text otherwise indicates, Parties to this Convention.

6. 'Regional economic integration organization' means an organization constituted by sovereign States of a given region which has competence in respect of matters governed by this Convention or its protocols and has been duly authorized, in accordance with its internal procedures, to sign, ratify, accept, approve or accede to the instruments concerned.

7. 'Protocols' means protocols to this Convention.

Article 2: General obligations

1. The Parties shall take appropriate measures in accordance with the provisions of this Convention and of those protocols in force to which they are party to protect human health and the environment against adverse effects resulting or likely to result from human activities which modify or are likely to modify the ozone layer.

2. To this end the Parties shall, in accordance with the means at their disposal and their capabilities:

(a) Co-operate by means of systematic observations, research and information exchange in order to better understand and assess the effects on human health and the environment from modification of the ozone layer;

(b) Adopt appropriate legislative or administrative measures and co-operate in harmonizing appropriate policies to control, limit, reduce or prevent human activities under their jurisdiction or control should it be found that these activities have or are likely to have adverse effects resulting from modification or likely modification of the ozone layer;

(c) Co-operate in the formulation of agreed measures, procedures and standards for the implementation of this Convention, with a view to the adoption of protocols and annexes;

(d) Co-operate with competent international bodies to implement effectively this Convention and protocols to which they are party.

3. The provisions of this Convention shall in no way affect the right of Parties to adopt, in accordance with international law, domestic measures additional to those referred to in paragraphs 1 and 2 above, nor shall they affect additional domestic measures already taken by a Party, provided that these measures are not incompatible with their obligations under this Convention.

4. The application of this article shall be based on relevant scientific and technical considerations.

Article 3: Research and systematic observations

1. The Parties undertake, as appropriate, to initiate and co-operate in, directly or through competent international bodies, the conduct of research and scientific assessments on:

(a) The physical and chemical processes that may affect the ozone layer;

(b) The human health and other biological effects deriving from any modifications of the ozone layer, particularly those resulting from changes in ultra-violet solar radiation having biological effects (UV-B);

(c) Climatic effects deriving from any modifications of the ozone layer;

(d) Effects deriving from any modifications of the ozone layer and any consequent change in UV-B radiation on natural and synthetic materials useful to mankind;

(e) Substances, practices, processes and activities that may affect the ozone layer, and their cumulative effects;

(f) Alternative substances and technologies;

(g) Related socio-economic matters;

and as further elaborated in annexes I and II.

2. The Parties undertake to promote or establish, as appropriate, directly or through competent international bodies and taking fully into account national legislation and relevant ongoing activities at both the national and international levels, joint or complementary programmes for systematic observation of the state of the ozone layer and other relevant parameters, as elaborated in annex I.

3. The Parties undertake to co-operate, directly or through competent international bodies, in ensuring the collection, validation and transmission of research and observational data through appropriate world data centers in a regular and timely fashion.

Article 4: Co-operation in the legal, scientific and technical fields

1. The Parties shall facilitate and encourage the exchange of scientific, technical, socio-economic, commercial and legal information relevant to this Convention as further elaborated in annex II. Such information shall be supplied to bodies agreed upon by the Parties. Any such body receiving information regarded as confidential by the supplying Party shall ensure that such information is not disclosed and shall aggregate it to protect its confidentiality before it is made available to all Parties.

2. The Parties shall co-operate, consistent with their national laws, regulations and practices and taking into account in particular the needs of the developing countries, in promoting, directly or through competent international bodies, the development and transfer of technology and knowledge. Such co-operation shall be carried out particularly through:

(a) Facilitation of the acquisition of alternative technologies by other Parties;
(b) Provision of information on alternative technologies and equipment, and supply of special manuals or guides to them;
(c) The supply of necessary equipment and facilities for research and systematic observations;
(d) Appropriate training of scientific and technical personnel.

Article 5: Transmission of information

The Parties shall transmit, through the secretariat, to the Conference of the Parties established under article 6 information on the measures adopted by them in implementation of this Convention and of protocols to which they are party in such form and at such intervals as the meetings of the parties to the relevant instruments may determine.

Article 6: Conference of the Parties

1. A Conference of the Parties is hereby established. The first meeting of the Conference of the Parties shall be convened by the secretariat designated on an interim basis under article 7 not later than one year after entry into force of this Convention. Thereafter, ordinary meetings of the Conference of the Parties shall be held at regular intervals to be determined by the Conference at its first meeting.

2. Extraordinary meetings of the Conference of the Parties shall be held at such other times as may be deemed necessary by the Conference, or at the written request of any Party, provided that, within six months of the request being communicated to them by the secretariat, it is supported by at least one third of the Parties.

3. The Conference of the Parties shall by consensus agree upon and adopt rules of procedure and financial rules for itself and for any subsidiary bodies it may establish, as well as financial provisions governing the functioning of the secretariat.

4. The Conference of the Parties shall keep under continuous review the implementation of this Convention, and, in addition, shall:

(a) Establish the form and the intervals for transmitting the information to be submitted in accordance with article 5 and consider such information as well as reports submitted by any subsidiary body;

(b) Review the scientific information on the ozone layer, on its possible modification and on possible effects of any such modification;

(c) Promote, in accordance with article 2, the harmonization of appropriate policies, strategies and measures for minimizing the release of substances causing or likely to cause modification of the ozone layer, and make recommendations on any other measures relating to this Convention;

(d) Adopt, in accordance with articles 3 and 4, programmes for research, systematic observations, scientific and technological co-operation, the exchange of information and the transfer of technology and knowledge;

(e) Consider and adopt, as required, in accordance with articles 9 and 10, amendments to this Convention and its annexes;

(f) Consider amendments to any protocol, as well as to any annexes thereto, and, if so decided, recommend their adoption to the parties to the protocol concerned;

(g) Consider and adopt, as required, in accordance with article 10, additional annexes to this Convention;

(h) Consider and adopt, as required, protocols in accordance with article 8;

(i) Establish such subsidiary bodies as are deemed necessary for the implementation of this Convention;

(j) Seek, where appropriate, the services of competent international bodies and scientific committees, in particular the World Meteorological Organization and the World Health Organization as well as the Co-ordinating Committee on the Ozone Layer, in scientific research, systematic observations and other activities pertinent to the objectives of this Convention, and make use as appropriate of information from these bodies and committees;

(k) Consider and undertake any additional action that may be required for the achievement of the purposes of this Convention.

5. The United Nations, its specialized agencies and the International Atomic Energy Agency, as well as any State not party to this Convention, may be represented at meetings of the Conference of the Parties by observers. Any body or

agency, whether national or international, governmental or non-governmental, qualified in fields relating to the protection of the ozone layer which has informed the secretariat of its wish to be represented at a meeting of the Conference of the Parties as an observer may be admitted unless at least one-third of the Parties present object. The admission and participation of observers shall be subject to the rules of procedure adopted by the Conference of the Parties.

Article 7: Secretariat

1. The functions of the secretariat shall be:

(a) To arrange for and service meetings provided for in articles 6, 8, 9 and 10;

(b) To prepare and transmit reports based upon information received in accordance with articles 4 and 5, as well as upon information derived from meetings of subsidiary bodies established under article 6;

(c) To perform the functions assigned to it by any protocol;

(d) To prepare reports on its activities carried out in implementation of its functions under this Convention and present them to the Conference of the Parties;

(e) To ensure the necessary co-ordination with other relevant international bodies, and in particular to enter into such administrative and contractual arrangements as may be required for the effective discharge of its functions;

(f) To perform such other functions as may be determined by the Conference of the Parties.

2. The secretariat functions will be carried out on an interim basis by the United Nations Environment Programme until the completion of the first ordinary meeting of the Conference of the Parties held pursuant to article 6. At its first ordinary meeting, the Conference of the Parties shall designate the secretariat from amongst those existing competent international organizations which have signified their willingness to carry out the secretariat functions under this Convention.

Article 8: Adoption of protocols

1. The Conference of the Parties may at a meeting adopt protocols pursuant to Article 2.

2. The text of any proposed protocol shall be communicated to the Parties by the secretariat at least six months before such a meeting.

Article 9: Amendment of the Convention or protocols

1. Any Party may propose amendments to this Convention or to any protocol. Such amendments shall take due account, *inter alia*, of relevant scientific and technical considerations.

2. Amendments to this Convention shall be adopted at a meeting of the Conference of the Parties. Amendments to any protocol shall be adopted at a meeting of the Parties to the protocol in question. The text of any proposed amendment to this Convention or to any protocol, except as may otherwise be provided in such protocol, shall be communicated to the Parties by the secretariat at least six months before the meeting at which it is proposed for adoption. The

secretariat shall also communicate proposed amendments to the signatories to this Convention for information.

3. The Parties shall make every effort to reach agreement on any proposed amendment to this Convention by consensus. If all efforts at consensus have been exhausted, and no agreement reached, the amendment shall as a last resort be adopted by a three-fourths majority vote of the Parties present and voting at the meeting, and shall be submitted by the Depositary to all Parties for ratification, approval or acceptance.

4. The procedure mentioned in paragraph 3 above shall apply to amendments to any protocol, except that a two-thirds majority of the parties to that protocol present and voting at the meeting shall suffice for their adoption.

5. Ratification, approval or acceptance of amendments shall be notified to the Depositary in writing. Amendments adopted in accordance with paragraphs 3 or 4 above shall enter into force between parties having accepted them on the ninetieth day after the receipt by the Depositary of notification of their ratification, approval or acceptance by at least three-fourths of the Parties to this Convention or by at least two-thirds of the parties to the protocol concerned, except as may otherwise be provided in such protocol. Thereafter the amendments shall enter into force for any other Party on the ninetieth day after that Party deposits its instrument of ratification, approval or acceptance of the amendments.

6. For the purposes of this article, 'Parties present and voting' means Parties present and casting an affirmative or negative vote.

Article 10: Adoption and amendment of annexes

1. The annexes to this Convention or to any protocol shall form an integral part of this Convention or of such protocol, as the case may be, and, unless expressly provided otherwise, a reference to this Convention or its protocols constitutes at the same time a reference to any annexes thereto. Such annexes shall be restricted to scientific, technical and administrative matters.

2. Except as may be otherwise provided in any protocol with respect to its annexes, the following procedure shall apply to the proposal, adoption and entry into force of additional annexes to this Convention or of annexes to a protocol:

(a) Annexes to this Convention shall be proposed and adopted according to the procedure laid down in article 9, paragraphs 2 and 3, while annexes to any protocol shall be proposed and adopted according to the procedure laid down in article 9, paragraphs 2 and 4;

(b) Any party that is unable to approve an additional annex to this Convention or annex to any protocol to which it is party shall so notify the Depositary, in writing, within six months from the date of the communication of the adoption by the Depositary. The Depositary shall without delay notify all Parties of any such notification received. A Party may at any time substitute an acceptance for a previous declaration of objection and the annexes shall thereupon enter into force for that Party;

(c) On the expiry of six months from the date of the circulation of the communication by the Depositary, the annex shall become effective for all Parties to this Convention or to any protocol concerned which have not submitted a notification in accordance with the provision of subparagraph (b) above.

3. The proposal, adoption and entry into force of amendments to annexes to this Convention or to any protocol shall be subject to the same procedure as for the proposal, adoption and entry into force of annexes to the Convention or annexes to a protocol. Annexes and amendments thereto shall take due account, *inter alia*, of relevant scientific and technical considerations.

4. If an additional annex or an amendment to an annex involves an amendment to this Convention or to any protocol, the additional annex or amended annex shall not enter into force until such time as the amendment to this Convention or to the protocol concerned enters into force.

Article 11: Settlement of disputes

1. In the event of a dispute between Parties concerning the interpretation or application of this Convention, the parties concerned shall seek solution by negotiation.

2. If the parties concerned cannot reach agreement by negotiation, they may jointly seek the good offices of, or request mediation by, a third party.

3. When ratifying, accepting, approving or acceding to this Convention, or at any time thereafter, a State or regional economic integration organization may declare in writing to the Depositary that for a dispute not resolved in accordance with paragraph 1 or paragraph 2 above, it accepts one or both of the following means of dispute settlement as compulsory:

(a) Arbitration in accordance with procedures to be adopted by the Conference of the Parties at its first ordinary meeting;

(b) Submission of the dispute to the International Court of Justice.

4. If the parties have not, in accordance with paragraph 3 above, accepted the same or any procedure, the dispute shall be submitted to conciliation in accordance with paragraph 5 below unless the parties otherwise agree.

5. A conciliation commission shall be created upon the request of one of the parties to the dispute. The commission shall be composed of an equal number of members appointed by each party concerned and a chairman chosen jointly by the members appointed by each party. The commission shall render a final and recommendatory award, which the parties shall consider in good faith.

6. The provisions of this Article shall apply with respect to any protocol except as provided in the protocol concerned.

[Articles 12-15 not reproduced]

Article 16: Relationship between the Convention and its protocols

1. A State or a regional economic integration organization may not become a party to a protocol unless it is, or becomes at the same time, a Party to the Convention.

2. Decisions concerning any protocol shall be taken only by the parties to the protocol concerned.

[Articles 17-21 not reproduced]

Annex I: Research and systematic observations; Annex II: Information exchange [not reproduced]

Montreal Protocol on Substances that Deplete the Ozone Layer[4]

Adopted on 16 September 1987 at Montreal. Entered into force on 1 January 1989. Source: 1522 *UNTS* 3 (the text reproduced incorporates amendments and/or adjustments adopted in London (1990), Copenhagen (1992), Vienna (1995), Montreal (1997) and Beijing (1999)). Number of parties: 186. Further information: Ozone Secretariat, Nairobi, Kenya, http://www.unep.org/ozone

Preamble

The Parties to this Protocol,

Being Parties to the Vienna Convention for the Protection of the Ozone Layer,

Mindful of their obligation under that Convention to take appropriate measures to protect human health and the environment against adverse effects resulting or likely to result from human activities which modify or are likely to modify the ozone layer,

Recognizing that world-wide emissions of certain substances can significantly deplete and otherwise modify the ozone layer in a manner that is likely to result in adverse effects on human health and the environment,

Conscious of the potential climatic effects of emissions of these substances,

Aware that measures taken to protect the ozone layer from depletion should be based on relevant scientific knowledge, taking into account technical and economic considerations,

Determined to protect the ozone layer by taking precautionary measures to control equitably total global emissions of substances that deplete it, with the ultimate objective of their elimination on the basis of developments in scientific knowledge,

---

4 The NCP for the Montreal Protocol is reproduced at p. 608.

taking into account technical and economic considerations and bearing in mind the developmental needs of developing countries,

Acknowledging that special provision is required to meet the needs of developing countries, including the provision of additional financial resources and access to relevant technologies, bearing in mind that the magnitude of funds necessary is predictable, and the funds can be expected to make a substantial difference in the world's ability to address the scientifically established problem of ozone depletion and its harmful effects,

Noting the precautionary measures for controlling emissions of certain chlorofluorocarbons that have already been taken at national and regional levels,

Considering the importance of promoting international co-operation in the research, development and transfer of alternative technologies relating to the control and reduction of emissions of substances that deplete the ozone layer, bearing in mind in particular the needs of developing countries,

Have agreed as follows:

Article 1: Definitions

For the purposes of this Protocol:

1. 'Convention' means the Vienna Convention for the Protection of the Ozone Layer, adopted on 22 March 1985.

2. 'Parties' means, unless the text otherwise indicates, Parties to this Protocol.

3. 'Secretariat' means the Secretariat of the Convention.

4. 'Controlled substance' means a substance in Annex A, Annex B, Annex C or Annex E to this Protocol, whether existing alone or in a mixture. It includes the isomers of any such substance, except as specified in the relevant Annex, but excludes any controlled substance or mixture which is in a manufactured product other than a container used for the transportation or storage of that substance.

5. 'Production' means the amount of controlled substances produced, minus the amount destroyed by technologies to be approved by the Parties and minus the amount entirely used as feedstock in the manufacture of other chemicals. The amount recycled and reused is not to be considered as 'production'.

6. 'Consumption' means production plus imports minus exports of controlled substances.

7. 'Calculated levels' of production, imports, exports and consumption means levels determined in accordance with Article 3.

8. 'Industrial rationalization' means the transfer of all or a portion of the calculated level of production of one Party to another, for the purpose of achieving economic efficiencies or responding to anticipated shortfalls in supply as a result of plant closures.

Article 2: Control measures

1. *Incorporated in Article 2A.*

2. *Replaced by Article 2B.*

3. *Replaced by Article 2A.*

4. *Replaced by Article 2A.*

5. Any Party may, for one or more control periods, transfer to another Party any portion of its calculated level of production set out in Articles 2A to 2F, and Article 2H, provided that the total combined calculated levels of production of the Parties concerned for any group of controlled substances do not exceed the production limits set out in those Articles for that group. Such transfer of production shall be notified to the Secretariat by each of the Parties concerned, stating the terms of such transfer and the period for which it is to apply.

5 *bis*. Any Party not operating under paragraph 1 of Article 5 may, for one or more control periods, transfer to another such Party any portion of its calculated level of consumption set out in Article 2F, provided that the calculated level of consumption of controlled substances in Group I of Annex A of the Party transferring the portion of its calculated level of consumption did not exceed 0.25 kilograms per capita in 1989 and that the total combined calculated levels of consumption of the Parties concerned do not exceed the consumption limits set out in Article 2F. Such transfer of consumption shall be notified to the Secretariat by each of the Parties concerned, stating the terms of such transfer and the period for which it is to apply.

6. Any Party not operating under Article 5, that has facilities for the production of Annex A or Annex B controlled substances under construction, or contracted for, prior to 16 September 1987, and provided for in national legislation prior to 1 January 1987, may add the production from such facilities to its 1986 production of such substances for the purposes of determining its calculated level of production for 1986, provided that such facilities are completed by 31 December 1990 and that such production does not raise that Party's annual calculated level of consumption of the controlled substances above 0.5 kilograms per capita.

7. Any transfer of production pursuant to paragraph 5 or any addition of production pursuant to paragraph 6 shall be notified to the Secretariat, no later than the time of the transfer or addition.

8. (a) Any Parties which are Member States of a regional economic integration organization as defined in Article 1 (6) of the Convention may agree that they shall jointly fulfil their obligations respecting consumption under this Article and Articles 2A to 2I provided that their total combined calculated level of consumption does not exceed the levels required by this Article and Articles 2A to 2I.

(b) The Parties to any such agreement shall inform the Secretariat of the terms of the agreement before the date of the reduction in consumption with which the agreement is concerned.

(c) Such agreement will become operative only if all Member States of the regional economic integration organization and the organization concerned are Parties to the Protocol and have notified the Secretariat of their manner of implementation.

9. (a) Based on the assessments made pursuant to Article 6, the Parties may decide whether:
   i) Adjustments to the ozone depleting potentials specified in Annex A, Annex B, Annex C and/or Annex E should be made and, if so, what the adjustments should be; and
   ii) Further adjustments and reductions of production or consumption of the controlled substances should be undertaken and, if so, what the scope, amount and timing of any such adjustments and reductions should be;

(b) Proposals for such adjustments shall be communicated to the Parties by the Secretariat at least six months before the meeting of the Parties at which they are proposed for adoption;

(c) In taking such decisions, the Parties shall make every effort to reach agreement by consensus. If all efforts at consensus have been exhausted, and no agreement reached, such decisions shall, as a last resort, be adopted by a two-thirds majority vote of the Parties present and voting representing a majority of the Parties operating under Paragraph 1 of Article 5 present and voting and a majority of the Parties not so operating present and voting;

(d) The decisions, which shall be binding on all Parties, shall forthwith be communicated to the Parties by the Depositary. Unless otherwise provided in the decisions, they shall enter into force on the expiry of six months from the date of the circulation of the communication by the Depositary.

10. Based on the assessments made pursuant to Article 6 of this Protocol and in accordance with the procedure set out in Article 9 of the Convention, the Parties may decide:

(a) whether any substances, and if so which, should be added to or removed from any annex to this Protocol, and

(b) the mechanism, scope and timing of the control measures that should apply to those substances;

11. Notwithstanding the provisions contained in this Article and Articles 2A to 2I Parties may take more stringent measures than those required by this Article and Articles 2A to 2I.

Article 2A: CFCs

1. Each Party shall ensure that for the twelve-month period commencing on the first day of the seventh month following the date of entry into force of this Protocol, and in each twelve-month period thereafter, its calculated level of consumption of the controlled substances in Group I of Annex A does not exceed its calculated level of consumption in 1986. By the end of the same period, each Party producing one or more of these substances shall ensure that its calculated level of production of the substances does not exceed its calculated level of production in 1986, except that such level may have increased by no more than ten per cent based on the 1986 level. Such increase shall be permitted only so as to

satisfy the basic domestic needs of the Parties operating under Article 5 and for the purposes of industrial rationalization between Parties.

2. Each Party shall ensure that for the period from 1 July 1991 to 31 December 1992 its calculated levels of consumption and production of the controlled substances in Group I of Annex A do not exceed 150 per cent of its calculated levels of production and consumption of those substances in 1986; with effect from 1 January 1993, the twelve-month control period for these controlled substances shall run from 1 January to 31 December each year.

3. Each Party shall ensure that for the twelve-month period commencing on 1 January 1994, and in each twelve-month period thereafter, its calculated level of consumption of the controlled substances in Group I of Annex A does not exceed, annually, twenty-five per cent of its calculated level of consumption in 1986. Each Party producing one or more of these substances shall, for the same periods, ensure that its calculated level of production of the substances does not exceed, annually, twenty-five per cent of its calculated level of production in 1986. However, in order to satisfy the basic domestic needs of the Parties operating under paragraph 1 of Article 5, its calculated level of production may exceed that limit by up to ten per cent of its calculated level of production in 1986.

4. Each Party shall ensure that for the twelve-month period commencing on 1 January 1996, and in each twelve-month period thereafter, its calculated level of consumption of the controlled substances in Group I of Annex A does not exceed zero. Each Party producing one or more of these substances shall, for the same periods, ensure that its calculated level of production of the substances does not exceed zero. However, in order to satisfy the basic domestic needs of the Parties operating under paragraph 1 of Article 5, its calculated level of production may exceed that limit by a quantity equal to the annual average of its production of the controlled substances in Group I of Annex A for basic domestic needs for the period 1995 to 1997 inclusive. This paragraph will apply save to the extent that the Parties decide to permit the level of production or consumption that is necessary to satisfy uses agreed by them to be essential.

5. Each Party shall ensure that for the twelve-month period commencing on 1 January 2003 and in each twelve-month period thereafter, its calculated level of production of the controlled substances in Group I of Annex A for the basic domestic needs of the Parties operating under paragraph 1 of Article 5 does not exceed eighty per cent of the annual average of its production of those substances for basic domestic needs for the period 1995 to 1997 inclusive.

6. Each Party shall ensure that for the twelve-month period commencing on 1 January 2005 and in each twelve-month period thereafter, its calculated level of production of the controlled substances in Group I of Annex A for the basic domestic needs of the Parties operating under paragraph 1 of Article 5 does not exceed fifty per cent of the annual average of its production of those substances for basic domestic needs for the period 1995 to 1997 inclusive.

7. Each Party shall ensure that for the twelve-month period commencing on 1 January 2007 and in each twelve-month period thereafter, its calculated level of production of the controlled substances in Group I of Annex A for the basic domestic needs of the Parties operating under paragraph 1 of Article 5 does not exceed fifteen per cent of the annual average of its production of those substances for basic domestic needs for the period 1995 to 1997 inclusive.

8. Each Party shall ensure that for the twelve-month period commencing on 1 January 2010 and in each twelve-month period thereafter, its calculated level of production of the controlled substances in Group I of Annex A for the basic domestic needs of the Parties operating under paragraph 1 of Article 5 does not exceed zero.

9. For the purposes of calculating basic domestic needs under paragraphs 4 to 8 of this Article, the calculation of the annual average of production by a Party includes any production entitlements that it has transferred in accordance with paragraph 5 of Article 2, and excludes any production entitlements that it has acquired in accordance with paragraph 5 of Article 2.

Article 2B: Halons

1. Each Party shall ensure that for the twelve-month period commencing on 1 January 1992, and in each twelve-month period thereafter, its calculated level of consumption of the controlled substances in Group II of Annex A does not exceed, annually, its calculated level of consumption in 1986. Each Party producing one or more of these substances shall, for the same periods, ensure that its calculated level of production of the substances does not exceed, annually, its calculated level of production in 1986. However, in order to satisfy the basic domestic needs of the Parties operating under paragraph 1 of Article 5, its calculated level of production may exceed that limit by up to ten per cent of its calculated level of production in 1986.

2. Each Party shall ensure that for the twelve-month period commencing on 1 January 1994, and in each twelve-month period thereafter, its calculated level of consumption of the controlled substances in Group II of Annex A does not exceed zero. Each Party producing one or more of these substances shall, for the same periods, ensure that its calculated level of production of the substances does not exceed zero. However, in order to satisfy the basic domestic needs of the Parties operating under paragraph 1 of Article 5, its calculated level of production may, until 1 January 2002 exceed that limit by up to fifteen per cent of its calculated level of production in 1986; thereafter, it may exceed that limit by a quantity equal to the annual average of its production of the controlled substances in Group II of Annex A for basic domestic needs for the period 1995 to 1997 inclusive. This paragraph will apply save to the extent that the Parties decide to permit the level of production or consumption that is necessary to satisfy uses agreed by them to be essential.

3. Each Party shall ensure that for the twelve-month period commencing on 1 January 2005 and in each twelve-month period thereafter, its calculated level of production of the controlled substances in Group II of Annex A for the basic domestic needs of the Parties operating under paragraph 1 of Article 5 does not exceed fifty per cent of the annual average of its production of those substances for basic domestic needs for the period 1995 to 1997 inclusive.

4. Each Party shall ensure that for the twelve-month period commencing on 1 January 2010 and in each twelve-month period thereafter, its calculated level of production of the controlled substances in Group II of Annex A for the basic domestic needs of the Parties operating under paragraph 1 of Article 5 does not exceed zero.

Article 2C: Other fully halogenated CFCs

1. Each Party shall ensure that for the twelve-month period commencing on 1 January 1993, its calculated level of consumption of the controlled substances in Group I of Annex B does not exceed, annually, eighty per cent of its calculated level of consumption in 1989. Each Party producing one or more of these substances shall, for the same period, ensure that its calculated level of production of the substances does not exceed, annually, eighty per cent of its calculated level of production in 1989. However, in order to satisfy the basic domestic needs of the Parties operating under paragraph 1 of Article 5, its calculated level of production may exceed that limit by up to ten per cent of its calculated level of production in 1989.

2. Each Party shall ensure that for the twelve-month period commencing on 1 January 1994, and in each twelve-month period thereafter, its calculated level of consumption of the controlled substances in Group I of Annex B does not exceed, annually, twenty-five per cent of its calculated level of consumption in 1989. Each Party producing one or more of these substances shall, for the same periods, ensure that its calculated level of production of the substances does not exceed, annually, twenty-five per cent of its calculated level of production in 1989. However, in order to satisfy the basic domestic needs of the Parties operating under paragraph 1 of Article 5, its calculated level of production may exceed that limit by up to ten per cent of its calculated level of production in 1989.

3. Each Party shall ensure that for the twelve-month period commencing on 1 January 1996, and in each twelve-month period thereafter, its calculated level of consumption of the controlled substances in Group I of Annex B does not exceed zero. Each Party producing one or more of these substances shall, for the same periods, ensure that its calculated level of production of the substances does not exceed zero. However, in order to satisfy the basic domestic needs of the Parties operating under paragraph 1 of Article 5, its calculated level of production may, until 1 January 2003 exceed that limit by up to fifteen per cent of its calculated level of production in 1989; thereafter, it may exceed that limit by a quantity equal to eighty per cent of the annual average of its production of the controlled

substances in Group I of Annex B for basic domestic needs for the period 1998 to 2000 inclusive. This paragraph will apply save to the extent that the Parties decide to permit the level of production or consumption that is necessary to satisfy uses agreed by them to be essential.

4. Each Party shall ensure that for the twelve-month period commencing on 1 January 2007 and in each twelve-month period thereafter, its calculated level of production of the controlled substances in Group I of Annex B for the basic domestic needs of the Parties operating under paragraph 1 of Article 5 does not exceed fifteen per cent of the annual average of its production of those substances for basic domestic needs for the period 1998 to 2000 inclusive.

5. Each Party shall ensure that for the twelve-month period commencing on 1 January 2010 and in each twelve-month period thereafter, its calculated level of production of the controlled substances in Group I of Annex B for the basic domestic needs of the Parties operating under paragraph 1 of Article 5 does not exceed zero.

Article 2D: Carbon tetrachloride

1. Each Party shall ensure that for the twelve-month period commencing on 1 January 1995, its calculated level of consumption of the controlled substance in Group II of Annex B does not exceed, annually, fifteen per cent of its calculated level of consumption in 1989. Each Party producing the substance shall, for the same period, ensure that its calculated level of production of the substance does not exceed, annually, fifteen per cent of its calculated level of production in 1989. However, in order to satisfy the basic domestic needs of the Parties operating under paragraph 1 of Article 5, its calculated level of production may exceed that limit by up to ten per cent of its calculated level of production in 1989.

2. Each Party shall ensure that for the twelve-month period commencing on 1 January 1996, and in each twelve-month period thereafter, its calculated level of consumption of the controlled substance in Group II of Annex B does not exceed zero. Each Party producing the substance shall, for the same periods, ensure that its calculated level of production of the substance does not exceed zero. However, in order to satisfy the basic domestic needs of the Parties operating under paragraph 1 of Article 5, its calculated level of production may exceed that limit by up to fifteen per cent of its calculated level of production in 1989. This paragraph will apply save to the extent that the Parties decide to permit the level of production or consumption that is necessary to satisfy uses agreed by them to be essential.

Article 2E: 1,1,1-Trichloroethane (Methyl chloroform)

1. Each Party shall ensure that for the twelve-month period commencing on 1 January 1993, its calculated level of consumption of the controlled substance in Group III of Annex B does not exceed, annually, its calculated level of consumption in 1989. Each Party producing the substance shall, for the same period, ensure that its calculated level of production of the substance does not exceed, annually, its calculated level of production in 1989. However, in order to

satisfy the basic domestic needs of the Parties operating under paragraph 1 of Article 5, its calculated level of production may exceed that limit by up to ten per cent of its calculated level of production in 1989.

2. Each Party shall ensure that for the twelve-month period commencing on 1 January 1994, and in each twelve-month period thereafter, its calculated level of consumption of the controlled substance in Group III of Annex B does not exceed, annually, fifty per cent of its calculated level of consumption in 1989. Each Party producing the substance shall, for the same periods, ensure that its calculated level of production of the substance does not exceed, annually, fifty per cent of its calculated level of production in 1989. However, in order to satisfy the basic domestic needs of the Parties operating under paragraph 1 of Article 5, its calculated level of production may exceed that limit by up to ten per cent of its calculated level of production in 1989.

3. Each Party shall ensure that for the twelve-month period commencing on 1 January 1996, and in each twelve-month period thereafter, its calculated level of consumption of the controlled substance in Group III of Annex B does not exceed zero. Each Party producing the substance shall, for the same periods, ensure that its calculated level of production of the substance does not exceed zero. However, in order to satisfy the basic domestic needs of the Parties operating under paragraph 1 of Article 5, its calculated level of production may exceed that limit by up to fifteen per cent of its calculated level of production for 1989. This paragraph will apply save to the extent that the Parties decide to permit the level of production or consumption that is necessary to satisfy uses agreed by them to be essential.

Article 2F: Hydrochlorofluorocarbons

1. Each Party shall ensure that for the twelve-month period commencing on 1 January 1996, and in each twelve-month period thereafter, its calculated level of consumption of the controlled substances in Group I of Annex C does not exceed, annually, the sum of:

(a) Two point eight per cent of its calculated level of consumption in 1989 of the controlled substances in Group I of Annex A; and

(b) Its calculated level of consumption in 1989 of the controlled substances in Group I of Annex C.

2. Each Party shall ensure that for the twelve month period commencing on 1 January 2004, and in each twelve-month period thereafter, its calculated level of consumption of the controlled substances in Group I of Annex C does not exceed, annually, sixty-five per cent of the sum referred to in paragraph 1 of this Article.

3. Each Party shall ensure that for the twelve-month period commencing on 1 January 2010, and in each twelve-month period thereafter, its calculated level of consumption of the controlled substances in Group I of Annex C does not exceed, annually, thirty-five per cent of the sum referred to in paragraph 1 of this Article.

4. Each Party shall ensure that for the twelve-month period commencing on 1 January 2015, and in each twelve-month period thereafter, its calculated level of

consumption of the controlled substances in Group I of Annex C does not exceed, annually, ten per cent of the sum referred to in paragraph 1 of this Article.

5. Each Party shall ensure that for the twelve-month period commencing on 1 January 2020, and in each twelve-month period thereafter, its calculated level of consumption of the controlled substances in Group I of Annex C does not exceed, annually, zero point five per cent of the sum referred to in paragraph 1 of this Article. Such consumption shall, however, be restricted to the servicing of refrigeration and air conditioning equipment existing at that date.

6. Each Party shall ensure that for the twelve-month period commencing on 1 January 2030, and in each twelve-month period thereafter, its calculated level of consumption of the controlled substances in Group I of Annex C does not exceed zero.

7. As of 1 January 1996, each Party shall endeavour to ensure that:

(a) The use of controlled substances in Group I of Annex C is limited to those applications where other more environmentally suitable alternative substances or technologies are not available;

(b) The use of controlled substances in Group I of Annex C is not outside the areas of application currently met by controlled substances in Annexes A, B and C, except in rare cases for the protection of human life or human health; and

(c) Controlled substances in Group I of Annex C are selected for use in a manner that minimizes ozone depletion, in addition to meeting other environmental, safety and economic considerations.

8. Each Party producing one or more of these substances shall ensure that for the twelve-month period commencing on 1 January 2004, and in each twelve-month period thereafter, its calculated level of production of the controlled substances in Group I of Annex C does not exceed, annually, the average of:

(a) The sum of its calculated level of consumption in 1989 of the controlled substances in Group I of Annex C and two point eight per cent of its calculated level of consumption in 1989 of the controlled substances in Group I of Annex A; and

(b) The sum of its calculated level of production in 1989 of the controlled substances in Group I of Annex C and two point eight per cent of its calculated level of production in 1989 of the controlled substances in Group I of Annex A.

However, in order to satisfy the basic domestic needs of the Parties operating under paragraph 1 of Article 5, its calculated level of production may exceed that limit by up to fifteen per cent of its calculated level of production of the controlled substances in Group I of Annex C as defined above.

Article 2G: Hydrobromofluorocarbons

Each Party shall ensure that for the twelve-month period commencing on 1 January 1996, and in each twelve-month period thereafter, its calculated level of consumption of the controlled substances in Group II of Annex C does not exceed zero. Each Party producing the substances shall, for the same periods, ensure that its calculated level of production of the substances does not exceed zero. This paragraph will apply save to the extent that the Parties decide to permit the level of production or consumption that is necessary to satisfy uses agreed by them to be essential.

Article 2H: Methyl bromide

1. Each Party shall ensure that for the twelve-month period commencing on 1 January 1995, and in each twelve-month period thereafter, its calculated level of consumption of the controlled substance in Annex E does not exceed, annually, its calculated level of consumption in 1991. Each Party producing the substance shall, for the same period, ensure that its calculated level of production of the substance does not exceed, annually, its calculated level of production in 1991. However, in order to satisfy the basic domestic needs of the Parties operating under paragraph 1 of Article 5, its calculated level of production may exceed that limit by up to ten per cent of its calculated level of production in 1991.

2. Each Party shall ensure that for the twelve-month period commencing on 1 January 1999, and in the twelve-month period thereafter, its calculated level of consumption of the controlled substance in Annex E does not exceed, annually, seventy-five per cent of its calculated level of consumption in 1991. Each Party producing the substance shall, for the same periods, ensure that its calculated level of production of the substance does not exceed, annually, seventy-five per cent of its calculated level of production in 1991. However, in order to satisfy the basic domestic needs of the Parties operating under paragraph 1 of Article 5, its calculated level of production may exceed that limit by up to ten per cent of its calculated level of production in 1991.

3. Each Party shall ensure that for the twelve-month period commencing on 1 January 2001, and in the twelve-month period thereafter, its calculated level of consumption of the controlled substance in Annex E does not exceed, annually, fifty per cent of its calculated level of consumption in 1991. Each Party producing the substance shall, for the same periods, ensure that its calculated level of production of the substance does not exceed, annually, fifty per cent of its calculated level of production in 1991. However, in order to satisfy the basic domestic needs of the Parties operating under paragraph 1 of Article 5, its calculated level of production may exceed that limit by up to ten per cent of its calculated level of production in 1991.

4. Each Party shall ensure that for the twelve-month period commencing on 1 January 2003, and in the twelve-month period thereafter, its calculated level of consumption of the controlled substance in Annex E does not exceed, annually, thirty per cent of its calculated level of consumption in 1991. Each Party producing the substance shall, for the same periods, ensure that its calculated level of production of the substance does not exceed, annually, thirty per cent of its calculated level of production in 1991. However, in order to satisfy the basic domestic needs of the Parties operating under paragraph 1 of Article 5, its

calculated level of production may exceed that limit by up to ten per cent of its calculated level of production in 1991.

5. Each Party shall ensure that for the twelve-month period commencing on 1 January 2005, and in each twelve-month period thereafter, its calculated level of consumption of the controlled substance in Annex E does not exceed zero. Each Party producing the substance hall, for the same periods, ensure that its calculated level of production of the substance does not exceed zero. However, in order to satisfy the basic domestic needs of the Parties operating under paragraph 1 of Article 5, its calculated level of production may, until 1 January 2002 exceed that limit by up to fifteen per cent of its calculated level of production in 1991; thereafter, it may exceed that limit by a quantity equal to the annual average of its production of the controlled substance in Annex E for basic domestic needs for the period 1995 to 1998 inclusive. This paragraph will apply save to the extent that the Parties decide to permit the level of production or consumption that is necessary to satisfy uses agreed by them to be critical uses.

5 *bis*. Each Party shall ensure that for the twelve-month period commencing on 1 January 2005 and in each twelve-month period thereafter, its calculated level of production of the controlled substance in Annex E for the basic domestic needs of the Parties operating under paragraph 1 of Article 5 does not exceed eighty per cent of the annual average of its production of the substance for basic domestic needs for the period 1995 to 1998 inclusive.

5 *ter*. Each Party shall ensure that for the twelve-month period commencing on 1 January 2015 and in each twelve-month period thereafter, its calculated level of production of the controlled substance in Annex E for the basic domestic needs of the Parties operating under paragraph 1 of Article 5 does not exceed zero.

6. The calculated levels of consumption and production under this Article shall not include the amounts used by the Party for quarantine and pre-shipment applications.

Article 2I: Bromochloromethane

Each Party shall ensure that for the twelve-month period commencing on 1 January 2002, and in each twelve-month period thereafter, its calculated level of consumption and production of the controlled substance in Group III of Annex C does not exceed zero. This paragraph will apply save to the extent that the Parties decide to permit the level of production or consumption that is necessary to satisfy uses agreed by them to be essential.

Article 3: Calculation of control levels

For the purposes of Articles 2, 2A to 2I and 5, each Party shall, for each group of substances in Annex A, Annex B, Annex C or Annex E determine its calculated levels of:

(a) Production by:

i) multiplying its annual production of each controlled substance by the ozone depleting potential specified in respect of it in Annex A, Annex B, Annex C or Annex E;

ii) adding together, for each such Group, the resulting figures;

(b) Imports and exports, respectively, by following, *mutatis mutandis*, the procedure set out in subparagraph (a); and

(c) Consumption by adding together its calculated levels of production and imports and subtracting its calculated level of exports as determined in accordance with subparagraphs (a) and (b). However, beginning on 1 January 1993, any export of controlled substances to non-Parties shall not be subtracted in calculating the consumption level of the exporting Party.

Article 4: Control of trade with non-Parties

1. As of 1 January 1990, each party shall ban the import of the controlled substances in Annex A from any State not party to this Protocol.

1 *bis*. Within one year of the date of the entry into force of this paragraph, each Party shall ban the import of the controlled substances in Annex B from any State not party to this Protocol.

1 *ter*. Within one year of the date of entry into force of this paragraph, each Party shall ban the import of any controlled substances in Group II of Annex C from any State not party to this Protocol.

1 *qua*. Within one year of the date of entry into force of this paragraph, each Party shall ban the import of the controlled substance in Annex E from any State not party to this Protocol.

1 *quin*. As of 1 January 2004, each Party shall ban the import of the controlled substances in Group I of Annex C from any State not party to this Protocol.

1 *sex*. Within one year of the date of entry into force of this paragraph, each Party shall ban the import of the controlled substance in Group III of Annex C from any State not party to this Protocol.

2. As of 1 January 1993, each Party shall ban the export of any controlled substances in Annex A to any State not party to this Protocol.

2 *bis*. Commencing one year after the date of entry into force of this paragraph, each Party shall ban the export of any controlled substances in Annex B to any State not party to this Protocol.

2 *ter*. Commencing one year after the date of entry into force of this paragraph, each Party shall ban the export of any controlled substances in Group II of Annex C to any State not party to this Protocol.

2 *qua*. Commencing one year of the date of entry into force of this paragraph, each Party shall ban the export of the controlled substance in Annex E to any State not party to this Protocol.

2 *quin*. As of 1 January 2004, each Party shall ban the export of the controlled substances in Group I of Annex C to any State not party to this Protocol.

2 *sex*. Within one year of the date of entry into force of this paragraph, each Party shall ban the export of the controlled substance in Group III of Annex C to any State not party to this Protocol.

3. By 1 January 1992, the Parties shall, following the procedures in Article 10 of the Convention, elaborate in an annex a list of products containing controlled substances in Annex A. Parties that have not objected to the annex in accordance with those procedures shall ban, within one year of the annex having become effective, the import of those products from any State not party to this Protocol.

3 *bis*. Within three years of the date of the entry into force of this paragraph, the Parties shall, following the procedures in Article 10 of the Convention, elaborate in an annex a list of products containing controlled substances in Annex B. Parties that have not objected to the annex in accordance with those procedures shall ban, within one year of the annex having become effective, the import of those products from any State not party to this Protocol.

3 *ter*. Within three years of the date of entry into force of this paragraph, the Parties shall, following the procedures in Article 10 of the Convention, elaborate in an annex a list of products containing controlled substances in Group II of Annex C. Parties that have not objected to the annex in accordance with those procedures shall ban, within one year of the annex having become effective, the import of those products from any State not party to this Protocol.

4. By 1 January 1994, the Parties shall determine the feasibility of banning or restricting, from States not party to this Protocol, the import of products produced with, but not containing, controlled substances in Annex A. If determined feasible, the Parties shall, following the procedures in Article 10 of the Convention, elaborate in an annex a list of such products. Parties that have not objected to the annex in accordance with those procedures shall ban, within one year of the annex having become effective, the import of those products from any State not party to this Protocol.

4 *bis*. Within five years of the date of the entry into force of this paragraph, the Parties shall determine the feasibility of banning or restricting, from States not party to this Protocol, the import of products produced with, but not containing, controlled substances in Annex B. If determined feasible, the Parties shall, following the procedures in Article 10 of the Convention, elaborate in an annex a list of such products. Parties that have not objected to the annex in accordance with those procedures shall ban or restrict, within one year of the annex having become effective, the import of those products from any State not party to this Protocol.

4 *ter*. Within five years of the date of entry into force of this paragraph, the Parties shall determine the feasibility of banning or restricting, from States not party to this Protocol, the import of products produced with, but not containing, controlled substances in Group II of Annex C. If determined feasible, the Parties shall,

following the procedures in Article 10 of the Convention, elaborate in an annex a list of such products. Parties that have not objected to the annex in accordance with those procedures shall ban or restrict, within one year of the annex having become effective, the import of those products from any State not party to this Protocol.

5. Each Party undertakes to the fullest practicable extent to discourage the export to any State not party to this Protocol of technology for producing and for utilizing controlled substances in Annexes A, B, C and E.

6. Each Party shall refrain from providing new subsidies, aid, credits, guarantees or insurance programmes for the export to States not party to this Protocol of products, equipment, plants or technology that would facilitate the production of controlled substances in Annexes A, B, C and E.

7. Paragraphs 5 and 6 shall not apply to products, equipment, plants or technology that improve the containment, recovery, recycling or destruction of controlled substances, promote the development of alternative substances, or otherwise contribute to the reduction of emissions of controlled substances in Annexes A, B, C and E.

8. Notwithstanding the provisions of this Article, imports and exports referred to in paragraphs 1 to 4 ter of this Article may be permitted from, or to, any State not party to this Protocol, if that State is determined, by a meeting of the Parties, to be in full compliance with Article 2, Articles 2A to 2I and this Article, and have submitted data to that effect as specified in Article 7.

9. For the purposes of this Article, the term 'State not party to this Protocol' shall include, with respect to a particular controlled substance, a State or regional economic integration organization that has not agreed to be bound by the control measures in effect for that substance.

10. By 1 January 1996, the Parties shall consider whether to amend this Protocol in order to extend the measures in this Article to trade in controlled substances in Group I of Annex C and in Annex E with States not party to the Protocol.

Article 4A: Control of trade with Parties

1. Where, after the phase-out date applicable to it for a controlled substance, a Party is unable, despite having taken all practicable steps to comply with its obligation under the Protocol, to cease production of that substance for domestic consumption, other than for uses agreed by the Parties to be essential, it shall ban the export of used, recycled and reclaimed quantities of that substance, other than for the purpose of destruction.

2. Paragraph 1 of this Article shall apply without prejudice to the operation of Article 11 of the Convention and the noncompliance procedure developed under Article 8 of the Protocol.

Article 4B: Licensing

1. Each Party shall, by 1 January 2000 or within three months of the date of entry into force of this Article for it, whichever is the later, establish and implement a

system for licensing the import and export of new, used, recycled and reclaimed controlled substances in Annexes A, B, C and E.

2. Notwithstanding paragraph 1 of this Article, any Party operating under paragraph 1 of Article 5 which decides it is not in a position to establish and implement a system for licensing the import and export of controlled substances in Annexes C and E, may delay taking those actions until 1 January 2005 and 1 January 2002, respectively.

3. Each Party shall, within three months of the date of introducing its licensing system, report to the Secretariat on the establishment and operation of that system.

4. The Secretariat shall periodically prepare and circulate to all Parties a list of the Parties that have reported to it on their licensing systems and shall forward this information to the Implementation Committee for consideration and appropriate recommendations to the Parties.

Article 5: Special situation of developing countries

1. Any Party that is a developing country and whose annual calculated level of consumption of the controlled substances in Annex A is less than 0.3 kilograms per capita on the date of the entry into force of the Protocol for it, or any time thereafter until 1 January 1999, shall, in order to meet its basic domestic needs, be entitled to delay for ten years its compliance with the control measures set out in Articles 2A to 2E, provided that any further amendments to the adjustments or Amendment adopted at the Second Meeting of the Parties in London, 29 June 1990, shall apply to the Parties operating under this paragraph after the review provided for in paragraph 8 of this Article has taken place and shall be based on the conclusions of that review.

1 *bis*. The Parties shall, taking into account the review referred to in paragraph 8 of this Article, the assessments made pursuant to Article 6 and any other relevant information, decide by 1 January 1996, through the procedure set forth in paragraph 9 of Article 2:

(a) With respect to paragraphs 1 to 6 of Article 2F, what base year, initial levels, control schedules and phase-out date for consumption of the controlled substances in Group I of Annex C will apply to Parties operating under paragraph 1 of this Article;
(b) With respect to Article 2G, what phase-out date for production and consumption of the controlled substances in Group II of Annex C will apply to Parties operating under paragraph 1 of this Article; and
(c) With respect to Article 2H, what base year, initial levels and control schedules for consumption and production of the controlled substance in Annex E will apply to Parties operating under paragraph 1 of this Article.

2. However, any Party operating under paragraph 1 of this Article shall exceed neither an annual calculated level of consumption of the controlled substances in Annex A of 0.3 kilograms per capita nor an annual calculated level of consumption of controlled substances of Annex B of 0.2 kilograms per capita.

3. When implementing the control measures set out in Articles 2A to 2E, any Party operating under paragraph 1 of this Article shall be entitled to use:

(a) For controlled substances under Annex A, either the average of its annual calculated level of consumption for the period 1995 to 1997 inclusive or a calculated level of consumption of 0.3 kilograms per capita, whichever is the lower, as the basis for determining its compliance with the control measures relating to consumption.

(b) For controlled substances under Annex B, the average of its annual calculated level of consumption for the period 1998 to 2000 inclusive or a calculated level of consumption of 0.2 kilograms per capita, whichever is the lower, as the basis for determining its compliance with the control measures relating to consumption.

(c) For controlled substances under Annex A, either the average of its annual calculated level of production for the period 1995 to 1997 inclusive or a calculated level of production of 0.3 kilograms per capita, whichever is the lower, as the basis for determining its compliance with the control measures relating to production.

(d) For controlled substances under Annex B, either the average of its annual calculated level of production for the period 1998 to 2000 inclusive or a calculated level of production of 0.2 kilograms per capita, whichever is the lower, as the basis for determining its compliance with the control measures relating to production.

4. If a Party operating under paragraph 1 of this Article, at any time before the control measures obligations in Articles 2A to 2I become applicable to it, finds itself unable to obtain an adequate supply of controlled substances, it may notify this to the Secretariat. The Secretariat shall forthwith transmit a copy of such notification to the Parties, which shall consider the matter at their next Meeting, and decide upon appropriate action to be taken.

5. Developing the capacity to fulfil the obligations of the Parties operating under paragraph 1 of this Article to comply with the control measures set out in Articles 2A to 2E and Article 2I, and any control measures in Articles 2F to 2H that are decided pursuant to paragraph 1 *bis* of this Article, and their implementation by those same Parties will depend upon the effective implementation of the financial co-operation as provided by Article 10 and the transfer of technology as provided by Article 10A.

6. Any Party operating under paragraph 1 of this Article may, at any time, notify the Secretariat in writing that, having taken all practicable steps it is unable to implement any or all of the obligations laid down in Articles 2A to 2E and Article 2I, or any or all obligations in Articles 2F to 2H that are decided pursuant to paragraph 1 *bis* of this Article, due to the inadequate implementation of Articles 10 and 10A. The Secretariat shall forthwith transmit a copy of the notification to the Parties, which shall consider the matter at their next Meeting, giving due

recognition to paragraph 5 of this Article and shall decide upon appropriate action to be taken.

7. During the period between notification and the Meeting of the Parties at which the appropriate action referred to in paragraph 6 above is to be decided, or for a further period if the Meeting of the Parties so decides, the non-compliance procedures referred to in Article 8 shall not be invoked against the notifying Party.

8. A Meeting of the Parties shall review, not later than 1995, the situation of the Parties operating under paragraph 1 of this Article, including the effective implementation of financial co-operation and transfer of technology to them, and adopt such revisions that may be deemed necessary regarding the schedule of control measures applicable to those Parties.

8 *bis*. Based on the conclusions of the review referred to in paragraph 8 above:

(a) With respect to the controlled substances in Annex A, a Party operating under paragraph 1 of this Article shall, in order to meet its basic domestic needs, be entitled to delay for ten years its compliance with the control measures adopted by the Second Meeting of the Parties in London, 29 June 1990, and reference by the Protocol to Articles 2A and 2B shall be read accordingly;

(b) With respect to the controlled substances in Annex B, a Party operating under paragraph 1 of this Article shall, in order to meet its basic domestic needs, be entitled to delay for ten years its compliance with the control measures adopted by the Second Meeting of the Parties in London, 29 June 1990, and reference by the Protocol to Articles 2C to 2E shall be read accordingly.

8 *ter*. Pursuant to paragraph 1 *bis* above:

(a) Each Party operating under paragraph 1 of this Article shall ensure that for the twelve-month period commencing on 1 January 2016, and in each twelve-month period thereafter, its calculated level of consumption of the controlled substances in Group I of Annex C does not exceed, annually, its calculated level of consumption in 2015. As of 1 January 2016 each Party operating under paragraph 1 of this Article shall comply with the control measures set out in paragraph 8 of Article 2F and, as the basis for its compliance with these control measures, it shall use the average of its calculated levels of production and consumption in 2015;

(b) Each Party operating under paragraph 1 of this Article shall ensure that for the twelve-month period commencing on 1 January 2040, and in each twelve-month period thereafter, its calculated level of consumption of the controlled substances in Group I of Annex C does not exceed zero;

(c) Each Party operating under paragraph 1 of this Article shall comply with Article 2G;

(d) With regard to the controlled substance contained in Annex E:

   i) As of 1 January 2002 each Party operating under paragraph 1 of this Article shall comply with the control measures set out in paragraph 1 of Article 2H and, as the basis for its compliance with these control measures, it shall use the average of its annual calculated level of consumption and production, respectively, for the period of 1995 to 1998 inclusive;

ii) Each Party operating under paragraph 1 of this Article shall ensure that for the twelve-month period commencing on 1 January 2005, and in each twelve-month period thereafter, its calculated levels of consumption and production of the controlled substance in Annex E do not exceed, annually, eighty per cent of the average of its annual calculated levels of consumption and production, respectively, for the period of 1995 to 1998 inclusive;

iii) Each Party operating under paragraph 1 of this Article shall ensure that for the twelve-month period commencing on 1 January 2015 and in each twelve-month period thereafter, its calculated levels of consumption and production of the controlled substance in Annex E do not exceed zero. This paragraph will apply save to the extent that the Parties decide to permit the level of production or consumption that is necessary to satisfy uses agreed by them to be critical uses;

iv) The calculated levels of consumption and production under this subparagraph shall not include the amounts used by the Party for quarantine and pre-shipment applications.

9. Decisions of the Parties referred to in paragraph 4, 6 and 7 of this Article shall be taken according to the same procedure applied to decision-making under Article 10.

Article 6: Assessment and review of control measures

Beginning in 1990, and at least every four years thereafter, the Parties shall assess the control measures provided for in Article 2 and Articles 2A to 2I on the basis of available scientific, environmental, technical and economic information. At least one year before each assessment, the Parties shall convene appropriate panels of experts qualified in the fields mentioned and determine the composition and terms of reference of any such panels. Within one year of being convened, the panels will report their conclusions, through the Secretariat, to the Parties.

Article 7: Reporting of data

1. Each Party shall provide to the Secretariat, within three months of becoming a Party, statistical data on its production, imports and exports of each of the controlled substances in Annex A for the year 1986, or the best possible estimates of such data where actual data are not available.

2. Each Party shall provide to the Secretariat statistical data on its production, imports and exports of each of the controlled substances

- in Annex B and Annexes I and II of Group C for the year 1989;
- in Annex E, for the year 1991,

or the best possible estimates of such data where actual data are not available, not later than three months after the date when the provisions set out in the Protocol with regard to the substances in Annexes B, C and E respectively enter into force for that Party.

3. Each Party shall provide to the Secretariat statistical data on its annual production (as defined in paragraph 5 of Article 1) of each of the controlled substances listed in Annexes A, B, C and E and, separately, for each substance,

- Amounts used for feedstocks,
- Amounts destroyed by technologies approved by the Parties, and
- Imports from and exports to Parties and non-Parties respectively,

for the year during which provisions concerning the substances in Annexes A, B, C and E respectively entered into force for that Party and for each year thereafter. Each Party shall provide to the Secretariat statistical data on the annual amount of the controlled substance listed in Annex E used for quarantine and pre-shipment applications. Data shall be forwarded not later than nine months after the end of the year to which the data relate.

3 *bis*. Each Party shall provide to the Secretariat separate statistical data of its annual imports and exports of each of the controlled substances listed in Group II of Annex A and Group I of Annex C that have been recycled.

4. For Parties operating under the provisions of paragraph 8 (a) of Article 2, the requirements in paragraphs 1, 2, 3 and 3 *bis* of this Article in respect of statistical data on imports and exports shall be satisfied if the regional economic integration organization concerned provides data on imports and exports between the organization and States that are not members of that organization.

Article 8: Non-compliance

The Parties, at their first meeting, shall consider and approve procedures and institutional mechanisms for determining noncompliance with the provisions of this Protocol and for treatment of Parties found to be in non-compliance.

Article 9: Research, development, public awareness and exchange of information

1. The Parties shall co-operate, consistent with their national laws, regulations and practices and taking into account in particular the needs of developing countries, in promoting, directly or through competent international bodies, research, development and exchange of information on:

(a) best technologies for improving the containment, recovery, recycling, or destruction of controlled substances or otherwise reducing their emissions;

(b) possible alternatives to controlled substances, to products containing such substances, and to products manufactured with them; and

(c) costs and benefits of relevant control strategies.

2. The Parties, individually, jointly or through competent international bodies, shall co-operate in promoting public awareness of the environmental effects of the emissions of controlled substances and other substances that deplete the ozone layer.

3. Within two years of the entry into force of this Protocol and every two years thereafter, each Party shall submit to the Secretariat a summary of the activities it has conducted pursuant to this Article.

Article 10: Financial mechanism

1. The Parties shall establish a mechanism for the purposes of providing financial and technical co-operation, including the transfer of technologies, to Parties operating under paragraph 1 of Article 5 of this Protocol to enable their compliance with the control measures set out in Articles 2A to 2E and Article 2I, and any control measures in Articles 2F to 2H that are decided pursuant to paragraph 1 *bis* of Article 5 of the Protocol. The mechanism, contributions to which shall be additional to other financial transfers to Parties operating under that paragraph, shall meet all agreed incremental costs of such Parties in order to enable their compliance with the control measures of the Protocol. An indicative list of the categories of incremental costs shall be decided by the meeting of the Parties.

2. The mechanism established under paragraph 1 shall include a Multilateral Fund. It may also include other means of multilateral, regional and bilateral co-operation.

3. The Multilateral Fund shall:

(a) Meet, on a grant or concessional basis as appropriate, and according to criteria to be decided upon by the Parties, the agreed incremental costs;

(b) Finance clearing-house functions to:

i) Assist Parties operating under paragraph 1 of Article 5, through country specific studies and other technical co-operation, to identify their needs for co-operation;

ii) Facilitate technical co-operation to meet these identified needs;

iii) Distribute, as provided for in Article 9, information and relevant materials, and hold workshops, training sessions, and other related activities, for the benefit of Parties that are developing countries; and

iv) Facilitate and monitor other multilateral, regional and bilateral co-operation available to Parties that are developing countries;

(c) Finance the secretarial services of the Multilateral Fund and related support costs.

4. The Multilateral Fund shall operate under the authority of the Parties who shall decide on its overall policies.

5. The Parties shall establish an Executive Committee to develop and monitor the implementation of specific operational policies, guidelines and administrative arrangements, including the disbursement of resources, for the purpose of achieving the objectives of the Multilateral Fund. The Executive Committee shall discharge its tasks and responsibilities, specified in its terms of reference as agreed by the Parties, with the co-operation and assistance of the International Bank for Reconstruction and Development (World Bank), the United Nations Environment Programme, the United Nations Development Programme or other appropriate agencies depending on their respective areas of expertise. The members of the

Executive Committee, which shall be selected on the basis of a balanced representation of the Parties operating under paragraph 1 of Article 5 and of the Parties not so operating, shall be endorsed by the Parties.

6. The Multilateral Fund shall be financed by contributions from Parties not operating under paragraph 1 of Article 5 in convertible currency or, in certain circumstances, in kind and/or in national currency, on the basis of the United Nations scale of assessments. Contributions by other Parties shall be encouraged. Bilateral and, in particular cases agreed by a decision of the Parties, regional co-operation may, up to a percentage and consistent with any criteria to be specified by decision of the Parties, be considered as a contribution to the Multilateral Fund, provided that such co-operation, as a minimum:

(a) Strictly relates to compliance with the provisions of this Protocol;

(b) Provides additional resources; and

(c) Meets agreed incremental costs.

7. The Parties shall decide upon the programme budget of the Multilateral Fund for each fiscal period and upon the percentage of contributions of the individual Parties thereto.

8. Resources under the Multilateral Fund shall be disbursed with the concurrence of the beneficiary Party.

9. Decisions by the Parties under this Article shall be taken by consensus whenever possible. If all efforts at consensus have been exhausted and no agreement reached, decisions shall be adopted by a two-thirds majority vote of the Parties present and voting, representing a majority of the Parties operating under paragraph 1 of Article 5 present and voting and a majority of the Parties not so operating present and voting.

10. The financial mechanism set out in this Article is without prejudice to any future arrangements that may be developed with respect to other environmental issues.

Article 10A: Transfer of technology

Each Party shall take every practicable step, consistent with the programmes supported by the financial mechanism, to ensure:

(a) that the best available, environmentally safe substitutes and related technologies are expeditiously transferred to Parties operating under paragraph 1 of Article 5; and

(b) that the transfers referred to in subparagraph (a) occur under fair and most favourable conditions.

Article 11: Meetings of the Parties

1. The Parties shall hold meetings at regular intervals. The Secretariat shall convene the first meeting of the Parties not later than one year after the date of the entry into force of this Protocol and in conjunction with a meeting of the

Conference of the Parties to the Convention, if a meeting of the latter is scheduled within that period.

2. Subsequent ordinary meetings of the parties shall be held, unless the Parties otherwise decide, in conjunction with meetings of the Conference of the Parties to the Convention. Extraordinary meetings of the Parties shall be held at such other times as may be deemed necessary by a meeting of the Parties, or at the written request of any Party, provided that within six months of such a request being communicated to them by the Secretariat, it is supported by at least one third of the Parties.

3. The Parties, at their first meeting, shall:

(a) adopt by consensus rules of procedure for their meetings;

(b) adopt by consensus the financial rules referred to in paragraph 2 of Article 13;

(c) establish the panels and determine the terms of reference referred to in Article 6;

(d) consider and approve the procedures and institutional mechanisms specified in Article 8; and

(e) begin preparation of workplans pursuant to paragraph 3 of Article 10.

4. The functions of the meetings of the Parties shall be to:

(a) review the implementation of this Protocol;

(b) decide on any adjustments or reductions referred to in paragraph 9 of Article 2;

(c) decide on any addition to, insertion in or removal from any annex of substances and on related control measures in accordance with paragraph 10 of Article 2;

(d) establish, where necessary, guidelines or procedures for reporting of information as provided for in Article 7 and paragraph 3 of Article 9;

(e) review requests for technical assistance submitted pursuant to paragraph 2 of Article 10;

(f) review reports prepared by the secretariat pursuant to subparagraph (c) of Article 12;

(g) assess, in accordance with Article 6, the control measures;

(h) consider and adopt, as required, proposals for amendment of this Protocol or any annex and for any new annex;

(i) consider and adopt the budget for implementing this Protocol; and

(j) consider and undertake any additional action that may be required for the achievement of the purposes of this Protocol.

5. The United Nations, its specialized agencies and the International Atomic Energy Agency, as well as any State not party to this Protocol, may be represented at meetings of the Parties as observers. Any body or agency, whether national or international, governmental or non-governmental, qualified in fields relating to the protection of the ozone layer which has informed the secretariat of its wish to be represented at a meeting of the Parties as an observer may be admitted unless at least one third of the Parties present object. The admission and participation of observers shall be subject to the rules of procedure adopted by the Parties.

Article 12: Secretariat

For the purposes of this Protocol, the Secretariat shall:

(a) arrange for and service meetings of the Parties as provided for in Article 11;

(b) receive and make available, upon request by a Party, data provided pursuant to Article 7;

(c) prepare and distribute regularly to the Parties reports based on information received pursuant to Articles 7 and 9;

(d) notify the Parties of any request for technical assistance received pursuant to Article 10 so as to facilitate the provision of such assistance;

(e) encourage non-Parties to attend the meetings of the Parties as observers and to act in accordance with the provisions of this Protocol;

(f) provide, as appropriate, the information and requests referred to in subparagraphs (c) and (d) to such non-party observers; and

(g) perform such other functions for the achievement of the purposes of this Protocol as may be assigned to it by the Parties.

Article 13: Financial provisions

1. The funds required for the operation of this Protocol, including those for the functioning of the Secretariat related to this Protocol, shall be charged exclusively against contributions from the Parties.

2. The Parties, at their first meeting, shall adopt by consensus financial rules for the operation of this Protocol.

Article 14: Relationship of this Protocol to the Convention

Except as otherwise provided in this Protocol, the provisions of the Convention relating to its protocols shall apply to this Protocol.

Article 15: Signature

This Protocol shall be open for signature by States and by regional economic integration organizations in Montreal on 16 September 1987, in Ottawa from 17 September 1987 to 16 January 1988, and at United Nations Headquarters in New York from 17 January 1988 to 15 September 1988.

Article 16: Entry into force

1. This Protocol shall enter into force on 1 January 1989, provided that at least eleven instruments of ratification, acceptance, approval of the Protocol or accession thereto have been deposited by States or regional economic integration organizations representing at least two-thirds of 1986 estimated global consumption of the controlled substances, and the provisions of paragraph 1 of Article 17 of the Convention have been fulfilled. In the event that these conditions have not been fulfilled by that date, the Protocol shall enter into force on the ninetieth day following the date on which the conditions have been fulfilled.

2. For the purposes of paragraph 1, any such instrument deposited by a regional economic integration organization shall not be counted as additional to those deposited by member States of such organization.

3. After the entry into force of this Protocol, any State or regional economic integration organization shall become a Party to it on the ninetieth day following the date of deposit of its instrument of ratification, acceptance, approval or accession.

Article 17: Parties joining after entry into force

Subject to Article 5, any State or regional economic integration organization which becomes a Party to this Protocol after the date of its entry into force, shall fulfil forthwith the sum of the obligations under Article 2, as well as under Articles 2A to 2I and Article 4, that apply at that date to the States and regional economic integration organizations that became Parties on the date the Protocol entered into force.

Article 18: Reservations

No reservations may be made to this Protocol.

Article 19: Withdrawal

Any Party may withdraw from this Protocol by giving written notification to the Depositary at any time after four years of assuming the obligations specified in paragraph 1 of Article 2A. Any such withdrawal shall take effect upon expiry of one year after the date of its receipt by the Depositary, or on such later date as may be specified in the notification of the withdrawal.

Article 20: Authentic texts

The original of this Protocol, of which the Arabic, Chinese, English, French, Russian and Spanish texts are equally authentic, shall be deposited with the Secretary-General of the United Nations.

In witness whereof the undersigned, being duly authorized to that effect, have signed this Protocol.

Done at Montreal this sixteenth day of September, one thousand nine hundred and eighty seven.

Annex A: Controlled substances; Annex B: Controlled substances; Annex C: Controlled substances; Annex D: A list of products containing controlled substances specified in Annex A; Annex E: Controlled substance [not reproduced]

Climate change

United Nations Framework Convention on Climate Change

Adopted on 9 May 1992 at New York. Entered into force on 21 March 1994. Source: 1771 *UNTS* 107 (the text reproduced includes the amendments to the Annexes adopted in 1997 and 2001). Number of parties: 188. Further information: UNFCCC Secretariat, Bonn, Germany, http://www.unfccc.int

The Parties to this Convention,

Acknowledging that change in the Earth's climate and its adverse effects are a common concern of humankind,

Concerned that human activities have been substantially increasing the atmospheric concentrations of greenhouse gases, that these increases enhance the natural greenhouse effect, and that this will result on average in an additional warming of the Earth's surface and atmosphere and may adversely affect natural ecosystems and humankind,

Noting that the largest share of historical and current global emissions of greenhouse gases has originated in developed countries, that per capita emissions in developing countries are still relatively low and that the share of global emissions originating in developing countries will grow to meet their social and development needs,

Aware of the role and importance in terrestrial and marine ecosystems of sinks and reservoirs of greenhouse gases,

Noting that there are many uncertainties in predictions of climate change, particularly with regard to the timing, magnitude and regional patterns thereof,

Acknowledging that the global nature of climate change calls for the widest possible cooperation by all countries and their participation in an effective and appropriate international response, in accordance with their common but differentiated responsibilities and respective capabilities and their social and economic conditions,

Recalling the pertinent provisions of the Declaration of the United Nations Conference on the Human Environment, adopted at Stockholm on 16 June 1972,

Recalling also that States have, in accordance with the Charter of the United Nations and the principles of international law, the sovereign right to exploit their own resources pursuant to their own environmental and developmental policies, and the responsibility to ensure that activities within their jurisdiction or control do not cause damage to the environment of other States or of areas beyond the limits of national jurisdiction,

Reaffirming the principle of sovereignty of States in international cooperation to address climate change,

Recognizing that States should enact effective environmental legislation, that environmental standards, management objectives and priorities should reflect the environmental and developmental context to which they apply, and that standards applied by some countries may be inappropriate and of unwarranted economic and social cost to other countries, in particular developing countries,

Recalling the provisions of General Assembly resolution 44/228 of 22 December 1989 on the United Nations Conference on Environment and Development, and resolutions 43/53 of 6 December 1988, 44/207 of 22 December 1989, 45/212 of 21 December 1990 and 46/169 of 19 December 1991 on protection of global climate for present and future generations of mankind,

Recalling also the provisions of General Assembly resolution 44/206 of 22 December 1989 on the possible adverse effects of sea-level rise on islands and coastal areas, particularly low-lying coastal areas and the pertinent provisions of General Assembly resolution 44/172 of 19 December 1989 on the implementation of the Plan of Action to Combat Desertification,

Recalling further the Vienna Convention for the Protection of the Ozone Layer, 1985, and the Montreal Protocol on Substances that Deplete the Ozone Layer, 1987, as adjusted and amended on 29 June 1990,

Noting the Ministerial Declaration of the Second World Climate Conference adopted on 7 November 1990,

Conscious of the valuable analytical work being conducted by many States on climate change and of the important contributions of the World Meteorological Organization, the United Nations Environment Programme and other organs, organizations and bodies of the United Nations system, as well as other international and intergovernmental bodies, to the exchange of results of scientific research and the coordination of research,

Recognizing that steps required to understand and address climate change will be environmentally, socially and economically most effective if they are based on relevant scientific, technical and economic considerations and continually re-evaluated in the light of new findings in these areas,

Recognizing that various actions to address climate change can be justified economically in their own right and can also help in solving other environmental problems,

Recognizing also the need for developed countries to take immediate action in a flexible manner on the basis of clear priorities, as a first step towards comprehensive response strategies at the global, national and, where agreed, regional levels that take into account all greenhouse gases, with due consideration of their relative contributions to the enhancement of the greenhouse effect,

Recognizing further that low-lying and other small island countries, countries with low-lying coastal, arid and semi-arid areas or areas liable to floods, drought and desertification, and developing countries with fragile mountainous ecosystems are particularly vulnerable to the adverse effects of climate change,

Recognizing the special difficulties of those countries, especially developing countries, whose economies are particularly dependent on fossil fuel production, use and exportation, as a consequence of action taken on limiting greenhouse gas emissions,

Affirming that responses to climate change should be coordinated with social and economic development in an integrated manner with a view to avoiding adverse impacts on the latter, taking into full account the legitimate priority needs of developing countries for the achievement of sustained economic growth and the eradication of poverty,

Recognizing that all countries, especially developing countries, need access to resources required to achieve sustainable social and economic development and that, in order for developing countries to progress towards that goal, their energy consumption will need to grow taking into account the possibilities for achieving greater energy efficiency and for controlling greenhouse gas emissions in general, including through the application of new technologies on terms which make such an application economically and socially beneficial,

Determined to protect the climate system for present and future generations,

Have agreed as follows:

Article 1: Definitions

For the purposes of this Convention:

1. 'Adverse effects of climate change' means changes in the physical environment or biota resulting from climate change which have significant deleterious effects on the composition, resilience or productivity of natural and managed ecosystems or on the operation of socio-economic systems or on human health and welfare.

2. 'Climate change' means a change of climate which is attributed directly or indirectly to human activity that alters the composition of the global atmosphere and which is in addition to natural climate variability observed over comparable time periods.

3. 'Climate system' means the totality of the atmosphere, hydrosphere, biosphere and geosphere and their interactions.

4. 'Emissions' means the release of greenhouse gases and/or their precursors into the atmosphere over a specified area and period of time.

5. 'Greenhouse gases' means those gaseous constituents of the atmosphere, both natural and anthropogenic, that absorb and re-emit infrared radiation.

6. 'Regional economic integration organization' means an organization constituted by sovereign States of a given region which has competence in respect of matters

governed by this Convention or its protocols and has been duly authorized, in accordance with its internal procedures, to sign, ratify, accept, approve or accede to the instruments concerned.

7. 'Reservoir' means a component or components of the climate system where a greenhouse gas or a precursor of a greenhouse gas is stored.

8. 'Sink' means any process, activity or mechanism which removes a greenhouse gas, an aerosol or a precursor of a greenhouse gas from the atmosphere.

9. 'Source' means any process or activity which releases a greenhouse gas, an aerosol or a precursor of a greenhouse gas into the atmosphere.

Article 2: Objective

The ultimate objective of this Convention and any related legal instruments that the Conference of the Parties may adopt is to achieve, in accordance with the relevant provisions of the Convention, stabilization of greenhouse gas concentrations in the atmosphere at a level that would prevent dangerous anthropogenic interference with the climate system. Such a level should be achieved within a time-frame sufficient to allow ecosystems to adapt naturally to climate change, to ensure that food production is not threatened and to enable economic development to proceed in a sustainable manner.

Article 3: Principles

In their actions to achieve the objective of the Convention and to implement its provisions, the Parties shall be guided, *inter alia*, by the following:

1. The Parties should protect the climate system for the benefit of present and future generations of humankind, on the basis of equity and in accordance with their common but differentiated responsibilities and respective capabilities. Accordingly, the developed country Parties should take the lead in combating climate change and the adverse effects thereof.

2. The specific needs and special circumstances of developing country Parties, especially those that are particularly vulnerable to the adverse effects of climate change, and of those Parties, especially developing country Parties, that would have to bear a disproportionate or abnormal burden under the Convention, should be given full consideration.

3. The Parties should take precautionary measures to anticipate, prevent or minimize the causes of climate change and mitigate its adverse effects. Where there are threats of serious or irreversible damage, lack of full scientific certainty should not be used as a reason for postponing such measures, taking into account that policies and measures to deal with climate change should be cost-effective so as to ensure global benefits at the lowest possible cost. To achieve this, such policies and measures should take into account different socio-economic contexts, be comprehensive, cover all relevant sources, sinks and reservoirs of greenhouse gases and adaptation, and comprise all economic sectors. Efforts to address climate change may be carried out cooperatively by interested Parties.

4. The Parties have a right to, and should, promote sustainable development. Policies and measures to protect the climate system against human-induced change should be appropriate for the specific conditions of each Party and should be integrated with national development programmes, taking into account that economic development is essential for adopting measures to address climate change.

5. The Parties should cooperate to promote a supportive and open international economic system that would lead to sustainable economic growth and development in all Parties, particularly developing country Parties, thus enabling them better to address the problems of climate change. Measures taken to combat climate change, including unilateral ones, should not constitute a means of arbitrary or unjustifiable discrimination or a disguised restriction on international trade.

Article 4: Commitments

1. All Parties, taking into account their common but differentiated responsibilities and their specific national and regional development priorities, objectives and circumstances, shall:

(a) Develop, periodically update, publish and make available to the Conference of the Parties, in accordance with Article 12, national inventories of anthropogenic emissions by sources and removals by sinks of all greenhouse gases not controlled by the Montreal Protocol, using comparable methodologies to be agreed upon by the Conference of the Parties;

(b) Formulate, implement, publish and regularly update national and, where appropriate, regional programmes containing measures to mitigate climate change by addressing anthropogenic emissions by sources and removals by sinks of all greenhouse gases not controlled by the Montreal Protocol, and measures to facilitate adequate adaptation to climate change;

(c) Promote and cooperate in the development, application and diffusion, including transfer, of technologies, practices and processes that control, reduce or prevent anthropogenic emissions of greenhouse gases not controlled by the Montreal Protocol in all relevant sectors, including the energy, transport, industry, agriculture, forestry and waste management sectors;

(d) Promote sustainable management, and promote and cooperate in the conservation and enhancement, as appropriate, of sinks and reservoirs of all greenhouse gases not controlled by the Montreal Protocol, including biomass, forests and oceans as well as other terrestrial, coastal and marine ecosystems;

(e) Cooperate in preparing for adaptation to the impacts of climate change; develop and elaborate appropriate and integrated plans for coastal zone management, water resources and agriculture, and for the protection and rehabilitation of areas, particularly in Africa, affected by drought and desertification, as well as floods;

(f) Take climate change considerations into account, to the extent feasible, in their relevant social, economic and environmental policies and actions, and employ appropriate methods, for example impact assessments, formulated and determined nationally, with a view to minimizing adverse effects on the economy, on public health and on the quality of the environment, of projects or measures undertaken by them to mitigate or adapt to climate change;

(g) Promote and cooperate in scientific, technological, technical, socio-economic and other research, systematic observation and development of data archives related to the climate system and intended to further the understanding and to reduce or eliminate the remaining uncertainties regarding the causes, effects, magnitude and timing of climate change and the economic and social consequences of various response strategies;

(h) Promote and cooperate in the full, open and prompt exchange of relevant scientific, technological, technical, socio-economic and legal information related to the climate system and climate change, and to the economic and social consequences of various response strategies;

(i) Promote and cooperate in education, training and public awareness related to climate change and encourage the widest participation in this process, including that of non-governmental organizations; and

(j) Communicate to the Conference of the Parties information related to implementation, in accordance with Article 12.

2. The developed country Parties and other Parties included in Annex I commit themselves specifically as provided for in the following:

(a) Each of these Parties shall adopt national* policies and take corresponding measures on the mitigation of climate change, by limiting its anthropogenic emissions of greenhouse gases and protecting and enhancing its greenhouse gas sinks and reservoirs. These policies and measures will demonstrate that developed countries are taking the lead in modifying longer-term trends in anthropogenic emissions consistent with the objective of the Convention, recognizing that the return by the end of the present decade to earlier levels of anthropogenic emissions of carbon dioxide and other greenhouse gases not controlled by the Montreal Protocol would contribute to such modification, and taking into account the differences in these Parties' starting points and approaches, economic structures and resource bases, the need to maintain strong and sustainable economic growth, available technologies and other individual circumstances, as well as the need for equitable and appropriate contributions by each of these Parties to the global effort regarding that objective. These Parties may implement such policies and measures jointly with other Parties and may assist other Parties in contributing to the achievement of the objective of the Convention and, in particular, that of this subparagraph;

(b) In order to promote progress to this end, each of these Parties shall communicate, within six months of the entry into force of the Convention for it and periodically thereafter, and in accordance with Article 12, detailed

---

* This includes policies and measures adopted by regional economic integration organizations.

information on its policies and measures referred to in subparagraph (a) above, as well as on its resulting projected anthropogenic emissions by sources and removals by sinks of greenhouse gases not controlled by the Montreal Protocol for the period referred to in subparagraph (a), with the aim of returning individually or jointly to their 1990 levels these anthropogenic emissions of carbon dioxide and other greenhouse gases not controlled by the Montreal Protocol. This information will be reviewed by the Conference of the Parties, at its first session and periodically thereafter, in accordance with Article 7;

(c) Calculations of emissions by sources and removals by sinks of greenhouse gases for the purposes of subparagraph (b) above should take into account the best available scientific knowledge, including of the effective capacity of sinks and the respective contributions of such gases to climate change. The Conference of the Parties shall consider and agree on methodologies for these calculations at its first session and review them regularly thereafter;

(d) The Conference of the Parties shall, at its first session, review the adequacy of subparagraphs (a) and (b) above. Such review shall be carried out in the light of the best available scientific information and assessment on climate change and its impacts, as well as relevant technical, social and economic information. Based on this review, the Conference of the Parties shall take appropriate action, which may include the adoption of amendments to the commitments in subparagraphs (a) and (b) above. The Conference of the Parties, at its first session, shall also take decisions regarding criteria for joint implementation as indicated in subparagraph (a) above. A second review of subparagraphs (a) and (b) shall take place not later than 31 December 1998, and thereafter at regular intervals determined by the Conference of the Parties, until the objective of the Convention is met;

(e) Each of these Parties shall:

  i) Coordinate as appropriate with other such Parties, relevant economic and administrative instruments developed to achieve the objective of the Convention; and

  ii) Identify and periodically review its own policies and practices which encourage activities that lead to greater levels of anthropogenic emissions of greenhouse gases not controlled by the Montreal Protocol than would otherwise occur;

(f) The Conference of the Parties shall review, not later than 31 December 1998, available information with a view to taking decisions regarding such amendments to the lists in Annexes I and II as may be appropriate, with the approval of the Party concerned;

(g) Any Party not included in Annex I may, in its instrument of ratification, acceptance, approval or accession, or at any time thereafter, notify the Depositary that it intends to be bound by subparagraphs (a) and (b) above. The Depositary shall inform the other signatories and Parties of any such notification.

3. The developed country Parties and other developed Parties included in Annex II shall provide new and additional financial resources to meet the agreed full costs incurred by developing country Parties in complying with their obligations under Article 12, paragraph 1. They shall also provide such financial resources, including for the transfer of technology, needed by the developing country Parties to meet the agreed full incremental costs of implementing measures that are covered by paragraph 1 of this Article and that are agreed between a developing country Party and the international entity or entities referred to in Article 11, in accordance with that Article. The implementation of these commitments shall take into account the need for adequacy and predictability in the flow of funds and the importance of appropriate burden sharing among the developed country Parties.

4. The developed country Parties and other developed Parties included in Annex II shall also assist the developing country Parties that are particularly vulnerable to the adverse effects of climate change in meeting costs of adaptation to those adverse effects.

5. The developed country Parties and other developed Parties included in Annex II shall take all practicable steps to promote, facilitate and finance, as appropriate, the transfer of, or access to, environmentally sound technologies and know-how to other Parties, particularly developing country Parties, to enable them to implement the provisions of the Convention. In this process, the developed country Parties shall support the development and enhancement of endogenous capacities and technologies of developing country Parties. Other Parties and organizations in a position to do so may also assist in facilitating the transfer of such technologies.

6. In the implementation of their commitments under paragraph 2 above, a certain degree of flexibility shall be allowed by the Conference of the Parties to the Parties included in Annex I undergoing the process of transition to a market economy, in order to enhance the ability of these Parties to address climate change, including with regard to the historical level of anthropogenic emissions of greenhouse gases not controlled by the Montreal Protocol chosen as a reference.

7. The extent to which developing country Parties will effectively implement their commitments under the Convention will depend on the effective implementation by developed country Parties of their commitments under the Convention related to financial resources and transfer of technology and will take fully into account that economic and social development and poverty eradication are the first and overriding priorities of the developing country Parties.

8. In the implementation of the commitments in this Article, the Parties shall give full consideration to what actions are necessary under the Convention, including actions related to funding, insurance and the transfer of technology, to meet the specific needs and concerns of developing country Parties arising from the adverse effects of climate change and/or the impact of the implementation of response measures, especially on:

(a) Small island countries;

(b) Countries with low-lying coastal areas;
(c) Countries with arid and semi-arid areas, forested areas and areas liable to forest decay;
(d) Countries with areas prone to natural disasters;
(e) Countries with areas liable to drought and desertification;
(f) Countries with areas of high urban atmospheric pollution;
(g) Countries with areas with fragile ecosystems, including mountainous ecosystems;
(h) Countries whose economies are highly dependent on income generated from the production, processing and export, and/or on consumption of fossil fuels and associated energy-intensive products; and
(i) Land-locked and transit countries.

Further, the Conference of the Parties may take actions, as appropriate, with respect to this paragraph.

9. The Parties shall take full account of the specific needs and special situations of the least developed countries in their actions with regard to funding and transfer of technology.

10. The Parties shall, in accordance with Article 10, take into consideration in the implementation of the commitments of the Convention the situation of Parties, particularly developing country Parties, with economies that are vulnerable to the adverse effects of the implementation of measures to respond to climate change. This applies notably to Parties with economies that are highly dependent on income generated from the production, processing and export, and/or consumption of fossil fuels and associated energy-intensive products and/or the use of fossil fuels for which such Parties have serious difficulties in switching to alternatives.

Article 5: Research and systematic observation

In carrying out their commitments under Article 4, paragraph 1(g), the Parties shall:

(a) Support and further develop, as appropriate, international and intergovernmental programmes and networks or organizations aimed at defining, conducting, assessing and financing research, data collection and systematic observation, taking into account the need to minimize duplication of effort;

(b) Support international and intergovernmental efforts to strengthen systematic observation and national scientific and technical research capacities and capabilities, particularly in developing countries, and to promote access to, and the exchange of, data and analyses thereof obtained from areas beyond national jurisdiction; and

(c) Take into account the particular concerns and needs of developing countries and cooperate in improving their endogenous capacities and capabilities to participate in the efforts referred to in subparagraphs (a) and (b) above.

Article 6: Education, training and public awareness

In carrying out their commitments under Article 4, paragraph 1(i), the Parties shall:

(a) Promote and facilitate at the national and, as appropriate, subregional and regional levels, and in accordance with national laws and regulations, and within their respective capacities:

i) The development and implementation of educational and public awareness programmes on climate change and its effects;

ii) Public access to information on climate change and its effects;

iii) Public participation in addressing climate change and its effects and developing adequate responses; and

iv) Training of scientific, technical and managerial personnel.

(b) Cooperate in and promote, at the international level, and, where appropriate, using existing bodies:

i) The development and exchange of educational and public awareness material on climate change and its effects; and

ii) The development and implementation of education and training programmes, including the strengthening of national institutions and the exchange or secondment of personnel to train experts in this field, in particular for developing countries.

Article 7: Conference of the Parties

1. A Conference of the Parties is hereby established.

2. The Conference of the Parties, as the supreme body of this Convention, shall keep under regular review the implementation of the Convention and any related legal instruments that the Conference of the Parties may adopt, and shall make, within its mandate, the decisions necessary to promote the effective implementation of the Convention. To this end, it shall:

(a) Periodically examine the obligations of the Parties and the institutional arrangements under the Convention, in the light of the objective of the Convention, the experience gained in its implementation and the evolution of scientific and technological knowledge;

(b) Promote and facilitate the exchange of information on measures adopted by the Parties to address climate change and its effects, taking into account the differing circumstances, responsibilities and capabilities of the Parties and their respective commitments under the Convention;

(c) Facilitate, at the request of two or more Parties, the coordination of measures adopted by them to address climate change and its effects, taking into account the differing circumstances, responsibilities and capabilities of the Parties and their respective commitments under the Convention;

(d) Promote and guide, in accordance with the objective and provisions of the Convention, the development and periodic refinement of comparable methodologies, to be agreed on by the Conference of the Parties, *inter alia*, for preparing inventories of greenhouse gas emissions by sources and removals by sinks, and for evaluating the effectiveness of measures to limit the emissions and enhance the removals of these gases;

(e) Assess, on the basis of all information made available to it in accordance with the provisions of the Convention, the implementation of the Convention by the Parties, the overall effects of the measures taken pursuant to the Convention, in particular environmental, economic and social effects as well as their cumulative impacts and the extent to which progress towards the objective of the Convention is being achieved;
(f) Consider and adopt regular reports on the implementation of the Convention and ensure their publication;
(g) Make recommendations on any matters necessary for the implementation of the Convention;
(h) Seek to mobilize financial resources in accordance with Article 4, paragraphs 3, 4 and 5, and Article 11;
(i) Establish such subsidiary bodies as are deemed necessary for the implementation of the Convention;
(j) Review reports submitted by its subsidiary bodies and provide guidance to them;
(k) Agree upon and adopt, by consensus, rules of procedure and financial rules for itself and for any subsidiary bodies;
(l) Seek and utilize, where appropriate, the services and cooperation of, and information provided by, competent international organizations and intergovernmental and non-governmental bodies; and
(m) Exercise such other functions as are required for the achievement of the objective of the Convention as well as all other functions assigned to it under the Convention.

3. The Conference of the Parties shall, at its first session, adopt its own rules of procedure as well as those of the subsidiary bodies established by the Convention, which shall include decision-making procedures for matters not already covered by decision-making procedures stipulated in the Convention. Such procedures may include specified majorities required for the adoption of particular decisions.

4. The first session of the Conference of the Parties shall be convened by the interim secretariat referred to in Article 21 and shall take place not later than one year after the date of entry into force of the Convention. Thereafter, ordinary sessions of the Conference of the Parties shall be held every year unless otherwise decided by the Conference of the Parties.

5. Extraordinary sessions of the Conference of the Parties shall be held at such other times as may be deemed necessary by the Conference, or at the written request of any Party, provided that, within six months of the request being communicated to the Parties by the secretariat, it is supported by at least one third of the Parties.

6. The United Nations, its specialized agencies and the International Atomic Energy Agency, as well as any State member thereof or observers thereto not Party to the Convention, may be represented at sessions of the Conference of the Parties as observers. Any body or agency, whether national or international, governmental

or non-governmental, which is qualified in matters covered by the Convention, and which has informed the secretariat of its wish to be represented at a session of the Conference of the Parties as an observer, may be so admitted unless at least one third of the Parties present object. The admission and participation of observers shall be subject to the rules of procedure adopted by the Conference of the Parties.

Article 8: Secretariat

1. A secretariat is hereby established.

2. The functions of the secretariat shall be:

(a) To make arrangements for sessions of the Conference of the Parties and its subsidiary bodies established under the Convention and to provide them with services as required;

(b) To compile and transmit reports submitted to it;

(c) To facilitate assistance to the Parties, particularly developing country Parties, on request, in the compilation and communication of information required in accordance with the provisions of the Convention;

(d) To prepare reports on its activities and present them to the Conference of the Parties;

(e) To ensure the necessary coordination with the secretariats of other relevant international bodies;

(f) To enter, under the overall guidance of the Conference of the Parties, into such administrative and contractual arrangements as may be required for the effective discharge of its functions; and

(g) To perform the other secretariat functions specified in the Convention and in any of its protocols and such other functions as may be determined by the Conference of the Parties.

3. The Conference of the Parties, at its first session, shall designate a permanent secretariat and make arrangements for its functioning.

Article 9: Subsidiary body for scientific and technological advice

1. A subsidiary body for scientific and technological advice is hereby established to provide the Conference of the Parties and, as appropriate, its other subsidiary bodies with timely information and advice on scientific and technological matters relating to the Convention. This body shall be open to participation by all Parties and shall be multidisciplinary. It shall comprise government representatives competent in the relevant field of expertise. It shall report regularly to the Conference of the Parties on all aspects of its work.

2. Under the guidance of the Conference of the Parties, and drawing upon existing competent international bodies, this body shall:

(a) Provide assessments of the state of scientific knowledge relating to climate change and its effects;

(b) Prepare scientific assessments on the effects of measures taken in the implementation of the Convention;

(c) Identify innovative, efficient and state-of-the-art technologies and know-how and advise on the ways and means of promoting development and/or transferring such technologies;
(d) Provide advice on scientific programmes, international cooperation in research and development related to climate change, as well as on ways and means of supporting endogenous capacity-building in developing countries; and
(e) Respond to scientific, technological and methodological questions that the Conference of the Parties and its subsidiary bodies may put to the body.

3. The functions and terms of reference of this body may be further elaborated by the Conference of the Parties.

Article 10: Subsidiary body for implementation

1. A subsidiary body for implementation is hereby established to assist the Conference of the Parties in the assessment and review of the effective implementation of the Convention. This body shall be open to participation by all Parties and comprise government representatives who are experts on matters related to climate change. It shall report regularly to the Conference of the Parties on all aspects of its work.

2. Under the guidance of the Conference of the Parties, this body shall:
(a) Consider the information communicated in accordance with Article 12, paragraph 1, to assess the overall aggregated effect of the steps taken by the Parties in the light of the latest scientific assessments concerning climate change;
(b) Consider the information communicated in accordance with Article 12, paragraph 2, in order to assist the Conference of the Parties in carrying out the reviews required by Article 4, paragraph 2(d); and
(c) Assist the Conference of the Parties, as appropriate, in the preparation and implementation of its decisions.

Article 11: Financial mechanism

1. A mechanism for the provision of financial resources on a grant or concessional basis, including for the transfer of technology, is hereby defined. It shall function under the guidance of and be accountable to the Conference of the Parties, which shall decide on its policies, programme priorities and eligibility criteria related to this Convention. Its operation shall be entrusted to one or more existing international entities.

2. The financial mechanism shall have an equitable and balanced representation of all Parties within a transparent system of governance.

3. The Conference of the Parties and the entity or entities entrusted with the operation of the financial mechanism shall agree upon arrangements to give effect to the above paragraphs, which shall include the following:
(a) Modalities to ensure that the funded projects to address climate change are in conformity with the policies, programme priorities and eligibility criteria established by the Conference of the Parties;

(b) Modalities by which a particular funding decision may be reconsidered in light of these policies, programme priorities and eligibility criteria;
(c) Provision by the entity or entities of regular reports to the Conference of the Parties on its funding operations, which is consistent with the requirement for accountability set out in paragraph 1 above; and
(d) Determination in a predictable and identifiable manner of the amount of funding necessary and available for the implementation of this Convention and the conditions under which that amount shall be periodically reviewed.

4. The Conference of the Parties shall make arrangements to implement the above-mentioned provisions at its first session, reviewing and taking into account the interim arrangements referred to in Article 21, paragraph 3, and shall decide whether these interim arrangements shall be maintained. Within four years thereafter, the Conference of the Parties shall review the financial mechanism and take appropriate measures.

5. The developed country Parties may also provide and developing country Parties avail themselves of, financial resources related to the implementation of the Convention through bilateral, regional and other multilateral channels.

Article 12: Communication of information related to implementation

1. In accordance with Article 4, paragraph 1, each Party shall communicate to the Conference of the Parties, through the secretariat, the following elements of information:
(a) A national inventory of anthropogenic emissions by sources and removals by sinks of all greenhouse gases not controlled by the Montreal Protocol, to the extent its capacities permit, using comparable methodologies to be promoted and agreed upon by the Conference of the Parties;
(b) A general description of steps taken or envisaged by the Party to implement the Convention; and
(c) Any other information that the Party considers relevant to the achievement of the objective of the Convention and suitable for inclusion in its communication, including, if feasible, material relevant for calculations of global emission trends.

2. Each developed country Party and each other Party included in Annex I shall incorporate in its communication the following elements of information:
(a) A detailed description of the policies and measures that it has adopted to implement its commitment under Article 4, paragraphs 2(a) and 2(b); and
(b) A specific estimate of the effects that the policies and measures referred to in subparagraph (a) immediately above will have on anthropogenic emissions by its sources and removals by its sinks of greenhouse gases during the period referred to in Article 4, paragraph 2(a).

3. In addition, each developed country Party and each other developed Party included in Annex II shall incorporate details of measures taken in accordance with Article 4, paragraphs 3, 4 and 5.

4. Developing country Parties may, on a voluntary basis, propose projects for financing, including specific technologies, materials, equipment, techniques or practices that would be needed to implement such projects, along with, if possible, an estimate of all incremental costs, of the reductions of emissions and increments of removals of greenhouse gases, as well as an estimate of the consequent benefits.

5. Each developed country Party and each other Party included in Annex I shall make its initial communication within six months of the entry into force of the Convention for that Party. Each Party not so listed shall make its initial communication within three years of the entry into force of the Convention for that Party, or of the availability of financial resources in accordance with Article 4, paragraph 3. Parties that are least developed countries may make their initial communication at their discretion. The frequency of subsequent communications by all Parties shall be determined by the Conference of the Parties, taking into account the differentiated timetable set by this paragraph.

6. Information communicated by Parties under this Article shall be transmitted by the secretariat as soon as possible to the Conference of the Parties and to any subsidiary bodies concerned. If necessary, the procedures for the communication of information may be further considered by the Conference of the Parties.

7. From its first session, the Conference of the Parties shall arrange for the provision to developing country Parties of technical and financial support, on request, in compiling and communicating information under this Article, as well as in identifying the technical and financial needs associated with proposed projects and response measures under Article 4. Such support may be provided by other Parties, by competent international organizations and by the secretariat, as appropriate.

8. Any group of Parties may, subject to guidelines adopted by the Conference of the Parties, and to prior notification to the Conference of the Parties, make a joint communication in fulfilment of their obligations under this Article, provided that such a communication includes information on the fulfilment by each of these Parties of its individual obligations under the Convention.

9. Information received by the secretariat that is designated by a Party as confidential, in accordance with criteria to be established by the Conference of the Parties, shall be aggregated by the secretariat to protect its confidentiality before being made available to any of the bodies involved in the communication and review of information.

10. Subject to paragraph 9 above, and without prejudice to the ability of any Party to make public its communication at any time, the secretariat shall make communications by Parties under this Article publicly available at the time they are submitted to the Conference of the Parties.

Article 13: Resolution of questions regarding implementation

The Conference of the Parties shall, at its first session, consider the establishment of a multilateral consultative process, available to Parties on their request, for the resolution of questions regarding the implementation of the Convention.

Article 14: Settlement of disputes

1. In the event of a dispute between any two or more Parties concerning the interpretation or application of the Convention, the Parties concerned shall seek a settlement of the dispute through negotiation or any other peaceful means of their own choice.

2. When ratifying, accepting, approving or acceding to the Convention, or at any time thereafter, a Party which is not a regional economic integration organization may declare in a written instrument submitted to the Depositary that, in respect of any dispute concerning the interpretation or application of the Convention, it recognizes as compulsory *ipso facto* and without special agreement, in relation to any Party accepting the same obligation:

(a) Submission of the dispute to the International Court of Justice, and/or

(b) Arbitration in accordance with procedures to be adopted by the Conference of the Parties as soon as practicable, in an annex on arbitration.

A Party which is a regional economic integration organization may make a declaration with like effect in relation to arbitration in accordance with the procedures referred to in subparagraph (b) above.

3. A declaration made under paragraph 2 above shall remain in force until it expires in accordance with its terms or until three months after written notice of its revocation has been deposited with the Depositary.

4. A new declaration, a notice of revocation or the expiry of a declaration shall not in any way affect proceedings pending before the International Court of Justice or the arbitral tribunal, unless the parties to the dispute otherwise agree.

5. Subject to the operation of paragraph 2 above, if after twelve months following notification by one Party to another that a dispute exists between them, the Parties concerned have not been able to settle their dispute through the means mentioned in paragraph 1 above, the dispute shall be submitted, at the request of any of the parties to the dispute, to conciliation.

6. A conciliation commission shall be created upon the request of one of the parties to the dispute. The commission shall be composed of an equal number of members appointed by each party concerned and a chairman chosen jointly by the members appointed by each party. The commission shall render a recommendatory award, which the parties shall consider in good faith.

7. Additional procedures relating to conciliation shall be adopted by the Conference of the Parties, as soon as practicable, in an annex on conciliation.

8. The provisions of this Article shall apply to any related legal instrument which the Conference of the Parties may adopt, unless the instrument provides otherwise.

Article 15: Amendments to the Convention

1. Any Party may propose amendments to the Convention.

2. Amendments to the Convention shall be adopted at an ordinary session of the Conference of the Parties. The text of any proposed amendment to the Convention shall be communicated to the Parties by the secretariat at least six months before the meeting at which it is proposed for adoption. The secretariat shall also communicate proposed amendments to the signatories to the Convention and, for information, to the Depositary.

3. The Parties shall make every effort to reach agreement on any proposed amendment to the Convention by consensus. If all efforts at consensus have been exhausted, and no agreement reached, the amendment shall as a last resort be adopted by a three-fourths majority vote of the Parties present and voting at the meeting. The adopted amendment shall be communicated by the secretariat to the Depositary, who shall circulate it to all Parties for their acceptance.

4. Instruments of acceptance in respect of an amendment shall be deposited with the Depositary. An amendment adopted in accordance with paragraph 3 above shall enter into force for those Parties having accepted it on the ninetieth day after the date of receipt by the Depositary of an instrument of acceptance by at least three fourths of the Parties to the Convention.

5. The amendment shall enter into force for any other Party on the ninetieth day after the date on which that Party deposits with the Depositary its instrument of acceptance of the said amendment.

6. For the purposes of this Article, 'Parties present and voting' means Parties present and casting an affirmative or negative vote.

Article 16: Adoption and amendment of annexes to the Convention

1. Annexes to the Convention shall form an integral part thereof and, unless otherwise expressly provided, a reference to the Convention constitutes at the same time a reference to any annexes thereto. Without prejudice to the provisions of Article 14, paragraphs 2(b) and 7, such annexes shall be restricted to lists, forms and any other material of a descriptive nature that is of a scientific, technical, procedural or administrative character.

2. Annexes to the Convention shall be proposed and adopted in accordance with the procedure set forth in Article 15, paragraphs 2, 3 and 4.

3. An annex that has been adopted in accordance with paragraph 2 above shall enter into force for all Parties to the Convention six months after the date of the communication by the Depositary to such Parties of the adoption of the annex, except for those Parties that have notified the Depositary, in writing, within that period of their non-acceptance of the annex. The annex shall enter into force for Parties which withdraw their notification of non-acceptance on the ninetieth day after the date on which withdrawal of such notification has been received by the Depositary.

4. The proposal, adoption and entry into force of amendments to annexes to the Convention shall be subject to the same procedure as that for the proposal, adoption and entry into force of annexes to the Convention in accordance with paragraphs 2 and 3 above.

5. If the adoption of an annex or an amendment to an annex involves an amendment to the Convention, that annex or amendment to an annex shall not enter into force until such time as the amendment to the Convention enters into force.

Article 17: Protocols

1. The Conference of the Parties may, at any ordinary session, adopt protocols to the Convention.

2. The text of any proposed protocol shall be communicated to the Parties by the secretariat at least six months before such a session.

3. The requirements for the entry into force of any protocol shall be established by that instrument.

4. Only Parties to the Convention may be Parties to a protocol.

5. Decisions under any protocol shall be taken only by the Parties to the protocol concerned.

Article 18: Right to vote

1. Each Party to the Convention shall have one vote, except as provided for in paragraph 2 below.

2. Regional economic integration organizations, in matters within their competence, shall exercise their right to vote with a number of votes equal to the number of their member States that are Parties to the Convention. Such an organization shall not exercise its right to vote if any of its member States exercises its right, and vice versa.

Article 19: Depositary

The Secretary-General of the United Nations shall be the Depositary of the Convention and of protocols adopted in accordance with Article 17.

Article 20: Signature

This Convention shall be open for signature by States Members of the United Nations or of any of its specialized agencies or that are Parties to the Statute of the International Court of Justice and by regional economic integration organizations at Rio de Janeiro, during the United Nations Conference on Environment and Development, and thereafter at United Nations Headquarters in New York from 20 June 1992 to 19 June 1993.

Article 21: Interim arrangements

1. The secretariat functions referred to in Article 8 will be carried out on an interim basis by the secretariat established by the General Assembly of the United

Nations in its resolution 45/212 of 21 December 1990, until the completion of the first session of the Conference of the Parties.

2. The head of the interim secretariat referred to in paragraph 1 above will cooperate closely with the Intergovernmental Panel on Climate Change to ensure that the Panel can respond to the need for objective scientific and technical advice. Other relevant scientific bodies could also be consulted.

3. The Global Environment Facility of the United Nations Development Programme, the United Nations Environment Programme and the International Bank for Reconstruction and Development shall be the international entity entrusted with the operation of the financial mechanism referred to in Article 11 on an interim basis. In this connection, the Global Environment Facility should be appropriately restructured and its membership made universal to enable it to fulfil the requirements of Article 11.

Article 22: Ratification, acceptance, approval or accession

1. The Convention shall be subject to ratification, acceptance, approval or accession by States and by regional economic integration organizations. It shall be open for accession from the day after the date on which the Convention is closed for signature. Instruments of ratification, acceptance, approval or accession shall be deposited with the Depositary.

2. Any regional economic integration organization which becomes a Party to the Convention without any of its member States being a Party shall be bound by all the obligations under the Convention. In the case of such organizations, one or more of whose member States is a Party to the Convention, the organization and its member States shall decide on their respective responsibilities for the performance of their obligations under the Convention. In such cases, the organization and the member States shall not be entitled to exercise rights under the Convention concurrently.

3. In their instruments of ratification, acceptance, approval or accession, regional economic integration organizations shall declare the extent of their competence with respect to the matters governed by the Convention. These organizations shall also inform the Depositary, who shall in turn inform the Parties, of any substantial modification in the extent of their competence.

Article 23: Entry into force

1. The Convention shall enter into force on the ninetieth day after the date of deposit of the fiftieth instrument of ratification, acceptance, approval or accession.

2. For each State or regional economic integration organization that ratifies, accepts or approves the Convention or accedes thereto after the deposit of the fiftieth instrument of ratification, acceptance, approval or accession, the Convention shall enter into force on the ninetieth day after the date of deposit by such State or regional economic integration organization of its instrument of ratification, acceptance, approval or accession.

3. For the purposes of paragraphs 1 and 2 above, any instrument deposited by a regional economic integration organization shall not be counted as additional to those deposited by States members of the organization.

Article 24: Reservations

No reservations may be made to the Convention.

Article 25: Withdrawal

1. At any time after three years from the date on which the Convention has entered into force for a Party, that Party may withdraw from the Convention by giving written notification to the Depositary.

2. Any such withdrawal shall take effect upon expiry of one year from the date of receipt by the Depositary of the notification of withdrawal, or on such later date as may be specified in the notification of withdrawal.

3. Any Party that withdraws from the Convention shall be considered as also having withdrawn from any protocol to which it is a Party.

Article 26: Authentic texts

The original of this Convention, of which the Arabic, Chinese, English, French, Russian and Spanish texts are equally authentic, shall be deposited with the Secretary-General of the United Nations.

In witness whereof the undersigned, being duly authorized to that effect, have signed this Convention.

Done at New York this ninth day of May one thousand nine hundred and ninety-two.

Annex I

Australia

Austria

Belarus[a/]

Belgium

Bulgaria[a/]

Canada

Croatia[a/]

Czech Republic[a/]

Denmark

European Union

Estonia[a/]

Finland

France

Germany

Greece
Hungary[a/]
Iceland
Ireland
Italy
Japan
Latvia[a/]
Liechtenstein
Lithuania[a/]
Luxembourg
Monaco
Netherlands
New Zealand
Norway
Poland[a/]
Portugal
Romania[a/]
Russian Federation[a/]
Slovakia[a/]
Slovenia[a/]
Spain
Sweden
Switzerland
Turkey
Ukraine[a/]
United Kingdom of Great Britain and Northern Ireland
United States of America

[a/] Countries that are undergoing the process of transition to a market economy.

Annex II

Australia
Austria
Belgium
Canada
Denmark
European Union

Finland
France
Germany
Greece
Iceland
Ireland
Italy
Japan
Luxembourg
Netherlands
New Zealand
Norway
Portugal
Spain
Sweden
Switzerland
United Kingdom of Great Britain and Northern Ireland
United States of America

Kyoto Protocol to the United Nations Framework Convention on Climate Change[5]

Adopted on 11 December 1997 at Kyoto. Not in force (122 ratifications). Source: Decision 1/CP.3 (Annex), Third Conference of the Parties to the UNFCCC, 1-11 December 1997, Doc. FCCC/CP/1997/7/Add.1. Further information: UNFCCC Secretariat, Bonn, Germany, http://www.unfccc.int

The Parties to this Protocol,
Being Parties to the United Nations Framework Convention on Climate Change, hereinafter referred to as 'the Convention',
In pursuit of the ultimate objective of the Convention as stated in its Article 2,
Recalling the provisions of the Convention,
Being guided by Article 3 of the Convention,
Pursuant to the Berlin Mandate adopted by decision 1/CP.1 of the Conference of the Parties to the Convention at its first session,

---

5 The text of the Kyoto Protocol's NCP is reproduced at p. 611.

Have agreed as follows:

Article 1

For the purposes of this Protocol, the definitions contained in Article 1 of the Convention shall apply. In addition:

1. 'Conference of the Parties' means the Conference of the Parties to the Convention.

2. 'Convention' means the United Nations Framework Convention on Climate Change, adopted in New York on 9 May 1992.

3. 'Intergovernmental Panel on Climate Change' means the Intergovernmental Panel on Climate Change established in 1988 jointly by the World Meteorological Organization and the United Nations Environment Programme.

4. 'Montreal Protocol' means the Montreal Protocol on Substances that Deplete the Ozone Layer, adopted in Montreal on 16 September 1987 and as subsequently adjusted and amended.

5. 'Parties present and voting' means Parties present and casting an affirmative or negative vote.

6. 'Party' means, unless the context otherwise indicates, a Party to this Protocol.

7. 'Party included in Annex I' means a Party included in Annex I to the Convention, as may be amended, or a Party which has made a notification under Article 4, paragraph 2(g), of the Convention.

Article 2

1. Each Party included in Annex I, in achieving its quantified emission limitation and reduction commitments under Article 3, in order to promote sustainable development, shall:

(a) Implement and/or further elaborate policies and measures in accordance with its national circumstances, such as:
   i) Enhancement of energy efficiency in relevant sectors of the national economy;
   ii) Protection and enhancement of sinks and reservoirs of greenhouse gases not controlled by the Montreal Protocol, taking into account its commitments under relevant international environmental agreements; promotion of sustainable forest management practices, afforestation and reforestation;
   iii) Promotion of sustainable forms of agriculture in light of climate change considerations;
   iv) Research on, and promotion, development and increased use of, new and renewable forms of energy, of carbon dioxide sequestration technologies and of advanced and innovative environmentally sound technologies;
   v) Progressive reduction or phasing out of market imperfections, fiscal incentives, tax and duty exemptions and subsidies in all greenhouse gas emitting sectors that run counter to the objective of the Convention and application of market instruments;

vi) Encouragement of appropriate reforms in relevant sectors aimed at promoting policies and measures which limit or reduce emissions of greenhouse gases not controlled by the Montreal Protocol;

vii) Measures to limit and/or reduce emissions of greenhouse gases not controlled by the Montreal Protocol in the transport sector;

viii) Limitation and/or reduction of methane emissions through recovery and use in waste management, as well as in the production, transport and distribution of energy;

(b) Cooperate with other such Parties to enhance the individual and combined effectiveness of their policies and measures adopted under this Article, pursuant to Article 4, paragraph 2(e)(i), of the Convention. To this end, these Parties shall take steps to share their experience and exchange information on such policies and measures, including developing ways of improving their comparability, transparency and effectiveness. The Conference of the Parties serving as the meeting of the Parties to this Protocol shall, at its first session or as soon as practicable thereafter, consider ways to facilitate such cooperation, taking into account all relevant information.

2. The Parties included in Annex I shall pursue limitation or reduction of emissions of greenhouse gases not controlled by the Montreal Protocol from aviation and marine bunker fuels, working through the International Civil Aviation Organization and the International Maritime Organization, respectively.

3. The Parties included in Annex I shall strive to implement policies and measures under this Article in such a way as to minimize adverse effects, including the adverse effects of climate change, effects on international trade, and social, environmental and economic impacts on other Parties, especially developing country Parties and in particular those identified in Article 4, paragraphs 8 and 9, of the Convention, taking into account Article 3 of the Convention. The Conference of the Parties serving as the meeting of the Parties to this Protocol may take further action, as appropriate, to promote the implementation of the provisions of this paragraph.

4. The Conference of the Parties serving as the meeting of the Parties to this Protocol, if it decides that it would be beneficial to coordinate any of the policies and measures in paragraph 1(a) above, taking into account different national circumstances and potential effects, shall consider ways and means to elaborate the coordination of such policies and measures.

Article 3

1. The Parties included in Annex I shall, individually or jointly, ensure that their aggregate anthropogenic carbon dioxide equivalent emissions of the greenhouse gases listed in Annex A do not exceed their assigned amounts, calculated pursuant to their quantified emission limitation and reduction commitments inscribed in Annex B and in accordance with the provisions of this Article, with a view to reducing their overall emissions of such gases by at least 5 per cent below 1990 levels in the commitment period 2008 to 2012.

2. Each Party included in Annex I shall, by 2005, have made demonstrable progress in achieving its commitments under this Protocol.

3. The net changes in greenhouse gas emissions by sources and removals by sinks resulting from direct human-induced land-use change and forestry activities, limited to afforestation, reforestation and deforestation since 1990, measured as verifiable changes in carbon stocks in each commitment period, shall be used to meet the commitments under this Article of each Party included in Annex I. The greenhouse gas emissions by sources and removals by sinks associated with those activities shall be reported in a transparent and verifiable manner and reviewed in accordance with Articles 7 and 8.

4. Prior to the first session of the Conference of the Parties serving as the meeting of the Parties to this Protocol, each Party included in Annex I shall provide, for consideration by the Subsidiary Body for Scientific and Technological Advice, data to establish its level of carbon stocks in 1990 and to enable an estimate to be made of its changes in carbon stocks in subsequent years. The Conference of the Parties serving as the meeting of the Parties to this Protocol shall, at its first session or as soon as practicable thereafter, decide upon modalities, rules and guidelines as to how, and which, additional human-induced activities related to changes in greenhouse gas emissions by sources and removals by sinks in the agricultural soils and the land-use change and forestry categories shall be added to, or subtracted from, the assigned amounts for Parties included in Annex I, taking into account uncertainties, transparency in reporting, verifiability, the methodological work of the Intergovernmental Panel on Climate Change, the advice provided by the Subsidiary Body for Scientific and Technological Advice in accordance with Article 5 and the decisions of the Conference of the Parties. Such a decision shall apply in the second and subsequent commitment periods. A Party may choose to apply such a decision on these additional human-induced activities for its first commitment period, provided that these activities have taken place since 1990.

5. The Parties included in Annex I undergoing the process of transition to a market economy whose base year or period was established pursuant to decision 9/CP.2 of the Conference of the Parties at its second session shall use that base year or period for the implementation of their commitments under this Article. Any other Party included in Annex I undergoing the process of transition to a market economy which has not yet submitted its first national communication under Article 12 of the Convention may also notify the Conference of the Parties serving as the meeting of the Parties to this Protocol that it intends to use an historical base year or period other than 1990 for the implementation of its commitments under this Article. The Conference of the Parties serving as the meeting of the Parties to this Protocol shall decide on the acceptance of such notification.

6. Taking into account Article 4, paragraph 6, of the Convention, in the implementation of their commitments under this Protocol other than those under this Article, a certain degree of flexibility shall be allowed by the Conference of the

Parties serving as the meeting of the Parties to this Protocol to the Parties included in Annex I undergoing the process of transition to a market economy.

7. In the first quantified emission limitation and reduction commitment period, from 2008 to 2012, the assigned amount for each Party included in Annex I shall be equal to the percentage inscribed for it in Annex B of its aggregate anthropogenic carbon dioxide equivalent emissions of the greenhouse gases listed in Annex A in 1990, or the base year or period determined in accordance with paragraph 5 above, multiplied by five. Those Parties included in Annex I for whom land-use change and forestry constituted a net source of greenhouse gas emissions in 1990 shall include in their 1990 emissions base year or period the aggregate anthropogenic carbon dioxide equivalent emissions by sources minus removals by sinks in 1990 from land-use change for the purposes of calculating their assigned amount.

8. Any Party included in Annex I may use 1995 as its base year for hydrofluorocarbons, perfluorocarbons and sulphur hexafluoride, for the purposes of the calculation referred to in paragraph 7 above.

9. Commitments for subsequent periods for Parties included in Annex I shall be established in amendments to Annex B to this Protocol, which shall be adopted in accordance with the provisions of Article 21, paragraph 7. The Conference of the Parties serving as the meeting of the Parties to this Protocol shall initiate the consideration of such commitments at least seven years before the end of the first commitment period referred to in paragraph 1 above.

10. Any emission reduction units, or any part of an assigned amount, which a Party acquires from another Party in accordance with the provisions of Article 6 or of Article 17 shall be added to the assigned amount for the acquiring Party.

11. Any emission reduction units, or any part of an assigned amount, which a Party transfers to another Party in accordance with the provisions of Article 6 or of Article 17 shall be subtracted from the assigned amount for the transferring Party.

12. Any certified emission reductions which a Party acquires from another Party in accordance with the provisions of Article 12 shall be added to the assigned amount for the acquiring Party.

13. If the emissions of a Party included in Annex I in a commitment period are less than its assigned amount under this Article, this difference shall, on request of that Party, be added to the assigned amount for that Party for subsequent commitment periods.

14. Each Party included in Annex I shall strive to implement the commitments mentioned in paragraph 1 above in such a way as to minimize adverse social, environmental and economic impacts on developing country Parties, particularly those identified in Article 4, paragraphs 8 and 9, of the Convention. In line with relevant decisions of the Conference of the Parties on the implementation of those paragraphs, the Conference of the Parties serving as the meeting of the Parties to this Protocol shall, at its first session, consider what actions are necessary to minimize the adverse effects of climate change and/or the impacts of response

measures on Parties referred to in those paragraphs. Among the issues to be considered shall be the establishment of funding, insurance and transfer of technology.

Article 4

1. Any Parties included in Annex I that have reached an agreement to fulfil their commitments under Article 3 jointly, shall be deemed to have met those commitments provided that their total combined aggregate anthropogenic carbon dioxide equivalent emissions of the greenhouse gases listed in Annex A do not exceed their assigned amounts calculated pursuant to their quantified emission limitation and reduction commitments inscribed in Annex B and in accordance with the provisions of Article 3. The respective emission level allocated to each of the Parties to the agreement shall be set out in that agreement.

2. The Parties to any such agreement shall notify the secretariat of the terms of the agreement on the date of deposit of their instruments of ratification, acceptance or approval of this Protocol, or accession thereto. The secretariat shall in turn inform the Parties and signatories to the Convention of the terms of the agreement.

3. Any such agreement shall remain in operation for the duration of the commitment period specified in Article 3, paragraph 7.

4. If Parties acting jointly do so in the framework of, and together with, a regional economic integration organization, any alteration in the composition of the organization after adoption of this Protocol shall not affect existing commitments under this Protocol. Any alteration in the composition of the organization shall only apply for the purposes of those commitments under Article 3 that are adopted subsequent to that alteration.

5. In the event of failure by the Parties to such an agreement to achieve their total combined level of emission reductions, each Party to that agreement shall be responsible for its own level of emissions set out in the agreement.

6. If Parties acting jointly do so in the framework of, and together with, a regional economic integration organization which is itself a Party to this Protocol, each member State of that regional economic integration organization individually, and together with the regional economic integration organization acting in accordance with Article 24, shall, in the event of failure to achieve the total combined level of emission reductions, be responsible for its level of emissions as notified in accordance with this Article.

Article 5

1. Each Party included in Annex I shall have in place, no later than one year prior to the start of the first commitment period, a national system for the estimation of anthropogenic emissions by sources and removals by sinks of all greenhouse gases not controlled by the Montreal Protocol. Guidelines for such national systems, which shall incorporate the methodologies specified in paragraph 2 below, shall be

decided upon by the Conference of the Parties serving as the meeting of the Parties to this Protocol at its first session.

2. Methodologies for estimating anthropogenic emissions by sources and removals by sinks of all greenhouse gases not controlled by the Montreal Protocol shall be those accepted by the Intergovernmental Panel on Climate Change and agreed upon by the Conference of the Parties at its third session. Where such methodologies are not used, appropriate adjustments shall be applied according to methodologies agreed upon by the Conference of the Parties serving as the meeting of the Parties to this Protocol at its first session. Based on the work of, *inter alia*, the Intergovernmental Panel on Climate Change and advice provided by the Subsidiary Body for Scientific and Technological Advice, the Conference of the Parties serving as the meeting of the Parties to this Protocol shall regularly review and, as appropriate, revise such methodologies and adjustments, taking fully into account any relevant decisions by the Conference of the Parties. Any revision to methodologies or adjustments shall be used only for the purposes of ascertaining compliance with commitments under Article 3 in respect of any commitment period adopted subsequent to that revision.

3. The global warming potentials used to calculate the carbon dioxide equivalence of anthropogenic emissions by sources and removals by sinks of greenhouse gases listed in Annex A shall be those accepted by the Intergovernmental Panel on Climate Change and agreed upon by the Conference of the Parties at its third session. Based on the work of, *inter alia*, the Intergovernmental Panel on Climate Change and advice provided by the Subsidiary Body for Scientific and Technological Advice, the Conference of the Parties serving as the meeting of the Parties to this Protocol shall regularly review and, as appropriate, revise the global warming potential of each such greenhouse gas, taking fully into account any relevant decisions by the Conference of the Parties. Any revision to a global warming potential shall apply only to commitments under Article 3 in respect of any commitment period adopted subsequent to that revision.

Article 6

1. For the purpose of meeting its commitments under Article 3, any Party included in Annex I may transfer to, or acquire from, any other such Party emission reduction units resulting from projects aimed at reducing anthropogenic emissions by sources or enhancing anthropogenic removals by sinks of greenhouse gases in any sector of the economy, provided that:

(a) Any such project has the approval of the Parties involved;

(b) Any such project provides a reduction in emissions by sources, or an enhancement of removals by sinks, that is additional to any that would otherwise occur;

(c) It does not acquire any emission reduction units if it is not in compliance with its obligations under Articles 5 and 7; and

(d) The acquisition of emission reduction units shall be supplemental to domestic actions for the purposes of meeting commitments under Article 3.

2. The Conference of the Parties serving as the meeting of the Parties to this Protocol may, at its first session or as soon as practicable thereafter, further elaborate guidelines for the implementation of this Article, including for verification and reporting.

3. A Party included in Annex I may authorize legal entities to participate, under its responsibility, in actions leading to the generation, transfer or acquisition under this Article of emission reduction units.

4. If a question of implementation by a Party included in Annex I of the requirements referred to in this Article is identified in accordance with the relevant provisions of Article 8, transfers and acquisitions of emission reduction units may continue to be made after the question has been identified, provided that any such units may not be used by a Party to meet its commitments under Article 3 until any issue of compliance is resolved.

Article 7

1. Each Party included in Annex I shall incorporate in its annual inventory of anthropogenic emissions by sources and removals by sinks of greenhouse gases not controlled by the Montreal Protocol, submitted in accordance with the relevant decisions of the Conference of the Parties, the necessary supplementary information for the purposes of ensuring compliance with Article 3, to be determined in accordance with paragraph 4 below.

2. Each Party included in Annex I shall incorporate in its national communication, submitted under Article 12 of the Convention, the supplementary information necessary to demonstrate compliance with its commitments under this Protocol, to be determined in accordance with paragraph 4 below.

3. Each Party included in Annex I shall submit the information required under paragraph 1 above annually, beginning with the first inventory due under the Convention for the first year of the commitment period after this Protocol has entered into force for that Party. Each such Party shall submit the information required under paragraph 2 above as part of the first national communication due under the Convention after this Protocol has entered into force for it and after the adoption of guidelines as provided for in paragraph 4 below. The frequency of subsequent submission of information required under this Article shall be determined by the Conference of the Parties serving as the meeting of the Parties to this Protocol, taking into account any timetable for the submission of national communications decided upon by the Conference of the Parties.

4. The Conference of the Parties serving as the meeting of the Parties to this Protocol shall adopt at its first session, and review periodically thereafter, guidelines for the preparation of the information required under this Article, taking into account guidelines for the preparation of national communications by Parties included in Annex I adopted by the Conference of the Parties. The Conference of the Parties serving as the meeting of the Parties to this Protocol shall also, prior to

the first commitment period, decide upon modalities for the accounting of assigned amounts.

Article 8

1. The information submitted under Article 7 by each Party included in Annex I shall be reviewed by expert review teams pursuant to the relevant decisions of the Conference of the Parties and in accordance with guidelines adopted for this purpose by the Conference of the Parties serving as the meeting of the Parties to this Protocol under paragraph 4 below. The information submitted under Article 7, paragraph 1, by each Party included in Annex I shall be reviewed as part of the annual compilation and accounting of emissions inventories and assigned amounts. Additionally, the information submitted under Article 7, paragraph 2, by each Party included in Annex I shall be reviewed as part of the review of communications.

2. Expert review teams shall be coordinated by the secretariat and shall be composed of experts selected from those nominated by Parties to the Convention and, as appropriate, by intergovernmental organizations, in accordance with guidance provided for this purpose by the Conference of the Parties.

3. The review process shall provide a thorough and comprehensive technical assessment of all aspects of the implementation by a Party of this Protocol. The expert review teams shall prepare a report to the Conference of the Parties serving as the meeting of the Parties to this Protocol, assessing the implementation of the commitments of the Party and identifying any potential problems in, and factors influencing, the fulfilment of commitments. Such reports shall be circulated by the secretariat to all Parties to the Convention. The secretariat shall list those questions of implementation indicated in such reports for further consideration by the Conference of the Parties serving as the meeting of the Parties to this Protocol.

4. The Conference of the Parties serving as the meeting of the Parties to this Protocol shall adopt at its first session, and review periodically thereafter, guidelines for the review of implementation of this Protocol by expert review teams taking into account the relevant decisions of the Conference of the Parties.

5. The Conference of the Parties serving as the meeting of the Parties to this Protocol shall, with the assistance of the Subsidiary Body for Implementation and, as appropriate, the Subsidiary Body for Scientific and Technological Advice, consider:

(a) The information submitted by Parties under Article 7 and the reports of the expert reviews thereon conducted under this Article; and

(b) Those questions of implementation listed by the secretariat under paragraph 3 above, as well as any questions raised by Parties.

6. Pursuant to its consideration of the information referred to in paragraph 5 above, the Conference of the Parties serving as the meeting of the Parties to this Protocol shall take decisions on any matter required for the implementation of this Protocol.

Article 9

1. The Conference of the Parties serving as the meeting of the Parties to this Protocol shall periodically review this Protocol in the light of the best available scientific information and assessments on climate change and its impacts, as well as relevant technical, social and economic information. Such reviews shall be coordinated with pertinent reviews under the Convention, in particular those required by Article 4, paragraph 2(d), and Article 7, paragraph 2(a), of the Convention. Based on these reviews, the Conference of the Parties serving as the meeting of the Parties to this Protocol shall take appropriate action.

2. The first review shall take place at the second session of the Conference of the Parties serving as the meeting of the Parties to this Protocol. Further reviews shall take place at regular intervals and in a timely manner.

Article 10

All Parties, taking into account their common but differentiated responsibilities and their specific national and regional development priorities, objectives and circumstances, without introducing any new commitments for Parties not included in Annex I, but reaffirming existing commitments under Article 4, paragraph 1, of the Convention, and continuing to advance the implementation of these commitments in order to achieve sustainable development, taking into account Article 4, paragraphs 3, 5 and 7, of the Convention, shall:

(a) Formulate, where relevant and to the extent possible, cost-effective national and, where appropriate, regional programmes to improve the quality of local emission factors, activity data and/or models which reflect the socio-economic conditions of each Party for the preparation and periodic updating of national inventories of anthropogenic emissions by sources and removals by sinks of all greenhouse gases not controlled by the Montreal Protocol, using comparable methodologies to be agreed upon by the Conference of the Parties, and consistent with the guidelines for the preparation of national communications adopted by the Conference of the Parties;

(b) Formulate, implement, publish and regularly update national and, where appropriate, regional programmes containing measures to mitigate climate change and measures to facilitate adequate adaptation to climate change:

i) Such programmes would, *inter alia*, concern the energy, transport and industry sectors as well as agriculture, forestry and waste management. Furthermore, adaptation technologies and methods for improving spatial planning would improve adaptation to climate change; and

ii) Parties included in Annex I shall submit information on action under this Protocol, including national programmes, in accordance with Article 7; and other Parties shall seek to include in their national communications, as appropriate, information on programmes which contain measures that the Party believes contribute to addressing climate change and its adverse impacts, including the abatement of increases in greenhouse gas emissions, and enhancement of and removals by sinks, capacity building and adaptation measures;

(c) Cooperate in the promotion of effective modalities for the development, application and diffusion of, and take all practicable steps to promote, facilitate and finance, as appropriate, the transfer of, or access to, environmentally sound technologies, know-how, practices and processes pertinent to climate change, in particular to developing countries, including the formulation of policies and programmes for the effective transfer of environmentally sound technologies that are publicly owned or in the public domain and the creation of an enabling environment for the private sector, to promote and enhance the transfer of, and access to, environmentally sound technologies;

(d) Cooperate in scientific and technical research and promote the maintenance and the development of systematic observation systems and development of data archives to reduce uncertainties related to the climate system, the adverse impacts of climate change and the economic and social consequences of various response strategies, and promote the development and strengthening of endogenous capacities and capabilities to participate in international and intergovernmental efforts, programmes and networks on research and systematic observation, taking into account Article 5 of the Convention;

(e) Cooperate in and promote at the international level, and, where appropriate, using existing bodies, the development and implementation of education and training programmes, including the strengthening of national capacity building, in particular human and institutional capacities and the exchange or secondment of personnel to train experts in this field, in particular for developing countries, and facilitate at the national level public awareness of, and public access to information on, climate change. Suitable modalities should be developed to implement these activities through the relevant bodies of the Convention, taking into account Article 6 of the Convention;

(f) Include in their national communications information on programmes and activities undertaken pursuant to this Article in accordance with relevant decisions of the Conference of the Parties; and

(g) Give full consideration, in implementing the commitments under this Article, to Article 4, paragraph 8, of the Convention.

Article 11

1. In the implementation of Article 10, Parties shall take into account the provisions of Article 4, paragraphs 4, 5, 7, 8 and 9, of the Convention.

2. In the context of the implementation of Article 4, paragraph 1, of the Convention, in accordance with the provisions of Article 4, paragraph 3, and Article 11 of the Convention, and through the entity or entities entrusted with the operation of the financial mechanism of the Convention, the developed country Parties and other developed Parties included in Annex II to the Convention shall:

(a) Provide new and additional financial resources to meet the agreed full costs incurred by developing country Parties in advancing the implementation of existing commitments under Article 4, paragraph 1(a), of the Convention that are covered in Article 10, subparagraph (a); and

(b) Also provide such financial resources, including for the transfer of technology, needed by the developing country Parties to meet the agreed full incremental costs of advancing the implementation of existing commitments under Article 4, paragraph 1, of the Convention that are covered by Article 10 and that are agreed between a developing country Party and the international entity or entities referred to in Article 11 of the Convention, in accordance with that Article.

The implementation of these existing commitments shall take into account the need for adequacy and predictability in the flow of funds and the importance of appropriate burden sharing among developed country Parties. The guidance to the entity or entities entrusted with the operation of the financial mechanism of the Convention in relevant decisions of the Conference of the Parties, including those agreed before the adoption of this Protocol, shall apply *mutatis mutandis* to the provisions of this paragraph.

3. The developed country Parties and other developed Parties in Annex II to the Convention may also provide, and developing country Parties avail themselves of, financial resources for the implementation of Article 10, through bilateral, regional and other multilateral channels.

Article 12

1. A clean development mechanism is hereby defined.

2. The purpose of the clean development mechanism shall be to assist Parties not included in Annex I in achieving sustainable development and in contributing to the ultimate objective of the Convention, and to assist Parties included in Annex I in achieving compliance with their quantified emission limitation and reduction commitments under Article 3.

3. Under the clean development mechanism:

(a) Parties not included in Annex I will benefit from project activities resulting in certified emission reductions; and

(b) Parties included in Annex I may use the certified emission reductions accruing from such project activities to contribute to compliance with part of their quantified emission limitation and reduction commitments under Article 3, as determined by the Conference of the Parties serving as the meeting of the Parties to this Protocol.

4. The clean development mechanism shall be subject to the authority and guidance of the Conference of the Parties serving as the meeting of the Parties to this Protocol and be supervised by an executive board of the clean development mechanism.

5. Emission reductions resulting from each project activity shall be certified by operational entities to be designated by the Conference of the Parties serving as the meeting of the Parties to this Protocol, on the basis of:

(a) Voluntary participation approved by each Party involved;

(b) Real, measurable, and long-term benefits related to the mitigation of climate change; and

(c) Reductions in emissions that are additional to any that would occur in the absence of the certified project activity.

6. The clean development mechanism shall assist in arranging funding of certified project activities as necessary.

7. The Conference of the Parties serving as the meeting of the Parties to this Protocol shall, at its first session, elaborate modalities and procedures with the objective of ensuring transparency, efficiency and accountability through independent auditing and verification of project activities.

8. The Conference of the Parties serving as the meeting of the Parties to this Protocol shall ensure that a share of the proceeds from certified project activities is used to cover administrative expenses as well as to assist developing country Parties that are particularly vulnerable to the adverse effects of climate change to meet the costs of adaptation.

9. Participation under the clean development mechanism, including in activities mentioned in paragraph 3(a) above and in the acquisition of certified emission reductions, may involve private and/or public entities, and is to be subject to whatever guidance may be provided by the executive board of the clean development mechanism.

10. Certified emission reductions obtained during the period from the year 2000 up to the beginning of the first commitment period can be used to assist in achieving compliance in the first commitment period.

Article 13

1. The Conference of the Parties, the supreme body of the Convention, shall serve as the meeting of the Parties to this Protocol.

2. Parties to the Convention that are not Parties to this Protocol may participate as observers in the proceedings of any session of the Conference of the Parties serving as the meeting of the Parties to this Protocol. When the Conference of the Parties serves as the meeting of the Parties to this Protocol, decisions under this Protocol shall be taken only by those that are Parties to this Protocol.

3. When the Conference of the Parties serves as the meeting of the Parties to this Protocol, any member of the Bureau of the Conference of the Parties representing a Party to the Convention but, at that time, not a Party to this Protocol, shall be replaced by an additional member to be elected by and from amongst the Parties to this Protocol.

4. The Conference of the Parties serving as the meeting of the Parties to this Protocol shall keep under regular review the implementation of this Protocol and shall make, within its mandate, the decisions necessary to promote its effective implementation. It shall perform the functions assigned to it by this Protocol and shall:

(a) Assess, on the basis of all information made available to it in accordance with the provisions of this Protocol, the implementation of this Protocol by the Parties, the overall effects of the measures taken pursuant to this Protocol, in particular environmental, economic and social effects as well as their cumulative impacts and the extent to which progress towards the objective of the Convention is being achieved;

(b) Periodically examine the obligations of the Parties under this Protocol, giving due consideration to any reviews required by Article 4, paragraph 2(d), and Article 7, paragraph 2, of the Convention, in the light of the objective of the Convention, the experience gained in its implementation and the evolution of scientific and technological knowledge, and in this respect consider and adopt regular reports on the implementation of this Protocol;

(c) Promote and facilitate the exchange of information on measures adopted by the Parties to address climate change and its effects, taking into account the differing circumstances, responsibilities and capabilities of the Parties and their respective commitments under this Protocol;

(d) Facilitate, at the request of two or more Parties, the coordination of measures adopted by them to address climate change and its effects, taking into account the differing circumstances, responsibilities and capabilities of the Parties and their respective commitments under this Protocol;

(e) Promote and guide, in accordance with the objective of the Convention and the provisions of this Protocol, and taking fully into account the relevant decisions by the Conference of the Parties, the development and periodic refinement of comparable methodologies for the effective implementation of this Protocol, to be agreed on by the Conference of the Parties serving as the meeting of the Parties to this Protocol;

(f) Make recommendations on any matters necessary for the implementation of this Protocol;

(g) Seek to mobilize additional financial resources in accordance with Article 11, paragraph 2;

(h) Establish such subsidiary bodies as are deemed necessary for the implementation of this Protocol;

(i) Seek and utilize, where appropriate, the services and cooperation of, and information provided by, competent international organizations and intergovernmental and non-governmental bodies; and

(j) Exercise such other functions as may be required for the implementation of this Protocol, and consider any assignment resulting from a decision by the Conference of the Parties.

5. The rules of procedure of the Conference of the Parties and financial procedures applied under the Convention shall be applied *mutatis mutandis* under this Protocol, except as may be otherwise decided by consensus by the Conference of the Parties serving as the meeting of the Parties to this Protocol.

6. The first session of the Conference of the Parties serving as the meeting of the Parties to this Protocol shall be convened by the secretariat in conjunction with the first session of the Conference of the Parties that is scheduled after the date of the entry into force of this Protocol. Subsequent ordinary sessions of the Conference of the Parties serving as the meeting of the Parties to this Protocol shall be held every year and in conjunction with ordinary sessions of the Conference of the Parties, unless otherwise decided by the Conference of the Parties serving as the meeting of the Parties to this Protocol.

7. Extraordinary sessions of the Conference of the Parties serving as the meeting of the Parties to this Protocol shall be held at such other times as may be deemed necessary by the Conference of the Parties serving as the meeting of the Parties to this Protocol, or at the written request of any Party, provided that, within six months of the request being communicated to the Parties by the secretariat, it is supported by at least one third of the Parties.

8. The United Nations, its specialized agencies and the International Atomic Energy Agency, as well as any State member thereof or observers thereto not party to the Convention, may be represented at sessions of the Conference of the Parties serving as the meeting of the Parties to this Protocol as observers. Any body or agency, whether national or international, governmental or non-governmental, which is qualified in matters covered by this Protocol and which has informed the secretariat of its wish to be represented at a session of the Conference of the Parties serving as the meeting of the Parties to this Protocol as an observer, may be so admitted unless at least one third of the Parties present object. The admission and participation of observers shall be subject to the rules of procedure, as referred to in paragraph 5 above.

Article 14

1. The secretariat established by Article 8 of the Convention shall serve as the secretariat of this Protocol.

2. Article 8, paragraph 2, of the Convention on the functions of the secretariat, and Article 8, paragraph 3, of the Convention on arrangements made for the functioning of the secretariat, shall apply *mutatis mutandis* to this Protocol. The secretariat shall, in addition, exercise the functions assigned to it under this Protocol.

Article 15

1. The Subsidiary Body for Scientific and Technological Advice and the Subsidiary Body for Implementation established by Articles 9 and 10 of the Convention shall serve as, respectively, the Subsidiary Body for Scientific and Technological Advice and the Subsidiary Body for Implementation of this Protocol. The provisions relating to the functioning of these two bodies under the

Convention shall apply *mutatis mutandis* to this Protocol. Sessions of the meetings of the Subsidiary Body for Scientific and Technological Advice and the Subsidiary Body for Implementation of this Protocol shall be held in conjunction with the meetings of, respectively, the Subsidiary Body for Scientific and Technological Advice and the Subsidiary Body for Implementation of the Convention.

2. Parties to the Convention that are not Parties to this Protocol may participate as observers in the proceedings of any session of the subsidiary bodies. When the subsidiary bodies serve as the subsidiary bodies of this Protocol, decisions under this Protocol shall be taken only by those that are Parties to this Protocol.

3. When the subsidiary bodies established by Articles 9 and 10 of the Convention exercise their functions with regard to matters concerning this Protocol, any member of the Bureaux of those subsidiary bodies representing a Party to the Convention but, at that time, not a party to this Protocol, shall be replaced by an additional member to be elected by and from amongst the Parties to this Protocol.

Article 16

The Conference of the Parties serving as the meeting of the Parties to this Protocol shall, as soon as practicable, consider the application to this Protocol of, and modify as appropriate, the multilateral consultative process referred to in Article 13 of the Convention, in the light of any relevant decisions that may be taken by the Conference of the Parties. Any multilateral consultative process that may be applied to this Protocol shall operate without prejudice to the procedures and mechanisms established in accordance with Article 18.

Article 17

The Conference of the Parties shall define the relevant principles, modalities, rules and guidelines, in particular for verification, reporting and accountability for emissions trading. The Parties included in Annex B may participate in emissions trading for the purposes of fulfilling their commitments under Article 3. Any such trading shall be supplemental to domestic actions for the purpose of meeting quantified emission limitation and reduction commitments under that Article.

Article 18

The Conference of the Parties serving as the meeting of the Parties to this Protocol shall, at its first session, approve appropriate and effective procedures and mechanisms to determine and to address cases of non-compliance with the provisions of this Protocol, including through the development of an indicative list of consequences, taking into account the cause, type, degree and frequency of non-compliance. Any procedures and mechanisms under this Article entailing binding consequences shall be adopted by means of an amendment to this Protocol.

Article 19

The provisions of Article 14 of the Convention on settlement of disputes shall apply *mutatis mutandis* to this Protocol.

Article 20

1. Any Party may propose amendments to this Protocol.

2. Amendments to this Protocol shall be adopted at an ordinary session of the Conference of the Parties serving as the meeting of the Parties to this Protocol. The text of any proposed amendment to this Protocol shall be communicated to the Parties by the secretariat at least six months before the meeting at which it is proposed for adoption. The secretariat shall also communicate the text of any proposed amendments to the Parties and signatories to the Convention and, for information, to the Depositary.

3. The Parties shall make every effort to reach agreement on any proposed amendment to this Protocol by consensus. If all efforts at consensus have been exhausted, and no agreement reached, the amendment shall as a last resort be adopted by a three-fourths majority vote of the Parties present and voting at the meeting. The adopted amendment shall be communicated by the secretariat to the Depositary, who shall circulate it to all Parties for their acceptance.

4. Instruments of acceptance in respect of an amendment shall be deposited with the Depositary. An amendment adopted in accordance with paragraph 3 above shall enter into force for those Parties having accepted it on the ninetieth day after the date of receipt by the Depositary of an instrument of acceptance by at least three fourths of the Parties to this Protocol.

5. The amendment shall enter into force for any other Party on the ninetieth day after the date on which that Party deposits with the Depositary its instrument of acceptance of the said amendment.

Article 21

1. Annexes to this Protocol shall form an integral part thereof and, unless otherwise expressly provided, a reference to this Protocol constitutes at the same time a reference to any annexes thereto. Any annexes adopted after the entry into force of this Protocol shall be restricted to lists, forms and any other material of a descriptive nature that is of a scientific, technical, procedural or administrative character.

2. Any Party may make proposals for an annex to this Protocol and may propose amendments to annexes to this Protocol.

3. Annexes to this Protocol and amendments to annexes to this Protocol shall be adopted at an ordinary session of the Conference of the Parties serving as the meeting of the Parties to this Protocol. The text of any proposed annex or amendment to an annex shall be communicated to the Parties by the secretariat at least six months before the meeting at which it is proposed for adoption. The secretariat shall also communicate the text of any proposed annex or amendment to an annex to the Parties and signatories to the Convention and, for information, to the Depositary.

4. The Parties shall make every effort to reach agreement on any proposed annex or amendment to an annex by consensus. If all efforts at consensus have been exhausted, and no agreement reached, the annex or amendment to an annex shall as a last resort be adopted by a three-fourths majority vote of the Parties present and voting at the meeting. The adopted annex or amendment to an annex shall be communicated by the secretariat to the Depositary, who shall circulate it to all Parties for their acceptance.

5. An annex, or amendment to an annex other than Annex A or B, that has been adopted in accordance with paragraphs 3 and 4 above shall enter into force for all Parties to this Protocol six months after the date of the communication by the Depositary to such Parties of the adoption of the annex or adoption of the amendment to the annex, except for those Parties that have notified the Depositary, in writing, within that period of their non-acceptance of the annex or amendment to the annex. The annex or amendment to an annex shall enter into force for Parties which withdraw their notification of non-acceptance on the ninetieth day after the date on which withdrawal of such notification has been received by the Depositary.

6. If the adoption of an annex or an amendment to an annex involves an amendment to this Protocol, that annex or amendment to an annex shall not enter into force until such time as the amendment to this Protocol enters into force.

7. Amendments to Annexes A and B to this Protocol shall be adopted and enter into force in accordance with the procedure set out in Article 20, provided that any amendment to Annex B shall be adopted only with the written consent of the Party concerned.

Article 22

1. Each Party shall have one vote, except as provided for in paragraph 2 below.

2. Regional economic integration organizations, in matters within their competence, shall exercise their right to vote with a number of votes equal to the number of their member States that are Parties to this Protocol. Such an organization shall not exercise its right to vote if any of its member States exercises its right, and vice versa.

Article 23

The Secretary-General of the United Nations shall be the Depositary of this Protocol.

Article 24

1. This Protocol shall be open for signature and subject to ratification, acceptance or approval by States and regional economic integration organizations which are Parties to the Convention. It shall be open for signature at United Nations Headquarters in New York from 16 March 1998 to 15 March 1999. This Protocol shall be open for accession from the day after the date on which it is closed for signature. Instruments of ratification, acceptance, approval or accession shall be deposited with the Depositary.

2. Any regional economic integration organization which becomes a Party to this Protocol without any of its member States being a Party shall be bound by all the obligations under this Protocol. In the case of such organizations, one or more of whose member States is a Party to this Protocol, the organization and its member States shall decide on their respective responsibilities for the performance of their obligations under this Protocol. In such cases, the organization and the member States shall not be entitled to exercise rights under this Protocol concurrently.

3. In their instruments of ratification, acceptance, approval or accession, regional economic integration organizations shall declare the extent of their competence with respect to the matters governed by this Protocol. These organizations shall also inform the Depositary, who shall in turn inform the Parties, of any substantial modification in the extent of their competence.

Article 25

1. This Protocol shall enter into force on the ninetieth day after the date on which not less than 55 Parties to the Convention, incorporating Parties included in Annex I which accounted in total for at least 55 per cent of the total carbon dioxide emissions for 1990 of the Parties included in Annex I, have deposited their instruments of ratification, acceptance, approval or accession.

2. For the purposes of this Article, 'the total carbon dioxide emissions for 1990 of the Parties included in Annex I' means the amount communicated on or before the date of adoption of this Protocol by the Parties included in Annex I in their first national communications submitted in accordance with Article 12 of the Convention.

3. For each State or regional economic integration organization that ratifies, accepts or approves this Protocol or accedes thereto after the conditions set out in paragraph 1 above for entry into force have been fulfilled, this Protocol shall enter into force on the ninetieth day following the date of deposit of its instrument of ratification, acceptance, approval or accession.

4. For the purposes of this Article, any instrument deposited by a regional economic integration organization shall not be counted as additional to those deposited by States members of the organization.

Article 26

No reservations may be made to this Protocol.

Article 27

1. At any time after three years from the date on which this Protocol has entered into force for a Party, that Party may withdraw from this Protocol by giving written notification to the Depositary.

2. Any such withdrawal shall take effect upon expiry of one year from the date of receipt by the Depositary of the notification of withdrawal, or on such later date as may be specified in the notification of withdrawal.

3. Any Party that withdraws from the Convention shall be considered as also having withdrawn from this Protocol.

Article 28

The original of this Protocol, of which the Arabic, Chinese, English, French, Russian and Spanish texts are equally authentic, shall be deposited with the Secretary-General of the United Nations.

Done at Kyoto this eleventh day of December one thousand nine hundred and ninety-seven.

In witness whereof the undersigned, being duly authorized to that effect, have affixed their signatures to this Protocol on the dates indicated.

Annex A

Greenhouse gases

Carbon dioxide (CO_2)

Methane (CH_4)

Nitrous oxide (N_2O)

Hydrofluorocarbons (HFCs)

Perfluorocarbons (PFCs)

Sulphur hexafluoride (SF_6)

Sectors/source categories

Energy
- Fuel combustion
  - Energy industries
  - Manufacturing industries and construction
  - Transport
  - Other sectors
  - Other
- Fugitive emissions from fuels
  - Solid fuels
  - Oil and natural gas
  - Other

Industrial processes
- Mineral products
- Chemical industry
- Metal production
- Other production
- Production of halocarbons and sulphur hexafluoride
- Consumption of halocarbons and sulphur hexafluoride
- Other

Solvent and other product use

Agriculture
- Enteric fermentation
- Manure management
- Rice cultivation
- Agricultural soils
- Prescribed burning of savannas
- Field burning of agricultural residues
- Other

Waste
- Solid waste disposal on land
- Wastewater handling
- Waste incineration
- Other

Annex B

Party	Quantified emission limitation or reduction commitment (percentage of base year or period)
Australia	108
Austria	92
Belgium	92
Bulgaria*	92
Canada	94
Croatia*	95
Czech Republic*	92
Denmark	92
Estonia*	92
European Community	92
Finland	92
France	92
Germany	92
Greece	92
Hungary*	94
Iceland	110
Ireland	92
Italy	92

Japan	94
Latvia*	92
Liechtenstein	92
Lithuania*	92
Luxembourg	92
Monaco	92
Netherlands	92
New Zealand	100
Norway	101
Poland*	94
Portugal	92
Romania*	92
Russian Federation*	100
Slovakia*	92
Slovenia*	92
Spain	92
Sweden	92
Switzerland	92
Ukraine*	100
United Kingdom of Great Britain and Northern Ireland	92
United States of America	93

* Countries that are undergoing the process of transition to a market economy.

Chapter 4

Biological Diversity

Introduction

This chapter, together with Chapter 5, provides a selection of the main treaties in the broad field of biodiversity law. This includes first of all the 1992 CBD, the umbrella agreement in this field. The CBD is characterised by the fact that it is a framework agreement that includes the basic principles guiding states' conservation and use policies in this field as well as a number of general obligations. It is not, however, hierarchically superior to other treaties in the field but only provides the missing general framework for biodiversity management. The Convention's significance derives from its broad membership and the ability of the Conference of the Parties to move beyond the very general framework to progressively examine specific issues such as agricultural biodiversity, traditional knowledge and access and benefit-sharing.

The section on biosafety includes two instruments in this field. The 2000 Biosafety Protocol, the main international regulatory framework, seeks to provide conditions for the safe use of genetic engineering. Its main significance is that its regulatory action is premised on the precautionary principle. In practice, the Protocol focuses mostly on transboundary movements of LMOs and provides a procedure for regulating international trade in LMOs. This section also reproduces parts of the 1994 SPS Agreement. This Agreement derives its main significance from the fact that it is one the treaties administered by the WTO and therefore binding on all WTO member states. It provides some scope for member states to adopt biosafety measures, including the possibility to temporarily rely on the precautionary principle.

Finally, this chapter reproduces the 2001 PGRFA Treaty which is one of the few treaties that specifically link environmental management and agriculture. In fact, the negotiation of the treaty was directly related to the adoption of the CBD, an element which is reflected in the basic objectives of the Treaty. In particular, one of the contributions of the PGRFA Treaty is to have developed some themes only briefly considered by the CBD by, for instance, adopting an access and benefit-sharing regime.

Selected readings

Biodiversity

Bowman, M. and Redgwell, C. (eds.), *International Law and the Conservation of Biological Diversity* (London: Kluwer Law International, 1996).

Kate, K.T. and Laird, S.A., *The Commercial Use of Biodiversity - Access to Genetic Resources and Benefit-Sharing* (London: Earthscan, 1999).

Le Prestre, P.G. (ed.), *Governing Global Biodiversity - The Evolution and Implementation of the Convention on Biological Diversity* (Aldershot: Ashgate, 2002).

Yongo, T., 'Development, Implementation, and Effectiveness of the CBD Process', *in* Schechter, M.G. (ed.), *United Nations-Sponsored World Conferences - Focus on Impact and Follow-up* (Tokyo: UN University, 2001), p. 85.

Biosafety

Bail, C., Falkner, R. and Marquard, H. (eds.), *The Cartagena Protocol on Biosafety - Reconciling Trade in Biotechnology with Environment and Development?* (London: Earthscan, 2002).

Boisson de Chazournes, L. and Thomas, U.P., 'The Biosafety Protocol: Regulatory Innovation and Emerging Trends', 10 *Swiss Rev. Int'l & European L.* 518 (2000).

Burgiel, S.W., 'The Cartagena Protocol on Biosafety: Taking the Steps from Negotiation to Implementation', 11 *RECIEL* 53 (2002).

Eggers, B. and Mackenzie, R., 'The Cartagena Protocol on Biosafety', 3 *J. Int'l Economic L.* 525 (2000).

Agriculture

Cooper, H.D., 'The International Treaty on Plant Genetic Resources for Food and Agriculture', 11 *RECIEL* 1 (2002).

Fowler, C., 'The Status of Public and Proprietary Germplasm and Information: An Assessment of Recent Developments at FAO', *IP Strategy Today* No. 7-2003.

Kameri-Mbote, P. and Cullet, P., 'Agro-biodiversity and International Law - A Conceptual Framework', 11 *JEL* 257 (1999).

Rose, G., 'International Law of Sustainable Agriculture in the 21st Century: The International Treaty on Plant Genetic Resources for Food and Agriculture', 15 *Georgetown Int'l Envtl L. Rev.* 583 (2003).

Biodiversity

Convention on Biological Diversity

Adopted on 5 June 1992 at Rio de Janeiro. Entered into force on 29 December 1993. Source: 1760 *UNTS* 79. Number of parties: 188. Further information: Secretariat, Montreal, Canada, http://www.biodiv.org

Preamble

The Contracting Parties,

Conscious of the intrinsic value of biological diversity and of the ecological, genetic, social, economic, scientific, educational, cultural, recreational and aesthetic values of biological diversity and its components,

Conscious also of the importance of biological diversity for evolution and for maintaining life sustaining systems of the biosphere,

Affirming that the conservation of biological diversity is a common concern of humankind,

Reaffirming that States have sovereign rights over their own biological resources,

Reaffirming also that States are responsible for conserving their biological diversity and for using their biological resources in a sustainable manner,

Concerned that biological diversity is being significantly reduced by certain human activities,

Aware of the general lack of information and knowledge regarding biological diversity and of the urgent need to develop scientific, technical and institutional capacities to provide the basic understanding upon which to plan and implement appropriate measures,

Noting that it is vital to anticipate, prevent and attack the causes of significant reduction or loss of biological diversity at source,

Noting also that where there is a threat of significant reduction or loss of biological diversity, lack of full scientific certainty should not be used as a reason for postponing measures to avoid or minimize such a threat,

Noting further that the fundamental requirement for the conservation of biological diversity is the *in-situ* conservation of ecosystems and natural habitats and the maintenance and recovery of viable populations of species in their natural surroundings,

Noting further that *ex-situ* measures, preferably in the country of origin, also have an important role to play,

Recognizing the close and traditional dependence of many indigenous and local communities embodying traditional lifestyles on biological resources, and the desirability of sharing equitably benefits arising from the use of traditional knowledge, innovations and practices relevant to the conservation of biological diversity and the sustainable use of its components,

Recognizing also the vital role that women play in the conservation and sustainable use of biological diversity and affirming the need for the full participation of women at all levels of policymaking and implementation for biological diversity conservation,

Stressing the importance of, and the need to promote, international, regional and global cooperation among States and intergovernmental organizations and the non-governmental sector for the conservation of biological diversity and the sustainable use of its components,

Acknowledging that the provision of new and additional financial resources and appropriate access to relevant technologies can be expected to make a substantial difference in the world's ability to address the loss of biological diversity,

Acknowledging further that special provision is required to meet the needs of developing countries, including the provision of new and additional financial resources and appropriate access to relevant technologies,

Noting in this regard the special conditions of the least developed countries and small island States,

Acknowledging that substantial investments are required to conserve biological diversity and that there is the expectation of a broad range of environmental, economic and social benefits from those investments,

Recognizing that economic and social development and poverty eradication are the first and overriding priorities of developing countries,

Aware that conservation and sustainable use of biological diversity is of critical importance for meeting the food, health and other needs of the growing world population, for which purpose access to and sharing of both genetic resources and technologies are essential,

Noting that, ultimately, the conservation and sustainable use of biological diversity will strengthen friendly relations among States and contribute to peace for humankind,

Desiring to enhance and complement existing international arrangements for the conservation of biological diversity and sustainable use of its components, and

Determined to conserve and sustainably use biological diversity for the benefit of present and future generations,

Have agreed as follows:

Article 1: Objectives

The objectives of this Convention, to be pursued in accordance with its relevant provisions, are the conservation of biological diversity, the sustainable use of its components and the fair and equitable sharing of the benefits arising out of the utilization of genetic resources, including by appropriate access to genetic resources and by appropriate transfer of relevant technologies, taking into account all rights over those resources and to technologies, and by appropriate funding.

Article 2: Use of terms

For the purposes of this Convention:

'*Biological diversity*' means the variability among living organisms from all sources including, *inter alia*, terrestrial, marine and other aquatic ecosystems and the ecological complexes of which they are part; this includes diversity within species, between species and of ecosystems.

'*Biological resources*' includes genetic resources, organisms or parts thereof, populations, or any other biotic component of ecosystems with actual or potential use or value for humanity.

'*Biotechnology*' means any technological application that uses biological systems, living organisms, or derivatives thereof, to make or modify products or processes for specific use.

'*Country of origin of genetic resources*' means the country which possesses those genetic resources in *in-situ* conditions.

'*Country providing genetic resources*' means the country supplying genetic resources collected from *in-situ* sources, including populations of both wild and domesticated species, or taken from *ex-situ* sources, which may or may not have originated in that country.

'*Domesticated or cultivated species*' means species in which the evolutionary process has been influenced by humans to meet their needs.

'*Ecosystem*' means a dynamic complex of plant, animal and micro-organism communities and their non-living environment interacting as a functional unit.

'*Ex-situ conservation*' means the conservation of components of biological diversity outside their natural habitats.

'*Genetic material*' means any material of plant, animal, microbial or other origin containing functional units of heredity.

'*Genetic resources*' means genetic material of actual or potential value.

'*Habitat*' means the place or type of site where an organism or population naturally occurs.

'*In-situ conditions*' means conditions where genetic resources exist within ecosystems and natural habitats, and, in the case of domesticated or cultivated species, in the surroundings where they have developed their distinctive properties.

'*In-situ conservation*' means the conservation of ecosystems and natural habitats and the maintenance and recovery of viable populations of species in their natural surroundings and, in the case of domesticated or cultivated species, in the surroundings where they have developed their distinctive properties.

'*Protected area*' means a geographically defined area which is designated or regulated and managed to achieve specific conservation objectives.

'*Regional economic integration organization*' means an organization constituted by sovereign States of a given region, to which its member States have transferred competence in respect of matters governed by this Convention and which has been duly authorized, in accordance with its internal procedures, to sign, ratify, accept, approve or accede to it.

'*Sustainable use*' means the use of components of biological diversity in a way and at a rate that does not lead to the long-term decline of biological diversity, thereby maintaining its potential to meet the needs and aspirations of present and future generations.

'*Technology*' includes biotechnology.

Article 3: Principle

States have, in accordance with the Charter of the United Nations and the principles of international law, the sovereign right to exploit their own resources pursuant to their own environmental policies, and the responsibility to ensure that activities within their jurisdiction or control do not cause damage to the environment of other States or of areas beyond the limits of national jurisdiction.

Article 4: Jurisdictional scope

Subject to the rights of other States, and except as otherwise expressly provided in this Convention, the provisions of this Convention apply, in relation to each Contracting Party:

a) In the case of components of biological diversity, in areas within the limits of its national jurisdiction; and

b) In the case of processes and activities, regardless of where their effects occur, carried out under its jurisdiction or control, within the area of its national jurisdiction or beyond the limits of national jurisdiction.

Article 5: Cooperation

Each Contracting Party shall, as far as possible and as appropriate, cooperate with other Contracting Parties, directly or, where appropriate, through competent international organizations, in respect of areas beyond national jurisdiction and on other matters of mutual interest, for the conservation and sustainable use of biological diversity.

Article 6: General measures for conservation and sustainable use

Each Contracting Party shall, in accordance with its particular conditions and capabilities:

a) Develop national strategies, plans or programmes for the conservation and sustainable use of biological diversity or adapt for this purpose existing strategies, plans or programmes which shall reflect, *inter alia*, the measures set out in this Convention relevant to the Contracting Party concerned; and

b) Integrate, as far as possible and as appropriate, the conservation and sustainable use of biological diversity into relevant sectoral or cross-sectoral plans, programmes and policies.

Article 7: Identification and monitoring

Each Contracting Party shall, as far as possible and as appropriate, in particular for the purposes of Articles 8 to 10:

a) Identify components of biological diversity important for its conservation and sustainable use having regard to the indicative list of categories set down in Annex I;

b) Monitor, through sampling and other techniques, the components of biological diversity identified pursuant to subparagraph (a) above, paying particular attention to those requiring urgent conservation measures and those which offer the greatest potential for sustainable use;

c) Identify processes and categories of activities which have or are likely to have significant adverse impacts on the conservation and sustainable use of biological diversity, and monitor their effects through sampling and other techniques; and

d) Maintain and organize, by any mechanism data, derived from identification and monitoring activities pursuant to subparagraphs (a), (b) and (c) above.

Article 8: *In-situ* conservation

Each Contracting Party shall, as far as possible and as appropriate:

a) Establish a system of protected areas or areas where special measures need to be taken to conserve biological diversity;

b) Develop, where necessary, guidelines for the selection, establishment and management of protected areas or areas where special measures need to be taken to conserve biological diversity;

c) Regulate or manage biological resources important for the conservation of biological diversity whether within or outside protected areas, with a view to ensuring their conservation and sustainable use;

d) Promote the protection of ecosystems, natural habitats and the maintenance of viable populations of species in natural surroundings;

e) Promote environmentally sound and sustainable development in areas adjacent to protected areas with a view to furthering protection of these areas;

f) Rehabilitate and restore degraded ecosystems and promote the recovery of threatened species, *inter alia*, through the development and implementation of plans or other management strategies;

g) Establish or maintain means to regulate, manage or control the risks associated with the use and release of living modified organisms resulting from biotechnology which are likely to have adverse environmental impacts that could affect the conservation and sustainable use of biological diversity, taking also into account the risks to human health;

h) Prevent the introduction of, control or eradicate those alien species which threaten ecosystems, habitats or species;

i) Endeavour to provide the conditions needed for compatibility between present uses and the conservation of biological diversity and the sustainable use of its components;

j) Subject to its national legislation, respect, preserve and maintain knowledge, innovations and practices of indigenous and local communities embodying traditional lifestyles relevant for the conservation and sustainable use of biological diversity and promote their wider application with the approval and involvement of the holders of such knowledge, innovations and practices and encourage the equitable sharing of the benefits arising from the utilization of such knowledge, innovations and practices;

k) Develop or maintain necessary legislation and/or other regulatory provisions for the protection of threatened species and populations;

l) Where a significant adverse effect on biological diversity has been determined pursuant to Article 7, regulate or manage the relevant processes and categories of activities; and

m) Cooperate in providing financial and other support for *in-situ* conservation outlined in subparagraphs (a) to (l) above, particularly to developing countries.

Article 9: *Ex-situ* conservation

Each Contracting Party shall, as far as possible and as appropriate, and predominantly for the purpose of complementing *in-situ* measures:

a) Adopt measures for the *ex-situ* conservation of components of biological diversity, preferably in the country of origin of such components;

b) Establish and maintain facilities for *ex-situ* conservation of and research on plants, animals and micro-organisms, preferably in the country of origin of genetic resources;

c) Adopt measures for the recovery and rehabilitation of threatened species and for their reintroduction into their natural habitats under appropriate conditions;

d) Regulate and manage collection of biological resources from natural habitats for *ex-situ* conservation purposes so as not to threaten ecosystems and *in-situ* populations of species, except where special temporary *ex-situ* measures are required under subparagraph (c) above; and

(e) Cooperate in providing financial and other support for *ex-situ* conservation outlined in subparagraphs (a) to (d) above and in the establishment and maintenance of *ex-situ* conservation facilities in developing countries.

Article 10: Sustainable use of components of biological diversity

Each Contracting Party shall, as far as possible and as appropriate:

a) Integrate consideration of the conservation and sustainable use of biological resources into national decision-making;

b) Adopt measures relating to the use of biological resources to avoid or minimize adverse impacts on biological diversity;

c) Protect and encourage customary use of biological resources in accordance with traditional cultural practices that are compatible with conservation or sustainable use requirements;

d) Support local populations to develop and implement remedial action in degraded areas where biological diversity has been reduced; and

e) Encourage cooperation between its governmental authorities and its private sector in developing methods for sustainable use of biological resources.

Article 11: Incentive measures

Each Contracting Party shall, as far as possible and as appropriate, adopt economically and socially sound measures that act as incentives for the conservation and sustainable use of components of biological diversity.

Article 12: Research and training

The Contracting Parties, taking into account the special needs of developing countries, shall:

a) Establish and maintain programmes for scientific and technical education and training in measures for the identification, conservation and sustainable use of biological diversity and its components and provide support for such education and training for the specific needs of developing countries;

b) Promote and encourage research which contributes to the conservation and sustainable use of biological diversity, particularly in developing countries, *inter alia*, in accordance with decisions of the Conference of the Parties taken in consequence of recommendations of the Subsidiary Body on Scientific, Technical and Technological Advice; and

c) In keeping with the provisions of Articles 16, 18 and 20, promote and cooperate in the use of scientific advances in biological diversity research in developing methods for conservation and sustainable use of biological resources.

Article 13: Public education and awareness

The Contracting Parties shall:

a) Promote and encourage understanding of the importance of, and the measures required for, the conservation of biological diversity, as well as its propagation through media, and the inclusion of these topics in educational programmes; and

b) Cooperate, as appropriate, with other States and international organizations in developing educational and public awareness programmes, with respect to conservation and sustainable use of biological diversity.

Article 14: Impact assessment and minimizing adverse impacts

1. Each Contracting Party, as far as possible and as appropriate, shall:

a) Introduce appropriate procedures requiring environmental impact assessment of its proposed projects that are likely to have significant adverse effects on biological diversity with a view to avoiding or minimizing such effects and, where appropriate, allow for public participation in such procedures;
b) Introduce appropriate arrangements to ensure that the environmental consequences of its programmes and policies that are likely to have significant adverse impacts on biological diversity are duly taken into account;
c) Promote, on the basis of reciprocity, notification, exchange of information and consultation on activities under their jurisdiction or control which are likely to significantly affect adversely the biological diversity of other States or areas beyond the limits of national jurisdiction, by encouraging the conclusion of bilateral, regional or multilateral arrangements, as appropriate;
d) In the case of imminent or grave danger or damage, originating under its jurisdiction or control, to biological diversity within the area under jurisdiction of other States or in areas beyond the limits of national jurisdiction, notify immediately the potentially affected States of such danger or damage, as well as initiate action to prevent or minimize such danger or damage; and
e) Promote national arrangements for emergency responses to activities or events, whether caused naturally or otherwise, which present a grave and imminent danger to biological diversity and encourage international cooperation to supplement such national efforts and, where appropriate and agreed by the States or regional economic integration organizations concerned, to establish joint contingency plans.

2. The Conference of the Parties shall examine, on the basis of studies to be carried out, the issue of liability and redress, including restoration and compensation, for damage to biological diversity, except where such liability is a purely internal matter.

Article 15: Access to genetic resources

1. Recognizing the sovereign rights of States over their natural resources, the authority to determine access to genetic resources rests with the national governments and is subject to national legislation.

2. Each Contracting Party shall endeavour to create conditions to facilitate access to genetic resources for environmentally sound uses by other Contracting Parties and not to impose restrictions that run counter to the objectives of this Convention.

3. For the purpose of this Convention, the genetic resources being provided by a Contracting Party, as referred to in this Article and Articles 16 and 19, are only those that are provided by Contracting Parties that are countries of origin of such resources or by the Parties that have acquired the genetic resources in accordance with this Convention.

4. Access, where granted, shall be on mutually agreed terms and subject to the provisions of this Article.

5. Access to genetic resources shall be subject to prior informed consent of the Contracting Party providing such resources, unless otherwise determined by that Party.

6. Each Contracting Party shall endeavour to develop and carry out scientific research based on genetic resources provided by other Contracting Parties with the full participation of, and where possible in, such Contracting Parties.

7. Each Contracting Party shall take legislative, administrative or policy measures, as appropriate, and in accordance with Articles 16 and 19 and, where necessary, through the financial mechanism established by Articles 20 and 21 with the aim of sharing in a fair and equitable way the results of research and development and the benefits arising from the commercial and other utilization of genetic resources with the Contracting Party providing such resources. Such sharing shall be upon mutually agreed terms.

Article 16: Access to and transfer of technology

1. Each Contracting Party, recognizing that technology includes biotechnology, and that both access to and transfer of technology among Contracting Parties are essential elements for the attainment of the objectives of this Convention, undertakes subject to the provisions of this Article to provide and/or facilitate access for and transfer to other Contracting Parties of technologies that are relevant to the conservation and sustainable use of biological diversity or make use of genetic resources and do not cause significant damage to the environment.

2. Access to and transfer of technology referred to in paragraph 1 above to developing countries shall be provided and/or facilitated under fair and most favourable terms, including on concessional and preferential terms where mutually agreed, and, where necessary, in accordance with the financial mechanism established by Articles 20 and 21. In the case of technology subject to patents and other intellectual property rights, such access and transfer shall be provided on terms which recognize and are consistent with the adequate and effective protection of intellectual property rights. The application of this paragraph shall be consistent with paragraphs 3, 4 and 5 below.

3. Each Contracting Party shall take legislative, administrative or policy measures, as appropriate, with the aim that Contracting Parties, in particular those that are developing countries, which provide genetic resources are provided access to and transfer of technology which makes use of those resources, on mutually agreed terms, including technology protected by patents and other intellectual property rights, where necessary, through the provisions of Articles 20 and 21 and in accordance with international law and consistent with paragraphs 4 and 5 below.

4. Each Contracting Party shall take legislative, administrative or policy measures, as appropriate, with the aim that the private sector facilitates access to, joint development and transfer of technology referred to in paragraph 1 above for the benefit of both governmental institutions and the private sector of developing

countries and in this regard shall abide by the obligations included in paragraphs 1, 2 and 3 above.

5. The Contracting Parties, recognizing that patents and other intellectual property rights may have an influence on the implementation of this Convention, shall cooperate in this regard subject to national legislation and international law in order to ensure that such rights are supportive of and do not run counter to its objectives.

Article 17: Exchange of information

1. The Contracting Parties shall facilitate the exchange of information, from all publicly available sources, relevant to the conservation and sustainable use of biological diversity, taking into account the special needs of developing countries.

2. Such exchange of information shall include exchange of results of technical, scientific and socio-economic research, as well as information on training and surveying programmes, specialized knowledge, indigenous and traditional knowledge as such and in combination with the technologies referred to in Article 16, paragraph 1. It shall also, where feasible, include repatriation of information.

Article 18: Technical and scientific cooperation

1. The Contracting Parties shall promote international technical and scientific cooperation in the field of conservation and sustainable use of biological diversity, where necessary, through the appropriate international and national institutions.

2. Each Contracting Party shall promote technical and scientific cooperation with other Contracting Parties, in particular developing countries, in implementing this Convention, *inter alia*, through the development and implementation of national policies. In promoting such cooperation, special attention should be given to the development and strengthening of national capabilities, by means of human resources development and institution building.

3. The Conference of the Parties, at its first meeting, shall determine how to establish a clearing-house mechanism to promote and facilitate technical and scientific cooperation.

4. The Contracting Parties shall, in accordance with national legislation and policies, encourage and develop methods of cooperation for the development and use of technologies, including indigenous and traditional technologies, in pursuance of the objectives of this Convention. For this purpose, the Contracting Parties shall also promote cooperation in the training of personnel and exchange of experts.

5. The Contracting Parties shall, subject to mutual agreement, promote the establishment of joint research programmes and joint ventures for the development of technologies relevant to the objectives of this Convention.

Article 19: Handling of biotechnology and distribution of its benefits

1. Each Contracting Party shall take legislative, administrative or policy measures, as appropriate, to provide for the effective participation in biotechnological research activities by those Contracting Parties, especially developing countries,

which provide the genetic resources for such research, and where feasible in such Contracting Parties.

2. Each Contracting Party shall take all practicable measures to promote and advance priority access on a fair and equitable basis by Contracting Parties, especially developing countries, to the results and benefits arising from biotechnologies based upon genetic resources provided by those Contracting Parties. Such access shall be on mutually agreed terms.

3. The Parties shall consider the need for and modalities of a protocol setting out appropriate procedures, including, in particular, advance informed agreement, in the field of the safe transfer, handling and use of any living modified organism resulting from biotechnology that may have adverse effect on the conservation and sustainable use of biological diversity.

4. Each Contracting Party shall, directly or by requiring any natural or legal person under its jurisdiction providing the organisms referred to in paragraph 3 above, provide any available information about the use and safety regulations required by that Contracting Party in handling such organisms, as well as any available information on the potential adverse impact of the specific organisms concerned to the Contracting Party into which those organisms are to be introduced.

Article 20: Financial resources

1. Each Contracting Party undertakes to provide, in accordance with its capabilities, financial support and incentives in respect of those national activities which are intended to achieve the objectives of this Convention, in accordance with its national plans, priorities and programmes.

2. The developed country Parties shall provide new and additional financial resources to enable developing country Parties to meet the agreed full incremental costs to them of implementing measures which fulfil the obligations of this Convention and to benefit from its provisions and which costs are agreed between a developing country Party and the institutional structure referred to in Article 21, in accordance with policy, strategy, programme priorities and eligibility criteria and an indicative list of incremental costs established by the Conference of the Parties. Other Parties, including countries undergoing the process of transition to a market economy, may voluntarily assume the obligations of the developed country Parties. For the purpose of this Article, the Conference of the Parties, shall at its first meeting establish a list of developed country Parties and other Parties which voluntarily assume the obligations of the developed country Parties. The Conference of the Parties shall periodically review and if necessary amend the list. Contributions from other countries and sources on a voluntary basis would also be encouraged. The implementation of these commitments shall take into account the need for adequacy, predictability and timely flow of funds and the importance of burden-sharing among the contributing Parties included in the list.

3. The developed country Parties may also provide, and developing country Parties avail themselves of, financial resources related to the implementation of this Convention through bilateral, regional and other multilateral channels.

4. The extent to which developing country Parties will effectively implement their commitments under this Convention will depend on the effective implementation by developed country Parties of their commitments under this Convention related to financial resources and transfer of technology and will take fully into account the fact that economic and social development and eradication of poverty are the first and overriding priorities of the developing country Parties.

5. The Parties shall take full account of the specific needs and special situation of least developed countries in their actions with regard to funding and transfer of technology.

6. The Contracting Parties shall also take into consideration the special conditions resulting from the dependence on, distribution and location of, biological diversity within developing country Parties, in particular small island States.

7. Consideration shall also be given to the special situation of developing countries, including those that are most environmentally vulnerable, such as those with arid and semi-arid zones, coastal and mountainous areas.

Article 21: Financial mechanism

1. There shall be a mechanism for the provision of financial resources to developing country Parties for purposes of this Convention on a grant or concessional basis the essential elements of which are described in this Article. The mechanism shall function under the authority and guidance of, and be accountable to, the Conference of the Parties for purposes of this Convention. The operations of the mechanism shall be carried out by such institutional structure as may be decided upon by the Conference of the Parties at its first meeting. For purposes of this Convention, the Conference of the Parties shall determine the policy, strategy, programme priorities and eligibility criteria relating to the access to and utilization of such resources. The contributions shall be such as to take into account the need for predictability, adequacy and timely flow of funds referred to in Article 20 in accordance with the amount of resources needed to be decided periodically by the Conference of the Parties and the importance of burden-sharing among the contributing Parties included in the list referred to in Article 20, paragraph 2. Voluntary contributions may also be made by the developed country Parties and by other countries and sources. The mechanism shall operate within a democratic and transparent system of governance.

2. Pursuant to the objectives of this Convention, the Conference of the Parties shall at its first meeting determine the policy, strategy and programme priorities, as well as detailed criteria and guidelines for eligibility for access to and utilization of the financial resources including monitoring and evaluation on a regular basis of such utilization. The Conference of the Parties shall decide on the arrangements to

give effect to paragraph 1 above after consultation with the institutional structure entrusted with the operation of the financial mechanism.

3. The Conference of the Parties shall review the effectiveness of the mechanism established under this Article, including the criteria and guidelines referred to in paragraph 2 above, not less than two years after the entry into force of this Convention and thereafter on a regular basis. Based on such review, it shall take appropriate action to improve the effectiveness of the mechanism if necessary.

4. The Contracting Parties shall consider strengthening existing financial institutions to provide financial resources for the conservation and sustainable use of biological diversity.

Article 22: Relationship with other international conventions

1. The provisions of this Convention shall not affect the rights and obligations of any Contracting Party deriving from any existing international agreement, except where the exercise of those rights and obligations would cause a serious damage or threat to biological diversity.

2. Contracting Parties shall implement this Convention with respect to the marine environment consistently with the rights and obligations of States under the law of the sea.

Article 23: Conference of the Parties

1. A Conference of the Parties is hereby established. The first meeting of the Conference of the Parties shall be convened by the Executive Director of the United Nations Environment Programme not later than one year after the entry into force of this Convention. Thereafter, ordinary meetings of the Conference of the Parties shall be held at regular intervals to be determined by the Conference at its first meeting.

2. Extraordinary meetings of the Conference of the Parties shall be held at such other times as may be deemed necessary by the Conference, or at the written request of any Party, provided that, within six months of the request being communicated to them by the Secretariat, it is supported by at least one third of the Parties.

3. The Conference of the Parties shall by consensus agree upon and adopt rules of procedure for itself and for any subsidiary body it may establish, as well as financial rules governing the funding of the Secretariat. At each ordinary meeting, it shall adopt a budget for the financial period until the next ordinary meeting.

4. The Conference of the Parties shall keep under review the implementation of this Convention, and, for this purpose, shall:

a) Establish the form and the intervals for transmitting the information to be submitted in accordance with Article 26 and consider such information as well as reports submitted by any subsidiary body;
b) Review scientific, technical and technological advice on biological diversity provided in accordance with Article 25;

c) Consider and adopt, as required, protocols in accordance with Article 28;
d) Consider and adopt, as required, in accordance with Articles 29 and 30, amendments to this Convention and its annexes;
e) Consider amendments to any protocol, as well as to any annexes thereto, and, if so decided, recommend their adoption to the parties to the protocol concerned;
f) Consider and adopt, as required, in accordance with Article 30, additional annexes to this Convention;
g) Establish such subsidiary bodies, particularly to provide scientific and technical advice, as are deemed necessary for the implementation of this Convention;
h) Contact, through the Secretariat, the executive bodies of conventions dealing with matters covered by this Convention with a view to establishing appropriate forms of cooperation with them; and
i) Consider and undertake any additional action that may be required for the achievement of the purposes of this Convention in the light of experience gained in its operation.

5. The United Nations, its specialized agencies and the International Atomic Energy Agency, as well as any State not Party to this Convention, may be represented as observers at meetings of the Conference of the Parties. Any other body or agency, whether governmental or non-governmental, qualified in fields relating to conservation and sustainable use of biological diversity, which has informed the Secretariat of its wish to be represented as an observer at a meeting of the Conference of the Parties, may be admitted unless at least one third of the Parties present object. The admission and participation of observers shall be subject to the rules of procedure adopted by the Conference of the Parties.

Article 24: Secretariat

1. A secretariat is hereby established. Its functions shall be:
a) To arrange for and service meetings of the Conference of the Parties provided for in Article 23;
b) To perform the functions assigned to it by any protocol;
c) To prepare reports on the execution of its functions under this Convention and present them to the Conference of the Parties;
d) To coordinate with other relevant international bodies and, in particular to enter into such administrative and contractual arrangements as may be required for the effective discharge of its functions; and
e) To perform such other functions as may be determined by the Conference of the Parties.

2. At its first ordinary meeting, the Conference of the Parties shall designate the secretariat from amongst those existing competent international organizations which have signified their willingness to carry out the secretariat functions under this Convention.

Article 25: Subsidiary Body on Scientific, Technical and Technological Advice

1. A subsidiary body for the provision of scientific, technical and technological advice is hereby established to provide the Conference of the Parties and, as appropriate, its other subsidiary bodies with timely advice relating to the implementation of this Convention. This body shall be open to participation by all Parties and shall be multidisciplinary. It shall comprise government representatives competent in the relevant field of expertise. It shall report regularly to the Conference of the Parties on all aspects of its work.

2. Under the authority of and in accordance with guidelines laid down by the Conference of the Parties, and upon its request, this body shall:

a) Provide scientific and technical assessments of the status of biological diversity;
b) Prepare scientific and technical assessments of the effects of types of measures taken in accordance with the provisions of this Convention;
c) Identify innovative, efficient and state-of-the-art technologies and know-how relating to the conservation and sustainable use of biological diversity and advise on the ways and means of promoting development and/or transferring such technologies;
d) Provide advice on scientific programmes and international cooperation in research and development related to conservation and sustainable use of biological diversity; and
e) Respond to scientific, technical, technological and methodological questions that the Conference of the Parties and its subsidiary bodies may put to the body.

3. The functions, terms of reference, organization and operation of this body may be further elaborated by the Conference of the Parties.

Article 26: Reports

Each Contracting Party shall, at intervals to be determined by the Conference of the Parties, present to the Conference of the Parties, reports on measures which it has taken for the implementation of the provisions of this Convention and their effectiveness in meeting the objectives of this Convention.

Article 27: Settlement of disputes

1. In the event of a dispute between Contracting Parties concerning the interpretation or application of this Convention, the parties concerned shall seek solution by negotiation.

2. If the parties concerned cannot reach agreement by negotiation, they may jointly seek the good offices of, or request mediation by, a third party.

3. When ratifying, accepting, approving or acceding to this Convention, or at any time thereafter, a State or regional economic integration organization may declare in writing to the Depositary that for a dispute not resolved in accordance with paragraph 1 or paragraph 2 above, it accepts one or both of the following means of dispute settlement as compulsory:

a) Arbitration in accordance with the procedure laid down in Part 1 of Annex II;

b) Submission of the dispute to the International Court of Justice.

4. If the parties to the dispute have not, in accordance with paragraph 3 above, accepted the same or any procedure, the dispute shall be submitted to conciliation in accordance with Part 2 of Annex II unless the parties otherwise agree.

5. The provisions of this Article shall apply with respect to any protocol except as otherwise provided in the protocol concerned.

Article 28: Adoption of protocols

1. The Contracting Parties shall cooperate in the formulation and adoption of protocols to this Convention.

2. Protocols shall be adopted at a meeting of the Conference of the Parties.

3. The text of any proposed protocol shall be communicated to the Contracting Parties by the Secretariat at least six months before such a meeting.

Article 29: Amendment of the Convention or protocols

1. Amendments to this Convention may be proposed by any Contracting Party. Amendments to any protocol may be proposed by any Party to that protocol.

2. Amendments to this Convention shall be adopted at a meeting of the Conference of the Parties. Amendments to any protocol shall be adopted at a meeting of the Parties to the Protocol in question. The text of any proposed amendment to this Convention or to any protocol, except as may otherwise be provided in such protocol, shall be communicated to the Parties to the instrument in question by the secretariat at least six months before the meeting at which it is proposed for adoption. The secretariat shall also communicate proposed amendments to the signatories to this Convention for information.

3. The Parties shall make every effort to reach agreement on any proposed amendment to this Convention or to any protocol by consensus. If all efforts at consensus have been exhausted, and no agreement reached, the amendment shall as a last resort be adopted by a two-third majority vote of the Parties to the instrument in question present and voting at the meeting, and shall be submitted by the Depositary to all Parties for ratification, acceptance or approval.

4. Ratification, acceptance or approval of amendments shall be notified to the Depositary in writing. Amendments adopted in accordance with paragraph 3 above shall enter into force among Parties having accepted them on the ninetieth day after the deposit of instruments of ratification, acceptance or approval by at least two thirds of the Contracting Parties to this Convention or of the Parties to the protocol concerned, except as may otherwise be provided in such protocol. Thereafter the amendments shall enter into force for any other Party on the ninetieth day after that Party deposits its instrument of ratification, acceptance or approval of the amendments.

5. For the purposes of this Article, 'Parties present and voting' means Parties present and casting an affirmative or negative vote.

Article 30: Adoption and amendment of annexes

1. The annexes to this Convention or to any protocol shall form an integral part of the Convention or of such protocol, as the case may be, and, unless expressly provided otherwise, a reference to this Convention or its protocols constitutes at the same time a reference to any annexes thereto. Such annexes shall be restricted to procedural, scientific, technical and administrative matters.

2. Except as may be otherwise provided in any protocol with respect to its annexes, the following procedure shall apply to the proposal, adoption and entry into force of additional annexes to this Convention or of annexes to any protocol:

a) Annexes to this Convention or to any protocol shall be proposed and adopted according to the procedure laid down in Article 29;
b) Any Party that is unable to approve an additional annex to this Convention or an annex to any protocol to which it is Party shall so notify the Depositary, in writing, within one year from the date of the communication of the adoption by the Depositary. The Depositary shall without delay notify all Parties of any such notification received. A Party may at any time withdraw a previous declaration of objection and the annexes shall thereupon enter into force for that Party subject to subparagraph (c) below;
c) On the expiry of one year from the date of the communication of the adoption by the Depositary, the annex shall enter into force for all Parties to this Convention or to any protocol concerned which have not submitted a notification in accordance with the provisions of subparagraph (b) above.

3. The proposal, adoption and entry into force of amendments to annexes to this Convention or to any protocol shall be subject to the same procedure as for the proposal, adoption and entry into force of annexes to the Convention or annexes to any protocol.

4. If an additional annex or an amendment to an annex is related to an amendment to this Convention or to any protocol, the additional annex or amendment shall not enter into force until such time as the amendment to the Convention or to the protocol concerned enters into force.

Article 31: Right to vote

1. Except as provided for in paragraph 2 below, each Contracting Party to this Convention or to any protocol shall have one vote.

2. Regional economic integration organizations, in matters within their competence, shall exercise their right to vote with a number of votes equal to the number of their member States which are Contracting Parties to this Convention or the relevant protocol. Such organizations shall not exercise their right to vote if their member States exercise theirs, and vice versa.

Article 32: Relationship between this Convention and its protocols

1. A State or a regional economic integration organization may not become a Party to a protocol unless it is, or becomes at the same time, a Contracting Party to this Convention.

2. Decisions under any protocol shall be taken only by the Parties to the protocol concerned. Any Contracting Party that has not ratified, accepted or approved a protocol may participate as an observer in any meeting of the parties to that protocol.

Article 33: Signature

This Convention shall be open for signature at Rio de Janeiro by all States and any regional economic integration organization from 5 June 1992 until 14 June 1992, and at the United Nations Headquarters in New York from 15 June 1992 to 4 June 1993.

Article 34: Ratification, acceptance or approval

1. This Convention and any protocol shall be subject to ratification, acceptance or approval by States and by regional economic integration organizations. Instruments of ratification, acceptance or approval shall be deposited with the Depositary.

2. Any organization referred to in paragraph 1 above which becomes a Contracting Party to this Convention or any protocol without any of its member States being a Contracting Party shall be bound by all the obligations under the Convention or the protocol, as the case may be. In the case of such organizations, one or more of whose member States is a Contracting Party to this Convention or relevant protocol, the organization and its member States shall decide on their respective responsibilities for the performance of their obligations under the Convention or protocol, as the case may be. In such cases, the organization and the member States shall not be entitled to exercise rights under the Convention or relevant protocol concurrently.

3. In their instruments of ratification, acceptance or approval, the organizations referred to in paragraph 1 above shall declare the extent of their competence with respect to the matters governed by the Convention or the relevant protocol. These organizations shall also inform the Depositary of any relevant modification in the extent of their competence.

Article 35: Accession

1. This Convention and any protocol shall be open for accession by States and by regional economic integration organizations from the date on which the Convention or the protocol concerned is closed for signature. The instruments of accession shall be deposited with the Depositary.

2. In their instruments of accession, the organizations referred to in paragraph 1 above shall declare the extent of their competence with respect to the matters governed by the Convention or the relevant protocol. These organizations shall also

inform the Depositary of any relevant modification in the extent of their competence.

3. The provisions of Article 34, paragraph 2, shall apply to regional economic integration organizations which accede to this Convention or any protocol.

Article 36: Entry into force

1. This Convention shall enter into force on the ninetieth day after the date of deposit of the thirtieth instrument of ratification, acceptance, approval or accession.

2. Any protocol shall enter into force on the ninetieth day after the date of deposit of the number of instruments of ratification, acceptance, approval or accession, specified in that protocol, has been deposited.

3. For each Contracting Party which ratifies, accepts or approves this Convention or accedes thereto after the deposit of the thirtieth instrument of ratification, acceptance, approval or accession, it shall enter into force on the ninetieth day after the date of deposit by such Contracting Party of its instrument of ratification, acceptance, approval or accession.

4. Any protocol, except as otherwise provided in such protocol, shall enter into force for a Contracting Party that ratifies, accepts or approves that protocol or accedes thereto after its entry into force pursuant to paragraph 2 above, on the ninetieth day after the date on which that Contracting Party deposits its instrument of ratification, acceptance, approval or accession, or on the date on which this Convention enters into force for that Contracting Party, whichever shall be the later.

5. For the purposes of paragraphs 1 and 2 above, any instrument deposited by a regional economic integration organization shall not be counted as additional to those deposited by member States of such organization.

Article 37: Reservations

No reservations may be made to this Convention.

Article 38: Withdrawals

1. At any time after two years from the date on which this Convention has entered into force for a Contracting Party, that Contracting Party may withdraw from the Convention by giving written notification to the Depositary.

2. Any such withdrawal shall take place upon expiry of one year after the date of its receipt by the Depositary, or on such later date as may be specified in the notification of the withdrawal.

3. Any Contracting Party which withdraws from this Convention shall be considered as also having withdrawn from any protocol to which it is party.

Article 39: Financial interim arrangements

Provided that it has been fully restructured in accordance with the requirements of Article 21, the Global Environment Facility of the United Nations Development Programme, the United Nations Environment Programme and the International

Bank for Reconstruction and Development shall be the institutional structure referred to in Article 21 on an interim basis, for the period between the entry into force of this Convention and the first meeting of the Conference of the Parties or until the Conference of the Parties decides which institutional structure will be designated in accordance with Article 21.

Article 40: Secretariat interim arrangements

The secretariat to be provided by the Executive Director of the United Nations Environment Programme shall be the secretariat referred to in Article 24, paragraph 2, on an interim basis for the period between the entry into force of this Convention and the first meeting of the Conference of the Parties.

Article 41: Depositary

The Secretary-General of the United Nations shall assume the functions of Depositary of this Convention and any protocols.

Article 42: Authentic Texts

The original of this Convention, of which the Arabic, Chinese, English, French, Russian and Spanish texts are equally authentic, shall be deposited with the Secretary-General of the United Nations.

In witness whereof the undersigned, being duly authorized to that effect, have signed this Convention.

Done at Rio de Janeiro on this fifth day of June, one thousand nine hundred and ninety-two.

Annex I: Identification and Monitoring; Annex II: Part 1: Arbitration; Part 2: Conciliation [not reproduced]

Biosafety

Cartagena Protocol on Biosafety to the Convention on Biological Diversity

Adopted on 20 January 2000 at Montreal. Entered into force on 11 September 2003. Number of parties: 94. Further information: CBD Secretariat, Montreal, Canada, http://www.biodiv.org

The Parties to this Protocol,

Being Parties to the Convention on Biological Diversity, hereinafter referred to as 'the Convention',

Recalling Article 19, paragraphs 3 and 4, and Articles 8 (g) and 17 of the Convention,

Recalling also decision II/5 of 17 November 1995 of the Conference of the Parties to the Convention to develop a Protocol on biosafety, specifically focusing on transboundary movement of any living modified organism resulting from modern biotechnology that may have adverse effect on the conservation and sustainable use of biological diversity, setting out for consideration, in particular, appropriate procedures for advance informed agreement,

Reaffirming the precautionary approach contained in Principle 15 of the Rio Declaration on Environment and Development,

Aware of the rapid expansion of modern biotechnology and the growing public concern over its potential adverse effects on biological diversity, taking also into account risks to human health,

Recognizing that modern biotechnology has great potential for human well-being if developed and used with adequate safety measures for the environment and human health,

Recognizing also the crucial importance to humankind of centres of origin and centres of genetic diversity,

Taking into account the limited capabilities of many countries, particularly developing countries, to cope with the nature and scale of known and potential risks associated with living modified organisms,

Recognizing that trade and environment agreements should be mutually supportive with a view to achieving sustainable development,

Emphasizing that this Protocol shall not be interpreted as implying a change in the rights and obligations of a Party under any existing international agreements,

Understanding that the above recital is not intended to subordinate this Protocol to other international agreements,

Have agreed as follows:

Article 1: Objective

In accordance with the precautionary approach contained in Principle 15 of the Rio Declaration on Environment and Development, the objective of this Protocol is to contribute to ensuring an adequate level of protection in the field of the safe transfer, handling and use of living modified organisms resulting from modern biotechnology that may have adverse effects on the conservation and sustainable use of biological diversity, taking also into account risks to human health, and specifically focusing on transboundary movements.

Article 2: General provisions

1. Each Party shall take necessary and appropriate legal, administrative and other measures to implement its obligations under this Protocol.

2. The Parties shall ensure that the development, handling, transport, use, transfer and release of any living modified organisms are undertaken in a manner that

prevents or reduces the risks to biological diversity, taking also into account risks to human health.

3. Nothing in this Protocol shall affect in any way the sovereignty of States over their territorial sea established in accordance with international law, and the sovereign rights and the jurisdiction which States have in their exclusive economic zones and their continental shelves in accordance with international law, and the exercise by ships and aircraft of all States of navigational rights and freedoms as provided for in international law and as reflected in relevant international instruments.

4. Nothing in this Protocol shall be interpreted as restricting the right of a Party to take action that is more protective of the conservation and sustainable use of biological diversity than that called for in this Protocol, provided that such action is consistent with the objective and the provisions of this Protocol and is in accordance with that Party's other obligations under international law.

5. The Parties are encouraged to take into account, as appropriate, available expertise, instruments and work undertaken in international forums with competence in the area of risks to human health.

Article 3: Use of terms

For the purposes of this Protocol:

(a) 'Conference of the Parties' means the Conference of the Parties to the Convention;

(b) 'Contained use' means any operation, undertaken within a facility, installation or other physical structure, which involves living modified organisms that are controlled by specific measures that effectively limit their contact with, and their impact on, the external environment;

(c) 'Export' means intentional transboundary movement from one Party to another Party;

(d) 'Exporter' means any legal or natural person, under the jurisdiction of the Party of export, who arranges for a living modified organism to be exported;

(e) 'Import' means intentional transboundary movement into one Party from another Party;

(f) 'Importer' means any legal or natural person, under the jurisdiction of the Party of import, who arranges for a living modified organism to be imported;

(g) 'Living modified organism' means any living organism that possesses a novel combination of genetic material obtained through the use of modern biotechnology;

(h) 'Living organism' means any biological entity capable of transferring or replicating genetic material, including sterile organisms, viruses and viroids;

(i) 'Modern biotechnology' means the application of:

a. In vitro nucleic acid techniques, including recombinant deoxyribonucleic acid (DNA) and direct injection of nucleic acid into cells or organelles, or

b. Fusion of cells beyond the taxonomic family,

that overcome natural physiological reproductive or recombination barriers and that are not techniques used in traditional breeding and selection;

(j) 'Regional economic integration organization' means an organization constituted by sovereign States of a given region, to which its member States have transferred competence in respect of matters governed by this Protocol and which has been duly authorized, in accordance with its internal procedures, to sign, ratify, accept, approve or accede to it;

(k) 'Transboundary movement' means the movement of a living modified organism from one Party to another Party, save that for the purposes of Articles 17 and 24 transboundary movement extends to movement between Parties and non-Parties.

Article 4: Scope

This Protocol shall apply to the transboundary movement, transit, handling and use of all living modified organisms that may have adverse effects on the conservation and sustainable use of biological diversity, taking also into account risks to human health.

Article 5: Pharmaceuticals

Notwithstanding Article 4 and without prejudice to any right of a Party to subject all living modified organisms to risk assessment prior to the making of decisions on import, this Protocol shall not apply to the transboundary movement of living modified organisms which are pharmaceuticals for humans that are addressed by other relevant international agreements or organisations.

Article 6: Transit and contained use

1. Notwithstanding Article 4 and without prejudice to any right of a Party of transit to regulate the transport of living modified organisms through its territory and make available to the Biosafety Clearing-House, any decision of that Party, subject to Article 2, paragraph 3, regarding the transit through its territory of a specific living modified organism, the provisions of this Protocol with respect to the advance informed agreement procedure shall not apply to living modified organisms in transit.

2. Notwithstanding Article 4 and without prejudice to any right of a Party to subject all living modified organisms to risk assessment prior to decisions on import and to set standards for contained use within its jurisdiction, the provisions of this Protocol with respect to the advance informed agreement procedure shall not apply to the transboundary movement of living modified organisms destined for contained use undertaken in accordance with the standards of the Party of import.

Article 7: Application of the advance informed agreement procedure

1. Subject to Articles 5 and 6, the advance informed agreement procedure in Articles 8 to 10 and 12 shall apply prior to the first intentional transboundary

movement of living modified organisms for intentional introduction into the environment of the Party of import.

2. 'Intentional introduction into the environment' in paragraph 1 above, does not refer to living modified organisms intended for direct use as food or feed, or for processing.

3. Article 11 shall apply prior to the first transboundary movement of living modified organisms intended for direct use as food or feed, or for processing.

4. The advance informed agreement procedure shall not apply to the intentional transboundary movement of living modified organisms identified in a decision of the Conference of the Parties serving as the meeting of the Parties to this Protocol as being not likely to have adverse effects on the conservation and sustainable use of biological diversity, taking also into account risks to human health.

Article 8: Notification

1. The Party of export shall notify, or require the exporter to ensure notification to, in writing, the competent national authority of the Party of import prior to the intentional transboundary movement of a living modified organism that falls within the scope of Article 7, paragraph 1. The notification shall contain, at a minimum, the information specified in Annex I.

2. The Party of export shall ensure that there is a legal requirement for the accuracy of information provided by the exporter.

Article 9: Acknowledgement of receipt of notification

1. The Party of import shall acknowledge receipt of the notification, in writing, to the notifier within ninety days of its receipt.

2. The acknowledgement shall state:

(a) The date of receipt of the notification;

(b) Whether the notification, prima facie, contains the information referred to in Article 8;

(c) Whether to proceed according to the domestic regulatory framework of the Party of import or according to the procedure specified in Article 10.

3. The domestic regulatory framework referred to in paragraph 2 (c) above, shall be consistent with this Protocol.

4. A failure by the Party of import to acknowledge receipt of a notification shall not imply its consent to an intentional transboundary movement.

Article 10: Decision procedure

1. Decisions taken by the Party of import shall be in accordance with Article 15.

2. The Party of import shall, within the period of time referred to in Article 9, inform the notifier, in writing, whether the intentional transboundary movement may proceed:

(a) Only after the Party of import has given its written consent; or

(b) After no less than ninety days without a subsequent written consent.

3. Within two hundred and seventy days of the date of receipt of notification, the Party of import shall communicate, in writing, to the notifier and to the Biosafety Clearing-House the decision referred to in paragraph 2 (a) above:

(a) Approving the import, with or without conditions, including how the decision will apply to subsequent imports of the same living modified organism;

(b) Prohibiting the import;

(c) Requesting additional relevant information in accordance with its domestic regulatory framework or Annex I; in calculating the time within which the Party of import is to respond, the number of days it has to wait for additional relevant information shall not be taken into account; or

(d) Informing the notifier that the period specified in this paragraph is extended by a defined period of time.

4. Except in a case in which consent is unconditional, a decision under paragraph 3 above, shall set out the reasons on which it is based.

5. A failure by the Party of import to communicate its decision within two hundred and seventy days of the date of receipt of the notification shall not imply its consent to an intentional transboundary movement.

6. Lack of scientific certainty due to insufficient relevant scientific information and knowledge regarding the extent of the potential adverse effects of a living modified organism on the conservation and sustainable use of biological diversity in the Party of import, taking also into account risks to human health, shall not prevent that Party from taking a decision, as appropriate, with regard to the import of the living modified organism in question as referred to in paragraph 3 above, in order to avoid or minimize such potential adverse effects.

7. The Conference of the Parties serving as the meeting of the Parties shall, at its first meeting, decide upon appropriate procedures and mechanisms to facilitate decision-making by Parties of import.

Article 11: Procedure for living modified organisms intended for direct use as food or feed, or for processing

1. A Party that makes a final decision regarding domestic use, including placing on the market, of a living modified organism that may be subject to transboundary movement for direct use as food or feed, or for processing shall, within fifteen days of making that decision, inform the Parties through the Biosafety Clearing-House. This information shall contain, at a minimum, the information specified in Annex II. The Party shall provide a copy of the information, in writing, to the national focal point of each Party that informs the Secretariat in advance that it does not have access to the Biosafety Clearing-House. This provision shall not apply to decisions regarding field trials.

2. The Party making a decision under paragraph 1 above, shall ensure that there is a legal requirement for the accuracy of information provided by the applicant.

3. Any Party may request additional information from the authority identified in paragraph (b) of Annex II.

4. A Party may take a decision on the import of living modified organisms intended for direct use as food or feed, or for processing, under its domestic regulatory framework that is consistent with the objective of this Protocol.

5. Each Party shall make available to the Biosafety Clearing-House copies of any national laws, regulations and guidelines applicable to the import of living modified organisms intended for direct use as food or feed, or for processing, if available.

6. A developing country Party or a Party with an economy in transition may, in the absence of the domestic regulatory framework referred to in paragraph 4 above, and in exercise of its domestic jurisdiction, declare through the Biosafety Clearing-House that its decision prior to the first import of a living modified organism intended for direct use as food or feed, or for processing, on which information has been provided under paragraph 1 above, will be taken according to the following:

(a) A risk assessment undertaken in accordance with Annex III; and

(b) A decision made within a predictable timeframe, not exceeding two hundred and seventy days.

7. Failure by a Party to communicate its decision according to paragraph 6 above, shall not imply its consent or refusal to the import of a living modified organism intended for direct use as food or feed, or for processing, unless otherwise specified by the Party.

8. Lack of scientific certainty due to insufficient relevant scientific information and knowledge regarding the extent of the potential adverse effects of a living modified organism on the conservation and sustainable use of biological diversity in the Party of import, taking also into account risks to human health, shall not prevent that Party from taking a decision, as appropriate, with regard to the import of that living modified organism intended for direct use as food or feed, or for processing, in order to avoid or minimize such potential adverse effects.

9. A Party may indicate its needs for financial and technical assistance and capacity-building with respect to living modified organisms intended for direct use as food or feed, or for processing. Parties shall cooperate to meet these needs in accordance with Articles 22 and 28.

Article 12: Review of decisions

1. A Party of import may, at any time, in light of new scientific information on potential adverse effects on the conservation and sustainable use of biological diversity, taking also into account the risks to human health, review and change a decision regarding an intentional transboundary movement. In such case, the Party shall, within thirty days, inform any notifier that has previously notified movements of the living modified organism referred to in such decision, as well as the Biosafety Clearing-House, and shall set out the reasons for its decision.

2. A Party of export or a notifier may request the Party of import to review a decision it has made in respect of it under Article 10 where the Party of export or the notifier considers that:

(a) A change in circumstances has occurred that may influence the outcome of the risk assessment upon which the decision was based; or
(b) Additional relevant scientific or technical information has become available.

3. The Party of import shall respond in writing to such a request within ninety days and set out the reasons for its decision.

4. The Party of import may, at its discretion, require a risk assessment for subsequent imports.

Article 13: Simplified procedure

1. A Party of import may, provided that adequate measures are applied to ensure the safe intentional transboundary movement of living modified organisms in accordance with the objective of this Protocol, specify in advance to the Biosafety Clearing-House:
(a) Cases in which intentional transboundary movement to it may take place at the same time as the movement is notified to the Party of import; and
(b) Imports of living modified organisms to it to be exempted from the advance informed agreement procedure.

Notifications under subparagraph (a) above, may apply to subsequent similar movements to the same Party.

2. The information relating to an intentional transboundary movement that is to be provided in the notifications referred to in paragraph 1 (a) above, shall be the information specified in Annex I.

Article 14: Bilateral, regional and multilateral agreements and arrangements

1. Parties may enter into bilateral, regional and multilateral agreements and arrangements regarding intentional transboundary movements of living modified organisms, consistent with the objective of this Protocol and provided that such agreements and arrangements do not result in a lower level of protection than that provided for by the Protocol.

2. The Parties shall inform each other, through the Biosafety Clearing-House, of any such bilateral, regional and multilateral agreements and arrangements that they have entered into before or after the date of entry into force of this Protocol.

3. The provisions of this Protocol shall not affect intentional transboundary movements that take place pursuant to such agreements and arrangements as between the parties to those agreements or arrangements.

4. Any Party may determine that its domestic regulations shall apply with respect to specific imports to it and shall notify the Biosafety Clearing-House of its decision.

Article 15: Risk assessment

1. Risk assessments undertaken pursuant to this Protocol shall be carried out in a scientifically sound manner, in accordance with Annex III and taking into account recognized risk assessment techniques. Such risk assessments shall be based, at a

minimum, on information provided in accordance with Article 8 and other available scientific evidence in order to identify and evaluate the possible adverse effects of living modified organisms on the conservation and sustainable use of biological diversity, taking also into account risks to human health.

2. The Party of import shall ensure that risk assessments are carried out for decisions taken under Article 10. It may require the exporter to carry out the risk assessment.

3. The cost of risk assessment shall be borne by the notifier if the Party of import so requires.

Article 16: Risk management

1. The Parties shall, taking into account Article 8 (g) of the Convention, establish and maintain appropriate mechanisms, measures and strategies to regulate, manage and control risks identified in the risk assessment provisions of this Protocol associated with the use, handling and transboundary movement of living modified organisms.

2. Measures based on risk assessment shall be imposed to the extent necessary to prevent adverse effects of the living modified organism on the conservation and sustainable use of biological diversity, taking also into account risks to human health, within the territory of the Party of import.

3. Each Party shall take appropriate measures to prevent unintentional transboundary movements of living modified organisms, including such measures as requiring a risk assessment to be carried out prior to the first release of a living modified organism.

4. Without prejudice to paragraph 2 above, each Party shall endeavour to ensure that any living modified organism, whether imported or locally developed, has undergone an appropriate period of observation that is commensurate with its life-cycle or generation time before it is put to its intended use.

5. Parties shall cooperate with a view to:

(a) Identifying living modified organisms or specific traits of living modified organisms that may have adverse effects on the conservation and sustainable use of biological diversity, taking also into account risks to human health; and

(b) Taking appropriate measures regarding the treatment of such living modified organisms or specific traits.

Article 17: Unintentional transboundary movements and emergency measures

1. Each Party shall take appropriate measures to notify affected or potentially affected States, the Biosafety Clearing-House and, where appropriate, relevant international organizations, when it knows of an occurrence under its jurisdiction resulting in a release that leads, or may lead, to an unintentional transboundary movement of a living modified organism that is likely to have significant adverse effects on the conservation and sustainable use of biological diversity, taking also

into account risks to human health in such States. The notification shall be provided as soon as the Party knows of the above situation.

2. Each Party shall, no later than the date of entry into force of this Protocol for it, make available to the Biosafety Clearing-House the relevant details setting out its point of contact for the purposes of receiving notifications under this Article.

3. Any notification arising from paragraph 1 above, should include:

(a) Available relevant information on the estimated quantities and relevant characteristics and/or traits of the living modified organism;

(b) Information on the circumstances and estimated date of the release, and on the use of the living modified organism in the originating Party;

(c) Any available information about the possible adverse effects on the conservation and sustainable use of biological diversity, taking also into account risks to human health, as well as available information about possible risk management measures;

(d) Any other relevant information; and

(e) A point of contact for further information.

4. In order to minimize any significant adverse effects on the conservation and sustainable use of biological diversity, taking also into account risks to human health, each Party, under whose jurisdiction the release of the living modified organism referred to in paragraph 1 above, occurs, shall immediately consult the affected or potentially affected States to enable them to determine appropriate responses and initiate necessary action, including emergency measures.

Article 18: Handling, transport, packaging and identification

1. In order to avoid adverse effects on the conservation and sustainable use of biological diversity, taking also into account risks to human health, each Party shall take necessary measures to require that living modified organisms that are subject to intentional transboundary movement within the scope of this Protocol are handled, packaged and transported under conditions of safety, taking into consideration relevant international rules and standards.

2. Each Party shall take measures to require that documentation accompanying:

(a) Living modified organisms that are intended for direct use as food or feed, or for processing, clearly identifies that they 'may contain' living modified organisms and are not intended for intentional introduction into the environment, as well as a contact point for further information. The Conference of the Parties serving as the meeting of the Parties to this Protocol shall take a decision on the detailed requirements for this purpose, including specification of their identity and any unique identification, no later than two years after the date of entry into force of this Protocol;

(b) Living modified organisms that are destined for contained use clearly identifies them as living modified organisms; and specifies any requirements for the safe handling, storage, transport and use, the contact point for further information, including the name and address of the individual and institution to whom the living modified organisms are consigned; and

(c) Living modified organisms that are intended for intentional introduction into the environment of the Party of import and any other living modified organisms within the scope of the Protocol, clearly identifies them as living modified organisms; specifies the identity and relevant traits and/or characteristics, any requirements for the safe handling, storage, transport and use, the contact point for further information and, as appropriate, the name and address of the importer and exporter; and contains a declaration that the movement is in conformity with the requirements of this Protocol applicable to the exporter.

3. The Conference of the Parties serving as the meeting of the Parties to this Protocol shall consider the need for and modalities of developing standards with regard to identification, handling, packaging and transport practices, in consultation with other relevant international bodies.

Article 19: Competent national authorities and national focal points

1. Each Party shall designate one national focal point to be responsible on its behalf for liaison with the Secretariat. Each Party shall also designate one or more competent national authorities, which shall be responsible for performing the administrative functions required by this Protocol and which shall be authorized to act on its behalf with respect to those functions. A Party may designate a single entity to fulfil the functions of both focal point and competent national authority.

2. Each Party shall, no later than the date of entry into force of this Protocol for it, notify the Secretariat of the names and addresses of its focal point and its competent national authority or authorities. Where a Party designates more than one competent national authority, it shall convey to the Secretariat, with its notification thereof, relevant information on the respective responsibilities of those authorities. Where applicable, such information shall, at a minimum, specify which competent authority is responsible for which type of living modified organism. Each Party shall forthwith notify the Secretariat of any changes in the designation of its national focal point or in the name and address or responsibilities of its competent national authority or authorities.

3. The Secretariat shall forthwith inform the Parties of the notifications it receives under paragraph 2 above, and shall also make such information available through the Biosafety Clearing-House.

Article 20: Information sharing and the Biosafety Clearing-House

1. A Biosafety Clearing-House is hereby established as part of the clearing-house mechanism under Article 18, paragraph 3, of the Convention, in order to:

(a) Facilitate the exchange of scientific, technical, environmental and legal information on, and experience with, living modified organisms; and

(b) Assist Parties to implement the Protocol, taking into account the special needs of developing country Parties, in particular the least developed and small island developing States among them, and countries with economies in transition as well as countries that are centres of origin and centres of genetic diversity.

2. The Biosafety Clearing-House shall serve as a means through which information is made available for the purposes of paragraph 1 above. It shall provide access to information made available by the Parties relevant to the implementation of the Protocol. It shall also provide access, where possible, to other international biosafety information exchange mechanisms.

3. Without prejudice to the protection of confidential information, each Party shall make available to the Biosafety Clearing-House any information required to be made available to the Biosafety Clearing-House under this Protocol, and:

(a) Any existing laws, regulations and guidelines for implementation of the Protocol, as well as information required by the Parties for the advance informed agreement procedure;

(b) Any bilateral, regional and multilateral agreements and arrangements;

(c) Summaries of its risk assessments or environmental reviews of living modified organisms generated by its regulatory process, and carried out in accordance with Article 15, including, where appropriate, relevant information regarding products thereof, namely, processed materials that are of living modified organism origin, containing detectable novel combinations of replicable genetic material obtained through the use of modern biotechnology;

(d) Its final decisions regarding the importation or release of living modified organisms; and

(e) Reports submitted by it pursuant to Article 33, including those on implementation of the advance informed agreement procedure.

4. The modalities of the operation of the Biosafety Clearing-House, including reports on its activities, shall be considered and decided upon by the Conference of the Parties serving as the meeting of the Parties to this Protocol at its first meeting, and kept under review thereafter.

Article 21: Confidential information

1. The Party of import shall permit the notifier to identify information submitted under the procedures of this Protocol or required by the Party of import as part of the advance informed agreement procedure of the Protocol that is to be treated as confidential. Justification shall be given in such cases upon request.

2. The Party of import shall consult the notifier if it decides that information identified by the notifier as confidential does not qualify for such treatment and shall, prior to any disclosure, inform the notifier of its decision, providing reasons on request, as well as an opportunity for consultation and for an internal review of the decision prior to disclosure.

3. Each Party shall protect confidential information received under this Protocol, including any confidential information received in the context of the advance informed agreement procedure of the Protocol. Each Party shall ensure that it has procedures to protect such information and shall protect the confidentiality of such

information in a manner no less favourable than its treatment of confidential information in connection with domestically produced living modified organisms.

4. The Party of import shall not use such information for a commercial purpose, except with the written consent of the notifier.

5. If a notifier withdraws or has withdrawn a notification, the Party of import shall respect the confidentiality of commercial and industrial information, including research and development information as well as information on which the Party and the notifier disagree as to its confidentiality.

6. Without prejudice to paragraph 5 above, the following information shall not be considered confidential:

(a) The name and address of the notifier;
(b) A general description of the living modified organism or organisms;
(c) A summary of the risk assessment of the effects on the conservation and sustainable use of biological diversity, taking also into account risks to human health; and
(d) Any methods and plans for emergency response.

Article 22: Capacity-building

1. The Parties shall cooperate in the development and/or strengthening of human resources and institutional capacities in biosafety, including biotechnology to the extent that it is required for biosafety, for the purpose of the effective implementation of this Protocol, in developing country Parties, in particular the least developed and small island developing States among them, and in Parties with economies in transition, including through existing global, regional, subregional and national institutions and organizations and, as appropriate, through facilitating private sector involvement.

2. For the purposes of implementing paragraph 1 above, in relation to cooperation, the needs of developing country Parties, in particular the least developed and small island developing States among them, for financial resources and access to and transfer of technology and know-how in accordance with the relevant provisions of the Convention, shall be taken fully into account for capacity-building in biosafety. Cooperation in capacity-building shall, subject to the different situation, capabilities and requirements of each Party, include scientific and technical training in the proper and safe management of biotechnology, and in the use of risk assessment and risk management for biosafety, and the enhancement of technological and institutional capacities in biosafety. The needs of Parties with economies in transition shall also be taken fully into account for such capacity-building in biosafety.

Article 23: Public awareness and participation

1. The Parties shall:

(a) Promote and facilitate public awareness, education and participation concerning the safe transfer, handling and use of living modified organisms in relation to the conservation and sustainable use of biological diversity, taking also into account risks to human health. In doing so, the Parties shall cooperate, as appropriate, with other States and international bodies;

(b) Endeavour to ensure that public awareness and education encompass access to information on living modified organisms identified in accordance with this Protocol that may be imported.

2. The Parties shall, in accordance with their respective laws and regulations, consult the public in the decision-making process regarding living modified organisms and shall make the results of such decisions available to the public, while respecting confidential information in accordance with Article 21.

3. Each Party shall endeavour to inform its public about the means of public access to the Biosafety Clearing-House.

Article 24: Non-Parties

1. Transboundary movements of living modified organisms between Parties and non-Parties shall be consistent with the objective of this Protocol. The Parties may enter into bilateral, regional and multilateral agreements and arrangements with non-Parties regarding such transboundary movements.

2. The Parties shall encourage non-Parties to adhere to this Protocol and to contribute appropriate information to the Biosafety Clearing-House on living modified organisms released in, or moved into or out of, areas within their national jurisdictions.

Article 25: Illegal transboundary movements

1. Each Party shall adopt appropriate domestic measures aimed at preventing and, if appropriate, penalizing transboundary movements of living modified organisms carried out in contravention of its domestic measures to implement this Protocol. Such movements shall be deemed illegal transboundary movements.

2. In the case of an illegal transboundary movement, the affected Party may request the Party of origin to dispose, at its own expense, of the living modified organism in question by repatriation or destruction, as appropriate.

3. Each Party shall make available to the Biosafety Clearing-House information concerning cases of illegal transboundary movements pertaining to it.

Article 26: Socio-economic considerations

1. The Parties, in reaching a decision on import under this Protocol or under its domestic measures implementing the Protocol, may take into account, consistent with their international obligations, socio-economic considerations arising from the impact of living modified organisms on the conservation and sustainable use of biological diversity, especially with regard to the value of biological diversity to indigenous and local communities.

2. The Parties are encouraged to cooperate on research and information exchange on any socio-economic impacts of living modified organisms, especially on indigenous and local communities.

Article 27: Liability and redress

The Conference of the Parties serving as the meeting of the Parties to this Protocol shall, at its first meeting, adopt a process with respect to the appropriate elaboration of international rules and procedures in the field of liability and redress for damage resulting from transboundary movements of living modified organisms, analysing and taking due account of the ongoing processes in international law on these matters, and shall endeavour to complete this process within four years.

Article 28: Financial mechanism and resources

1. In considering financial resources for the implementation of this Protocol, the Parties shall take into account the provisions of Article 20 of the Convention.

2. The financial mechanism established in Article 21 of the Convention shall, through the institutional structure entrusted with its operation, be the financial mechanism for this Protocol.

3. Regarding the capacity-building referred to in Article 22 of this Protocol, the Conference of the Parties serving as the meeting of the Parties to this Protocol, in providing guidance with respect to the financial mechanism referred to in paragraph 2 above, for consideration by the Conference of the Parties, shall take into account the need for financial resources by developing country Parties, in particular the least developed and the small island developing States among them.

4. In the context of paragraph 1 above, the Parties shall also take into account the needs of the developing country Parties, in particular the least developed and the small island developing States among them, and of the Parties with economies in transition, in their efforts to identify and implement their capacity-building requirements for the purposes of the implementation of this Protocol.

5. The guidance to the financial mechanism of the Convention in relevant decisions of the Conference of the Parties, including those agreed before the adoption of this Protocol, shall apply, *mutatis mutandis*, to the provisions of this Article.

6. The developed country Parties may also provide, and the developing country Parties and the Parties with economies in transition avail themselves of, financial and technological resources for the implementation of the provisions of this Protocol through bilateral, regional and multilateral channels.

Article 29: Conference of the Parties serving as the Meeting of the Parties to this Protocol

1. The Conference of the Parties shall serve as the meeting of the Parties to this Protocol.

2. Parties to the Convention that are not Parties to this Protocol may participate as observers in the proceedings of any meeting of the Conference of the Parties serving as the meeting of the Parties to this Protocol. When the Conference of the Parties serves as the meeting of the Parties to this Protocol, decisions under this Protocol shall be taken only by those that are Parties to it.

3. When the Conference of the Parties serves as the meeting of the Parties to this Protocol, any member of the bureau of the Conference of the Parties representing a Party to the Convention but, at that time, not a Party to this Protocol, shall be substituted by a member to be elected by and from among the Parties to this Protocol.

4. The Conference of the Parties serving as the meeting of the Parties to this Protocol shall keep under regular review the implementation of this Protocol and shall make, within its mandate, the decisions necessary to promote its effective implementation. It shall perform the functions assigned to it by this Protocol and shall:

(a) Make recommendations on any matters necessary for the implementation of this Protocol;

(b) Establish such subsidiary bodies as are deemed necessary for the implementation of this Protocol;

(c) Seek and utilize, where appropriate, the services and cooperation of, and information provided by, competent international organizations and intergovernmental and non-governmental bodies;

(d) Establish the form and the intervals for transmitting the information to be submitted in accordance with Article 33 of this Protocol and consider such information as well as reports submitted by any subsidiary body;

(e) Consider and adopt, as required, amendments to this Protocol and its annexes, as well as any additional annexes to this Protocol, that are deemed necessary for the implementation of this Protocol; and

(f) Exercise such other functions as may be required for the implementation of this Protocol.

5. The rules of procedure of the Conference of the Parties and financial rules of the Convention shall be applied, *mutatis mutandis*, under this Protocol, except as may be otherwise decided by consensus by the Conference of the Parties serving as the meeting of the Parties to this Protocol.

6. The first meeting of the Conference of the Parties serving as the meeting of the Parties to this Protocol shall be convened by the Secretariat in conjunction with the first meeting of the Conference of the Parties that is scheduled after the date of the entry into force of this Protocol. Subsequent ordinary meetings of the Conference of the Parties serving as the meeting of the Parties to this Protocol shall be held in conjunction with ordinary meetings of the Conference of the Parties, unless otherwise decided by the Conference of the Parties serving as the meeting of the Parties to this Protocol.

7. Extraordinary meetings of the Conference of the Parties serving as the meeting of the Parties to this Protocol shall be held at such other times as may be deemed necessary by the Conference of the Parties serving as the meeting of the Parties to this Protocol, or at the written request of any Party, provided that, within six months of the request being communicated to the Parties by the Secretariat, it is supported by at least one third of the Parties.

8. The United Nations, its specialized agencies and the International Atomic Energy Agency, as well as any State member thereof or observers thereto not party to the Convention, may be represented as observers at meetings of the Conference of the Parties serving as the meeting of the Parties to this Protocol. Any body or agency, whether national or international, governmental or non-governmental, that is qualified in matters covered by this Protocol and that has informed the Secretariat of its wish to be represented at a meeting of the Conference of the Parties serving as a meeting of the Parties to this Protocol as an observer, may be so admitted, unless at least one third of the Parties present object. Except as otherwise provided in this Article, the admission and participation of observers shall be subject to the rules of procedure, as referred to in paragraph 5 above.

Article 30: Subsidiary bodies

1. Any subsidiary body established by or under the Convention may, upon a decision by the Conference of the Parties serving as the meeting of the Parties to this Protocol, serve the Protocol, in which case the meeting of the Parties shall specify which functions that body shall exercise.

2. Parties to the Convention that are not Parties to this Protocol may participate as observers in the proceedings of any meeting of any such subsidiary bodies. When a subsidiary body of the Convention serves as a subsidiary body to this Protocol, decisions under the Protocol shall be taken only by the Parties to the Protocol.

3. When a subsidiary body of the Convention exercises its functions with regard to matters concerning this Protocol, any member of the bureau of that subsidiary body representing a Party to the Convention but, at that time, not a Party to the Protocol, shall be substituted by a member to be elected by and from among the Parties to the Protocol.

Article 31: Secretariat

1. The Secretariat established by Article 24 of the Convention shall serve as the secretariat to this Protocol.

2. Article 24, paragraph 1, of the Convention on the functions of the Secretariat shall apply, *mutatis mutandis*, to this Protocol.

3. To the extent that they are distinct, the costs of the secretariat services for this Protocol shall be met by the Parties hereto. The Conference of the Parties serving as the meeting of the Parties to this Protocol shall, at its first meeting, decide on the necessary budgetary arrangements to this end.

Article 32: Relationship with the Convention

Except as otherwise provided in this Protocol, the provisions of the Convention relating to its protocols shall apply to this Protocol.

Article 33: Monitoring and reporting

Each Party shall monitor the implementation of its obligations under this Protocol, and shall, at intervals to be determined by the Conference of the Parties serving as the meeting of the Parties to this Protocol, report to the Conference of the Parties serving as the meeting of the Parties to this Protocol on measures that it has taken to implement the Protocol.

Article 34: Compliance

The Conference of the Parties serving as the meeting of the Parties to this Protocol shall, at its first meeting, consider and approve cooperative procedures and institutional mechanisms to promote compliance with the provisions of this Protocol and to address cases of non-compliance. These procedures and mechanisms shall include provisions to offer advice or assistance, where appropriate. They shall be separate from, and without prejudice to, the dispute settlement procedures and mechanisms established by Article 27 of the Convention.

Article 35: Assessment and review

The Conference of the Parties serving as the meeting of the Parties to this Protocol shall undertake, five years after the entry into force of this Protocol and at least every five years thereafter, an evaluation of the effectiveness of the Protocol, including an assessment of its procedures and annexes.

Article 36: Signature

This Protocol shall be open for signature at the United Nations Office at Nairobi by States and regional economic integration organizations from 15 to 26 May 2000, and at United Nations Headquarters in New York from 5 June 2000 to 4 June 2001.

Article 37: Entry into force

1. This Protocol shall enter into force on the ninetieth day after the date of deposit of the fiftieth instrument of ratification, acceptance, approval or accession by States or regional economic integration organizations that are Parties to the Convention.

2. This Protocol shall enter into force for a State or regional economic integration organization that ratifies, accepts or approves this Protocol or accedes thereto after its entry into force pursuant to paragraph 1 above, on the ninetieth day after the date on which that State or regional economic integration organization deposits its instrument of ratification, acceptance, approval or accession, or on the date on which the Convention enters into force for that State or regional economic integration organization, whichever shall be the later.

3. For the purposes of paragraphs 1 and 2 above, any instrument deposited by a regional economic integration organization shall not be counted as additional to those deposited by member States of such organization.

Article 38: Reservations

No reservations may be made to this Protocol.

Article 39: Withdrawal

1. At any time after two years from the date on which this Protocol has entered into force for a Party, that Party may withdraw from the Protocol by giving written notification to the Depositary.

2. Any such withdrawal shall take place upon expiry of one year after the date of its receipt by the Depositary, or on such later date as may be specified in the notification of the withdrawal.

Article 40: Authentic texts

The original of this Protocol, of which the Arabic, Chinese, English, French, Russian and Spanish texts are equally authentic, shall be deposited with the Secretary-General of the United Nations.

In witness whereof the undersigned, being duly authorized to that effect, have signed this Protocol.

Done at Montreal on this twenty-ninth day of January, two thousand.

Annex I: Information required in notifications under Articles 8, 10 and 13; Annex II: Information required concerning living modified organisms intended for direct use as food or feed, or for processing under Article 11; Annex III: Risk assessment [not reproduced]

Agreement on the Application of Sanitary and Phytosanitary Measures [excerpts]

Adopted on 15 April 1994 at Marrakesh. Entered into force on 1 January 1995. Source: 1867 *UNTS* 3 (the text reproduced does not incorporate the footnotes). Number of parties: 147. Further information: WTO, Geneva, Switzerland, http://www.wto.org

[Preamble not reproduced]

Article 1: General provisions

1. This Agreement applies to all sanitary and phytosanitary measures which may, directly or indirectly, affect international trade. Such measures shall be developed and applied in accordance with the provisions of this Agreement.

[Paragraphs 2-4 not reproduced]

Article 2: Basic rights and obligations

1. Members have the right to take sanitary and phytosanitary measures necessary for the protection of human, animal or plant life or health, provided that such measures are not inconsistent with the provisions of this Agreement.

2. Members shall ensure that any sanitary or phytosanitary measure is applied only to the extent necessary to protect human, animal or plant life or health, is based on scientific principles and is not maintained without sufficient scientific evidence, except as provided for in paragraph 7 of Article 5.

3. Members shall ensure that their sanitary and phytosanitary measures do not arbitrarily or unjustifiably discriminate between Members where identical or

similar conditions prevail, including between their own territory and that of other Members. Sanitary and phytosanitary measures shall not be applied in a manner which would constitute a disguised restriction on international trade.

4. Sanitary or phytosanitary measures which conform to the relevant provisions of this Agreement shall be presumed to be in accordance with the obligations of the Members under the provisions of GATT 1994 which relate to the use of sanitary or phytosanitary measures, in particular the provisions of Article XX(b).

[Articles 3-4 not reproduced]

Article 5: Assessment of risk and determination of the appropriate level of sanitary or phytosanitary protection

1. Members shall ensure that their sanitary or phytosanitary measures are based on an assessment, as appropriate to the circumstances, of the risks to human, animal or plant life or health, taking into account risk assessment techniques developed by the relevant international organizations.

2. In the assessment of risks, Members shall take into account available scientific evidence; relevant processes and production methods; relevant inspection, sampling and testing methods; prevalence of specific diseases or pests; existence of pest- or disease-free areas; relevant ecological and environmental conditions; and quarantine or other treatment.

3. In assessing the risk to animal or plant life or health and determining the measure to be applied for achieving the appropriate level of sanitary or phytosanitary protection from such risk, Members shall take into account as relevant economic factors: the potential damage in terms of loss of production or sales in the event of the entry, establishment or spread of a pest or disease; the costs of control or eradication in the territory of the importing Member; and the relative cost-effectiveness of alternative approaches to limiting risks.

4. Members should, when determining the appropriate level of sanitary or phytosanitary protection, take into account the objective of minimizing negative trade effects.

5. With the objective of achieving consistency in the application of the concept of appropriate level of sanitary or phytosanitary protection against risks to human life or health, or to animal and plant life or health, each Member shall avoid arbitrary or unjustifiable distinctions in the levels it considers to be appropriate in different situations, if such distinctions result in discrimination or a disguised restriction on international trade. Members shall cooperate in the Committee, in accordance with paragraphs 1, 2 and 3 of Article 12, to develop guidelines to further the practical implementation of this provision. In developing the guidelines, the Committee shall take into account all relevant factors, including the exceptional character of human health risks to which people voluntarily expose themselves.

6. Without prejudice to paragraph 2 of Article 3, when establishing or maintaining sanitary or phytosanitary measures to achieve the appropriate level of sanitary or

phytosanitary protection, Members shall ensure that such measures are not more trade-restrictive than required to achieve their appropriate level of sanitary or phytosanitary protection, taking into account technical and economic feasibility.

7. In cases where relevant scientific evidence is insufficient, a Member may provisionally adopt sanitary or phytosanitary measures on the basis of available pertinent information, including that from the relevant international organizations as well as from sanitary or phytosanitary measures applied by other Members. In such circumstances, Members shall seek to obtain the additional information necessary for a more objective assessment of risk and review the sanitary or phytosanitary measure accordingly within a reasonable period of time.

8. When a Member has reason to believe that a specific sanitary or phytosanitary measure introduced or maintained by another Member is constraining, or has the potential to constrain, its exports and the measure is not based on the relevant international standards, guidelines or recommendations, or such standards, guidelines or recommendations do not exist, an explanation of the reasons for such sanitary or phytosanitary measure may be requested and shall be provided by the Member maintaining the measure.

[Articles 6-14 not reproduced]

Annex A: Definitions; Annex B: Transparency of sanitary and phytosanitary regulations; Annex C: Control, inspection and approval procedures [not reproduced]

Agriculture

International Treaty on Plant Genetic Resources for Food and Agriculture

Adopted on 3 November 2001 at Rome. Entered into force on 29 June 2004. Source: Doc. Y3159/E. Number of parties: 48. Further information: Commission on Genetic Resources for Food and Agriculture, FAO, Rome, Italy, http://www.fao.org/ag/cgrfa/

Preamble

The Contracting Parties,

Convinced of the special nature of plant genetic resources for food and agriculture, their distinctive features and problems needing distinctive solutions;

Alarmed by the continuing erosion of these resources;

Cognizant that plant genetic resources for food and agriculture are a common concern of all countries, in that all countries depend very largely on plant genetic resources for food and agriculture that originated elsewhere;

Acknowledging that the conservation, exploration, collection, characterization, evaluation and documentation of plant genetic resources for food and agriculture are essential in meeting the goals of the Rome Declaration on World Food Security and the World Food Summit Plan of Action and for sustainable agricultural development for this and future generations, and that the capacity of developing countries and countries with economies in transition to undertake such tasks needs urgently to be reinforced;

Noting that the Global Plan of Action for the Conservation and Sustainable Use of Plant Genetic Resources for Food and Agriculture is an internationally agreed framework for such activities;

Acknowledging further that plant genetic resources for food and agriculture are the raw material indispensable for crop genetic improvement, whether by means of farmers' selection, classical plant breeding or modern biotechnologies, and are essential in adapting to unpredictable environmental changes and future human needs;

Affirming that the past, present and future contributions of farmers in all regions of the world, particularly those in centres of origin and diversity, in conserving, improving and making available these resources, is the basis of Farmers' Rights;

Affirming also that the rights recognized in this Treaty to save, use, exchange and sell farm-saved seed and other propagating material, and to participate in decision-making regarding, and in the fair and equitable sharing of the benefits arising from, the use of plant genetic resources for food and agriculture, are fundamental to the realization of Farmers' Rights, as well as the promotion of Farmers' Rights at national and international levels;

Recognizing that this Treaty and other international agreements relevant to this Treaty should be mutually supportive with a view to sustainable agriculture and food security;

Affirming that nothing in this Treaty shall be interpreted as implying in any way a change in the rights and obligations of the Contracting Parties under other international agreements;

Understanding that the above recital is not intended to create a hierarchy between this Treaty and other international agreements;

Aware that questions regarding the management of plant genetic resources for food and agriculture are at the meeting point between agriculture, the environment and commerce, and convinced that there should be synergy among these sectors;

Aware of their responsibility to past and future generations to conserve the World's diversity of plant genetic resources for food and agriculture;

Recognizing that, in the exercise of their sovereign rights over their plant genetic resources for food and agriculture, states may mutually benefit from the creation of an effective multilateral system for facilitated access to a negotiated selection of these resources and for the fair and equitable sharing of the benefits arising from their use; and

Desiring to conclude an international agreement within the framework of the Food and Agriculture Organization of the United Nations, hereinafter referred to as FAO, under Article XIV of the FAO Constitution;

Have agreed as follows:

Part I: Introduction

Article 1: Objectives

1. The objectives of this Treaty are the conservation and sustainable use of plant genetic resources for food and agriculture and the fair and equitable sharing of the benefits arising out of their use, in harmony with the Convention on Biological Diversity, for sustainable agriculture and food security.

2. These objectives will be attained by closely linking this Treaty to the Food and Agriculture Organization of the United Nations and to the Convention on Biological Diversity.

Article 2: Use of terms

For the purpose of this Treaty, the following terms shall have the meanings hereunder assigned to them. These definitions are not intended to cover trade in commodities:

'*In situ* conservation' means the conservation of ecosystems and natural habitats and the maintenance and recovery of viable populations of species in their natural surroundings and, in the case of domesticated or cultivated plant species, in the surroundings where they have developed their distinctive properties.

'*Ex situ* conservation' means the conservation of plant genetic resources for food and agriculture outside their natural habitat.

'Plant genetic resources for food and agriculture' means any genetic material of plant origin of actual or potential value for food and agriculture.

'Genetic material' means any material of plant origin, including reproductive and vegetative propagating material, containing functional units of heredity.

'Variety' means a plant grouping, within a single botanical taxon of the lowest known rank, defined by the reproducible expression of its distinguishing and other genetic characteristics.

'*Ex situ* collection' means a collection of plant genetic resources for food and agriculture maintained outside their natural habitat.

'Centre of origin' means a geographical area where a plant species, either domesticated or wild, first developed its distinctive properties.

'Centre of crop diversity' means a geographic area containing a high level of genetic diversity for crop species in *in situ* conditions.

Article 3: Scope

This Treaty relates to plant genetic resources for food and agriculture.

Part II: General provisions

Article 4: General obligations

Each Contracting Party shall ensure the conformity of its laws, regulations and procedures with its obligations as provided in this Treaty.

Article 5: Conservation, exploration, collection, characterization, evaluation and documentation of plant genetic resources for food and agriculture

1. Each Contracting Party shall, subject to national legislation, and in cooperation with other Contracting Parties where appropriate, promote an integrated approach to the exploration, conservation and sustainable use of plant genetic resources for food and agriculture and shall in particular, as appropriate:

(a) Survey and inventory plant genetic resources for food and agriculture, taking into account the status and degree of variation in existing populations, including those that are of potential use and, as feasible, assess any threats to them;

(b) Promote the collection of plant genetic resources for food and agriculture and relevant associated information on those plant genetic resources that are under threat or are of potential use;

(c) Promote or support, as appropriate, farmers and local communities' efforts to manage and conserve on-farm their plant genetic resources for food and agriculture;

(d) Promote *in situ* conservation of wild crop relatives and wild plants for food production, including in protected areas, by supporting, *inter alia*, the efforts of indigenous and local communities;

(e) Cooperate to promote the development of an efficient and sustainable system of *ex situ* conservation, giving due attention to the need for adequate documentation, characterization, regeneration and evaluation, and promote the development and transfer of appropriate technologies for this purpose with a view to improving the sustainable use of plant genetic resources for food and agriculture;

(f) Monitor the maintenance of the viability, degree of variation, and the genetic integrity of collections of plant genetic resources for food and agriculture.

2. The Contracting Parties shall, as appropriate, take steps to minimize or, if possible, eliminate threats to plant genetic resources for food and agriculture.

Article 6: Sustainable use of plant genetic resources

1. The Contracting Parties shall develop and maintain appropriate policy and legal measures that promote the sustainable use of plant genetic resources for food and agriculture.

2. The sustainable use of plant genetic resources for food and agriculture may include such measures as:

(a) pursuing fair agricultural policies that promote, as appropriate, the development and maintenance of diverse farming systems that enhance the sustainable use of agricultural biological diversity and other natural resources;

(b) strengthening research which enhances and conserves biological diversity by maximizing intra- and inter-specific variation for the benefit of farmers, especially those who generate and use their own varieties and apply ecological principles in maintaining soil fertility and in combating diseases, weeds and pests;

(c) promoting, as appropriate, plant breeding efforts which, with the participation of farmers, particularly in developing countries, strengthen the capacity to develop varieties particularly adapted to social, economic and ecological conditions, including in marginal areas;

(d) broadening the genetic base of crops and increasing the range of genetic diversity available to farmers;

(e) promoting, as appropriate, the expanded use of local and locally adapted crops, varieties and underutilized species;

(f) supporting, as appropriate, the wider use of diversity of varieties and species in on-farm management, conservation and sustainable use of crops and creating strong links to plant breeding and agricultural development in order to reduce crop vulnerability and genetic erosion, and promote increased world food production compatible with sustainable development; and

(g) reviewing, and, as appropriate, adjusting breeding strategies and regulations concerning variety release and seed distribution.

Article 7: National commitments and international cooperation

1. Each Contracting Party shall, as appropriate, integrate into its agriculture and rural development policies and programmes, activities referred to in Articles 5 and 6, and cooperate with other Contracting Parties, directly or through FAO and other relevant international organizations, in the conservation and sustainable use of plant genetic resources for food and agriculture.

2. International cooperation shall, in particular, be directed to:

(a) establishing or strengthening the capabilities of developing countries and countries with economies in transition with respect to conservation and sustainable use of plant genetic resources for food and agriculture;

(b) enhancing international activities to promote conservation, evaluation, documentation, genetic enhancement, plant breeding, seed multiplication; and sharing, providing access to, and exchanging, in conformity with Part IV, plant genetic resources for food and agriculture and appropriate information and technology;

(c) maintaining and strengthening the institutional arrangements provided for in Part V; and

(d) implement the funding strategy of Article 18.

Article 8: Technical assistance

The Contracting Parties agree to promote the provision of technical assistance to Contracting Parties, especially those that are developing countries or countries with economies in transition, either bilaterally or through the appropriate international organizations, with the objective of facilitating the implementation of this Treaty.

Part III: Farmers' rights

Article 9: Farmers' rights

1. The Contracting Parties recognize the enormous contribution that the local and indigenous communities and farmers of all regions of the world, particularly those in the centres of origin and crop diversity, have made and will continue to make for the conservation and development of plant genetic resources which constitute the basis of food and agriculture production throughout the world.

2. The Contracting Parties agree that the responsibility for realizing Farmers' Rights, as they relate to plant genetic resources for food and agriculture, rests with national governments. In accordance with their needs and priorities, each Contracting Party should, as appropriate, and subject to its national legislation, take measures to protect and promote Farmers' Rights, including:
(a) protection of traditional knowledge relevant to plant genetic resources for food and agriculture;
(b) the right to equitably participate in sharing benefits arising from the utilization of plant genetic resources for food and agriculture; and
(c) the right to participate in making decisions, at the national level, on matters related to the conservation and sustainable use of plant genetic resources for food and agriculture.

3. Nothing in this Article shall be interpreted to limit any rights that farmers have to save, use, exchange and sell farm-saved seed/propagating material, subject to national law and as appropriate.

Part IV: The Multilateral System of access and benefit-sharing

Article 10: Multilateral System of access and benefit-sharing

1. In their relationships with other States, the Contracting Parties recognize the sovereign rights of States over their own plant genetic resources for food and agriculture, including that the authority to determine access to those resources rests with national governments and is subject to national legislation.

2. In the exercise of their sovereign rights, the Contracting Parties agree to establish a multilateral system, which is efficient, effective, and transparent, both to facilitate access to plant genetic resources for food and agriculture, and to share, in a fair and equitable way, the benefits arising from the utilization of these resources, on a complementary and mutually reinforcing basis.

Article 11: Coverage of the Multilateral System

1. In furtherance of the objectives of conservation and sustainable use of plant genetic resources for food and agriculture and the fair and equitable sharing of benefits arising out of their use, as stated in Article 1, the Multilateral System shall cover the plant genetic resources or food and agriculture listed in Annex I, established according to criteria of food security and interdependence.

2. The Multilateral System, as identified in Article 11.1, shall include all plant genetic resources for food and agriculture listed in Annex I that are under the management and control of the Contracting Parties and in the public domain. With a view to achieving the fullest possible coverage of the Multilateral System, the Contracting Parties invite all other holders of the plant genetic resources for food and agriculture listed in Annex I to include these plant genetic resources for food and agriculture in the Multilateral System.

3. Contracting Parties also agree to take appropriate measures to encourage natural and legal persons within their jurisdiction who hold plant genetic resources for food and agriculture listed in Annex I to include such plant genetic resources for food and agriculture in the Multilateral System.

4. Within two years of the entry into force of the Treaty, the Governing Body shall assess the progress in including the plant genetic resources for food and agriculture referred to in paragraph 11.3 in the Multilateral System. Following this assessment, the Governing Body shall decide whether access shall continue to be facilitated to those natural and legal persons referred to in paragraph 11.3 that have not included these plant genetic resources for food and agriculture in the Multilateral System, or take such other measures as it deems appropriate.

5. The Multilateral System shall also include the plant genetic resources for food and agriculture listed in Annex I and held in the *ex situ* collections of the International Agricultural Research Centres of the Consultative Group on International Agricultural Research (CGIAR), as provided in Article 15.1a, and in other international institutions, in accordance with Article 15.5.

Article 12: Facilitated access to plant genetic resources for food and agriculture within the Multilateral System

1. The Contracting Parties agree that facilitated access to plant genetic resources for food and agriculture under the Multilateral System, as defined in Article 11, shall be in accordance with the provisions of this Treaty.

2. The Contracting Parties agree to take the necessary legal or other appropriate measures to provide such access to other Contracting Parties through the Multilateral System. To this effect, such access shall also be provided to legal and natural persons under the jurisdiction of any Contracting Party, subject to the provisions of Article 11.4.

3. Such access shall be provided in accordance with the conditions below:

(a) Access shall be provided solely for the purpose of utilization and conservation for research, breeding and training for food and agriculture, provided that such purpose does not include chemical, pharmaceutical and/or other non-food/feed industrial uses. In the case of multiple-use crops (food and non-food), their importance for food security should be the determinant for their inclusion in the Multilateral System and availability for facilitated access.

(b) Access shall be accorded expeditiously, without the need to track individual accessions and free of charge, or, when a fee is charged, it shall not exceed the minimal cost involved;

(c) All available passport data and, subject to applicable law, any other associated available non-confidential descriptive information, shall be made available with the plant genetic resources for food and agriculture provided;

(d) Recipients shall not claim any intellectual property or other rights that limit the facilitated access to the plant genetic resources for food and agriculture, or their genetic parts or components, in the form received from the Multilateral System;

(e) Access to plant genetic resources for food and agriculture under development, including material being developed by farmers, shall be at the discretion of its developer, during the period of its development;

(f) Access to plant genetic resources for food and agriculture protected by intellectual and other property rights shall be consistent with relevant international agreements, and with relevant national laws;

(g) Plant genetic resources for food and agriculture accessed under the Multilateral System and conserved shall continue to be made available to the Multilateral System by the recipients of those plant genetic resources for food and agriculture, under the terms of this Treaty; and

(h) Without prejudice to the other provisions under this Article, the Contracting Parties agree that access to plant genetic resources for food and agriculture found in *in situ* conditions will be provided according to national legislation or, in the absence of such legislation, in accordance with such standards as may be set by the Governing Body.

4. To this effect, facilitated access, in accordance with Articles 12.2 and 12.3 above, shall be provided pursuant to a standard material transfer agreement (MTA), which shall be adopted by the Governing Body and contain the provisions of Articles 12.3a, d and g, as well as the benefit-sharing provisions set forth in Article 13.2d(ii) and other relevant provisions of this Treaty, and the provision that the recipient of the plant genetic resources for food and agriculture shall require that the conditions of the MTA shall apply to the transfer of plant genetic resources for food and agriculture to another person or entity, as well as to any subsequent transfers of those plant genetic resources for food and agriculture.

5. Contracting Parties shall ensure that an opportunity to seek recourse is available, consistent with applicable jurisdictional requirements, under their legal systems, in case of contractual disputes arising under such MTAs, recognizing that

obligations arising under such MTAs rest exclusively with the parties to those MTAs.

6. In emergency disaster situations, the Contracting Parties agree to provide facilitated access to appropriate plant genetic resources for food and agriculture in the Multilateral System for the purpose of contributing to the re-establishment of agricultural systems, in cooperation with disaster relief co-ordinators.

Article 13: Benefit-sharing in the Multilateral System

1. The Contracting Parties recognize that facilitated access to plant genetic resources for food and agriculture which are included in the Multilateral System constitutes itself a major benefit of the Multilateral System and agree that benefits accruing therefrom shall be shared fairly and equitably in accordance with the provisions of this Article.

2. The Contracting Parties agree that benefits arising from the use, including commercial, of plant genetic resources for food and agriculture under the Multilateral System shall be shared fairly and equitably through the following mechanisms: the exchange of information, access to and transfer of technology, capacity-building, and the sharing of the benefits arising from commercialization, taking into account the priority activity areas in the rolling Global Plan of Action, under the guidance of the Governing Body:

(a) *Exchange of information*

The Contracting Parties agree to make available information which shall, *inter alia*, encompass catalogues and inventories, information on technologies, results of technical, scientific and socio-economic research, including characterization, evaluation and utilization, regarding those plant genetic resources for food and agriculture under the Multilateral System. Such information shall be made available, where non-confidential, subject to applicable law and in accordance with national capabilities. Such information shall be made available to all Contracting Parties to this Treaty through the information system, provided for in Article 17.

(b) *Access to and transfer of technology*

i) The Contracting Parties undertake to provide and/or facilitate access to technologies for the conservation, characterization, evaluation and use of plant genetic resources for food and agriculture which are under the Multilateral System. Recognizing that some technologies can only be transferred through genetic material, the Contracting Parties shall provide and/or facilitate access to such technologies and genetic material which is under the Multilateral System and to improved varieties and genetic material developed through the use of plant genetic resources for food and agriculture under the Multilateral System, in conformity with the provisions of Article 12. Access to these technologies, improved varieties and genetic material shall be provided and/or facilitated, while respecting applicable property rights and access laws, and in accordance with national capabilities.

ii) Access to and transfer of technology to countries, especially to developing countries and countries with economies in transition, shall be carried out through a set of measures, such as the establishment and maintenance of, and participation in, crop-based thematic groups on utilization of plant genetic resources for food and agriculture, all types of partnership in research and development and in commercial joint ventures relating to the material received, human resource development, and effective access to research facilities.

iii) Access to and transfer of technology as referred to in (i) and (ii) above, including that protected by intellectual property rights, to developing countries that are Contracting Parties, in particular least developed countries, and countries with economies in transition, shall be provided and/or facilitated under fair and most favourable terms, in particular in the case of technologies for use in conservation as well as technologies for the benefit of farmers in developing countries, especially in least developed countries, and countries with economies in transition, including on concessional and preferential terms where mutually agreed, *inter alia*, through partnerships in research and development under the Multilateral System. Such access and transfer shall be provided on terms which recognize and are consistent with the adequate and effective protection of intellectual property rights.

(c) *Capacity-building*

Taking into account the needs of developing countries and countries with economies in transition, as expressed through the priority they accord to building capacity in plant genetic resources for food and agriculture in their plans and programmes, when in place, in respect of those plant genetic resources for food and agriculture covered by the Multilateral System, the Contracting Parties agree to give priority to (i) establishing and/or strengthening programmes for scientific and technical education and training in conservation and sustainable use of plant genetic resources for food and agriculture, (ii) developing and strengthening facilities for conservation and sustainable use of plant genetic resources for food and agriculture, in particular in developing countries, and countries with economies in transition, and (iii) carrying out scientific research preferably, and where possible, in developing countries and countries with economies in transition, in cooperation with institutions of such countries, and developing capacity for such research in fields where they are needed.

(d) *Sharing of monetary and other benefits of commercialization*

i) The Contracting Parties agree, under the Multilateral System, to take measures in order to achieve commercial benefit-sharing, through the involvement of the private and public sectors in activities identified under this Article, through partnerships and collaboration, including with the private sector in developing countries and countries with economies in transition, in research and technology development;

ii) The Contracting Parties agree that the standard Material Transfer Agreement referred to in Article 12.4 shall include a requirement that a recipient who commercializes a product that is a plant genetic resource for food and agriculture and that incorporates material accessed from the Multilateral System, shall pay to the mechanism referred to in Article 19.3f, an equitable share of the benefits arising from the commercialization of that product, except whenever such a product is available without restriction to others for further research and breeding, in which case the recipient who commercializes shall be encouraged to make such payment.

The Governing Body shall, at its first meeting, determine the level, form and manner of the payment, in line with commercial practice. The Governing Body may decide to establish different levels of payment for various categories of recipients who commercialize such products; it may also decide on the need to exempt from such payments small farmers in developing countries and in countries with economies in transition. The Governing Body may, from time to time, review the levels of payment with a view to achieving fair and equitable sharing of benefits, and it may also assess, within a period of five years from the entry into force of this Treaty, whether the mandatory payment requirement in the MTA shall apply also in cases where such commercialized products are available without restriction to others for further research and breeding.

3. The Contracting Parties agree that benefits arising from the use of plant genetic resources for food and agriculture that are shared under the Multilateral System should flow primarily, directly and indirectly, to farmers in all countries, especially in developing countries, and countries with economies in transition, who conserve and sustainably utilize plant genetic resources for food and agriculture.

4. The Governing Body shall, at its first meeting, consider relevant policy and criteria for specific assistance under the agreed funding strategy established under Article 18 for the conservation of plant genetic resources for food and agriculture in developing countries, and countries with economies in transition whose contribution to the diversity of plant genetic resources for food and agriculture in the Multilateral System is significant and/or which have special needs.

5. The Contracting Parties recognize that the ability to fully implement the Global Plan of Action, in particular of developing countries and countries with economies in transition, will depend largely upon the effective implementation of this Article and of the funding strategy as provided in Article 18.

6. The Contracting Parties shall consider modalities of a strategy of voluntary benefit-sharing contributions whereby Food Processing Industries that benefit from plant genetic resources for food and agriculture shall contribute to the Multilateral System.

[Articles 14-35 not reproduced]

Annex I: List of crops covered under the Multilateral System; Annex II: Part 1: Arbitration; Part 2: Conciliation [not reproduced]

Chapter 5

Species and Habitats

Introduction

This chapter sets forth the main global instruments in the field of biodiversity law that relate more specifically to the conservation of different types of species and habitats.[1] A first set of international agreements reproduced here has as its main objective the conservation of particular groups of vulnerable species. The focus of CITES, adopted in 1973, is the prohibition or regulation of international trade in endangered species of fauna and flora listed in three Appendices to the Convention. For this purpose, CITES sets up a regulatory system for the import, export and re-export of listed species through a licensing system managed by the national authorities of states parties.[2] Terrestrial, marine and avian migratory species and their habitats are protected under the 1979 Bonn Convention, which contains obligations for parties to provide strict protection for endangered migratory species found in Appendix I and to conclude multilateral agreements for the conservation and management of migratory species listed in Appendix II.

A second range of instruments on the international level deals more specifically with the protection of different types of habitats.[3] The 1971 Ramsar Convention, which covers all aspects of wetland conservation and wise use, maintains a List of Wetlands of International Importance containing wetlands of significance in terms of ecology, botany, zoology, limnology or hydrology. The World Heritage Convention, negotiated under the auspices of UNESCO in 1972, notably addresses the conservation and protection of the natural heritage, including habitats of

---

1 See Chapter 4 on the conservation of biological diversity and Chapter 8 on the protection of marine-based species.

2 Trade in endangered species is, for instance, regulated on a regional basis under the Agreement on Co-operative Enforcement Operations Directed at Illegal Trade in Wild Fauna and Flora, Lusaka, 8 September 1994, 1950 *UNTS* 35, which is open to all African states.

3 At the regional level, *see, e.g.*, the Convention on Nature Protection and Wildlife Preservation in the Western Hemisphere, Washington, DC, 12 October 1940, 161 *UNTS* 193; Convention on the Conservation of European Wildlife and Natural Habitats, Berne, 19 September 1979, *European Treaty Series* 104, ASEAN Agreement on the Conservation of Nature and Natural Resources, Kuala Lumpur, 9 July 1985, available at http://www.aseansec.org/6080.htm, African Convention on the Conservation of Nature and Natural Resources, Maputo, 11 July 2003.

threatened species of animals and plants of outstanding universal value from the scientific and conservation perspective. The Convention maintains the World Heritage List of protected sites that includes both marine and terrestrial sites.

This chapter also contains specific sub-sections devoted to desertification, forests and Antarctica. The 1994 Desertification Convention aims to combat desertification and mitigate the effects of drought while focusing especially on states experiencing serious drought in Africa. While forests are significant in providing natural habitats for wildlife, reservoirs of biodiversity, fuel and timber, as well as carbon-absorbing sinks, there is as yet no comprehensive international legal framework for the conservation of forests. Instead, the lack of international consensus on the subject has led to the adoption of a legally non-binding instrument, the 1992 Forest Principles. On the other hand, the 1994 ITTA is a commodity agreement bringing together producer and consumer states of tropical timber, rather than a conservation treaty.[4] Finally, the protection of the Antarctic environment has benefited from the establishment of a comprehensive framework of international regulation based on the particular status of the continent. The 1980 CCAMLR extends its scope to all marine living resources within the Antarctic ecosystem on the basis of a holistic approach.[5] Also reproduced here is the 1991 Protocol to the 1959 Antarctic Treaty,[6] which endeavours to provide an integrated environmental protection regime for Antarctica, and effectively designates Antarctica as a natural reserve.

Selected readings

Species

Bowman, M., Davies P. and Redgwell, C., *Lyster's International Wildlife Law* (Cambridge: Cambridge University Press, 2nd edn. 2005).

Lyster, S., 'The Convention on the Conservation of Migratory Species of Wild Animals (The "Bonn Convention")', 29 *Natural Resources J.* 979 (1989).

---

4 The ITTA, which superseded the previous Agreement adopted on 18 November 1983 at Geneva, is currently being renegotiated. See Report of the Second Session of the Preparatory Committee for the Negotiation of a Successor Agreement to the International Tropical Timber Agreement, 1994, 10-12 November 2003, Doc. ITTA/3/PrepCom(II)/3, Rev.1.

5 CCAMLR explicitly excludes from its scope seals and whales, whose conservation is addressed under the Convention for the Conservation of Antarctic Seals, London, 11 February 1972, 11 *ILM* 251 (1972) and the International Whaling Convention (reproduced at p. 476), respectively.

6 Antarctic Treaty, Washington, DC, 1 December 1959, 402 *UNTS* 71, available at http://www.ats.org.ar/treaty.htm

Reeve, R., *Policing the International Trade in Endangered Species: The CITES Treaty and Compliance* (London: Earthscan, 2002).

Sand, P.H., 'Whither CITES? The Evolution of a Treaty Regime in the Borderland of Trade and Environment', 1 *EJIL* 29 (1997).

Habitats

Atherton, T.-A. and Atherton, T.C., 'The Power and the Glory: National Sovereignty and the World Heritage Convention', 69 *Australian L.J.* 631 (1995).

Bowman, M.J., 'The Ramsar Convention Comes of Age', XLII *Netherlands Int'l L. Rev.* 1 (1995).

Farrier, D. and Tucker, L., 'Wise Use of Wetlands Under the Ramsar Convention: A Challenge for Meaningful Implementation of International Law', 12 *JEL* 21 (2000).

Kunich, J.C., 'World Heritage in Danger in the Hotspots', 78 *Indiana L.J.* 619 (2003).

Desertification

Konate, A., 'L'Afrique et la Convention des Nations Unies sur la lutte contre la désertification', 12 *African J. Int'l & Comparative L.* 718 (2000).

Bassett, C. and Talafré, J., 'Implementing the UNCCD: Towards a Recipe for Success', 12 *RECIEL* 133 (2003).

Kjellén, B., 'The Saga of the Convention to Combat Desertification: The Rio/Johannesburg Process and the Global Responsibility for the Drylands', 12 *RECIEL* 127 (2003).

Forests

Schally, H., 'Forests: Towards an International Legal Regime?', 4 *YbIEL* 30 (1993).

Schulte zu Sogingen, B., 'Sustainable Forest Management - Progresses since Rio and Challenges for the Future', 63 *ZaöRV* 397 (2003).

Tarasofsky, R.G., 'The Global Regime for the Conservation and Sustainable Use of Forests: An Assessment of Progress to Date', 56 *ZaöRV* 668 (1996).

Antarctica

Rothwell, D.R., 'Polar Environmental Protection and International Law: The 1991 Antarctic Protocol', 11 *EJIL* 591 (2000).

Verhoeven, J., Sands, P. and Bruce, M. (eds.), *The Antarctic Environment and International Law* (London: Graham & Trotman, 1992).

Vidas, D. (ed.), *Protecting the Polar Marine Environment: Law and Policy for Pollution Prevention* (Cambridge: Cambridge University Press, 2000).

Wood, K.R., 'The Uncertain Fate of the Madrid Protocol to the Antarctic Treaty in the Maritime Area', 34 *Ocean Development & Int'l L.* 139 (2003).

Species

Convention on International Trade in Endangered Species of Wild Fauna and Flora

Adopted on 3 March 1973 at Washington, DC. Entered into force on 1 July 1975. Source: 993 *UNTS* 243 (the text reproduced incorporates the Bonn Amendment adopted on 22 June 1979).[7] Number of parties: 164. Further information: Secretariat, Geneva, Switzerland, http://www.cites.org

The Contracting States,

Recognizing that wild fauna and flora in their many beautiful and varied forms are an irreplaceable part of the natural systems of the earth which must be protected for this and the generations to come;

Conscious of the ever-growing value of wild fauna and flora from aesthetic, scientific, cultural, recreational and economic points of view;

Recognizing that peoples and States are and should be the best protectors of their own wild fauna and flora;

Recognizing, in addition, that international co-operation is essential for the protection of certain species of wild fauna and flora against over-exploitation through international trade;

Convinced of the urgency of taking appropriate measures to this end;

Have agreed as follows:

Article I: Definitions

For the purpose of the present Convention, unless the context otherwise requires:

(a) 'Species' means any species, subspecies, or geographically separate population thereof;

(b) 'Specimen' means:

i) any animal or plant, whether alive or dead;

ii) in the case of an animal: for species included in Appendices I and II, any readily recognizable part or derivative thereof; and for species included in Appendix III, any readily recognizable part or derivative thereof specified in Appendix III in relation to the species; and

iii) in the case of a plant: for species included in Appendix I, any readily recognizable part or derivative thereof; and for species included in Appendices II and III, any readily recognizable part or derivative thereof specified in Appendices II and III in relation to the species;

---

7 The Gabarone Amendment adopted on 30 April 1983 is not in force.

(c) 'Trade' means export, re-export, import and introduction from the sea;

(d) 'Re-export' means export of any specimen that has previously been imported;

(e) 'Introduction from the sea' means transportation into a State of specimens of any species which were taken in the marine environment not under the jurisdiction of any State;

(f) 'Scientific Authority' means a national scientific authority designated in accordance with Article IX;

(g) 'Management Authority' means a national management authority designated in accordance with Article IX;

(h) 'Party' means a State for which the present Convention has entered into force.

Article II: Fundamental principles

1. Appendix I shall include all species threatened with extinction which are or may be affected by trade. Trade in specimens of these species must be subject to particularly strict regulation in order not to endanger further their survival and must only be authorized in exceptional circumstances.

2. Appendix II shall include:

(a) all species which although not necessarily now threatened with extinction may become so unless trade in specimens of such species is subject to strict regulation in order to avoid utilization incompatible with their survival; and

(b) other species which must be subject to regulation in order that trade in specimens of certain species referred to in sub-paragraph (a) of this paragraph may be brought under effective control.

3. Appendix III shall include all species which any Party identifies as being subject to regulation within its jurisdiction for the purpose of preventing or restricting exploitation, and as needing the co-operation of other Parties in the control of trade.

4. The Parties shall not allow trade in specimens of species included in Appendices I, II and III except in accordance with the provisions of the present Convention.

Article III: Regulation of trade in specimens of species included in Appendix I

1. All trade in specimens of species included in Appendix I shall be in accordance with the provisions of this Article.

2. The export of any specimen of a species included in Appendix I shall require the prior grant and presentation of an export permit. An export permit shall only be granted when the following conditions have been met:

(a) a Scientific Authority of the State of export has advised that such export will not be detrimental to the survival of that species;

(b) a Management Authority of the State of export is satisfied that the specimen was not obtained in contravention of the laws of that State for the protection of fauna and flora;

(c) a Management Authority of the State of export is satisfied that any living specimen will be so prepared and shipped as to minimize the risk of injury, damage to health or cruel treatment; and
(d) a Management Authority of the State of export is satisfied that an import permit has been granted for the specimen.

3. The import of any specimen of a species included in Appendix I shall require the prior grant and presentation of an import permit and either an export permit or a re-export certificate. An import permit shall only be granted when the following conditions have been met:
(a) a Scientific Authority of the State of import has advised that the import will be for purposes which are not detrimental to the survival of the species involved;
(b) a Scientific Authority of the State of import is satisfied that the proposed recipient of a living specimen is suitably equipped to house and care for it; and
(c) a Management Authority of the State of import is satisfied that the specimen is not to be used for primarily commercial purposes.

4. The re-export of any specimen of a species included in Appendix I shall require the prior grant and presentation of a re-export certificate. A re-export certificate shall only be granted when the following conditions have been met:
(a) a Management Authority of the State of re-export is satisfied that the specimen was imported into that State in accordance with the provisions of the present Convention;
(b) a Management Authority of the State of re-export is satisfied that any living specimen will be so prepared and shipped as to minimize the risk of injury, damage to health or cruel treatment; and
(c) a Management Authority of the State of re-export is satisfied that an import permit has been granted for any living specimen.

5. The introduction from the sea of any specimen of a species included in Appendix I shall require the prior grant of a certificate from a Management Authority of the State of introduction. A certificate shall only be granted when the following conditions have been met:
(a) a Scientific Authority of the State of introduction advises that the introduction will not be detrimental to the survival of the species involved;
(b) a Management Authority of the State of introduction is satisfied that the proposed recipient of a living specimen is suitably equipped to house and care for it; and
(c) a Management Authority of the State of introduction is satisfied that the specimen is not to be used for primarily commercial purposes.

Article IV: Regulation of trade in specimens of species included in Appendix II

1. All trade in specimens of species included in Appendix II shall be in accordance with the provisions of this Article.

2. The export of any specimen of a species included in Appendix II shall require the prior grant and presentation of an export permit. An export permit shall only be granted when the following conditions have been met:

(a) a Scientific Authority of the State of export has advised that such export will not be detrimental to the survival of that species;

(b) a Management Authority of the State of export is satisfied that the specimen was not obtained in contravention of the laws of that State for the protection of fauna and flora; and

(c) a Management Authority of the State of export is satisfied that any living specimen will be so prepared and shipped as to minimize the risk of injury, damage to health or cruel treatment.

3. A Scientific Authority in each Party shall monitor both the export permits granted by that State for specimens of species included in Appendix II and the actual exports of such specimens. Whenever a Scientific Authority determines that the export of specimens of any such species should be limited in order to maintain that species throughout its range at a level consistent with its role in the ecosystems in which it occurs and well above the level at which that species might become eligible for inclusion in Appendix I, the Scientific Authority shall advise the appropriate Management Authority of suitable measures to be taken to limit the grant of export permits for specimens of that species.

4. The import of any specimen of a species included in Appendix II shall require the prior presentation of either an export permit or a re-export certificate.

5. The re-export of any specimen of a species included in Appendix II shall require the prior grant and presentation of a re-export certificate. A re-export certificate shall only be granted when the following conditions have been met:

(a) a Management Authority of the State of re-export is satisfied that the specimen was imported into that State in accordance with the provisions of the present Convention; and

(b) a Management Authority of the State of re-export is satisfied that any living specimen will be so prepared and shipped as to minimize the risk of injury, damage to health or cruel treatment.

6. The introduction from the sea of any specimen of a species included in Appendix II shall require the prior grant of a certificate from a Management Authority of the State of introduction. A certificate shall only be granted when the following conditions have been met:

(a) a Scientific Authority of the State of introduction advises that the introduction will not be detrimental to the survival of the species involved; and

(b) a Management Authority of the State of introduction is satisfied that any living specimen will be so handled as to minimize the risk of injury, damage to health or cruel treatment.

7. Certificates referred to in paragraph 6 of this Article may be granted on the advice of a Scientific Authority, in consultation with other national scientific

authorities or, when appropriate, international scientific authorities, in respect of periods not exceeding one year for total numbers of specimens to be introduced in such periods.

Article V: Regulation of trade in specimens of species included in Appendix III

1. All trade in specimens of species included in Appendix III shall be in accordance with the provisions of this Article.

2. The export of any specimen of a species included in Appendix III from any State which has included that species in Appendix III shall require the prior grant and presentation of an export permit. An export permit shall only be granted when the following conditions have been met:

(a) a Management Authority of the State of export is satisfied that the specimen was not obtained in contravention of the laws of that State for the protection of fauna and flora; and

(b) a Management Authority of the State of export is satisfied that any living specimen will be so prepared and shipped as to minimize the risk of injury, damage to health or cruel treatment.

3. The import of any specimen of a species included in Appendix III shall require, except in circumstances to which paragraph 4 of this Article applies, the prior presentation of a certificate of origin and, where the import is from a State which has included that species in Appendix III, an export permit.

4. In the case of re-export, a certificate granted by the Management Authority of the State of re-export that the specimen was processed in that State or is being re-exported shall be accepted by the State of import as evidence that the provisions of the present Convention have been complied with in respect of the specimen concerned.

Article VI: Permits and certificates

1. Permits and certificates granted under the provisions of Articles III, IV, and V shall be in accordance with the provisions of this Article.

2. An export permit shall contain the information specified in the model set forth in Appendix IV, and may only be used for export within a period of six months from the date on which it was granted.

3. Each permit or certificate shall contain the title of the present Convention, the name and any identifying stamp of the Management Authority granting it and a control number assigned by the Management Authority.

4. Any copies of a permit or certificate issued by a Management Authority shall be clearly marked as copies only and no such copy may be used in place of the original, except to the extent endorsed thereon.

5. A separate permit or certificate shall be required for each consignment of specimens.

6. A Management Authority of the State of import of any specimen shall cancel and retain the export permit or re-export certificate and any corresponding import permit presented in respect of the import of that specimen.

7. Where appropriate and feasible a Management Authority may affix a mark upon any specimen to assist in identifying the specimen. For these purposes 'mark' means any indelible imprint, lead seal or other suitable means of identifying a specimen, designed in such a way as to render its imitation by unauthorized persons as difficult as possible.

Article VII: Exemptions and other special provisions relating to trade

1. The provisions of Articles III, IV and V shall not apply to the transit or transhipment of specimens through or in the territory of a Party while the specimens remain in Customs control.

2. Where a Management Authority of the State of export or re-export is satisfied that a specimen was acquired before the provisions of the present Convention applied to that specimen, the provisions of Articles III, IV and V shall not apply to that specimen where the Management Authority issues a certificate to that effect.

3. The provisions of Articles III, IV and V shall not apply to specimens that are personal or household effects. This exemption shall not apply where:

(a) in the case of specimens of a species included in Appendix I, they were acquired by the owner outside his State of usual residence, and are being imported into that State; or

(b) in the case of specimens of species included in Appendix II:

   i) they were acquired by the owner outside his State of usual residence and in a State where removal from the wild occurred;

   ii) they are being imported into the owner's State of usual residence; and

   iii) the State where removal from the wild occurred requires the prior grant of export permits before any export of such specimens; unless a Management Authority is satisfied that the specimens were acquired before the provisions of the present Convention applied to such specimens.

4. Specimens of an animal species included in Appendix I bred in captivity for commercial purposes, or of a plant species included in Appendix I artificially propagated for commercial purposes, shall be deemed to be specimens of species included in Appendix II.

5. Where a Management Authority of the State of export is satisfied that any specimen of an animal species was bred in captivity or any specimen of a plant species was artificially propagated, or is a part of such an animal or plant or was derived therefrom, a certificate by that Management Authority to that effect shall be accepted in lieu of any of the permits or certificates required under the provisions of Article III, IV or V.

6. The provisions of Articles III, IV and V shall not apply to the non-commercial loan, donation or exchange between scientists or scientific institutions registered by a Management Authority of their State, of herbarium specimens, other preserved,

dried or embedded museum specimens, and live plant material which carry a label issued or approved by a Management Authority.

7. A Management Authority of any State may waive the requirements of Articles III, IV and V and allow the movement without permits or certificates of specimens which form part of a travelling zoo, circus, menagerie, plant exhibition or other travelling exhibition provided that:

(a) the exporter or importer registers full details of such specimens with that Management Authority;
(b) the specimens are in either of the categories specified in paragraph 2 or 5 of this Article; and
(c) the Management Authority is satisfied that any living specimen will be so transported and cared for as to minimize the risk of injury, damage to health or cruel treatment.

Article VIII: Measures to be taken by the Parties

1. The Parties shall take appropriate measures to enforce the provisions of the present Convention and to prohibit trade in specimens in violation thereof. These shall include measures:

(a) to penalize trade in, or possession of, such specimens, or both; and
(b) to provide for the confiscation or return to the State of export of such specimens.

2. In addition to the measures taken under paragraph 1 of this Article, a Party may, when it deems it necessary, provide for any method of internal reimbursement for expenses incurred as a result of the confiscation of a specimen traded in violation of the measures taken in the application of the provisions of the present Convention.

3. As far as possible, the Parties shall ensure that specimens shall pass through any formalities required for trade with a minimum of delay. To facilitate such passage, a Party may designate ports of exit and ports of entry at which specimens must be presented for clearance. The Parties shall ensure further that all living specimens, during any period of transit, holding or shipment, are properly cared for so as to minimize the risk of injury, damage to health or cruel treatment.

4. Where a living specimen is confiscated as a result of measures referred to in paragraph 1 of this Article:

(a) the specimen shall be entrusted to a Management Authority of the State of confiscation;
(b) the Management Authority shall, after consultation with the State of export, return the specimen to that State at the expense of that State, or to a rescue centre or such other place as the Management Authority deems appropriate and consistent with the purposes of the present Convention; and
(c) the Management Authority may obtain the advice of a Scientific Authority, or may, whenever it considers it desirable, consult the Secretariat in order to

facilitate the decision under sub-paragraph (b) of this paragraph, including the choice of a rescue centre or other place.

5. A rescue centre as referred to in paragraph 4 of this Article means an institution designated by a Management Authority to look after the welfare of living specimens, particularly those that have been confiscated.

6. Each Party shall maintain records of trade in specimens of species included in Appendices I, II and III which shall cover:
(a) the names and addresses of exporters and importers; and
(b) the number and type of permits and certificates granted; the States with which such trade occurred; the numbers or quantities and types of specimens, names of species as included in Appendices I, II and III and, where applicable, the size and sex of the specimens in question.

7. Each Party shall prepare periodic reports on its implementation of the present Convention and shall transmit to the Secretariat:
(a) an annual report containing a summary of the information specified in sub-paragraph (b) of paragraph 6 of this Article; and
(b) a biennial report on legislative, regulatory and administrative measures taken to enforce the provisions of the present Convention.

8. The information referred to in paragraph 7 of this Article shall be available to the public where this is not inconsistent with the law of the Party concerned.

Article IX: Management and Scientific Authorities

1. Each Party shall designate for the purposes of the present Convention:
(a) one or more Management Authorities competent to grant permits or certificates on behalf of that Party; and
(b) one or more Scientific Authorities.

2. A State depositing an instrument of ratification, acceptance, approval or accession shall at that time inform the Depositary Government of the name and address of the Management Authority authorized to communicate with other Parties and with the Secretariat.

3. Any changes in the designations or authorizations under the provisions of this Article shall be communicated by the Party concerned to the Secretariat for transmission to all other Parties.

4. Any Management Authority referred to in paragraph 2 of this Article shall, if so requested by the Secretariat or the Management Authority of another Party, communicate to it impression of stamps, seals or other devices used to authenticate permits or certificates.

Article X: Trade with States not Party to the Convention

Where export or re-export is to, or import is from, a State not a Party to the present Convention, comparable documentation issued by the competent authorities in that State which substantially conforms with the requirements of the present Convention for permits and certificates may be accepted in lieu thereof by any Party.

Article XI: Conference of the Parties

1. The Secretariat shall call a meeting of the Conference of the Parties not later than two years after the entry into force of the present Convention.

2. Thereafter the Secretariat shall convene regular meetings at least once every two years, unless the Conference decides otherwise, and extraordinary meetings at any time on the written request of at least one-third of the Parties.

3. At meetings, whether regular or extraordinary, the Parties shall review the implementation of the present Convention and may:

(a) make such provision as may be necessary to enable the Secretariat to carry out its duties, and adopt financial provisions;
(b) consider and adopt amendments to Appendices I and II in accordance with Article XV;
(c) review the progress made towards the restoration and conservation of the species included in Appendices I, II and III;
(d) receive and consider any reports presented by the Secretariat or by any Party; and
(e) where appropriate, make recommendations for improving the effectiveness of the present Convention.

4. At each regular meeting, the Parties may determine the time and venue of the next regular meeting to be held in accordance with the provisions of paragraph 2 of this Article.

5. At any meeting, the Parties may determine and adopt rules of procedure for the meeting.

6. The United Nations, its Specialized Agencies and the International Atomic Energy Agency, as well as any State not a Party to the present Convention, may be represented at meetings of the Conference by observers, who shall have the right to participate but not to vote.

7. Any body or agency technically qualified in protection, conservation or management of wild fauna and flora, in the following categories, which has informed the Secretariat of its desire to be represented at meetings of the Conference by observers, shall be admitted unless at least one-third of the Parties present object:

(a) international agencies or bodies, either governmental or non-governmental, and national governmental agencies and bodies; and
(b) national non-governmental agencies or bodies which have been approved for this purpose by the State in which they are located. Once admitted, these observers shall have the right to participate but not to vote.

Article XII: The Secretariat

1. Upon entry into force of the present Convention, a Secretariat shall be provided by the Executive Director of the United Nations Environment Programme. To the extent and in the manner he considers appropriate, he may be assisted by suitable

inter-governmental or non-governmental international or national agencies and bodies technically qualified in protection, conservation and management of wild fauna and flora.

2. The functions of the Secretariat shall be:

(a) to arrange for and service meetings of the Parties;

(b) to perform the functions entrusted to it under the provisions of Articles XV and XVI of the present Convention;

(c) to undertake scientific and technical studies in accordance with programmes authorized by the Conference of the Parties as will contribute to the implementation of the present Convention, including studies concerning standards for appropriate preparation and shipment of living specimens and the means of identifying specimens;

(d) to study the reports of Parties and to request from Parties such further information with respect thereto as it deems necessary to ensure implementation of the present Convention;

(e) to invite the attention of the Parties to any matter pertaining to the aims of the present Convention;

(f) to publish periodically and distribute to the Parties current editions of Appendices I, II and III together with any information which will facilitate identification of specimens of species included in those Appendices;

(g) to prepare annual reports to the Parties on its work and on the implementation of the present Convention and such other reports as meetings of the Parties may request;

(h) to make recommendations for the implementation of the aims and provisions of the present Convention, including the exchange of information of a scientific or technical nature;

(i) to perform any other function as may be entrusted to it by the Parties.

Article XIII: International measures

1. When the Secretariat in the light of information received is satisfied that any species included in Appendix I or II is being affected adversely by trade in specimens of that species or that the provisions of the present Convention are not being effectively implemented, it shall communicate such information to the authorized Management Authority of the Party or Parties concerned.

2. When any Party receives a communication as indicated in paragraph 1 of this Article, it shall, as soon as possible, inform the Secretariat of any relevant facts insofar as its laws permit and, where appropriate, propose remedial action. Where the Party considers that an inquiry is desirable, such inquiry may be carried out by one or more persons expressly authorized by the Party.

3. The information provided by the Party or resulting from any inquiry as specified in paragraph 2 of this Article shall be reviewed by the next Conference of the Parties which may make whatever recommendations it deems appropriate.

Article XIV: Effect on domestic legislation and international conventions

1. The provisions of the present Convention shall in no way affect the right of Parties to adopt:

(a) stricter domestic measures regarding the conditions for trade, taking, possession or transport of specimens of species included in Appendices I, II and III, or the complete prohibition thereof; or

(b) domestic measures restricting or prohibiting trade, taking, possession or transport of species not included in Appendix I, II or III.

2. The provisions of the present Convention shall in no way affect the provisions of any domestic measures or the obligations of Parties deriving from any treaty, convention, or international agreement relating to other aspects of trade, taking, possession or transport of specimens which is in force or subsequently may enter into force for any Party including any measure pertaining to the Customs, public health, veterinary or plant quarantine fields.

3. The provisions of the present Convention shall in no way affect the provisions of, or the obligations deriving from, any treaty, convention or international agreement concluded or which may be concluded between States creating a union or regional trade agreement establishing or maintaining a common external Customs control and removing Customs control between the parties thereto insofar as they relate to trade among the States members of that union or agreement.

4. A State party to the present Convention, which is also a party to any other treaty, convention or international agreement which is in force at the time of the coming into force of the present Convention and under the provisions of which protection is afforded to marine species included in Appendix II, shall be relieved of the obligations imposed on it under the provisions of the present Convention with respect to trade in specimens of species included in Appendix II that are taken by ships registered in that State and in accordance with the provisions of such other treaty, convention or international agreement.

5. Notwithstanding the provisions of Articles III, IV and V, any export of a specimen taken in accordance with paragraph 4 of this Article shall only require a certificate from a Management Authority of the State of introduction to the effect that the specimen was taken in accordance with the provisions of the other treaty, convention or international agreement in question.

6. Nothing in the present Convention shall prejudice the codification and development of the law of the sea by the United Nations Conference on the Law of the Sea convened pursuant to Resolution 2750 C (XXV) of the General Assembly of the United Nations nor the present or future claims and legal views of any State concerning the law of the sea and the nature and extent of coastal and flag State jurisdiction.

Article XV: Amendments to Appendices I and II

1. The following provisions shall apply in relation to amendments to Appendices I and II at meetings of the Conference of the Parties:

(a) Any Party may propose an amendment to Appendix I or II for consideration at the next meeting. The text of the proposed amendment shall be communicated to the Secretariat at least 150 days before the meeting. The Secretariat shall consult the other Parties and interested bodies on the amendment in accordance with the provisions of sub-paragraphs (b) and (c) of paragraph 2 of this Article and shall communicate the response to all Parties not later than 30 days before the meeting.

(b) Amendments shall be adopted by a two-thirds majority of Parties present and voting. For these purposes 'Parties present and voting' means Parties present and casting an affirmative or negative vote. Parties abstaining from voting shall not be counted among the two-thirds required for adopting an amendment.

(c) Amendments adopted at a meeting shall enter into force 90 days after that meeting for all Parties except those which make a reservation in accordance with paragraph 3 of this Article.

2. The following provisions shall apply in relation to amendments to Appendices I and II between meetings of the Conference of the Parties:

(a) Any Party may propose an amendment to Appendix I or II for consideration between meetings by the postal procedures set forth in this paragraph.

(b) For marine species, the Secretariat shall, upon receiving the text of the proposed amendment, immediately communicate it to the Parties. It shall also consult inter-governmental bodies having a function in relation to those species especially with a view to obtaining scientific data these bodies may be able to provide and to ensuring co-ordination with any conservation measures enforced by such bodies. The Secretariat shall communicate the views expressed and data provided by these bodies and its own findings and recommendations to the Parties as soon as possible.

(c) For species other than marine species, the Secretariat shall, upon receiving the text of the proposed amendment, immediately communicate it to the Parties, and, as soon as possible thereafter, its own recommendations.

(d) Any Party may, within 60 days of the date on which the Secretariat communicated its recommendations to the Parties under sub-paragraph (b) or (c) of this paragraph, transmit to the Secretariat any comments on the proposed amendment together with any relevant scientific data and information.

(e) The Secretariat shall communicate the replies received together with its own recommendations to the Parties as soon as possible.

(f) If no objection to the proposed amendment is received by the Secretariat within 30 days of the date the replies and recommendations were communicated under the provisions of sub-paragraph (e) of this paragraph, the amendment shall enter into force 90 days later for all Parties except those which make a reservation in accordance with paragraph 3 of this Article.

(g) If an objection by any Party is received by the Secretariat, the proposed amendment shall be submitted to a postal vote in accordance with the provisions of sub-paragraphs (h) , (i) and (j) of this paragraph.

(h) The Secretariat shall notify the Parties that notification of objection has been received.
(i) Unless the Secretariat receives the votes for, against or in abstention from at least one-half of the Parties within 60 days of the date of notification under sub-paragraph (h) of this paragraph, the proposed amendment shall be referred to the next meeting of the Conference for further consideration.
(j) Provided that votes are received from one-half of the Parties, the amendment shall be adopted by a two-thirds majority of Parties casting an affirmative or negative vote.
(k) The Secretariat shall notify all Parties of the result of the vote.
(l) If the proposed amendment is adopted it shall enter into force 90 days after the date of the notification by the Secretariat of its acceptance for all Parties except those which make a reservation in accordance with paragraph 3 of this Article.

3. During the period of 90 days provided for by sub-paragraph (c) of paragraph 1 or sub-paragraph (l) of paragraph 2 of this Article any Party may by notification in writing to the Depositary Government make a reservation with respect to the amendment. Until such reservation is withdrawn the Party shall be treated as a State not a Party to the present Convention with respect to trade in the species concerned.

Article XVI: Appendix III and amendments thereto

1. Any Party may at any time submit to the Secretariat a list of species which it identifies as being subject to regulation within its jurisdiction for the purpose mentioned in paragraph 3 of Article II. Appendix III shall include the names of the Parties submitting the species for inclusion therein, the scientific names of the species so submitted, and any parts or derivatives of the animals or plants concerned that are specified in relation to the species for the purposes of sub-paragraph (b) of Article I.

2. Each list submitted under the provisions of paragraph 1 of this Article shall be communicated to the Parties by the Secretariat as soon as possible after receiving it. The list shall take effect as part of Appendix III 90 days after the date of such communication. At any time after the communication of such list, any Party may by notification in writing to the Depositary Government enter a reservation with respect to any species or any parts or derivatives, and until such reservation is withdrawn, the State shall be treated as a State not a Party to the present Convention with respect to trade in the species or part or derivative concerned.

3. A Party which has submitted a species for inclusion in Appendix III may withdraw it at any time by notification to the Secretariat which shall communicate the withdrawal to all Parties. The withdrawal shall take effect 30 days after the date of such communication.

4. Any Party submitting a list under the provisions of paragraph 1 of this Article shall submit to the Secretariat a copy of all domestic laws and regulations applicable to the protection of such species, together with any interpretations which the Party may deem appropriate or the Secretariat may request. The Party shall, for

as long as the species in question is included in Appendix III, submit any amendments of such laws and regulations or any interpretations as they are adopted.

Article XVII: Amendment of the Convention

1. An extraordinary meeting of the Conference of the Parties shall be convened by the Secretariat on the written request of at least one-third of the Parties to consider and adopt amendments to the present Convention. Such amendments shall be adopted by a two-thirds majority of Parties present and voting. For these purposes 'Parties present and voting' means Parties present and casting an affirmative or negative vote. Parties abstaining from voting shall not be counted among the two-thirds required for adopting an amendment.

2. The text of any proposed amendment shall be communicated by the Secretariat to all Parties at least 90 days before the meeting.

3. An amendment shall enter into force for the Parties which have accepted it 60 days after two-thirds of the Parties have deposited an instrument of acceptance of the amendment with the Depositary Government. Thereafter, the amendment shall enter into force for any other Party 60 days after that Party deposits its instrument of acceptance of the amendment.

Article XVIII: Resolution of disputes

1. Any dispute which may arise between two or more Parties with respect to the interpretation or application of the provisions of the present Convention shall be subject to negotiation between the Parties involved in the dispute.

2. If the dispute can not be resolved in accordance with paragraph 1 of this Article, the Parties may, by mutual consent, submit the dispute to arbitration, in particular that of the Permanent Court of Arbitration at The Hague, and the Parties submitting the dispute shall be bound by the arbitral decision.

Article XIX: Signature

The present Convention shall be open for signature at Washington until 30th April 1973 and thereafter at Berne until 31st December 1974.

Article XX: Ratification, acceptance, approval

The present Convention shall be subject to ratification, acceptance or approval. Instruments of ratification, acceptance or approval shall be deposited with the Government of the Swiss Confederation which shall be the Depositary Government.

Article XXI: Accession

The present Convention shall be open indefinitely for accession. Instruments of accession shall be deposited with the Depositary Government.

Article XXII: Entry into force

1. The present Convention shall enter into force 90 days after the date of deposit of the tenth instrument of ratification, acceptance, approval or accession, with the Depositary Government.

2. For each State which ratifies, accepts or approves the present Convention or accedes thereto after the deposit of the tenth instrument of ratification, acceptance, approval or accession, the present Convention shall enter into force 90 days after the deposit by such State of its instrument of ratification, acceptance, approval or accession.

Article XXIII: Reservations

1. The provisions of the present Convention shall not be subject to general reservations. Specific reservations may be entered in accordance with the provisions of this Article and Articles XV and XVI.

2. Any State may, on depositing its instrument of ratification, acceptance, approval or accession, enter a specific reservation with regard to:
(a) any species included in Appendix I, II or III; or
(b) any parts or derivatives specified in relation to a species included in Appendix III.

3. Until a Party withdraws its reservation entered under the provisions of this Article, it shall be treated as a State not a Party to the present Convention with respect to trade in the particular species or parts or derivatives specified in such reservation.

Article XXIV: Denunciation

Any Party may denounce the present Convention by written notification to the Depositary Government at any time. The denunciation shall take effect twelve months after the Depositary Government has received the notification.

Article XXV: Depositary

1. The original of the present Convention, in the Chinese, English, French, Russian and Spanish languages, each version being equally authentic, shall be deposited with the Depositary Government, which shall transmit certified copies thereof to all States that have signed it or deposited instruments of accession to it.

2. The Depositary Government shall inform all signatory and acceding States and the Secretariat of signatures, deposit of instruments of ratification, acceptance, approval or accession, entry into force of the present Convention, amendments thereto, entry and withdrawal of reservations and notifications of denunciation.

3. As soon as the present Convention enters into force, a certified copy thereof shall be transmitted by the Depositary Government to the Secretariat of the United Nations for registration and publication in accordance with Article 102 of the Charter of the United Nations.

In witness whereof the undersigned Plenipotentiaries, being duly authorized to that effect, have signed the present Convention.

Done at Washington this third day of March, One Thousand Nine Hundred and Seventy-three.

Appendices I, II and III [not reproduced]

Convention on the Conservation of Migratory Species of Wild Animals

Adopted on 23 June 1979 at Bonn. Entered into force on 1 November 1983. Source: 1651 *UNTS* 356. Number of parties: 85. Further information: Secretariat, Bonn, Germany, http://www.wcmc.org.uk/cms

The Contracting Parties,

Recognizing that wild animals in their innumerable forms are an irreplaceable part of the earth's natural system which must be conserved for the good of mankind;

Aware that each generation of man holds the resources of the earth for future generations and has an obligation to ensure that this legacy is conserved and, where utilized, is used wisely;

Conscious of the ever-growing value of wild animals from environmental, ecological, genetic, scientific, aesthetic, recreational, cultural, educational, social and economic points of view;

Concerned particularly with those species of wild animals that migrate across or outside national jurisdictional boundaries;

Recognizing that the States are and must be the protectors of the migratory species of wild animals that live within or pass through their national jurisdictional boundaries;

Convinced that conservation and effective management of migratory species of wild animals require the concerted action of all States within the national jurisdictional boundaries of which such species spend any part of their life cycle;

Recalling Recommendation 32 of the Action Plan adopted by the United Nations Conference on the Human Environment (Stockholm, 1972) and noted with satisfaction at the Twenty-seventh Session of the General Assembly of the United Nations,

Have agreed as follows:

Article I: Interpretation

1. For the purpose of this Convention:

a) 'Migratory species' means the entire population or any geographically separate part of the population of any species or lower taxon of wild animals, a significant proportion of whose members cyclically and predictably cross one or more national jurisdictional boundaries;
b) 'Conservation status of a migratory species' means the sum of the influences acting on the migratory species that may affect its long-term distribution and abundance;
c) 'Conservation status' will be taken as 'favourable' when:
   (1) population dynamics data indicate that the migratory species is maintaining itself on a long-term basis as a viable component of its ecosystems;
   (2) the range of the migratory species is neither currently being reduced, nor is likely to be reduced, on a long-term basis;
   (3) there is, and will be in the foreseeable future sufficient habitat to maintain the population of the migratory species on a long-term basis; and
   (4) the distribution and abundance of the migratory species approach historic coverage and levels to the extent that potentially suitable ecosystems exist and to the extent consistent with wise wildlife management;
d) 'Conservation status' will be taken as 'unfavourable' if any of the conditions set out in sub-paragraph (c) of this paragraph is not met;
e) 'Endangered' in relation to a particular migratory species means that the migratory species is in danger of extinction throughout all or a significant portion of its range;
f) 'Range' means all the areas of land or water that a migratory species inhabits, stays in temporarily, crosses or overflies at any time on its normal migration route;
g) 'Habitat' means any area in the range of a migratory species which contains suitable living conditions for that species;
h) 'Range State' in relation to a particular migratory species means any State (and where appropriate any other Party referred to under subparagraph (k) of this paragraph) that exercises jurisdiction over any part of the range of that migratory species, or a State, flag vessels of which are engaged outside national jurisdictional limits in taking that migratory species;
i) 'Taking' means taking, hunting, fishing capturing, harassing, deliberate killing, or attempting to engage in any such conduct;
j) 'Agreement' means an international agreement relating to the conservation of one or more migratory species as provided for in Articles IV and V of this Convention; and
k) 'Party' means a State or any regional economic integration organization constituted by sovereign States which has competence in respect of the negotiation, conclusion and application of international Agreements in matters covered by this Convention for which this Convention is in force.

2. In matters within their competence, the regional economic integration organizations which are Parties to this Convention shall in their own name exercise the rights and fulfil the responsibilities which this Convention attributes to their

member States. In such cases the member States of these organizations shall not be entitled to exercise such rights individually.

3. Where this Convention provides for a decision to be taken by either a two-thirds majority or a unanimous decision of 'the Parties present and voting' this shall mean 'the Parties present and casting an affirmative or negative vote'. Those abstaining from voting shall not be counted amongst 'the Parties present and voting' in determining the majority.

Article II: Fundamental principles

1. The Parties acknowledge the importance of migratory species being conserved and of Range States agreeing to take action to this end whenever possible and appropriate, paying special attention to migratory species the conservation status of which is unfavourable, and taking individually or in co-operation appropriate and necessary steps to conserve such species and their habitat.

2. The Parties acknowledge the need to take action to avoid any migratory species becoming endangered.

3. In particular, the Parties:

a) should promote, co-operate in and support research relating to migratory species;
b) shall endeavour to provide immediate protection for migratory species included in Appendix I; and
c) shall endeavour to conclude Agreements covering the conservation and management of migratory species included in Appendix II.

Article III: Endangered migratory species: Appendix I

1. Appendix I shall list migratory species which are endangered.

2. A migratory species may be listed in Appendix I provided that reliable evidence, including the best scientific evidence available, indicates that the species is endangered.

3. A migratory species may be removed from Appendix I when the Conference of the Parties determines that:

a) reliable evidence, including the best scientific evidence available, indicates that the species is no longer endangered, and
b) the species is not likely to become endangered again because of loss of protection due to its removal from Appendix I.

4. Parties that are Range States of a migratory species listed in Appendix I shall endeavour:

a) to conserve and, where feasible and appropriate, restore those habitats of the species which are of importance in removing the species from danger of extinction;
b) to prevent, remove, compensate for or minimize, as appropriate, the adverse effects of activities or obstacles that seriously impede or prevent the migration of the species; and

c) to the extent feasible and appropriate, to prevent, reduce or control factors that are endangering or are likely to further endanger the species, including strictly controlling the introduction of, or controlling or eliminating, already introduced exotic species.

5. Parties that are Range States of a migratory species listed in Appendix I shall prohibit the taking of animals belonging to such species. Exceptions may be made to this prohibition only if:

a) the taking is for scientific purposes;
b) the taking is for the purpose of enhancing the propagation or survival of the affected species;
c) the taking is to accommodate the needs of traditional subsistence users of such species; or
d) extraordinary circumstances so require; provided that such exceptions are precise as to content and limited in space and time. Such taking should not operate to the disadvantage of the species.

6. The Conferences of the Parties may recommend to the Parties that are Range States of a migratory species listed in Appendix I that they take further measures considered appropriate to benefit the species.

7. The Parties shall as soon as possible inform the Secretariat of any exceptions made pursuant to paragraph 5 of this Article.

Article IV: Migratory species to be the subject of agreements: Appendix II

1. Appendix II shall list migratory species which have an unfavourable conservation status and which require international agreements for their conservation and management, as well as those which have a conservation status which would significantly benefit from the international cooperation that could be achieved by an international agreement.

2. If the circumstances so warrant, a migratory species may be listed both in Appendix I and Appendix II.

3. Parties that are Range States of migratory species listed in Appendix II shall endeavour to conclude Agreements where these should benefit the species and should give priority to those species in an unfavourable conservation status.

4. Parties are encouraged to take action with a view to concluding agreements for any population or any geographically separate part of the population of any species or lower taxon of wild animals, members of which periodically cross one or more national jurisdiction boundaries.

5. The Secretariat shall be provided with a copy of each Agreement concluded pursuant to the provisions of this Article.

Article V: Guidelines for Agreements

1. The object of each Agreement shall be to restore the migratory species concerned to a favourable conservation status or to maintain it in such a status.

Each Agreement should deal with those aspects of the conservation and management of the migratory species concerned which serve to achieve that object.

2. Each Agreement should cover the whole of the range of the migratory species concerned and should be open to accession by all Range States of that species, whether or not they are Parties to this Convention.

3. An Agreement should, wherever possible, deal with more than one migratory species.

4. Each Agreement should:

a) identify the migratory species covered;
b) describe the range and migration route of the migratory species;
c) provide for each Party to designate its national authority concerned with the implementation of the Agreement.
d) establish, if necessary, appropriate machinery to assist in carrying out the aims of the Agreement, to monitor its effectiveness, and to prepare reports for the Conference of the Parties;
e) provide for procedures for the settlement of disputes between Parties to the Agreement; and
f) at a minimum, prohibit, in relation to a migratory species of the Order Cetacea, any taking that is not permitted for that migratory species under any other multilateral Agreement and provide for accession to the Agreement by States that are not Range States of that migratory species.

5. Where appropriate and feasible, each Agreement should provide for but not be limited to:

a) periodic review of the conservation status of the migratory species concerned and the identification of the factors which may be harmful to that status;
b) co-ordinated conservation and management plans;
c) research into the ecology and population dynamics of the migratory species concerned, with special regard to migration;
d) the exchange of information on the migratory species concerned, special regard being paid to the exchange of the results of research and of relevant statistics;
e) conservation and, where required and feasible, restoration of the habitats of importance in maintaining a favourable conservation status, and protection of such habitats from disturbances, including strict control of the introduction of, or control of already introduced, exotic species detrimental to the migratory species;
f) maintenance of a network of suitable habitats appropriately disposed in relation to the migration routes;
g) where it appears desirable, the provision of new habitats favourable to the migratory species or reintroduction of the migratory species into favourable habitats;
h) elimination of, to the maximum extent possible, or compensation for activities and obstacles which hinder or impede migration;

i) prevention, reduction or control of the release into the habitat of the migratory species of substances harmful to that migratory species;
j) measures based on sound ecological principles to control and manage the taking of the migratory species;
k) procedures for co-ordinating action to suppress illegal taking;
l) exchange of information on substantial threats to the migratory species;
m) emergency procedures whereby conservation action would be considerably and rapidly strengthened when the conservation status of the migratory species is seriously affected; and
n) making the general public aware of the contents and aims of the Agreement.

Article VI: Range States

1. A list of the Range States of migratory species listed in Appendices I and II shall be kept up to date by the Secretariat using information it has received from the Parties.

2. The Parties shall keep the Secretariat informed in regard to which of the migratory species listed in Appendices I and II they consider themselves to be Range States, including provision of information on their flag vessels engaged outside national jurisdictional limits in taking the migratory species concerned and, where possible, future plans in respect of such taking.

3. The Parties which are Range States for migratory species listed in Appendix I or Appendix II should inform the Conference of the Parties through the Secretariat, at least six months prior to each ordinary meeting of the Conference, on measures that they are taking to implement the provisions of this Convention for these species.

Article VII: The Conference of the Parties

1. The Conference of the Parties shall be the decision-making organ of this Convention.

2. The Secretariat shall call a meeting of the Conference of the Parties not later than two years after the entry into force of this Convention.

3. Thereafter the Secretariat shall convene ordinary meetings of the Conference of the Parties at intervals of not more than three years, unless the Conference decides otherwise, and extraordinary meetings at any time on the written request of at least one-third of the Parties.

4. The Conference of the Parties shall establish and keep under review the financial regulations of this Convention. The Conference of the Parties shall, at each of its ordinary meetings, adopt the budget for the next financial period. Each Party shall contribute to this budget according to a scale to be agreed upon by the Conference. Financial regulations, including the provisions on the budget and the scale of contributions as well as their modifications, shall be adopted by unanimous vote of the Parties present and voting.

5. At each of its meetings the Conference of the Parties shall review the implementation of this Convention and may in particular:

a) review and assess the conservation status of migratory species;
b) review the progress made towards the conservation of migratory species, especially those listed in Appendices I and II;
c) make such provision and provide such guidance as may be necessary to enable the Scientific Council and the Secretariat to carry out their duties;
d) receive and consider any reports presented by the Scientific Council, the Secretariat, any Party or any standing body established pursuant to an Agreement;
e) make recommendations to the Parties for improving the conservation status of migratory species and review the progress being made under Agreements;
f) in those cases where an Agreement has not been concluded, make recommendations for the convening of meetings of the Parties that are Range States of a migratory species or group of migratory species to discuss measures to improve the conservation status of the species;
g) make recommendations to the Parties for improving the effectiveness of this Convention; and
h) decide on any additional measure that should be taken to implement the objectives of this Convention.

6. Each meeting of the Conference of the Parties should determine the time and venue of the next meeting.

7. Any meeting of the Conference of the Parties shall determine and adopt rules of procedure for that meeting. Decisions at a meeting of the Conference of the Parties shall require a two-thirds majority of the Parties present and voting, except where otherwise provided for by this Convention.

8. The United Nations, its Specialized Agencies, the International Atomic Energy Agency, as well as any State not a party to this Convention and, for each Agreement, the body designated by the parties to that Agreement, may be represented by observers at meetings of the Conference of the Parties.

9. Any agency or body technically qualified in protection, conservation and management of migratory species, in the following categories, which has informed the Secretariat of its desire to be represented at meetings of the Conference of the Parties by observers, shall be admitted unless at least one-third of the Parties present object:

a) international agencies or bodies, either governmental or non-governmental, and national governmental agencies and bodies; and
b) national non-governmental agencies or bodies which have been approved for this purpose by the State in which they are located.

Once admitted, these observers shall have the right to participate but not to vote.

Article VIII: The Scientific Council

1. At its first meeting, the Conference of the Parties shall establish a Scientific Council to provide advice on scientific matters.

2. Any Party may appoint a qualified expert as a member of the Scientific Council. In addition, the Scientific Council shall include as members qualified experts selected and appointed by the Conference of the Parties; the number of these experts, the criteria for their selection and the terms of their appointments shall be as determined by the Conference of the Parties.

3. The Scientific Council shall meet at the request of the Secretariat as required by the Conference of the Parties.

4. Subject to the approval of the Conference of the Parties, the Scientific Council shall establish its own rules of procedure.

5. The Conference of the Parties shall determine the functions of the Scientific Council, which may include:

a) providing scientific advice to the Conference of the Parties, to the Secretariat, and, if approved by the Conference of the Parties, to any body set up under this Convention or an Agreement or to any Party;
b) recommending research and the co-ordination of research on migratory species, evaluating the results of such research in order to ascertain the conservation status of migratory species and reporting to the Conference of the Parties on such status and measures for its improvement;
c) making recommendations to the Conference of the Parties as to the migratory species to be included in Appendices I and II, together with an indication of the range of such migratory species;
d) making recommendations to the Conference of the Parties as to specific conservation and management measures to be included in Agreements on migratory species; and
e) recommending to the Conference of the Parties solutions to problems relating to the scientific aspects of the implementation of this Convention, in particular with regard to the habitats of migratory species.

Article IX: The Secretariat

1. For the purposes of this Convention a Secretariat shall be established.

2. Upon entry into force of this Convention, the Secretariat is provided by the Executive Director of the United Nations Environment Programme. To the extent and in the manner he considers appropriate, he may be assisted by suitable intergovernmental or non-governmental, international or national agencies and bodies technically qualified in protection, conservation and management of wild animals.

3. If the United Nations Environment Programme is no longer able to provide the Secretariat, the Conference of the Parties shall make alternative arrangements for the Secretariat.

4. The functions of the Secretariat shall be:

a) to arrange for and service meetings: (i) of the Conference of the Parties, and (ii) of the Scientific Council;
b) to maintain liaison with and promote liaison between the Parties, the standing bodies set up under Agreements and other international organizations concerned with migratory species;
c) to obtain from any appropriate source reports and other information which will further the objectives and implementation of this Convention and to arrange for the appropriate dissemination of such information;
d) to invite the attention of the Conference of the Parties to any matter pertaining to the objectives of this Convention;
e) to prepare for the Conference of the Parties reports on the work of the Secretariat and on the implementation of this Convention;
f) to maintain and publish a list of Range States of all migratory species included in Appendices I and II;
g) to promote, under the direction of the Conference of the Parties, the conclusion of Agreements,
h) to maintain and make available to the Parties a list of Agreements and, if so required by the Conference of the Parties, to provide any information on such Agreements;
i) to maintain and publish a list of the recommendations made by the Conference of the Parties pursuant to sub-paragraphs (e), (f) and (g) of paragraph 5 of Article VII or of decisions made pursuant to sub-paragraph (h) of that paragraph;
j) to provide for the general public information concerning this Convention and its objectives; and
k) to perform any other function entrusted to it under this Convention or by the Conference of the Parties.

Article X: Amendment of the Convention

1. This Convention may be amended at any ordinary or extraordinary meeting of the Conference of the Parties.

2. Proposals for amendment may be made by any Party.

3. The text of any proposed amendment and the reasons for it shall be communicated to the Secretary at least one hundred and fifty days before the meeting at which it is to be considered and shall promptly be communicated by the Secretary to all Parties. Any comments on the text by the Parties shall be communicated to the Secretariat not less than sixty days before the meeting begins. The Secretariat shall, immediately after the last day for submission of comments, communicate to the Parties all comments submitted by that day.

4. Amendments shall be adopted by a two-thirds majority of Parties present and voting.

5. An amendment adopted shall enter into force for all Parties which have accepted it on the first day of the third month following the date on which two-thirds of the Parties have deposited an instrument of acceptance with the Depositary. For each Party which deposits an instrument of acceptance after the date on which two-thirds of the Parties have deposited an instrument of acceptance, the amendment shall enter into force for that Party on the first day of the third month following the deposit of its instrument of acceptance.

Article XI: Amendment of the Appendices

1. Appendices I and II may be amended at any ordinary or extraordinary meeting of the Conference of the Parties.

2. Proposals for amendment may be made by any Party.

3. The text of any proposed amendment and the reasons for it, based on the best scientific evidence available, shall be communicated to the Secretariat at least one hundred and fifty days before the meeting and shall promptly be communicated by the Secretariat to all Parties. Any comments on the text by the Parties shall be communicated to the Secretariat not less than sixty days before the meeting begins. The Secretariat shall, immediately after the last day for submission of comments, communicate to the Parties all comments submitted by that day.

4. Amendments shall be adopted by a two-thirds majority of Parties present and voting.

5. An amendment to the Appendices shall enter into force for all Parties ninety days after the meeting of the Conference of the Parties at which it was adopted, except for those Parties which make a reservation in accordance with paragraph 6 of this Article.

6. During the period of ninety days provided for in paragraph 5 of this Article, any Party may by notification in writing to the Depositary make a reservation with respect to the amendment. A reservation to an amendment may be withdrawn by written notification to the Depositary and thereupon the amendment shall enter into force for that Party ninety days after the reservation is withdrawn.

Article XII: Effect on international conventions and other legislation

1. Nothing in this Convention shall prejudice the codification and development of the law of the sea by the United Nations Conference on the Law of the Sea convened pursuant to Resolution 2750 C (XXV) of the General Assembly of the United Nations nor the present or future claims and legal views of any State concerning the law of the sea and the nature and extent of coastal and flag State jurisdiction.

2. The provisions of this Convention shall in no way affect the rights or obligations of any Party deriving from any existing treaty, convention or Agreement.

3. The provisions of this Convention shall in no way affect the right of Parties to adopt stricter domestic measures concerning the conservation of migratory species

listed in Appendices I and II or to adopt domestic measures concerning the conservation of species not listed in Appendices I and II.

Article XIII: Settlement of disputes

1. Any dispute which may arise between two or more Parties with respect to the interpretation or application of the provisions of this Convention shall be subject to negotiation between the Parties involved in the dispute.

2. If the dispute cannot be resolved in accordance with paragraph 1 of this Article, the Parties may, by mutual consent, submit the dispute to arbitration, in particular that of the Permanent Court of Arbitration at The Hague, and the Parties submitting the dispute shall be bound by the arbitral decision.

Article XIV: Reservations

1. The provisions of this Convention shall not be subject to general reservations. Specific reservations may be entered in accordance with the provisions of this Article and Article XI.

2. Any State or regional economic integration organization may, on depositing its instrument of ratification, acceptance, approval or accession, enter a specific reservation with regard to the presence on either Appendix I or Appendix II or both, of any migratory species and shall then not be regarded as a Party in regard to the subject of that reservation until ninety days after the Depositary has transmitted to the Parties notification that such reservation has been withdrawn.

Article XV: Signature

This Convention shall be open for signature at Bonn for all States and any regional economic integration organization until the twenty-second day of June, 1980.

Article XVI: Ratification, acceptance, approval

This Convention shall be subject to ratification, acceptance or approval. Instruments of ratification, acceptance or approval shall be deposited with the Government of the Federal Republic of Germany, which shall be the Depositary.

Article XVII: Accession

After the twenty-second day of June 1980 this Convention shall be open for accession by all non-signatory States and any regional economic integration organization. Instruments of accession shall be deposited with the Depositary.

Article XVIII: Entry into force

1. This Convention shall enter into force on the first day of the third month following the date of deposit of the fifteenth instrument of ratification, acceptance, approval or accession with the Depositary.

2. For each State or each regional economic integration organization which ratifies, accepts or approves this Convention or accedes thereto after the deposit of the fifteenth instrument of ratification, acceptance, approval or accession, this Convention shall enter into force on the first day of the third month following the

deposit by such State or such organization of its instrument of ratification, acceptance, approval or accession.

Article XIX: Denunciation

Any Party may denounce this Convention by written notification to the Depositary at any time. The denunciation shall take effect twelve months after the Depositary has received the notification.

Article XX: Depositary

1. The original of this Convention, in the English, French, German, Russian and Spanish languages, each version being equally authentic, shall be deposited with the Depositary. The Depositary shall transmit certified copies of each of these versions to all States and all regional economic integration organizations that have signed the Convention or deposited instruments of accession to it.

2. The Depositary shall, after consultation with the Governments concerned, prepare official versions of the text of this Convention in the Arabic and Chinese languages.

3. The Depositary shall inform all signatory and acceding States and all signatory and acceding regional economic integration organizations and the Secretariat of signatures, deposit of instruments of ratification, acceptance, approval or accession, entry into force of this Convention, amendments thereto, specific reservations and notifications of denunciation.

4. As soon as this Convention enters into force, a certified copy thereof shall be transmitted by the Depositary to the Secretariat of the United Nations for registration and publication in accordance with Article 102 of the Charter of the United Nations. In witness whereof the undersigned, being duly authorized to that effect, have signed this Convention.

Done at Bonn on 23 June 1979.

Appendices I and II [not reproduced]

Habitats

Convention on Wetlands of International Importance Especially as Waterfowl Habitat

Adopted on 2 February 1971 at Ramsar. Entered into force on 21 December 1975. Source: 996 *UNTS* 245 (the text reproduced incorporates the amendments adopted in the Protocol of 3 December 1982 and on 28 May 1987). Number of parties: 138. Further information: Secretariat, Gland, Switzerland, http://www.ramsar.org

The Contracting Parties,

Recognizing the interdependence of Man and his environment;

Considering the fundamental ecological functions of wetlands as regulators of water regimes and as habitats supporting a characteristic flora and fauna, especially waterfowl;

Being convinced that wetlands constitute a resource of great economic, cultural, scientific, and recreational value, the loss of which would be irreparable;

Desiring to stem the progressive encroachment on and loss of wetlands now and in the future;

Recognizing that waterfowl in their seasonal migrations may transcend frontiers and so should be regarded as an international resource;

Being confident that the conservation of wetlands and their flora and fauna can be ensured by combining far-sighted national policies with co-ordinated international action;

Have agreed as follows:

Article 1

1. For the purpose of this Convention wetlands are areas of marsh, fen, peatland or water, whether natural or artificial, permanent or temporary, with water that is static or flowing, fresh, brackish or salt, including areas of marine water the depth of which at low tide does not exceed six metres.

2. For the purpose of this Convention waterfowl are birds ecologically dependent on wetlands.

Article 2

1. Each Contracting Party shall designate suitable wetlands within its territory for inclusion in a List of Wetlands of International Importance, hereinafter referred to as 'the List' which is maintained by the bureau established under Article 8. The boundaries of each wetland shall be precisely described and also delimited on a map and they may incorporate riparian and coastal zones adjacent to the wetlands, and islands or bodies of marine water deeper than six metres at low tide lying within the wetlands, especially where these have importance as waterfowl habitat.

2. Wetlands should be selected for the List on account of their international significance in terms of ecology, botany, zoology, limnology or hydrology. In the first instance wetlands of international importance to waterfowl at any season should be included.

3. The inclusion of a wetland in the List does not prejudice the exclusive sovereign rights of the Contracting Party in whose territory the wetland is situated.

4. Each Contracting Party shall designate at least one wetland to be included in the List when signing this Convention or when depositing its instrument of ratification or accession, as provided in Article 9.

5. Any Contracting Party shall have the right to add to the List further wetlands situated within its territory, to extend the boundaries of those wetlands already included by it in the List, or, because of its urgent national interests, to delete or restrict the boundaries of wetlands already included by it in the List and shall, at the earliest possible time, inform the organization or government responsible for the continuing bureau duties specified in Article 8 of any such changes.

6. Each Contracting Party shall consider its international responsibilities for the conservation, management and wise use of migratory stocks of waterfowl, both when designating entries for the List and when exercising its right to change entries in the List relating to wetlands within its territory.

Article 3

1. The Contracting Parties shall formulate and implement their planning so as to promote the conservation of the wetlands included in the List, and as far as possible the wise use of wetlands in their territory.

2. Each Contracting Party shall arrange to be informed at the earliest possible time if the ecological character of any wetland in its territory and included in the List has changed, is changing or is likely to change as the result of technological developments, pollution or other human interference. Information on such changes shall be passed without delay to the organization or government responsible for the continuing bureau duties specified in Article 8.

Article 4

1. Each Contracting Party shall promote the conservation of wetlands and waterfowl by establishing nature reserves on wetlands, whether they are included in the List or not, and provide adequately for their wardening.

2. Where a Contracting Party in its urgent national interest, deletes or restricts the boundaries of a wetland included in the List, it should as far as possible compensate for any loss of wetland resources, and in particular it should create additional nature reserves for waterfowl and for the protection, either in the same area or elsewhere, of an adequate portion of the original habitat.

3. The Contracting Parties shall encourage research and the exchange of data and publications regarding wetlands and their flora and fauna.

4. The Contracting Parties shall endeavour through management to increase waterfowl populations on appropriate wetlands.

5. The Contracting Parties shall promote the training of personnel competent in the fields of wetland research, management and wardening.

Article 5

1. The Contracting Parties shall consult with each other about implementing obligations arising from the Convention especially in the case of a wetland extending over the territories of more than one Contracting Party or where a water system is shared by Contracting Parties. They shall at the same time endeavour to

coordinate and support present and future policies and regulations concerning the conservation of wetlands and their flora and fauna.

Article 6

1. There shall be established a Conference of the Contracting Parties to review and promote the implementation of this Convention. The Bureau referred to in Article 8, paragraph 1, shall convene ordinary meetings of the Conference of the Contracting Parties at intervals of not more than three years, unless the Conference decides otherwise, and extraordinary meetings at the written requests of at least one third of the Contracting Parties. Each ordinary meeting of the Conference of the Contracting Parties shall determine the time and venue of the next ordinary meeting.

2. The Conference of the Contracting Parties shall be competent:

a. to discuss the implementation of this Convention;
b. to discuss additions to and changes in the List;
c. to consider information regarding changes in the ecological character of wetlands included in the List provided in accordance with paragraph 2 of Article 3;
d. to make general or specific recommendations to the Contracting Parties regarding the conservation, management and wise use of wetlands and their flora and fauna;
e. to request relevant international bodies to prepare reports and statistics on matters which are essentially international in character affecting wetlands;
f. to adopt other recommendations, or resolutions, to promote the functioning of this Convention.

3. The Contracting Parties shall ensure that those responsible at all levels for wetlands management shall be informed of, and take into consideration, recommendations of such Conferences concerning the conservation, management and wise use of wetlands and their flora and fauna.

4. The Conference of the Contracting Parties shall adopt rules of procedure for each of its meetings.

5. The Conference of the Contracting Parties shall establish and keep under review the financial regulations of this Convention. At each of its ordinary meetings, it shall adopt the budget for the next financial period by a two-third majority of Contracting Parties present and voting.

6. Each Contracting Party shall contribute to the budget according to a scale of contributions adopted by unanimity of the Contracting Parties present and voting at a meeting of the ordinary Conference of the Contracting Parties.

Article 7

1. The representatives of the Contracting Parties at such Conferences should include persons who are experts on wetlands or waterfowl by reason of knowledge and experience gained in scientific, administrative or other appropriate capacities.

2. Each of the Contracting Parties represented at a Conference shall have one vote, recommendations, resolutions and decisions being adopted by a simple majority of the Contracting Parties present and voting, unless otherwise provided for in this Convention.

Article 8

1. The International Union for Conservation of Nature and Natural Resources shall perform the continuing bureau duties under this Convention until such time as another organization or government is appointed by a majority of two-thirds of all Contracting Parties.

2. The continuing bureau duties shall be, inter alia:

a. to assist in the convening and organizing of Conferences specified in Article 6;
b. to maintain the List of Wetlands of International Importance and to be informed by the Contracting Parties of any additions, extensions, deletions or restrictions concerning wetlands included in the List provided in accordance with paragraph 5 of Article 2;
c. to be informed by the Contracting Parties of any changes in the ecological character of wetlands included in the List provided in accordance with paragraph 2 of Article 3;
d. to forward notification of any alterations to the List, or changes in character of wetlands included therein, to all Contracting Parties and to arrange for these matters to be discussed at the next Conference;
e. to make known to the Contracting Party concerned, the recommendations of the Conferences in respect of such alterations to the List or of changes in the character of wetlands included therein.

Article 9

1. This Convention shall remain open for signature indefinitely.

2. Any member of the United Nations or of one of the Specialized Agencies or of the International Atomic Energy Agency or Party to the Statute of the International Court of Justice may become a Party to this Convention by:

a. signature without reservation as to ratification;
b. signature subject to ratification followed by ratification;
c. accession.

3. Ratification or accession shall be effected by the deposit of an instrument of ratification or accession with the Director-General of the United Nations Educational, Scientific and Cultural Organization (hereinafter referred to as 'the Depositary').

Article 10

1. This Convention shall enter into force four months after seven States have become Parties to this Convention in accordance with paragraph 2 of Article 9.

2. Thereafter this Convention shall enter into force for each Contracting Party four months after the day of its signature without reservation as to ratification, or its deposit of an instrument of ratification or accession.

Article 10 bis

1. This Convention may be amended at a meeting of the Contracting Parties convened for that purpose in accordance with this article.

2. Proposals for amendment may be made by any Contracting Party.

3. The text of any proposed amendment and the reasons for it shall be communicated to the organization or government performing the continuing bureau duties under the Convention (hereinafter referred to as 'the Bureau') and shall promptly be communicated by the Bureau to all Contracting Parties. Any comments on the text by the Contracting Parties shall be communicated to the Bureau within three months of the date on which the amendments were communicated to the Contracting Parties by the Bureau. The Bureau shall, immediately after the last day for submission of comments, communicate to the Contracting Parties all comments submitted by that day.

4. A meeting of Contracting Parties to consider an amendment communicated in accordance with paragraph 3 shall be convened by the Bureau upon the written request of one third of the Contracting Parties. The Bureau shall consult the Parties concerning the time and venue of the meeting.

5. Amendments shall be adopted by a two-thirds majority of the Contracting Parties present and voting.

6. An amendment adopted shall enter into force for the Contracting Parties which have accepted it on the first day of the fourth month following the date on which two thirds of the Contracting Parties have deposited an instrument of acceptance with the Depositary. For each Contracting Party which deposits an instrument of acceptance after the date on which two thirds of the Contracting Parties have deposited an instrument of acceptance, the amendment shall enter into force on the first day of the fourth month following the date of the deposit of its instrument of acceptance.

Article 11

1. This Convention shall continue in force for an indefinite period.

2. Any Contracting Party may denounce this Convention after a period of five years from the date on which it entered into force for that party by giving written notice thereof to the Depositary. Denunciation shall take effect four months after the day on which notice thereof is received by the Depositary.

Article 12

1. The Depositary shall inform all States that have signed and acceded to this Convention as soon as possible of:

a. signatures to the Convention;

b. deposits of instruments of ratification of this Convention;
c. deposits of instruments of accession to this Convention;
d. the date of entry into force of this Convention;
e. notifications of denunciation of this Convention.

2. When this Convention has entered into force, the Depositary shall have it registered with the Secretariat of the United Nations in accordance with Article 102 of the Charter.

In witness whereof, the undersigned, being duly authorized to that effect, have signed this Convention.

Done at Ramsar this 2nd day of February 1971, in a single original in the English, French, German and Russian languages, all texts being equally authentic which shall be deposited with the Depositary which shall send true copies thereof to all Contracting Parties.

Convention for the Protection of the World Cultural and Natural Heritage

Adopted on 23 November 1972 at Paris. Entered into force on 17 December 1975. Source: 1037 *UNTS* 151. Number of parties: 177. Further information: Secretariat, Paris, France, http://whc.unesco.org

The General Conference of the United Nations Educational, Scientific and Cultural Organization meeting in Paris from 17 October to 21 November 1972, at its seventeenth session,

Noting that the cultural heritage and the natural heritage are increasingly threatened with destruction not only by the traditional causes of decay, but also by changing social and economic conditions which aggravate the situation with even more formidable phenomena of damage or destruction,

Considering that deterioration or disappearance of any item of the cultural or natural heritage constitutes a harmful impoverishment of the heritage of all the nations of the world,

Considering that protection of this heritage at the national level often remains incomplete because of the scale of the resources which it requires and of the insufficient economic, scientific, and technological resources of the country where the property to be protected is situated,

Recalling that the Constitution of the Organization provides that it will maintain, increase, and diffuse knowledge, by assuring the conservation and protection of the world's heritage, and recommending to the nations concerned the necessary international conventions,

Considering that the existing international conventions, recommendations and resolutions concerning cultural and natural property demonstrate the importance, for all the peoples of the world, of safeguarding this unique and irreplaceable property, to whatever people it may belong,

Considering that parts of the cultural or natural heritage are of outstanding interest and therefore need to be preserved as part of the world heritage of mankind as a whole,

Considering that, in view of the magnitude and gravity of the new dangers threatening them, it is incumbent on the international community as a whole to participate in the protection of the cultural and natural heritage of outstanding universal value, by the granting of collective assistance which, although not taking the place of action by the State concerned, will serve as an efficient complement thereto,

Considering that it is essential for this purpose to adopt new provisions in the form of a convention establishing an effective system of collective protection of the cultural and natural heritage of outstanding universal value, organized on a permanent basis and in accordance with modern scientific methods,

Having decided, at its sixteenth session, that this question should be made the subject of an international convention,

Adopts this sixteenth day of November 1972 this Convention.

I. Definition of the cultural and natural heritage

Article 1

For the purposes of this Convention, the following shall be considered as 'cultural heritage':

monuments: architectural works, works of monumental sculpture and painting, elements or structures of an archaeological nature, inscriptions, cave dwellings and combinations of features, which are of outstanding universal value from the point of view of history, art or science;

groups of buildings: groups of separate or connected buildings which, because of their architecture, their homogeneity or their place in the landscape, are of outstanding universal value from the point of view of history, art or science;

sites: works of man or the combined works of nature and man, and areas including archaeological sites which are of outstanding universal value from the historical, aesthetic, ethnological or anthropological point of view.

Article 2

For the purposes of this Convention, the following shall be considered as 'natural heritage':

natural features consisting of physical and biological formations or groups of such formations, which are of outstanding universal value from the aesthetic or scientific point of view;

geological and physiographical formations and precisely delineated areas which constitute the habitat of threatened species of animals and plants of outstanding universal value from the point of view of science or conservation;

natural sites or precisely delineated natural areas of outstanding universal value from the point of view of science, conservation or natural beauty.

Article 3

It is for each State Party to this Convention to identify and delineate the different properties situated on its territory mentioned in Articles 1 and 2 above.

II. National protection and international protection of the cultural and natural heritage

Article 4

Each State Party to this Convention recognizes that the duty of ensuring the identification, protection, conservation, presentation and transmission to future generations of the cultural and natural heritage referred to in Articles 1 and 2 and situated on its territory, belongs primarily to that State. It will do all it can to this end, to the utmost of its own resources and, where appropriate, with any international assistance and co-operation, in particular, financial, artistic, scientific and technical, which it may be able to obtain.

Article 5

To ensure that effective and active measures are taken for the protection, conservation and presentation of the cultural and natural heritage situated on its territory, each State Party to this Convention shall endeavor, in so far as possible, and as appropriate for each country:

a. to adopt a general policy which aims to give the cultural and natural heritage a function in the life of the community and to integrate the protection of that heritage into comprehensive planning programmes;

b. to set up within its territories, where such services do not exist, one or more services for the protection, conservation and presentation of the cultural and natural heritage with an appropriate staff and possessing the means to discharge their functions;

c. to develop scientific and technical studies and research and to work out such operating methods as will make the State capable of counteracting the dangers that threaten its cultural or natural heritage;

d. to take the appropriate legal, scientific, technical, administrative and financial measures necessary for the identification, protection, conservation, presentation and rehabilitation of this heritage; and

e. to foster the establishment or development of national or regional centres for training in the protection, conservation and presentation of the cultural and natural heritage and to encourage scientific research in this field.

Article 6

1. Whilst fully respecting the sovereignty of the States on whose territory the cultural and natural heritage mentioned in Articles 1 and 2 is situated, and without prejudice to property right provided by national legislation, the States Parties to this Convention recognize that such heritage constitutes a world heritage for whose protection it is the duty of the international community as a whole to co-operate.

2. The States Parties undertake, in accordance with the provisions of this Convention, to give their help in the identification, protection, conservation and presentation of the cultural and natural heritage referred to in paragraphs 2 and 4 of Article 11 if the States on whose territory it is situated so request.

3. Each State Party to this Convention undertakes not to take any deliberate measures which might damage directly or indirectly the cultural and natural heritage referred to in Articles 1 and 2 situated on the territory of other States Parties to this Convention.

Article 7

For the purpose of this Convention, international protection of the world cultural and natural heritage shall be understood to mean the establishment of a system of international co-operation and assistance designed to support States Parties to the Convention in their efforts to conserve and identify that heritage.

III. Intergovernmental Committee for the Protection of the World Cultural and Natural Heritage

Article 8

1. An Intergovernmental Committee for the Protection of the Cultural and Natural Heritage of Outstanding Universal Value, called 'the World Heritage Committee', is hereby established within the United Nations Educational, Scientific and Cultural Organization. It shall be composed of 15 States Parties to the Convention, elected by States Parties to the Convention meeting in general assembly during the ordinary session of the General Conference of the United Nations Educational, Scientific and Cultural Organization. The number of States members of the Committee shall be increased to 21 as from the date of the ordinary session of the General Conference following the entry into force of this Convention for at least 40 States.

2. Election of members of the Committee shall ensure an equitable representation of the different regions and cultures of the world.

3. A representative of the International Centre for the Study of the Preservation and Restoration of Cultural Property (Rome Centre), a representative of the International Council of Monuments and Sites (ICOMOS) and a representative of the International Union for Conservation of Nature and Natural Resources (IUCN), to whom may be added, at the request of States Parties to the Convention meeting in general assembly during the ordinary sessions of the General Conference of the United Nations Educational, Scientific and Cultural Organization, representatives

of other intergovernmental or non-governmental organizations, with similar objectives, may attend the meetings of the Committee in an advisory capacity.

Article 9

1. The term of office of States members of the World Heritage Committee shall extend from the end of the ordinary session of the General Conference during which they are elected until the end of its third subsequent ordinary session.

2. The term of office of one-third of the members designated at the time of the first election shall, however, cease at the end of the first ordinary session of the General Conference following that at which they were elected; and the term of office of a further third of the members designated at the same time shall cease at the end of the second ordinary session of the General Conference following that at which they were elected. The names of these members shall be chosen by lot by the President of the General Conference of the United Nations Educational, Scientific and Cultural Organization after the first election.

3. States members of the Committee shall choose as their representatives persons qualified in the field of the cultural or natural heritage.

Article 10

1. The World Heritage Committee shall adopt its Rules of Procedure.

2. The Committee may at any time invite public or private organizations or individuals to participate in its meetings for consultation on particular problems.

3. The Committee may create such consultative bodies as it deems necessary for the performance of its functions.

Article 11

1. Every State Party to this Convention shall, in so far as possible, submit to the World Heritage Committee an inventory of property forming part of the cultural and natural heritage, situated in its territory and suitable for inclusion in the list provided for in paragraph 2 of this Article. This inventory, which shall not be considered exhaustive, shall include documentation about the location of the property in question and its significance.

2. On the basis of the inventories submitted by States in accordance with paragraph 1, the Committee shall establish, keep up to date and publish, under the title of 'World Heritage List,' a list of properties forming part of the cultural heritage and natural heritage, as defined in Articles 1 and 2 of this Convention, which it considers as having outstanding universal value in terms of such criteria as it shall have established. An updated list shall be distributed at least every two years.

3. The inclusion of a property in the World Heritage List requires the consent of the State concerned. The inclusion of a property situated in a territory, sovereignty or jurisdiction over which is claimed by more than one State shall in no way prejudice the rights of the parties to the dispute.

4. The Committee shall establish, keep up to date and publish, whenever circumstances shall so require, under the title of 'List of World Heritage in Danger', a list of the property appearing in the World Heritage List for the conservation of which major operations are necessary and for which assistance has been requested under this Convention. This list shall contain an estimate of the cost of such operations. The list may include only such property forming part of the cultural and natural heritage as is threatened by serious and specific dangers, such as the threat of disappearance caused by accelerated deterioration, large-scale public or private projects or rapid urban or tourist development projects; destruction caused by changes in the use or ownership of the land; major alterations due to unknown causes; abandonment for any reason whatsoever; the outbreak or the threat of an armed conflict; calamities and cataclysms; serious fires, earthquakes, landslides; volcanic eruptions; changes in water level, floods and tidal waves. The Committee may at any time, in case of urgent need, make a new entry in the List of World Heritage in Danger and publicize such entry immediately.

5. The Committee shall define the criteria on the basis of which a property belonging to the cultural or natural heritage may be included in either of the lists mentioned in paragraphs 2 and 4 of this article.

6. Before refusing a request for inclusion in one of the two lists mentioned in paragraphs 2 and 4 of this article, the Committee shall consult the State Party in whose territory the cultural or natural property in question is situated.

7. The Committee shall, with the agreement of the States concerned, co-ordinate and encourage the studies and research needed for the drawing up of the lists referred to in paragraphs 2 and 4 of this article.

Article 12

The fact that a property belonging to the cultural or natural heritage has not been included in either of the two lists mentioned in paragraphs 2 and 4 of Article 11 shall in no way be construed to mean that it does not have an outstanding universal value for purposes other than those resulting from inclusion in these lists.

Article 13

1. The World Heritage Committee shall receive and study requests for international assistance formulated by States Parties to this Convention with respect to property forming part of the cultural or natural heritage, situated in their territories, and included or potentially suitable for inclusion in the lists mentioned referred to in paragraphs 2 and 4 of Article 11. The purpose of such requests may be to secure the protection, conservation, presentation or rehabilitation of such property.

2. Requests for international assistance under paragraph 1 of this article may also be concerned with identification of cultural or natural property defined in Articles 1 and 2, when preliminary investigations have shown that further inquiries would be justified.

3. The Committee shall decide on the action to be taken with regard to these requests, determine where appropriate, the nature and extent of its assistance, and authorize the conclusion, on its behalf, of the necessary arrangements with the government concerned.

4. The Committee shall determine an order of priorities for its operations. It shall in so doing bear in mind the respective importance for the world cultural and natural heritage of the property requiring protection, the need to give international assistance to the property most representative of a natural environment or of the genius and the history of the peoples of the world, the urgency of the work to be done, the resources available to the States on whose territory the threatened property is situated and in particular the extent to which they are able to safeguard such property by their own means.

5. The Committee shall draw up, keep up to date and publicize a list of property for which international assistance has been granted.

6. The Committee shall decide on the use of the resources of the Fund established under Article 15 of this Convention. It shall seek ways of increasing these resources and shall take all useful steps to this end.

7. The Committee shall co-operate with international and national governmental and non-governmental organizations having objectives similar to those of this Convention. For the implementation of its programmes and projects, the Committee may call on such organizations, particularly the International Centre for the Study of the Preservation and Restoration of cultural Property (the Rome Centre), the International Council of Monuments and Sites (ICOMOS) and the International Union for Conservation of Nature and Natural Resources (IUCN), as well as on public and private bodies and individuals.

8. Decisions of the Committee shall be taken by a majority of two-thirds of its members present and voting. A majority of the members of the Committee shall constitute a quorum.

Article 14

1. The World Heritage Committee shall be assisted by a Secretariat appointed by the Director-General of the United Nations Educational, Scientific and Cultural Organization.

2. The Director-General of the United Nations Educational, Scientific and Cultural Organization, utilizing to the fullest extent possible the services of the International Centre for the Study of the Preservation and the Restoration of Cultural Property (the Rome Centre), the International Council of Monuments and Sites (ICOMOS) and the International Union for Conservation of Nature and Natural Resources (IUCN) in their respective areas of competence and capability, shall prepare the Committee's documentation and the agenda of its meetings and shall have the responsibility for the implementation of its decisions.

IV. Fund for the Protection of the World Cultural and Natural Heritage

Article 15

1. A Fund for the Protection of the World Cultural and Natural Heritage of Outstanding Universal Value, called 'the World Heritage Fund', is hereby established.

2. The Fund shall constitute a trust fund, in conformity with the provisions of the Financial Regulations of the United Nations Educational, Scientific and Cultural Organization.

3. The resources of the Fund shall consist of:

a. compulsory and voluntary contributions made by States Parties to this Convention,
b. Contributions, gifts or bequests which may be made by:
   i. other States;
   ii. the United Nations Educational, Scientific and Cultural Organization, other organizations of the United Nations system, particularly the United Nations Development Programme or other intergovernmental organizations;
   iii. public or private bodies or individuals;
c. any interest due on the resources of the Fund;
d. funds raised by collections and receipts from events organized for the benefit of the fund; and
e. all other resources authorized by the Fund's regulations, as drawn up by the World Heritage Committee.

4. Contributions to the Fund and other forms of assistance made available to the Committee may be used only for such purposes as the Committee shall define. The Committee may accept contributions to be used only for a certain programme or project, provided that the Committee shall have decided on the implementation of such programme or project. No political conditions may be attached to contributions made to the Fund.

Article 16

1. Without prejudice to any supplementary voluntary contribution, the States Parties to this Convention undertake to pay regularly, every two years, to the World Heritage Fund, contributions, the amount of which, in the form of a uniform percentage applicable to all States, shall be determined by the General Assembly of States Parties to the Convention, meeting during the sessions of the General Conference of the United Nations Educational, Scientific and Cultural Organization. This decision of the General Assembly requires the majority of the States Parties present and voting, which have not made the declaration referred to in paragraph 2 of this Article. In no case shall the compulsory contribution of States Parties to the Convention exceed 1% of the contribution to the regular budget of the United Nations Educational, Scientific and Cultural Organization.

2. However, each State referred to in Article 31 or in Article 32 of this Convention may declare, at the time of the deposit of its instrument of ratification, acceptance

or accession, that it shall not be bound by the provisions of paragraph 1 of this Article.

3. A State Party to the Convention which has made the declaration referred to in paragraph 2 of this Article may at any time withdraw the said declaration by notifying the Director-General of the United Nations Educational, Scientific and Cultural Organization. However, the withdrawal of the declaration shall not take effect in regard to the compulsory contribution due by the State until the date of the subsequent General Assembly of States parties to the Convention.

4. In order that the Committee may be able to plan its operations effectively, the contributions of States Parties to this Convention which have made the declaration referred to in paragraph 2 of this Article, shall be paid on a regular basis, at least every two years, and should not be less than the contributions which they should have paid if they had been bound by the provisions of paragraph 1 of this Article.

5. Any State Party to the Convention which is in arrears with the payment of its compulsory or voluntary contribution for the current year and the calendar year immediately preceding it shall not be eligible as a Member of the World Heritage Committee, although this provision shall not apply to the first election.

The terms of office of any such State which is already a member of the Committee shall terminate at the time of the elections provided for in Article 8, paragraph 1 of this Convention.

Article 17

The States Parties to this Convention shall consider or encourage the establishment of national public and private foundations or associations whose purpose is to invite donations for the protection of the cultural and natural heritage as defined in Articles 1 and 2 of this Convention.

Article 18

The States Parties to this Convention shall give their assistance to international fund-raising campaigns organized for the World Heritage Fund under the auspices of the United Nations Educational, Scientific and Cultural Organization. They shall facilitate collections made by the bodies mentioned in paragraph 3 of Article 15 for this purpose.

V. Conditions and arrangements for international assistance

Article 19

Any State Party to this Convention may request international assistance for property forming part of the cultural or natural heritage of outstanding universal value situated within its territory. It shall submit with its request such information and documentation provided for in Article 21 as it has in its possession and as will enable the Committee to come to a decision.

Article 20

Subject to the provisions of paragraph 2 of Article 13, sub-paragraph (c) of Article 22 and Article 23, international assistance provided for by this Convention may be granted only to property forming part of the cultural and natural heritage which the World Heritage Committee has decided, or may decide, to enter in one of the lists mentioned in paragraphs 2 and 4 of Article 11.

Article 21

1. The World Heritage Committee shall define the procedure by which requests to it for international assistance shall be considered and shall specify the content of the request, which should define the operation contemplated, the work that is necessary, the expected cost thereof, the degree of urgency and the reasons why the resources of the State requesting assistance do not allow it to meet all the expenses. Such requests must be supported by experts' reports whenever possible.

2. Requests based upon disasters or natural calamities should, by reasons of the urgent work which they may involve, be given immediate, priority consideration by the Committee, which should have a reserve fund at its disposal against such contingencies.

3. Before coming to a decision, the Committee shall carry out such studies and consultations as it deems necessary.

Article 22

Assistance granted by the World Heritage Committee may take the following forms:

a. studies concerning the artistic, scientific and technical problems raised by the protection, conservation, presentation and rehabilitation of the cultural and natural heritage, as defined in paragraphs 2 and 4 of Article 11 of this Convention;

b. provisions of experts, technicians and skilled labour to ensure that the approved work is correctly carried out;

c. training of staff and specialists at all levels in the field of identification, protection, conservation, presentation and rehabilitation of the cultural and natural heritage;

d. supply of equipment which the State concerned does not possess or is not in a position to acquire;

e. low-interest or interest-free loans which might be repayable on a long-term basis;

f. the granting, in exceptional cases and for special reasons, of non-repayable subsidies.

Article 23

The World Heritage Committee may also provide international assistance to national or regional centres for the training of staff and specialists at all levels in the field of identification, protection, conservation, presentation and rehabilitation of the cultural and natural heritage.

Article 24

International assistance on a large scale shall be preceded by detailed scientific, economic and technical studies. These studies shall draw upon the most advanced techniques for the protection, conservation, presentation and rehabilitation of the natural and cultural heritage and shall be consistent with the objectives of this Convention. The studies shall also seek means of making rational use of the resources available in the State concerned.

Article 25

As a general rule, only part of the cost of work necessary shall be borne by the international community. The contribution of the State benefiting from international assistance shall constitute a substantial share of the resources devoted to each programme or project, unless its resources do not permit this.

Article 26

The World Heritage Committee and the recipient State shall define in the agreement they conclude the conditions in which a programme or project for which international assistance under the terms of this Convention is provided, shall be carried out. It shall be the responsibility of the State receiving such international assistance to continue to protect, conserve and present the property so safeguarded, in observance of the conditions laid down by the agreement.

VI. Educational programmes

Article 27

1. The States Parties to this Convention shall endeavor by all appropriate means, and in particular by educational and information programmes, to strengthen appreciation and respect by their peoples of the cultural and natural heritage defined in Articles 1 and 2 of the Convention.

2. They shall undertake to keep the public broadly informed of the dangers threatening this heritage and of the activities carried on in pursuance of this Convention.

Article 28

States Parties to this Convention which receive international assistance under the Convention shall take appropriate measures to make known the importance of the property for which assistance has been received and the role played by such assistance.

VII. Reports

Article 29

1. The States Parties to this Convention shall, in the reports which they submit to the General Conference of the United Nations Educational, Scientific and Cultural Organization on dates and in a manner to be determined by it, give information on the legislative and administrative provisions which they have adopted and other action which they have taken for the application of this Convention, together with details of the experience acquired in this field.

2. These reports shall be brought to the attention of the World Heritage Committee.

3. The Committee shall submit a report on its activities at each of the ordinary sessions of the General Conference of the United Nations Educational, Scientific and Cultural Organization.

VIII. Final clauses

Article 30

This Convention is drawn up in Arabic, English, French, Russian and Spanish, the five texts being equally authoritative.

Article 31

1. This Convention shall be subject to ratification or acceptance by States members of the United Nations Educational, Scientific and Cultural Organization in accordance with their respective constitutional procedures.

2. The instruments of ratification or acceptance shall be deposited with the Director-General of the United Nations Educational, Scientific and Cultural Organization.

Article 32

1. This Convention shall be open to accession by all States not members of the United Nations Educational, Scientific and Cultural Organization which are invited by the General Conference of the Organization to accede to it.

2. Accession shall be effected by the deposit of an instrument of accession with the Director-General of the United Nations Educational, Scientific and Cultural Organization.

Article 33

This Convention shall enter into force three months after the date of the deposit of the twentieth instrument of ratification, acceptance or accession, but only with respect to those States which have deposited their respective instruments of ratification, acceptance or accession on or before that date. It shall enter into force with respect to any other State three months after the deposit of its instrument of ratification, acceptance or accession.

Article 34

The following provisions shall apply to those States Parties to this Convention which have a federal or non-unitary constitutional system:

a. with regard to the provisions of this Convention, the implementation of which comes under the legal jurisdiction of the federal or central legislative power, the obligations of the federal or central government shall be the same as for those States parties which are not federal States;

b. with regard to the provisions of this Convention, the implementation of which comes under the legal jurisdiction of individual constituent States, countries, provinces or cantons that are not obliged by the constitutional system of the federation to take legislative measures, the federal government shall inform the competent authorities of such States, countries, provinces or cantons of the said provisions, with its recommendation for their adoption.

Article 35

1. Each State Party to this Convention may denounce the Convention.

2. The denunciation shall be notified by an instrument in writing, deposited with the Director-General of the United Nations Educational, Scientific and Cultural Organization.

3. The denunciation shall take effect twelve months after the receipt of the instrument of denunciation. It shall not affect the financial obligations of the denouncing State until the date on which the withdrawal takes effect.

Article 36

The Director-General of the United Nations Educational, Scientific and Cultural Organization shall inform the States members of the Organization, the States not members of the Organization which are referred to in Article 32, as well as the United Nations, of the deposit of all the instruments of ratification, acceptance, or accession provided for in Articles 31 and 32, and of the denunciations provided for in Article 35.

Article 37

1. This Convention may be revised by the General Conference of the United Nations Educational, Scientific and Cultural Organization. Any such revision shall, however, bind only the States which shall become Parties to the revising convention.

2. If the General Conference should adopt a new convention revising this Convention in whole or in part, then, unless the new convention otherwise provides, this Convention shall cease to be open to ratification, acceptance or accession, as from the date on which the new revising convention enters into force.

Article 38

In conformity with Article 102 of the Charter of the United Nations, this Convention shall be registered with the Secretariat of the United Nations at the request of the Director-General of the United Nations Educational, Scientific and Cultural Organization.

Done in Paris, this twenty-third day of November 1972, in two authentic copies bearing the signature of the President of the seventeenth session of the General Conference and of the Director-General of the United Nations Educational, Scientific and Cultural Organization, which shall be deposited in the archives of the United Nations Educational, Scientific and Cultural Organization, and certified true copies of which shall be delivered to all the States referred to in Articles 31 and 32 as well as to the United Nations.

Desertification

United Nations Convention to Combat Desertification in Those Countries Experiencing Serious Drought and/or Desertification, Particularly in Africa

Adopted on 17 June 1994 at Paris. Entered into force on 26 December 1996. Source: 1954 *UNTS* 3. Number of parties: 191. Further information: Secretariat, Bonn, Germany, http://www.unccd.int

The Parties to this Convention,

Affirming that human beings in affected or threatened areas are at the centre of concerns to combat desertification and mitigate the effects of drought,

Reflecting the urgent concern of the international community, including States and international organizations, about the adverse impacts of desertification and drought,

Aware that arid, semi-arid and dry sub-humid areas together account for a significant proportion of the Earth's land area and are the habitat and source of livelihood for a large segment of its population,

Acknowledging that desertification and drought are problems of global dimension in that they affect all regions of the world and that joint action of the international community is needed to combat desertification and/or mitigate the effects of drought,

Noting the high concentration of developing countries, notably the least developed countries, among those experiencing serious drought and/or desertification, and the particularly tragic consequences of these phenomena in Africa,

Noting also that desertification is caused by complex interactions among physical, biological, political, social, cultural and economic factors,

Considering the impact of trade and relevant aspects of international economic relations on the ability of affected countries to combat desertification adequately,

Conscious that sustainable economic growth, social development and poverty eradication are priorities of affected developing countries, particularly in Africa, and are essential to meeting sustainability objectives,

Mindful that desertification and drought affect sustainable development through their interrelationships with important social problems such as poverty, poor health and nutrition, lack of food security, and those arising from migration, displacement of persons and demographic dynamics,

Appreciating the significance of the past efforts and experience of States and international organizations in combating desertification and mitigating the effects of drought, particularly in implementing the Plan of Action to Combat Desertification which was adopted at the United Nations Conference on Desertification in 1977,

Realizing that, despite efforts in the past, progress in combating desertification and mitigating the effects of drought has not met expectations and that a new and more effective approach is needed at all levels within the framework of sustainable development,

Recognizing the validity and relevance of decisions adopted at the United Nations Conference on Environment and Development, particularly of Agenda 21 and its chapter 12, which provide a basis for combating desertification,

Reaffirming in this light the commitments of developed countries as contained in paragraph 13 of chapter 33 of Agenda 21,

Recalling General Assembly resolution 47/188, particularly the priority in it prescribed for Africa, and all other relevant United Nations resolutions, decisions and programmes on desertification and drought, as well as relevant declarations by African countries and those from other regions,

Reaffirming the Rio Declaration on Environment and Development which states, in its Principle 2, that States have, in accordance with the Charter of the United Nations and the principles of international law, the sovereign right to exploit their own resources pursuant to their own environmental and developmental policies, and the responsibility to ensure that activities within their jurisdiction or control do not cause damage to the environment of other States or of areas beyond the limits of national jurisdiction,

Recognizing that national Governments play a critical role in combating desertification and mitigating the effects of drought and that progress in that respect depends on local implementation of action programmes in affected areas,

Recognizing also the importance and necessity of international cooperation and partnership in combating desertification and mitigating the effects of drought,

Recognizing further the importance of the provision to affected developing countries, particularly in Africa, of effective means, *inter alia* substantial financial resources, including new and additional funding, and access to technology, without which it will be difficult for them to implement fully their commitments under this Convention,

Expressing concern over the impact of desertification and drought on affected countries in Central Asia and the Transcaucasus,

Stressing the important role played by women in regions affected by desertification and/or drought, particularly in rural areas of developing countries, and the importance of ensuring the full participation of both men and women at all levels in programmes to combat desertification and mitigate the effects of drought,

Emphasizing the special role of non-governmental organizations and other major groups in programmes to combat desertification and mitigate the effects of drought,

Bearing in mind the relationship between desertification and other environmental problems of global dimension facing the international and national communities,

Bearing also in mind the contribution that combating desertification can make to achieving the objectives of the United Nations Framework Convention on Climate Change, the Convention on Biological Diversity and other related environmental conventions,

Believing that strategies to combat desertification and mitigate the effects of drought will be most effective if they are based on sound systematic observation and rigorous scientific knowledge and if they are continuously re-evaluated,

Recognizing the urgent need to improve the effectiveness and coordination of international cooperation to facilitate the implementation of national plans and priorities,

Determined to take appropriate action in combating desertification and mitigating the effects of drought for the benefit of present and future generations,

Have agreed as follows:

Part I: Introduction

Article 1: Use of terms

For the purposes of this Convention:

(a) 'desertification' means land degradation in arid, semi-arid and dry sub-humid areas resulting from various factors, including climatic variations and human activities;

(b) 'combating desertification' includes activities which are part of the integrated development of land in arid, semi-arid and dry sub-humid areas for sustainable development which are aimed at:

i) prevention and/or reduction of land degradation;
ii) rehabilitation of partly degraded land; and
iii) reclamation of desertified land;

(c) 'drought' means the naturally occurring phenomenon that exists when precipitation has been significantly below normal recorded levels, causing serious hydrological imbalances that adversely affect land resource production systems;

(d) 'mitigating the effects of drought' means activities related to the prediction of drought and intended to reduce the vulnerability of society and natural systems to drought as it relates to combating desertification;

(e) 'land' means the terrestrial bio-productive system that comprises soil, vegetation, other biota, and the ecological and hydrological processes that operate within the system;

(f) 'land degradation' means reduction or loss, in arid, semi-arid and dry sub-humid areas, of the biological or economic productivity and complexity of rainfed cropland, irrigated cropland, or range, pasture, forest and woodlands resulting from land uses or from a process or combination of processes, including processes arising from human activities and habitation patterns, such as:

i) soil erosion caused by wind and/or water;
ii) deterioration of the physical, chemical and biological or economic properties of soil; and
iii) long-term loss of natural vegetation;

(g) 'arid, semi-arid and dry sub-humid areas' means areas, other than polar and sub-polar regions, in which the ratio of annual precipitation to potential evapotranspiration falls within the range from 0.05 to 0.65;

(h) 'affected areas' means arid, semi-arid and/or dry sub-humid areas affected or threatened by desertification;

(i) 'affected countries' means countries whose lands include, in whole or in part, affected areas;

(j) 'regional economic integration organization' means an organization constituted by sovereign States of a given region which has competence in respect of matters governed by this Convention and has been duly authorized, in accordance with its internal procedures, to sign, ratify, accept, approve or accede to this Convention;

(k) 'developed country Parties' means developed country Parties and regional economic integration organizations constituted by developed countries.

Article 2: Objective

1. The objective of this Convention is to combat desertification and mitigate the effects of drought in countries experiencing serious drought and/or desertification, particularly in Africa, through effective action at all levels, supported by international cooperation and partnership arrangements, in the framework of an integrated approach which is consistent with Agenda 21, with a view to contributing to the achievement of sustainable development in affected areas.

2. Achieving this objective will involve long-term integrated strategies that focus simultaneously, in affected areas, on improved productivity of land, and the rehabilitation, conservation and sustainable management of land and water

resources, leading to improved living conditions, in particular at the community level.

Article 3: Principles

In order to achieve the objective of this Convention and to implement its provisions, the Parties shall be guided, *inter alia*, by the following:

(a) the Parties should ensure that decisions on the design and implementation of programmes to combat desertification and/or mitigate the effects of drought are taken with the participation of populations and local communities and that an enabling environment is created at higher levels to facilitate action at national and local levels;

(b) the Parties should, in a spirit of international solidarity and partnership, improve cooperation and coordination at subregional, regional and international levels, and better focus financial, human, organizational and technical resources where they are needed;

(c) the Parties should develop, in a spirit of partnership, cooperation among all levels of government, communities, non-governmental organizations and landholders to establish a better understanding of the nature and value of land and scarce water resources in affected areas and to work towards their sustainable use; and

(d) the Parties should take into full consideration the special needs and circumstances of affected developing country Parties, particularly the least developed among them.

Part II: General provisions

Article 4: General obligations

1. The Parties shall implement their obligations under this Convention, individually or jointly, either through existing or prospective bilateral and multilateral arrangements or a combination thereof, as appropriate, emphasizing the need to coordinate efforts and develop a coherent long-term strategy at all levels.

2. In pursuing the objective of this Convention, the Parties shall:

(a) adopt an integrated approach addressing the physical, biological and socio-economic aspects of the processes of desertification and drought;

(b) give due attention, within the relevant international and regional bodies, to the situation of affected developing country Parties with regard to international trade, marketing arrangements and debt with a view to establishing an enabling international economic environment conducive to the promotion of sustainable development;

(c) integrate strategies for poverty eradication into efforts to combat desertification and mitigate the effects of drought;

(d) promote cooperation among affected country Parties in the fields of environmental protection and the conservation of land and water resources, as they relate to desertification and drought;
(e) strengthen subregional, regional and international cooperation;
(f) cooperate within relevant intergovernmental organizations;
(g) determine institutional mechanisms, if appropriate, keeping in mind the need to avoid duplication; and
(h) promote the use of existing bilateral and multilateral financial mechanisms and arrangements that mobilize and channel substantial financial resources to affected developing country Parties in combating desertification and mitigating the effects of drought.

3. Affected developing country Parties are eligible for assistance in the implementation of the Convention.

Article 5: Obligations of affected country Parties

In addition to their obligations pursuant to article 4, affected country Parties undertake to:

(a) give due priority to combating desertification and mitigating the effects of drought, and allocate adequate resources in accordance with their circumstances and capabilities;

(b) establish strategies and priorities, within the framework of sustainable development plans and/or policies, to combat desertification and mitigate the effects of drought;

(c) address the underlying causes of desertification and pay special attention to the socio-economic factors contributing to desertification processes;

(d) promote awareness and facilitate the participation of local populations, particularly women and youth, with the support of non-governmental organizations, in efforts to combat desertification and mitigate the effects of drought; and

(e) provide an enabling environment by strengthening, as appropriate, relevant existing legislation and, where they do not exist, enacting new laws and establishing long-term policies and action programmes.

Article 6: Obligations of developed country Parties

In addition to their general obligations pursuant to article 4, developed country Parties undertake to:

(a) actively support, as agreed, individually or jointly, the efforts of affected developing country Parties, particularly those in Africa, and the least developed countries, to combat desertification and mitigate the effects of drought;

(b) provide substantial financial resources and other forms of support to assist affected developing country Parties, particularly those in Africa, effectively to develop and implement their own long-term plans and strategies to combat desertification and mitigate the effects of drought;

(c) promote the mobilization of new and additional funding pursuant to article 20, paragraph 2 (b);

(d) encourage the mobilization of funding from the private sector and other non-governmental sources; and

(e) promote and facilitate access by affected country Parties, particularly affected developing country Parties, to appropriate technology, knowledge and know-how.

Article 7: Priority for Atrica

In implementing this Convention, the Parties shall give priority to affected African country Parties, in the light of the particular situation prevailing in that region, while not neglecting affected developing country Parties in other regions.

Article 8: Relationship with other conventions

1. The Parties shall encourage the coordination of activities carried out under this Convention and, if they are Parties to them, under other relevant international agreements, particularly the United Nations Framework Convention on Climate Change and the Convention on Biological Diversity, in order to derive maximum benefit from activities under each agreement while avoiding duplication of effort. The Parties shall encourage the conduct of joint programmes, particularly in the fields of research, training, systematic observation and information collection and exchange, to the extent that such activities may contribute to achieving the objectives of the agreements concerned.

2. The provisions of this Convention shall not affect the rights and obligations of any Party deriving from a bilateral, regional or international agreement into which it has entered prior to the entry into force of this Convention for it.

Part III: Action programmes, scientific and technical cooperation and supporting measures

Section 1: Action programmes

Article 9: Basic approach

1. In carrying out their obligations pursuant to article 5, affected developing country Parties and any other affected country Party in the framework of its regional implementation annex or, otherwise, that has notified the Permanent Secretariat in writing of its intention to prepare a national action programme, shall, as appropriate, prepare, make public and implement national action programmes, utilizing and building, to the extent possible, on existing relevant successful plans and programmes, and subregional and regional action programmes, as the central element of the strategy to combat desertification and mitigate the effects of drought. Such programmes shall be updated through a continuing participatory process on the basis of lessons from field action, as well as the results of research. The preparation of national action programmes shall be closely interlinked with other efforts to formulate national policies for sustainable development.

2. In the provision by developed country Parties of different forms of assistance under the terms of article 6, priority shall be given to supporting, as agreed, national, subregional and regional action programmes of affected developing country Parties, particularly those in Africa, either directly or through relevant multilateral organizations or both.

3. The Parties shall encourage organs, funds and programmes of the United Nations system and other relevant intergovernmental organizations, academic institutions, the scientific community and non-governmental organizations in a position to cooperate, in accordance with their mandates and capabilities, to support the elaboration, implementation and follow-up of action programmes.

Article 10: National action programmes

1. The purpose of national action programmes is to identify the factors contributing to desertification and practical measures necessary to combat desertification and mitigate the effects of drought.

2. National action programmes shall specify the respective roles of government, local communities and land users and the resources available and needed. They shall, *inter alia*:

(a) incorporate long-term strategies to combat desertification and mitigate the effects of drought, emphasize implementation and be integrated with national policies for sustainable development;
(b) allow for modifications to be made in response to changing circumstances and be sufficiently flexible at the local level to cope with different socio-economic, biological and geo-physical conditions;
(c) give particular attention to the implementation of preventive measures for lands that are not yet degraded or which are only slightly degraded;
(d) enhance national climatological, meteorological and hydrological capabilities and the means to provide for drought early warning;
(e) promote policies and strengthen institutional frameworks which develop cooperation and coordination, in a spirit of partnership, between the donor community, governments at all levels, local populations and community groups, and facilitate access by local populations to appropriate information and technology;
(f) provide for effective participation at the local, national and regional levels of non-governmental organizations and local populations, both women and men, particularly resource users, including farmers and pastoralists and their representative organizations, in policy planning, decision-making, and implementation and review of national action programmes; and
(g) require regular review of, and progress reports on, their implementation.

3. National action programmes may include, *inter alia*, some or all of the following measures to prepare for and mitigate the effects of drought:

(a) establishment and/or strengthening, as appropriate, of early warning systems, including local and national facilities and joint systems at the subregional and regional levels, and mechanisms for assisting environmentally displaced persons;

(b) strengthening of drought preparedness and management, including drought contingency plans at the local, national, subregional and regional levels, which take into consideration seasonal to interannual climate predictions;

(c) establishment and/or strengthening, as appropriate, of food security systems, including storage and marketing facilities, particularly in rural areas;

(d) establishment of alternative livelihood projects that could provide incomes in drought prone areas; and

(e) development of sustainable irrigation programmes for both crops and livestock.

4. Taking into account the circumstances and requirements specific to each affected country Party, national action programmes include, as appropriate, *inter alia*, measures in some or all of the following priority fields as they relate to combating desertification and mitigating the effects of drought in affected areas and to their populations: promotion of alternative livelihoods and improvement of national economic environments with a view to strengthening programmes aimed at the eradication of poverty and at ensuring food security; demographic dynamics; sustainable management of natural resources; sustainable agricultural practices; development and efficient use of various energy sources; institutional and legal frameworks; strengthening of capabilities for assessment and systematic observation, including hydrological and meteorological services, and capacity building, education and public awareness.

Article 11: Subregional and regional action programmes

Affected country Parties shall consult and cooperate to prepare, as appropriate, in accordance with relevant regional implementation annexes, subregional and/or regional action programmes to harmonize, complement and increase the efficiency of national programmes. The provisions of article 10 shall apply *mutatis mutandis* to subregional and regional programmes. Such cooperation may include agreed joint programmes for the sustainable management of transboundary natural resources, scientific and technical cooperation, and strengthening of relevant institutions.

Article 12: International cooperation

Affected country Parties, in collaboration with other Parties and the international community, should cooperate to ensure the promotion of an enabling international environment in the implementation of the Convention. Such cooperation should also cover fields of technology transfer as well as scientific research and development, information collection and dissemination and financial resources.

Article 13: Support for the elaboration and implementation of action programmes

1. Measures to support action programmes pursuant to article 9 include, *inter alia*:

(a) financial cooperation to provide predictability for action programmes, allowing for necessary long-term planning;

(b) elaboration and use of cooperation mechanisms which better enable support at the local level, including action through non-governmental organizations, in order to promote the replicability of successful pilot programme activities where relevant;

(c) increased flexibility in project design, funding and implementation in keeping with the experimental, iterative approach indicated for participatory action at the local community level; and

(d) as appropriate, administrative and budgetary procedures that increase the efficiency of cooperation and of support programmes.

2. In providing such support to affected developing country Parties, priority shall be given to African country Parties and to least developed country Parties.

Article 14: Coordination in the elaboration and implementation of action programmes

1. The Parties shall work closely together, directly and through relevant intergovernmental organizations, in the elaboration and implementation of action programmes.

2. The Parties shall develop operational mechanisms, particularly at the national and field levels, to ensure the fullest possible coordination among developed country Parties, developing country Parties and relevant intergovernmental and non-governmental organizations, in order to avoid duplication, harmonize interventions and approaches, and maximize the impact of assistance. In affected developing country Parties, priority will be given to coordinating activities related to international cooperation in order to maximize the efficient use of resources, to ensure responsive assistance, and to facilitate the implementation of national action programmes and priorities under this Convention.

Article 15: Regional implementation annexes

Elements for incorporation in action programmes shall be selected and adapted to the socio-economic, geographical and climatic factors applicable to affected country Parties or regions, as well as to their level of development. Guidelines for the preparation of action programmes and their exact focus and content for particular subregions and regions are set out in the regional implementation annexes.

Section 2: Scientific and technical cooperation

Article 16: Information collection, analysis and exchange

The Parties agree, according to their respective capabilities, to integrate and coordinate the collection, analysis and exchange of relevant short term and long term data and information to ensure systematic observation of land degradation in affected areas and to understand better and assess the processes and effects of drought and desertification. This would help accomplish, *inter alia*, early warning and advance planning for periods of adverse climatic variation in a form suited for practical application by users at all levels, including especially local populations. To this end, they shall, as appropriate:

(a) facilitate and strengthen the functioning of the global network of institutions and facilities for the collection, analysis and exchange of information, as well as for systematic observation at all levels, which shall, *inter alia*:

i) aim to use compatible standards and systems;
ii) encompass relevant data and stations, including in remote areas;
iii) use and disseminate modern technology for data collection, transmission and assessment on land degradation; and
iv) link national, subregional and regional data and information centres more closely with global information sources;

(b) ensure that the collection, analysis and exchange of information address the needs of local communities and those of decision makers, with a view to resolving specific problems, and that local communities are involved in these activities;

(c) support and further develop bilateral and multilateral programmes and projects aimed at defining, conducting, assessing and financing the collection, analysis and exchange of data and information, including, *inter alia*, integrated sets of physical, biological, social and economic indicators;

(d) make full use of the expertise of competent intergovernmental and non-governmental organizations, particularly to disseminate relevant information and experiences among target groups in different regions;

(e) give full weight to the collection, analysis and exchange of socio-economic data, and their integration with physical and biological data;

(f) exchange and make fully, openly and promptly available information from all publicly available sources relevant to combating desertification and mitigating the effects of drought; and

(g) subject to their respective national legislation and/or policies, exchange information on local and traditional knowledge, ensuring adequate protection for it and providing appropriate return from the benefits derived from it, on an equitable basis and on mutually agreed terms, to the local populations concerned.

Article 17: Research and development

1. The Parties undertake, according to their respective capabilities, to promote technical and scientific cooperation in the fields of combating desertification and mitigating the effects of drought through appropriate national, subregional, regional and international institutions. To this end, they shall support research activities that:

(a) contribute to increased knowledge of the processes leading to desertification and drought and the impact of, and distinction between, causal factors, both natural and human, with a view to combating desertification and mitigating the effects of drought, and achieving improved productivity as well as sustainable use and management of resources;

(b) respond to well defined objectives, address the specific needs of local populations and lead to the identification and implementation of solutions that improve the living standards of people in affected areas;
(c) protect, integrate, enhance and validate traditional and local knowledge, know-how and practices, ensuring, subject to their respective national legislation and/or policies, that the owners of that knowledge will directly benefit on an equitable basis and on mutually agreed terms from any commercial utilization of it or from any technological development derived from that knowledge;
(d) develop and strengthen national, subregional and regional research capabilities in affected developing country Parties, particularly in Africa, including the development of local skills and the strengthening of appropriate capacities, especially in countries with a weak research base, giving particular attention to multidisciplinary and participative socio-economic research;
(e) take into account, where relevant, the relationship between poverty, migration caused by environmental factors, and desertification;
(f) promote the conduct of joint research programmes between national, subregional, regional and international research organizations, in both the public and private sectors, for the development of improved, affordable and accessible technologies for sustainable development through effective participation of local populations and communities; and
(g) enhance the availability of water resources in affected areas, by means of, *inter alia*, cloud-seeding.

2. Research priorities for particular regions and subregions, reflecting different local conditions, should be included in action programmes. The Conference of the Parties shall review research priorities periodically on the advice of the Committee on Science and Technology.

Article 18: Transfer, acquisition, adaptation and development of technology

1. The Parties undertake, as mutually agreed and in accordance with their respective national legislation and/or policies, to promote, finance and/or facilitate the financing of the transfer, acquisition, adaptation and development of environmentally sound, economically viable and socially acceptable technologies relevant to combating desertification and/or mitigating the effects of drought, with a view to contributing to the achievement of sustainable development in affected areas. Such cooperation shall be conducted bilaterally or multilaterally, as appropriate, making full use of the expertise of intergovernmental and non-governmental organizations. The Parties shall, in particular:
(a) fully utilize relevant existing national, subregional, regional and international information systems and clearing-houses for the dissemination of information on available technologies, their sources, their environmental risks and the broad terms under which they may be acquired;
(b) facilitate access, in particular by affected developing country Parties, on favourable terms, including on concessional and preferential terms, as mutually agreed, taking into account the need to protect intellectual property rights, to

technologies most suitable to practical application for specific needs of local populations, paying special attention to the social, cultural, economic and environmental impact of such technology;

(c) facilitate technology cooperation among affected country Parties through financial assistance or other appropriate means;

(d) extend technology cooperation with affected developing country Parties, including, where relevant, joint ventures, especially to sectors which foster alternative livelihoods; and

(e) take appropriate measures to create domestic market conditions and incentives, fiscal or otherwise, conducive to the development, transfer, acquisition and adaptation of suitable technology, knowledge, know-how and practices, including measures to ensure adequate and effective protection of intellectual property rights.

2. The Parties shall, according to their respective capabilities, and subject to their respective national legislation and/or policies, protect, promote and use in particular relevant traditional and local technology, knowledge, know-how and practices and, to that end, they undertake to:

(a) make inventories of such technology, knowledge, know-how and practices and their potential uses with the participation of local populations, and disseminate such information, where appropriate, in cooperation with relevant intergovernmental and non-governmental organizations;

(b) ensure that such technology, knowledge, know-how and practices are adequately protected and that local populations benefit directly, on an equitable basis and as mutually agreed, from any commercial utilization of them or from any technological development derived therefrom;

(c) encourage and actively support the improvement and dissemination of such technology, knowledge, know-how and practices or of the development of new technology based on them; and

(d) facilitate, as appropriate, the adaptation of such technology, knowledge, know-how and practices to wide use and integrate them with modern technology, as appropriate.

Section 3: Supporting measures

Article 19: Capacity building, education and public awareness

1. The Parties recognize the significance of capacity building - that is to say, institution building, training and development of relevant local and national capacities - in efforts to combat desertification and mitigate the effects of drought. They shall promote, as appropriate, capacity-building:

(a) through the full participation at all levels of local people, particularly at the local level, especially women and youth, with the cooperation of non-governmental and local organizations;

(b) by strengthening training and research capacity at the national level in the field of desertification and drought;

(c) by establishing and/or strengthening support and extension services to disseminate relevant technology methods and techniques more effectively, and by training field agents and members of rural organizations in participatory approaches for the conservation and sustainable use of natural resources;
(d) by fostering the use and dissemination of the knowledge, know-how and practices of local people in technical cooperation programmes, wherever possible;
(e) by adapting, where necessary, relevant environmentally sound technology and traditional methods of agriculture and pastoralism to modern socio-economic conditions;
(f) by providing appropriate training and technology in the use of alternative energy sources, particularly renewable energy resources, aimed particularly at reducing dependence on wood for fuel;
(g) through cooperation, as mutually agreed, to strengthen the capacity of affected developing country Parties to develop and implement programmes in the field of collection, analysis and exchange of information pursuant to article 16;
(h) through innovative ways of promoting alternative livelihoods, including training in new skills;
(i) by training of decision makers, managers, and personnel who are responsible for the collection and analysis of data for the dissemination and use of early warning information on drought conditions and for food production;
(j) through more effective operation of existing national institutions and legal frameworks and, where necessary, creation of new ones, along with strengthening of strategic planning and management; and
(k) by means of exchange visitor programmes to enhance capacity building in affected country Parties through a long-term, interactive process of learning and study.

2. Affected developing country Parties shall conduct, in cooperation with other Parties and competent intergovernmental and non-governmental organizations, as appropriate, an interdisciplinary review of available capacity and facilities at the local and national levels, and the potential for strengthening them.

3. The Parties shall cooperate with each other and through competent intergovernmental organizations, as well as with non-governmental organizations, in undertaking and supporting public awareness and educational programmes in both affected and, where relevant, unaffected country Parties to promote understanding of the causes and effects of desertification and drought and of the importance of meeting the objective of this Convention. To that end, they shall:
(a) organize awareness campaigns for the general public;
(b) promote, on a permanent basis, access by the public to relevant information, and wide public participation in education and awareness activities;
(c) encourage the establishment of associations that contribute to public awareness;
(d) develop and exchange educational and public awareness material, where possible in local languages, exchange and second experts to train personnel of

affected developing country Parties in carrying out relevant education and awareness programmes, and fully utilize relevant educational material available in competent international bodies;

(e) assess educational needs in affected areas, elaborate appropriate school curricula and expand, as needed, educational and adult literacy programmes and opportunities for all, in particular for girls and women, on the identification, conservation and sustainable use and management of the natural resources of affected areas; and

(f) develop interdisciplinary participatory programmes integrating desertification and drought awareness into educational systems and in non-formal, adult, distance and practical educational programmes.

4. The Conference of the Parties shall establish and/or strengthen networks of regional education and training centres to combat desertification and mitigate the effects of drought. These networks shall be coordinated by an institution created or designated for that purpose, in order to train scientific, technical and management personnel and to strengthen existing institutions responsible for education and training in affected country Parties, where appropriate, with a view to harmonizing programmes and to organizing exchanges of experience among them. These networks shall cooperate closely with relevant intergovernmental and non-governmental organizations to avoid duplication of effort.

Article 20: Financial resources

1. Given the central importance of financing to the achievement of the objective of the Convention, the Parties, taking into account their capabilities, shall make every effort to ensure that adequate financial resources are available for programmes to combat desertification and mitigate the effects of drought.

2. In this connection, developed country Parties, while giving priority to affected African country Parties without neglecting affected developing country Parties in other regions, in accordance with article 7, undertake to:

(a) mobilize substantial financial resources, including grants and concessional loans, in order to support the implementation of programmes to combat desertification and mitigate the effects of drought;

(b) promote the mobilization of adequate, timely and predictable financial resources, including new and additional funding from the Global Environment Facility of the agreed incremental costs of those activities concerning desertification that relate to its four focal areas, in conformity with the relevant provisions of the Instrument establishing the Global Environment Facility;

(c) facilitate through international cooperation the transfer of technology, knowledge and know-how; and

(d) explore, in cooperation with affected developing country Parties, innovative methods and incentives for mobilizing and channelling resources, including those of foundations, non-governmental organizations and other private sector entities, particularly debt swaps and other innovative means which increase financing by reducing the external debt burden of affected developing country Parties, particularly those in Africa.

3. Affected developing country Parties, taking into account their capabilities, undertake to mobilize adequate financial resources for the implementation of their national action programmes.

4. In mobilizing financial resources, the Parties shall seek full use and continued qualitative improvement of all national, bilateral and multilateral funding sources and mechanisms, using consortia, joint programmes and parallel financing, and shall seek to involve private sector funding sources and mechanisms, including those of non-governmental organizations. To this end, the Parties shall fully utilize the operational mechanisms developed pursuant to article 14.

5. In order to mobilize the financial resources necessary for affected developing country Parties to combat desertification and mitigate the effects of drought, the Parties shall:

(a) rationalize and strengthen the management of resources already allocated for combating desertification and mitigating the effects of drought by using them more effectively and efficiently, assessing their successes and shortcomings, removing hindrances to their effective use and, where necessary, reorienting programmes in light of the integrated long-term approach adopted pursuant to this Convention;

(b) give due priority and attention within the governing bodies of multilateral financial institutions, facilities and funds, including regional development banks and funds, to supporting affected developing country Parties, particularly those in Africa, in activities which advance implementation of the Convention, notably action programmes they undertake in the framework of regional implementation annexes; and

(c) examine ways in which regional and subregional cooperation can be strengthened to support efforts undertaken at the national level.

6. Other Parties are encouraged to provide, on a voluntary basis, knowledge, know-how and techniques related to desertification and/or financial resources to affected developing country Parties.

7. The full implementation by affected developing country Parties, particularly those in Africa, of their obligations under the Convention will be greatly assisted by the fulfilment by developed country Parties of their obligations under the Convention, including in particular those regarding financial resources and transfer of technology. In fulfilling their obligations, developed country Parties should take fully into account that economic and social development and poverty eradication are the first priorities of affected developing country Parties, particularly those in Africa.

Article 21: Financial mechanisms

1. The Conference of the Parties shall promote the availability of financial mechanisms and shall encourage such mechanisms to seek to maximize the

availability of funding for affected developing country Parties, particularly those in Africa, to implement the Convention. To this end, the Conference of the Parties shall consider for adoption *inter alia* approaches and policies that:

(a) facilitate the provision of necessary funding at the national, subregional, regional and global levels for activities pursuant to relevant provisions of the Convention;

(b) promote multiple-source funding approaches, mechanisms and arrangements and their assessment, consistent with article 20;

(c) provide on a regular basis, to interested Parties and relevant intergovernmental and non-governmental organizations, information on available sources of funds and on funding patterns in order to facilitate coordination among them;

(d) facilitate the establishment, as appropriate, of mechanisms, such as national desertification funds, including those involving the participation of non-governmental organizations, to channel financial resources rapidly and efficiently to the local level in affected developing country Parties; and

(e) strengthen existing funds and financial mechanisms at the subregional and regional levels, particularly in Africa, to support more effectively the implementation of the Convention.

2. The Conference of the Parties shall also encourage the provision, through various mechanisms within the United Nations system and through multilateral financial institutions, of support at the national, subregional and regional levels to activities that enable developing country Parties to meet their obligations under the Convention.

3. Affected developing country Parties shall utilize, and where necessary, establish and/or strengthen, national coordinating mechanisms, integrated in national development programmes, that would ensure the efficient use of all available financial resources. They shall also utilize participatory processes involving non-governmental organizations, local groups and the private sector, in raising funds, in elaborating as well as implementing programmes and in assuring access to funding by groups at the local level. These actions can be enhanced by improved coordination and flexible programming on the part of those providing assistance.

4. In order to increase the effectiveness and efficiency of existing financial mechanisms, a Global Mechanism to promote actions leading to the mobilization and channelling of substantial financial resources, including for the transfer of technology, on a grant basis, and/or on concessional or other terms, to affected developing country Parties, is hereby established. This Global Mechanism shall function under the authority and guidance of the Conference of the Parties and be accountable to it.

5. The Conference of the Parties shall identify, at its first ordinary session, an organization to house the Global Mechanism. The Conference of the Parties and the organization it has identified shall agree upon modalities for this Global Mechanism to ensure *inter alia* that such Mechanism:

(a) identifies and draws up an inventory of relevant bilateral and multilateral cooperation programmes that are available to implement the Convention;
(b) provides advice, on request, to Parties on innovative methods of financing and sources of financial assistance and on improving the coordination of cooperation activities at the national level;
(c) provides interested Parties and relevant intergovernmental and non-governmental organizations with information on available sources of funds and on funding patterns in order to facilitate coordination among them; and
(d) reports to the Conference of the Parties, beginning at its second ordinary session, on its activities.

6. The Conference of the Parties shall, at its first session, make appropriate arrangements with the organization it has identified to house the Global Mechanism for the administrative operations of such Mechanism, drawing to the extent possible on existing budgetary and human resources.

7. The Conference of the Parties shall, at its third ordinary session, review the policies, operational modalities and activities of the Global Mechanism accountable to it pursuant to paragraph 4, taking into account the provisions of article 7. On the basis of this review, it shall consider and take appropriate action.

Part IV: Institutions

Article 22: Conference of the Parties

1. A Conference of the Parties is hereby established.

2. The Conference of the Parties is the supreme body of the Convention. It shall make, within its mandate, the decisions necessary to promote its effective implementation. In particular, it shall:
(a) regularly review the implementation of the Convention and the functioning of its institutional arrangements in the light of the experience gained at the national, subregional, regional and international levels and on the basis of the evolution of scientific and technological knowledge;
(b) promote and facilitate the exchange of information on measures adopted by the Parties, and determine the form and timetable for transmitting the information to be submitted pursuant to article 26, review the reports and make recommendations on them;
(c) establish such subsidiary bodies as are deemed necessary for the implementation of the Convention;
(d) review reports submitted by its subsidiary bodies and provide guidance to them;
(e) agree upon and adopt, by consensus, rules of procedure and financial rules for itself and any subsidiary bodies;
(f) adopt amendments to the Convention pursuant to articles 30 and 31;
(g) approve a programme and budget for its activities, including those of its subsidiary bodies, and undertake necessary arrangements for their financing;

(h) as appropriate, seek the cooperation of, and utilize the services of and information provided by, competent bodies or agencies, whether national or international, intergovernmental or non-governmental;
(i) promote and strengthen the relationship with other relevant conventions while avoiding duplication of effort; and
(j) exercise such other functions as may be necessary for the achievement of the objective of the Convention.

3. The Conference of the Parties shall, at its first session, adopt its own rules of procedure, by consensus, which shall include decision-making procedures for matters not already covered by decision-making procedures stipulated in the Convention. Such procedures may include specified majorities required for the adoption of particular decisions.

4. The first session of the Conference of the Parties shall be convened by the interim secretariat referred to in article 35 and shall take place not later than one year after the date of entry into force of the Convention. Unless otherwise decided by the Conference of the Parties, the second, third and fourth ordinary sessions shall be held yearly, and thereafter, ordinary sessions shall be held every two years.

5. Extraordinary sessions of the Conference of the Parties shall be held at such other times as may be decided either by the Conference of the Parties in ordinary session or at the written request of any Party, provided that, within three months of the request being communicated to the Parties by the Permanent Secretariat, it is supported by at least one third of the Parties.

6. At each ordinary session, the Conference of the Parties shall elect a Bureau. The structure and functions of the Bureau shall be determined in the rules of procedure. In appointing the Bureau, due regard shall be paid to the need to ensure equitable geographical distribution and adequate representation of affected country Parties, particularly those in Africa.

7. The United Nations, its specialized agencies and any State member thereof or observers thereto not Party to the Convention, may be represented at sessions of the Conference of the Parties as observers. Any body or agency, whether national or international, governmental or non-governmental, which is qualified in matters covered by the Convention, and which has informed the Permanent Secretariat of its wish to be represented at a session of the Conference of the Parties as an observer, may be so admitted unless at least one third of the Parties present object. The admission and participation of observers shall be subject to the rules of procedure adopted by the Conference of the Parties.

8. The Conference of the Parties may request competent national and international organizations which have relevant expertise to provide it with information relevant to article 16, paragraph (g), article 17, paragraph 1 (c) and article 18, paragraph 2(b).

Article 23: Permanent Secretariat

1. A Permanent Secretariat is hereby established.

2. The functions of the Permanent Secretariat shall be:

(a) to make arrangements for sessions of the Conference of the Parties and its subsidiary bodies established under the Convention and to provide them with services as required;

(b) to compile and transmit reports submitted to it;

(c) to facilitate assistance to affected developing country Parties, on request, particularly those in Africa, in the compilation and communication of information required under the Convention;

(d) to coordinate its activities with the secretariats of other relevant international bodies and conventions;

(e) to enter, under the guidance of the Conference of the Parties, into such administrative and contractual arrangements as may be required for the effective discharge of its functions;

(f) to prepare reports on the execution of its functions under this Convention and present them to the Conference of the Parties; and

(g) to perform such other secretariat functions as may be determined by the Conference of the Parties.

3. The Conference of the Parties, at its first session, shall designate a Permanent Secretariat and make arrangements for its functioning.

Article 24: Committee on Science and Technology

1. A Committee on Science and Technology is hereby established as a subsidiary body of the Conference of the Parties to provide it with information and advice on scientific and technological matters relating to combating desertification and mitigating the effects of drought. The Committee shall meet in conjunction with the ordinary sessions of the Conference of the Parties and shall be multidisciplinary and open to the participation of all Parties. It shall be composed of government representatives competent in the relevant fields of expertise. The Conference of the Parties shall decide, at its first session, on the terms of reference of the Committee.

2. The Conference of the Parties shall establish and maintain a roster of independent experts with expertise and experience in the relevant fields. The roster shall be based on nominations received in writing from the Parties, taking into account the need for a multidisciplinary approach and broad geographical representation.

3. The Conference of the Parties may, as necessary, appoint ad hoc panels to provide it, through the Committee, with information and advice on specific issues regarding the state of the art in fields of science and technology relevant to combating desertification and mitigating the effects of drought. These panels shall be composed of experts whose names are taken from the roster, taking into account the need for a multidisciplinary approach and broad geographical representation. These experts shall have scientific backgrounds and field experience and shall be appointed by the Conference of the Parties on the recommendation of the

Committee. The Conference of the Parties shall decide on the terms of reference and the modalities of work of these panels.

Article 25: Networking of institutions, agencies and bodies

1. The Committee on Science and Technology shall, under the supervision of the Conference of the Parties, make provision for the undertaking of a survey and evaluation of the relevant existing networks, institutions, agencies and bodies willing to become units of a network. Such a network shall support the implementation of the Convention.

2. On the basis of the results of the survey and evaluation referred to in paragraph 1, the Committee on Science and Technology shall make recommendations to the Conference of the Parties on ways and means to facilitate and strengthen networking of the units at the local, national and other levels, with a view to ensuring that the thematic needs set out in articles 16 to 19 are addressed.

3. Taking into account these recommendations, the Conference of the Parties shall:
(a) identify those national, subregional, regional and international units that are most appropriate for networking, and recommend operational procedures, and a time frame, for them; and
(b) identify the units best suited to facilitating and strengthening such networking at all levels.

Part V: Procedures

Article 26: Communication of information

1. Each Party shall communicate to the Conference of the Parties for consideration at its ordinary sessions, through the Permanent Secretariat, reports on the measures which it has taken for the implementation of the Convention. The Conference of the Parties shall determine the timetable for submission and the format of such reports.

2. Affected country Parties shall provide a description of the strategies established pursuant to article 5 and of any relevant information on their implementation.

3. Affected country Parties which implement action programmes pursuant to articles 9 to 15 shall provide a detailed description of the programmes and of their implementation.

4. Any group of affected country Parties may make a joint communication on measures taken at the subregional and/or regional levels in the framework of action programmes.

5. Developed country Parties shall report on measures taken to assist in the preparation and implementation of action programmes, including information on the financial resources they have provided, or are providing, under the Convention.

6. Information communicated pursuant to paragraphs 1 to 4 shall be transmitted by the Permanent Secretariat as soon as possible to the Conference of the Parties and to any relevant subsidiary body.

7. The Conference of the Parties shall facilitate the provision to affected developing countries, particularly those in Africa, on request, of technical and financial support in compiling and communicating information in accordance with this article, as well as identifying the technical and financial needs associated with action programmes.

Article 27: Measures to resolve questions on implementation

The Conference of the Parties shall consider and adopt procedures and institutional mechanisms for the resolution of questions that may arise with regard to the implementation of the Convention.

Article 28: Settlement of disputes

1. Parties shall settle any dispute between them concerning the interpretation or application of the Convention through negotiation or other peaceful means of their own choice.

2. When ratifying, accepting, approving, or acceding to the Convention, or at any time thereafter, a Party which is not a regional economic integration organization may declare in a written instrument submitted to the Depositary that, in respect of any dispute concerning the interpretation or application of the Convention, it recognizes one or both of the following means of dispute settlement as compulsory in relation to any Party accepting the same obligation:

(a) arbitration in accordance with procedures adopted by the Conference of the Parties in an annex as soon as practicable;

(b) submission of the dispute to the International Court of Justice.

3. A Party which is a regional economic integration organization may make a declaration with like effect in relation to arbitration in accordance with the procedure referred to in paragraph 2 (a).

4. A declaration made pursuant to paragraph 2 shall remain in force until it expires in accordance with its terms or until three months after written notice of its revocation has been deposited with the Depositary.

5. The expiry of a declaration, a notice of revocation or a new declaration shall not in any way affect proceedings pending before an arbitral tribunal or the International Court of Justice unless the Parties to the dispute otherwise agree.

6. If the Parties to a dispute have not accepted the same or any procedure pursuant to paragraph 2 and if they have not been able to settle their dispute within twelve months following notification by one Party to another that a dispute exists between them, the dispute shall be submitted to conciliation at the request of any Party to the dispute, in accordance with procedures adopted by the Conference of the Parties in an annex as soon as practicable.

Article 29: Status of annexes

1. Annexes form an integral part of the Convention and, unless expressly provided otherwise, a reference to the Convention also constitutes a reference to its annexes.

2. The Parties shall interpret the provisions of the annexes in a manner that is in conformity with their rights and obligations under the articles of this Convention.

Article 30: Amendments to the Convention

1. Any Party may propose amendments to the Convention.

2. Amendments to the Convention shall be adopted at an ordinary session of the Conference of the Parties. The text of any proposed amendment shall be communicated to the Parties by the Permanent Secretariat at least six months before the meeting at which it is proposed for adoption. The Permanent Secretariat shall also communicate proposed amendments to the signatories to the Convention.

3. The Parties shall make every effort to reach agreement on any proposed amendment to the Convention by consensus. If all efforts at consensus have been exhausted and no agreement reached, the amendment shall, as a last resort, be adopted by a two-thirds majority vote of the Parties present and voting at the meeting. The adopted amendment shall be communicated by the Permanent Secretariat to the Depositary, who shall circulate it to all Parties for their ratification, acceptance, approval or accession.

4. Instruments of ratification, acceptance, approval or accession in respect of an amendment shall be deposited with the Depositary. An amendment adopted pursuant to paragraph 3 shall enter into force for those Parties having accepted it on the ninetieth day after the date of receipt by the Depositary of an instrument of ratification, acceptance, approval or accession by at least two thirds of the Parties to the Convention which were Parties at the time of the adoption of the amendment.

5. The amendment shall enter into force for any other Party on the ninetieth day after the date on which that Party deposits with the Depositary its instrument of ratification, acceptance or approval of, or accession to the said amendment.

6. For the purposes of this article and article 31, 'Parties present and voting' means Parties present and casting an affirmative or negative vote.

Article 31: Adoption and amendment of annexes

1. Any additional annex to the Convention and any amendment to an annex shall be proposed and adopted in accordance with the procedure for amendment of the Convention set forth in article 30, provided that, in adopting an additional regional implementation annex or amendment to any regional implementation annex, the majority provided for in that article shall include a two-thirds majority vote of the Parties of the region concerned present and voting. The adoption or amendment of an annex shall be communicated by the Depositary to all Parties.

2. An annex, other than an additional regional implementation annex, or an amendment to an annex, other than an amendment to any regional implementation annex, that has been adopted in accordance with paragraph 1, shall enter into force for all Parties to the Convention six months after the date of communication by the Depositary to such Parties of the adoption of such annex or amendment, except for those Parties that have notified the Depositary in writing within that period of their

non-acceptance of such annex or amendment. Such annex or amendment shall enter into force for Parties which withdraw their notification of non-acceptance on the ninetieth day after the date on which withdrawal of such notification has been received by the Depositary.

3. An additional regional implementation annex or amendment to any regional implementation annex that has been adopted in accordance with paragraph 1, shall enter into force for all Parties to the Convention six months after the date of the communication by the Depositary to such Parties of the adoption of such annex or amendment, except with respect to:

(a) any Party that has notified the Depositary in writing, within such six month period, of its non-acceptance of that additional regional implementation annex or of the amendment to the regional implementation annex, in which case such annex or amendment shall enter into force for Parties which withdraw their notification of non-acceptance on the ninetieth day after the date on which withdrawal of such notification has been received by the Depositary; and

(b) any Party that has made a declaration with respect to additional regional implementation annexes or amendments to regional implementation annexes in accordance with article 34, paragraph 4, in which case any such annex or amendment shall enter into force for such a Party on the ninetieth day after the date of deposit with the Depositary of its instrument of ratification, acceptance, approval or accession with respect to such annex or amendment.

4. If the adoption of an annex or an amendment to an annex involves an amendment to the Convention, that annex or amendment to an annex shall not enter into force until such time as the amendment to the Convention enters into force.

Article 32: Right to vote

1. Except as provided for in paragraph 2, each Party to the Convention shall have one vote.

2. Regional economic integration organizations, in matters within their competence, shall exercise their right to vote with a number of votes equal to the number of their member States that are Parties to the Convention. Such an organization shall not exercise its right to vote if any of its member States exercises its right, and vice versa.

Part VI: Final provisions

Article 33: Signature

This Convention shall be opened for signature at Paris, on 14-15 October 1994, by States Members of the United Nations or any of its specialized agencies or that are Parties to the Statute of the International Court of Justice and by regional economic integration organizations. It shall remain open for signature, thereafter, at the United Nations Headquarters in New York until 13 October 1995.

Article 34: Ratification, acceptance, approval and accession

1. The Convention shall be subject to ratification, acceptance, approval or accession by States and by regional economic integration organizations. It shall be open for accession from the day after the date on which the Convention is closed for signature. Instruments of ratification, acceptance, approval or accession shall be deposited with the Depositary.

2. Any regional economic integration organization which becomes a Party to the Convention without any of its member States being a Party to the Convention shall be bound by all the obligations under the Convention. Where one or more member States of such an organization are also Party to the Convention, the organization and its member States shall decide on their respective responsibilities for the performance of their obligations under the Convention. In such cases, the organization and the member States shall not be entitled to exercise rights under the Convention concurrently.

3. In their instruments of ratification, acceptance, approval or accession, regional economic integration organizations shall declare the extent of their competence with respect to the matters governed by the Convention. They shall also promptly inform the Depositary, who shall in turn inform the Parties, of any substantial modification in the extent of their competence.

4. In its instrument of ratification, acceptance, approval or accession, any Party may declare that, with respect to it, any additional regional implementation annex or any amendment to any regional implementation annex shall enter into force only upon the deposit of its instrument of ratification, acceptance, approval or accession with respect thereto.

Article 35: Interim arrangements

The secretariat functions referred to in article 23 will be carried out on an interim basis by the secretariat established by the General Assembly of the United Nations in its resolution 47/188 of 22 December 1992, until the completion of the first session of the Conference of the Parties.

Article 36: Entry into force

1. The Convention shall enter into force on the ninetieth day after the date of deposit of the fiftieth instrument of ratification, acceptance, approval or accession.

2. For each State or regional economic integration organization ratifying, accepting, approving or acceding to the Convention after the deposit of the fiftieth instrument of ratification, acceptance, approval or accession, the Convention shall enter into force on the ninetieth day after the date of deposit by such State or regional economic integration organization of its instrument of ratification, acceptance, approval or accession.

3. For the purposes of paragraphs 1 and 2, any instrument deposited by a regional economic integration organization shall not be counted as additional to those deposited by States members of the organization.

Article 37: Reservations

No reservations may be made to this Convention.

Article 38: Withdrawal

1. At any time after three years from the date on which the Convention has entered into force for a Party, that Party may withdraw from the Convention by giving written notification to the Depositary.

2. Any such withdrawal shall take effect upon expiry of one year from the date of receipt by the Depositary of the notification of withdrawal, or on such later date as may be specified in the notification of withdrawal.

Article 39: Depositary

The Secretary-General of the United Nations shall be the Depositary of the Convention.

Article 40: Authentic texts

The original of the present Convention, of which the Arabic, Chinese, English, French, Russian and Spanish texts are equally authentic, shall be deposited with the Secretary-General of the United Nations.

In witness whereof the undersigned, being duly authorized to that effect, have signed the present Convention.

Done at Paris, this 17th day of June one thousand nine hundred and ninety-four.

Annex I: Regional Implementation Annex for Africa; Annex II: Regional Implementation Annex for Asia; Annex III: Regional Implementation Annex for Latin America and the Caribbean; Annex IV: Regional Implementation Annex for the Northern Mediterranean; Annex V: Regional Implementation Annex for Central and Eastern Europe [not reproduced]

Forests

Non-Legally Binding Authoritative Statement of Principles for a Global Consensus on the Management, Conservation and Sustainable Development of All Types of Forests

Adopted on 14 June 1992 at Rio de Janeiro. Source: Report of the UNCED, Doc. A/CONF.151/26 (Vol. I), Annex II (1992). Further information: CSD, New York, USA, http://www.un.org/esa/sustdev/csd/csd.htm

Preamble

(a) The subject of forests is related to the entire range of environmental and development issues and opportunities, including the right to socio-economic development on a sustainable basis.

(b) The guiding objective of these principles is to contribute to the management, conservation and sustainable development of forests and to provide for their multiple and complementary functions and uses.

(c) Forestry issues and opportunities should be examined in a holistic and balanced manner within the overall context of environment and development, taking into consideration the multiple functions and uses of forests, including traditional uses, and the likely economic and social stress when these uses are constrained or restricted, as well as the potential for development that sustainable forest management can offer.

(d) These principles reflect a first global consensus on forests. In committing themselves to the prompt implementation of these principles, countries also decide to keep them under assessment for their adequacy with regard to further international cooperation on forest issues.

(e) These principles should apply to all types of forests, both natural and planted, in all geographical regions and climatic zones, including austral, boreal, subtemperate, temperate, subtropical and tropical.

(f) All types of forests embody complex and unique ecological processes which are the basis for their present and potential capacity to provide resources to satisfy human needs as well as environmental values, and as such their sound management and conservation is of concern to the Governments of the countries to which they belong and are of value to local communities and to the environment as a whole.

(g) Forests are essential to economic development and the maintenance of all forms of life.

(h) Recognizing that the responsibility for forest management, conservation and sustainable development is in many States allocated among federal/national, state/provincial and local levels of government, each State, in accordance with its constitution and/or national legislation, should pursue these principles at the appropriate level of government.

Principles/Elements

1. (a) States have, in accordance with the Charter of the United Nations and the principles of international law, the sovereign right to exploit their own resources pursuant to their own environmental policies and have the responsibility to ensure that activities within their jurisdiction or control do not cause damage to the environment of other States or of areas beyond the limits of national jurisdiction.

(b) The agreed full incremental cost of achieving benefits associated with forest conservation and sustainable development requires increased international cooperation and should be equitably shared by the international community.

2. (a) States have the sovereign and inalienable right to utilize, manage and develop their forests in accordance with their development needs and level of socio-economic development and on the basis of national policies consistent with sustainable development and legislation, including the conversion of such areas for other uses within the overall socio-economic development plan and based on rational land-use policies.

(b) Forest resources and forest lands should be sustainably managed to meet the social, economic, ecological, cultural and spiritual needs of present and future generations. These needs are for forest products and services, such as wood and wood products, water, food, fodder, medicine, fuel, shelter, employment, recreation, habitats for wildlife, landscape diversity, carbon sinks and reservoirs, and for other forest products. Appropriate measures should be taken to protect forests against harmful effects of pollution, including air-borne pollution, fires, pests and diseases, in order to maintain their full multiple value.

(c) The provision of timely, reliable and accurate information on forests and forest ecosystems is essential for public understanding and informed decision-making and should be ensured.

(d) Governments should promote and provide opportunities for the participation of interested parties, including local communities and indigenous people, industries, labour, non-governmental organizations and individuals, forest dwellers and women, in the development, implementation and planning of national forest policies.

3. (a) National policies and strategies should provide a framework for increased efforts, including the development and strengthening of institutions and programmes for the management, conservation and sustainable development of forests and forest lands.

(b) International institutional arrangements, building on those organizations and mechanisms already in existence, as appropriate, should facilitate international cooperation in the field of forests.

(c) All aspects of environmental protection and social and economic development as they relate to forests and forest lands should be integrated and comprehensive.

4. The vital role of all types of forests in maintaining the ecological processes and balance at the local, national, regional and global levels through, inter alia, their role in protecting fragile ecosystems, watersheds and freshwater resources and as rich storehouses of biodiversity and biological resources and sources of genetic material for biotechnology products, as well as photosynthesis, should be recognized.

5. (a) National forest policies should recognize and duly support the identity, culture and the rights of indigenous people, their communities and other

communities and forest dwellers. Appropriate conditions should be promoted for these groups to enable them to have an economic stake in forest use, perform economic activities, and achieve and maintain cultural identity and social organization, as well as adequate levels of livelihood and well-being, through, inter alia, those land tenure arrangements which serve as incentives for the sustainable management of forests.

(b) The full participation of women in all aspects of the management, conservation and sustainable development of forests should be actively promoted.

6. (a) All types of forests play an important role in meeting energy requirements through the provision of a renewable source of bio-energy, particularly in developing countries, and the demands for fuelwood for household and industrial needs should be met through sustainable forest management, afforestation and reforestation. To this end, the potential contribution of plantations of both indigenous and introduced species for the provision of both fuel and industrial wood should be recognized.

(b) National policies and programmes should take into account the relationship, where it exists, between the conservation, management and sustainable development of forests and all aspects related to the production, consumption, recycling and/or final disposal of forest products.

(c) Decisions taken on the management, conservation and sustainable development of forest resources should benefit, to the extent practicable, from a comprehensive assessment of economic and non-economic values of forest goods and services and of the environmental costs and benefits. The development and improvement of methodologies for such evaluations should be promoted.

(d) The role of planted forests and permanent agricultural crops as sustainable and environmentally sound sources of renewable energy and industrial raw material should be recognized, enhanced and promoted. Their contribution to the maintenance of ecological processes, to offsetting pressure on primary/old-growth forest and to providing regional employment and development with the adequate involvement of local inhabitants should be recognized and enhanced.

(e) Natural forests also constitute a source of goods and services, and their conservation, sustainable management and use should be promoted.

7. (a) Efforts should be made to promote a supportive international economic climate conducive to sustained and environmentally sound development of forests in all countries, which include, inter alia, the promotion of sustainable patterns of production and consumption, the eradication of poverty and the promotion of food security.

(b) Specific financial resources should be provided to developing countries with significant forest areas which establish programmes for the conservation of forests including protected natural forest areas. These resources should be directed notably to economic sectors which would stimulate economic and social substitution activities.

8. (a) Efforts should be undertaken towards the greening of the world. All countries, notably developed countries, should take positive and transparent action towards reforestation, afforestation and forest conservation, as appropriate.
(b) Efforts to maintain and increase forest cover and forest productivity should be undertaken in ecologically, economically and socially sound ways through the rehabilitation, reforestation and re-establishment of trees and forests on unproductive, degraded and deforested lands, as well as through the management of existing forest resources.
(c) The implementation of national policies and programmes aimed at forest management, conservation and sustainable development, particularly in developing countries, should be supported by international financial and technical cooperation, including through the private sector, where appropriate.
(d) Sustainable forest management and use should be carried out in accordance with national development policies and priorities and on the basis of environmentally sound national guidelines. In the formulation of such guidelines, account should be taken, as appropriate and if applicable, of relevant internationally agreed methodologies and criteria.
(e) Forest management should be integrated with management of adjacent areas so as to maintain ecological balance and sustainable productivity.
(f) National policies and/or legislation aimed at management, conservation and sustainable development of forests should include the protection of ecologically viable representative or unique examples of forests, including primary/old-growth forests, cultural, spiritual, historical, religious and other unique and valued forests of national importance.
(g) Access to biological resources, including genetic material, shall be with due regard to the sovereign rights of the countries where the forests are located and to the sharing on mutually agreed terms of technology and profits from biotechnology products that are derived from these resources.
(h) National policies should ensure that environmental impact assessments should be carried out where actions are likely to have significant adverse impacts on important forest resources, and where such actions are subject to a decision of a competent national authority.

9. (a) The efforts of developing countries to strengthen the management, conservation and sustainable development of their forest resources should be supported by the international community, taking into account the importance of redressing external indebtedness, particularly where aggravated by the net transfer of resources to developed countries, as well as the problem of achieving at least the replacement value of forests through improved market access for forest products, especially processed products. In this respect, special attention should also be given to the countries undergoing the process of transition to market economies.
(b) The problems that hinder efforts to attain the conservation and sustainable use of forest resources and that stem from the lack of alternative options available

to local communities, in particular the urban poor and poor rural populations who are economically and socially dependent on forests and forest resources, should be addressed by Governments and the international community.

(c) National policy formulation with respect to all types of forests should take account of the pressures and demands imposed on forest ecosystems and resources from influencing factors outside the forest sector, and intersectoral means of dealing with these pressures and demands should be sought.

10. New and additional financial resources should be provided to developing countries to enable them to sustainably manage, conserve and develop their forest resources, including through afforestation, reforestation and combating deforestation and forest and land degradation.

11. In order to enable, in particular, developing countries to enhance their endogenous capacity and to better manage, conserve and develop their forest resources, the access to and transfer of environmentally sound technologies and corresponding know-how on favourable terms, including on concessional and preferential terms, as mutually agreed, in accordance with the relevant provisions of Agenda 21, should be promoted, facilitated and financed, as appropriate.

12. (a) Scientific research, forest inventories and assessments carried out by national institutions which take into account, where relevant, biological, physical, social and economic variables, as well as technological development and its application in the field of sustainable forest management, conservation and development, should be strengthened through effective modalities, including international cooperation. In this context, attention should also be given to research and development of sustainably harvested non-wood products.

(b) National and, where appropriate, regional and international institutional capabilities in education, training, science, technology, economics, anthropology and social aspects of forests and forest management are essential to the conservation and sustainable development of forests and should be strengthened.

(c) International exchange of information on the results of forest and forest management research and development should be enhanced and broadened, as appropriate, making full use of education and training institutions, including those in the private sector.

(d) Appropriate indigenous capacity and local knowledge regarding the conservation and sustainable development of forests should, through institutional and financial support and in collaboration with the people in the local communities concerned, be recognized, respected, recorded, developed and, as appropriate, introduced in the implementation of programmes. Benefits arising from the utilization of indigenous knowledge should therefore be equitably shared with such people.

13. (a) Trade in forest products should be based on non-discriminatory and multilaterally agreed rules and procedures consistent with international trade

law and practices. In this context, open and free international trade in forest products should be facilitated.

(b) Reduction or removal of tariff barriers and impediments to the provision of better market access and better prices for higher value-added forest products and their local processing should be encouraged to enable producer countries to better conserve and manage their renewable forest resources.

(c) Incorporation of environmental costs and benefits into market forces and mechanisms, in order to achieve forest conservation and sustainable development, should be encouraged both domestically and internationally.

(d) Forest conservation and sustainable development policies should be integrated with economic, trade and other relevant policies.

(e) Fiscal, trade, industrial, transportation and other policies and practices that may lead to forest degradation should be avoided. Adequate policies, aimed at management, conservation and sustainable development of forests, including, where appropriate, incentives, should be encouraged.

14. Unilateral measures, incompatible with international obligations or agreements, to restrict and/or ban international trade in timber or other forest products should be removed or avoided, in order to attain long-term sustainable forest management.

15. Pollutants, particularly air-borne pollutants, including those responsible for acidic deposition, that are harmful to the health of forest ecosystems at the local, national, regional and global levels should be controlled.

International Tropical Timber Agreement

Adopted on 26 January 1994 at Geneva. Entered into force on 1 January 1997. Source: 1955 *UNTS* 81. Number of parties: 60. Further information: ITTO, Yokohama, Japan, http://www.itto.or.jp

The Parties to this Agreement,

Recalling the Declaration and the Programme of Action on the Establishment of A New International Economic Order; the Integrated Programme for Commodities; A New Partnership for Development; the Cartagena Commitment and the relevant objectives contained in the Spirit of Cartagena,

Recalling the International Tropical Timber Agreement, 1983, and *recognizing* the work of the International Tropical Timber Organization and its achievements since its inception, including a strategy for achieving international trade in tropical timber from sustainably managed sources,

Recalling further the Rio Declaration on Environment and Development, the Non-Legally Binding Authoritative Statement of Principles for a Global Consensus on the Management, Conservation and Sustainable Development of all Types of

Forests, and the relevant Chapters of Agenda 21 as adopted by the United Nations Conference on Environment and Development in June 1992, in Rio de Janeiro; the United Nations Framework Convention on Climate Change; and the Convention on Biological Diversity,

Recognizing the importance of timber to the economies of countries with timber-producing forests,

Further recognizing the need to promote and apply comparable and appropriate guidelines and criteria for the management, conservation and sustainable development of all types of timber-producing forests,

Taking into account the linkages of tropical timber trade and the international timber market and the need for taking a global perspective in order to improve transparency in the international timber market,

Noting the commitment of all members, made in Bali, Indonesia, in May 1990, to achieve exports of tropical timber products from sustainably managed sources by the year 2000 and *recognizing* Principle 10 of the Non-Legally Binding Authoritative Statement of Principles for a Global Consensus on the Management, Conservation and Sustainable Development of all Types of Forests which states that new and additional financial resources should be provided to developing countries to enable them to sustainably manage, conserve and develop their forests, including through afforestation, reforestation and combating deforestation and forest and land degradation,

Noting also the statement of commitment to maintain, or achieve by the year 2000, the sustainable management of their respective forests made by consuming members who are parties to the International Tropical Timber Agreement, 1983 at the fourth session of the United Nations Conference for the Negotiation of a Successor Agreement to the International Tropical Timber Agreement, 1983 in Geneva on 21 January 1994,

Desiring to strengthen the framework of international cooperation and policy development between members in finding solutions to the problems facing the tropical timber economy,

Have agreed as follows:

Chapter I: Objectives

Article 1: Objectives

Recognizing the sovereignty of members over their natural resources, as defined in Principle 1 (a) of the Non-Legally Binding Authoritative Statement of Principles for a Global Consensus on the Management, Conservation and Sustainable Development of all Types of Forests, the objectives of the International Tropical Timber Agreement, 1994 (hereinafter referred to as 'this Agreement') are:

(a) To provide an effective framework for consultation, international cooperation and policy development among all members with regard to all relevant aspects of the world timber economy;

(b) To provide a forum for consultation to promote non-discriminatory timber trade practices;

(c) To contribute to the process of sustainable development;

(d) To enhance the capacity of members to implement a strategy for achieving exports of tropical timber and timber products from sustainably managed sources by the year 2000;

(e) To promote the expansion and diversification of international trade in tropical timber from sustainable sources by improving the structural conditions in international markets, by taking into account, on the one hand, a long-term increase in consumption and continuity of supplies, and, on the other, prices which reflect the costs of sustainable forest management and which are remunerative and equitable for members, and the improvement of market access;

(f) To promote and support research and development with a view to improving forest management and efficiency of wood utilization as well as increasing the capacity to conserve and enhance other forest values in timber producing tropical forests;

(g) To develop and contribute towards mechanisms for the provision of new and additional financial resources and expertise needed to enhance the capacity of producing members to attain the objectives of this Agreement;

(h) To improve market intelligence with a view to ensuring greater transparency in the international timber market, including the gathering, compilation, and dissemination of trade related data, including data related to species being traded;

(i) To promote increased and further processing of tropical timber from sustainable sources in producing member countries with a view to promoting their industrialization and thereby increasing their employment opportunities and export earnings;

(j) To encourage members to support and develop industrial tropical timber reforestation and forest management activities as well as rehabilitation of degraded forest land, with due regard for the interests of local communities dependent on forest resources;

(k) To improve marketing and distribution of tropical timber exports from sustainably managed sources;

(l) To encourage members to develop national policies aimed at sustainable utilization and conservation of timber producing forests and their genetic resources and at maintaining the ecological balance in the regions concerned, in the context of tropical timber trade;

(m) To promote the access to, and transfer of, technologies and technical cooperation to implement the objectives of this Agreement, including on concessional and preferential terms and conditions, as mutually agreed; and

(n) To encourage information-sharing on the international timber market.

Chapter II: Definitions

Article 2: Definitions

For the purposes of this Agreement:

1. 'Tropical timber' means non-coniferous tropical wood for industrial uses, which grows or is produced in the countries situated between the Tropic of Cancer and the Tropic of Capricorn. The term covers logs, sawnwood, veneer sheets and plywood. Plywood which includes in some measure conifers of tropical origin shall also be covered by this definition.

2. 'Further processing' means the transformation of logs into primary wood products, semi-finished and finished products made wholly or almost wholly of tropical timber.

3. 'Member' means a Government or an intergovernmental organization referred to in article 5 which has consented to be bound by this Agreement whether it is in force provisionally or definitively.

4. 'Producing member' means any country with tropical forest resources and/or a net exporter of tropical timber in volume terms which is listed in annex A and which becomes a party to this Agreement, or any country with tropical forest resources and/or a net exporter of tropical timber in volume terms which is not so listed and which becomes a party to this Agreement and which the Council, with the consent of that country, declares to be a producing member.

5. 'Consuming member' means any country listed in annex B which becomes a party to this Agreement, or any country not so listed which becomes a party to this Agreement and which the Council, with the consent of that country, declares to be a consuming member.

6. 'Organization' means the International Tropical Timber Organization established in accordance with article 3.

7. 'Council' means the International Tropical Timber Council established in accordance with article 6.

8. 'Special vote' means a vote requiring at least two thirds of the votes cast by producing members present and voting and at least 60 per cent of the votes cast by consuming members present and voting, counted separately, on condition that these votes are cast by at least half of the producing members present and voting and at least half of the consuming members present and voting.

9. 'Simple distributed majority vote' means a vote requiring more than half of the votes cast by producing members present and voting and more than half of the votes cast by consuming members present and voting, counted separately.

10. 'Financial year' means the period from 1 January to 31 December inclusive.

11. 'Freely usable currencies' means the Deutsche mark, the French franc, the Japanese yen, the pound sterling, the United States dollar and any other currency which has been designated from time to time by a competent international monetary organization as being in fact widely used to make payments for international transactions and widely traded in the principal exchange markets.

Chapter III: Organization and administration

Article 3: Establishment, headquarters and structure of the International Tropical Timber Organization

1. The International Tropical Timber Organization established by the International Tropical Timber Agreement, 1983 shall continue in being for the purposes of administering the provisions and supervising the operation of this Agreement.

2. The Organization shall function through the Council established under article 6, the committees and other subsidiary bodies referred to in article 26 and the Executive Director and staff.

3. The headquarters of the Organization shall be in Yokohama, unless the Council, by special vote, decides otherwise.

4. The headquarters of the Organization shall at all times be located in the territory of a member.

Article 4: Membership in the Organization

There shall be two categories of membership in the Organization, namely:

(a) Producing; and

(b) Consuming.

Article 5: Membership by intergovernmental organizations

1. Any reference in this Agreement to 'Governments' shall be construed as including the European Community and any other intergovernmental organization having responsibilities in respect of the negotiation, conclusion and application of international agreements, in particular commodity agreements. Accordingly, any reference in this Agreement to signature, ratification, acceptance or approval, or to notification of provisional application, or to accession shall, in the case of such intergovernmental organizations, be construed as including a reference to signature, ratification, acceptance or approval, or to notification of provisional application, or to accession, by such intergovernmental organizations.

2. In the case of voting on matters within their competence, such intergovernmental organizations shall vote with a number of votes equal to the total number of votes attributable to their member States in accordance with article 10. In such cases, the member States of such intergovernmental organizations shall not be entitled to exercise their individual voting rights.

Chapter IV: International Tropical Timber Council

Article 6: Composition of the International Tropical Timber Council

1. The highest authority of the Organization shall be the International Tropical Timber Council, which shall consist of all the members of the Organization.

2. Each member shall be represented in the Council by one representative and may designate alternates and advisers to attend sessions of the Council.

3. An alternate representative shall be empowered to act and vote on behalf of the representative during the latter's absence or in special circumstances.

Article 7: Powers and functions of the Council

1. The Council shall exercise all such powers and perform or arrange for the performance of all such functions as are necessary to carry out the provisions of this Agreement.

2. The Council shall, by special vote, adopt such rules and regulations as are necessary to carry out the provisions of this Agreement and as are consistent therewith, including its own rules of procedure and the financial rules and staff regulations of the Organization. Such financial rules shall, *inter alia*, govern the receipt and expenditure of funds under the Administrative Account, the Special Account and the Bali Partnership Fund. The Council may, in its rules of procedure, provide for a procedure whereby it may, without meeting, decide specific questions.

3. The Council shall keep such records as are required for the performance of its functions under this Agreement.

Article 8: Chairman and Vice-Chairman of the Council

1. The Council shall elect for each calendar year a Chairman and a Vice-Chairman, whose salaries shall not be paid by the Organization.

2. The Chairman and the Vice-Chairman shall be elected, one from among the representatives of producing members and the other from among the representatives of consuming members. These offices shall alternate each year between the two categories of members, provided, however, that this shall not prohibit the re-election of either or both, under exceptional circumstances, by special vote of the Council.

3. In the temporary absence of the Chairman, the Vice-Chairman shall act in his place. In the temporary absence of both the Chairman and the Vice-Chairman, or in the absence of one or both of them for the rest of the term for which they were elected, the Council may elect new officers from among the representatives of the producing members and/or from among the representatives of the consuming members, as the case may be, on a temporary basis or for the rest of the term for which the predecessor or predecessors were elected.

Article 9: Sessions of the Council

1. As a general rule, the Council shall hold at least one regular session a year.

2. The Council shall meet in special session whenever it so decides or at the request of:
(a) The Executive Director, in agreement with the Chairman of the Council; or
(b) A majority of producing members or a majority of consuming members; or
(c) Members holding at least 500 votes.

3. Sessions of the Council shall be held at the headquarters of the Organization unless the Council, by special vote, decides otherwise. If on the invitation of any member the Council meets elsewhere than at the headquarters of the Organization, that member shall pay the additional cost of holding the meeting away from headquarters.

4. Notice of any sessions and the agenda for such sessions shall be communicated to members by the Executive Director at least six weeks in advance, except in cases of emergency, when notice shall be communicated at least seven days in advance.

Article 10: Distribution of votes

1. The producing members shall together hold 1,000 votes and the consuming members shall together hold 1,000 votes.

2. The votes of the producing members shall be distributed as follows:
(a) Four hundred votes shall be distributed equally among the three producing regions of Africa, Asia-Pacific and Latin America. The votes thus allocated to each of these regions shall then be distributed equally among the producing members of that region;
(b) Three hundred votes shall be distributed among the producing members in accordance with their respective shares of the total tropical forest resources of all producing members; and
(c) Three hundred votes shall be distributed among the producing members in proportion to the average of the values of their respective net exports of tropical timber during the most recent three-year period for which definitive figures are available.

3. Notwithstanding the provisions of paragraph 2 of this article, the total votes allocated to the producing members from the African region, calculated in accordance with paragraph 2 of this article, shall be distributed equally among all producing members from the African region. If there are any remaining votes, each of these votes shall be allocated to a producing member from the African region: the first to the producing member which is allocated the highest number of votes calculated in accordance with paragraph 2 of this article, the second to the producing member which is allocated the second highest number of votes, and so on until all the remaining votes have been distributed.

4. For purposes of the calculation of the distribution of votes under paragraph 2 (b) of this article, 'tropical forest resources' means productive closed broadleaved forests as defined by the Food and Agriculture Organization (FAO).

5. The votes of the consuming members shall be distributed as follows: each consuming member shall have 10 initial votes: the remaining votes shall be

distributed among the consuming members in proportion to the average volume of their respective net imports of tropical timber during the three-year period commencing four calendar years prior to the distribution of votes.

6. The Council shall distribute the votes for each financial year at the beginning of its first session of that year in accordance with the provisions of this article. Such distribution shall remain in effect for the rest of that year, except as provided for in paragraph 7 of this article.

7. Whenever the membership of the Organization changes or when any member has its voting rights suspended or restored under any provision of this Agreement, the Council shall redistribute the votes within the affected category or categories of members in accordance with the provisions of this article. The Council shall, in that event, decide when such redistribution shall become effective.

8. There shall be no fractional votes.

Article 11: Voting procedure of the Council

1. Each member shall be entitled to cast the number of votes it holds and no member shall be entitled to divide its votes. A member may, however, cast differently from such votes any votes which it is authorized to cast under paragraph 2 of this article.

2. By written notification to the Chairman of the Council, any producing member may authorize, under its own responsibility, any other producing member, and any consuming member may authorize, under its own responsibility, any other consuming member, to represent its interests and to cast its votes at any meeting of the Council.

3. When abstaining, a member shall be deemed not to have cast its votes.

Article 12: Decisions and recommendations of the Council

1. The Council shall endeavour to take all decisions and to make all recommendations by consensus. If consensus cannot be reached, the Council shall take all decisions and make all recommendations by a simple distributed majority vote, unless this Agreement provides for a special vote.

2. Where a member avails itself of the provisions of article 11, paragraph 2, and its votes are cast at a meeting of the Council, such member shall, for the purposes of paragraph 1 of this article, be considered as present and voting.

Article 13: Quorum for the Council

1. The quorum for any meeting of the Council shall be the presence of a majority of members of each category referred to in article 4, provided that such members hold at least two thirds of the total votes in their respective categories.

2. If there is no quorum in accordance with paragraph 1 of this article on the day fixed for the meeting and on the following day, the quorum on the subsequent days of the session shall be the presence of a majority of members of each category

referred to in article 4, provided that such members hold a majority of the total votes in their respective categories.

3. Representation in accordance with article 11, paragraph 2, shall be considered as presence.

Article 14: Cooperation and co-ordination with other organizations

1. The Council shall make arrangements as appropriate for consultations and cooperation with the United Nations and its organs, including the United Nations Conference on Trade and Development (UNCTAD) and the Commission on Sustainable Development (CSD), intergovernmental organizations, including the General Agreement on Tariffs and Trade (GATT) and the Convention on International Trade in Endangered Species of Wild Fauna and Flora (CITES), and non-governmental organizations.

2. The Organization shall, to the maximum extent possible, utilize the facilities, services and expertise of existing intergovernmental, governmental or non-governmental organizations, in order to avoid duplication of efforts in achieving the objectives of this Agreement and to enhance the complementarity and the efficiency of their activities.

Article 15: Admission of observers

The Council may invite any non-member Government or any of the organizations referred to in article 14, article 20 and article 29, interested in the activities of the Organization to attend as observers any of the meetings of the Council.

Article 16: Executive Director and staff

1. The Council shall, by special vote, appoint the Executive Director.

2. The terms and conditions of appointment of the Executive Director shall be determined by the Council.

3. The Executive Director shall be the chief administrative officer of the Organization and shall be responsible to the Council for the administration and operation of this Agreement in accordance with decisions of the Council.

4. The Executive Director shall appoint the staff in accordance with regulations to be established by the Council. The Council shall, by special vote, decide the number of executive and professional staff the Executive Director may appoint. Any changes in the number of executive and professional staff shall be decided by the Council by special vote. The staff shall be responsible to the Executive Director.

5. Neither the Executive Director nor any member of the staff shall have any financial interest in the timber industry or trade, or associated commercial activities.

6. In the performance of their duties, the Executive Director and staff shall not seek or receive instructions from any member or from any authority external to the Organization. They shall refrain from any action which might reflect adversely on

their positions as international officials ultimately responsible to the Council. Each member shall respect the exclusively international character of the responsibilities of the Executive Director and staff and shall not seek to influence them in the discharge of their responsibilities.

[Chapter V: Privileges and immunities; Chapter VI: Finance; Chapter VII: Operational activities; Chapter VIII: Relationship with the Common Fund for Commodities; Chapter IX: Statistics, studies and information, Chapter X: Miscellaneous; Chapter XI: Final provisions, not reproduced]

Annex A: List of producing countries; Annex B: List of consuming countries [not reproduced]

Antarctica

Convention on the Conservation of Antarctic Marine Living Resources

Adopted on 20 May 1980 at Canberra. Entered into force on 7 April 1982. Source: 1329 *UNTS* 47. Number of parties: 31. Further information: Commission for the Conservation of Antarctic Marine Living Resources, Hobart, Tasmania, Australia, http://www.ccamlr.org

The Contracting Parties,

Recognising the importance of safeguarding the environment and protecting the integrity of the ecosystem of the seas surrounding Antarctica;

Noting the concentration of marine living resources found in Antarctic waters and the increased interest in the possibilities offered by the utilization of these resources as a source of protein;

Conscious of the urgency of ensuring the conservation of Antarctic marine living resources;

Considering that it is essential to increase knowledge of the Antarctic marine ecosystem and its components so as to be able to base decisions on harvesting on sound scientific information;

Believing that the conservation of Antarctic marine living resources calls for international cooperation with due regard for the provisions of the Antarctic Treaty and with the active involvement of all States engaged in research or harvesting activities in Antarctic waters;

Recognising the prime responsibilities of the Antarctic Treaty Consultative Parties for the protection and preservation of the Antarctic environment and, in particular, their responsibilities under Article IX, paragraph 1(f) of the Antarctic Treaty in respect of the preservation and conservation of living resources in Antarctica;

Recalling the action already taken by the Antarctic Treaty Consultative Parties including in particular the Agreed Measures for the Conservation of Antarctic Fauna and Flora, as well as the provisions of the Convention for the Conservation of Antarctic Seals;

Bearing in mind the concern regarding the conservation of Antarctic marine living resources expressed by the Consultative Parties at the Ninth Consultative Meeting of the Antarctic Treaty and the importance of the provisions of Recommendation IX-2 which led to the establishment of the present Convention;

Believing that it is in the interest of all mankind to preserve the waters surrounding the Antarctic continent for peaceful purposes only and to prevent their becoming the scene or object of international discord;

Recognising, in the light of the foregoing, that it is desirable to establish suitable machinery for recommending, promoting, deciding upon and coordinating the measures and scientific studies needed to ensure the conservation of Antarctic marine living organisms;

Have agreed as follows:

Article I

1. This Convention applies to the Antarctic marine living resources of the area south of 60° South latitude and to the Antarctic marine living resources of the area between that latitude and the Antarctic Convergence which form part of the Antarctic marine ecosystem.

2. Antarctic marine living resources means the populations of fin fish, molluscs, crustaceans and all other species of living organisms, including birds, found south of the Antarctic Convergence.

3. The Antarctic marine ecosystem means the complex of relationships of Antarctic marine living resources with each other and with their physical environment.

4. The Antarctic Convergence shall be deemed to be a line joining the following points along parallels of latitude and meridians of longitude:

50°S, 0°; 50°S, 30°E; 45°S, 30°E; 45°S, 80°E; 55°S, 80°E; 55°S, 150°E; 60°S, 150°E; 60°S, 50°W; 50°S, 50°W; 50°S, 0°.

Article II

1. The objective of this Convention is the conservation of Antarctic marine living resources.

2. For the purposes of this Convention, the term 'conservation' includes rational use.

3. Any harvesting and associated activities in the area to which this Convention applies shall be conducted in accordance with the provisions of this Convention and with the following principles of conservation:

(a) prevention of decrease in the size of any harvested population to levels below those which ensure its stable recruitment. For this purpose its size should not be allowed to fall below a level close to that which ensures the greatest net annual increment;

(b) maintenance of the ecological relationships between harvested, dependent and related populations of Antarctic marine living resources and the restoration of depleted populations to the levels defined in sub-paragraph (a) above; and

(c) prevention of changes or minimization of the risk of changes in the marine ecosystem which are not potentially reversible over two or three decades, taking into account the state of available knowledge of the direct and indirect impact of harvesting, the effect of the introduction of alien species, the effects of associated activities on the marine ecosystem and of the effects of environmental changes, with the aim of making possible the sustained conservation of Antarctic marine living resources.

Article III

The Contracting Parties, whether or not they are Parties to the Antarctic Treaty, agree that they will not engage in any activities in the Antarctic Treaty area contrary to the principles and purposes of that Treaty and that, in their relations with each other, they are bound by the obligations contained in Articles I and V of the Antarctic Treaty.

Article IV

1. With respect to the Antarctic Treaty area, all Contracting Parties, whether or not they are Parties to the Antarctic Treaty, are bound by Articles IV and VI of the Antarctic Treaty in their relations with each other.

2. Nothing in this Convention and no acts or activities taking place while the present Convention is in force shall:

(a) constitute a basis for asserting, supporting or denying a claim to territorial sovereignty in the Antarctic Treaty area or create any rights of sovereignty in the Antarctic Treaty area;

(b) be interpreted as a renunciation or diminution by any Contracting Party of, or as prejudicing, any right or claim on basis of claim to exercise coastal State jurisdiction under international law within the area to which this Convention applies;

(c) be interpreted as prejudicing the position of any Contracting Party as regards its recognition or non-recognition of any such right, claim or basis of claim;

(d) affect the provision of Article IV, paragraph 2, of the Antarctic Treaty that no new claim, or enlargement of an existing claim, to territorial sovereignty in Antarctica shall be asserted while the Antarctic Treaty is in force.

Article V

1. The Contracting Parties which are not Parties to the Antarctic Treaty acknowledge the special obligations and responsibilities of the Antarctic Treaty Consultative Parties for the protection and preservation of the environment of the Antarctic Treaty area.

2. The Contracting Parties which are not Parties to the Antarctic Treaty agree that, in their activities in the Antarctic Treaty area, they will observe as and when appropriate the Agreed Measures for the Conservation of Antarctic Fauna and Flora and such other measures as have been recommended by the Antarctic Treaty Consultative Parties in fulfilment of their responsibility for the protection of the Antarctic environment from all forms of harmful human interference.

3. For the purposes of this Convention, 'Antarctic Treaty Consultative Parties' means the Contracting Parties to the Antarctic Treaty whose Representatives participate in meetings under Article IX of the Antarctic Treaty.

Article VI

Nothing in this Convention shall derogate from the rights and obligations of Contracting Parties under the International Convention for the Regulation of Whaling and the Convention for the Conservation of Antarctic Seals.

Article VII

1. The Contracting Parties hereby establish and agree to maintain the Commission for the Conservation of Antarctic Marine Living Resources (hereinafter referred to as 'the Commission').

2. Membership in the Commission shall be as follows:

(a) each Contracting Party which participated in the meeting at which this Convention was adopted shall be a Member of the Commission;

(b) each State Party which has acceded to this Convention pursuant to Article XXIX shall be entitled to be a Member of the Commission during such time as that acceding party is engaged in research or harvesting activities in relation to the marine living resources to which this Convention applies;

(c) each regional economic integration organization which has acceded to this Convention pursuant to Article XXIX shall be entitled to be a Member of the Commission during such time as its States members are so entitled;

(d) a Contracting Party seeking to participate in the work of the Commission pursuant to sub-paragraphs (b) and (c) above shall notify the Depositary of the basis upon which it seeks to become a Member of the Commission and of its willingness to accept conservation measures in force. The Depositary shall communicate to each Member of the Commission such notification and accompanying information. Within two months of receipt of such communication from the Depositary, any Member of the Commission may request that a special meeting of the Commission be held to consider the matter. Upon receipt of such request, the Depositary shall call such a meeting. If there is no request for a meeting, the Contracting Party submitting the notification shall be deemed to have satisfied the requirements for Commission Membership.

3. Each Member of the Commission shall be represented by one representative who may be accompanied by alternate representatives and advisers.

Article VIII

The Commission shall have legal personality and shall enjoy in the territory of each of the States Parties such legal capacity as may be necessary to perform its function and achieve the purposes of this Convention. The privileges and immunities to be enjoyed by the Commission and its staff in the territory of a State Party shall be determined by agreement between the Commission and the State Party concerned.

Article IX

1. The function of the Commission shall be to give effect to the objective and principles set out in Article II of this Convention. To this end, it shall:

(a) facilitate research into and comprehensive studies of Antarctic marine living resources and of the Antarctic marine ecosystem;

(b) compile data on the status of and changes in population of Antarctic marine living resources and on factors affecting the distribution, abundance and productivity of harvested species and dependent or related species or populations;

(c) ensure the acquisition of catch and effort statistics on harvested populations;

(d) analyse, disseminate and publish the information referred to in sub-paragraphs (b) and (c) above and the reports of the Scientific Committee:

(e) identify conservation needs and analyse the effectiveness of conservation measures;

(f) formulate, adopt and revise conservation measures on the basis of the best scientific evidence available, subject to the provisions of paragraph 5 of this Article;

(g) implement the system of observation and inspection established under Article XXIV of this Convention;

(h) carry out such other activities as are necessary to fulfil the objective of this Convention.

2. The conservation measures referred to in paragraph 1(f) above include the following:

(a) the designation of the quantity of any species which may be harvested in the area to which this Convention applies;

(b) the designation of regions and sub-regions based on the distribution of populations of Antarctic marine living resources;

(c) the designation of the quantity which may be harvested from the populations of regions and sub-regions;

(d) the designation of protected species;

(e) the designation of the size, age and, as appropriate, sex of species which may be harvested;

(f) the designation of open and closed seasons for harvesting;
(g) the designation of the opening and closing of areas, regions or sub-regions for purposes of scientific study or conservation, including special areas for protection and scientific study;
(h) regulation of the effort employed and methods of harvesting, including fishing gear, with a view, inter alia, to avoiding undue concentration of harvesting in any region or sub-region;
(i) the taking of such other conservation measures as the Commission considers necessary for the fulfilment of the objective of this Convention, including measures concerning the effects of harvesting and associated activities on components of the marine ecosystem other than the harvested populations.

3. The Commission shall publish and maintain a record of all conservation measures in force.

4. In exercising its functions under paragraph 1 above, the Commission shall take full account of the recommendations and advice of the Scientific Committee.

5. The Commission shall take full account of any relevant measures or regulations established or recommended by the Consultative Meetings pursuant to Article IX of the Antarctic Treaty or by existing fisheries commissions responsible for species which may enter the area to which this Convention applies, in order that there shall be no inconsistency between the rights and obligations of a Contracting Party under such regulations or measures and conservation measures which may be adopted by the Commission.

6. Conservation measures adopted by the Commission in accordance with this Convention shall be implemented by Members of the Commission in the following manner:
(a) the Commission shall notify conservation measures to all Members of the Commission;
(b) conservation measures shall become binding upon all Members of the Commission 180 days after such notification, except as provided in subparagraphs (c) and (d) below:
(c) if a Member of the Commission, within ninety days following the notification specified in subparagraph (a), notifies the Commission that it is unable to accept the conservation measure, in whole or in part, the measure shall not, to the extent stated, be binding upon that Member of the Commission;
(d) in the event that any Member of the Commission invokes the procedure set forth in subparagraph (c) above, the Commission shall meet at the request of any Member of the Commission to review the conservation measure. At the time of such meeting and within thirty days following the meeting, any Member of the Commission shall have the right to declare that it is no longer able to accept the conservation measure, in which case the Member shall no longer be bound by such measure.

Article X

1. The Commission shall draw the attention of any State which is not a Party to this Convention to any activity undertaken by its nationals or vessels which, in the opinion of the Commission, affects the implementation of the objective of this Convention.

2. The Commission shall draw the attention of all Contracting Parties to any activity which, in the opinion of the Commission, affects the implementation by a Contracting Party of the objective of this Convention or the compliance by that Contracting Party with its obligations under this Convention.

Article XI

The Commission shall seek to co-operate with Contracting Parties which may exercise jurisdiction in marine areas adjacent to the area to which this Convention applies in respect of the conservation of any stock or stocks of associated species which occur both within those areas and the area to which this Convention applies, with a view to harmonizing the conservation measures adopted in respect of such stocks.

Article XII

1. Decisions of the Commission on matters of substance shall be taken by consensus. The question of whether a matter is one of substance shall be treated as a matter of substance.

2. Decisions on matters other than those referred to in paragraph 1 above shall be taken by a simple majority of the Members of the Commission present and voting.

3. In Commission consideration of any item requiring a decision, it shall be made clear whether a regional economic integration organization will participate in the taking of the decision and, if so, whether any of its member States will also participate. The number of Contracting Parties so participating shall not exceed the number of member States of the regional economic integration organization which are Members of the Commission.

4. In the taking of decisions pursuant to this Article, a regional economic integration organization shall have only one vote.

Article XIII

1. The headquarters of the Commission shall be established at Hobart, Tasmania, Australia.

2. The Commission shall hold a regular annual meeting. Other meetings shall also be held at the request of one-third of its members and as otherwise provided in this Convention. The first meeting of the Commission shall be held within three months of the entry into force of this Convention, provided that among the Contracting Parties there are at least two States conducting harvesting activities within the area to which this Convention applies. The first meeting shall, in any event, be held within one year of the entry into force of this Convention. The Depositary shall

consult with the signatory States regarding the first Commission meeting, taking into account that a broad representation of such States is necessary for the effective operation of the Commission.

3. The Depositary shall convene the first meeting of the Commission at the headquarters of the Commission. Thereafter, meetings of the Commission shall be held at its headquarters, unless it decides otherwise.

4. The Commission shall elect from among its members a Chairman and Vice-Chairman, each of whom shall serve for a term of two years and shall be eligible for re-election for one additional term. The first Chairman shall, however, be elected for an initial term of three years. The Chairman and Vice-Chairman shall not be representatives of the same Contracting Party.

5. The Commission shall adopt and amend as necessary the rules of procedure for the conduct of its meetings, except with respect to the matters dealt with in Article XII of this Convention.

6. The Commission may establish such subsidiary bodies as are necessary for the performance of its functions.

Article XIV

1. The Contracting Parties hereby establish the Scientific Committee for the Conservation of Antarctic Marine Living Resources (hereinafter referred to as the 'Scientific Committee') which shall be a consultative body to the Commission. The Scientific Committee shall normally meet at the headquarters of the Commission unless the Scientific Committee decides otherwise.

2. Each Member of the Commission shall be a member of the Scientific Committee and shall appoint a representative with suitable scientific qualifications who may be accompanied by other experts and advisers.

3. The Scientific Committee may seek the advice of other scientists and experts as may be required on an *ad hoc* basis.

Article XV

1. The Scientific Committee shall provide a forum for consultation and co-operation concerning the collection, study and exchange of information with respect to the marine living resources to which this Convention applies. It shall encourage and promote co-operation in the field of scientific research in order to extend knowledge of the marine living resources of the Antarctic marine ecosystem.

2. The Scientific Committee shall conduct such activities as the Commission may direct in pursuance of the objective of this Convention and shall:

(a) establish criteria and methods to be used for determinations concerning the conservation measures referred to in Article IX of this Convention;

(b) regularly assess the status and trends of the populations of Antarctic marine living resources;

(c) analyse data concerning the direct and indirect effects of harvesting on the populations of Antarctic marine living resources;
(d) assess the effects of proposed changes in the methods or levels of harvesting and proposed conservation measures;
(e) transmit assessments, analyses, reports and recommendations to the Commission as requested or on its own initiative regarding measures and research to implement the objective of this Convention;
(f) formulate proposals for the conduct of international and national programs of research into Antarctic marine living resources.

3. In carrying out its functions, the Scientific Committee shall have regard to the work of other relevant technical and scientific organizations and to the scientific activities conducted within the framework of the Antarctic Treaty.

Article XVI

1. The first meeting of the Scientific Committee shall be held within three months of the first meeting of the Commission. The Scientific Committee shall meet thereafter as often as may be necessary to fulfil its functions.

2. The Scientific Committee shall adopt and amend as necessary its rules of procedure. The rules and any amendments thereto shall be approved by the Commission. The rules shall include procedures for the presentation of minority reports.

3. The Scientific Committee may establish, with the approval of the Commission, such subsidiary bodies as are necessary for the performance of its functions.

Article XVII

1. The Commission shall appoint an Executive Secretary to serve the Commission and Scientific Committee according to such procedures and on such terms and conditions as the Commission may determine. His term of office shall be for four years and he shall be eligible for re-appointment.

2. The Commission shall authorize such staff establishment for the Secretariat as may be necessary and the Executive Secretary shall appoint, direct and supervise such staff according to such rules and procedures and on such terms and conditions as the Commission may determine.

3. The Executive Secretary and Secretariat shall perform the functions entrusted to them by the Commission.

Article XVIII

The official languages of the Commission and of the Scientific Committee shall be English, French, Russian and Spanish.

Article XIX

1. At each annual meeting, the Commission shall adopt by consensus its budget and the budget of the Scientific Committee.

2. A draft budget for the Commission and the Scientific Committee and any subsidiary bodies shall be prepared by the Executive Secretary and submitted to the Members of the Commission at least sixty days before the annual meeting of the Commission.

3. Each Member of the Commission shall contribute to the budget. Until the expiration of five years after the entry into force of this Convention, the contribution of each Member of the Commission shall be equal. Thereafter the contribution shall be determined in accordance with two criteria: the amount harvested and an equal sharing among all Members of the Commission. The Commission shall determine by consensus the proportion in which these two criteria shall apply.

4. The financial activities of the Commission and Scientific Committee shall be conducted in accordance with financial regulations adopted by the Commission and shall be subject to an annual audit by external auditors selected by the Commission.

5. Each Member of the Commission shall meet its own expenses arising from attendance at meetings of the Commission and of the Scientific Committee.

6. A Member of the Commission that fails to pay its contributions for two consecutive years shall not, during the period of its default, have the right to participate in the taking of decisions in the Commission.

Article XX

1. The Members of the Commission shall, to the greatest extent possible, provide annually to the Commission and to the Scientific Committee such statistical, biological and other data and information as the Commission and Scientific Committee may require in the exercise of their functions.

2. The Members of the Commission shall provide, in the manner and at such intervals as may be prescribed, information about their harvesting activities, including fishing areas and vessels, so as to enable reliable catch and effort statistics to be compiled.

3. The Members of the Commission shall provide to the Commission at such intervals as may be prescribed information on steps taken to implement the conservation measures adopted by the Commission.

4. The Members of the Commission agree that in any of their harvesting activities, advantage shall be taken of opportunities to collect data needed to assess the impact of harvesting.

Article XXI

1. Each Contracting Party shall take appropriate measures within its competence to ensure compliance with the provisions of this Convention and with conservation measures adopted by the Commission to which the Party is bound in accordance with Article IX of this Convention.

2. Each Contracting Party shall transmit to the Commission information on measures taken pursuant to paragraph 1 above, including the imposition of sanctions for any violation.

Article XXII

1. Each Contracting Party undertakes to exert appropriate efforts, consistent with the Charter of the United Nations, to the end that no one engages in any activity contrary to the objective of this Convention.

2. Each Contracting Party shall notify the Commission of any such activity which comes to its attention.

Article XXIII

1. The Commission and the Scientific Committee shall co-operate with the Antarctic Treaty Consultative Parties on matters falling within the competence of the latter.

2. The Commission and the Scientific Committee shall co-operate, as appropriate, with the Food and Agriculture Organization of the United Nations and with other Specialised Agencies.

3. The Commission and the Scientific Committee shall seek to develop co-operative working relationships, as appropriate, with inter-governmental and non-governmental organizations which could contribute to their work, including the Scientific Committee on Antarctic Research, the Scientific Committee on Oceanic Research and the International Whaling Commission.

4. The Commission may enter into agreements with the organizations referred to in this Article and with other organizations as may be appropriate. The Commission and the Scientific Committee may invite such organizations to send observers to their meetings and to meetings of their subsidiary bodies.

Article XXIV

1. In order to promote the objective and ensure observance of the provisions of this Convention, the Contracting Parties agree that a system of observation and inspection shall be established.

2. The system of observation and inspection shall be elaborated by the Commission on the basis of the following principles:

(a) Contracting Parties shall co-operate with each other to ensure the effective implementation of the system of observation and inspection, taking account of the existing international practice. This system shall include, inter alia, procedures for boarding and inspection by observers and inspectors designated by the Members of the Commission and procedures for flag State prosecution and sanctions on the basis of evidence resulting from such boarding and inspections. A report of such prosecutions and sanctions imposed shall be included in the information referred to in Article XXI of this Convention;

(b) in order to verify compliance with measures adopted under this Convention, observation and inspection shall be carried out on board vessels engaged in scientific research or harvesting of marine living resources in the area to which this Convention applies, through observers and inspectors designated by the Members of the Commission and operating under terms and conditions to be established by the Commission;

(c) designated observers and inspectors shall remain subject to the jurisdiction of the Contracting Party of which they are nationals. They shall report to the Member of the Commission by which they have been designated which in turn shall report to the Commission.

3. Pending the establishment of the system of observation and inspection, the Members of the Commission shall seek to establish interim arrangements to designate observers and inspectors and such designated observers and inspectors shall be entitled to carry out inspections in accordance with the principles set out in paragraph 2 above.

Article XXV

1. If any dispute arises between two or more of the Contracting Parties concerning the interpretation or application of this Convention, those Contracting Parties shall consult among themselves with a view to having the dispute resolved by negotiation, inquiry, mediation, conciliation, arbitration, judicial settlement or other peaceful means of their own choice.

2. Any dispute of this character not so resolved shall, with the consent in each case of all Parties to the dispute, be referred for settlement to the International Court of Justice or to arbitration; but failure to reach agreement on reference to the International Court or to arbitration shall not absolve Parties to the dispute from the responsibility of continuing to seek to resolve it by any of the various peaceful means referred to in paragraph 1 above.

3. In cases where the dispute is referred to arbitration, the arbitral tribunal shall be constituted as provided in the Annex to this Convention.

[Articles XXVI- XXXIII not reproduced]

Annex for an arbitral tribunal; Statement by the Chairman of the Conference on the Conservation of Antarctic Marine Living Resources [not reproduced]

Protocol on Environmental Protection to the Antarctic Treaty

Adopted on 4 October 1991 at Madrid. Entered into force on 14 January 1998. Source: *Australian Treaty Series* 1998 No. 6. Number of parties: 30. Further information: Committee for Environmental Protection (CEP), Kingston, Tasmania, Australia, http://www.cep.aq and Antarctic Treaty Secretariat, Buenos Aires, Argentina, http://www.ats.org.ar

Preamble

The States Parties to this Protocol to the Antarctic Treaty, hereinafter referred to as the Parties,

Convinced of the need to enhance the protection of the Antarctic environment and dependent and associated ecosystems;

Convinced of the need to strengthen the Antarctic Treaty system so as to ensure that Antarctic shall continue forever to be used exclusively for peaceful purposes and shall not become the scene or object of international discord;

Bearing in mind the special legal and political status of Antarctic and the special responsibility of the Antarctic Treaty Consultative Parties to ensure that all activities in Antarctic are consistent with the purposes and principles of the Antarctic Treaty;

Recalling the designation of Antarctic as a Special Conservation Area and other measures adopted under the Antarctic Treaty system to protect the Antarctic environment and dependent and associated ecosystems;

Acknowledging further the unique opportunities Antarctic offers for scientific monitoring of and research on processes of global as well as regional importance;

Reaffirming the conservation principles of the Convention on the Conservation of Antarctic Marine Living Resources;

Convinced that the development of a comprehensive regime for the protection of the Antarctic environment and dependent and associated ecosystems is in the interest of mankind as a whole;

Desiring to supplement the Antarctic Treaty to this end;

Have agreed as follows:

Article 1: Definitions

For the purposes of this Protocol:

(a) 'The Antarctic Treaty' means the Antarctic Treaty done at Washington on 1 December 1959;

(b) 'Antarctic Treaty area' means the area to which the provisions of the Antarctic Treaty apply in accordance with Article VI of that Treaty;

(c) 'Antarctic Treaty Consultative Meetings' means the meetings referred to in Article IX of the Antarctic Treaty;

(d) 'Antarctic Treaty Consultative Parties' means the Contracting Parties to the Antarctic Treaty entitled to appoint representatives to participate in the meetings referred to in Article IX of that Treaty;

(e) 'Antarctic Treaty system' means the Antarctic Treaty, the measures in effect under that Treaty, its associated separate international instruments in force and the measures in effect under those instruments;

(f) 'Arbitral Tribunal' means the Arbitral Tribunal established in accordance with the Schedule to this Protocol, which forms an integral part thereof;

(g) 'Committee' means the Committee for Environmental Protection established in accordance with Article 11.

Article 2: Objective and designation

The Parties commit themselves to the comprehensive protection of the Antarctic environment and dependent and associated ecosystems and hereby designate Antarctica as a natural reserve, devoted to peace and science.

Article 3: Environmental principles

1. The protection of the Antarctic environment and dependent and associated ecosystems and the intrinsic value of Antarctica, including its wilderness and aesthetic values and its value as an area for the conduct of scientific research, in particular research essential to understanding the global environment, shall be fundamental considerations in the planning and conduct of all activities in the Antarctic Treaty area.

2. To this end:

(a) activities in the Antarctic Treaty area shall be planned and conducted so as to limit adverse impacts on the Antarctic environment and dependent and associated ecosystems;

(b) activities in the Antarctic Treaty area shall be planned and conducted so as to avoid:

i) adverse effects on climate or weather patterns;

ii) significant adverse effects on air or water quality;

iii) significant changes in the atmospheric, terrestrial (including aquatic), glacial or marine environments;

iv) detrimental changes in the distribution, abundance or productivity of species or populations of species of fauna and flora;

v) further jeopardy to endangered or threatened species or populations of such species; or

vi) degradation of, or substantial risk to, areas of biological, scientific, historic, aesthetic or wilderness significance;

(c) activities in the Antarctic Treaty area shall be planned and conducted on the basis of information sufficient to allow prior assessments of, and informed judgments about, their possible impacts on the Antarctic environment and dependent and associated ecosystems and on the value of Antarctic for the conduct of scientific research; such judgments shall take full account of:

i) the scope of the activity, including its area, duration and intensity;

ii) the cumulative impacts of the activity, both by itself and in combination with other activities in the Antarctic Treaty area;

iii) whether the activity will detrimentally affect any other activity in the Antarctic Treaty area;

iv) whether technology and procedures are available to provide for environmentally safe operations;
v) whether there exists the capacity to monitor key environmental parameters and ecosystem components so as to identify and provide early warning of any adverse effects of the activity and to provide for such modification of operating procedures as may be necessary in the light of the results of monitoring or increased knowledge of the Antarctic environment and dependent and associated ecosystems; and
vi) whether there exists the capacity to respond promptly and effectively to accidents, particularly those with potential environmental effects;

(d) regular and effective monitoring shall take place to allow assessment of the impacts of ongoing activities, including the verification of predicted impacts;
(e) regular and effective monitoring shall take place to facilitate early detection of the possible unforeseen effects of activities carried on both within and outside the Antarctic Treaty area on the Antarctic environment and dependent and associated ecosystems.

3. Activities shall be planned and conducted in the Antarctic Treaty area so as to accord priority to scientific research and to preserve the value of Antarctica as an area for the conduct of such research, including research essential to understanding the global environment.

4. Activities undertaken in the Antarctic Treaty area pursuant to scientific research programmes, tourism and all other governmental and non-governmental activities in the Antarctic Treaty area for which advance notice is required in accordance with Article VII (5) of the Antarctic Treaty, including associated logistic support activities, shall:
(a) take place in a manner consistent with the principles in this Article; and
(b) be modified, suspended or cancelled if they result in or threaten to result in impacts upon the Antarctic environment or dependent or associated ecosystems inconsistent with those principles.

Article 4: Relationship with the other components of the Antarctic Treaty system

1. This Protocol shall supplement the Antarctic Treaty and shall neither modify nor amend that Treaty.

2. Nothing in this Protocol shall derogate from the rights and obligations of the Parties to this Protocol under the other international instruments in force within the Antarctic Treaty system.

Article 5: Consistency with the other components of the Antarctic Treaty system

The Parties shall consult and co-operate with the Contracting Parties to the other international instruments in force within the Antarctic Treaty system and their respective institutions with a view to ensuring the achievement of the objectives and principles of this Protocol and avoiding any interference with the achievement of the objectives and principles of those instruments or any inconsistency between the implementation of those instruments and of this Protocol.

Article 6: Co-operation

1. The Parties shall co-operate in the planning and conduct of activities in the Antarctic Treaty area. To this end, each Party shall endeavour to:

(a) promote co-operative programmes of scientific, technical and educational value, concerning the protection of the Antarctic environment and dependent and associated ecosystems;

(b) provide appropriate assistance to other Parties in the preparation of environmental impact assessments;

(c) provide to other Parties upon request information relevant to any potential environmental risk and assistance to minimize the effects of accidents which may damage the Antarctic environment or dependent and associated ecosystems;

(d) consult with other Parties with regard to the choice of sites for prospective stations and other facilities so as to avoid the cumulative impacts caused by their excessive concentration in any location;

(e) where appropriate, undertake joint expeditions and share the use of stations and other facilities; and

(f) carry out such steps as may be agreed upon at Antarctic Treaty Consultative Meetings.

2. Each Party undertakes, to the extent possible, to share information that maybe helpful to other Parties in planning and conducting their activities in the Antarctic Treaty area, with a view to the protection of the Antarctic environment and dependent and associated ecosystems.

3. The Parties shall co-operate with those Parties which may exercise jurisdiction in areas adjacent to the Antarctic Treaty area with a view to ensuring that activities in the Antarctic Treaty area do not have adverse environmental impacts on those areas.

Article 7: Prohibition of mineral resource activities

Any activity relating to mineral resources, other than scientific research, shall be prohibited.

Article 8: Environmental impact assessment

1. Proposed activities referred to in paragraph 2 below shall be subject to the procedures set out in Annex I for prior assessment of the impacts of those activities on the Antarctic environment or on dependent or associated ecosystems according to whether those activities are identified as having:

(a) less than a minor or transitory impact;

(b) a minor or transitory impact; or

(c) more than a minor or transitory impact.

2. Each Party shall ensure that the assessment procedures set out in Annex I are applied in the planning processes leading to decisions about any activities undertaken in the Antarctic Treaty area pursuant to scientific research programmes, tourism and all other governmental and non-governmental activities in the Antarctic Treaty area for which advance notice is required under Article VII (5) of the Antarctic Treaty, including associated logistic support activities.

3. The assessment procedures set out in Annex I shall apply to any change in an activity whether the change arises from an increase or decrease in the intensity of an existing activity, from the addition of an activity, the decommissioning of a facility, or otherwise.

4. Where activities are planned jointly by more than one Party, the Parties involved shall nominate one of their number to coordinate the implementation of the environmental impact assessment procedures set out in Annex I.

Article 9: Annexes

1. The Annexes to this Protocol shall form an integral part thereof.

2. Annexes, additional to Annexes I-IV, may be adopted and become effective in accordance with Article IX of the Antarctic Treaty.

3. Amendments and modifications to Annexes may be adopted and become effective in accordance with Article IX of the Antarctic Treaty, provided that any Annex may itself make provision for amendments and modifications to become effective on an accelerated basis.

4. Annexes and any amendments and modifications thereto which have become effective in accordance with paragraphs 2 and 3 above shall, unless an Annex itself provides otherwise in respect of the entry into effect of any amendment or modification thereto, become effective for a Contracting Party to the Antarctic Treaty which is not an Antarctic Treaty Consultative Party, or which was not an Antarctic Treaty Consultative Party at the time of the adoption, when notice of approval of that Contracting Party has been received by the Depositary.

5. Annexes shall, except to the extent that an Annex provides otherwise, be subject to the procedures for dispute settlement set out in Articles 18 to 20.

Article 10: Antarctic Treaty Consultative Meetings

1. Antarctic Treaty Consultative Meetings shall, drawing upon the best scientific and technical advice available:

(a) define, in accordance with the provisions of this Protocol, the general policy for the comprehensive protection of the Antarctic environment and dependent and associated ecosystems; and

(b) adopt measures under Article IX of the Antarctic Treaty for the implementation of this Protocol.

2. Antarctic Treaty Consultative Meetings shall review the work of the Committee and shall draw fully upon its advice and recommendations in carrying out the tasks

referred to in paragraph 1 above, as well as upon the advice of the Scientific Committee on Antarctic Research.

Article 11: Committee for Environmental Protection

1. There is hereby established the Committee for Environmental Protection.

2. Each Party shall be entitled to be a member of the Committee and to appoint a representative who may be accompanied by experts and advisers.

3. Observer status in the Committee shall be open to any Contracting Party to the Antarctic Treaty which is not a Party to this Protocol.

4. The Committee shall invite the President of the Scientific Committee on Antarctic Research and the Chairman of the Scientific Committee for the Conservation of Antarctic Marine Living Resources to participate as observers at its sessions. The Committee may also, with the approval of the Antarctic Treaty Consultative Meeting, invite such other relevant scientific, environmental and technical organisations which can contribute to its work to participate as observers at its sessions.

5. The Committee shall present a report on each of its sessions to the Antarctic Treaty Consultative Meeting. The report shall cover all matters considered at the session and shall reflect the views expressed. The report shall be circulated to the Parties and to observers attending the session, and shall thereupon be made publicly available.

6. The Committee shall adopt its rules of procedure which shall be subject to approval by the Antarctic Treaty Consultative Meeting.

Article 12: Functions of the Committee

1. The functions of the Committee shall be to provide advice and formulate recommendations to the Parties in connection with the implementation of this Protocol, including the operation of its Annexes, for consideration at Antarctic Treaty Consultative Meetings, and to perform such other functions as may be referred to it by the Antarctic Treaty Consultative Meetings. In particular, it shall provide advice on:

(a) the effectiveness of measures taken pursuant to this Protocol;
(b) the need to update, strengthen or otherwise improve such measures;
(c) the need for additional measures, including the need for additional Annexes, where appropriate;
(d) the application and implementation of the environmental impact assessment procedures set out in Article 8 and Annex I;
(e) means of minimising or mitigating environmental impacts of activities in the Antarctic Treaty area;
(f) procedures for situations requiring urgent action, including response action in environmental emergencies;
(g) the operation and further elaboration of the Antarctic Protected Area system;

(h) inspection procedures, including formats for inspection reports and checklists for the conduct of inspections;
(i) the collection, archiving, exchange and evaluation of information related to environmental protection;
(j) the state of the Antarctic environment; and
(k) the need for scientific research, including environmental monitoring, related to the implementation of this Protocol.

2. In carrying out its functions, the Committee shall, as appropriate, consult with the Scientific Committee on Antarctic Research, the Scientific Committee for the Conservation of Antarctic Marine Living Resources and other relevant scientific, environmental and technical organizations.

Article 13: Compliance with this Protocol

1. Each Party shall take appropriate measures within its competence, including the adoption of laws and regulations, administrative actions and enforcement measures, to ensure compliance with this Protocol.

2. Each Party shall exert appropriate efforts, consistent with the Charter of the United Nations, to the end that no one engages in any activity contrary to this Protocol.

3. Each Party shall notify all other Parties of the measures it takes pursuant to paragraphs 1 and 2 above.

4. Each Party shall draw the attention of all other Parties to any activity which in its opinion affects the implementation of the objectives and principles of this Protocol.

5. The Antarctic Treaty Consultative Meetings shall draw the attention of any State which is not a Party to this Protocol to any activity undertaken by that State, its agencies, instrumentalities, natural or juridical persons, ships, aircraft or other means of transport which affects the implementation of the objectives and principles of this Protocol.

Article 14: Inspection

1. In order to promote the protection of the Antarctic environment and dependent and associated ecosystems, and to ensure compliance with this Protocol, the Antarctic Treaty Consultative Parties shall arrange, individually or collectively, for inspections by observers to be made in accordance with Article VII of the Antarctic Treaty.

2. Observers are:
(a) observers designated by any Antarctic Treaty Consultative Party who shall be nationals of that Party; and
(b) any observers designated at Antarctic Treaty Consultative Meetings to carry out inspections under procedures to be established by an Antarctic Treaty Consultative Meeting.

3. Parties shall co-operate fully with observers undertaking inspections, and shall ensure that during inspections, observers are given access to all parts of stations, installations, equipment, ships and aircraft open to inspection under Article VII (3) of the Antarctic Treaty, as well as to all records maintained thereon which are called for pursuant to this Protocol.

4. Reports of inspections shall be sent to the Parties whose stations, installations, equipment, ships or aircraft are covered by the reports. After those Parties have been given the opportunity to comment, the reports and any comments thereon shall be circulated to all the Parties and to the Committee, considered at the next Antarctic Treaty Consultative Meeting, and thereafter made publicly available.

Article 15: Emergency response action

1. In order to respond to environmental emergencies in the Antarctic Treaty area, each Party agrees to:

(a) provide for prompt and effective response action to such emergencies which might arise in the performance of scientific research programmes, tourism and all other governmental and nongovernmental activities in the Antarctic Treaty area for which advance notice is required under Article VII (5) of the Antarctic Treaty, including associated logistic support activities; and

(b) establish contingency plans for response to incidents with potential adverse effects on the Antarctic environment or dependent and associated ecosystems.

2. To this end, the Parties shall:

(a) co-operate in the formulation and implementation of such contingency plans; and

(b) establish procedures for immediate notification of, and co-operative response to, environmental emergencies.

3. In the implementation of this Article, the Parties shall draw upon the advice of the appropriate international organisations.

Article 16: Liability

Consistent with the objectives of this Protocol for the comprehensive protection of the Antarctic environment and dependent and associated ecosystems, the Parties undertake to elaborate rules and procedures relating to liability for damage arising from activities taking place in the Antarctic Treaty area and covered by this Protocol. Those rules and procedures shall be included in one or more Annexes to be adopted in accordance with Article 9 (2).

Article 17: Annual report by Parties

1. Each Party shall report annually on the steps taken to implement this Protocol. Such reports shall include notifications made in accordance with Article 13 (3), contingency plans established in accordance with Article 15 and any other notifications and information called for pursuant to this Protocol for which there is no other provision concerning the circulation and exchange of information.

2. Reports made in accordance with paragraph 1 above shall be circulated to all Parties and to the Committee, considered at the next Antarctic Treaty Consultative Meeting, and made publicly available.

Article 18: Dispute settlement

If a dispute arises concerning the interpretation or application of this Protocol, the parties to the dispute shall, at the request of any one of them, consult among themselves as soon as possible with a view to having the dispute resolved by negotiation, inquiry, mediation, conciliation, arbitration, judicial settlement or other peaceful means to which the parties to the dispute agree.

Article 19: Choice of dispute settlement procedure

1. Each Party, when signing, ratifying, accepting, approving or acceding to this Protocol, or at any time thereafter, may choose, by written declaration, one or both of the following means for the settlement of disputes concerning the interpretation or application of Articles 7, 8 and 15 and, except to the extent that an Annex provides otherwise, the provisions of any Annex and, insofar as it relates to these Articles and provisions, Article 13:
(a) the International Court of Justice;
(b) the Arbitral Tribunal.

2. A declaration made under paragraph 1 above shall not affect the operation of Article 18 and Article 20(2).

3. A Party which has not made a declaration under paragraph 1 above or in respect of which a declaration is no longer in force shall be deemed to have accepted the competence of the Arbitral Tribunal.

4. If the parties to a dispute have accepted the same means for the settlement of a dispute, the dispute may be submitted only to that procedure, unless the parties otherwise agree.

5. If the parties to a dispute have not accepted the same means for the settlement of a dispute, or if they have both accepted both means, the dispute may be submitted only to the Arbitral Tribunal, unless the parties otherwise agree.

6. A declaration made under paragraph 1 above shall remain in force until it expires in accordance with its terms or until three months after written notice of revocation has been deposited with the Depositary.

7. A new declaration, a notice of revocation or the expiry of a declaration shall not in any way affect proceedings pending before the International Court of Justice or the Arbitral Tribunal, unless the parties to the dispute otherwise agree.

8. Declarations and notices referred to in this Article shall be deposited with the Depositary who shall transmit copies thereof to all Parties.

Article 20: Dispute settlement procedure

1. If the parties to a dispute concerning the interpretation or application of Articles 7, 8 or 15 or, except to the extent that an Annex provides otherwise, the provisions

of any Annex or, insofar as it relates to these Articles and provisions, Article 13, have not agreed on a means for resolving it within 12 months of the request for consultation pursuant to Article 18, the dispute shall be referred, at the request of any party to the dispute, for settlement in accordance with the procedure determined by Article 19 (4) and (5).

2. The Arbitral Tribunal shall not be competent to decide or rule upon any matter within the scope of Article IV of the Antarctic Treaty. In addition, nothing in this Protocol shall be interpreted as conferring competence or jurisdiction on the International Court of Justice or any other tribunal established for the purpose of settling disputes between Parties to decide or otherwise rule upon any matter within the scope of Article IV of the Antarctic Treaty.

[Articles 21-27 not reproduced]

Schedule: Arbitration; Annex I: Environmental impact assessment; Annex II: Conservation of Antarctic fauna and flora; Annex III: Waste disposal and waste management; Annex IV: Prevention of marine pollution; Annex V: Area protection and management [not reproduced]

Chapter 6

Hazardous Wastes, Chemicals and Pesticides, and Nuclear Energy

Introduction

The three global conventions covered in the first section of this chapter address the problems caused by different types of hazardous substances, namely wastes, chemicals and pesticides that are dangerous for human health and the environment. The 1989 Basel Convention is concerned with hazardous wastes and their transboundary movements.[1] It imposes obligations on states parties to ensure that such wastes are managed and disposed of in an environmentally sound manner while permitting countries to prohibit imports. The 1998 Rotterdam Convention is noteworthy in that it seeks to address the harm caused by certain hazardous chemicals and pesticides by creating legally binding obligations for the implementation of a prior informed consent (PIC) procedure.[2] The PIC procedure established under the Convention requires exporters trading in a list of hazardous substances to obtain the consent of importers before proceeding with the trade of

1 For a non-binding instrument on the topic, *see* UNEP's Cairo Guidelines and Principles for the Environmentally Sound Management of Hazardous Wastes, Doc. UNEP/GC.14/17 (Annex II), 1987. Regional agreements addressing the transboundary movements of hazardous wastes include, *e.g.*, Convention on the Ban of the Import into Africa and the Control of Transboundary Movement and Management of Hazardous Wastes Within Africa, Bamako, 29 January 1991, 30 *ILM* 773 (1991); Protocol on the Prevention of Pollution of the Mediterranean Sea by Transboundary Movements of Hazardous Wastes and their Disposal, Izmir, 1 October 1996, available at http://www.unep.ch/seas/main/med/medhaz.html; Convention to Ban the Importation into Forum Island Countries of Hazardous and Radioactive Wastes and to Control the Transboundary Movement and Management of Hazardous Wastes within the South Pacific Region, Waigani, 16 September 1995, available at http://www.basel.int/misclinks/waigani.html

2 Providing voluntary PIC procedures, *see* UNEP London Guidelines for the Exchange of Information on Chemicals in International Trade, UNEP Governing Council Decision 14/27 (1987), as amended in 1989, available at http://www.chem.unep.ch/ethics/english/longuien.htm: and FAO International Code of Conduct on the Distribution and Use of Pesticides, FAO Conference Resolution 10/85 (1985), as revised in 2002, available at http://www.fao.org/waicent/FaoInfo/Agricult/AGP/AGPP/Pesticid/Code/PM_Code.htm

the substance. Persistent organic pollutants (POPs) are chemicals that are highly toxic, persistent, bioaccumulate and become widely distributed geographically in the environment. The 2001 Stockholm Convention aims at the elimination or restriction of the production and use of all intentionally produced POPs, as well as the continuing minimization and, where feasible, ultimate elimination of the release of unintentionally produced POPs.[3]

The second section of this chapter deals with instruments tackling the environmental risks created by modern nuclear technology, including radioactive contamination and the spread of toxic substances. The Convention on Nuclear Safety and the Joint Convention, adopted under the auspices of the IAEA in 1994 and 1997, respectively, are two global treaties committing states to control the risks of nuclear energy in view of environmental objectives.[4] These conventions give binding force to some of the IAEA's minimum standards on nuclear safety regarding the management of civil nuclear power plants, radioactive waste management and spent fuel disposal and reprocessing.

Selected readings

Hazardous wastes, chemicals and pesticides

Kummer, K., *International Management of Hazardous Wastes: The Basel Convention and Related Rules* (Oxford: Clarendon Press, 1995).

Mintz, J.A., 'Two Cheers for Global POPs: A Summary and Assessment of the Stockholm Convention on Persistent Organic Pollutants', 14 *Georgetown Int'l Envtl L. Rev.* 319 (2001).

Redgwell, C., 'Regulating Trade in Dangerous Substances: Prior Informed Consent under the 1998 Rotterdam Convention', *in* Kiss, A., Shelton, D. and Ishibashi, K. (eds.), *Economic Globalization and Compliance with International Environmental Agreements* (The Hague: Kluwer Law International, 2003), p. 75.

Sanders, A. and Bowal, P., 'International Trade in Hazardous Wastes and the Basel Convention', 11 *J. Envtl L. & Practice* 143 (2001).

---

[3] POPs are regulated on a regional basis under the Århus Protocol on Persistent Organic Pollutants to the Air Pollution Convention, cited at p. 83, n. 1.

[4] Other relevant treaties on nuclear safety include the Convention on Physical Protection of Nuclear Material, Vienna, 26 October 1979, 18 *ILM* 1419 (1979); Convention on Assistance in the Case of a Nuclear Accident or Radiological Emergency, Vienna, 26 September 1986, 25 *ILM* 1377 (1986); and Convention on Early Notification of a Nuclear Accident, Vienna, 26 September 1986, 25 *ILM* 1370 (1986). The Convention on Civil Liability for Nuclear Damage is reproduced at p. 557.

Nuclear safety

de la Fayette, L., 'International Environmental Law and the Problem of Nuclear Safety', 5 *JEL* 31 (1993).

de Kageneck, A. and Pinel, C., 'The Joint Convention on the Safety of Spent Fuel Management and on the Safety of Radioactive Waste Management', 47 *ICLQ* 409 (1998).

Kamminga, M.T., 'The IAEA Convention on Nuclear Safety', 44 *ICLQ* 872 (1995).

Hazardous wastes, chemicals and pesticides

Basel Convention on the Control of Transboundary Movements of Hazardous Wastes and Their Disposal[5]

Adopted on 22 March 1989 at Basel. Entered into force on 5 May 1992. Source: 1673 *UNTS* 126 (the text reproduced does not incorporate the Ban Amendment adopted by Decision III/1 of 22 September 1995, which is not in force). Number of parties: 160. Further information: Secretariat, Geneva, Switzerland, http://www.basel.int

Preamble

The Parties to this Convention,

Aware of the risk of damage to human health and the environment caused by hazardous wastes and other wastes and the transboundary movement thereof,

Mindful of the growing threat to human health and the environment posed by the increased generation and complexity, and transboundary movement of hazardous wastes and other wastes,

Mindful also that the most effective way of protecting human health and the environment from the dangers posed by such wastes is the reduction of their generation to a minimum in terms of quantity and/or hazard potential,

Convinced that States should take necessary measures to ensure that the management of hazardous wastes and other wastes including their transboundary movement and disposal is consistent with the protection of human health and the environment whatever the place of disposal,

Noting that States should ensure that the generator should carry out duties with regards to the transport and disposal of hazardous wastes and other wastes in a

---

5 The Basel Convention's Protocol on Liability and Compensation is reproduced at p. 573 and its mechanism for promoting implementation and compliance at p. 628.

manner that is consistent with the protection of the environment, whatever the place of disposal.

Fully recognizing that any State has the sovereign right to ban the entry or disposal of foreign hazardous wastes and other wastes in its territory,

Recognizing also the increasing desire for the prohibition of transboundary movements of hazardous wastes and their disposal in other States, especially developing countries,

Convinced that hazardous wastes and other wastes should, as far as is compatible with environmentally sound and efficient management, be disposed of in the State where they were generated,

Aware also that transboundary movements of such wastes from the State of their generation to any other State should be permitted only when conducted under conditions which do not endanger human health and the environment, and under conditions in conformity with the provisions of this Convention,

Considering that enhanced control of transboundary movement of hazardous wastes and other wastes will act as an incentive for their environmentally sound management and for the reduction of the volume of such transboundary movement,

Convinced that States should take measures for the proper exchange of information on and control of the transboundary movement of hazardous wastes and other wastes from and to those States,

Noting that a number of international and regional agreements have addressed the issue of protection and preservation of the environment with regard to the transit of dangerous goods,

Taking into account the Declaration of the United Nations Conference on the Human Environment (Stockholm, 1972), the Cairo Guidelines and Principles for the Environmentally Sound Management of Hazardous Wastes adopted by the Governing Council of the United Nations Environment Programme (UNEP) by decision 14/30 of 17 June 1987, the Recommendations of the United Nations Committee of Experts on the Transport of Dangerous Goods (formulated in 1957 and updated biennially), relevant recommendations, declarations, instruments and regulations adopted within the United Nations system and the work and studies done within other international and regional organizations,

Mindful of the spirit, principles, aims and functions of the World Charter for Nature adopted by the General Assembly of the United Nations at its thirty-seventh session (1982) as the rule of ethics in respect of the protection of the human environment and the conservation of natural resources,

Affirming that States are responsible for the fulfilment of their international obligations concerning the protection of human health and protection and preservation of the environment, and are liable in accordance with international law,

Recognizing that in the case of a material breach of the provisions of this Convention or any protocol thereto the relevant international law of treaties shall apply,

Aware of the need to continue the development and implementation of environmentally sound low-waste technologies, recycling options, good house-keeping and management systems with a view to reducing to a minimum the generation of hazardous wastes and other wastes,

Aware also of the growing international concern about the need for stringent control of transboundary movement of hazardous wastes and other wastes, and of the need as far as possible to reduce such movement to a minimum,

Concerned about the problem of illegal transboundary traffic in hazardous wastes and other wastes,

Taking into account also the limited capabilities of the developing countries to manage hazardous wastes and other wastes,

Recognizing the need to promote the transfer of technology for the sound management of hazardous wastes and other wastes produced locally, particularly to the developing countries in accordance with the spirit of the Cairo Guidelines and decision 14/16 of the Governing Council of UNEP on Promotion of the transfer of environmental protection technology,

Recognizing also that hazardous wastes and other wastes should be transported in accordance with relevant international conventions and recommendations,

Convinced also that the transboundary movement of hazardous wastes and other wastes should be permitted only when the transport and the ultimate disposal of such wastes is environmentally sound, and

Determined to protect, by strict control, human health and the environment against the adverse effects which may result from the generation and management of hazardous wastes and other wastes,

Have agreed as follows:

Article 1: Scope of the Convention

1. The following wastes that are subject to transboundary movement shall be 'hazardous wastes' for the purposes of this Convention:

(a) Wastes that belong to any category contained in Annex I, unless they do not possess any of the characteristics contained in Annex III; and

(b) Wastes that are not covered under paragraph (a) but are defined as, or are considered to be, hazardous wastes by the domestic legislation of the Party of export, import or transit.

2. Wastes that belong to any category contained in Annex II that are subject to transboundary movement shall be 'other wastes' for the purposes of this Convention.

3. Wastes which, as a result of being radioactive, are subject to other international control systems, including international instruments, applying specifically to radioactive materials, are excluded from the scope of this Convention.

4. Wastes which derive from the normal operations of a ship, the discharge of which is covered by another international instrument, are excluded from the scope of this Convention.

Article 2: Definitions

For the purposes of this Convention:

1. 'Wastes' are substances or objects which are disposed of or are intended to be disposed of or are required to be disposed of by the provisions of national law;

2. 'Management' means the collection, transport and disposal of hazardous wastes or other wastes, including after-care of disposal sites;

3. 'Transboundary movement' means any movement of hazardous wastes or other wastes from an area under the national jurisdiction of one State to or through an area under the national jurisdiction of another State or to or through an area not under the national jurisdiction of any State, provided at least two States are involved in the movement;

4. 'Disposal' means any operation specified in Annex IV to this Convention;

5. 'Approved site or facility' means a site or facility for the disposal of hazardous wastes or other wastes which is authorized or permitted to operate for this purpose by a relevant authority of the State where the site or facility is located;

6. 'Competent authority' means one governmental authority designated by a Party to be responsible, within such geographical areas as the Party may think fit, for receiving the notification of a transboundary movement of hazardous wastes or other wastes, and any information related to it, and for responding to such a notification, as provided in Article 6;

7. 'Focal point' means the entity of a Party referred to in Article 5 responsible for receiving and submitting information as provided for in Articles 13 and 16;

8. 'Environmentally sound management of hazardous wastes or other wastes' means taking all practicable steps to ensure that hazardous wastes or other wastes are managed in a manner which will protect human health and the environment against the adverse effects which may result from such wastes;

9. 'Area under the national jurisdiction of a State' means any land, marine area or air space within which a State exercises administrative and regulatory responsibility in accordance with international law in regard to the protection of human health or the environment;

10. 'State of export' means a Party from which a transboundary movement of hazardous wastes or other wastes is planned to be initiated or is initiated;

11. 'State of import' means a Party to which a transboundary movement of hazardous wastes or other wastes is planned or takes place for the purpose of

disposal therein or for the purpose of loading prior to disposal in an area not under the national jurisdiction of any State;

12. 'State of transit' means any State, other than the State of export or import, through which a movement of hazardous wastes or other wastes is planned or takes place;

13. 'States concerned' means Parties which are States of export or import, or transit States, whether or not Parties;

14. 'Person' means any natural or legal person;

15. 'Exporter' means any person under the jurisdiction of the State of export who arranges for hazardous wastes or other wastes to be exported;

16. 'Importer' means any person under the jurisdiction of the State of import who arranges for hazardous wastes or other wastes to be imported;

17. 'Carrier' means any person who carries out the transport of hazardous wastes or other wastes;

18. 'Generator' means any person whose activity produces hazardous wastes or other wastes or, if that person is not known, the person who is in possession and/or control of those wastes;

19. 'Disposer' means any person to whom hazardous wastes or other wastes are shipped and who carries out the disposal of such wastes;

20. 'Political and/or economic integration organization' means an organization constituted by sovereign States to which its member States have transferred competence in respect of matters governed by this Convention and which has been duly authorized, in accordance with its internal procedures, to sign, ratify, accept, approve, formally confirm or accede to it;

21. 'Illegal traffic' means any transboundary movement of hazardous wastes or other wastes as specified in Article 9.

Article 3: National definitions of hazardous wastes

1. Each Party shall, within six months of becoming a Party to this Convention, inform the Secretariat of the Convention of the wastes, other than those listed in Annexes I and II, considered or defined as hazardous under its national legislation and of any requirements concerning transboundary movement procedures applicable to such wastes.

2. Each Party shall subsequently inform the Secretariat of any significant changes to the information it has provided pursuant to paragraph 1.

3. The Secretariat shall forthwith inform all Parties of the information it has received pursuant to paragraphs 1 and 2.

4. Parties shall be responsible for making the information transmitted to them by the Secretariat under paragraph 3 available to their exporters.

Article 4: General obligations

1. (a) Parties exercising their right to prohibit the import of hazardous wastes or other wastes for disposal shall inform the other Parties of their decision pursuant to Article 13.

(b) Parties shall prohibit or shall not permit the export of hazardous wastes and other wastes to the Parties which have prohibited the import of such wastes, when notified pursuant to subparagraph (a) above.

(c) Parties shall prohibit or shall not permit the export of hazardous wastes and other wastes if the State of import does not consent in writing to the specific import, in the case where that State of import has not prohibited the import of such wastes.

2. Each Party shall take the appropriate measures to:

(a) Ensure that the generation of hazardous wastes and other wastes within it is reduced to a minimum, taking into account social, technological and economic aspects;

(b) Ensure the availability of adequate disposal facilities, for the environmentally sound management of hazardous wastes and other wastes, that shall be located, to the extent possible, within it, whatever the place of their disposal;

(c) Ensure that persons involved in the management of hazardous wastes or other wastes within it take such steps as are necessary to prevent pollution due to hazardous wastes and other wastes arising from such management and, if such pollution occurs, to minimize the consequences thereof for human health and the environment;

(d) Ensure that the transboundary movement of hazardous wastes and other wastes is reduced to the minimum consistent with the environmentally sound and efficient management of such wastes, and is conducted in a manner which will protect human health and the environment against the adverse effects which may result from such movement;

(e) Not allow the export of hazardous wastes or other wastes to a State or group of States belonging to an economic and/or political integration organization that are Parties, particularly developing countries, which have prohibited by their legislation all imports, or if it has reason to believe that the wastes in question will not be managed in an environmentally sound manner, according to criteria to be decided on by the Parties at their first meeting.

(f) Require that information about a proposed transboundary movement of hazardous wastes and other wastes be provided to the States concerned, according to Annex V A, to state clearly the effects of the proposed movement on human health and the environment;

(g) Prevent the import of hazardous wastes and other wastes if it has reason to believe that the wastes in question will not be managed in an environmentally sound manner;

(h) Co-operate in activities with other Parties and interested organizations, directly and through the Secretariat, including the dissemination of information on the transboundary movement of hazardous wastes and other wastes, in order to improve the environmentally sound management of such wastes and to achieve the prevention of illegal traffic.

3. The Parties consider that illegal traffic in hazardous wastes or other wastes is criminal.

4. Each Party shall take appropriate legal, administrative and other measures to implement and enforce the provisions of this Convention, including measures to prevent and punish conduct in contravention of the Convention.

5. A Party shall not permit hazardous wastes or other wastes to be exported to a non-Party or to be imported from a non-Party.

6. The Parties agree not to allow the export of hazardous wastes or other wastes for disposal within the area south of 60° South latitude, whether or not such wastes are subject to transboundary movement.

7. Furthermore, each Party shall:

(a) Prohibit all persons under its national jurisdiction from transporting or disposing of hazardous wastes or other wastes unless such persons are authorized or allowed to perform such types of operations;

(b) Require that hazardous wastes and other wastes that are to be the subject of a transboundary movement be packaged, labelled, and transported in conformity with generally accepted and recognized international rules and standards in the field of packaging, labelling, and transport, and that due account is taken of relevant internationally recognized practices;

(c) Require that hazardous wastes and other wastes be accompanied by a movement document from the point at which a transboundary movement commences to the point of disposal.

8. Each Party shall require that hazardous wastes or other wastes, to be exported, are managed in an environmentally sound manner in the State of import or elsewhere. Technical guidelines for the environmentally sound management of wastes subject to this Convention shall be decided by the Parties at their first meeting.

9. Parties shall take the appropriate measures to ensure that the transboundary movement of hazardous wastes and other wastes only be allowed if:

(a) The State of export does not have the technical capacity and the necessary facilities, capacity or suitable disposal sites in order to dispose of the wastes in question in an environmentally sound and efficient manner; or

(b) The wastes in question are required as a raw material for recycling or recovery industries in the State of import; or

(c) The transboundary movement in question is in accordance with other criteria to be decided by the Parties, provided those criteria do not differ from the objectives of this Convention.

10. The obligation under this Convention of States in which hazardous wastes and other wastes are generated to require that those wastes are managed in an

environmentally sound manner may not under any circumstances be transferred to the States of import or transit.

11. Nothing in this Convention shall prevent a Party from imposing additional requirements that are consistent with the provisions of this Convention, and are in accordance with the rules of international law, in order better to protect human health and the environment.

12. Nothing in this Convention shall affect in any way the sovereignty of States over their territorial sea established in accordance with international law, and the sovereign rights and the jurisdiction which States have in their exclusive economic zones and their continental shelves in accordance with international law, and the exercise by ships and aircraft of all States of navigational rights and freedoms as provided for in international law and as reflected in relevant international instruments.

13. Parties shall undertake to review periodically the possibilities for the reduction of the amount and/or the pollution potential of hazardous wastes and other wastes which are exported to other States, in particular to developing countries.

Article 5: Designation of competent authorities and focal point

To facilitate the implementation of this Convention, the Parties shall:

1. Designate or establish one or more competent authorities and one focal point. One competent authority shall be designated to receive the notification in case of a State of transit.

2. Inform the Secretariat, within three months of the date of the entry into force of this Convention for them, which agencies they have designated as their focal point and their competent authorities.

3. Inform the Secretariat, within one month of the date of decision, of any changes regarding the designation made by them under paragraph 2 above.

Article 6: Transboundary movement between Parties

1. The State of export shall notify, or shall require the generator or exporter to notify, in writing, through the channel of the competent authority of the State of export, the competent authority of the States concerned of any proposed transboundary movement of hazardous wastes or other wastes. Such notification shall contain the declarations and information specified in Annex V A, written in a language acceptable to the State of import. Only one notification needs to be sent to each State concerned.

2. The State of import shall respond to the notifier in writing, consenting to the movement with or without conditions, denying permission for the movement, or requesting additional information. A copy of the final response of the State of import shall be sent to the competent authorities of the States concerned which are Parties.

3. The State of export shall not allow the generator or exporter to commence the transboundary movement until it has received written confirmation that:

(a) The notifier has received the written consent of the State of import; and
(b) The notifier has received from the State of import confirmation of the existence of a contract between the exporter and the disposer specifying environmentally sound management of the wastes in question.

4. Each State of transit which is a Party shall promptly acknowledge to the notifier receipt of the notification. It may subsequently respond to the notifier in writing, within 60 days, consenting to the movement with or without conditions, denying permission for the movement, or requesting additional information. The State of export shall not allow the transboundary movement to commence until it has received the written consent of the State of transit. However, if at any time a Party decides not to require prior written consent, either generally or under specific conditions, for transit transboundary movements of hazardous wastes or other wastes, or modifies its requirements in this respect, it shall forthwith inform the other Parties of its decision pursuant to Article 13. In this latter case, if no response is received by the State of export within 60 days of the receipt of a given notification by the State of transit, the State of export may allow the export to proceed through the State of transit.

5. In the case of a transboundary movement of wastes where the wastes are legally defined as or considered to be hazardous wastes only:
(a) By the State of export, the requirements of paragraph 9 of this Article that apply to the importer or disposer and the State of import shall apply *mutatis mutandis* to the exporter and State of export, respectively;
(b) By the State of import, or by the States of import and transit which are Parties, the requirements of paragraphs 1, 3, 4 and 6 of this Article that apply to the exporter and State of export shall apply *mutatis mutandis* to the importer or disposer and State of import, respectively; or
(c) By any State of transit which is a Party, the provisions of paragraph 4 shall apply to such State.

6. The State of export may, subject to the written consent of the States concerned, allow the generator or the exporter to use a general notification where hazardous wastes or other wastes having the same physical and chemical characteristics are shipped regularly to the same disposer via the same customs office of exit of the State of export via the same customs office of entry of the State of import, and, in the case of transit, via the same customs office of entry and exit of the State or States of transit.

7. The States concerned may make their written consent to the use of the general notification referred to in paragraph 6 subject to the supply of certain information, such as the exact quantities or periodical lists of hazardous wastes or other wastes to be shipped.

8. The general notification and written consent referred to in paragraphs 6 and 7 may cover multiple shipments of hazardous wastes or other wastes during a maximum period of 12 months.

9. The Parties shall require that each person who takes charge of a transboundary movement of hazardous wastes or other wastes sign the movement document either upon delivery or receipt of the wastes in question. They shall also require that the disposer inform both the exporter and the competent authority of the State of export of receipt by the disposer of the wastes in question and, in due course, of the completion of disposal as specified in the notification. If no such information is received within the State of export, the competent authority of the State of export or the exporter shall so notify the State of import.

10. The notification and response required by this Article shall be transmitted to the competent authority of the Parties concerned or to such governmental authority as may be appropriate in the case of non-Parties.

11. Any transboundary movement of hazardous wastes or other wastes shall be covered by insurance, bond or other guarantee as may be required by the State of import or any State of transit which is a Party.

Article 7: Transboundary movement from a Party through States which are not Parties

Paragraph 1 of Article 6 of the Convention shall apply *mutatis mutandis* to transboundary movement of hazardous wastes or other wastes from a Party through a State or States which are not Parties.

Article 8: Duty to re-import

When a transboundary movement of hazardous wastes or other wastes to which the consent of the States concerned has been given, subject to the provisions of this Convention, cannot be completed in accordance with the terms of the contract, the State of export shall ensure that the wastes in question are taken back into the State of export, by the exporter, if alternative arrangements cannot be made for their disposal in an environmentally sound manner, within 90 days from the time that the importing State informed the State of export and the Secretariat, or such other period of time as the States concerned agree. To this end, the State of export and any Party of transit shall not oppose, hinder or prevent the return of those wastes to the State of export.

Article 9: Illegal traffic

1. For the purpose of this Convention, any transboundary movement of hazardous wastes or other wastes:

(a) without notification pursuant to the provisions of this Convention to all States concerned; or
(b) without the consent pursuant to the provisions of this Convention of a State concerned; or
(c) with consent obtained from States concerned through falsification, misrepresentation or fraud; or
(d) that does not conform in a material way with the documents; or

(e) that results in deliberate disposal (e.g. dumping) of hazardous wastes or other wastes in contravention of this Convention and of general principles of international law,

shall be deemed to be illegal traffic.

2. In case of a transboundary movement of hazardous wastes or other wastes deemed to be illegal traffic as the result of conduct on the part of the exporter or generator, the State of export shall ensure that the wastes in question are:

(a) taken back by the exporter or the generator or, if necessary, by itself into the State of export, or, if impracticable,

(b) are otherwise disposed of in accordance with the provisions of this Convention,

within 30 days from the time the State of export has been informed about the illegal traffic or such other period of time as States concerned may agree. To this end the Parties concerned shall not oppose, hinder or prevent the return of those wastes to the State of export.

3. In the case of a transboundary movement of hazardous wastes or other wastes deemed to be illegal traffic as the result of conduct on the part of the importer or disposer, the State of import shall ensure that the wastes in question are disposed of in an environmentally sound manner by the importer or disposer or, if necessary, by itself within 30 days from the time the illegal traffic has come to the attention of the State of import or such other period of time as the States concerned may agree. To this end, the Parties concerned shall co-operate, as necessary, in the disposal of the wastes in an environmentally sound manner.

4. In cases where the responsibility for the illegal traffic cannot be assigned either to the exporter or generator or to the importer or disposer, the Parties concerned or other Parties, as appropriate, shall ensure, through co-operation, that the wastes in question are disposed of as soon as possible in an environmentally sound manner either in the State of export or the State of import or elsewhere as appropriate.

5. Each Party shall introduce appropriate national/domestic legislation to prevent and punish illegal traffic. The Parties shall co-operate with a view to achieving the objects of this Article.

Article 10: International co-operation

1. The Parties shall co-operate with each other in order to improve and achieve environmentally sound management of hazardous wastes and other wastes.

2. To this end, the Parties shall:

(a) Upon request, make available information, whether on a bilateral or multilateral basis, with a view to promoting the environmentally sound management of hazardous wastes and other wastes, including harmonization of technical standards and practices for the adequate management of hazardous wastes and other wastes;

(b) Co-operate in monitoring the effects of the management of hazardous wastes on human health and the environment;

(c) Co-operate, subject to their national laws, regulations and policies, in the development and implementation of new environmentally sound low-waste technologies and the improvement of existing technologies with a view to eliminating, as far as practicable, the generation of hazardous wastes and other wastes and achieving more effective and efficient methods of ensuring their management in an environmentally sound manner, including the study of the economic, social and environmental effects of the adoption of such new or improved technologies;

(d) Co-operate actively, subject to their national laws, regulations and policies, in the transfer of technology and management systems related to the environmentally sound management of hazardous wastes and other wastes. They shall also co-operate in developing the technical capacity among Parties, especially those which may need and request technical assistance in this field;

(e) Co-operate in developing appropriate technical guidelines and/or codes of practice.

3. The Parties shall employ appropriate means to co-operate in order to assist developing countries in the implementation of subparagraphs a, b, c and d of paragraph 2 of Article 4.

4. Taking into account the needs of developing countries, co-operation between Parties and the competent international organizations is encouraged to promote, *inter alia*, public awareness, the development of sound management of hazardous wastes and other wastes and the adoption of new low-waste technologies.

Article 11: Bilateral, multilateral and regional agreements

1. Notwithstanding the provisions of Article 4 paragraph 5, Parties may enter into bilateral, multilateral, or regional agreements or arrangements regarding transboundary movement of hazardous wastes or other wastes with Parties or non-Parties provided that such agreements or arrangements do not derogate from the environmentally sound management of hazardous wastes and other wastes as required by this Convention. These agreements or arrangements shall stipulate provisions which are not less environmentally sound than those provided for by this Convention in particular taking into account the interests of developing countries.

2. Parties shall notify the Secretariat of any bilateral, multilateral or regional agreements or arrangements referred to in paragraph 1 and those which they have entered into prior to the entry into force of this Convention for them, for the purpose of controlling transboundary movements of hazardous wastes and other wastes which take place entirely among the Parties to such agreements. The provisions of this Convention shall not affect transboundary movements which take place pursuant to such agreements provided that such agreements are compatible with the environmentally sound management of hazardous wastes and other wastes as required by this Convention.

Article 12: Consultations on liability

The Parties shall co-operate with a view to adopting, as soon as practicable, a protocol setting out appropriate rules and procedures in the field of liability and compensation for damage resulting from the transboundary movement and disposal of hazardous wastes and other wastes.

Article 13: Transmission of information

1. The Parties shall, whenever it comes to their knowledge, ensure that, in the case of an accident occurring during the transboundary movement of hazardous wastes or other wastes or their disposal, which are likely to present risks to human health and the environment in other States, those states are immediately informed.

2. The Parties shall inform each other, through the Secretariat, of:

(a) Changes regarding the designation of competent authorities and/or focal points, pursuant to Article 5;

(b) Changes in their national definition of hazardous wastes, pursuant to Article 3;

and, as soon as possible,

(c) Decisions made by them not to consent totally or partially to the import of hazardous wastes or other wastes for disposal within the area under their national jurisdiction;

(d) Decisions taken by them to limit or ban the export of hazardous wastes or other wastes;

(e) Any other information required pursuant to paragraph 4 of this Article.

3. The Parties, consistent with national laws and regulations, shall transmit, through the Secretariat, to the Conference of the Parties established under Article 15, before the end of each calendar year, a report on the previous calendar year, containing the following information:

(a) Competent authorities and focal points that have been designated by them pursuant to Article 5;

(b) Information regarding transboundary movements of hazardous wastes or other wastes in which they have been involved, including:

   i) The amount of hazardous wastes and other wastes exported, their category, characteristics, destination, any transit country and disposal method as stated on the response to notification;

   ii) The amount of hazardous wastes and other wastes imported, their category, characteristics, origin, and disposal methods;

   iii) Disposals which did not proceed as intended;

   iv) Efforts to achieve a reduction of the amount of hazardous wastes or other wastes subject to transboundary movement;

(c) Information on the measures adopted by them in implementation of this Convention;

(d) Information on available qualified statistics which have been compiled by them on the effects on human health and the environment of the generation, transportation and disposal of hazardous wastes or other wastes;

(e) Information concerning bilateral, multilateral and regional agreements and arrangements entered into pursuant to Article 11 of this Convention;
(f) Information on accidents occurring during the transboundary movement and disposal of hazardous wastes and other wastes and on the measures undertaken to deal with them;
(g) Information on disposal options operated within the area of their national jurisdiction;
(h) Information on measures undertaken for development of technologies for the reduction and/or elimination of production of hazardous wastes and other wastes; and
(i) Such other matters as the Conference of the Parties shall deem relevant.

4. The Parties, consistent with national laws and regulations, shall ensure that copies of each notification concerning any given transboundary movement of hazardous wastes or other wastes, and the response to it, are sent to the Secretariat when a Party considers that its environment may be affected by that transboundary movement has requested that this should be done.

Article 14: Financial aspects

1. The Parties agree that, according to the specific needs of different regions and subregions, regional or sub-regional centres for training and technology transfers regarding the management of hazardous wastes and other wastes and the minimization of their generation should be established. The Parties shall decide on the establishment of appropriate funding mechanisms of a voluntary nature.

2. The Parties shall consider the establishment of a revolving fund to assist on an interim basis in case of emergency situations to minimize damage from accidents arising from transboundary movements of hazardous wastes and other wastes or during the disposal of those wastes.

Article 15: Conference of the Parties

1. A Conference of the Parties is hereby established. The first meeting of the Conference of the Parties shall be convened by the Executive Director of UNEP not later than one year after the entry into force of this Convention. Thereafter, ordinary meetings of the Conference of the Parties shall be held at regular intervals to be determined by the Conference at its first meeting.

2. Extraordinary meetings of the Conference of the Parties shall be held at such other times as may be deemed necessary by the Conference, or at the written request of any Party, provided that, within six months of the request being communicated to them by the Secretariat, it is supported by at least one third of the Parties.

3. The Conference of the Parties shall by consensus agree upon and adopt rules of procedure for itself and for any subsidiary body it may establish, as well as financial rules to determine in particular the financial participation of the Parties under this Convention.

4. The Parties at their first meeting shall consider any additional measures needed to assist them in fulfilling their responsibilities with respect to the protection and the preservation of the marine environment in the context of this Convention.

5. The Conference of the Parties shall keep under continuous review and evaluation the effective implementation of this Convention, and, in addition, shall:

(a) Promote the harmonization of appropriate policies, strategies and measures for minimizing harm to human health and the environment by hazardous wastes and other wastes;

(b) Consider and adopt, as required, amendments to this Convention and its annexes, taking into consideration, *inter alia*, available scientific, technical, economic and environmental information;

(c) Consider and undertake any additional action that may be required for the achievement of the purposes of this Convention in the light of experience gained in its operation and in the operation of the agreements and arrangements envisaged in Article 11;

(d) Consider and adopt protocols as required; and

(e) Establish such subsidiary bodies as are deemed necessary for the implementation of this Convention.

6. The United Nations, its specialized agencies, as well as any State not Party to this Convention, may be represented as observers at meetings of the Conference of the Parties. Any other body or agency, whether national or international, governmental or non-governmental, qualified in fields relating to hazardous wastes or other wastes which has informed the Secretariat of its wish to be represented as an observer at a meeting of the Conference of Parties, may be admitted unless at least one third of the Parties present object. The admission and participation of observers shall be subject to the rules of procedure adopted by the Conference of the Parties.

7. The Conference of the Parties shall undertake three years after the entry into force of this Convention, and at least every six years thereafter, an evaluation of its effectiveness and, if deemed necessary, to consider the adoption of a complete or partial ban of transboundary movements of hazardous wastes and other wastes in light of the latest scientific, environmental, technical and economic information.

Article 16: Secretariat

1. The functions of the Secretariat shall be:

(a) To arrange for and service meetings provided for in Articles 15 and 17;

(b) To prepare and transmit reports based upon information received in accordance with Articles 3, 4, 6, 11 and 13 as well as upon information derived from meetings of subsidiary bodies established under Article 15 as well as upon, as appropriate, information provided by relevant intergovernmental and non-governmental entities;

(c) To prepare reports on its activities carried out in implementation of its functions under this Convention and present them to the Conference of the Parties;

(d) To ensure the necessary coordination with relevant international bodies, and in particular to enter into such administrative and contractual arrangements as may be required for the effective discharge of its function;

(e) To communicate with Focal Points and Competent Authorities established by the Parties in accordance with Article 5 of this Convention;

(f) To compile information concerning authorized national sites and facilities of Parties available for the disposal of their hazardous wastes and other wastes and to circulate this information among Parties;

(g) To receive and convey information from and to Parties on:

- sources of technical assistance and training;
- available technical and scientific know-how;
- sources of advice and expertise; and
- availability of resources

with a view to assisting them, upon request, in such areas as:

- the handling of the notification system of this Convention;
- the management of hazardous wastes and other wastes;
- environmentally sound technologies relating to hazardous wastes and other wastes; such as low- and non-waste technology;
- the assessment of disposal capabilities and sites;
- the monitoring of hazardous wastes and other wastes; and
- emergency responses;

(h) To provide Parties, upon request, with information on consultants or consulting firms having the necessary technical competence in the field, which can assist them to examine a notification for a transboundary movement, the concurrence of a shipment of hazardous wastes or other wastes with the relevant notification, and/or the fact that the proposed disposal facilities for hazardous wastes or other wastes are environmentally sound, when they have reason to believe that the wastes in question will not be managed in an environmentally sound manner. Any such examination would not be at the expense of the Secretariat;

(i) To assist Parties upon request in their identification of cases of illegal traffic and to circulate immediately to the Parties concerned any information it has received regarding illegal traffic;

(j) To co-operate with Parties and with relevant and competent international organizations and agencies in the provision of experts and equipment for the purpose of rapid assistance to States in the event of an emergency situation; and

(k) To perform such other functions relevant to the purposes of this Convention as may be determined by the Conference of the Parties.

2. The Secretariat functions will be carried out on an interim basis by UNEP until the completion of the first meeting of the Conference of the Parties held pursuant to Article 15.

3. At its first meeting, the Conference of the Parties shall designate the Secretariat from among those existing competent intergovernmental organizations which have signified their willingness to carry out the Secretariat functions under this

Convention. At this meeting, the Conference of the Parties shall also evaluate the implementation by the interim Secretariat of the functions assigned to it, in particular under paragraph 1 above, and decide upon the structures appropriate for those functions.

Article 17: Amendment of the Convention

1. Any Party may propose amendments to this Convention and any Party to a protocol may propose amendments to that protocol. Such amendments shall take due account, *inter alia*, of relevant scientific and technical considerations.

2. Amendments to this Convention shall be adopted at a meeting of the Conference of the Parties. Amendments to any protocol shall be adopted at a meeting of the Parties to the protocol in question. The text of any proposed amendment to this Convention or to any protocol, except as may otherwise be provided in such protocol, shall be communicated to the Parties by the Secretariat at least six months before the meeting at which it is proposed for adoption. The Secretariat shall also communicate proposed amendments to the Signatories to this Convention for information.

3. The Parties shall make every effort to reach agreement on any proposed amendment to this Convention by consensus. If all efforts at consensus have been exhausted, and no agreement reached, the amendment shall as a last resort be adopted by a three-fourths majority of the Parties present and voting at the meeting, and shall be submitted by the Depositary to all Parties for ratification, approval, formal confirmation or acceptance.

4. The procedure mentioned in paragraph 3 above shall apply to amendments to any protocol, except that a two-thirds majority of the Parties to that protocol present and voting at the meeting shall suffice for their adoption.

5. Instruments of ratification, approval, formal confirmation or acceptance of amendments shall be deposited with the Depositary. Amendments adopted in accordance with paragraphs 3 or 4 above shall enter into force between Parties having accepted them on the ninetieth day after the receipt by the Depositary of their instrument of ratification, approval, formal confirmation or acceptance by at least three-fourths of the Parties who accepted them or by at least two thirds of the Parties to the protocol concerned who accepted them, except as may otherwise be provided in such protocol. The amendments shall enter into force for any other Party on the ninetieth day after that Party deposits its instrument of ratification, approval, formal confirmation or acceptance of the amendments.

6. For the purpose of this Article, 'Parties present and voting' means Parties present and casting an affirmative or negative vote.

Article 18: Adoption and amendment of annexes

1. The annexes to this Convention or to any protocol shall form an integral part of this Convention or of such protocol, as the case may be and, unless expressly provided otherwise, a reference to this Convention or its protocols constitutes at the

same time a reference to any annexes thereto. Such annexes shall be restricted to scientific, technical and administrative matters.

2. Except as may be otherwise provided in any protocol with respect to its annexes, the following procedure shall apply to the proposal, adoption and entry into force of additional annexes to this Convention or of annexes to a protocol:

(a) Annexes to this Convention and its protocols shall be proposed and adopted according to the procedure laid down in Article 17, paragraphs 2, 3 and 4;

(b) Any Party that is unable to accept an additional annex to this Convention or an annex to any protocol to which it is party shall so notify the Depositary, in writing, within six months from the date of the communication of the adoption by the Depositary. The Depositary shall without delay notify all Parties of any such notification received. A Party may at any time substitute an acceptance for a previous declaration of objection and the annexes shall thereupon enter into force for that Party;

(c) On the expiry of six months from the date of the circulation of the communication by the Depositary, the annex shall become effective for all Parties to this Convention or to any protocol concerned, which have not submitted a notification in accordance with the provision of subparagraph (b) above.

3. The proposal, adoption and entry into force of amendments to annexes to this Convention or to any protocol shall be subject to the same procedure as for the proposal, adoption and entry into force of annexes to the Convention or annexes to a protocol. Annexes and amendments thereto shall take due account, *inter alia*, of relevant scientific and technical considerations.

4. If an additional annex or an amendment to an annex involves an amendment to this Convention or to any protocol, the additional annex or amended annex shall not enter into force until such time the amendment to this Convention or to the protocol enters into force.

Article 19: Verification

Any Party which has reason to believe that another Party is acting or has acted in breach of its obligations under this Convention may inform the Secretariat thereof, and in such an event, shall simultaneously and immediately inform, directly or through the Secretariat, the Party against whom the allegations are made. All relevant information should be submitted by the Secretariat to the Parties.

Article 20: Settlement of disputes

1. In case of a dispute between Parties as to the interpretation or application of, or compliance with, this Convention or any protocol thereto, they shall seek a settlement of the dispute through negotiation or any other peaceful means of their own choice.

2. If the Parties concerned cannot settle their dispute through the means mentioned in the preceding paragraph, the dispute, if the Parties to the dispute agree, shall be submitted to the International Court of Justice or to arbitration under the conditions

set out in Annex VI on Arbitration. However, failure to reach common agreement on submission of the dispute to the International Court of Justice or to arbitration shall not absolve the Parties from the responsibility of continuing to seek to resolve it by the means referred to in paragraph 1.

3. When ratifying, accepting, approving, formally confirming or acceding to this Convention, or at any time thereafter, a State or political and/or economic integration organization may declare that it recognizes as compulsory *ipso facto* and without special agreement, in relation to any Party accepting the same obligation:

(a) submission of the dispute to the International Court of Justice; and/or

(b) arbitration in accordance with the procedures set out in Annex VI.

Such declaration shall be notified in writing to the Secretariat which shall communicate it to the Parties.

Article 21: Signature

This Convention shall be open for signature by States, by Namibia, represented by the United Nations Council for Namibia, and by political and/or economic integration organizations, in Basel on 22 March 1989, at the Federal Department of Foreign Affairs of Switzerland in Berne from 23 March 1989 to 30 June 1989 and at United Nations Headquarters in New York from 1 July 1989 to 22 March 1990.

Article 22: Ratification, acceptance, formal confirmation or approval

1. This Convention shall be subject to ratification, acceptance or approval by States and by Namibia, represented by the United Nations Council for Namibia, and to formal confirmation or approval by political and/or economic integration organizations. Instruments of ratification, acceptance, formal confirmation, or approval shall be deposited with the Depositary.

2. Any organization referred to in paragraph 1 above which becomes a Party to this Convention without any of its members States being a Party shall be bound by all the obligations under the Convention. In the case of such organizations, one or more of whose member States is a Party to the Convention, the organization and its member States shall decide on their respective responsibilities for the performance of their obligations under the Convention. In such cases, the organization and the member States shall not be entitled to exercise rights under the Convention concurrently.

3. In their instruments of formal confirmation or approval, the organizations referred to in paragraph 1 above shall declare the extent of their competence with respect to the matters governed by the Convention. These organizations shall also inform the Depositary, who will inform the Parties of any substantial modification in the extent of their competence.

Article 23: Accession

1. This Convention shall be open for accession by States, by Namibia, represented by the United Nations Council for Namibia, and by political and/or economic

integration organizations from the day after the date on which the Convention is closed for signature. The instruments of accession shall be deposited with the Depositary.

2. In their instruments of accession, the organizations referred to in paragraph 1 above shall declare the extent of their competence with respect to the matters governed by the Convention. These organizations shall also inform the Depositary of any substantial modification in the extent of their competence.

3. The provisions of Article 22, paragraph 2, shall apply to political and/or economic integration organizations which accede to this Convention.

Article 24: Right to vote

1. Except as provided for in paragraph 2 below, each Contracting Party to this Convention shall have one vote.

2. Political and/or economic integration organizations, in matters within their competence, in accordance with Article 22, paragraph 3, and Article 23, paragraph 2, shall exercise their right to vote with a number of votes equal to the number of their member States which are Parties to the Convention or the relevant protocol. Such organizations shall not exercise their right to vote if their member States exercise theirs, and vice versa.

Article 25: Entry into force

1. This Convention shall enter into force on the ninetieth day after the day of deposit of the twentieth instrument of ratification, acceptance, formal confirmation, approval or accession.

2. For each State or political and/or economic integration organization which ratifies, accepts, approves or formally confirms this Convention or accedes thereto after the date of the deposit of the twentieth instrument of ratification, acceptance, approval, formal confirmation or accession, it shall enter into force on the ninetieth day after the date of deposit by such State or political and/or economic integration organization of its instrument of ratification, acceptance, approval, formal confirmation or accession.

3. For the purpose of paragraphs 1 and 2 above, any instrument deposited by a political and/or economic integration organization shall not be counted as additional to those deposited by member States of such organization.

Article 26: Reservations and declarations

1. No reservation or exception may be made to this Convention.

2. Paragraph 1 of this Article does not preclude a State or political and/or economic integration organization, when signing, ratifying, accepting, approving, formally confirming or acceding to this Convention, from making declarations or statements, however phrased or named, with a view, *inter alia*, to the harmonization of its laws and regulations with the provisions of this Convention, provided that such declarations or statements do not purport to exclude or to

modify the legal effects of the provisions of the Convention in their application to that State.

Article 27: Withdrawal

1. At any time after three years from the date on which this Convention has entered into force for a Party, that Party may withdraw from the Convention by giving written notification to the Depositary.

2. Withdrawal shall be effective one year from receipt of notification by the Depositary, or on such later date as may be specified in the notification.

Article 28: Depository

The Secretary-General of the United Nations shall be the Depository of this Convention and of any protocol thereto.

Article 29: Authentic texts

The original Arabic, Chinese, English, French, Russian and Spanish texts of this Convention are equally authentic.

In witness whereof the undersigned, being duly authorized to that effect, have signed this Convention.

Done at Basel on the 22nd day of March 1989.

Annex I: Categories of wastes to be controlled; Annex II: Categories of wastes requiring special consideration; Annex III: List of hazardous characteristics; Annex IV: Disposal operations; Annex V A: Information to be provided on notification; Annex V B: Information to be provided on the movement document; Annex VI: Arbitration; Annex VIII: List A; Annex IX: List B [not reproduced]

Annex VII

[not yet entered into force]

Decision III/1 (Amendment to the Basel Convention)

The Conference,

Decides to adopt the following amendment to the Convention:

'Insert new preambular paragraph 7 bis:

Recognizing that transboundary movements of hazardous wastes, especially to developing countries, have a high risk of not constituting an environmentally sound management of hazardous wastes as required by this Convention;

Insert new Article 4A:

1. Each Party listed in Annex VII shall prohibit all transboundary movements of hazardous wastes which are destined for operations according to Annex IV A, to States not listed in Annex VII.

2. Each Party listed in Annex VII shall phase out by 31 December 1997, and prohibit as of that date, all transboundary movements of hazardous wastes under

Article 1, paragraph 1 (a) of the Convention which are destined for operations according to Annex IV B to States not listed in Annex VII. Such transboundary movements shall not be prohibited unless the wastes in question are characterized as hazardous under the Convention.

Annex VII

Parties and other States which are members of OECD, EC, Liechtenstein'.

Rotterdam Convention on the Prior Informed Consent Procedure for Certain Hazardous Chemicals and Pesticides in International Trade

Adopted on 10 September 1998 at Rotterdam. Entered into force on 24 February 2004. Source: Doc. UNEP/FAO/PIC/CONF/5. Number of parties: 63. Further information: Secretariat, Geneva, Switzerland, http://www.pic.int

The Parties to this Convention,

Aware of the harmful impact on human health and the environment from certain hazardous chemicals and pesticides in international trade,

Recalling the pertinent provisions of the Rio Declaration on Environment and Development and chapter 19 of Agenda 21 on 'Environmentally sound management of toxic chemicals, including prevention of illegal international traffic in toxic and dangerous products',

Mindful of the work undertaken by the United Nations Environment Programme (UNEP) and the Food and Agriculture Organization of the United Nations (FAO) in the operation of the voluntary Prior Informed Consent procedure, as set out in the UNEP Amended London Guidelines for the Exchange of Information on Chemicals in International Trade (hereinafter referred to as the 'Amended London Guidelines') and the FAO International Code of Conduct on the Distribution and Use of Pesticides (hereinafter referred to as the 'International Code of Conduct'),

Taking into account the circumstances and particular requirements of developing countries and countries with economies in transition, in particular the need to strengthen national capabilities and capacities for the management of chemicals, including transfer of technology, providing financial and technical assistance and promoting cooperation among the Parties,

Noting the specific needs of some countries for information on transit movements,

Recognizing that good management practices for chemicals should be promoted in all countries, taking into account, *inter alia*, the voluntary standards laid down in the International Code of Conduct and the UNEP Code of Ethics on the International Trade in Chemicals,

Desiring to ensure that hazardous chemicals that are exported from their territory are packaged and labelled in a manner that is adequately protective of human health and the environment, consistent with the principles of the Amended London Guidelines and the International Code of Conduct,

Recognizing that trade and environmental policies should be mutually supportive with a view to achieving sustainable development,

Emphasizing that nothing in this Convention shall be interpreted as implying in any way a change in the rights and obligations of a Party under any existing international agreement applying to chemicals in international trade or to environmental protection,

Understanding that the above recital is not intended to create a hierarchy between this Convention and other international agreements,

Determined to protect human health, including the health of consumers and workers, and the environment against potentially harmful impacts from certain hazardous chemicals and pesticides in international trade,

Have agreed as follows:

Article 1: Objective

The objective of this Convention is to promote shared responsibility and cooperative efforts among Parties in the international trade of certain hazardous chemicals in order to protect human health and the environment from potential harm and to contribute to their environmentally sound use, by facilitating information exchange about their characteristics, by providing for a national decision-making process on their import and export and by disseminating these decisions to Parties.

Article 2: Definitions

For the purposes of this Convention:

(a) 'Chemical' means a substance whether by itself or in a mixture or preparation and whether manufactured or obtained from nature, but does not include any living organism. It consists of the following categories: pesticide (including severely hazardous pesticide formulations) and industrial;

(b) 'Banned chemical' means a chemical all uses of which within one or more categories have been prohibited by final regulatory action, in order to protect human health or the environment. It includes a chemical that has been refused approval for first-time use or has been withdrawn by industry either from the domestic market or from further consideration in the domestic approval process and where there is clear evidence that such action has been taken in order to protect human health or the environment;

(c) 'Severely restricted chemical' means a chemical virtually all use of which within one or more categories has been prohibited by final regulatory action in order to protect human health or the environment, but for which certain specific uses remain allowed. It includes a chemical that has, for virtually all use, been refused for approval or been withdrawn by industry either from the domestic market or from further consideration in the domestic approval process, and where there is clear evidence that such action has been taken in order to protect human health or the environment;

(d) 'Severely hazardous pesticide formulation' means a chemical formulated for pesticidal use that produces severe health or environmental effects observable within a short period of time after single or multiple exposure, under conditions of use;

(e) 'Final regulatory action' means an action taken by a Party, that does not require subsequent regulatory action by that Party, the purpose of which is to ban or severely restrict a chemical;

(f) 'Export' and 'import' mean, in their respective connotations, the movement of a chemical from one Party to another Party, but exclude mere transit operations;

(g) 'Party' means a State or regional economic integration organization that has consented to be bound by this Convention and for which the Convention is in force;

(h) 'Regional economic integration organization' means an organization constituted by sovereign States of a given region to which its member States have transferred competence in respect of matters governed by this Convention and which has been duly authorized, in accordance with its internal procedures, to sign, ratify, accept, approve or accede to this Convention;

(i) 'Chemical Review Committee' means the subsidiary body referred to in paragraph 6 of Article 18.

Article 3: Scope of the Convention

1. This Convention applies to:

(a) Banned or severely restricted chemicals; and

(b) Severely hazardous pesticide formulations.

2. This Convention does not apply to:

(a) Narcotic drugs and psychotropic substances;

(b) Radioactive materials;

(c) Wastes;

(d) Chemical weapons;

(e) Pharmaceuticals, including human and veterinary drugs;

(f) Chemicals used as food additives;

(g) Food;

(h) Chemicals in quantities not likely to affect human health or the environment provided they are imported:

i) For the purpose of research or analysis; or

ii) By an individual for his or her own personal use in quantities reasonable for such use.

Article 4: Designated national authorities

1. Each Party shall designate one or more national authorities that shall be authorized to act on its behalf in the performance of the administrative functions required by this Convention.

2. Each Party shall seek to ensure that such authority or authorities have sufficient resources to perform their tasks effectively.

3. Each Party shall, no later than the date of the entry into force of this Convention for it, notify the name and address of such authority or authorities to the Secretariat. It shall forthwith notify the Secretariat of any changes in the name and address of such authority or authorities.

4. The Secretariat shall forthwith inform the Parties of the notifications it receives under paragraph 3.

Article 5: Procedures for banned or severely restricted chemicals

1. Each Party that has adopted a final regulatory action shall notify the Secretariat in writing of such action. Such notification shall be made as soon as possible, and in any event no later than ninety days after the date on which the final regulatory action has taken effect, and shall contain the information required by Annex I, where available.

2. Each Party shall, at the date of entry into force of this Convention for it, notify the Secretariat in writing of its final regulatory actions in effect at that time, except that each Party that has submitted notifications of final regulatory actions under the Amended London Guidelines or the International Code of Conduct need not resubmit those notifications.

3. The Secretariat shall, as soon as possible, and in any event no later than six months after receipt of a notification under paragraphs 1 and 2, verify whether the notification contains the information required by Annex I. If the notification contains the information required, the Secretariat shall forthwith forward to all Parties a summary of the information received. If the notification does not contain the information required, it shall inform the notifying Party accordingly.

4. The Secretariat shall every six months communicate to the Parties a synopsis of the information received pursuant to paragraphs 1 and 2, including information regarding those notifications which do not contain all the information required by Annex I.

5. When the Secretariat has received at least one notification from each of two Prior Informed Consent regions regarding a particular chemical that it has verified meet the requirements of Annex I, it shall forward them to the Chemical Review Committee. The composition of the Prior Informed Consent regions shall be defined in a decision to be adopted by consensus at the first meeting of the Conference of the Parties.

6. The Chemical Review Committee shall review the information provided in such notifications and, in accordance with the criteria set out in Annex II, recommend to

the Conference of the Parties whether the chemical in question should be made subject to the Prior Informed Consent procedure and, accordingly, be listed in Annex III.

Article 6: Procedures for severely hazardous pesticide formulations

1. Any Party that is a developing country or a country with an economy in transition and that is experiencing problems caused by a severely hazardous pesticide formulation under conditions of use in its territory, may propose to the Secretariat the listing of the severely hazardous pesticide formulation in Annex III. In developing a proposal, the Party may draw upon technical expertise from any relevant source. The proposal shall contain the information required by part 1 of Annex IV.

2. The Secretariat shall, as soon as possible, and in any event no later than six months after receipt of a proposal under paragraph 1, verify whether the proposal contains the information required by part 1 of Annex IV. If the proposal contains the information required, the Secretariat shall forthwith forward to all Parties a summary of the information received. If the proposal does not contain the information required, it shall inform the proposing Party accordingly.

3. The Secretariat shall collect the additional information set out in part 2 of Annex IV regarding the proposal forwarded under paragraph 2.

4. When the requirements of paragraphs 2 and 3 above have been fulfilled with regard to a particular severely hazardous pesticide formulation, the Secretariat shall forward the proposal and the related information to the Chemical Review Committee.

5. The Chemical Review Committee shall review the information provided in the proposal and the additional information collected and, in accordance with the criteria set out in part 3 of Annex IV, recommend to the Conference of the Parties whether the severely hazardous pesticide formulation in question should be made subject to the Prior Informed Consent procedure and, accordingly, be listed in Annex III.

Article 7: Listing of chemicals in Annex III

1. For each chemical that the Chemical Review Committee has decided to recommend for listing in Annex III, it shall prepare a draft decision guidance document. The decision guidance document should, at a minimum, be based on the information specified in Annex I, or, as the case may be, Annex IV, and include information on uses of the chemical in a category other than the category for which the final regulatory action applies.

2. The recommendation referred to in paragraph 1 together with the draft decision guidance document shall be forwarded to the Conference of the Parties. The Conference of the Parties shall decide whether the chemical should be made subject to the Prior Informed Consent procedure and, accordingly, list the chemical in Annex III and approve the draft decision guidance document.

3. When a decision to list a chemical in Annex III has been taken and the related decision guidance document has been approved by the Conference of the Parties, the Secretariat shall forthwith communicate this information to all Parties.

Article 8: Chemicals in the voluntary Prior Informed Consent procedure

For any chemical, other than a chemical listed in Annex III, that has been included in the voluntary Prior Informed Consent procedure before the date of the first meeting of the Conference of the Parties, the Conference of the Parties shall decide at that meeting to list the chemical in Annex III, provided that it is satisfied that all the requirements for listing in that Annex have been fulfilled.

Article 9: Removal of chemicals from Annex III

1. If a Party submits to the Secretariat information that was not available at the time of the decision to list a chemical in Annex III and that information indicates that its listing may no longer be justified in accordance with the relevant criteria in Annex II or, as the case may be, Annex IV, the Secretariat shall forward the information to the Chemical Review Committee.

2. The Chemical Review Committee shall review the information it receives under paragraph 1. For each chemical that the Chemical Review Committee decides, in accordance with the relevant criteria in Annex II or, as the case may be, Annex IV, to recommend for removal from Annex III, it shall prepare a revised draft decision guidance document.

3. A recommendation referred to in paragraph 2 shall be forwarded to the Conference of the Parties and be accompanied by a revised draft decision guidance document. The Conference of the Parties shall decide whether the chemical should be removed from Annex III and whether to approve the revised draft decision guidance document.

4. When a decision to remove a chemical from Annex III has been taken and the revised decision guidance document has been approved by the Conference of the Parties, the Secretariat shall forthwith communicate this information to all Parties.

Article 10: Obligations in relation to imports of chemicals listed in Annex III

1. Each Party shall implement appropriate legislative or administrative measures to ensure timely decisions with respect to the import of chemicals listed in Annex III.

2. Each Party shall transmit to the Secretariat, as soon as possible, and in any event no later than nine months after the date of dispatch of the decision guidance document referred to in paragraph 3 of Article 7, a response concerning the future import of the chemical concerned. If a Party modifies this response, it shall forthwith submit the revised response to the Secretariat.

3. The Secretariat shall, at the expiration of the time period in paragraph 2, forthwith address to a Party that has not provided such a response, a written request to do so. Should the Party be unable to provide a response, the Secretariat shall,

where appropriate, help it to provide a response within the time period specified in the last sentence of paragraph 2 of Article 11.

4. A response under paragraph 2 shall consist of either:
(a) A final decision, pursuant to legislative or administrative measures:
   i) To consent to import;
   ii) Not to consent to import; or
   iii) To consent to import only subject to specified conditions; or
(b) An interim response, which may include:
   i) An interim decision consenting to import with or without specified conditions, or not consenting to import during the interim period;
   ii) A statement that a final decision is under active consideration;
   iii) A request to the Secretariat, or to the Party that notified the final regulatory action, for further information;
   iv) A request to the Secretariat for assistance in evaluating the chemical.

5. A response under subparagraphs (a) or (b) of paragraph 4 shall relate to the category or categories specified for the chemical in Annex III.

6. A final decision should be accompanied by a description of any legislative or administrative measures upon which it is based.

7. Each Party shall, no later than the date of entry into force of this Convention for it, transmit to the Secretariat responses with respect to each chemical listed in Annex III. A Party that has provided such responses under the Amended London Guidelines or the International Code of Conduct need not resubmit those responses.

8. Each Party shall make its responses under this Article available to those concerned within its jurisdiction, in accordance with its legislative or administrative measures.

9. A Party that, pursuant to paragraphs 2 and 4 above and paragraph 2 of Article 11, takes a decision not to consent to import of a chemical or to consent to its import only under specified conditions shall, if it has not already done so, simultaneously prohibit or make subject to the same conditions:
(a) Import of the chemical from any source; and
(b) Domestic production of the chemical for domestic use.

10. Every six months the Secretariat shall inform all Parties of the responses it has received. Such information shall include a description of the legislative or administrative measures on which the decisions have been based, where available. The Secretariat shall, in addition, inform the Parties of any cases of failure to transmit a response.

Article 11: Obligations in relation to exports of chemicals listed in Annex III

1. Each exporting Party shall:
(a) Implement appropriate legislative or administrative measures to communicate the responses forwarded by the Secretariat in accordance with paragraph 10 of Article 10 to those concerned within its jurisdiction;

(b) Take appropriate legislative or administrative measures to ensure that exporters within its jurisdiction comply with decisions in each response no later than six months after the date on which the Secretariat first informs the Parties of such response in accordance with paragraph 10 of Article 10;

(c) Advise and assist importing Parties, upon request and as appropriate:

i) To obtain further information to help them to take action in accordance with paragraph 4 of Article 10 and paragraph 2 (c) below; and

ii) To strengthen their capacities and capabilities to manage chemicals safely during their life-cycle.

2. Each Party shall ensure that a chemical listed in Annex III is not exported from its territory to any importing Party that, in exceptional circumstances, has failed to transmit a response or has transmitted an interim response that does not contain an interim decision, unless:

(a) It is a chemical that, at the time of import, is registered as a chemical in the importing Party; or

(b) It is a chemical for which evidence exists that it has previously been used in, or imported into, the importing Party and in relation to which no regulatory action to prohibit its use has been taken; or

(c) Explicit consent to the import has been sought and received by the exporter through a designated national authority of the importing Party. The importing Party shall respond to such a request within sixty days and shall promptly notify the Secretariat of its decision.

The obligations of exporting Parties under this paragraph shall apply with effect from the expiration of a period of six months from the date on which the Secretariat first informs the Parties, in accordance with paragraph 10 of Article 10, that a Party has failed to transmit a response or has transmitted an interim response that does not contain an interim decision, and shall apply for one year.

Article 12: Export notification

1. Where a chemical that is banned or severely restricted by a Party is exported from its territory, that Party shall provide an export notification to the importing Party. The export notification shall include the information set out in Annex V.

2. The export notification shall be provided for that chemical prior to the first export following adoption of the corresponding final regulatory action. Thereafter, the export notification shall be provided before the first export in any calendar year. The requirement to notify before export may be waived by the designated national authority of the importing Party.

3. An exporting Party shall provide an updated export notification after it has adopted a final regulatory action that results in a major change concerning the ban or severe restriction of that chemical.

4. The importing Party shall acknowledge receipt of the first export notification received after the adoption of the final regulatory action. If the exporting Party does not receive the acknowledgement within thirty days of the dispatch of the export

notification, it shall submit a second notification. The exporting Party shall make reasonable efforts to ensure that the importing Party receives the second notification.

5. The obligations of a Party set out in paragraph 1 shall cease when:
(a) The chemical has been listed in Annex III;
(b) The importing Party has provided a response for the chemical to the Secretariat in accordance with paragraph 2 of Article 10; and
(c) The Secretariat has distributed the response to the Parties in accordance with paragraph 10 of Article 10.

Article 13: Information to accompany exported chemicals

1. The Conference of the Parties shall encourage the World Customs Organization to assign specific Harmonized System customs codes to the individual chemicals or groups of chemicals listed in Annex III, as appropriate. Each Party shall require that, whenever a code has been assigned to such a chemical, the shipping document for that chemical bears the code when exported.

2. Without prejudice to any requirements of the importing Party, each Party shall require that both chemicals listed in Annex III and chemicals banned or severely restricted in its territory are, when exported, subject to labelling requirements that ensure adequate availability of information with regard to risks and/or hazards to human health or the environment, taking into account relevant international standards.

3. Without prejudice to any requirements of the importing Party, each Party may require that chemicals subject to environmental or health labelling requirements in its territory are, when exported, subject to labelling requirements that ensure adequate availability of information with regard to risks and/or hazards to human health or the environment, taking into account relevant international standards.

4. With respect to the chemicals referred to in paragraph 2 that are to be used for occupational purposes, each exporting Party shall require that a safety data sheet that follows an internationally recognized format, setting out the most up-to-date information available, is sent to each importer.

5. The information on the label and on the safety data sheet should, as far as practicable, be given in one or more of the official languages of the importing Party.

Article 14: Information exchange

1. Each Party shall, as appropriate and in accordance with the objective of this Convention, facilitate:
(a) The exchange of scientific, technical, economic and legal information concerning the chemicals within the scope of this Convention, including toxicological, ecotoxicological and safety information;
(b) The provision of publicly available information on domestic regulatory actions relevant to the objectives of this Convention; and

(c) The provision of information to other Parties, directly or through the Secretariat, on domestic regulatory actions that substantially restrict one or more uses of the chemical, as appropriate.

2. Parties that exchange information pursuant to this Convention shall protect any confidential information as mutually agreed.

3. The following information shall not be regarded as confidential for the purposes of this Convention:

(a) The information referred to in Annexes I and IV, submitted pursuant to Articles 5 and 6 respectively;
(b) The information contained in the safety data sheet referred to in paragraph 4 of Article 13;
(c) The expiry date of the chemical;
(d) Information on precautionary measures, including hazard classification, the nature of the risk and the relevant safety advice; and
(e) The summary results of the toxicological and ecotoxicological tests.

4. The production date of the chemical shall generally not be considered confidential for the purposes of this Convention.

5. Any Party requiring information on transit movements through its territory of chemicals listed in Annex III may report its need to the Secretariat, which shall inform all Parties accordingly.

Article 15: Implementation of the Convention

1. Each Party shall take such measures as may be necessary to establish and strengthen its national infrastructures and institutions for the effective implementation of this Convention. These measures may include, as required, the adoption or amendment of national legislative or administrative measures and may also include:

(a) The establishment of national registers and databases including safety information for chemicals;
(b) The encouragement of initiatives by industry to promote chemical safety; and
(c) The promotion of voluntary agreements, taking into consideration the provisions of Article 16.

2. Each Party shall ensure, to the extent practicable, that the public has appropriate access to information on chemical handling and accident management and on alternatives that are safer for human health or the environment than the chemicals listed in Annex III.

3. The Parties agree to cooperate, directly or, where appropriate, through competent international organizations, in the implementation of this Convention at the subregional, regional and global levels.

4. Nothing in this Convention shall be interpreted as restricting the right of the Parties to take action that is more stringently protective of human health and the environment than that called for in this Convention, provided that such action is

consistent with the provisions of this Convention and is in accordance with international law.

Article 16: Technical assistance

The Parties shall, taking into account in particular the needs of developing countries and countries with economies in transition, cooperate in promoting technical assistance for the development of the infrastructure and the capacity necessary to manage chemicals to enable implementation of this Convention. Parties with more advanced programmes for regulating chemicals should provide technical assistance, including training, to other Parties in developing their infrastructure and capacity to manage chemicals throughout their life-cycle.

Article 17: Non-compliance

The Conference of the Parties shall, as soon as practicable, develop and approve procedures and institutional mechanisms for determining non-compliance with the provisions of this Convention and for treatment of Parties found to be in non-compliance.

Article 18: Conference of the Parties

1. A Conference of the Parties is hereby established.

2. The first meeting of the Conference of the Parties shall be convened by the Executive Director of UNEP and the Director-General of FAO, acting jointly, no later than one year after the entry into force of this Convention. Thereafter, ordinary meetings of the Conference of the Parties shall be held at regular intervals to be determined by the Conference.

3. Extraordinary meetings of the Conference of the Parties shall be held at such other times as may be deemed necessary by the Conference, or at the written request of any Party provided that it is supported by at least one third of the Parties.

4. The Conference of the Parties shall by consensus agree upon and adopt at its first meeting rules of procedure and financial rules for itself and any subsidiary bodies, as well as financial provisions governing the functioning of the Secretariat.

5. The Conference of the Parties shall keep under continuous review and evaluation the implementation of this Convention. It shall perform the functions assigned to it by the Convention and, to this end, shall:

(a) Establish, further to the requirements of paragraph 6 below, such subsidiary bodies, as it considers necessary for the implementation of the Convention;
(b) Cooperate, where appropriate, with competent international organizations and intergovernmental and non-governmental bodies; and
(c) Consider and undertake any additional action that may be required for the achievement of the objectives of the Convention.

6. The Conference of the Parties shall, at its first meeting, establish a subsidiary body, to be called the Chemical Review Committee, for the purposes of performing the functions assigned to that Committee by this Convention. In this regard:

(a) The members of the Chemical Review Committee shall be appointed by the Conference of the Parties. Membership of the Committee shall consist of a limited number of government-designated experts in chemicals management. The members of the Committee shall be appointed on the basis of equitable geographical distribution, including ensuring a balance between developed and developing Parties;

(b) The Conference of the Parties shall decide on the terms of reference, organization and operation of the Committee;

(c) The Committee shall make every effort to make its recommendations by consensus. If all efforts at consensus have been exhausted, and no consensus reached, such recommendation shall as a last resort be adopted by a two-thirds majority vote of the members present and voting.

7. The United Nations, its specialized agencies and the International Atomic Energy Agency, as well as any State not Party to this Convention, may be represented at meetings of the Conference of the Parties as observers. Any body or agency, whether national or international, governmental or non-governmental, qualified in matters covered by the Convention, and which has informed the Secretariat of its wish to be represented at a meeting of the Conference of the Parties as an observer may be admitted unless at least one third of the Parties present object. The admission and participation of observers shall be subject to the rules of procedure adopted by the Conference of the Parties.

Article 19: Secretariat

1. A Secretariat is hereby established.

2. The functions of the Secretariat shall be:

(a) To make arrangements for meetings of the Conference of the Parties and its subsidiary bodies and to provide them with services as required;

(b) To facilitate assistance to the Parties, particularly developing Parties and Parties with economies in transition, on request, in the implementation of this Convention;

(c) To ensure the necessary coordination with the secretariats of other relevant international bodies;

(d) To enter, under the overall guidance of the Conference of the Parties, into such administrative and contractual arrangements as may be required for the effective discharge of its functions; and

(e) To perform the other secretariat functions specified in this Convention and such other functions as may be determined by the Conference of the Parties.

3. The secretariat functions for this Convention shall be performed jointly by the Executive Director of UNEP and the Director-General of FAO, subject to such arrangements as shall be agreed between them and approved by the Conference of the Parties.

4. The Conference of the Parties may decide, by a three-fourths majority of the Parties present and voting, to entrust the secretariat functions to one or more other

competent international organizations, should it find that the Secretariat is not functioning as intended.

Article 20: Settlement of disputes

1. Parties shall settle any dispute between them concerning the interpretation or application of this Convention through negotiation or other peaceful means of their own choice.

2. When ratifying, accepting, approving or acceding to this Convention, or at any time thereafter, a Party that is not a regional economic integration organization may declare in a written instrument submitted to the Depositary that, with respect to any dispute concerning the interpretation or application of the Convention, it recognizes one or both of the following means of dispute settlement as compulsory in relation to any Party accepting the same obligation:

(a) Arbitration in accordance with procedures to be adopted by the Conference of the Parties in an annex as soon as practicable; and

(b) Submission of the dispute to the International Court of Justice.

3. A Party that is a regional economic integration organization may make a declaration with like effect in relation to arbitration in accordance with the procedure referred to in paragraph 2 (a).

4. A declaration made pursuant to paragraph 2 shall remain in force until it expires in accordance with its terms or until three months after written notice of its revocation has been deposited with the Depositary.

5. The expiry of a declaration, a notice of revocation or a new declaration shall not in any way affect proceedings pending before an arbitral tribunal or the International Court of Justice unless the parties to the dispute otherwise agree.

6. If the parties to a dispute have not accepted the same or any procedure pursuant to paragraph 2, and if they have not been able to settle their dispute within twelve months following notification by one party to another that a dispute exists between them, the dispute shall be submitted to a conciliation commission at the request of any party to the dispute. The conciliation commission shall render a report with recommendations. Additional procedures relating to the conciliation commission shall be included in an annex to be adopted by the Conference of the Parties no later than the second meeting of the Conference.

Article 21: Amendments to the Convention

1. Amendments to this Convention may be proposed by any Party.

2. Amendments to this Convention shall be adopted at a meeting of the Conference of the Parties. The text of any proposed amendment shall be communicated to the Parties by the Secretariat at least six months before the meeting at which it is proposed for adoption. The Secretariat shall also communicate the proposed amendment to the signatories to this Convention and, for information, to the Depositary.

3. The Parties shall make every effort to reach agreement on any proposed amendment to this Convention by consensus. If all efforts at consensus have been exhausted, and no agreement reached, the amendment shall as a last resort be adopted by a three-fourths majority vote of the Parties present and voting at the meeting.

4. The amendment shall be communicated by the Depositary to all Parties for ratification, acceptance or approval.

5. Ratification, acceptance or approval of an amendment shall be notified to the Depositary in writing. An amendment adopted in accordance with paragraph 3 shall enter into force for the Parties having accepted it on the ninetieth day after the date of deposit of instruments of ratification, acceptance or approval by at least three fourths of the Parties. Thereafter, the amendment shall enter into force for any other Party on the ninetieth day after the date on which that Party deposits its instrument of ratification, acceptance or approval of the amendment.

Article 22: Adoption and amendment of annexes

1. Annexes to this Convention shall form an integral part thereof and, unless expressly provided otherwise, a reference to this Convention constitutes at the same time a reference to any annexes thereto.

2. Annexes shall be restricted to procedural, scientific, technical or administrative matters.

3. The following procedure shall apply to the proposal, adoption and entry into force of additional annexes to this Convention:

(a) Additional annexes shall be proposed and adopted according to the procedure laid down in paragraphs 1, 2 and 3 of Article 21;

(b) Any Party that is unable to accept an additional annex shall so notify the Depositary, in writing, within one year from the date of communication of the adoption of the additional annex by the Depositary. The Depositary shall without delay notify all Parties of any such notification received. A Party may at any time withdraw a previous notification of non-acceptance in respect of an additional annex and the annex shall thereupon enter into force for that Party subject to subparagraph (c) below; and

(c) On the expiry of one year from the date of the communication by the Depositary of the adoption of an additional annex, the annex shall enter into force for all Parties that have not submitted a notification in accordance with the provisions of subparagraph (b) above.

4. Except in the case of Annex III, the proposal, adoption and entry into force of amendments to annexes to this Convention shall be subject to the same procedures as for the proposal, adoption and entry into force of additional annexes to the Convention.

5. The following procedure shall apply to the proposal, adoption and entry into force of amendments to Annex III:

(a) Amendments to Annex III shall be proposed and adopted according to the procedure laid down in Articles 5 to 9 and paragraph 2 of Article 21;
(b) The Conference of the Parties shall take its decisions on adoption by consensus;
(c) A decision to amend Annex III shall forthwith be communicated to the Parties by the Depositary. The amendment shall enter into force for all Parties on a date to be specified in the decision.

6. If an additional annex or an amendment to an annex is related to an amendment to this Convention, the additional annex or amendment shall not enter into force until such time as the amendment to the Convention enters into force.

Article 23: Voting

1. Each Party to this Convention shall have one vote, except as provided for in paragraph 2 below.

2. A regional economic integration organization, on matters within its competence, shall exercise its right to vote with a number of votes equal to the number of its member States that are Parties to this Convention. Such an organization shall not exercise its right to vote if any of its member States exercises its right to vote, and vice versa.

3. For the purposes of this Convention, 'Parties present and voting' means Parties present and casting an affirmative or negative vote.

Article 24: Signature

This Convention shall be open for signature at Rotterdam by all States and regional economic integration organizations on 11 September 1998, and at United Nations Headquarters in New York from 12 September 1998 to 10 September 1999.

Article 25: Ratification, acceptance, approval or accession

1. This Convention shall be subject to ratification, acceptance or approval by States and by regional economic integration organizations. It shall be open for accession by States and by regional economic integration organizations from the day after the date on which the Convention is closed for signature. Instruments of ratification, acceptance, approval or accession shall be deposited with the Depositary.

2. Any regional economic integration organization that becomes a Party to this Convention without any of its member States being a Party shall be bound by all the obligations under the Convention. In the case of such organizations, one or more of whose member States is a Party to this Convention, the organization and its member States shall decide on their respective responsibilities for the performance of their obligations under the Convention. In such cases, the organization and the member States shall not be entitled to exercise rights under the Convention concurrently.

3. In its instrument of ratification, acceptance, approval or accession, a regional economic integration organization shall declare the extent of its competence in respect of the matters governed by this Convention. Any such organization shall

also inform the Depositary, who shall in turn inform the Parties, of any relevant modification in the extent of its competence.

Article 26: Entry into force

1. This Convention shall enter into force on the ninetieth day after the date of deposit of the fiftieth instrument of ratification, acceptance, approval or accession.

2. For each State or regional economic integration organization that ratifies, accepts or approves this Convention or accedes thereto after the deposit of the fiftieth instrument of ratification, acceptance, approval or accession, the Convention shall enter into force on the ninetieth day after the date of deposit by such State or regional economic integration organization of its instrument of ratification, acceptance, approval or accession.

3. For the purpose of paragraphs 1 and 2, any instrument deposited by a regional economic integration organization shall not be counted as additional to those deposited by member States of that organization.

Article 27: Reservations

No reservations may be made to this Convention.

Article 28: Withdrawal

1. At any time after three years from the date on which this Convention has entered into force for a Party, that Party may withdraw from the Convention by giving written notification to the Depositary.

2. Any such withdrawal shall take effect upon expiry of one year from the date of receipt by the Depositary of the notification of withdrawal, or on such later date as may be specified in the notification of withdrawal.

Article 29: Depositary

The Secretary-General of the United Nations shall be the Depositary of this Convention.

Article 30: Authentic texts

The original of this Convention, of which the Arabic, Chinese, English, French, Russian and Spanish texts are equally authentic, shall be deposited with the Secretary-General of the United Nations.

In witness whereof the undersigned, being duly authorized to that effect, have signed this Convention.

Done at Rotterdam on this tenth day of September, one thousand nine hundred and ninety-eight.

Annex I: Information requirements for notifications made pursuant to Article 5; Annex II: Criteria for listing banned or severely restricted chemicals in Annex III; Annex III: Chemicals subject to the Prior Informed Consent procedure; Annex IV: Information and criteria for listing severely hazardous pesticide formulations in Annex III; Annex V: Information requirements for export notification [not reproduced]

Stockholm Convention on Persistent Organic Pollutants

Adopted on 23 May 2001 at Stockholm. Entered into force on 17 May 2004. Source: Doc. UNEP/POPS/CONF/4 (Appendix II). Number of parties: 56. Further information: Secretariat, Geneva, Switzerland, http://www.pops.int

The Parties to this Convention,

Recognizing that persistent organic pollutants possess toxic properties, resist degradation, bioaccumulate and are transported, through air, water and migratory species, across international boundaries and deposited far from their place of release, where they accumulate in terrestrial and aquatic ecosystems,

Aware of the health concerns, especially in developing countries, resulting from local exposure to persistent organic pollutants, in particular impacts upon women and, through them, upon future generations,

Acknowledging that the Arctic ecosystems and indigenous communities are particularly at risk because of the biomagnification of persistent organic pollutants and that contamination of their traditional foods is a public health issue,

Conscious of the need for global action on persistent organic pollutants,

Mindful of decision 19/13 C of 7 February 1997 of the Governing Council of the United Nations Environment Programme to initiate international action to protect human health and the environment through measures which will reduce and/or eliminate emissions and discharges of persistent organic pollutants,

Recalling the pertinent provisions of the relevant international environmental conventions, especially the Rotterdam Convention on the Prior Informed Consent Procedure for Certain Hazardous Chemicals and Pesticides in International Trade, and the Basel Convention on the Control of Transboundary Movements of Hazardous Wastes and their Disposal including the regional agreements developed within the framework of its Article 11,

Recalling also the pertinent provisions of the Rio Declaration on Environment and Development and Agenda 21,

Acknowledging that precaution underlies the concerns of all the Parties and is embedded within this Convention,

Recognizing that this Convention and other international agreements in the field of trade and the environment are mutually supportive,

Reaffirming that States have, in accordance with the Charter of the United Nations and the principles of international law, the sovereign right to exploit their own resources pursuant to their own environmental and developmental policies, and the responsibility to ensure that activities within their jurisdiction or control do not cause damage to the environment of other States or of areas beyond the limits of national jurisdiction,

Taking into account the circumstances and particular requirements of developing countries, in particular the least developed among them, and countries with economies in transition, especially the need to strengthen their national capabilities for the management of chemicals, including through the transfer of technology, the provision of financial and technical assistance and the promotion of cooperation among the Parties,

Taking full account of the Programme of Action for the Sustainable Development of Small Island Developing States, adopted in Barbados on 6 May 1994,

Noting the respective capabilities of developed and developing countries, as well as the common but differentiated responsibilities of States as set forth in Principle 7 of the Rio Declaration on Environment and Development,

Recognizing the important contribution that the private sector and non-governmental organizations can make to achieving the reduction and/or elimination of emissions and discharges of persistent organic pollutants,

Underlining the importance of manufacturers of persistent organic pollutants taking responsibility for reducing adverse effects caused by their products and for providing information to users, Governments and the public on the hazardous properties of those chemicals,

Conscious of the need to take measures to prevent adverse effects caused by persistent organic pollutants at all stages of their life cycle,

Reaffirming Principle 16 of the Rio Declaration on Environment and Development which states that national authorities should endeavour to promote the internalization of environmental costs and the use of economic instruments, taking into account the approach that the polluter should, in principle, bear the cost of pollution, with due regard to the public interest and without distorting international trade and investment,

Encouraging Parties not having regulatory and assessment schemes for pesticides and industrial chemicals to develop such schemes,

Recognizing the importance of developing and using environmentally sound alternative processes and chemicals,

Determined to protect human health and the environment from the harmful impacts of persistent organic pollutants,

Have agreed as follows:

Article 1: Objective

Mindful of the precautionary approach as set forth in Principle 15 of the Rio Declaration on Environment and Development, the objective of this Convention is to protect human health and the environment from persistent organic pollutants.

Article 2: Definitions

For the purposes of this Convention:

(a) 'Party' means a State or regional economic integration organization that has consented to be bound by this Convention and for which the Convention is in force;

(b) 'Regional economic integration organization' means an organization constituted by sovereign States of a given region to which its member States have transferred competence in respect of matters governed by this Convention and which has been duly authorized, in accordance with its internal procedures, to sign, ratify, accept, approve or accede to this Convention;

(c) 'Parties present and voting' means Parties present and casting an affirmative or negative vote.

Article 3: Measures to reduce or eliminate releases from intentional production and use

1. Each Party shall:

(a) Prohibit and/or take the legal and administrative measures necessary to eliminate:

i) Its production and use of the chemicals listed in Annex A subject to the provisions of that Annex; and

ii) Its import and export of the chemicals listed in Annex A in accordance with the provisions of paragraph 2; and

(b) Restrict its production and use of the chemicals listed in Annex B in accordance with the provisions of that Annex.

2. Each Party shall take measures to ensure:

(a) That a chemical listed in Annex A or Annex B is imported only:

i) For the purpose of environmentally sound disposal as set forth in paragraph 1 (d) of Article 6; or

ii) For a use or purpose which is permitted for that Party under Annex A or Annex B;

(b) That a chemical listed in Annex A for which any production or use specific exemption is in effect or a chemical listed in Annex B for which any production or use specific exemption or acceptable purpose is in effect, taking into account any relevant provisions in existing international prior informed consent instruments, is exported only:

i) For the purpose of environmentally sound disposal as set forth in paragraph 1 (d) of Article 6;

ii) To a Party which is permitted to use that chemical under Annex A or Annex B; or

iii) To a State not Party to this Convention which has provided an annual certification to the exporting Party. Such certification shall specify the intended use of the chemical and include a statement that, with respect to that chemical, the importing State is committed to:

a. Protect human health and the environment by taking the necessary measures to minimize or prevent releases;

b. Comply with the provisions of paragraph 1 of Article 6; and

c. Comply, where appropriate, with the provisions of paragraph 2 of Part II of Annex B.

The certification shall also include any appropriate supporting documentation, such as legislation, regulatory instruments, or administrative or policy guidelines. The exporting Party shall transmit the certification to the Secretariat within sixty days of receipt.

(c) That a chemical listed in Annex A, for which production and use specific exemptions are no longer in effect for any Party, is not exported from it except for the purpose of environmentally sound disposal as set forth in paragraph 1 (d) of Article 6;

(d) For the purposes of this paragraph, the term 'State not Party to this Convention' shall include, with respect to a particular chemical, a State or regional economic integration organization that has not agreed to be bound by the Convention with respect to that chemical.

3. Each Party that has one or more regulatory and assessment schemes for new pesticides or new industrial chemicals shall take measures to regulate with the aim of preventing the production and use of new pesticides or new industrial chemicals which, taking into consideration the criteria in paragraph 1 of Annex D, exhibit the characteristics of persistent organic pollutants.

4. Each Party that has one or more regulatory and assessment schemes for pesticides or industrial chemicals shall, where appropriate, take into consideration within these schemes the criteria in paragraph 1 of Annex D when conducting assessments of pesticides or industrial chemicals currently in use.

5. Except as otherwise provided in this Convention, paragraphs 1 and 2 shall not apply to quantities of a chemical to be used for laboratory-scale research or as a reference standard.

6. Any Party that has a specific exemption in accordance with Annex A or a specific exemption or an acceptable purpose in accordance with Annex B shall take appropriate measures to ensure that any production or use under such exemption or purpose is carried out in a manner that prevents or minimizes human exposure and release into the environment. For exempted uses or acceptable purposes that involve intentional release into the environment under conditions of normal use, such release shall be to the minimum extent necessary, taking into account any applicable standards and guidelines.

Article 4: Register of specific exemptions

1. A Register is hereby established for the purpose of identifying the Parties that have specific exemptions listed in Annex A or Annex B. It shall not identify Parties that make use of the provisions in Annex A or Annex B that may be exercised by all Parties. The Register shall be maintained by the Secretariat and shall be available to the public.

2. The Register shall include:

(a) A list of the types of specific exemptions reproduced from Annex A and Annex B;

(b) A list of the Parties that have a specific exemption listed under Annex A or Annex B; and

(c) A list of the expiry dates for each registered specific exemption.

3. Any State may, on becoming a Party, by means of a notification in writing to the Secretariat, register for one or more types of specific exemptions listed in Annex A or Annex B.

4. Unless an earlier date is indicated in the Register by a Party, or an extension is granted pursuant to paragraph 7, all registrations of specific exemptions shall expire five years after the date of entry into force of this Convention with respect to a particular chemical.

5. At its first meeting, the Conference of the Parties shall decide upon its review process for the entries in the Register.

6. Prior to a review of an entry in the Register, the Party concerned shall submit a report to the Secretariat justifying its continuing need for registration of that exemption. The report shall be circulated by the Secretariat to all Parties. The review of a registration shall be carried out on the basis of all available information. Thereupon, the Conference of the Parties may make such recommendations to the Party concerned as it deems appropriate.

7. The Conference of the Parties may, upon request from the Party concerned, decide to extend the expiry date of a specific exemption for a period of up to five years. In making its decision, the Conference of the Parties shall take due account of the special circumstances of the developing country Parties and Parties with economies in transition.

8. A Party may, at any time, withdraw an entry from the Register for a specific exemption upon written notification to the Secretariat. The withdrawal shall take effect on the date specified in the notification.

9. When there are no longer any Parties registered for a particular type of specific exemption, no new registrations may be made with respect to it.

Article 5: Measures to reduce or eliminate releases from unintentional production

Each Party shall at a minimum take the following measures to reduce the total releases derived from anthropogenic sources of each of the chemicals listed in

Annex C, with the goal of their continuing minimization and, where feasible, ultimate elimination:

(a) Develop an action plan or, where appropriate, a regional or subregional action plan within two years of the date of entry into force of this Convention for it, and subsequently implement it as part of its implementation plan specified in Article 7, designed to identify, characterize and address the release of the chemicals listed in Annex C and to facilitate implementation of subparagraphs (b) to (e). The action plan shall include the following elements:

i) An evaluation of current and projected releases, including the development and maintenance of source inventories and release estimates, taking into consideration the source categories identified in Annex C;
ii) An evaluation of the efficacy of the laws and policies of the Party relating to the management of such releases;
iii) Strategies to meet the obligations of this paragraph, taking into account the evaluations in (i) and (ii);
iv) Steps to promote education and training with regard to, and awareness of, those strategies;
v) A review every five years of those strategies and of their success in meeting the obligations of this paragraph; such reviews shall be included in reports submitted pursuant to Article 15;
vi) A schedule for implementation of the action plan, including for the strategies and measures identified therein;

(b) Promote the application of available, feasible and practical measures that can expeditiously achieve a realistic and meaningful level of release reduction or source elimination;

(c) Promote the development and, where it deems appropriate, require the use of substitute or modified materials, products and processes to prevent the formation and release of the chemicals listed in Annex C, taking into consideration the general guidance on prevention and release reduction measures in Annex C and guidelines to be adopted by decision of the Conference of the Parties;

(d) Promote and, in accordance with the implementation schedule of its action plan, require the use of best available techniques for new sources within source categories which a Party has identified as warranting such action in its action plan, with a particular initial focus on source categories identified in Part II of Annex C. In any case, the requirement to use best available techniques for new sources in the categories listed in Part II of that Annex shall be phased in as soon as practicable but no later than four years after the entry into force of the Convention for that Party. For the identified categories, Parties shall promote the use of best environmental practices. When applying best available techniques and best environmental practices, Parties should take into consideration the general guidance on prevention and release reduction measures in that Annex and guidelines on best available techniques and best environmental practices to be adopted by decision of the Conference of the Parties;

(e) Promote, in accordance with its action plan, the use of best available techniques and best environmental practices:

i) For existing sources, within the source categories listed in Part II of Annex C and within source categories such as those in Part III of that Annex; and
ii) For new sources, within source categories such as those listed in Part III of Annex C which a Party has not addressed under subparagraph (d).

When applying best available techniques and best environmental practices, Parties should take into consideration the general guidance on prevention and release reduction measures in Annex C and guidelines on best available techniques and best environmental practices to be adopted by decision of the Conference of the Parties;

(f) For the purposes of this paragraph and Annex C:

i) 'Best available techniques' means the most effective and advanced stage in the development of activities and their methods of operation which indicate the practical suitability of particular techniques for providing in principle the basis for release limitations designed to prevent and, where that is not practicable, generally to reduce releases of chemicals listed in Part I of Annex C and their impact on the environment as a whole. In this regard:
ii) 'Techniques' includes both the technology used and the way in which the installation is designed, built, maintained, operated and decommissioned;
iii) 'Available' techniques means those techniques that are accessible to the operator and that are developed on a scale that allows implementation in the relevant industrial sector, under economically and technically viable conditions, taking into consideration the costs and advantages; and
iv) 'Best' means most effective in achieving a high general level of protection of the environment as a whole;
v) 'Best environmental practices' means the application of the most appropriate combination of environmental control measures and strategies;
vi) 'New source' means any source of which the construction or substantial modification is commenced at least one year after the date of:
    a. Entry into force of this Convention for the Party concerned; or
    b. Entry into force for the Party concerned of an amendment to Annex C where the source becomes subject to the provisions of this Convention only by virtue of that amendment.

g) Release limit values or performance standards may be used by a Party to fulfill its commitments for best available techniques under this paragraph.

Article 6: Measures to reduce or eliminate releases from stockpiles and wastes

1. In order to ensure that stockpiles consisting of or containing chemicals listed either in Annex A or Annex B and wastes, including products and articles upon becoming wastes, consisting of, containing or contaminated with a chemical listed in Annex A, B or C, are managed in a manner protective of human health and the environment, each Party shall:

(a) Develop appropriate strategies for identifying:
  i) Stockpiles consisting of or containing chemicals listed either in Annex A or Annex B; and
  ii) Products and articles in use and wastes consisting of, containing or contaminated with a chemical listed in Annex A, B or C;

(b) Identify, to the extent practicable, stockpiles consisting of or containing chemicals listed either in Annex A or Annex B on the basis of the strategies referred to in subparagraph (a);

(c) Manage stockpiles, as appropriate, in a safe, efficient and environmentally sound manner. Stockpiles of chemicals listed either in Annex A or Annex B, after they are no longer allowed to be used according to any specific exemption specified in Annex A or any specific exemption or acceptable purpose specified in Annex B, except stockpiles which are allowed to be exported according to paragraph 2 of Article 3, shall be deemed to be waste and shall be managed in accordance with subparagraph (d);

(d) Take appropriate measures so that such wastes, including products and articles upon becoming wastes, are:
  i) Handled, collected, transported and stored in an environmentally sound manner;
  ii) Disposed of in such a way that the persistent organic pollutant content is destroyed or irreversibly transformed so that they do not exhibit the characteristics of persistent organic pollutants or otherwise disposed of in an environmentally sound manner when destruction or irreversible transformation does not represent the environmentally preferable option or the persistent organic pollutant content is low, taking into account international rules, standards, and guidelines, including those that may be developed pursuant to paragraph 2, and relevant global and regional regimes governing the management of hazardous wastes;
  iii) Not permitted to be subjected to disposal operations that may lead to recovery, recycling, reclamation, direct reuse or alternative uses of persistent organic pollutants; and
  iv) Not transported across international boundaries without taking into account relevant international rules, standards and guidelines;

(e) Endeavour to develop appropriate strategies for identifying sites contaminated by chemicals listed in Annex A, B or C; if remediation of those sites is undertaken it shall be performed in an environmentally sound manner.

2. The Conference of the Parties shall cooperate closely with the appropriate bodies of the Basel Convention on the Control of Transboundary Movements of Hazardous Wastes and their Disposal to, *inter alia*:

(a) Establish levels of destruction and irreversible transformation necessary to ensure that the characteristics of persistent organic pollutants as specified in paragraph 1 of Annex D are not exhibited;

(b) Determine what they consider to be the methods that constitute environmentally sound disposal referred to above; and

(c) Work to establish, as appropriate, the concentration levels of the chemicals listed in Annexes A, B and C in order to define the low persistent organic pollutant content referred to in paragraph 1 (d)(ii).

Article 7: Implementation plans

1. Each Party shall:

(a) Develop and endeavour to implement a plan for the implementation of its obligations under this Convention;

(b) Transmit its implementation plan to the Conference of the Parties within two years of the date on which this Convention enters into force for it; and

(c) Review and update, as appropriate, its implementation plan on a periodic basis and in a manner to be specified by a decision of the Conference of the Parties.

2. The Parties shall, where appropriate, cooperate directly or through global, regional and subregional organizations, and consult their national stakeholders, including women's groups and groups involved in the health of children, in order to facilitate the development, implementation and updating of their implementation plans.

3. The Parties shall endeavour to utilize and, where necessary, establish the means to integrate national implementation plans for persistent organic pollutants in their sustainable development strategies where appropriate.

Article 8: Listing of chemicals in Annexes A, B and C

1. A Party may submit a proposal to the Secretariat for listing a chemical in Annexes A, B and/or C. The proposal shall contain the information specified in Annex D. In developing a proposal, a Party may be assisted by other Parties and/or by the Secretariat.

2. The Secretariat shall verify whether the proposal contains the information specified in Annex D. If the Secretariat is satisfied that the proposal contains the information so specified, it shall forward the proposal to the Persistent Organic Pollutants Review Committee.

3. The Committee shall examine the proposal and apply the screening criteria specified in Annex D in a flexible and transparent way, taking all information provided into account in an integrative and balanced manner.

4. If the Committee decides that:

(a) It is satisfied that the screening criteria have been fulfilled, it shall, through the Secretariat, make the proposal and the evaluation of the Committee available to all Parties and observers and invite them to submit the information specified in Annex E; or

(b) It is not satisfied that the screening criteria have been fulfilled, it shall, through the Secretariat, inform all Parties and observers and make the proposal and the evaluation of the Committee available to all Parties and the proposal shall be set aside.

5. Any Party may resubmit a proposal to the Committee that has been set aside by the Committee pursuant to paragraph 4. The resubmission may include any concerns of the Party as well as a justification for additional consideration by the Committee. If, following this procedure, the Committee again sets the proposal aside, the Party may challenge the decision of the Committee and the Conference of the Parties shall consider the matter at its next session. The Conference of the Parties may decide, based on the screening criteria in Annex D and taking into account the evaluation of the Committee and any additional information provided by any Party or observer, that the proposal should proceed.

6. Where the Committee has decided that the screening criteria have been fulfilled, or the Conference of the Parties has decided that the proposal should proceed, the Committee shall further review the proposal, taking into account any relevant additional information received, and shall prepare a draft risk profile in accordance with Annex E. It shall, through the Secretariat, make that draft available to all Parties and observers, collect technical comments from them and, taking those comments into account, complete the risk profile.

7. If, on the basis of the risk profile conducted in accordance with Annex E, the Committee decides:

(a) That the chemical is likely as a result of its long-range environmental transport to lead to significant adverse human health and/or environmental effects such that global action is warranted, the proposal shall proceed. Lack of full scientific certainty shall not prevent the proposal from proceeding. The Committee shall, through the Secretariat, invite information from all Parties and observers relating to the considerations specified in Annex F. It shall then prepare a risk management evaluation that includes an analysis of possible control measures for the chemical in accordance with that Annex; or

(b) That the proposal should not proceed, it shall, through the Secretariat, make the risk profile available to all Parties and observers and set the proposal aside.

8. For any proposal set aside pursuant to paragraph 7 (b), a Party may request the Conference of the Parties to consider instructing the Committee to invite additional information from the proposing Party and other Parties during a period not to exceed one year. After that period and on the basis of any information received, the Committee shall reconsider the proposal pursuant to paragraph 6 with a priority to be decided by the Conference of the Parties. If, following this procedure, the Committee again sets the proposal aside, the Party may challenge the decision of the Committee and the Conference of the Parties shall consider the matter at its next session. The Conference of the Parties may decide, based on the risk profile prepared in accordance with Annex E and taking into account the evaluation of the Committee and any additional information provided by any Party or observer, that the proposal should proceed. If the Conference of the Parties decides that the proposal shall proceed, the Committee shall then prepare the risk management evaluation.

9. The Committee shall, based on the risk profile referred to in paragraph 6 and the risk management evaluation referred to in paragraph 7 (a) or paragraph 8, recommend whether the chemical should be considered by the Conference of the Parties for listing in Annexes A, B and/or C. The Conference of the Parties, taking due account of the recommendations of the Committee, including any scientific uncertainty, shall decide, in a precautionary manner, whether to list the chemical, and specify its related control measures, in Annexes A, B and/or C.

Article 9: Information exchange

1. Each Party shall facilitate or undertake the exchange of information relevant to:
(a) The reduction or elimination of the production, use and release of persistent organic pollutants; and
(b) Alternatives to persistent organic pollutants, including information relating to their risks as well as to their economic and social costs.

2. The Parties shall exchange the information referred to in paragraph 1 directly or through the Secretariat.

3. Each Party shall designate a national focal point for the exchange of such information.

4. The Secretariat shall serve as a clearing-house mechanism for information on persistent organic pollutants, including information provided by Parties, intergovernmental organizations and nongovernmental organizations.

5. For the purposes of this Convention, information on health and safety of humans and the environment shall not be regarded as confidential. Parties that exchange other information pursuant to this Convention shall protect any confidential information as mutually agreed.

Article 10: Public information, awareness and education

1. Each Party shall, within its capabilities, promote and facilitate:
(a) Awareness among its policy and decision makers with regard to persistent organic pollutants;
(b) Provision to the public of all available information on persistent organic pollutants, taking into account paragraph 5 of Article 9;
(c) Development and implementation, especially for women, children and the least educated, of educational and public awareness programmes on persistent organic pollutants, as well as on their health and environmental effects and on their alternatives;
(d) Public participation in addressing persistent organic pollutants and their health and environmental effects and in developing adequate responses, including opportunities for providing input at the national level regarding implementation of this Convention;
(e) Training of workers, scientists, educators and technical and managerial personnel;
(f) Development and exchange of educational and public awareness materials at the national and international levels; and

(g) Development and implementation of education and training programmes at the national and international levels.

2. Each Party shall, within its capabilities, ensure that the public has access to the public information referred to in paragraph 1 and that the information is kept up-to-date.

3. Each Party shall, within its capabilities, encourage industry and professional users to promote and facilitate the provision of the information referred to in paragraph 1 at the national level and, as appropriate, subregional, regional and global levels.

4. In providing information on persistent organic pollutants and their alternatives, Parties may use safety data sheets, reports, mass media and other means of communication, and may establish information centres at national and regional levels.

5. Each Party shall give sympathetic consideration to developing mechanisms, such as pollutant release and transfer registers, for the collection and dissemination of information on estimates of the annual quantities of the chemicals listed in Annex A, B or C that are released or disposed of.

Article 11: Research, development and monitoring

1. The Parties shall, within their capabilities, at the national and international levels, encourage and/or undertake appropriate research, development, monitoring and cooperation pertaining to persistent organic pollutants and, where relevant, to their alternatives and to candidate persistent organic pollutants, including on their:
(a) Sources and releases into the environment;
(b) Presence, levels and trends in humans and the environment;
(c) Environmental transport, fate and transformation;
(d) Effects on human health and the environment;
(e) Socio-economic and cultural impacts;
(f) Release reduction and/or elimination; and
(g) Harmonized methodologies for making inventories of generating sources and analytical techniques for the measurement of releases.

2. In undertaking action under paragraph 1, the Parties shall, within their capabilities:
(a) Support and further develop, as appropriate, international programmes, networks and organizations aimed at defining, conducting, assessing and financing research, data collection and monitoring, taking into account the need to minimize duplication of effort;
(b) Support national and international efforts to strengthen national scientific and technical research capabilities, particularly in developing countries and countries with economies in transition, and to promote access to, and the exchange of, data and analyses;
(c) Take into account the concerns and needs, particularly in the field of financial and technical resources, of developing countries and countries with economies

in transition and cooperate in improving their capability to participate in the efforts referred to in subparagraphs (a) and (b);

(d) Undertake research work geared towards alleviating the effects of persistent organic pollutants on reproductive health;

(e) Make the results of their research, development and monitoring activities referred to in this paragraph accessible to the public on a timely and regular basis; and

(f) Encourage and/or undertake cooperation with regard to storage and maintenance of information generated from research, development and monitoring.

Article 12: Technical assistance

1. The Parties recognize that rendering of timely and appropriate technical assistance in response to requests from developing country Parties and Parties with economies in transition is essential to the successful implementation of this Convention.

2. The Parties shall cooperate to provide timely and appropriate technical assistance to developing country Parties and Parties with economies in transition, to assist them, taking into account their particular needs, to develop and strengthen their capacity to implement their obligations under this Convention.

3. In this regard, technical assistance to be provided by developed country Parties, and other Parties in accordance with their capabilities, shall include, as appropriate and as mutually agreed, technical assistance for capacity-building relating to implementation of the obligations under this Convention. Further guidance in this regard shall be provided by the Conference of the Parties.

4. The Parties shall establish, as appropriate, arrangements for the purpose of providing technical assistance and promoting the transfer of technology to developing country Parties and Parties with economies in transition relating to the implementation of this Convention. These arrangements shall include regional and subregional centres for capacity-building and transfer of technology to assist developing country Parties and Parties with economies in transition to fulfil their obligations under this Convention. Further guidance in this regard shall be provided by the Conference of the Parties.

5. The Parties shall, in the context of this Article, take full account of the specific needs and special situation of least developed countries and small island developing states in their actions with regard to technical assistance.

Article 13: Financial resources and mechanisms

1. Each Party undertakes to provide, within its capabilities, financial support and incentives in respect of those national activities that are intended to achieve the objective of this Convention in accordance with its national plans, priorities and programmes.

2. The developed country Parties shall provide new and additional financial resources to enable developing country Parties and Parties with economies in transition to meet the agreed full incremental costs of implementing measures which fulfill their obligations under this Convention as agreed between a recipient Party and an entity participating in the mechanism described in paragraph 6. Other Parties may also on a voluntary basis and in accordance with their capabilities provide such financial resources. Contributions from other sources should also be encouraged. The implementation of these commitments shall take into account the need for adequacy, predictability, the timely flow of funds and the importance of burden sharing among the contributing Parties.

3. Developed country Parties, and other Parties in accordance with their capabilities and in accordance with their national plans, priorities and programmes, may also provide and developing country Parties and Parties with economies in transition avail themselves of financial resources to assist in their implementation of this Convention through other bilateral, regional and multilateral sources or channels.

4. The extent to which the developing country Parties will effectively implement their commitments under this Convention will depend on the effective implementation by developed country Parties of their commitments under this Convention relating to financial resources, technical assistance and technology transfer. The fact that sustainable economic and social development and eradication of poverty are the first and overriding priorities of the developing country Parties will be taken fully into account, giving due consideration to the need for the protection of human health and the environment.

5. The Parties shall take full account of the specific needs and special situation of the least developed countries and the small island developing states in their actions with regard to funding.

6. A mechanism for the provision of adequate and sustainable financial resources to developing country Parties and Parties with economies in transition on a grant or concessional basis to assist in their implementation of the Convention is hereby defined. The mechanism shall function under the authority, as appropriate, and guidance of, and be accountable to the Conference of the Parties for the purposes of this Convention. Its operation shall be entrusted to one or more entities, including existing international entities, as may be decided upon by the Conference of the Parties. The mechanism may also include other entities providing multilateral, regional and bilateral financial and technical assistance. Contributions to the mechanism shall be additional to other financial transfers to developing country Parties and Parties with economies in transition as reflected in, and in accordance with, paragraph 2.

7. Pursuant to the objectives of this Convention and paragraph 6, the Conference of the Parties shall at its first meeting adopt appropriate guidance to be provided to the mechanism and shall agree with the entity or entities participating in the

financial mechanism upon arrangements to give effect thereto. The guidance shall address, *inter alia*:

(a) The determination of the policy, strategy and programme priorities, as well as clear and detailed criteria and guidelines regarding eligibility for access to and utilization of financial resources including monitoring and evaluation on a regular basis of such utilization;
(b) The provision by the entity or entities of regular reports to the Conference of the Parties on adequacy and sustainability of funding for activities relevant to the implementation of this Convention;
(c) The promotion of multiple-source funding approaches, mechanisms and arrangements;
(d) The modalities for the determination in a predictable and identifiable manner of the amount of funding necessary and available for the implementation of this Convention, keeping in mind that the phasing out of persistent organic pollutants might require sustained funding, and the conditions under which that amount shall be periodically reviewed; and
(e) The modalities for the provision to interested Parties of assistance with needs assessment, information on available sources of funds and on funding patterns in order to facilitate coordination among them.

8. The Conference of the Parties shall review, not later than its second meeting and thereafter on a regular basis, the effectiveness of the mechanism established under this Article, its ability to address the changing needs of the developing country Parties and Parties with economies in transition, the criteria and guidance referred to in paragraph 7, the level of funding as well as the effectiveness of the performance of the institutional entities entrusted to operate the financial mechanism. It shall, based on such review, take appropriate action, if necessary, to improve the effectiveness of the mechanism, including by means of recommendations and guidance on measures to ensure adequate and sustainable funding to meet the needs of the Parties.

Article 14: Interim financial arrangements

The institutional structure of the Global Environment Facility, operated in accordance with the Instrument for the Establishment of the Restructured Global Environment Facility, shall, on an interim basis, be the principal entity entrusted with the operations of the financial mechanism referred to in Article 13, for the period between the date of entry into force of this Convention and the first meeting of the Conference of the Parties, or until such time as the Conference of the Parties decides which institutional structure will be designated in accordance with Article 13. The institutional structure of the Global Environment Facility should fulfill this function through operational measures related specifically to persistent organic pollutants taking into account that new arrangements for this area may be needed.

Article 15: Reporting

1. Each Party shall report to the Conference of the Parties on the measures it has taken to implement the provisions of this Convention and on the effectiveness of such measures in meeting the objectives of the Convention.

2. Each Party shall provide to the Secretariat:

(a) Statistical data on its total quantities of production, import and export of each of the chemicals listed in Annex A and Annex B or a reasonable estimate of such data; and

(b) To the extent practicable, a list of the States from which it has imported each such substance and the States to which it has exported each such substance.

3. Such reporting shall be at periodic intervals and in a format to be decided by the Conference of the Parties at its first meeting.

Article 16: Effectiveness evaluation

1. Commencing four years after the date of entry into force of this Convention, and periodically thereafter at intervals to be decided by the Conference of the Parties, the Conference shall evaluate the effectiveness of this Convention.

2. In order to facilitate such evaluation, the Conference of the Parties shall, at its first meeting, initiate the establishment of arrangements to provide itself with comparable monitoring data on the presence of the chemicals listed in Annexes A, B and C as well as their regional and global environmental transport. These arrangements:

(a) Should be implemented by the Parties on a regional basis when appropriate, in accordance with their technical and financial capabilities, using existing monitoring programmes and mechanisms to the extent possible and promoting harmonization of approaches;

(b) May be supplemented where necessary, taking into account the differences between regions ad their capabilities to implement monitoring activities; and

(c) Shall include reports to the Conference of the Parties on the results of the monitoring activities on a regional and global basis at intervals to be specified by the Conference of the Parties.

3. The evaluation described in paragraph 1 shall be conducted on the basis of available scientific, environmental, technical and economic information, including:

(a) Reports and other monitoring information provided pursuant to paragraph 2;

(b) National reports submitted pursuant to Article 15; and

(c) Non-compliance information provided pursuant to the procedures established under Article 17.

Article 17: Non-compliance

The Conference of the Parties shall, as soon as practicable, develop and approve procedures and institutional mechanisms for determining non-compliance with the provisions of this Convention and for the treatment of Parties found to be in non-compliance.

Article 18: Settlement of disputes

1. Parties shall settle any dispute between them concerning the interpretation or application of this Convention through negotiation or other peaceful means of their own choice.

2. When ratifying, accepting, approving or acceding to the Convention, or at any time thereafter, a Party that is not a regional economic integration organization may declare in a written instrument submitted to the depositary that, with respect to any dispute concerning the interpretation or application of the Convention, it recognizes one or both of the following means of dispute settlement as compulsory in relation to any Party accepting the same obligation:

(a) Arbitration in accordance with procedures to be adopted by the Conference of the Parties in an annex as soon as practicable;

(b) Submission of the dispute to the International Court of Justice.

3. A Party that is a regional economic integration organization may make a declaration with like effect in relation to arbitration in accordance with the procedure referred to in paragraph 2 (a).

4. A declaration made pursuant to paragraph 2 or paragraph 3 shall remain in force until it expires in accordance with its terms or until three months after written notice of its revocation has been deposited with the depositary.

5. The expiry of a declaration, a notice of revocation or a new declaration shall not in any way affect proceedings pending before an arbitral tribunal or the International Court of Justice unless the parties to the dispute otherwise agree.

6. If the parties to a dispute have not accepted the same or any procedure pursuant to paragraph 2, and if they have not been able to settle their dispute within twelve months following notification by one party to another that a dispute exists between them, the dispute shall be submitted to a conciliation commission at the request of any party to the dispute. The conciliation commission shall render a report with recommendations. Additional procedures relating to the conciliation commission shall be included in an annex to be adopted by the Conference of the Parties no later than at its second meeting.

Article 19: Conference of the Parties

1. A Conference of the Parties is hereby established.

2. The first meeting of the Conference of the Parties shall be convened by the Executive Director of the United Nations Environment Programme no later than one year after the entry into force of this Convention. Thereafter, ordinary meetings of the Conference of the Parties shall be held at regular intervals to be decided by the Conference.

3. Extraordinary meetings of the Conference of the Parties shall be held at such other times as may be deemed necessary by the Conference, or at the written request of any Party provided that it is supported by at least one third of the Parties.

4. The Conference of the Parties shall by consensus agree upon and adopt at its first meeting rules of procedure and financial rules for itself and any subsidiary bodies, as well as financial provisions governing the functioning of the Secretariat.

5. The Conference of the Parties shall keep under continuous review and evaluation the implementation of this Convention. It shall perform the functions assigned to it by the Convention and, to this end, shall:

(a) Establish, further to the requirements of paragraph 6, such subsidiary bodies as it considers necessary for the implementation of the Convention;
(b) Cooperate, where appropriate, with competent international organizations and intergovernmental and non-governmental bodies; and
(c) Regularly review all information made available to the Parties pursuant to Article 15, including consideration of the effectiveness of paragraph 2 (b) (iii) of Article 3;
(d) Consider and undertake any additional action that may be required for the achievement of the objectives of the Convention.

6. The Conference of the Parties shall, at its first meeting, establish a subsidiary body to be called the Persistent Organic Pollutants Review Committee for the purposes of performing the functions assigned to that Committee by this Convention. In this regard:

(a) The members of the Persistent Organic Pollutants Review Committee shall be appointed by the Conference of the Parties. Membership of the Committee shall consist of government-designated experts in chemical assessment or management. The members of the Committee shall be appointed on the basis of equitable geographical distribution;
(b) The Conference of the Parties shall decide on the terms of reference, organization and operation of the Committee; and
(c) The Committee shall make every effort to adopt its recommendations by consensus. If all efforts at consensus have been exhausted, and no consensus reached, such recommendation shall as a last resort be adopted by a two-thirds majority vote of the members present and voting.

7. The Conference of the Parties shall, at its third meeting, evaluate the continued need for the procedure contained in paragraph 2 (b) of Article 3, including consideration of its effectiveness.

8. The United Nations, its specialized agencies and the International Atomic Energy Agency, as well as any State not Party to this Convention, may be represented at meetings of the Conference of the Parties as observers. Any body or agency, whether national or international, governmental or non-governmental, qualified in matters covered by the Convention, and which has informed the Secretariat of its wish to be represented at a meeting of the Conference of the Parties as an observer may be admitted unless at least one third of the Parties present object. The admission and participation of observers shall be subject to the rules of procedure adopted by the Conference of the Parties.

Article 20: Secretariat

1. A Secretariat is hereby established.

2. The functions of the Secretariat shall be:

(a) To make arrangements for meetings of the Conference of the Parties and its subsidiary bodies and to provide them with services as required;

(b) To facilitate assistance to the Parties, particularly developing country Parties and Parties with economies in transition, on request, in the implementation of this Convention;

(c) To ensure the necessary coordination with the secretariats of other relevant international bodies;

(d) To prepare and make available to the Parties periodic reports based on information received pursuant to Article 15 and other available information;

(e) To enter, under the overall guidance of the Conference of the Parties, into such administrative and contractual arrangements as may be required for the effective discharge of its functions; and

(f) To perform the other secretariat functions specified in this Convention and such other functions as may be determined by the Conference of the Parties.

3. The secretariat functions for this Convention shall be performed by the Executive Director of the United Nations Environment Programme, unless the Conference of the Parties decides, by a three-fourths majority of the Parties present and voting, to entrust the secretariat functions to one or more other international organizations.

Article 21: Amendments to the Convention

1. Amendments to this Convention may be proposed by any Party.

2. Amendments to this Convention shall be adopted at a meeting of the Conference of the Parties. The text of any proposed amendment shall be communicated to the Parties by the Secretariat at least six months before the meeting at which it is proposed for adoption. The Secretariat shall also communicate proposed amendments to the signatories to this Convention and, for information, to the depositary.

3. The Parties shall make every effort to reach agreement on any proposed amendment to this Convention by consensus. If all efforts at consensus have been exhausted, and no agreement reached, the amendment shall as a last resort be adopted by a three-fourths majority vote of the Parties present and voting.

4. The amendment shall be communicated by the depositary to all Parties for ratification, acceptance or approval.

5. Ratification, acceptance or approval of an amendment shall be notified to the depositary in writing. An amendment adopted in accordance with paragraph 3 shall enter into force for the Parties having accepted it on the ninetieth day after the date of deposit of instruments of ratification, acceptance or approval by at least three-fourths of the Parties. Thereafter, the amendment shall enter into force for any other

Party on the ninetieth day after the date on which that Party deposits its instrument of ratification, acceptance or approval of the amendment.

Article 22: Adoption and amendment of annexes

1. Annexes to this Convention shall form an integral part thereof and, unless expressly provided otherwise, a reference to this Convention constitutes at the same time a reference to any annexes thereto.

2. Any additional annexes shall be restricted to procedural, scientific, technical or administrative matters.

3. The following procedure shall apply to the proposal, adoption and entry into force of additional annexes to this Convention:

(a) Additional annexes shall be proposed and adopted according to the procedure laid down in paragraphs 1, 2 and 3 of Article 21;

(b) Any Party that is unable to accept an additional annex shall so notify the depositary, in writing, within one year from the date of communication by the depositary of the adoption of the additional annex. The depositary shall without delay notify all Parties of any such notification received. A Party may at any time withdraw a previous notification of non-acceptance in respect of any additional annex, and the annex shall thereupon enter into force for that Party subject to subparagraph (c); and

(c) On the expiry of one year from the date of the communication by the depositary of the adoption of an additional annex, the annex shall enter into force for all Parties that have not submitted a notification in accordance with the provisions of subparagraph (b).

4. The proposal, adoption and entry into force of amendments to Annex A, B or C shall be subject to the same procedures as for the proposal, adoption and entry into force of additional annexes to this Convention, except that an amendment to Annex A, B or C shall not enter into force with respect to any Party that has made a declaration with respect to amendment to those Annexes in accordance with paragraph 4 of Article 25, in which case any such amendment shall enter into force for such a Party on the ninetieth day after the date of deposit with the depositary of its instrument of ratification, acceptance, approval or accession with respect to such amendment.

5. The following procedure shall apply to the proposal, adoption and entry into force of an amendment to Annex D, E or F:

(a) Amendments shall be proposed according to the procedure in paragraphs 1 and 2 of Article 21;

(b) The Parties shall take decisions on an amendment to Annex D, E or F by consensus; and

(c) A decision to amend Annex D, E or F shall forthwith be communicated to the Parties by the depositary. The amendment shall enter into force for all Parties on a date to be specified in the decision.

6. If an additional annex or an amendment to an annex is related to an amendment to this Convention, the additional annex or amendment shall not enter into force until such time as the amendment to the Convention enters into force.

Article 23: Right to vote

1. Each Party to this Convention shall have one vote, except as provided for in paragraph 2.

2. A regional economic integration organization, on matters within its competence, shall exercise its right to vote with a number of votes equal to the number of its member States that are Parties to this Convention. Such an organization shall not exercise its right to vote if any of its member States exercises its right to vote, and vice versa.

Article 24: Signature

This Convention shall be open for signature at Stockholm by all States and regional economic integration organizations on 23 May 2001, and at the United Nations Headquarters in New York from 24 May 2001 to 22 May 2002.

Article 25: Ratification, acceptance, approval or accession

1. This Convention shall be subject to ratification, acceptance or approval by States and by regional economic integration organizations. It shall be open for accession by States and by regional economic integration organizations from the day after the date on which the Convention is closed for signature. Instruments of ratification, acceptance, approval or accession shall be deposited with the depositary.

2. Any regional economic integration organization that becomes a Party to this Convention without any of its member States being a Party shall be bound by all the obligations under the Convention. In the case of such organizations, one or more of whose member States is a Party to this Convention, the organization and its member States shall decide on their respective responsibilities for the performance of their obligations under the Convention. In such cases, the organization and the member States shall not be entitled to exercise rights under the Convention concurrently.

3. In its instrument of ratification, acceptance, approval or accession, a regional economic integration organization shall declare the extent of its competence in respect of the matters governed by this Convention. Any such organization shall also inform the depositary, who shall in turn inform the Parties, of any relevant modification in the extent of its competence.

4. In its instrument of ratification, acceptance, approval or accession, any Party may declare that, with respect to it, any amendment to Annex A, B or C shall enter into force only upon the deposit of its instrument of ratification, acceptance, approval or accession with respect thereto.

Article 26: Entry into force

1. This Convention shall enter into force on the ninetieth day after the date of deposit of the fiftieth instrument of ratification, acceptance, approval or accession.

2. For each State or regional economic integration organization that ratifies, accepts or approves this Convention or accedes thereto after the deposit of the fiftieth instrument of ratification, acceptance, approval or accession, the Convention shall enter into force on the ninetieth day after the date of deposit by such State or regional economic integration organization of its instrument of ratification, acceptance, approval or accession.

3. For the purpose of paragraphs 1 and 2, any instrument deposited by a regional economic integration organization shall not be counted as additional to those deposited by member States of that organization.

Article 27: Reservations

No reservations may be made to this Convention.

Article 28: Withdrawal

1. At any time after three years from the date on which this Convention has entered into force for a Party, that Party may withdraw from the Convention by giving written notification to the depositary.

2. Any such withdrawal shall take effect upon the expiry of one year from the date of receipt by the depositary of the notification of withdrawal, or on such later date as may be specified in the notification of withdrawal.

Article 29: Depositary

The Secretary-General of the United Nations shall be the depositary of this Convention.

Article 30: Authentic texts

The original of this Convention, of which the Arabic, Chinese, English, French, Russian and Spanish texts are equally authentic, shall be deposited with the Secretary-General of the United Nations.

In witness whereof the undersigned, being duly authorized to that effect, have signed this Convention.

Done at Stockholm on this twenty-second day of May, two thousand and one.

Annex A: Elimination; Annex B: Restriction; Annex C: Unintentional production; Annex D: Information requirements and screening criteria; Annex E: Information requirements for the risk profile; Annex F: Information on socio-economic considerations [not reproduced]

Nuclear energy

Convention on Nuclear Safety

Adopted on 17 June 1994 at Vienna. Entered into force on 24 October 1996. Source: 1963 *UNTS* 317. Number of parties: 55. Further information: IAEA, Vienna, Austria, http://www.iaea.org/

Preamble

The Contracting Parties

i. Aware of the importance to the international community of ensuring that the use of nuclear energy is safe, well regulated and environmentally sound;

ii. Reaffirming the necessity of continuing to promote a high level of nuclear safety worldwide;

iii. Reaffirming that responsibility for nuclear safety rests with the State having jurisdiction over a nuclear installation;

iv. Desiring to promote an effective nuclear safety culture;

v. Aware that accidents at nuclear installations have the potential for transboundary impacts;

vi. Keeping in mind the Convention on the Physical Protection of Nuclear Material (1979), the Convention on Early Notification of a Nuclear Accident (1986), and the Convention on Assistance in the Case of a Nuclear Accident or Radiological Emergency (1986);

vii. Affirming the importance of international co-operation for the enhancement of nuclear safety through existing bilateral and multilateral mechanisms and the establishment of this incentive Convention;

viii. Recognizing that this Convention entails a commitment to the application of fundamental safety principles for nuclear installations rather than of detailed safety standards and that there are internationally formulated safety guidelines which are updated from time to time and so can provide guidance on contemporary means of achieving a high level of safety;

ix. Affirming the need to begin promptly the development of an international convention on the safety of radioactive waste management as soon as the ongoing process to develop waste management safety fundamentals has resulted in broad international agreement;

x. Recognizing the usefulness of further technical work in connection with the safety of other parts of the nuclear fuel cycle, and that this work may, in time, facilitate the development of current or future international instruments;

Have agreed as follows:

Chapter 1: Objectives, definitions and scope of application

Article 1: Objectives

The objectives of this Convention are:

i. to achieve and maintain a high level of nuclear safety worldwide through the enhancement of national measures and international co-operation including, where appropriate, safety-related technical co-operation;

ii. to establish and maintain effective defences in nuclear installations against potential radiological hazards in order to protect individuals, society and the environment from harmful effects of ionizing radiation from such installations;

iii. to prevent accidents with radiological consequences and to mitigate such consequences should they occur.

Article 2: Definitions

For the purpose of this Convention:

i. 'nuclear installation' means for each Contracting Party any land-based civil nuclear power plant under its jurisdiction including such storage, handling and treatment facilities for radioactive materials as are on the same site and are directly related to the operation of the nuclear power plant. Such a plant ceases to be a nuclear installation when all nuclear fuel elements have been removed permanently from the reactor core and have been stored safely in accordance with approved procedures, and a decommissioning programme has been agreed to by the regulatory body.

ii. 'regulatory body' means for each Contracting Party any body or bodies given the legal authority by that Contracting Party to grant licences and to regulate the siting, design, construction, commissioning, operation or decommissioning of nuclear installations.

iii. 'licence' means any authorization granted by the regulatory body to the applicant to have the responsibility for the siting, design, construction, commissioning, operation or decommissioning of a nuclear installation.

Article 3: Scope of application

This Convention shall apply to the safety of nuclear installations.

Chapter 2: Obligations

A. General provisions

Article 4: Implementing measures

Each Contracting Party shall take, within the framework of its national law, the legislative, regulatory and administrative measures and other steps necessary for implementing its obligations under this Convention.

Article 5: Reporting

Each Contracting Party shall submit for review, prior to each meeting referred to in Article 20, a report on the measures it has taken to implement each of the obligations of this Convention.

Article 6: Existing nuclear installations

Each Contracting Party shall take the appropriate steps to ensure that the safety of nuclear installations existing at the time the Convention enters into force for that Contracting Party is reviewed as soon as possible. When necessary in the context of this Convention, the Contracting Party shall ensure that all reasonably practicable improvements are made as a matter of urgency to upgrade the safety of the nuclear installation. If such upgrading cannot be achieved, plans should be implemented to shut down the nuclear installation as soon as practically possible. The timing of the shut-down may take into account the whole energy context and possible alternatives as well as the social, environmental and economic impact.

B. Legislation and regulation

Article 7: Legislative and regulatory framework

1. Each Contracting Party shall establish and maintain a legislative and regulatory framework to govern the safety of nuclear installations.
2. The legislative and regulatory framework shall provide for:

i. the establishment of applicable national safety requirements and regulations;
ii. a system of licensing with regard to nuclear installations and the prohibition of the operation of a nuclear installation without a licence:
iii. a system of regulatory inspection and assessment of nuclear installations to ascertain compliance with applicable regulations and the terms of licences;
iv. the enforcement of applicable regulations and of the terms of licences, including suspension, modification or revocation.

Article 8: Regulatory body

1. Each Contracting Party shall establish or designate a regulatory body entrusted with the implementation of the legislative and regulatory framework referred to in Article 7, and provided with adequate authority, competence and financial and human resources to fulfil its assigned responsibilities.

2. Each Contracting Party shall take the appropriate steps to ensure an effective separation between the functions of the regulatory body and those of any other body or organization concerned with the promotion or utilization of nuclear energy.

Article 9: Responsibility of the licence holder

Each Contracting Party shall ensure that prime responsibility for the safety of a nuclear installation rests with the holder of the relevant licence and shall take the appropriate steps to ensure that each such licence holder meets its responsibility.

C. General safety considerations

Article 10: Priority to safety

Each Contracting Party shall take the appropriate steps to ensure that all organizations engaged in activities directly related to nuclear installations shall establish policies that give due priority to nuclear safety.

Article 11: Financial and human resources

1. Each Contracting Party shall take the appropriate steps to ensure that adequate financial resources are available to support the safety of each nuclear installation throughout its life.
2. Each Contracting Party shall take the appropriate steps to ensure that sufficient numbers of qualified staff with appropriate education, training and retraining are available for all safety-related activities in or for each nuclear installation, throughout its life.

Article 12: Human factors

Each Contracting Party shall take the appropriate steps to ensure that the capabilities and limitations of human performance are taken into account throughout the life of a nuclear installation.

Article 13: Quality assurance

Each Contracting Party shall take the appropriate steps to ensure that quality assurance programmes are established and implemented with a view to providing confidence that specified requirements for all activities important to nuclear safety are satisfied throughout the life of a nuclear installation.

Article 14: Assessment and verification of safety

Each Contracting Party shall take the appropriate steps to ensure that:

i. comprehensive and systematic safety assessments are carried out before the construction and commissioning of a nuclear installation and throughout its life. Such assessments shall be well documented, subsequently updated in the light of operating experience and significant new safety information, and reviewed under the authority of the regulatory body;

ii. verification by analysis, surveillance, testing and inspection is carried out to ensure that the physical state and the operation of a nuclear installation continue to be in accordance with its design, applicable national safety requirements, and operational limits and conditions.

Article 15: Radiation protection

Each Contracting Party shall take the appropriate steps to ensure that in all operational states the radiation exposure to the workers and the public caused by a nuclear installation shall be kept as low as reasonably achievable and that no individual shall be exposed to radiation doses which exceed prescribed national dose limits.

Article 16: Emergency preparedness

1. Each Contracting Party shall take the appropriate steps to ensure that there are on-site and off-site emergency plans that are routinely tested for nuclear installations and cover the activities to be carried out in the event of an emergency.

For any new nuclear installation, such plans shall be prepared and tested before it commences operation above a low power level agreed by the regulatory body.

2. Each Contracting Party shall take the appropriate steps to ensure that, insofar as they are likely to be affected by a radiological emergency, its own population and the competent authorities of the States in the vicinity of the nuclear installation are provided with appropriate information for emergency planning and response.

3. Contracting Parties which do not have a nuclear installation on their territory, insofar as they are likely to be affected in the event of a radiological emergency at a nuclear installation in the vicinity, shall take the appropriate steps for the preparation and testing of emergency plans for their territory that cover the activities to be carried out in the event of such an emergency.

D. Safety of installations

Article 17: Siting

Each Contracting Party shall take the appropriate steps to ensure that appropriate procedures are established and implemented:

i. for evaluating all relevant site-related factors likely to affect the safety of a nuclear installation for its projected lifetime;

ii. for evaluating the likely safety impact of a proposed nuclear installation on individuals, society and the environment;

iii. for re-evaluating as necessary all relevant factors referred to in sub-paragraphs (i) and (ii) so as to ensure the continued safety acceptability of the nuclear installation;

iv. for consulting Contracting Parties in the vicinity of a proposed nuclear installation, insofar as they are likely to be affected by that installation and, upon request providing the necessary information to such Contracting Parties, in order to enable them to evaluate and make their own assessment of the likely safety impact on their own territory of the nuclear installation.

Article 18: Design and construction

Each Contracting Party shall take the appropriate steps to ensure that:

i. the design and construction of a nuclear installation provides for several reliable levels and methods of protection (defense in depth) against the release of radioactive materials, with a view to preventing the occurrence of accidents and to mitigating their radiological consequences should they occur;

ii. the technologies incorporated in the design and construction of a nuclear installation are proven by experience or qualified by testing or analysis;

iii. the design of a nuclear installation allows for reliable, stable and easily manageable operation, with specific consideration of human factors and the man-machine interface.

Article 19: Operation

Each Contracting Party shall take the appropriate steps to ensure that:

i. the initial authorization to operate a nuclear installation is based upon an appropriate safety analysis and a commissioning programme demonstrating that the installation, as constructed, is consistent with design and safety requirements;

ii. operational limits and conditions derived from the safety analysis, tests and operational experience are defined and revised as necessary for identifying safe boundaries for operation;

iii. operation, maintenance, inspection and testing of a nuclear installation are conducted in accordance with approved procedures;

iv. procedures are established for responding to anticipated operational occurrences and to accidents;

v. necessary engineering and technical support in all safety-related fields is available throughout the lifetime of a nuclear installation;

vi. incidents significant to safety are reported in a timely manner by the holder of the relevant licence to the regulatory body;

vii. programmes to collect and analyse operating experience are established, the results obtained and the conclusions drawn are acted upon and that existing mechanisms are used to share important experience with international bodies and with other operating organizations and regulatory bodies;

viii. the generation of radioactive waste resulting from the operation of a nuclear installation is kept to the minimum practicable for the process concerned, both in activity and in volume, and any necessary treatment and storage of spent fuel and waste directly related to the operation and on the same site as that of the nuclear installation take into consideration conditioning and disposal.

Chapter 3: Meetings of the Contracting Parties

Article 20: Review meetings

1. The Contracting Parties shall hold meetings (hereinafter referred to as 'review meetings') for the purpose of reviewing the reports submitted pursuant to Article 5 in accordance with the procedures adopted under Article 22.

2. Subject to the provisions of Article 24 sub-groups comprised of representatives of Contracting Parties may be established and may function during the review meetings as deemed necessary for the purpose of reviewing specific subjects contained in the reports.

3. Each Contracting Party shall have a reasonable opportunity to discuss the reports submitted by other Contracting Parties and to seek clarification of such reports.

Article 21: Timetable

1. A preparatory meeting of the Contracting Parties shall be held not later than six months after the date of entry into force of this Convention.

2. At this preparatory meeting, the Contracting Parties shall determine the date for the first review meeting. This review meeting shall be held as soon as possible, but not later than thirty months after the date of entry into force of this Convention.

3. At each review meeting, the Contracting Parties shall determine the date for the next such meeting. The interval between review meetings shall not exceed three years.

Article 22: Procedural arrangements

1. At the preparatory meeting held pursuant to Article 21 the Contracting Parties shall prepare and adopt by consensus Rules of Procedure and Financial Rules. The Contracting Parties shall establish in particular and in accordance with the Rules of Procedure:

i. guidelines regarding the form and structure of the reports to be submitted pursuant to Article 5;
ii. a date for the submission of such reports;
iii. the process for reviewing such reports.

2. At review meetings the Contracting Parties may, if necessary, review the arrangements established pursuant to sub-paragraphs (i)-(iii) above, and adopt revisions by consensus unless otherwise provided for in the Rules of Procedure. They may also amend the Rules of Procedure and the Financial Rules, by consensus.

Article 23: Extraordinary meetings

An extraordinary meeting of the Contracting Parties shall be held:

i. if so agreed by a majority of the Contracting Parties present and voting at a meeting, abstentions being considered as voting; or

ii. at the written request of a Contracting Party, within six months of this request having been communicated to the Contracting Parties and notification having been received by the secretariat referred to in Article 28, that the request has been supported by a majority of the Contracting Parties.

Article 24: Attendance

1. Each Contracting Party shall attend meetings of the Contracting Parties and be represented at such meetings by one delegate, and by such alternates, experts and advisers as it deems necessary.

2. The Contracting Parties may invite, by consensus, any intergovernmental organization which is competent in respect of matters governed by this Convention

to attend, as an observer, any meeting, or specific sessions thereof. Observers shall be required to accept in writing, and in advance, the provisions of Article 27.

Article 25: Summary reports

The Contracting Parties shall adopt, by consensus, and make available to the public a document addressing issues discussed and conclusions reached during a meeting.

Article 26: Languages

1. The languages of meetings of the Contracting Parties shall be Arabic, Chinese, English, French, Russian and Spanish unless otherwise provided in the Rules of Procedure.

2. Reports submitted pursuant to Article 5 shall be prepared in the national language of the submitting Contracting Party or in a single designated language to be agreed in the Rules of Procedure. Should the report be submitted in a national language other than the designated language, a translation of the report into the designated language shall be provided by the Contracting Party.

3. Notwithstanding the provisions of paragraph 2, if compensated, the secretariat will assume the translation into the designated language of reports submitted in any other language of the meeting.

Article 27: Confidentiality

1. The provisions of this Convention shall not affect the rights and obligations of the Contracting Parties under their law to protect information from disclosure. For the purposes of this Article, 'information' includes, inter alia, (i) personal data; (ii) information protected by intellectual property rights or by industrial or commercial confidentiality; and (iii) information relating to national security or to the physical protection of nuclear materials or nuclear installations.

2. When, in the context of this Convention, a Contracting Party provides information identified by it as protected as described in paragraph 1, such information shall be used only for the purposes for which it has been provided and its confidentiality shall be respected.

3. The content of the debates during the reviewing of the reports by the Contracting Parties at each meeting shall be confidential.

Article 28: Secretariat

1. The International Atomic Energy Agency, (hereinafter referred to as the 'Agency') shall provide the secretariat for the meetings of the Contracting Parties.

2. The secretariat shall:

i. convene, prepare and service the meetings of the Contracting Parties;

ii. transmit to the Contracting Parties information received or prepared in accordance with the provisions of this Convention.

The costs incurred by the Agency in carrying out the functions referred to in sub-paragraphs (i) and (ii) above shall be borne by the Agency as part of its regular budget.

3. The Contracting Parties may, by consensus, request the Agency to provide other services in support of meetings of the Contracting Parties. The Agency may provide such services if they can be undertaken within its programme and regular budget. Should this not be possible, the Agency may provide such services if voluntary funding is provided from another source.

[Chapter 4: Final clauses and other provisions, not reproduced]

Joint Convention on the Safety of Spent Fuel Management and on the Safety of Radioactive Waste Management

Adopted on 5 September 1997 at Vienna. Entered into force on 18 June 2001. Source: 2153 *UNTS* 357. Number of parties: 34. Further information: IAEA, Vienna, Austria, http://www.iaea.org

Preamble

The Contracting Parties

i. Recognizing that the operation of nuclear reactors generates spent fuel and radioactive waste and that other applications of nuclear technologies also generate radioactive waste;

ii. Recognizing that the same safety objectives apply both to spent fuel and radioactive waste management;

iii. Reaffirming the importance to the international community of ensuring that sound practices are planned and implemented for the safety of spent fuel and radioactive waste management;

iv. Recognizing the importance of informing the public on issues regarding the safety of spent fuel and radioactive waste management;

v. Desiring to promote an effective nuclear safety culture worldwide;

vi. Reaffirming that the ultimate responsibility for ensuring the safety of spent fuel and radioactive waste management rests with the State;

vii. Recognizing that the definition of a fuel cycle policy rests with the State, some States considering spent fuel as a valuable resource that may be reprocessed, others electing to dispose of it;

viii. Recognizing that spent fuel and radioactive waste excluded from the present Convention because they are within military or defence programmes should be managed in accordance with the objectives stated in this Convention;

ix. Affirming the importance of international co-operation in enhancing the safety of spent fuel and radioactive waste management through bilateral and multilateral mechanisms, and through this incentive Convention;

x. Mindful of the needs of developing countries, and in particular the least developed countries, and of States with economies in transition and of the need to facilitate existing mechanisms to assist in the fulfillment of their rights and obligations set out in this incentive Convention;

xi. Convinced that radioactive waste should, as far as is compatible with the safety of the management of such material, be disposed of in the State in which it was generated, whilst recognizing that, in certain circumstances, safe and efficient management of spent fuel and radioactive waste might be fostered through agreements among Contracting Parties to use facilities in one of them for the benefit of the other Parties, particularly where waste originates from joint projects;

xii. Recognizing that any State has the right to ban import into its territory of foreign spent fuel and radioactive waste;

xiii. Keeping in mind the Convention on Nuclear Safety (1994), the Convention on Early Notification of a Nuclear Accident (1986), the Convention on Assistance in the Case of a Nuclear Accident or Radiological Emergency (1986), the Convention on the Physical Protection of Nuclear Material (1980), the Convention on the Prevention of Marine Pollution by Dumping of Wastes and Other Matter as amended (1994) and other relevant international instruments;

xiv. Keeping in mind the principles contained in the interagency 'International Basic Safety Standards for Protection against Ionizing Radiation and for the Safety of Radiation Sources' (1996), in the IAEA Safety Fundamentals entitled 'The Principles of Radioactive Waste Management' (1995), and in the existing international standards relating to the safety of the transport of radioactive materials;

xv. Recalling Chapter 22 of Agenda 21 by the United Nations Conference on Environment and Development in Rio de Janeiro adopted in 1992, which reaffirms the paramount importance of the safe and environmentally sound management of radioactive waste;

xvi. Recognizing the desirability of strengthening the international control system applying specifically to radioactive materials as referred to in Article 1(3) of the Basel Convention on the Control of Transboundary Movements of Hazardous Wastes and Their Disposal (1989);

Have agreed as follows:

Chapter 1: Objectives, definitions and scope of application

Article 1: Objectives

The objectives of this Convention are:

i. to achieve and maintain a high level of safety worldwide in spent fuel and radioactive waste management, through the enhancement of national measures and international co-operation, including where appropriate, safety-related technical co-operation;

ii. to ensure that during all stages of spent fuel and radioactive waste management there are effective defenses against potential hazards so that individuals, society and the environment are protected from harmful effects of ionizing radiation, now and in the future, in such a way that the needs and aspirations of the present generation are met without compromising the ability of future generations to meet their needs and aspirations;

iii. to prevent accidents with radiological consequences and to mitigate their consequences should they occur during any stage of spent fuel or radioactive waste management.

Article 2: Definitions

For the purposes of this Convention:

a. '*closure*' means the completion of all operations at some time after the emplacement of spent fuel or radioactive waste in a disposal facility. This includes the final engineering or other work required to bring the facility to a condition that will be safe in the long term;

b. '*decommissioning*' means all steps leading to the release of a nuclear facility, other than a disposal facility, from regulatory control. These steps include the processes of decontamination and dismantling;

c. '*discharges*' means planned and controlled releases into the environment, as a legitimate practice, within limits authorized by the regulatory body, of liquid or gaseous radioactive materials that originate from regulated nuclear facilities during normal operation;

d. '*disposal*' means the emplacement of spent fuel or radioactive waste in an appropriate facility without the intention of retrieval;

e. '*licence*' means any authorization, permission or certification granted by a regulatory body to carry out any activity related to management of spent fuel or of radioactive waste;

f. '*nuclear facility*' means a civilian facility and its associated land, buildings and equipment in which radioactive materials are produced, processed, used, handled, stored or disposed of on such a scale that consideration of safety is required;

g. '*operating lifetime*' means the period during which a spent fuel or a radioactive waste management facility is used for its intended purpose. In the case of a disposal facility, the period begins when spent fuel or radioactive waste is first emplaced in the facility and ends upon closure of the facility;

h. '*radioactive waste*' means radioactive material in gaseous, liquid or solid form for which no further use is foreseen by the Contracting Party or by a natural or legal person whose decision is accepted by the Contracting Party, and which is controlled as radioactive waste by a regulatory body under the legislative and regulatory framework of the Contracting Party;

i. '*radioactive waste management*' means all activities, including decommissioning activities, that relate to the handling, pretreatment, treatment, conditioning, storage, or disposal of radioactive waste, excluding off-site transportation. It may also involve discharges;

j. '*radioactive waste management facility*' means any facility or installation the primary purpose of which is radioactive waste management, including a nuclear facility in the process of being decommissioned only if it is designated by the Contracting Party as a radioactive waste management facility;

k. '*regulatory body*' means any body or bodies given the legal authority by the Contracting Party to regulate any aspect of the safety of spent fuel or radioactive waste management including the granting of licences;

l. '*reprocessing*' means a process or operation, the purpose of which is to extract radioactive isotopes from spent fuel for further use;

m. '*sealed source*' means radioactive material that is permanently sealed in a capsule or closely bonded and in a solid form, excluding reactor fuel elements;

n. '*spent fuel*' means nuclear fuel that has been irradiated in and permanently removed from a reactor core;

o. '*spent fuel management*' means all activities that relate to the handling or storage of spent fuel, excluding off-site transportation. It may also involve discharges;

p. '*spent fuel management facility*' means any facility or installation the primary purpose of which is spent fuel management;

q. '*State of destination*' means a State to which a transboundary movement is planned or takes place;

r. '*State of origin*' means a State from which a transboundary movement is planned to be initiated or is initiated;

s. '*State of transit*' means any State, other than a State of origin or a State of destination, through whose territory a transboundary movement is planned or takes place;

t. '*storage*' means the holding of spent fuel or of radioactive waste in a facility that provides for its containment, with the intention of retrieval;

u. '*transboundary movement*' means any shipment of spent fuel or of radioactive waste from a State of origin to a State of destination.

Article 3: Scope of application

1. This Convention shall apply to the safety of spent fuel management when the spent fuel results from the operation of civilian nuclear reactors. Spent fuel held at reprocessing facilities as part of a reprocessing activity is not covered in the scope of this Convention unless the Contracting Party declares reprocessing to be part of spent fuel management.

2. This Convention shall also apply to the safety of radioactive waste management when the radioactive waste results from civilian applications. However, this Convention shall not apply to waste that contains only naturally occurring

radioactive materials and that does not originate from the nuclear fuel cycle, unless it constitutes a disused sealed source or it is declared as radioactive waste for the purposes of this Convention by the Contracting Party.

3. This Convention shall not apply to the safety of management of spent fuel or radioactive waste within military or defence programmes, unless declared as spent fuel or radioactive waste for the purposes of this Convention by the Contracting Party. However, this Convention shall apply to the safety of management of spent fuel and radioactive waste from military or defence programmes if and when such materials are transferred permanently to and managed within exclusively civilian programmes.

4. This Convention shall also apply to discharges as provided for in Articles 4, 7, 11, 14, 24 and 26.

Chapter 2: Safety of spent fuel management

Article 4: General safety requirements

Each Contracting Party shall take the appropriate steps to ensure that at all stages of spent fuel management, individuals, society and the environment are adequately protected against radiological hazards.

In so doing, each Contracting Party shall take the appropriate steps to:

i. ensure that criticality and removal of residual heat generated during spent fuel management are adequately addressed;

ii. ensure that the generation of radioactive waste associated with spent fuel management is kept to the minimum practicable, consistent with the type of fuel cycle policy adopted;

iii. take into account interdependencies among the different steps in spent fuel management;

iv. provide for effective protection of individuals, society and the environment, by applying at the national level suitable protective methods as approved by the regulatory body, in the framework of its national legislation which has due regard to internationally endorsed criteria and standards;

v. take into account the biological, chemical and other hazards that may be associated with spent fuel management;

vi. strive to avoid actions that impose reasonably predictable impacts on future generations greater than those permitted for the current generation;

vii. aim to avoid imposing undue burdens on future generations.

Article 5: Existing facilities

Each Contracting Party shall take the appropriate steps to review the safety of any spent fuel management facility existing at the time the Convention enters into force for that Contracting Party and to ensure that, if necessary, all reasonably practicable improvements are made to upgrade the safety of such a facility.

Article 6: Siting of proposed facilities

1. Each Contracting Party shall take the appropriate steps to ensure that procedures are established and implemented for a proposed spent fuel management facility:

i. to evaluate all relevant site-related factors likely to affect the safety of such a facility during its operating lifetime;

ii. to evaluate the likely safety impact of such a facility on individuals, society and the environment;

iii. to make information on the safety of such a facility available to members of the public;

iv. to consult Contracting Parties in the vicinity of such a facility, insofar as they are likely to be affected by that facility, and provide them, upon their request, with general data relating to the facility to enable them to evaluate the likely safety impact of the facility upon their territory.

2. In so doing, each Contracting Party shall take the appropriate steps to ensure that such facilities shall not have unacceptable effects on other Contracting Parties by being sited in accordance with the general safety requirements of Article 4.

Article 7: Design and construction of facilities

Each Contracting Party shall take the appropriate steps to ensure that:

i. the design and construction of a spent fuel management facility provide for suitable measures to limit possible radiological impacts on individuals, society and the environment, including those from discharges or uncontrolled releases;

ii. at the design stage, conceptual plans and, as necessary, technical provisions for the decommissioning of a spent fuel management facility are taken into account;

iii. the technologies incorporated in the design and construction of a spent fuel management facility are supported by experience, testing or analysis.

Article 8: Assessment of safety of facilities

Each Contracting Party shall take the appropriate steps to ensure that:

i. before construction of a spent fuel management facility, a systematic safety assessment and an environmental assessment appropriate to the hazard presented by the facility and covering its operating lifetime shall be carried out;

ii. before the operation of a spent fuel management facility, updated and detailed versions of the safety assessment and of the environmental assessment shall be prepared when deemed necessary to complement the assessments referred to in paragraph (i).

Article 9: Operation of facilities

Each Contracting Party shall take the appropriate steps to ensure that:

i. the licence to operate a spent fuel management facility is based upon appropriate assessments as specified in Article 8 and is conditional on the completion of a commissioning programme demonstrating that the facility, as constructed, is consistent with design and safety requirements;

ii. operational limits and conditions derived from tests, operational experience and the assessments, as specified in Article 8, are defined and revised as necessary;

iii. operation, maintenance, monitoring, inspection and testing of a spent fuel management facility are conducted in accordance with established procedures;

iv. engineering and technical support in all safety-related fields are available throughout the operating lifetime of a spent fuel management facility;

v. incidents significant to safety are reported in a timely manner by the holder of the licence to the regulatory body;

vi. programmes to collect and analyse relevant operating experience are established and that the results are acted upon, where appropriate;

vii. decommissioning plans for a spent fuel management facility are prepared and updated, as necessary, using information obtained during the operating lifetime of that facility, and are reviewed by the regulatory body.

Article 10: Disposal of spent fuel

If, pursuant to its own legislative and regulatory framework, a Contracting Party has designated spent fuel for disposal, the disposal of such spent fuel shall be in accordance with the obligations of Chapter 3 relating to the disposal of radioactive waste.

Chapter 3: Safety of radioactive waste management

Article 11: General safety requirements

Each Contracting Party shall take the appropriate steps to ensure that at all stages of radioactive waste management individuals, society and the environment are adequately protected against radiological and other hazards.

In so doing, each Contracting Party shall take the appropriate steps to:

i. ensure that criticality and removal of residual heat generated during radioactive waste management are adequately addressed;

ii. ensure that the generation of radioactive waste is kept to the minimum practicable;

iii. take into account interdependencies among the different steps in radioactive waste management;

iv. provide for effective protection of individuals, society and the environment, by applying at the national level suitable protective methods as approved by the regulatory body, in the framework of its national legislation which has due regard to internationally endorsed criteria and standards;

v. take into account the biological, chemical and other hazards that may be associated with radioactive waste management;

vi. strive to avoid actions that impose reasonably predictable impacts on future generations greater than those permitted for the current generation;

vii. aim to avoid imposing undue burdens on future generations.

Article 12: Existing facilities and past practices

Each Contracting Party shall in due course take the appropriate steps to review:

i. the safety of any radioactive waste management facility existing at the time the Convention enters into force for that Contracting Party and to ensure that, if necessary, all reasonably practicable improvements are made to upgrade the safety of such a facility;

ii. the results of past practices in order to determine whether any intervention is needed for reasons of radiation protection bearing in mind that the reduction in detriment resulting from the reduction in dose should be sufficient to justify the harm and the costs, including the social costs, of the intervention.

Article 13: Siting of proposed facilities

1. Each Contracting Party shall take the appropriate steps to ensure that procedures are established and implemented for a proposed radioactive waste management facility:

i. to evaluate all relevant site-related factors likely to affect the safety of such a facility during its operating lifetime as well as that of a disposal facility after closure;

ii. to evaluate the likely safety impact of such a facility on individuals, society and the environment, taking into account possible evolution of the site conditions of disposal facilities after closure;

iii. to make information on the safety of such a facility available to members of the public;

iv. to consult Contracting Parties in the vicinity of such a facility, insofar as they are likely to be affected by that facility, and provide them, upon their request, with general data relating to the facility to enable them to evaluate the likely safety impact of the facility upon their territory.

2. In so doing, each Contracting Party shall take the appropriate steps to ensure that such facilities shall not have unacceptable effects on other Contracting Parties by being sited in accordance with the general safety requirements of Article 11.

Article 14: Design and construction of facilities

Each Contracting Party shall take the appropriate steps to ensure that:

i. the design and construction of a radioactive waste management facility provide for suitable measures to limit possible radiological impacts on individuals, society and the environment, including those from discharges or uncontrolled releases;

ii. at the design stage, conceptual plans and, as necessary, technical provisions for the decommissioning of a radioactive waste management facility other than a disposal facility are taken into account;

iii. at the design stage, technical provisions for the closure of a disposal facility are prepared;

iv. the technologies incorporated in the design and construction of a radioactive waste management facility are supported by experience, testing or analysis.

Article 15: Assessment of safety of facilities

Each Contracting Party shall take the appropriate steps to ensure that:

i. before construction of a radioactive waste management facility, a systematic safety assessment and an environmental assessment appropriate to the hazard presented by the facility and covering its operating lifetime shall be carried out;

ii. in addition, before construction of a disposal facility, a systematic safety assessment and an environmental assessment for the period following closure shall be carried out and the results evaluated against the criteria established by the regulatory body;

iii. before the operation of a radioactive waste management facility, updated and detailed versions of the safety assessment and of the environmental assessment shall be prepared when deemed necessary to complement the assessments referred to in paragraph (i).

Article 16: Operation of facilities

Each Contracting Party shall take the appropriate steps to ensure that:

i. the licence to operate a radioactive waste management facility is based upon appropriate assessments as specified in Article 15 and is conditional on the completion of a commissioning programme demonstrating that the facility, as constructed, is consistent with design and safety requirements;

ii. operational limits and conditions, derived from tests, operational experience and the assessments as specified in Article 15 are defined and revised as necessary;

iii. operation, maintenance, monitoring, inspection and testing of a radioactive waste management facility are conducted in accordance with established procedures. For a disposal facility the results thus obtained shall be used to verify and to review the validity of assumptions made and to update the assessments as specified in Article 15 for the period after closure;

iv. engineering and technical support in all safety-related fields are available throughout the operating lifetime of a radioactive waste management facility;

v. procedures for characterization and segregation of radioactive waste are applied;

vi. incidents significant to safety are reported in a timely manner by the holder of the licence to the regulatory body;

vii. programmes to collect and analyse relevant operating experience are established and that the results are acted upon, where appropriate;

viii. decommissioning plans for a radioactive waste management facility other than a disposal facility are prepared and updated, as necessary, using information obtained during the operating lifetime of that facility, and are reviewed by the regulatory body;

ix. plans for the closure of a disposal facility are prepared and updated, as necessary, using information obtained during the operating lifetime of that facility and are reviewed by the regulatory body.

Article 17: Institutional measures after closure

Each Contracting Party shall take the appropriate steps to ensure that after closure of a disposal facility:

i. records of the location, design and inventory of that facility required by the regulatory body are preserved;

ii. active or passive institutional controls such as monitoring or access restrictions are carried out, if required; and

iii. if, during any period of active institutional control, an unplanned release of radioactive materials into the environment is detected, intervention measures are implemented, if necessary.

Chapter 4: General safety provisions

Article 18: Implementing measures

Each Contracting Party shall take, within the framework of its national law, the legislative, regulatory and administrative measures and other steps necessary for implementing its obligations under this Convention.

Article 19: Legislative and regulatory framework

1. Each Contracting Party shall establish and maintain a legislative and regulatory framework to govern the safety of spent fuel and radioactive waste management.

2. This legislative and regulatory framework shall provide for:

i. the establishment of applicable national safety requirements and regulations for radiation safety;

ii. a system of licensing of spent fuel and radioactive waste management activities;

iii. a system of prohibition of the operation of a spent fuel or radioactive waste management facility without a licence;

iv. a system of appropriate institutional control, regulatory inspection and documentation and reporting;

v. the enforcement of applicable regulations and of the terms of the licences;

vi. a clear allocation of responsibilities of the bodies involved in the different steps of spent fuel and of radioactive waste management.

3. When considering whether to regulate radioactive materials as radioactive waste, Contracting Parties shall take due account of the objectives of this Convention.

Article 20: Regulatory body

1. Each Contracting Party shall establish or designate a regulatory body entrusted with the implementation of the legislative and regulatory framework referred to in Article 19, and provided with adequate authority, competence and financial and human resources to fulfill its assigned responsibilities.

2. Each Contracting Party, in accordance with its legislative and regulatory framework, shall take the appropriate steps to ensure the effective independence of the regulatory functions from other functions where organizations are involved in both spent fuel or radioactive waste management and in their regulation.

Article 21: Responsibility of the licence holder

1. Each Contracting Party shall ensure that prime responsibility for the safety of spent fuel or radioactive waste management rests with the holder of the relevant licence and shall take the appropriate steps to ensure that each such licence holder meets its responsibility.

2. If there is no such licence holder or other responsible party, the responsibility rests with the Contracting Party which has jurisdiction over the spent fuel or over the radioactive waste.

Article 22: Human and financial resources

Each Contracting Party shall take the appropriate steps to ensure that:

i. qualified staff are available as needed for safety-related activities during the operating lifetime of a spent fuel and a radioactive waste management facility;

ii. adequate financial resources are available to support the safety of facilities for spent fuel and radioactive waste management during their operating lifetime and for decommissioning;

iii. financial provision is made which will enable the appropriate institutional controls and monitoring arrangements to be continued for the period deemed necessary following the closure of a disposal facility.

Article 23: Quality assurance

Each Contracting Party shall take the necessary steps to ensure that appropriate quality assurance programmes concerning the safety of spent fuel and radioactive waste management are established and implemented.

Article 24: Operational radiation protection

1. Each Contracting Party shall take the appropriate steps to ensure that during the operating lifetime of a spent fuel or radioactive waste management facility:

i. the radiation exposure of the workers and the public caused by the facility shall be kept as low as reasonably achievable, economic and social factors being taken into account;

ii. no individual shall be exposed, in normal situations, to radiation doses which exceed national prescriptions for dose limitation which have due regard to internationally endorsed standards on radiation protection; and

iii. measures are taken to prevent unplanned and uncontrolled releases of radioactive materials into the environment.

2. Each Contracting Party shall take appropriate steps to ensure that discharges shall be limited:

i. to keep exposure to radiation as low as reasonably achievable, economic and social factors being taken into account; and

ii. so that no individual shall be exposed, in normal situations, to radiation doses which exceed national prescriptions for dose limitation which have due regard to internationally endorsed standards on radiation protection.

3. Each Contracting Party shall take appropriate steps to ensure that during the operating lifetime of a regulated nuclear facility, in the event that an unplanned or uncontrolled release of radioactive materials into the environment occurs, appropriate corrective measures are implemented to control the release and mitigate its effects.

Article 25: Emergency preparedness

1. Each Contracting Party shall ensure that before and during operation of a spent fuel or radioactive waste management facility there are appropriate on-site and, if necessary, off-site emergency plans. Such emergency plans should be tested at an appropriate frequency.

2. Each Contracting Party shall take the appropriate steps for the preparation and testing of emergency plans for its territory insofar as it is likely to be affected in the event of a radiological emergency at a spent fuel or radioactive waste management facility in the vicinity of its territory.

Article 26: Decommissioning

Each Contracting Party shall take the appropriate steps to ensure the safety of decommissioning of a nuclear facility. Such steps shall ensure that:

i. qualified staff and adequate financial resources are available;

ii. the provisions of Article 24 with respect to operational radiation protection, discharges and unplanned and uncontrolled releases are applied;

iii. the provisions of Article 25 with respect to emergency preparedness are applied; and

iv. records of information important to decommissioning are kept.

Chapter 5: Miscellaneous provisions

Article 27: Transboundary movement

1. Each Contracting Party involved in transboundary movement shall take the appropriate steps to ensure that such movement is undertaken in a manner consistent with the provisions of this Convention and relevant binding international instruments.

In so doing:

i. a Contracting Party which is a State of origin shall take the appropriate steps to ensure that transboundary movement is authorized and takes place only with the prior notification and consent of the State of destination;
ii. transboundary movement through States of transit shall be subject to those international obligations which are relevant to the particular modes of transport utilized;
iii. a Contracting Party which is a State of destination shall consent to a transboundary movement only if it has the administrative and technical capacity, as well as the regulatory structure, needed to manage the spent fuel or the radioactive waste in a manner consistent with this Convention;
iv. a Contracting Party which is a State of origin shall authorize a transboundary movement only if it can satisfy itself in accordance with the consent of the State of destination that the requirements of subparagraph (iii) are met prior to transboundary movement;
v. a Contracting Party which is a State of origin shall take the appropriate steps to permit re-entry into its territory, if a transboundary movement is not or cannot be completed in conformity with this Article, unless an alternative safe arrangement can be made.

2. A Contracting Party shall not licence the shipment of its spent fuel or radioactive waste to a destination south of latitude 60 degrees South for storage or disposal.

3. Nothing in this Convention prejudices or affects:
i. the exercise, by ships and aircraft of all States, of maritime, river and air navigation rights and freedoms, as provided for in international law;
ii. rights of a Contracting Party to which radioactive waste is exported for processing to return, or provide for the return of, the radioactive waste and other products after treatment to the State of origin;
iii. the right of a Contracting Party to export its spent fuel for reprocessing;
iv. rights of a Contracting Party to which spent fuel is exported for reprocessing to return, or provide for the return of, radioactive waste and other products resulting from reprocessing operations to the State of origin.

Article 28: Disused sealed sources

1. Each Contracting Party shall, in the framework of its national law, take the appropriate steps to ensure that the possession, remanufacturing or disposal of disused sealed sources takes place in a safe manner.

2. A Contracting Party shall allow for reentry into its territory of disused sealed sources if, in the framework of its national law, it has accepted that they be returned to a manufacturer qualified to receive and possess the disused sealed sources.

Chapter 6: Meetings of the Contracting Parties

Article 29: Preparatory meeting

1. A preparatory meeting of the Contracting Parties shall be held not later than six months after the date of entry into force of this Convention.

2. At this meeting, the Contracting Parties shall:

i. determine the date for the first review meeting as referred to in Article 30. This review meeting shall be held as soon as possible, but not later than thirty months after the date of entry into force of this Convention;

ii. prepare and adopt by consensus Rules of Procedure and Financial Rules;

iii. establish in particular and in accordance with the Rules of Procedure:

a. guidelines regarding the form and structure of the national reports to be submitted pursuant to Article 32;

b. a date for the submission of such reports;

c. the process for reviewing such reports.

3. Any State or regional organization of an integration or other nature which ratifies, accepts, approves, accedes to or confirms this Convention and for which the Convention is not yet in force, may attend the preparatory meeting as if it were a Party to this Convention.

Article 30: Review meetings

1. The Contracting Parties shall hold meetings for the purpose of reviewing the reports submitted pursuant to Article 32.

2. At each review meeting the Contracting Parties:

i. shall determine the date for the next such meeting, the interval between review meetings not exceeding three years;

ii. may review the arrangements established pursuant to paragraph 2 of Article 29, and adopt revisions by consensus unless otherwise provided for in the Rules of Procedure. They may also amend the Rules of Procedure and Financial Rules by consensus.

3. At each review meeting each Contracting Party shall have a reasonable opportunity to discuss the reports submitted by other Contracting Parties and to seek clarification of such reports.

Article 31: Extraordinary meetings

An extraordinary meeting of the Contracting Parties shall be held:

i. if so agreed by a majority of the Contracting Parties present and voting at a meeting; or

ii. at the written request of a Contracting Party, within six months of this request having been communicated to the Contracting Parties and notification having been received by the secretariat referred to in Article 37 that the request has been supported by a majority of the Contracting Parties.

Article 32: Reporting

1. In accordance with the provisions of Article 30, each Contracting Party shall submit a national report to each review meeting of Contracting Parties. This report shall address the measures taken to implement each of the obligations of the Convention. For each Contracting Party the report shall also address its:

i. spent fuel management policy;
ii. spent fuel management practices;
iii. radioactive waste management policy;
iv. radioactive waste management practices;
v. criteria used to define and categorize radioactive waste.

2. This report shall also include:

i. a list of the spent fuel management facilities subject to this Convention, their location, main purpose and essential features;
ii. an inventory of spent fuel that is subject to this Convention and that is being held in storage and of that which has been disposed of. This inventory shall contain a description of the material and, if available, give information on its mass and its total activity;
iii. a list of the radioactive waste management facilities subject to this Convention, their location, main purpose and essential features;
iv. an inventory of radioactive waste that is subject to this Convention that:
    a. is being held in storage at radioactive waste management and nuclear fuel cycle facilities;
    b. has been disposed of; or
    c. has resulted from past practices.

    This inventory shall contain a description of the material and other appropriate information available, such as volume or mass, activity and specific radionuclides;
v. a list of nuclear facilities in the process of being decommissioned and the status of decommissioning activities at those facilities.

Article 33: Attendance

1. Each Contracting Party shall attend meetings of the Contracting Parties and be represented at such meetings by one delegate, and by such alternates, experts and advisers as it deems necessary.

2. The Contracting Parties may invite, by consensus, any intergovernmental organization which is competent in respect of matters governed by this Convention to attend, as an observer, any meeting, or specific sessions thereof. Observers shall be required to accept in writing, and in advance, the provisions of Article 36.

Article 34: Summary reports

The Contracting Parties shall adopt, by consensus, and make available to the public a document addressing issues discussed and conclusions reached during meetings of the Contracting Parties.

Article 35: Languages

1. The languages of meetings of the Contracting Parties shall be Arabic, Chinese, English, French, Russian and Spanish unless otherwise provided in the Rules of Procedure.

2. Reports submitted pursuant to Article 32 shall be prepared in the national language of the submitting Contracting Party or in a single designated language to be agreed in the Rules of Procedure. Should the report be submitted in a national language other than the designated language, a translation of the report into the designated language shall be provided by the Contracting Party.

3. Notwithstanding the provisions of paragraph 2, the secretariat, if compensated, will assume the translation of reports submitted in any other language of the meeting into the designated language.

Article 36: Confidentiality

1. The provisions of this Convention shall not affect the rights and obligations of the Contracting Parties under their laws to protect information from disclosure. For the purposes of this Article, 'information' includes, inter alia, information relating to national security or to the physical protection of nuclear materials, information protected by intellectual property rights or by industrial or commercial confidentiality, and personal data.

2. When, in the context of this Convention, a Contracting Party provides information identified by it as protected as described in paragraph 1, such information shall be used only for the purposes for which it has been provided and its confidentiality shall be respected.

3. With respect to information relating to spent fuel or radioactive waste falling within the scope of this Convention by virtue of paragraph 3 of Article 3, the provisions of this Convention shall not affect the exclusive discretion of the Contracting Party concerned to decide:

i. whether such information is classified or otherwise controlled to preclude release;
ii. whether to provide information referred to in sub-paragraph (i) above in the context of the Convention; and
iii. what conditions of confidentiality are attached to such information if it is provided in the context of this Convention.

4. The content of the debates during the reviewing of the national reports at each review meeting held pursuant to Article 30 shall be confidential.

Article 37: Secretariat

1. The International Atomic Energy Agency, (hereinafter referred to as 'the Agency') shall provide the secretariat for the meetings of the Contracting Parties.

2. The secretariat shall:

i. convene, prepare and service the meetings of the Contracting Parties referred to in Articles 29, 30 and 31;

ii. transmit to the Contracting Parties information received or prepared in accordance with the provisions of this Convention.

The costs incurred by the Agency in carrying out the functions referred to in sub-paragraphs (i) and (ii) above shall be borne by the Agency as part of its regular budget.

3. The Contracting Parties may, by consensus, request the Agency to provide other services in support of meetings of the Contracting Parties. The Agency may provide such services if they can be undertaken within its programme and regular budget. Should this not be possible, the Agency may provide such services if voluntary funding is provided from another source.

[Chapter 7: Final clauses and other provisions, not reproduced]

Chapter 7

Military Activities

The present chapter examines international instruments that place limitations on the deliberate infliction of environmental damage for military purposes or during armed conflict. On the one hand, the 1949 Geneva Conventions[1] and Protocols have sought to protect persons and property from the impacts of military activities. While there is no specific protocol for the protection of the environment in times of armed conflict, the 1977 Protocol I to the Geneva Conventions prohibits methods or means of warfare intended or expected to cause widespread, long-term and severe damage to the natural environment, as well as attacks against the natural environment by way of reprisals. Conversely, ENMOD, adopted in 1976, addresses directly the question of environmental harm resulting from military activities by prohibiting the hostile use of environmental modification techniques having widespread, long-lasting or severe effects.

The environmental consequences of armed conflict have also been addressed in the framework of the UN Charter after Iraq's 1990 invasion of Kuwait. This led the Security Council to consider for the first time the responsibility of a state for environmental harm caused by unlawful military activities. Security Council Resolution 687 holds Iraq liable for, *inter alia*, environmental damage and the depletion of natural resources arising out of its unlawful invasion and occupation of Kuwait. Further consideration of the environmental impacts of armed conflict has been made by the UNCC, which was established by the Security Council as a mechanism for the processing of claims and the payment of compensation for losses resulting from Iraq's invasion and occupation of Kuwait, including losses or expenses resulting from direct environmental damage and the depletion of natural resources.[2]

---

1 Convention for the Amelioration of the Condition of the Wounded and Sick in Armed Forces in the Field, 12 August 1949, 75 *UNTS* 31; Convention for the Amelioration of the Condition of Wounded, Sick and Ship-wrecked Members of Armed Forces at Sea, 12 August 1949, 75 *UNTS* 85; Convention relative to the Treatment of Prisoners of War, 12 August 1949, 75 *UNTS* 135; and Convention relative to the Protection of Civilian Persons in Time of War, 12 August 1949, 75 *UNTS* 287.

2 The UNCC is a subsidiary organ of the Security Council established by Security Council Resolution 692 of 20 May 1991.

Selected readings

Austin, J.E. and Bruch, C.E. (eds.), *The Environmental Consequences of War* (Cambridge: Cambridge University Press, 2000).

Henckaerts, J.-M., 'Towards Better Protection for the Environment in Armed Conflict: Recent Developments in International Humanitarian Law', 9 *RECIEL* 13 (2000).

Kazazi, M., 'Environmental Damage in the Practice of the UN Compensation Commission', *in* Bowman, M. and Boyle, A. (eds.), *Environmental Damage in International and Comparative Law* (Oxford: Oxford University Press, 2002), p. 111.

Momtaz, D., 'Les règles relatives à la protection de l'environnement au cours des conflits armés à l'épreuve du conflit entre l'Irak et le Koweit', 37 *Annuaire français de droit international* 203 (1991).

Tarasofsky, R.G., 'Legal Protection of the Environment during International Armed Conflict', 24 *Netherlands Ybk Int'l L.* 17 (1993).

Convention on the Prohibition of Military or Any Other Hostile Use of Environmental Modification Techniques

Adopted on 10 December 1976 at Geneva. Entered into force on 5 October 1978. Source: 1108 *UNTS* 151. Number of parties: 69. Further information: UN, New York, USA, http://www.un.org

The States Parties to this Convention,

Guided by the interest of consolidating peace, and wishing to contribute to the cause of halting the arms race, and of bringing about general and complete disarmament under strict and effective international control, and of saving mankind from the danger of using new means of warfare,

Determined to continue negotiations with a view to achieving effective progress towards further measures in the field of disarmament,

Recognizing that scientific and technical advances may open new possibilities with respect to modification of the environment,

Recalling the Declaration of the United Nations Conference on the Human Environment adopted at Stockholm on 16 June 1972,

Realizing that the use of environmental modification techniques for peaceful purposes could improve the interrelationship of man and nature and contribute to the preservation and improvement of the environment for the benefit of present and future generations,

Recognizing, however, that military or any other hostile use of such techniques could have effects extremely harmful to human welfare,

Desiring to prohibit effectively military or any other hostile use of environmental modification techniques in order to eliminate the dangers to mankind from such use, and affirming their willingness to work towards the achievement of this objective,

Desiring also to contribute to the strengthening of trust among nations and to the further improvement of the international situation in accordance with the purposes and principles of the Charter of the United Nations,

Have agreed as follows:

Article I

1. Each State Party to this Convention undertakes not to engage in military or any other hostile use of environmental modification techniques having widespread, long-lasting or severe effects as the means of destruction, damage or injury to any other State Party.

2. Each State Party to this Convention undertakes not to assist, encourage or induce any State, group of States or international organization to engage in activities contrary to the provisions of paragraph 1 of this article.

Article II

As used in Article I, the term 'environmental modification techniques' refers to any technique for changing - through the deliberate manipulation of natural processes - the dynamics, composition or structure of the Earth, including its biota, lithosphere, hydrosphere and atmosphere, or of outer space.

Article III

1. The provisions of this Convention shall not hinder the use of environmental modification techniques for peaceful purposes and shall be without prejudice to the generally recognized principles and applicable rules of international law concerning such use.

2. The States Parties to this Convention undertake to facilitate, and have the right to participate in, the fullest possible exchange of scientific and technological information on the use of environmental modification techniques for peaceful purposes. States Parties in a position to do so shall contribute, alone or together with other States or international organizations, to international economic and scientific co-operation in the preservation, improvement, and peaceful utilization of the environment, with due consideration for the needs of the developing areas of the world.

Article IV

Each State Party to this Convention undertakes to take any measures it considers necessary in accordance with its constitutional processes to prohibit and prevent any activity in violation of the provisions of the Convention anywhere under its jurisdiction or control.

Article V

1. The States Parties to this Convention undertake to consult one another and to cooperate in solving any problems which may arise in relation to the objectives of,

or in the application of the provisions of, the Convention. Consultation and cooperation pursuant to this article may also be undertaken through appropriate international procedures within the framework of the United Nations and in accordance with its Charter. These international procedures may include the services of appropriate international organizations, as well as of a Consultative Committee of Experts as provided for in paragraph 2 of this article.

2. For the purposes set forth in paragraph 1 of this article, the Depositary shall, within one month of the receipt of a request from any State Party to this Convention, convene a Consultative Committee of Experts. Any State Party may appoint an expert to the Committee whose functions and rules of procedure are set out in the annex, which constitutes an integral part of this Convention. The Committee shall transmit to the Depositary a summary of its findings of fact, incorporating all views and information presented to the Committee during its proceedings. The Depositary shall distribute the summary to all States Parties.

3. Any State Party to this Convention which has reason to believe that any other State Party is acting in breach of obligations deriving from the provisions of the Convention may lodge a complaint with the Security Council of the United Nations. Such a complaint should include all relevant information as well as all possible evidence supporting its validity.

4. Each State Party to this Convention undertakes to cooperate in carrying out any investigation which the Security Council may initiate, in accordance with the provisions of the Charter of the United Nations, on the basis of the complaint received by the Council. The Security Council shall inform the States Parties of the results of the investigation.

5. Each State Party to this Convention undertakes to provide or support assistance, in accordance with the provisions of the Charter of the United Nations, to any State Party which so requests, if the Security Council decides that such Party has been harmed or is likely to be harmed as a result of violation of the Convention.

Article VI

1. Any State Party to this Convention may propose amendments to the Convention. The text of any proposed amendment shall be submitted to the Depositary who shall promptly circulate it to all States Parties.

2. An amendment shall enter into force for all States Parties to this Convention which have accepted it, upon the deposit with the Depositary of instruments of acceptance by a majority of States Parties. Thereafter it shall enter into force for any remaining State Party on the date of deposit of its instrument of acceptance.

Article VII

This Convention shall be of unlimited duration.

Article VIII

1. Five years after the entry into force of this Convention, a conference of the States Parties to the Convention shall be convened by the Depositary at Geneva,

Switzerland. The conference shall review the operation of the Convention with a view to ensuring that its purposes and provisions are being realized, and shall in particular examine the effectiveness of the provisions of paragraph 1 of Article I in eliminating the dangers of military or any other hostile use of environmental modification techniques.

2. At intervals of not less than five years thereafter, a majority of the States Parties to the Convention may obtain, by submitting a proposal to this effect to the Depositary, the convening of a conference with the same objectives.

3. If no conference has been convened pursuant to paragraph 2 of this article within ten years following the conclusion of a previous conference, the Depositary shall solicit the views of all States Parties to the Convention, concerning the convening of such a conference. If one third or ten of the States Parties, whichever number is less, respond affirmatively, the Depositary shall take immediate steps to convene the conference.

Article IX

1. This Convention shall be open to all States for signature. Any State which does not sign the Convention before its entry into force in accordance with paragraph 3 of this article may accede to it at any time.

2. This Convention shall be subject to ratification by signatory States. Instruments of ratification or accession shall be deposited with the Secretary-General of the United Nations.

3. This Convention shall enter into force upon the deposit of instruments of ratification by twenty Governments in accordance with paragraph 2 of this article.

4. For those States whose instruments of ratification or accession are deposited after the entry into force of this Convention, it shall enter into force on the date of the deposit of their instruments of ratification or accession.

5. The Depositary shall promptly inform all signatory and acceding States of the date of each signature, the date of deposit of each instrument of ratification or accession and the date of the entry into force of this Convention and of any amendments thereto, as well as of the receipt of other notices.

6. This Convention shall be registered by the Depositary in accordance with Article 102 of the Charter of the United Nations.

Article X

This Convention, of which the English, Arabic, Chinese, French, Russian, and Spanish texts are equally authentic, shall be deposited with the Secretary-General of the United Nations, who shall send certified copies thereof to the Governments of the signatory and acceding States.

In witness whereof, the undersigned, being duly authorized thereto by their respective governments, have signed this Convention, opened for signature at Geneva on the eighteenth day of May, one thousand nine hundred and seventy-seven.

Annex: Consultative Committee of Experts [not reproduced]

Protocol Additional to the Geneva Conventions of 12 August 1949, and Relating to the Protection of Victims of International Armed Conflicts (Protocol I) [excerpts]

Adopted on 8 June 1977 at Geneva. Entered into force on 7 December 1978. Source: 1125 *UNTS* 3. Number of parties: 161. Further information: International Committee of the Red Cross, Geneva, Switzerland, http://www.icrc.org

Part III: Methods and means of warfare

Combatant and prisoners-of-war

Section I: Methods and means of warfare

Article 35: Basic rules

[Paragraphs 1-2 not reproduced]

3. It is prohibited to employ methods or means of warfare which are intended, or may be expected, to cause widespread, long-term and severe damage to the natural environment.

Article 55: Protection of the natural environment

1. Care shall be taken in warfare to protect the natural environment against widespread, long-term and severe damage. This protection includes a prohibition of the use of methods or means of warfare which are intended or may be expected to cause such damage to the natural environment and thereby to prejudice the health or survival of the population.

2. Attacks against the natural environment by way of reprisals are prohibited.

United Nations Security Council Resolution 687 [excerpts]

Adopted on 3 April 1991 at New York. Source: 2981st Meeting of the UN Security Council, Doc. S/RES/687. Further information: UN, New York, USA, http://www.un.org

The Security Council,

E.

16. *Reaffirms* that Iraq, without prejudice to the debts and obligations of Iraq arising prior to 2 August 1990, which will be addressed through the normal

mechanisms, is liable under international law for any direct loss, damage, including environmental damage and the depletion of natural resources, or injury to foreign Governments, nationals and corporations, as a result of Iraq's unlawful invasion and occupation of Kuwait;

[Paragraph 17 not reproduced]

18. *Decides* also to create a fund to pay compensation for claims that fall within paragraph 16 above and to establish a Commission that will administer the fund;

19. *Directs* the Secretary-General to develop and present to the Security Council for decision, no later than thirty days following the adoption of the present resolution, recommendations for the fund to meet the requirement for the payment of claims established in accordance with paragraph 18 above and for a programme to implement the decisions in paragraphs 16, 17 and 18 above, including: administration of the fund; mechanisms for determining the appropriate level of Iraq's contribution to the fund based on a percentage of the value of the exports of petroleum and petroleum products from Iraq not to exceed a figure to be suggested to the Council by the Secretary-General, taking into account the requirements of the people of Iraq, Iraq's payment capacity as assessed in conjunction with the international financial institutions taking into consideration external debt service, and the needs of the Iraqi economy; arrangements for ensuring that payments are made to the fund; the process by which funds will be allocated and claims paid; appropriate procedures for evaluating losses, listing claims and verifying their validity and resolving disputed claims in respect of Iraq's liability as specified in paragraph 16 above; and the composition of the Commission designated above;

United Nations Compensation Commission, Decision 7, Criteria for Additional Categories of Claims [excerpts]

Source: 3rd Session of the Governing Council of the UNCC, 16-20 March 1992, Doc. S/AC.26/1991/7/Rev.1. Further information: UNCC, Geneva, Switzerland, http://www.unog.ch/uncc

III. Criteria for processing claims of governments and international organizations[3]

Claims covered

35. These payments are available with respect to direct environmental damage and the depletion of natural resources as a result of Iraq's unlawful invasion and occupation of Kuwait. This will include losses or expenses resulting from:

(a) Abatement and prevention of environmental damage, including expenses directly relating to fighting oil fires and stemming the flow of oil in coastal and international waters;
(b) Reasonable measures already taken to clean and restore the environment or future measures which can be documented as reasonably necessary to clean and restore the environment;
(c) Reasonable monitoring and assessment of the environmental damage for the purposes of evaluating and abating the harm and restoring the environment;
(d) Reasonable monitoring of public health and performing medical screenings for the purposes of investigation and combating increased health risks as a result of the environmental damage; and
(e) Depletion of or damage to natural resources.

---

3 *Editors' note*: According to paragraph 30 of Decision 7, the 'following criteria will govern the submission of claims of Governments and international organizations pursuant to resolution 687 (1991)'.

Chapter 8

Marine Environment, Marine Resources and International Watercourses

Introduction

This chapter first includes a selection of treaties related to the protection of the marine environment and the management of marine resources. Traditionally, the law relating to the marine environment and marine resources has been a separate field of international law because it deals mostly with areas beyond the sovereignty of states. Over time, a great number of treaties concerning the management of the marine environment and marine resources have been adopted by states. A number of them are relevant in the context of international environmental law because they include environmental aspects even though their main focus may not be environmental. Since an entire volume could easily be devoted to these treaties, this compilation cannot do more than include some of the more salient and/or recent instruments in this field to illustrate the nexus between the law of the sea and international environmental law.

Concerning the protection of the marine environment, this chapter first reproduces the part of the 1982 UNCLOS that deals specifically with the marine environment. It goes on to include two specific instruments concerning marine pollution as an illustration of the work of the IMO in this field: MARPOL 73/78 and the 1996 Protocol to the London Convention.

The second section focuses on the exploitation of marine resources. It first includes some of the relevant parts of the UNCLOS, in particular extracts from Parts V and VII which define the legal framework for the exploitation of marine resources in the exclusive economic zone and in the high seas. It also includes extracts from Part XI which defines the legal regime for deep seabed and whose main significance is the recognition that the management of the Area is based on the principle of the common heritage of humankind. This section also contains an Agreement linked to the UNCLOS which seeks to define more precisely the obligations of states with regard to the conservation and management of straddling and highly migratory fish stocks. Further, it incorporates the 1946 International Whaling Convention, one of the most important treaties concerning the protection of marine mammals as well as a relatively old treaty, which has followed a very interesting evolution from a focus on the regulation of takings in the 1940s to a conservationist one in recent years.

The last section on international watercourses reproduces the only existing global convention on international watercourses. The 1997 Convention on the Law of the Non-navigational Uses of International Watercourses is significant because it incorporates most of the basic principles of international watercourse law. Besides the 1997 Convention, there exist a plethora of bilateral and regional river and river basin treaties.[1] These instruments are not reproduced because this compilation focuses on instruments of international application and because international watercourse law is also a specific field of international law which is partly but not completely concerned with environmental management and which merits specific consideration on its own.

Selected readings

Marine environment

Charney, J., 'The Marine Environment and the 1982 United Nations Convention on the Law of the Sea', 28 *Int'l Lawyer* 879 (1994).

Churchill, R.R. and Lowe, A.V., *The Law of the Sea* (Manchester: Manchester University Press, 3rd edn. 1999).

Van Dyke, J. M., 'The Legal Regime Governing Sea Transport of Ultrahazardous Radioactive Materials', 33 *Ocean Development & Int'l L.* 77 (2002).

VanderZwaag, D., 'The Precautionary Principle and Marine Environmental Protection: Slippery Shores, Rough Seas, and Rising Normative Tides', 33 *Ocean Development & Int'l L.* 165 (2002).

Marine resources

Burke, W.T., *The New International Law of Fisheries - UNCLOS 1982 and Beyond* (Oxford: Clarendon, 1994).

Burns, W.C.G. and Wandesforde-Smith, G., 'The International Whaling Commission and the Future of Cetaceans in a Changing World', 11 *RECIEL* 199 (2002).

Kaye, S.M., *International Fisheries Management* (The Hague: Kluwer Law International, 2001).

---

1 For a general regional regime, *see, e.g.*, Convention on the Protection and Use of Transboundary Watercourses and International Lakes, Helsinki, 17 March 1992, 31 *ILM* 1312 (1992). For specific regimes, *see, e.g.*, Agreement on the Action Plan for The Environmentally Sound Management of the Common Zambezi River System, Harare, 28 May 1987, 27 *ILM* 1109 (1988); and Agreement on the Cooperation for the Sustainable Development of the Mekong River Basin, Chiang Rai (Thailand), 5 April 1995, 34 *ILM* 864 (1995).

Vicuña, F.O., *The Changing International Law of High Seas Fisheries* (Cambridge: Cambridge University Press, 1998).

Watercourses

Fuentes, X., 'Sustainable Development and the Equitable Utilization of International Watercourses', 69 *BYIL* 119 (1999).

McCaffrey, S., *The Law of International Watercourses* (Oxford: Oxford University Press, 2001).

McIntyre, O., 'The Emergence of an 'Ecosystem Approach' to the Protection of International Watercourses under International Law', 13/1 *RECIEL* 1 (2004).

Tanzi, A., 'The UN Convention on International Watercourses as a Framework for the Avoidance and Settlement of Waterlaw Disputes', 11/3 *Leiden J. Int'l L.* 441 (1998).

Marine environment

United Nations Convention on the Law of the Sea, Part XII: Protection and Preservation of the Marine Environment[2]

Adopted on 10 December 1982 at Montego Bay. Entered into force on 16 November 1994. Source: 1833 *UNTS* 3. Number of parties: 145. Further information: Division for Ocean Affairs and the Law of the Sea, UN, New York, USA, http://www.un.org/Depts/los

Section 1: General provisions

Article 192: General obligation

States have the obligation to protect and preserve the marine environment.

Article 193: Sovereign right of States to exploit their natural resources

States have the sovereign right to exploit their natural resources pursuant to their environmental policies and in accordance with their duty to protect and preserve the marine environment.

[2] This compilation also reproduces Part XV of the UNCLOS. at p. 590.

Article 194: Measures to prevent, reduce and control pollution of the marine environment[3]

1. States shall take, individually or jointly as appropriate, all measures consistent with this Convention that are necessary to prevent, reduce and control pollution of the marine environment from any source, using for this purpose the best practicable means at their disposal and in accordance with their capabilities, and they shall endeavour to harmonize their policies in this connection.

2. States shall take all measures necessary to ensure that activities under their jurisdiction or control are so conducted as not to cause damage by pollution to other States and their environment, and that pollution arising from incidents or activities under their jurisdiction or control does not spread beyond the areas where they exercise sovereign rights in accordance with this Convention.

3. The measures taken pursuant to this Part shall deal with all sources of pollution of the marine environment. These measures shall include, *inter alia*, those designed to minimize to the fullest possible extent:

(a) the release of toxic, harmful or noxious substances, especially those which are persistent, from land-based sources, from or through the atmosphere or by dumping;[4]

(b) pollution from vessels, in particular measures for preventing accidents and dealing with emergencies, ensuring the safety of operations at sea, preventing intentional and unintentional discharges, and regulating the design, construction, equipment, operation and manning of vessels;

(c) pollution from installations and devices used in exploration or exploitation of the natural resources of the seabed and subsoil, in particular measures for preventing accidents and dealing with emergencies, ensuring the safety of operations at sea, and regulating the design, construction, equipment, operation and manning of such installations or devices;

(d) pollution from other installations and devices operating in the marine environment, in particular measures for preventing accidents and dealing with emergencies, ensuring the safety of operations at sea, and regulating the design, construction, equipment, operation and manning of such installations or devices.

---

3 *Editors' note*: As per Article 1(4) of the UNCLOS, 'pollution of the marine environment' means the introduction by man, directly or indirectly, of substances or energy into the marine environment, including estuaries, which results or is likely to result in such deleterious effects as harm to living resources and marine life, hazards to human health, hindrance to marine activities, including fishing and other legitimate uses of the sea, impairment of quality for use of sea water and reduction of amenities.

4 *Editors' note*: As per Article 1(5)a of the UNCLOS, 'dumping' means: (i) any deliberate disposal of wastes or other matter from vessels, aircraft, platforms or other man made structures at sea; (ii) any deliberate disposal of vessels, aircraft, platforms or other man made structures at sea.

4. In taking measures to prevent, reduce or control pollution of the marine environment, States shall refrain from unjustifiable interference with activities carried out by other States in the exercise of their rights and in pursuance of their duties in conformity with this Convention.

5. The measures taken in accordance with this Part shall include those necessary to protect and preserve rare or fragile ecosystems as well as the habitat of depleted, threatened or endangered species and other forms of marine life.

Article 195: Duty not to transfer damage or hazards or transform one type of pollution into another

In taking measures to prevent, reduce and control pollution of the marine environment, States shall act so as not to transfer, directly or indirectly, damage or hazards from one area to another or transform one type of pollution into another.

Article 196: Use of technologies or introduction of alien or new species

1. States shall take all measures necessary to prevent, reduce and control pollution of the marine environment resulting from the use of technologies under their jurisdiction or control, or the intentional or accidental introduction of species, alien or new, to a particular part of the marine environment, which may cause significant and harmful changes thereto.

2. This article does not affect the application of this Convention regarding the prevention, reduction and control of pollution of the marine environment.

Section 2: Global and regional cooperation

Article 197: Cooperation on a global or regional basis

States shall cooperate on a global basis and, as appropriate, on a regional basis, directly or through competent international organizations, in formulating and elaborating international rules, standards and recommended practices and procedures consistent with this Convention, for the protection and preservation of the marine environment, taking into account characteristic regional features.

Article 198: Notification of imminent or actual damage

When a State becomes aware of cases in which the marine environment is in imminent danger of being damaged or has been damaged by pollution, it shall immediately notify other States it deems likely to be affected by such damage, as well as the competent international organizations.

Article 199: Contingency plans against pollution

In the cases referred to in article 198, States in the area affected, in accordance with their capabilities, and the competent international organizations shall cooperate, to the extent possible, in eliminating the effects of pollution and preventing or minimizing the damage. To this end, States shall jointly develop and promote contingency plans for responding to pollution incidents in the marine environment.

Article 200: Studies, research programmes and exchange of information and data

States shall cooperate, directly or through competent international organizations, for the purpose of promoting studies, undertaking programmes of scientific research and encouraging the exchange of information and data acquired about pollution of the marine environment. They shall endeavour to participate actively in regional and global programmes to acquire knowledge for the assessment of the nature and extent of pollution, exposure to it, and its pathways, risks and remedies.

Article 201: Scientific criteria for regulations

In the light of the information and data acquired pursuant to article 200, States shall cooperate, directly or through competent international organizations, in establishing appropriate scientific criteria for the formulation and elaboration of rules, standards and recommended practices and procedures for the prevention, reduction and control of pollution of the marine environment.

Section 3: Technical assistance

Article 202: Scientific and technical assistance to developing States

States shall, directly or through competent international organizations:

(a) promote programmes of scientific, educational, technical and other assistance to developing States for the protection and preservation of the marine environment and the prevention, reduction and control of marine pollution. Such assistance shall include, *inter alia*:

i) training of their scientific and technical personnel;
ii) facilitating their participation in relevant international programmes;
iii) supplying them with necessary equipment and facilities;
iv) enhancing their capacity to manufacture such equipment;
v) advice on and developing facilities for research, monitoring, educational and other programmes;

(b) provide appropriate assistance, especially to developing States, for the minimization of the effects of major incidents which may cause serious pollution of the marine environment;

(c) provide appropriate assistance, especially to developing States, concerning the preparation of environmental assessments.

Article 203: Preferential treatment for developing States

Developing States shall, for the purposes of prevention, reduction and control of pollution of the marine environment or minimization of its effects, be granted preference by international organizations in:

(a) the allocation of appropriate funds and technical assistance; and

(b) the utilization of their specialized services.

Section 4: Monitoring and environmental assessment

Article 204: Monitoring of the risks or effects of pollution

1. States shall, consistent with the rights of other States, endeavour, as far as practicable, directly or through the competent international organizations, to observe, measure, evaluate and analyse, by recognized scientific methods, the risks or effects of pollution of the marine environment.

2. In particular, States shall keep under surveillance the effects of any activities which they permit or in which they engage in order to determine whether these activities are likely to pollute the marine environment.

Article 205: Publication of reports

States shall publish reports of the results obtained pursuant to article 204 or provide such reports at appropriate intervals to the competent international organizations, which should make them available to all States.

Article 206: Assessment of potential effects of activities

When States have reasonable grounds for believing that planned activities under their jurisdiction or control may cause substantial pollution of or significant and harmful changes to the marine environment, they shall, as far as practicable, assess the potential effects of such activities on the marine environment and shall communicate reports of the results of such assessments in the manner provided in article 205.

Section 5: International rules and national legislation to prevent, reduce and control pollution of the marine environment

Article 207: Pollution from land-based sources

1. States shall adopt laws and regulations to prevent, reduce and control pollution of the marine environment from land-based sources, including rivers, estuaries, pipelines and outfall structures, taking into account internationally agreed rules, standards and recommended practices and procedures.

2. States shall take other measures as may be necessary to prevent, reduce and control such pollution.

3. States shall endeavour to harmonize their policies in this connection at the appropriate regional level.

4. States, acting especially through competent international organizations or diplomatic conference, shall endeavour to establish global and regional rules, standards and recommended practices and procedures to prevent, reduce and control pollution of the marine environment from land-based sources, taking into account characteristic regional features, the economic capacity of developing States and their need for economic development. Such rules, standards and recommended practices and procedures shall be re-examined from time to time as necessary.

5. Laws, regulations, measures, rules, standards and recommended practices and procedures referred to in paragraphs 1, 2 and 4 shall include those designed to

minimize, to the fullest extent possible, the release of toxic, harmful or noxious substances, especially those which are persistent, into the marine environment.

Article 208: Pollution from sea-bed activities subject to national jurisdiction

1. Coastal States shall adopt laws and regulations to prevent, reduce and control pollution of the marine environment arising from or in connection with seabed activities subject to their jurisdiction and from artificial islands, installations and structures under their jurisdiction, pursuant to articles 60 and 80.

2. States shall take other measures as may be necessary to prevent, reduce and control such pollution.

3. Such laws, regulations and measures shall be no less effective than international rules, standards and recommended practices and procedures.

4. States shall endeavour to harmonize their policies in this connection at the appropriate regional level.

5. States, acting especially through competent international organizations or diplomatic conference, shall establish global and regional rules, standards and recommended practices and procedures to prevent, reduce and control pollution of the marine environment referred to in paragraph l. Such rules, standards and recommended practices and procedures shall be re-examined from time to time as necessary.

Article 209: Pollution from activities in the Area

1. International rules, regulations and procedures shall be established in accordance with Part XI to prevent, reduce and control pollution of the marine environment from activities in the Area. Such rules, regulations and procedures shall be re-examined from time to time as necessary.

2. Subject to the relevant provisions of this section, States shall adopt laws and regulations to prevent, reduce and control pollution of the marine environment from activities in the Area undertaken by vessels, installations, structures and other devices flying their flag or of their registry or operating under their authority, as the case may be. The requirements of such laws and regulations shall be no less effective than the international rules, regulations and procedures referred to in paragraph 1.

Article 210: Pollution by dumping

1. States shall adopt laws and regulations to prevent, reduce and control pollution of the marine environment by dumping.

2. States shall take other measures as may be necessary to prevent, reduce and control such pollution.

3. Such laws, regulations and measures shall ensure that dumping is not carried out without the permission of the competent authorities of States.

4. States, acting especially through competent international organizations or diplomatic conference, shall endeavour to establish global and regional rules,

standards and recommended practices and procedures to prevent, reduce and control such pollution. Such rules, standards and recommended practices and procedures shall be re-examined from time to time as necessary.

5. Dumping within the territorial sea and the exclusive economic zone or onto the continental shelf shall not be carried out without the express prior approval of the coastal State, which has the right to permit, regulate and control such dumping after due consideration of the matter with other States which by reason of their geographical situation may be adversely affected thereby.

6. National laws, regulations and measures shall be no less effective in preventing, reducing and controlling such pollution than the global rules and standards.

Article 211: Pollution from vessels

1. States, acting through the competent international organization or general diplomatic conference, shall establish international rules and standards to prevent, reduce and control pollution of the marine environment from vessels and promote the adoption, in the same manner, wherever appropriate, of routeing systems designed to minimize the threat of accidents which might cause pollution of the marine environment, including the coastline, and pollution damage to the related interests of coastal States. Such rules and standards shall, in the same manner, be re-examined from time to time as necessary.

2. States shall adopt laws and regulations for the prevention, reduction and control of pollution of the marine environment from vessels flying their flag or of their registry. Such laws and regulations shall at least have the same effect as that of generally accepted international rules and standards established through the competent international organization or general diplomatic conference.

3. States which establish particular requirements for the prevention, reduction and control of pollution of the marine environment as a condition for the entry of foreign vessels into their ports or internal waters or for a call at their off-shore terminals shall give due publicity to such requirements and shall communicate them to the competent international organization. Whenever such requirements are established in identical form by two or more coastal States in an endeavour to harmonize policy, the communication shall indicate which States are participating in such cooperative arrangements. Every State shall require the master of a vessel flying its flag or of its registry, when navigating within the territorial sea of a State participating in such cooperative arrangements, to furnish, upon the request of that State, information as to whether it is proceeding to a State of the same region participating in such cooperative arrangements and, if so, to indicate whether it complies with the port entry requirements of that State. This article is without prejudice to the continued exercise by a vessel of its right of innocent passage or to the application of article 25, paragraph 2.

4. Coastal States may, in the exercise of their sovereignty within their territorial sea, adopt laws and regulations for the prevention, reduction and control of marine pollution from foreign vessels, including vessels exercising the right of innocent

passage. Such laws and regulations shall, in accordance with Part II, section 3, not hamper innocent passage of foreign vessels.

5. Coastal States, for the purpose of enforcement as provided for in section 6, may in respect of their exclusive economic zones adopt laws and regulations for the prevention, reduction and control of pollution from vessels conforming to and giving effect to generally accepted international rules and standards established through the competent international organization or general diplomatic conference.

6. (a) Where the international rules and standards referred to in paragraph 1 are inadequate to meet special circumstances and coastal States have reasonable grounds for believing that a particular, clearly defined area of their respective exclusive economic zones is an area where the adoption of special mandatory measures for the prevention of pollution from vessels is required for recognized technical reasons in relation to its oceanographical and ecological conditions, as well as its utilization or the protection of its resources and the particular character of its traffic, the coastal States, after appropriate consultations through the competent international organization with any other States concerned, may, for that area, direct a communication to that organization, submitting scientific and technical evidence in support and information on necessary reception facilities. Within 12 months after receiving such a communication, the organization shall determine whether the conditions in that area correspond to the requirements set out above. If the organization so determines, the coastal States may, for that area, adopt laws and regulations for the prevention, reduction and control of pollution from vessels implementing such international rules and standards or navigational practices as are made applicable, through the organization, for special areas. These laws and regulations shall not become applicable to foreign vessels until 15 months after the submission of the communication to the organization.

(b) The coastal States shall publish the limits of any such particular, clearly defined area.

(c) If the coastal States intend to adopt additional laws and regulations for the same area for the prevention, reduction and control of pollution from vessels, they shall, when submitting the aforesaid communication, at the same time notify the organization thereof. Such additional laws and regulations may relate to discharges or navigational practices but shall not require foreign vessels to observe design, construction, manning or equipment standards other than generally accepted international rules and standards; they shall become applicable to foreign vessels 15 months after the submission of the communication to the organization, provided that the organization agrees within 12 months after the submission of the communication.

7. The international rules and standards referred to in this article should include *inter alia* those relating to prompt notification to coastal States, whose coastline or related interests may be affected by incidents, including maritime casualties, which involve discharges or probability of discharges.

Article 212: Pollution from or through the atmosphere

1. States shall adopt laws and regulations to prevent, reduce and control pollution of the marine environment from or through the atmosphere, applicable to the air space under their sovereignty and to vessels flying their flag or vessels or aircraft of their registry, taking into account internationally agreed rules, standards and recommended practices and procedures and the safety of air navigation.

2. States shall take other measures as may be necessary to prevent, reduce and control such pollution.

3. States, acting especially through competent international organizations or diplomatic conference, shall endeavour to establish global and regional rules, standards and recommended practices and procedures to prevent, reduce and control such pollution.

Section 6: Enforcement

Article 213: Enforcement with respect to pollution from land-based sources

States shall enforce their laws and regulations adopted in accordance with article 207 and shall adopt laws and regulations and take other measures necessary to implement applicable international rules and standards established through competent international organizations or diplomatic conference to prevent, reduce and control pollution of the marine environment from land-based sources.

Article 214: Enforcement with respect to pollution from sea-bed activities

States shall enforce their laws and regulations adopted in accordance with article 208 and shall adopt laws and regulations and take other measures necessary to implement applicable international rules and standards established through competent international organizations or diplomatic conference to prevent, reduce and control pollution of the marine environment arising from or in connection with sea-bed activities subject to their jurisdiction and from artificial islands, installations and structures under their jurisdiction, pursuant to articles 60 and 80.

Article 215: Enforcement with respect to pollution from activities in the Area

Enforcement of international rules, regulations and procedures established in accordance with Part XI to prevent, reduce and control pollution of the marine environment from activities in the Area shall be governed by that Part.

Article 216: Enforcement with respect to pollution by dumping

1. Laws and regulations adopted in accordance with this Convention and applicable international rules and standards established through competent international organizations or diplomatic conference for the prevention, reduction and control of pollution of the marine environment by dumping shall be enforced:

(a) by the coastal State with regard to dumping within its territorial sea or its exclusive economic zone or onto its continental shelf;

(b) by the flag State with regard to vessels flying its flag or vessels or aircraft of its registry;

(c) by any State with regard to acts of loading of wastes or other matter occurring within its territory or at its off-shore terminals.

2. No State shall be obliged by virtue of this article to institute proceedings when another State has already instituted proceedings in accordance with this article.

Article 217: Enforcement by flag States

1. States shall ensure compliance by vessels flying their flag or of their registry with applicable international rules and standards, established through the competent international organization or general diplomatic conference, and with their laws and regulations adopted in accordance with this Convention for the prevention, reduction and control of pollution of the marine environment from vessels and shall accordingly adopt laws and regulations and take other measures necessary for their implementation. Flag States shall provide for the effective enforcement of such rules, standards, laws and regulations, irrespective of where a violation occurs.

2. States shall, in particular, take appropriate measures in order to ensure that vessels flying their flag or of their registry are prohibited from sailing, until they can proceed to sea in compliance with the requirements of the international rules and standards referred to in paragraph 1, including requirements in respect of design, construction, equipment and manning of vessels.

3. States shall ensure that vessels flying their flag or of their registry carry on board certificates required by and issued pursuant to international rules and standards referred to in paragraph 1. States shall ensure that vessels flying their flag are periodically inspected in order to verify that such certificates are in conformity with the actual condition of the vessels. These certificates shall be accepted by other States as evidence of the condition of the vessels and shall be regarded as having the same force as certificates issued by them, unless there are clear grounds for believing that the condition of the vessel does not correspond substantially with the particulars of the certificates.

4. If a vessel commits a violation of rules and standards established through the competent international organization or general diplomatic conference, the flag State, without prejudice to articles 218, 220 and 228, shall provide for immediate investigation and where appropriate institute proceedings in respect of the alleged violation irrespective of where the violation occurred or where the pollution caused by such violation has occurred or has been spotted.

5. Flag States conducting an investigation of the violation may request the assistance of any other State whose co-operation could be useful in clarifying the circumstances of the case. States shall endeavour to meet appropriate requests of flag States.

6. States shall, at the written request of any State, investigate any violation alleged to have been committed by vessels flying their flag. If satisfied that sufficient evidence is available to enable proceedings to be brought in respect of the alleged violation, flag States shall without delay institute such proceedings in accordance with their laws.

7. Flag States shall promptly inform the requesting State and the competent international organization of the action taken and its outcome. Such information shall be available to all States.

8. Penalties provided for by the laws and regulations of States for vessels flying their flag shall be adequate in severity to discourage violations wherever they occur.

Article 218: Enforcement by port States

1. When a vessel is voluntarily within a port or at an off-shore terminal of a State, that State may undertake investigations and, where the evidence so warrants, institute proceedings in respect of any discharge from that vessel outside the internal waters, territorial sea or exclusive economic zone of that State in violation of applicable international rules and standards established through the competent international organization or general diplomatic conference.

2. No proceedings pursuant to paragraph 1 shall be instituted in respect of a discharge violation in the internal waters, territorial sea or exclusive economic zone of another State unless requested by that State, the flag State, or a State damaged or threatened by the discharge violation, or unless the violation has caused or is likely to cause pollution in the internal waters, territorial sea or exclusive economic zone of the State instituting the proceedings.

3. When a vessel is voluntarily within a port or at an off-shore terminal of a State, that State shall, as far as practicable, comply with requests from any State for investigation of a discharge violation referred to in paragraph 1, believed to have occurred in, caused, or threatened damage to the internal waters, territorial sea or exclusive economic zone of the requesting State. It shall likewise, as far as practicable, comply with requests from the flag State for investigation of such a violation, irrespective of where the violation occurred.

4. The records of the investigation carried out by a port State pursuant to this article shall be transmitted upon request to the flag State or to the coastal State. Any proceedings instituted by the port State on the basis of such an investigation may, subject to section 7, be suspended at the request of the coastal State when the violation has occurred within its internal waters, territorial sea or exclusive economic zone. The evidence and records of the case, together with any bond or other financial security posted with the authorities of the port State, shall in that event be transmitted to the coastal State. Such transmittal shall preclude the continuation of proceedings in the port State.

Article 219: Measures relating to seaworthiness of vessels to avoid pollution

Subject to section 7, States which, upon request or on their own initiative, have ascertained that a vessel within one of their ports or at one of their off-shore terminals is in violation of applicable international rules and standards relating to seaworthiness of vessels and thereby threatens damage to the marine environment shall, as far as practicable, take administrative measures to prevent the vessel from sailing. Such States may permit the vessel to proceed only to the nearest appropriate repair yard and, upon removal of the causes of the violation, shall permit the vessel to continue immediately.

Article 220: Enforcement by coastal States

1. When a vessel is voluntarily within a port or at an off-shore terminal of a State, that State may, subject to section 7, institute proceedings in respect of any violation of its laws and regulations adopted in accordance with this Convention or applicable international rules and standards for the prevention, reduction and control of pollution from vessels when the violation has occurred within the territorial sea or the exclusive economic zone of that State.

2. Where there are clear grounds for believing that a vessel navigating in the territorial sea of a State has, during its passage therein, violated laws and regulations of that State adopted in accordance with this Convention or applicable international rules and standards for the prevention, reduction and control of pollution from vessels, that State, without prejudice to the application of the relevant provisions of Part II, section 3, may undertake physical inspection of the vessel relating to the violation and may, where the evidence so warrants, institute proceedings, including detention of the vessel, in accordance with its laws, subject to the provisions of section 7.

3. Where there are clear grounds for believing that a vessel navigating in the exclusive economic zone or the territorial sea of a State has, in the exclusive economic zone, committed a violation of applicable international rules and standards for the prevention, reduction and control of pollution from vessels or laws and regulations of that State conforming and giving effect to such rules and standards, that State may require the vessel to give information regarding its identity and port of registry, its last and its next port of call and other relevant information required to establish whether a violation has occurred.

4. States shall adopt laws and regulations and take other measures so that vessels flying their flag comply with requests for information pursuant to paragraph 3.

5. Where there are clear grounds for believing that a vessel navigating in the exclusive economic zone or the territorial sea of a State has, in the exclusive economic zone, committed a violation referred to in paragraph 3 resulting in a substantial discharge causing or threatening significant pollution of the marine environment, that State may undertake physical inspection of the vessel for matters relating to the violation if the vessel has refused to give information or if the information supplied by the vessel is manifestly at variance with the evident factual situation and if the circumstances of the case justify such inspection.

6. Where there is clear objective evidence that a vessel navigating in the exclusive economic zone or the territorial sea of a State has, in the exclusive economic zone, committed a violation referred to in paragraph 3 resulting in a discharge causing major damage or threat of major damage to the coastline or related interests of the coastal State, or to any resources of its territorial sea or exclusive economic zone,

that State may, subject to section 7, provided that the evidence so warrants, institute proceedings, including detention of the vessel, in accordance with its laws.

7. Notwithstanding the provisions of paragraph 6, whenever appropriate procedures have been established, either through the competent international organization or as otherwise agreed, whereby compliance with requirements for bonding or other appropriate financial security has been assured, the coastal State if bound by such procedures shall allow the vessel to proceed.

8. The provisions of paragraphs 3, 4, 5, 6 and 7 also apply in respect of national laws and regulations adopted pursuant to article 211, paragraph 6.

Article 221: Measures to avoid pollution arising from maritime casualties

1. Nothing in this Part shall prejudice the right of States, pursuant to international law, both customary and conventional, to take and enforce measures beyond the territorial sea proportionate to the actual or threatened damage to protect their coastline or related interests, including fishing, from pollution or threat of pollution following upon a maritime casualty or acts relating to such a casualty, which may reasonably be expected to result in major harmful consequences.

2. For the purposes of this article, 'maritime casualty' means a collision of vessels, stranding or other incident of navigation, or other occurrence on board a vessel or external to it resulting in material damage or imminent threat of material damage to a vessel or cargo.

Article 222: Enforcement with respect to pollution from or through the atmosphere

States shall enforce, within the air space under their sovereignty or with regard to vessels flying their flag or vessels or aircraft of their registry, their laws and regulations adopted in accordance with article 212, paragraph 1, and with other provisions of this Convention and shall adopt laws and regulations and take other measures necessary to implement applicable international rules and standards established through competent international organizations or diplomatic conference to prevent, reduce and control pollution of the marine environment from or through the atmosphere, in conformity with all relevant international rules and standards concerning the safety of air navigation.

Section 7: Safeguards

Article 223: Measures to facilitate proceedings

In proceedings instituted pursuant to this Part, States shall take measures to facilitate the hearing of witnesses and the admission of evidence submitted by authorities of another State, or by the competent international organization, and shall facilitate the attendance at such proceedings of official representatives of the competent international organization, the flag State and any State affected by pollution arising out of any violation. The official representatives attending such proceedings shall have such rights and duties as may be provided under national laws and regulations or international law.

Article 224: Exercise of powers of enforcement

The powers of enforcement against foreign vessels under this Part may only be exercised by officials or by warships, military aircraft, or other ships or aircraft clearly marked and identifiable as being on government service and authorized to that effect.

Article 225: Duty to avoid adverse consequences in the exercise of the powers of enforcement

In the exercise under this Convention of their powers of enforcement against foreign vessels, States shall not endanger the safety of navigation or otherwise create any hazard to a vessel, or bring it to an unsafe port or anchorage, or expose the marine environment to an unreasonable risk.

Article 226: Investigation of foreign vessels

1. (a) States shall not delay a foreign vessel longer than is essential for purposes of the investigations provided for in articles 216, 218 and 220. Any physical inspection of a foreign vessel shall be limited to an examination of such certificates, records or other documents as the vessel is required to carry by generally accepted international rules and standards or of any similar documents which it is carrying; further physical inspection of the vessel may be undertaken only after such an examination and only when:
   i) there are clear grounds for believing that the condition of the vessel or its equipment does not correspond substantially with the particulars of those documents;
   ii) the contents of such documents are not sufficient to confirm or verify a suspected violation; or
   iii) the vessel is not carrying valid certificates and records.

(b) If the investigation indicates a violation of applicable laws and regulations or international rules and standards for the protection and preservation of the marine environment, release shall be made promptly subject to reasonable procedures such as bonding or other appropriate financial security.

(c) Without prejudice to applicable international rules and standards relating to the seaworthiness of vessels, the release of a vessel may, whenever it would present an unreasonable threat of damage to the marine environment, be refused or made conditional upon proceeding to the nearest appropriate repair yard. Where release has been refused or made conditional, the flag State of the vessel must be promptly notified, and may seek release of the vessel in accordance with Part XV.

2. States shall co-operate to develop procedures for the avoidance of unnecessary physical inspection of vessels at sea.

Article 227: Non-discrimination with respect to foreign vessels

In exercising their rights and performing their duties under this Part, States shall not discriminate in form or in fact against vessels of any other State.

Article 228: Suspension and restrictions on institution of proceedings

1. Proceedings to impose penalties in respect of any violation of applicable laws and regulations or international rules and standards relating to the prevention, reduction and control of pollution from vessels committed by a foreign vessel beyond the territorial sea of the State instituting proceedings shall be suspended upon the taking of proceedings to impose penalties in respect of corresponding charges by the flag State within six months of the date on which proceedings were first instituted, unless those proceedings relate to a case of major damage to the coastal State or the flag State in question has repeatedly disregarded its obligation to enforce effectively the applicable international rules and standards in respect of violations committed by its vessels. The flag State shall in due course make available to the State previously instituting proceedings a full dossier of the case and the records of the proceedings, whenever the flag State has requested the suspension of proceedings in accordance with this article. When proceedings instituted by the flag State have been brought to a conclusion, the suspended proceedings shall be terminated. Upon payment of costs incurred in respect of such proceedings, any bond posted or other financial security provided in connection with the suspended proceedings shall be released by the coastal State.

2. Proceedings to impose penalties on foreign vessels shall not be instituted after the expiry of three years from the date on which the violation was committed, and shall not be taken by any State in the event of proceedings having been instituted by another State subject to the provisions set out in paragraph 1.

3. The provisions of this article are without prejudice to the right of the flag State to take any measures, including proceedings to impose penalties, according to its laws irrespective of prior proceedings by another State.

Article 229: Institution of civil proceedings

Nothing in this Convention affects the institution of civil proceedings in respect of any claim for loss or damage resulting from pollution of the marine environment.

Article 230: Monetary penalties and the observance of recognized rights of the accused

1. Monetary penalties only may be imposed with respect to violations of national laws and regulations or applicable international rules and standards for the prevention, reduction and control of pollution of the marine environment, committed by foreign vessels beyond the territorial sea.

2. Monetary penalties only may be imposed with respect to violations of national laws and regulations or applicable international rules and standards for the prevention, reduction and control of pollution of the marine environment, committed by foreign vessels in the territorial sea, except in the case of a wilful and serious act of pollution in the territorial sea.

3. In the conduct of proceedings in respect of such violations committed by a foreign vessel which may result in the imposition of penalties, recognized rights of the accused shall be observed.

Article 231: Notification to the flag State and other States concerned

States shall promptly notify the flag State and any other State concerned of any measures taken pursuant to section 6 against foreign vessels, and shall submit to the flag State all official reports concerning such measures. However, with respect to violations committed in the territorial sea, the foregoing obligations of the coastal State apply only to such measures as are taken in proceedings. The diplomatic agents or consular officers and where possible the maritime authority of the flag State, shall be immediately informed of any such measures taken pursuant to section 6 against foreign vessels.

Article 232: Liability of States arising from enforcement measures

States shall be liable for damage or loss attributable to them arising from measures taken pursuant to section 6 when such measures are unlawful or exceed those reasonably required in the light of available information. States shall provide for recourse in their courts for actions in respect of such damage or loss.

Article 233: Safeguards with respect to straits used for international navigation

Nothing in sections 5, 6 and 7 affects the legal regime of straits used for international navigation. However, if a foreign ship other than those referred to in section 10 has committed a violation of the laws and regulations referred to in article 42, paragraph 1(a) and (b), causing or threatening major damage to the marine environment of the straits, the States bordering the straits may take appropriate enforcement measures and if so shall respect *mutatis mutandis* the provisions of this section.

Section 8: Ice-covered areas

Article 234: Ice-covered areas

Coastal States have the right to adopt and enforce non-discriminatory laws and regulations for the prevention, reduction and control of marine pollution from vessels in ice-covered areas within the limits of the exclusive economic zone, where particularly severe climatic conditions and the presence of ice covering such areas for most of the year create obstructions or exceptional hazards to navigation, and pollution of the marine environment could cause major harm to or irreversible disturbance of the ecological balance. Such laws and regulations shall have due regard to navigation and the protection and preservation of the marine environment based on the best available scientific evidence.

Section 9: Responsibility and liability

Article 235: Responsibility and liability

1. States are responsible for the fulfilment of their international obligations concerning the protection and preservation of the marine environment. They shall be liable in accordance with international law.

2. States shall ensure that recourse is available in accordance with their legal systems for prompt and adequate compensation or other relief in respect of damage caused by pollution of the marine environment by natural or juridical persons under their jurisdiction.

3. With the objective of assuring prompt and adequate compensation in respect of all damage caused by pollution of the marine environment, States shall co-operate in the implementation of existing international law and the further development of international law relating to responsibility and liability for the assessment of and compensation for damage and the settlement of related disputes, as well as, where appropriate, development of criteria and procedures for payment of adequate compensation, such as compulsory insurance or compensation funds.

Section 10: Sovereign immunity

Article 236: Sovereign immunity

The provisions of this Convention regarding the protection and preservation of the marine environment do not apply to any warship, naval auxiliary, other vessels or aircraft owned or operated by a State and used, for the time being, only on government non-commercial service. However, each State shall ensure, by the adoption of appropriate measures not impairing operations or operational capabilities of such vessels or aircraft owned or operated by it, that such vessels or aircraft act in a manner consistent, so far as is reasonable and practicable, with this Convention.

Section 11: Obligations under other conventions on the protection and preservation of the marine environment

Article 237: Obligations under other conventions on the protection and preservation of the marine environment

1. The provisions of this Part are without prejudice to the specific obligations assumed by States under special conventions and agreements concluded previously which relate to the protection and preservation of the marine environment and to agreements which may be concluded in furtherance of the general principles set forth in this Convention.

2. Specific obligations assumed by States under special conventions, with respect to the protection and preservation of the marine environment, should be carried out in a manner consistent with the general principles and objectives of this Convention.

International Convention for the Prevention of Pollution from Ships, 1973 as modified by the Protocol of 1978 relating thereto (MARPOL 73/78)

Adopted on 2 November 1973 at London. Entered into force on 2 October 1983. Source: 1340 *UNTS* 61 and 1340 *UNTS* 184 (the text reproduced includes the amendments introduced by the Protocol of 17 February 1978 as subsequently amended in 1984 and 1985). Number of parties: 127. Further information: IMO, London, UK, http://www.imo.org

The Parties to the Convention,

Being conscious of the need to preserve the human environment in general and the marine environment in particular,

Recognizing that deliberate, negligent or accidental release of oil and other harmful substances from ships constitutes a serious source of pollution,

Recognizing also the importance of the International Convention for the Prevention of Pollution of the Sea by Oil 1954, as being the first multilateral instrument to be concluded with the prime objective of protecting the environment, and appreciating the significant contribution which that Convention has made in preserving the seas and coastal environment from pollution,

Desiring to achieve the complete elimination of intentional pollution of the marine environment by oil and other harmful substances and the minimization of accidental discharge of such substances,

Considering that this object may best be achieved by establishing rules not limited to oil pollution having a universal purport,

Have agreed as follows:

The parties to the present Protocol,

Recognizing the significant contribution which can be made by the International Convention for the Prevention of Pollution from Ships, 1973, to the protection of the marine environment from pollution from ships,

Recognizing also the need to improve further the prevention and control of marine pollution from ships, particularly oil tankers,

Recognizing further the need for implementing the Regulations for the Prevention of Pollution by Oil contained in Annex I of that Convention as early and as widely as possible,

Acknowledging however the need to defer the application of Annex II of that Convention until certain technical problems have been satisfactorily resolved,

Considering that these objectives may best be achieved by the conclusion of a Protocol relating to the International Convention for the Prevention of Pollution from Ships, 1973,

Have agreed as follows:

Article 1: General obligations under the Convention

(1) The Parties to the Convention undertake to give effect to the provisions of the present Convention and those Annexes thereto by which they are bound, in order to prevent the pollution of the marine environment by the discharge of harmful substances or effluents containing such substances in contravention of the Convention.

(2) Unless expressly provided otherwise, a reference to the present Convention constitutes at the same time a reference to its Protocols and to the Annexes.

Article I (Protocol): General obligations

1. The Parties to the present Protocol undertake to give effect to the provisions of:
(a) the present Protocol and the Annex hereto which shall constitute an integral part of the present Protocol; and
(b) the International Convention for the Prevention of Pollution from Ships, 1973 (hereinafter referred to as 'the Convention'), subject to the modifications and additions set out in the present Protocol.

2. The provisions of the Convention and the present Protocol shall be read and interpreted together as one single instrument.

3. Every reference to the present Protocol constitutes at the same time a reference to the Annex hereto.

Article 2: Definitions

For the purposes of the present Convention, unless expressly provided otherwise:

(1) 'Regulations' means the Regulations contained in the Annexes to the present Convention.

(2) 'Harmful substance' means any substance which, if introduced into the sea, is liable to create hazards to human health, to harm living resources and marine life, to damage amenities or to interfere with other legitimate uses of the sea, and includes any substance subject to control by the present Convention.

(3) (a) 'Discharge', in relation to harmful substances or effluents containing such substances, means any release howsoever caused from a ship and includes any escape, disposal, spilling, leaking, pumping, emitting or emptying;
(b) 'Discharge' does not include:
i) dumping within the meaning of the Convention on the Prevention of Marine Pollution by Dumping of Wastes and Other Matter, done at London on 13 November 1972; or
ii) release of harmful substances directly arising from the exploration, exploitation and associated off-shore processing of sea-bed mineral resources; or
iii) release of harmful substances for purposes of legitimate scientific research into pollution abatement or control.

(4) 'Ship' means a vessel of any type whatsoever operating in the marine environment and includes hydrofoil boats, air-cushion vehicles, submersibles, floating craft and fixed or floating platforms.

(5) 'Administration' means the Government of the State under whose authority the ship is operating. With respect to a ship entitled to fly a flag of any State, the Administration is the Government of that State. With respect to fixed or floating platforms engaged in exploration and exploitation of the sea-bed and subsoil thereof adjacent to the coast over which the coastal State exercises sovereign rights for the purposes of exploration and exploitation of their natural resources, the Administration is the Government of the coastal State concerned.

(6) 'Incident' means an event involving the actual or probable discharge into the sea of a harmful substance, or effluents containing such a substance.

(7) 'Organization' means the Inter-Governmental Maritime Consultative Organization.

Article 3: Application

(1) The present Convention shall apply to:
(a) ships entitled to fly the flag of a Party to the Convention; and
(b) ships not entitled to fly the flag of a party but which operate under the authority of a Party.

(2) Nothing in the present Article shall be construed as derogating from or extending the sovereign rights of the Parties under international law over the sea-bed and subsoil thereof adjacent to their coasts for the purposes of exploration and exploitation of their natural resources.

(3) The present Convention shall not apply to any warship, naval auxiliary or other ship owned or operated by a State and used, for the time being only on government non-commercial service. However, each Party shall ensure by the adoption of appropriate measures not impairing the operations or operational capabilities of such ships owned or operated by it, that such ships act in a manner consistent, so far as is reasonable and practicable, with the present Convention.

Article 4: Violation

(1) Any violation of the requirements of the present Convention shall be prohibited and sanctions shall be established therefor under the law of the Administration of the ship concerned wherever the violation occurs. If the Administration is informed of such a violation and is satisfied that sufficient evidence is available to enable proceedings to be brought in respect of the alleged violation, it shall cause such proceedings to be taken as soon as possible, in accordance with its law.

(2) Any violation of the requirements of the present Convention within the jurisdiction of any Party to the Convention shall be prohibited and sanctions shall be established therefor under the law of that Party. Whenever such a violation occurs, that Party shall either:
(a) cause proceedings to be taken in accordance with its law; or

(b) furnish to the Administration of the ship such information and evidence as may be in its possession that a violation has occurred.

(3) Where information or evidence with respect to any violation of the present Convention by a ship is furnished to the Administration of that ship, the Administration shall promptly inform the Party which has furnished the information or evidence and the Organization, of the action taken.

(4) The penalties specified under the law of a Party pursuant to the present Article shall be adequate in severity to discourage violations of the present Convention and shall be equally severe irrespective of where the violations occur.

Article 5: Certificates and special rules on inspection of ships

(1) Subject to the provisions of paragraph (2) of the present Article a certificate issued under the authority of a Party to the Convention in accordance with the provisions of the Regulations shall be accepted by the other Parties and regarded for all purposes covered by the present Convention as having the same validity as a certificate issued by them.

(2) A ship required to hold a certificate in accordance with the provisions of the Regulations is subject, while in the ports or off-shore terminals under the jurisdiction of a Party, to inspection by officers duly authorized by that Party. Any such inspection shall be limited to verifying that there is on board a valid certificate, unless there are clear grounds for believing that the condition of the ship or its equipment does not correspond substantially with the particulars of that certificate. In that case, or if the ship does not carry a valid certificate the Party carrying out the inspection shall take such steps as will ensure that the ship shall not sail until it can proceed to sea without presenting an unreasonable threat of harm to the marine environment. That Party may, however, grant such a ship permission to leave the port or off-shore terminal for the purpose of proceeding to the nearest appropriate repair yard available.

(3) If a Party denies a foreign ship entry to the ports or off-shore terminals under its jurisdiction or takes any action against such a ship for the reasons that the ship does not comply with the provisions of the present Convention, the Party shall immediately inform the consul or diplomatic representative of the Party whose flag the ship is entitled to fly, or if this is not possible, the Administration of the ship concerned. Before denying entry or taking such action the Party may request consultation with the Administration of the ship concerned. Information shall also be given to the Administration when a ship does not carry a valid certificate in accordance with the provisions of the Regulations.

(4) With respect to the ships of non-Parties to the Convention, Parties shall apply the requirements of the present Convention as may be necessary to ensure that no more favourable treatment is given to such ships.

Article 6: Detection of violations and enforcement of the Convention

(1) Parties to the Convention shall co-operate in the detection of violations and the enforcement of the provisions of the present Convention, using all appropriate and practicable measures of detection and environmental monitoring, adequate procedures for reporting and accumulation of evidence.

(2) A ship to which the present Convention applies may, in any port or off-shore terminal of a Party, be subject to inspection by officers appointed or authorized by that Party for the purpose of verifying whether the ship has discharged any harmful substances in violation of the provisions of the Regulations. If an inspection indicates a violation of the Convention, a report shall be forwarded to the Administration for any appropriate action.

(3) Any Party shall furnish to the Administration evidence, if any, that the ship has discharged harmful substances or effluents containing such substances in violation of the provisions of the Regulations. If it is practicable to do so, the competent authority of the former Party shall notify the Master of the ship of the alleged violation.

(4) Upon receiving such evidence, the Administration so informed shall investigate the matter, and may request the other Party to furnish further or better evidence of the alleged contravention. If the Administration is satisfied that sufficient evidence is available to enable proceedings to be brought in respect of the alleged violation, it shall cause such proceedings to be taken in accordance with its law as soon as possible. The Administration shall promptly inform the Party which has reported the alleged violation, as well as the Organization, of the action taken.

(5) A Party may also inspect a ship to which the present Convention applies when it enters the ports or off-shore terminals under its jurisdiction, if a request for an investigation is received from any Party together with sufficient evidence that the ship has discharged harmful substances or effluents containing such substances in any place. The report of such investigation shall be sent to the Party requesting it and to the Administration so that the appropriate action may be taken under the present Convention.

Article 7: Undue delay to ships

(1) All possible efforts shall be made to avoid a ship being unduly detained or delayed under Article 4, 5 or 6 of the present Convention.

(2) When a ship is unduly detained or delayed under Article 4, 5 or 6 of the present Convention, it shall be entitled to compensation for any loss or damage suffered.

Article 8: Reports on incidents involving harmful substances

(1) A report of an incident shall be made without delay to the fullest extent possible in accordance with the provisions of Protocol I to the present Convention.

(2) Each Party to the Convention shall:

(a) make all arrangements necessary for an appropriate officer or agency to receive and process all reports on incidents; and

(b) notify the Organization with complete details of such arrangements for circulation to other Parties and Member States of the Organization.

(3) Whenever a Party receives a report under the provisions of the present Article, that Party shall relay the report without delay to:

(a) the Administration of the ship involved; and

(b) any other State which may be affected.

(4) Each Party to the Convention undertakes to issue instructions to its maritime inspection vessels and aircraft and to other appropriate services, to report to its authorities any incident referred to in Protocol I to the present Convention. That Party shall, if it considers it appropriate, report accordingly to the Organization and to any other party concerned.

Article 9: Other treaties and interpretation

(1) Upon its entry into force, the present Convention supersedes the International Convention for the Prevention of Pollution of the Sea by Oil, 1954, as amended, as between Parties to that Convention.

(2) Nothing in the present Convention shall prejudice the codification and development of the law of the sea by the United Nations Conference on the Law of the Sea convened pursuant to Resolution 2750 C (XXV) of the General Assembly of the United Nations nor the present or future claims and legal views of any State concerning the law of the sea and the nature and extent of coastal and flag State jurisdiction.

(3) The term 'jurisdiction' in the present Convention shall be construed in the light of international law in force at the time of application or interpretation of the present Convention.

Article 10: Settlement of disputes

Any dispute between two or more Parties to the Convention concerning the interpretation or application of the present Convention shall, if settlement by negotiation between the Parties involved has not been possible, and if these Parties do not otherwise agree, be submitted upon request of any of them to arbitration as set out in Protocol II to the present Convention.

Article 11: Communication of information

(1) The Parties to the Convention undertake to communicate to the Organization:

(a) the text of laws, orders, decrees and regulations and other instruments which have been promulgated on the various matters within the scope of the present Convention;

(b) a list of nominated surveyors or recognized organizations which are authorized to act on their behalf in the administration of matters relating to the design, construction, equipment and operation of ships carrying harmful substances in accordance with the provisions of the Regulations for circulation to the Parties for information of their officers. The Administration shall therefore notify the

Organization of the specific responsibilities and conditions of the authority delegated to nominated surveyors or recognized organizations.

(c) a sufficient number of specimens of their certificates issued under the provisions of the Regulations;

(d) a list of reception facilities including their location, capacity and available facilities and other characteristics;

(e) official reports or summaries of official reports in so far as they show the results of the application of the present Convention; and

(f) an annual statistical report, in a form standardized by the Organization, of penalties actually imposed for infringement of the present Convention.

(2) The Organization shall notify Parties of the receipt of any communications under the present Article and circulate to all Parties any information communicated to it under sub-paragraphs (1)(b) to (f) of the present Article.

Article 12: Casualties to ships

(1) Each Administration undertakes to conduct an investigation of any casualty occurring to any of its ships subject to the provisions of the Regulations if such casualty has produced a major deleterious effect upon the marine environment.

(2) Each Party to the Convention undertakes to supply the Organization with information concerning the findings of such investigation, when it judges that such information may assist in determining what changes in the present Convention might be desirable.

[Article 13 not reproduced]

Article 14: Optional Annexes

(1) A State may at the time of signing, ratifying, accepting, approving or acceding to the present Convention declare that it does not accept any one or all of Annexes III, IV and V (hereinafter referred to as 'Optional Annexes') of the present Convention. Subject to the above, Parties to the Convention shall be bound by any Annex in its entirety.

(2) A State which has declared that it is not bound by an Optional Annex may at any time accept such Annex by depositing with the Organization an instrument of the kind referred to in Article 13(2) of the present Convention.

(3) A State which makes a declaration under paragraph (1) of the present Article in respect of an Optional Annex and which has not subsequently accepted that Annex in accordance with paragraph (2) of the present Article shall not be under any obligation nor entitled to claim any privileges under the present Convention in respect of matters related to such Annex and all references to Parties in the present Convention shall not include that State in so far as matters related to such Annex are concerned.

(4) The Organization shall inform the States which have signed or acceded to the present Convention of any declaration under the present Article as well as the

receipt of any instrument deposited in accordance with the provisions of paragraph (2) of the present Article.

[Articles 15-20 not reproduced]

Annex I: Prevention of pollution by oil; Annex II: Control of pollution by noxious liquid substances, Annex III: Prevention of pollution by hazardous substances carried in packaged form; Annex IV: Prevention of pollution by sewage from ships; Annex V: Prevention of pollution by garbage from ships; Annex VI: Prevention of pollution by air pollution from ships [not reproduced]

Protocol I: Provisions concerning reports on incidents involving harmful substances; Protocol II: Arbitration [not reproduced]

Protocol to the Convention on the Prevention of Marine Pollution by Dumping of Wastes and other Matter, 1972

Adopted on 17 November 1996 at London. Not in force (19 ratifications). Source: Doc. LC/SM.1/6. Further information: Office for the London Convention 1972, IMO, London, UK, http://www.londonconvention.org/

The Contracting Parties to this Protocol,

Stressing the need to protect the marine environment and to promote the sustainable use and conservation of marine resources,

Noting in this regard the achievements within the framework of the Convention on the Prevention of Marine Pollution by Dumping of Wastes and Other Matter, 1972 and especially the evolution towards approaches based on precaution and prevention,

Noting further the contribution in this regard by complementary regional and national instruments which aim to protect the marine environment and which take account of specific circumstances and needs of those regions and States,

Reaffirming the value of a global approach to these matters and in particular the importance of continuing co-operation and collaboration between Contracting Parties in implementing the Convention and the Protocol,

Recognizing that it may be desirable to adopt, on a national or regional level, more stringent measures with respect to prevention and elimination of pollution of the marine environment from dumping at sea than are provided for in international conventions or other types of agreements with a global scope,

Taking into account relevant international agreements and actions, especially the United Nations Convention on the Law of the Sea, 1982, the Rio Declaration on Environment and Development and Agenda 21,

Recognizing also the interests and capacities of developing States and in particular small island developing States,

Being convinced that further international action to prevent, reduce and where practicable eliminate pollution of the sea caused by dumping can and must be taken without delay to protect and preserve the marine environment and to manage human activities in such a manner that the marine ecosystem will continue to sustain the legitimate uses of the sea and will continue to meet the needs of present and future generations,

Have agreed as follows:

Article 1: Definitions

For the purposes of this Protocol:

1 'Convention' means the Convention on the Prevention of Marine Pollution by Dumping of Wastes and Other Matter, 1972, as amended.

2 'Organization' means the International Maritime Organization.

3 'Secretary-General' means the Secretary-General of the Organization.

4.1 'Dumping' means:

.1 any deliberate disposal into the sea of wastes or other matter from vessels, aircraft, platforms or other man-made structures at sea;

.2 any deliberate disposal into the sea of vessels, aircraft, platforms or other man-made structures at sea;

.3 any storage of wastes or other matter in the seabed and the subsoil thereof from vessels, aircraft, platforms or other man-made structures at sea; and

.4 any abandonment or toppling at site of platforms or other man-made structures at sea, for the sole purpose of deliberate disposal.

4.2 'Dumping' does not include:

.1 the disposal into the sea of wastes or other matter incidental to, or derived from the normal operations of vessels, aircraft, platforms or other man-made structures at sea and their equipment, other than wastes or other matter transported by or to vessels, aircraft, platforms or other man-made structures at sea, operating for the purpose of disposal of such matter or derived from the treatment of such wastes or other matter on such vessels, aircraft, platforms or other man-made structures;

.2 placement of matter for a purpose other than the mere disposal thereof, provided that such placement is not contrary to the aims of this Protocol; and

.3 notwithstanding paragraph 4.1.4, abandonment in the sea of matter (e.g., cables, pipelines and marine research devices) placed for a purpose other than the mere disposal thereof.

.3 The disposal or storage of wastes or other matter directly arising from, or related to the exploration, exploitation and associated off-shore processing of seabed mineral resources is not covered by the provisions of this Protocol.

5.1 'Incineration at sea' means the combustion on board a vessel, platform or other man-made structure at sea of wastes or other matter for the purpose of their deliberate disposal by thermal destruction.

.2 'Incineration at sea' does not include the incineration of wastes or other matter on board a vessel, platform, or other man-made structure at sea if such wastes or other matter were generated during the normal operation of that vessel, platform or other man-made structure at sea.

6 'Vessels and aircraft' means waterborne or airborne craft of any type whatsoever. This expression includes air-cushioned craft and floating craft, whether self-propelled or not.

7 'Sea' means all marine waters other than the internal waters of States, as well as the seabed and the subsoil thereof; it does not include sub-seabed repositories accessed only from land.

8 'Wastes or other matter' means material and substance of any kind, form or description.

9 'Permit' means permission granted in advance and in accordance with relevant measures adopted pursuant to article 4.1.2 or 8.2.

10 'Pollution' means the introduction, directly or indirectly, by human activity, of wastes or other matter into the sea which results or is likely to result in such deleterious effects as harm to living resources and marine ecosystems, hazards to human health, hindrance to marine activities, including fishing and other legitimate uses of the sea, impairment of quality for use of sea water and reduction of amenities.

Article 2: Objectives

Contracting Parties shall individually and collectively protect and preserve the marine environment from all sources of pollution and take effective measures, according to their scientific, technical and economic capabilities, to prevent, reduce and where practicable eliminate pollution caused by dumping or incineration at sea of wastes or other matter. Where appropriate, they shall harmonize their policies in this regard.

Article 3: General obligations

1 In implementing this Protocol, Contracting Parties shall apply a precautionary approach to environmental protection from dumping of wastes or other matter whereby appropriate preventative measures are taken when there is reason to believe that wastes or other matter introduced into the marine environment are likely to cause harm even when there is no conclusive evidence to prove a causal relation between inputs and their effects.

2 Taking into account the approach that the polluter should, in principle, bear the cost of pollution, each Contracting Party shall endeavour to promote practices whereby those it has authorized to engage in dumping or incineration at sea bear

the cost of meeting the pollution prevention and control requirements for the authorized activities, having due regard to the public interest.

3 In implementing the provisions of this Protocol, Contracting Parties shall act so as not to transfer, directly or indirectly, damage or likelihood of damage from one part of the environment to another or transform one type of pollution into another.

4 No provision of this Protocol shall be interpreted as preventing Contracting Parties from taking, individually or jointly, more stringent measures in accordance with international law with respect to the prevention, reduction and where practicable elimination of pollution.

Article 4: Dumping of wastes or other matter

1.1 Contracting Parties shall prohibit the dumping of any wastes or other matter with the exception of those listed in Annex 1.

.2 The dumping of wastes or other matter listed in Annex 1 shall require a permit. Contracting Parties shall adopt administrative or legislative measures to ensure that issuance of permits and permit conditions comply with provisions of Annex 2. Particular attention shall be paid to opportunities to avoid dumping in favour of environmentally preferable alternatives.

2 No provision of this Protocol shall be interpreted as preventing a Contracting Party from prohibiting, insofar as that Contracting Party is concerned, the dumping of wastes or other matter mentioned in Annex 1. That Contracting Party shall notify the Organization of such measures.

Article 5: Incineration at sea

Contracting Parties shall prohibit incineration at sea of wastes or other matter.

Article 6: Export of wastes or other matter

Contracting Parties shall not allow the export of wastes or other matter to other countries for dumping or incineration at sea.

Article 7: Internal waters

1 Notwithstanding any other provision of this Protocol, this Protocol shall relate to internal waters only to the extent provided for in paragraphs 2 and 3.

2 Each Contracting Party shall at its discretion either apply the provisions of this Protocol or adopt other effective permitting and regulatory measures to control the deliberate disposal of wastes or other matter in marine internal waters where such disposal would be 'dumping' or 'incineration at sea' within the meaning of article 1, if conducted at sea.

3 Each Contracting Party should provide the Organization with information on legislation and institutional mechanisms regarding implementation, compliance and enforcement in marine internal waters. Contracting Parties should also use their best efforts to provide on a voluntary basis summary reports on the type and nature of the materials dumped in marine internal waters.

Article 8: Exceptions

1 The provisions of articles 4.1 and 5 shall not apply when it is necessary to secure the safety of human life or of vessels, aircraft, platforms or other man-made structures at sea in cases of force majeure caused by stress of weather, or in any case which constitutes a danger to human life or a real threat to vessels, aircraft, platforms or other man-made structures at sea, if dumping or incineration at sea appears to be the only way of averting the threat and if there is every probability that the damage consequent upon such dumping or incineration at sea will be less than would otherwise occur. Such dumping or incineration at sea shall be conducted so as to minimize the likelihood of damage to human or marine life and shall be reported forthwith to the Organization.

2 A Contracting Party may issue a permit as an exception to articles 4.1 and 5, in emergencies posing an unacceptable threat to human health, safety, or the marine environment and admitting of no other feasible solution. Before doing so the Contracting Party shall consult any other country or countries that are likely to be affected and the Organization which, after consulting other Contracting Parties, and competent international organizations as appropriate, shall, in accordance with article 18.6 promptly recommend to the Contracting Party the most appropriate procedures to adopt. The Contracting Party shall follow these recommendations to the maximum extent feasible consistent with the time within which action must be taken and with the general obligation to avoid damage to the marine environment and shall inform the Organization of the action it takes. The Contracting Parties pledge themselves to assist one another in such situations.

3 Any Contracting Party may waive its rights under paragraph 2 at the time of, or subsequent to ratification of, or accession to this Protocol.

Article 9: Issuance of permits and reporting

1 Each Contracting Party shall designate an appropriate authority or authorities to:

.1 issue permits in accordance with this Protocol;

.2 keep records of the nature and quantities of all wastes or other matter for which dumping permits have been issued and where practicable the quantities actually dumped and the location, time and method of dumping; and

.3 monitor individually, or in collaboration with other Contracting Parties and competent international organizations, the condition of the sea for the purposes of this Protocol.

2 The appropriate authority or authorities of a Contracting Party shall issue permits in accordance with this Protocol in respect of wastes or other matter intended for dumping or, as provided for in article 8.2, incineration at sea:

.1 loaded in its territory; and

.2 loaded onto a vessel or aircraft registered in its territory or flying its flag, when the loading occurs in the territory of a State not a Contracting Party to this Protocol.

3 In issuing permits, the appropriate authority or authorities shall comply with the requirements of article 4, together with such additional criteria, measures and requirements as they may consider relevant.

4 Each Contracting Party, directly or through a secretariat established under a regional agreement, shall report to the Organization and where appropriate to other Contracting Parties:

.1 the information specified in paragraphs 1.2 and 1.3;

.2 the administrative and legislative measures taken to implement the provisions of this Protocol, including a summary of enforcement measures; and

.3 the effectiveness of the measures referred to in paragraph 4.2 and any problems encountered in their application.

The information referred to in paragraphs 1.2 and 1.3 shall be submitted on an annual basis. The information referred to in paragraphs 4.2 and 4.3 shall be submitted on a regular basis.

5 Reports submitted under paragraphs 4.2 and 4.3 shall be evaluated by an appropriate subsidiary body as determined by the Meeting of Contracting Parties. This body will report its conclusions to an appropriate Meeting or Special Meeting of Contracting Parties.

Article 10: Application and enforcement

1 Each Contracting Party shall apply the measures required to implement this Protocol to all:

.1 vessels and aircraft registered in its territory or flying its flag;

.2 vessels and aircraft loading in its territory the wastes or other matter which are to be dumped or incinerated at sea; and

.3 vessels, aircraft and platforms or other man-made structures believed to be engaged in dumping or incineration at sea in areas within which it is entitled to exercise jurisdiction in accordance with international law.

2 Each Contracting Party shall take appropriate measures in accordance with international law to prevent and if necessary punish acts contrary to the provisions of this Protocol.

3 Contracting Parties agree to co-operate in the development of procedures for the effective application of this Protocol in areas beyond the jurisdiction of any State, including procedures for the reporting of vessels and aircraft observed dumping or incinerating at sea in contravention of this Protocol.

4 This Protocol shall not apply to those vessels and aircraft entitled to sovereign immunity under international law. However, each Contracting Party shall ensure by the adoption of appropriate measures that such vessels and aircraft owned or operated by it act in a manner consistent with the object and purpose of this Protocol and shall inform the Organization accordingly.

5 A State may, at the time it expresses its consent to be bound by this Protocol, or at any time thereafter, declare that it shall apply the provisions of this Protocol to

its vessels and aircraft referred to in paragraph 4, recognising that only that State may enforce those provisions against such vessels and aircraft.

Article 11: Compliance procedures

1 No later than two years after the entry into force of this Protocol, the Meeting of Contracting Parties shall establish those procedures and mechanisms necessary to assess and promote compliance with this Protocol. Such procedures and mechanisms shall be developed with a view to allowing for the full and open exchange of information, in a constructive manner.

2 After full consideration of any information submitted pursuant to this Protocol and any recommendations made through procedures or mechanisms established under paragraph 1, the Meeting of Contracting Parties may offer advice, assistance or co-operation to Contracting Parties and non-Contracting Parties.

Article 12: Regional co-operation

In order to further the objectives of this Protocol, Contracting Parties with common interests to protect the marine environment in a given geographical area shall endeavour, taking into account characteristic regional features, to enhance regional co-operation including the conclusion of regional agreements consistent with this Protocol for the prevention, reduction and where practicable elimination of pollution caused by dumping or incineration at sea of wastes or other matter. Contracting Parties shall seek to co-operate with the parties to regional agreements in order to develop harmonized procedures to be followed by Contracting Parties to the different conventions concerned.

Article 13: Technical co-operation and assistance

1 Contracting Parties shall, through collaboration within the Organization and in co-ordination with other competent international organizations, promote bilateral and multilateral support for the prevention, reduction and where practicable elimination of pollution caused by dumping as provided for in this Protocol to those Contracting Parties that request it for:

.1 training of scientific and technical personnel for research, monitoring and enforcement, including as appropriate the supply of necessary equipment and facilities, with a view to strengthening national capabilities;

.2 advice on implementation of this Protocol;

.3 information and technical co-operation relating to waste minimization and clean production processes;

.4 information and technical co-operation relating to the disposal and treatment of waste and other measures to prevent, reduce and where practicable eliminate pollution caused by dumping; and

.5 access to and transfer of environmentally sound technologies and corresponding know-how, in particular to developing countries and countries in transition to market economies, on favourable terms, including on concessional and preferential terms, as mutually agreed, taking into account the need to protect intellectual property rights as well as the special needs of developing countries and countries in transition to market economies.

2 The Organization shall perform the following functions:

.1 forward requests from Contracting Parties for technical co-operation to other Contracting Parties, taking into account such factors as technical capabilities;

.2 co-ordinate requests for assistance with other competent international organizations, as appropriate; and

.3 subject to the availability of adequate resources, assist developing countries and those in transition to market economies, which have declared their intention to become Contracting Parties to this Protocol, to examine the means necessary to achieve full implementation.

Article 14: Scientific and technical research

1 Contracting Parties shall take appropriate measures to promote and facilitate scientific and technical research on the prevention, reduction and where practicable elimination of pollution by dumping and other sources of marine pollution relevant to this Protocol. In particular, such research should include observation, measurement, evaluation and analysis of pollution by scientific methods.

2 Contracting Parties shall, to achieve the objectives of this Protocol, promote the availability of relevant information to other Contracting Parties who request it on:

.1 scientific and technical activities and measures undertaken in accordance with this Protocol;

.2 marine scientific and technological programmes and their objectives; and

.3 the impacts observed from the monitoring and assessment conducted pursuant to article 9.1.3.

Article 15: Responsibility and liability

In accordance with the principles of international law regarding State responsibility for damage to the environment of other States or to any other area of the environment, the Contracting Parties undertake to develop procedures regarding liability arising from the dumping or incineration at sea of wastes or other matter.

Article 16: Settlement of disputes

1 Any disputes regarding the interpretation or application of this Protocol shall be resolved in the first instance through negotiation, mediation or conciliation, or other peaceful means chosen by parties to the dispute.

2 If no resolution is possible within twelve months after one Contracting Party has notified another that a dispute exists between them, the dispute shall be settled, at the request of a party to the dispute, by means of the Arbitral Procedure set forth in Annex 3, unless the parties to the dispute agree to use one of the procedures listed in paragraph 1 of Article 287 of the 1982 United Nations Convention on the Law of the Sea. The parties to the dispute may so agree, whether or not they are also States Parties to the 1982 United Nations Convention on the Law of the Sea.

3 In the event an agreement to use one of the procedures listed in paragraph 1 of Article 287 of the 1982 United Nations Convention on the Law of the Sea is reached, the provisions set forth in Part XV of that Convention that are related to the chosen procedure would also apply, *mutatis mutandis*.

4 The twelve month period referred to in paragraph 2 may be extended for another twelve months by mutual consent of the parties concerned.

5 Notwithstanding paragraph 2, any State may, at the time it expresses its consent to be bound by this Protocol, notify the Secretary-General that, when it is a party to a dispute about the interpretation or application of article 3.1 or 3.2, its consent will be required before the dispute may be settled by means of the Arbitral Procedure set forth in Annex 3.

Article 17: International co-operation

Contracting Parties shall promote the objectives of this Protocol within the competent international organizations.

[Articles 18-29 not reproduced]

Annex 1: Wastes or other matter that may be considered for dumping; Annex 2: Assessment of wastes or other matter that may be considered for dumping; Annex 3: Arbitral procedure [not reproduced]

Marine resources

United Nations Convention on the Law of the Sea, Part V: Exclusive Economic Zone; Part VII: High seas; Part XI: The Area

Adopted on 10 December 1982 at Montego Bay. Entered into force on 16 November 1994. Source: 1833 *UNTS* 3. Number of parties: 145. Further information: Division for Ocean Affairs and the Law of the Sea, UN, New York, USA, http://www.un.org/Depts/los

Part V: Exclusive economic zone

Article 55: Specific legal regime of the exclusive economic zone

The exclusive economic zone is an area beyond and adjacent to the territorial sea, subject to the specific legal regime established in this Part, under which the rights and jurisdiction of the coastal State and the rights and freedoms of other States are governed by the relevant provisions of this Convention.

Article 56: Rights, jurisdiction and duties of the coastal State in the exclusive economic zone

1. In the exclusive economic zone, the coastal State has:

(a) sovereign rights for the purpose of exploring and exploiting, conserving and managing the natural resources, whether living or non-living, of the waters superjacent to the sea-bed and of the sea-bed and its subsoil, and with regard to other activities for the economic exploitation and exploration of the zone, such as the production of energy from the water, currents and winds;

(b) jurisdiction as provided for in the relevant provisions of this Convention with regard to:

i) the establishment and use of artificial islands, installations and structures;

ii) marine scientific research;

iii) the protection and preservation of the marine environment;

(c) other rights and duties provided for in this Convention.

2. In exercising its rights and performing its duties under this Convention in the exclusive economic zone, the coastal State shall have due regard to the rights and duties of other States and shall act in a manner compatible with the provisions of this Convention.

3. The rights set out in this article with respect to the seabed and subsoil shall be exercised in accordance with Part VI.

Article 57: Breadth of the exclusive economic zone

The exclusive economic zone shall not extend beyond 200 nautical miles from the baselines from which the breadth of the territorial sea is measured.

Article 58: Rights and duties of other States in the exclusive economic zone

1. In the exclusive economic zone, all States, whether coastal or land-locked, enjoy, subject to the relevant provisions of this Convention, the freedoms referred to in article 87 of navigation and overflight and of the laying of submarine cables and pipelines, and other internationally lawful uses of the sea related to these freedoms, such as those associated with the operation of ships, aircraft and submarine cables and pipelines, and compatible with the other provisions of this Convention.

2. Articles 88 to 115 and other pertinent rules of international law apply to the exclusive economic zone in so far as they are not incompatible with this Part.

3. In exercising their rights and performing their duties under this Convention in the exclusive economic zone, States shall have due regard to the rights and duties of the coastal State and shall comply with the laws and regulations adopted by the coastal State in accordance with the provisions of this Convention and other rules of international law in so far as they are not incompatible with this Part.

Article 59: Basis for the resolution of conflicts regarding the attribution of rights and jurisdiction in the exclusive economic zone

In cases where this Convention does not attribute rights or jurisdiction to the coastal State or to other States within the exclusive economic zone, and a conflict arises between the interests of the coastal State and any other State or States, the conflict should be resolved on the basis of equity and in the light of all the relevant circumstances, taking into account the respective importance of the interests involved to the parties as well as to the international community as a whole.

Article 60: Artificial islands, installations and structures in the exclusive economic zone

1. In the exclusive economic zone, the coastal State shall have the exclusive right to construct and to authorize and regulate the construction, operation and use of:
(a) artificial islands;
(b) installations and structures for the purposes provided for in article 56 and other economic purposes;
(c) installations and structures which may interfere with the exercise of the rights of the coastal State in the zone.

2. The coastal State shall have exclusive jurisdiction over such artificial islands, installations and structures, including jurisdiction with regard to customs, fiscal, health, safety and immigration laws and regulations.

3. Due notice must be given of the construction of such artificial islands, installations or structures, and permanent means for giving warning of their presence must be maintained. Any installations or structures which are abandoned or disused shall be removed to ensure safety of navigation, taking into account any generally accepted international standards established in this regard by the competent international organization. Such removal shall also have due regard to fishing, the protection of the marine environment and the rights and duties of other States. Appropriate publicity shall be given to the depth, position and dimensions of any installations or structures not entirely removed.

4. The coastal State may, where necessary, establish reasonable safety zones around such artificial islands, installations and structures in which it may take appropriate measures to ensure the safety both of navigation and of the artificial islands, installations and structures.

5. The breadth of the safety zones shall be determined by the coastal State, taking into account applicable international standards. Such zones shall be designed to ensure that they are reasonably related to the nature and function of the artificial islands, installations or structures, and shall not exceed a distance of 500 metres around them, measured from each point of their outer edge, except as authorized by generally accepted international standards or as recommended by the competent international organization. Due notice shall be given of the extent of safety zones.

6. All ships must respect these safety zones and shall comply with generally accepted international standards regarding navigation in the vicinity of artificial islands, installations, structures and safety zones.

7. Artificial islands, installations and structures and the safety zones around them may not be established where interference may be caused to the use of recognized sea lanes essential to international navigation.

8. Artificial islands, installations and structures do not possess the status of islands. They have no territorial sea of their own, and their presence does not affect the delimitation of the territorial sea, the exclusive economic zone or the continental shelf.

Article 61: Conservation of the living resources

1. The coastal State shall determine the allowable catch of the living resources in its exclusive economic zone.

2. The coastal State, taking into account the best scientific evidence available to it, shall ensure through proper conservation and management measures that the maintenance of the living resources in the exclusive economic zone is not endangered by over-exploitation. As appropriate, the coastal State and competent international organizations, whether subregional, regional or global, shall co-operate to this end.

3. Such measures shall also be designed to maintain or restore populations of harvested species at levels which can produce the maximum sustainable yield, as qualified by relevant environmental and economic factors, including the economic needs of coastal fishing communities and the special requirements of developing States, and taking into account fishing patterns, the interdependence of stocks and any generally recommended international minimum standards, whether subregional, regional or global.

4. In taking such measures the coastal State shall take into consideration the effects on species associated with or dependent upon harvested species with a view to maintaining or restoring populations of such associated or dependent species above levels at which their reproduction may become seriously threatened.

5. Available scientific information, catch and fishing effort statistics, and other data relevant to the conservation of fish stocks shall be contributed and exchanged on a regular basis through competent international organizations, whether subregional, regional or global, where appropriate and with participation by all States concerned, including States whose nationals are allowed to fish in the exclusive economic zone.

Article 62: Utilization of the living resources

1. The coastal State shall promote the objective of optimum utilization of the living resources in the exclusive economic zone without prejudice to article 61.

2. The coastal State shall determine its capacity to harvest the living resources of the exclusive economic zone. Where the coastal State does not have the capacity to

harvest the entire allowable catch, it shall, through agreements or other arrangements and pursuant to the terms, conditions, laws and regulations referred to in paragraph 4, give other States access to the surplus of the allowable catch, having particular regard to the provisions of articles 69 and 70, especially in relation to the developing States mentioned therein.

3. In giving access to other States to its exclusive economic zone under this article, the coastal State shall take into account all relevant factors, including, *inter alia*, the significance of the living resources of the area to the economy of the coastal State concerned and its other national interests, the provisions of articles 69 and 70, the requirements of developing States in the subregion or region in harvesting part of the surplus and the need to minimize economic dislocation in States whose nationals have habitually fished in the zone or which have made substantial efforts in research and identification of stocks.

4. Nationals of other States fishing in the exclusive economic zone shall comply with the conservation measures and with the other terms and conditions established in the laws and regulations of the coastal State. These laws and regulations shall be consistent with this Convention and may relate, *inter alia*, to the following:

(a) licensing of fishermen, fishing vessels and equipment, including payment of fees and other forms of remuneration, which, in the case of developing coastal States, may consist of adequate compensation in the field of financing, equipment and technology relating to the fishing industry;

(b) determining the species which may be caught, and fixing quotas of catch, whether in relation to particular stocks or groups of stocks or catch per vessel over a period of time or to the catch by nationals of any State during a specified period;

(c) regulating seasons and areas of fishing, the types, sizes and amount of gear, and the types, sizes and number of fishing vessels that may be used;

(d) fixing the age and size of fish and other species that may be caught;

(e) specifying information required of fishing vessels, including catch and effort statistics and vessel position reports;

(f) requiring, under the authorization and control of the coastal State, the conduct of specified fisheries research programmes and regulating the conduct of such research, including the sampling of catches, disposition of samples and reporting of associated scientific data;

(g) the placing of observers or trainees on board such vessels by the coastal State;

(h) the landing of all or any part of the catch by such vessels in the ports of the coastal State;

(i) terms and conditions relating to joint ventures or other cooperative arrangements;

(j) requirements for the training of personnel and the transfer of fisheries technology, including enhancement of the coastal State's capability of undertaking fisheries research;

(k) enforcement procedures.

5. Coastal States shall give due notice of conservation and management laws and regulations.

Article 63: Stocks occurring within the exclusive economic zones of two or more coastal States or both within the exclusive economic zone and in an area beyond and adjacent to it

1. Where the same stock or stocks of associated species occur within the exclusive economic zones of two or more coastal States, these States shall seek, either directly or through appropriate subregional or regional organizations, to agree upon the measures necessary to co-ordinate and ensure the conservation and development of such stocks without prejudice to the other provisions of this Part.

2. Where the same stock or stocks of associated species occur both within the exclusive economic zone and in an area beyond and adjacent to the zone, the coastal State and the States fishing for such stocks in the adjacent area shall seek, either directly or through appropriate subregional or regional organizations, to agree upon the measures necessary for the conservation of these stocks in the adjacent area.

Article 64: Highly migratory species

1. The coastal State and other States whose nationals fish in the region for the highly migratory species listed in Annex I shall co-operate directly or through appropriate international organizations with a view to ensuring conservation and promoting the objective of optimum utilization of such species throughout the region, both within and beyond the exclusive economic zone. In regions for which no appropriate international organization exists, the coastal State and other States whose nationals harvest these species in the region shall co-operate to establish such an organization and participate in its work.

2. The provisions of paragraph 1 apply in addition to the other provisions of this Part.

Article 65: Marine mammals

Nothing in this Part restricts the right of a coastal State or the competence of an international organization, as appropriate, to prohibit, limit or regulate the exploitation of marine mammals more strictly than provided for in this Part. States shall co-operate with a view to the conservation of marine mammals and in the case of cetaceans shall in particular work through the appropriate international organizations for their conservation, management and study.

Article 66: Anadromous stocks

1. States in whose rivers anadromous stocks originate shall have the primary interest in and responsibility for such stocks.

2. The State of origin of anadromous stocks shall ensure their conservation by the establishment of appropriate regulatory measures for fishing in all waters landward of the outer limits of its exclusive economic zone and for fishing provided for in paragraph 3(b). The State of origin may, after consultations with the other States

referred to in paragraphs 3 and 4 fishing these stocks, establish total allowable catches for stocks originating in its rivers.

3. (a) Fisheries for anadromous stocks shall be conducted only in waters landward of the outer limits of exclusive economic zones, except in cases where this provision would result in economic dislocation for a State other than the State of origin. With respect to such fishing beyond the outer limits of the exclusive economic zone, States concerned shall maintain consultations with a view to achieving agreement on terms and conditions of such fishing giving due regard to the conservation requirements and the needs of the State of origin in respect of these stocks.

(b) The State of origin shall cooperate in minimizing economic dislocation in such other States fishing these stocks, taking into account the normal catch and the mode of operations of such States, and all the areas in which such fishing has occurred.

(c) States referred to in subparagraph (b), participating by agreement with the State of origin in measures to renew anadromous stocks, particularly by expenditures for that purpose, shall be given special consideration by the State of origin in the harvesting of stocks originating in its rivers.

(d) Enforcement of regulations regarding anadromous stocks beyond the exclusive economic zone shall be by agreement between the State of origin and the other States concerned.

4. In cases where anadromous stocks migrate into or through the waters landward of the outer limits of the exclusive economic zone of a State other than the State of origin, such State shall cooperate with the State of origin with regard to the conservation and management of such stocks.

5. The State of origin of anadromous stocks and other States fishing these stocks shall make arrangements for the implementation of the provisions of this article, where appropriate, through regional organizations.

Article 67: Catadromous species

1. A coastal State in whose waters catadromous species spend the greater part of their life cycle shall have responsibility for the management of these species and shall ensure the ingress and egress of migrating fish.

2. Harvesting of catadromous species shall be conducted only in waters landward of the outer limits of exclusive economic zones. When conducted in exclusive economic zones, harvesting shall be subject to this article and the other provisions of this Convention concerning fishing in these zones.

3. In cases where catadromous fish migrate through the exclusive economic zone of another State, whether as juvenile or maturing fish, the management, including harvesting, of such fish shall be regulated by agreement between the State mentioned in paragraph 1 and the other State concerned. Such agreement shall ensure the rational management of the species and take into account the

responsibilities of the State mentioned in paragraph 1 for the maintenance of these species.

Article 68: Sedentary species

This Part does not apply to sedentary species as defined in article 77, paragraph 4.

Article 69: Right of land-locked States

1. Land-locked States shall have the right to participate, on an equitable basis, in the exploitation of an appropriate part of the surplus of the living resources of the exclusive economic zones of coastal States of the same subregion or region, taking into account the relevant economic and geographical circumstances of all the States concerned and in conformity with the provisions of this article and of articles 61 and 62.

2. The terms and modalities of such participation shall be established by the States concerned through bilateral, subregional or regional agreements taking into account, *inter alia*:

(a) the need to avoid effects detrimental to fishing communities or fishing industries of the coastal State;
(b) the extent to which the land-locked State, in accordance with the provisions of this article, is participating or is entitled to participate under existing bilateral, subregional or regional agreements in the exploitation of living resources of the exclusive economic zones of other coastal States;
(c) the extent to which other land-locked States and geographically disadvantaged States are participating in the exploitation of the living resources of the exclusive economic zone of the coastal State and the consequent need to avoid a particular burden for any single coastal State or a part of it;
(d) the nutritional needs of the populations of the respective States.

3. When the harvesting capacity of a coastal State approaches a point which would enable it to harvest the entire allowable catch of the living resources in its exclusive economic zone, the coastal State and other States concerned shall co-operate in the establishment of equitable arrangements on a bilateral, subregional or regional basis to allow for participation of developing land-locked States of the same subregion or region in the exploitation of the living resources of the exclusive economic zones of coastal States of the subregion or region, as may be appropriate in the circumstances and on terms satisfactory to all parties. In the implementation of this provision the factors mentioned in paragraph 2 shall also be taken into account.

4. Developed land-locked States shall, under the provisions of this article, be entitled to participate in the exploitation of living resources only in the exclusive economic zones of developed coastal States of the same subregion or region having regard to the extent to which the coastal State, in giving access to other States to the living resources of its exclusive economic zone, has taken into account the need to minimize detrimental effects on fishing communities and economic dislocation in States whose nationals have habitually fished in the zone.

5. The above provisions are without prejudice to arrangements agreed upon in subregions or regions where the coastal States may grant to land-locked States of the same subregion or region equal or preferential rights for the exploitation of the living resources in the exclusive economic zones.

Article 70: Right of geographically disadvantaged States

1. Geographically disadvantaged States shall have the right to participate, on an equitable basis, in the exploitation of an appropriate part of the surplus of the living resources of the exclusive economic zones of coastal States of the same subregion or region, taking into account the relevant economic and geographical circumstances of all the States concerned and in conformity with the provisions of this article and of articles 61 and 62.

2. For the purposes of this Part, 'geographically disadvantaged States' means coastal States, including States bordering enclosed or semi-enclosed seas, whose geographical situation makes them dependent upon the exploitation of the living resources of the exclusive economic zones of other States in the subregion or region for adequate supplies of fish for the nutritional purposes of their populations or parts thereof, and coastal States which can claim no exclusive economic zones of their own.

3. The terms and modalities of such participation shall be established by the States concerned through bilateral, subregional or regional agreements taking into account, *inter alia*:

(a) the need to avoid effects detrimental to fishing communities or fishing industries of the coastal State;

(b) the extent to which the geographically disadvantaged State, in accordance with the provisions of this article, is participating or is entitled to participate under existing bilateral, subregional or regional agreements in the exploitation of living resources of the exclusive economic zones of other coastal States;

(c) the extent to which other geographically disadvantaged States and land-locked States are participating in the exploitation of the living resources of the exclusive economic zone of the coastal State and the consequent need to avoid a particular burden for any single coastal State or a part of it;

(d) the nutritional needs of the populations of the respective States.

4. When the harvesting capacity of a coastal State approaches a point which would enable it to harvest the entire allowable catch of the living resources in its exclusive economic zone, the coastal State and other States concerned shall co-operate in the establishment of equitable arrangements on a bilateral, subregional or regional basis to allow for participation of developing geographically disadvantaged States of the same subregion or region in the exploitation of the living resources of the exclusive economic zones of coastal States of the subregion or region, as may be appropriate in the circumstances and on terms satisfactory to all parties. In the implementation of this provision the factors mentioned in paragraph 3 shall also be taken into account.

5. Developed geographically disadvantaged States shall, under the provisions of this article, be entitled to participate in the exploitation of living resources only in the exclusive economic zones of developed coastal States of the same subregion or region having regard to the extent to which the coastal State, in giving access to other States to the living resources of its exclusive economic zone, has taken into account the need to minimize detrimental effects on fishing communities and economic dislocation in States whose nationals have habitually fished in the zone.

6. The above provisions are without prejudice to arrangements agreed upon in subregions or regions where the coastal States may grant to geographically disadvantaged States of the same subregion or region equal or preferential rights for the exploitation of the living resources in the exclusive economic zones.

Article 71: Non-applicability of articles 69 and 70

The provisions of articles 69 and 70 do not apply in the case of a coastal State whose economy is overwhelmingly dependent on the exploitation of the living resources of its exclusive economic zone.

[Articles 72-75 not reproduced]

Part VII: High seas

Section 1: General provisions

Article 86: Application of the provisions of this Part

The provisions of this Part apply to all parts of the sea that are not included in the exclusive economic zone, in the territorial sea or in the internal waters of a State, or in the archipelagic waters of an archipelagic State. This article does not entail any abridgement of the freedoms enjoyed by all States in the exclusive economic zone in accordance with article 58.

Article 87: Freedom of the high seas

1. The high seas are open to all States, whether coastal or land-locked. Freedom of the high seas is exercised under the conditions laid down by this Convention and by other rules of international law. It comprises, *inter alia*, both for coastal and land-locked States:

(a) freedom of navigation;
(b) freedom of overflight;
(c) freedom to lay submarine cables and pipelines, subject to Part VI;
(d) freedom to construct artificial islands and other installations permitted under international law, subject to Part VI;
(e) freedom of fishing, subject to the conditions laid down in section 2;
(f) freedom of scientific research, subject to Parts VI and XIII.

2. These freedoms shall be exercised by all States with due regard for the interests of other States in their exercise of the freedom of the high seas, and also with due regard for the rights under this Convention with respect to activities in the Area.

Article 88: Reservation of the high seas for peaceful purposes

The high seas shall be reserved for peaceful purposes.

Article 89: Invalidity of claims of sovereignty over the high seas

No State may validly purport to subject any part of the high seas to its sovereignty.

[Articles 90-115 not reproduced]

Section 2: Conservation and management of the living resources of the high seas

Article 116: Right to fish on the high seas

All States have the right for their nationals to engage in fishing on the high seas subject to:

(a) their treaty obligations;

(b) the rights and duties as well as the interests of coastal States provided for, *inter alia*, in article 63, paragraph 2, and articles 64 to 67; and

(c) the provisions of this section.

Article 117: Duty of States to adopt with respect to their nationals measures for the conservation of the living resources of the high seas

All States have the duty to take, or to cooperate with other States in taking, such measures for their respective nationals as may be necessary for the conservation of the living resources of the high seas.

Article 118: Co-operation of States in the conservation and management of living resources

States shall co-operate with each other in the conservation and management of living resources in the areas of the high seas. States whose nationals exploit identical living resources, or different living resources in the same area, shall enter into negotiations with a view to taking the measures necessary for the conservation of the living resources concerned. They shall, as appropriate, co-operate to establish subregional or regional fisheries organizations to this end.

Article 119: Conservation of the living resources of the high seas

1. In determining the allowable catch and establishing other conservation measures for the living resources in the high seas, States shall:

(a) take measures which are designed, on the best scientific evidence available to the States concerned, to maintain or restore populations of harvested species at levels which can produce the maximum sustainable yield, as qualified by relevant environmental and economic factors, including the special requirements of developing States, and taking into account fishing patterns, the interdependence of stocks and any generally recommended international minimum standards, whether subregional, regional or global;

(b) take into consideration the effects on species associated with or dependent upon harvested species with a view to maintaining or restoring populations of such associated or dependent species above levels at which their reproduction may become seriously threatened.

2. Available scientific information, catch and fishing effort statistics, and other data relevant to the conservation of fish stocks shall be contributed and exchanged on a regular basis through competent international organizations, whether subregional, regional or global, where appropriate and with participation by all States concerned.

3. States concerned shall ensure that conservation measures and their implementation do not discriminate in form or in fact against the fishermen of any State.

Article 120: Marine mammals

Article 65 also applies to the conservation and management of marine mammals in the high seas.

Part XI: The Area[5]

Section 1: General provisions [not reproduced]

Section 2: Principles governing the Area[6]

Article 136: Common heritage of mankind

The Area and its resources are the common heritage of mankind.

Article 137: Legal status of the Area and its resources

1. No State shall claim or exercise sovereignty or sovereign rights over any part of the Area or its resources, nor shall any State or natural or juridical person appropriate any part thereof. No such claim or exercise of sovereignty or sovereign rights nor such appropriation shall be recognized.

2. All rights in the resources of the Area are vested in mankind as a whole, on whose behalf the Authority shall act. These resources are not subject to alienation. The minerals recovered from the Area, however, may only be alienated in accordance with this Part and the rules, regulations and procedures of the Authority.

3. No State or natural or juridical person shall claim, acquire or exercise rights with respect to the minerals recovered from the Area except in accordance with this Part. Otherwise, no such claim, acquisition or exercise of such rights shall be recognized.

---

5 *Editors' note*: This part should be read in conjunction with the 1994 Agreement relating to the implementation of Part XI of the United Nations Convention on the Law of the Sea of 10 December 1982. *See* United Nations General Assembly Resolution 48/263, Doc. A/RES/48/263, Annex (1994).

6 *Editors' note*: as per Article 1(1)1 of the UNCLOS 'Area' means the sea bed and ocean floor and subsoil thereof, beyond the limits of national jurisdiction.

[Articles 138-139 not reproduced]

Article 140: Benefit of mankind

1. Activities in the Area shall, as specifically provided for in this Part, be carried out for the benefit of mankind as a whole, irrespective of the geographical location of States, whether coastal or land-locked, and taking into particular consideration the interests and needs of developing States and of peoples who have not attained full independence or other self-governing status recognized by the United Nations in accordance with General Assembly resolution 1514 (XV) and other relevant General Assembly resolutions.

2. The Authority shall provide for the equitable sharing of financial and other economic benefits derived from activities in the Area through any appropriate mechanism, on a non-discriminatory basis, in accordance with article 160, paragraph 2(f)(i).

[Articles 141-144 not reproduced]

Article 145: Protection of the marine environment

Necessary measures shall be taken in accordance with this Convention with respect to activities in the Area to ensure effective protection for the marine environment from harmful effects which may arise from such activities. To this end the Authority shall adopt appropriate rules, regulations and procedures for *inter alia*:

(a) the prevention, reduction and control of pollution and other hazards to the marine environment, including the coastline, and of interference with the ecological balance of the marine environment, particular attention being paid to the need for protection from harmful effects of such activities as drilling, dredging, excavation, disposal of waste, construction and operation or maintenance of installations, pipelines and other devices related to such activities;

(b) the protection and conservation of the natural resources of the Area and the prevention of damage to the flora and fauna of the marine environment.

[Articles 146-191 not reproduced]

Agreement for the Implementation of the Provisions of the United Nations Convention on the Law of the Sea of 10 December 1982 Relating to the Conservation and Management of Straddling Fish Stocks and Highly Migratory Fish Stocks [excerpts]

Adopted on 4 August 1995 at New York. Entered into force on 11 December 2001. Source: Doc. A/CONF.164/37. Number of parties: 51. Further information: Division for Ocean Affairs and the Law of the Sea, UN, New York, USA, http://www.un.org/Depts/los

The States Parties to this Agreement,

Recalling the relevant provisions of the United Nations Convention on the Law of the Sea of 10 December 1982,

Determined to ensure the long-term conservation and sustainable use of straddling fish stocks and highly migratory fish stocks,

Resolved to improve cooperation between States to that end,

Calling for more effective enforcement by flag States, port States and coastal States of the conservation and management measures adopted for such stocks,

Seeking to address in particular the problems identified in chapter 17, programme area C, of Agenda 21 adopted by the United Nations Conference on Environment and Development, namely, that the management of high seas fisheries is inadequate in many areas and that some resources are overutilized; noting that there are problems of unregulated fishing, over-capitalization, excessive fleet size, vessel reflagging to escape controls, insufficiently selective gear, unreliable databases and lack of sufficient cooperation between States,

Committing themselves to responsible fisheries,

Conscious of the need to avoid adverse impacts on the marine environment, preserve biodiversity, maintain the integrity of marine ecosystems and minimize the risk of long-term or irreversible effects of fishing operations,

Recognizing the need for specific assistance, including financial, scientific and technological assistance, in order that developing States can participate effectively in the conservation, management and sustainable use of straddling fish stocks and highly migratory fish stocks,

Convinced that an agreement for the implementation of the relevant provisions of the Convention would best serve these purposes and contribute to the maintenance of international peace and security,

Affirming that matters not regulated by the Convention or by this Agreement continue to be governed by the rules and principles of general international law,

Have agreed as follows:

Part I: General provisions

Article 1: Use of terms and scope

1. For the purposes of this Agreement:

(a) 'Convention' means the United Nations Convention on the Law of the Sea of 10 December 1982;

(b) 'conservation and management measures' means measures to conserve and manage one or more species of living marine resources that are adopted and applied consistent with the relevant rules of international law as reflected in the Convention and this Agreement;

(c) 'fish' includes molluscs and crustaceans except those belonging to sedentary species as defined in article 77 of the Convention; and

(d) 'arrangement' means a co-operative mechanism established in accordance with the Convention and this Agreement by two or more States for the purpose, *inter alia*, of establishing conservation and management measures in a subregion or region for one or more straddling fish stocks or highly migratory fish stocks.

2. (a) 'States Parties' means States which have consented to be bound by this Agreement and for which the Agreement is in force.

(b) This Agreement applies *mutatis mutandis*:

i) to any entity referred to in article 305, paragraph 1 (c), (d) and (e), of the Convention and

ii) subject to article 47, to any entity referred to as an 'international organization' in Annex IX, article 1, of the Convention

which becomes a Party to this Agreement, and to that extent 'States Parties' refers to those entities.

3. This Agreement applies *mutatis mutandis* to other fishing entities whose vessels fish on the high seas.

Article 2: Objective

The objective of this Agreement is to ensure the long-term conservation and sustainable use of straddling fish stocks and highly migratory fish stocks through effective implementation of the relevant provisions of the Convention.

Article 3: Application

1. Unless otherwise provided, this Agreement applies to the conservation and management of straddling fish stocks and highly migratory fish stocks beyond areas under national jurisdiction, except that articles 6 and 7 apply also to the conservation and management of such stocks within areas under national jurisdiction, subject to the different legal regimes that apply within areas under national jurisdiction and in areas beyond national jurisdiction as provided for in the Convention.

2. In the exercise of its sovereign rights for the purpose of exploring and exploiting, conserving and managing straddling fish stocks and highly migratory fish stocks within areas under national jurisdiction, the coastal State shall apply *mutatis mutandis* the general principles enumerated in article 5.

3. States shall give due consideration to the respective capacities of developing States to apply articles 5, 6 and 7 within areas under national jurisdiction and their need for assistance as provided for in this Agreement. To this end, Part VII applies *mutatis mutandis* in respect of areas under national jurisdiction.

Article 4: Relationship between this Agreement and the Convention

Nothing in this Agreement shall prejudice the rights, jurisdiction and duties of States under the Convention. This Agreement shall be interpreted and applied in the context of and in a manner consistent with the Convention.

Part II: Conservation and management of straddling fish stocks and highly migratory fish stocks

Article 5: General principles

In order to conserve and manage straddling fish stocks and highly migratory fish stocks, coastal States and States fishing on the high seas shall, in giving effect to their duty to co-operate in accordance with the Convention:

(a) adopt measures to ensure long-term sustainability of straddling fish stocks and highly migratory fish stocks and promote the objective of their optimum utilization;

(b) ensure that such measures are based on the best scientific evidence available and are designed to maintain or restore stocks at levels capable of producing maximum sustainable yield, as qualified by relevant environmental and economic factors, including the special requirements of developing States, and taking into account fishing patterns, the interdependence of stocks and any generally recommended international minimum standards, whether subregional, regional or global;

(c) apply the precautionary approach in accordance with article 6;

(d) assess the impacts of fishing, other human activities and environmental factors on target stocks and species belonging to the same ecosystem or associated with or dependent upon the target stocks;

(e) adopt, where necessary, conservation and management measures for species belonging to the same ecosystem or associated with or dependent upon the target stocks, with a view to maintaining or restoring populations of such species above levels at which their reproduction may become seriously threatened;

(f) minimize pollution, waste, discards, catch by lost or abandoned gear, catch of non-target species, both fish and non-fish species, (hereinafter referred to as non-target species) and impacts on associated or dependent species, in particular endangered species, through measures including, to the extent practicable, the development and use of selective, environmentally safe and cost-effective fishing gear and techniques;

(g) protect biodiversity in the marine environment;

(h) take measures to prevent or eliminate overfishing and excess fishing capacity and to ensure that levels of fishing effort do not exceed those commensurate with the sustainable use of fishery resources;

(i) take into account the interests of artisanal and subsistence fishers;

(j) collect and share, in a timely manner, complete and accurate data concerning fishing activities on, *inter alia*, vessel position, catch of target and non-target species and fishing effort, as set out in Annex I, as well as information from national and international research programmes;

(k) promote and conduct scientific research and develop appropriate technologies in support of fishery conservation and management; and

(l) implement and enforce conservation and management measures through effective monitoring, control and surveillance.

Article 6: Application of the precautionary approach

1. States shall apply the precautionary approach widely to conservation, management and exploitation of straddling fish stocks and highly migratory fish stocks in order to protect the living marine resources and preserve the marine environment.

2. States shall be more cautious when information is uncertain, unreliable or inadequate. The absence of adequate scientific information shall not be used as a reason for postponing or failing to take conservation and management measures.

3. In implementing the precautionary approach, States shall:

(a) improve decision-making for fishery resource conservation and management by obtaining and sharing the best scientific information available and implementing improved techniques for dealing with risk and uncertainty;

(b) apply the guidelines set out in Annex II and determine, on the basis of the best scientific information available, stock-specific reference points and the action to be taken if they are exceeded;

(c) take into account, *inter alia*, uncertainties relating to the size and productivity of the stocks, reference points, stock condition in relation to such reference points, levels and distribution of fishing mortality and the impact of fishing activities on non-target and associated or dependent species, as well as existing and predicted oceanic, environmental and socio-economic conditions; and

(d) develop data collection and research programmes to assess the impact of fishing on non-target and associated or dependent species and their environment, and adopt plans which are necessary to ensure the conservation of such species and to protect habitats of special concern.

4. States shall take measures to ensure that, when reference points are approached, they will not be exceeded. In the event that they are exceeded, States shall, without delay, take the action determined under paragraph 3 (b) to restore the stocks.

5. Where the status of target stocks or non-target or associated or dependent species is of concern, States shall subject such stocks and species to enhanced monitoring in order to review their status and the efficacy of conservation and management measures. They shall revise those measures regularly in the light of new information.

6. For new or exploratory fisheries, States shall adopt as soon as possible cautious conservation and management measures, including, *inter alia*, catch limits and effort limits. Such measures shall remain in force until there are sufficient data to allow assessment of the impact of the fisheries on the long-term sustainability of the stocks, whereupon conservation and management measures based on that assessment shall be implemented. The latter measures shall, if appropriate, allow for the gradual development of the fisheries.

7. If a natural phenomenon has a significant adverse impact on the status of straddling fish stocks or highly migratory fish stocks, States shall adopt conservation and management measures on an emergency basis to ensure that

fishing activity does not exacerbate such adverse impact. States shall also adopt such measures on an emergency basis where fishing activity presents a serious threat to the sustainability of such stocks. Measures taken on an emergency basis shall be temporary and shall be based on the best scientific evidence available.

Article 7: Compatibility of conservation and management measures

1. Without prejudice to the sovereign rights of coastal States for the purpose of exploring and exploiting, conserving and managing the living marine resources within areas under national jurisdiction as provided for in the Convention, and the right of all States for their nationals to engage in fishing on the high seas in accordance with the Convention:

(a) with respect to straddling fish stocks, the relevant coastal States and the States whose nationals fish for such stocks in the adjacent high seas area shall seek, either directly or through the appropriate mechanisms for cooperation provided for in Part III, to agree upon the measures necessary for the conservation of these stocks in the adjacent high seas area;

(b) with respect to highly migratory fish stocks, the relevant coastal States and other States whose nationals fish for such stocks in the region shall cooperate, either directly or through the appropriate mechanisms for cooperation provided for in Part III, with a view to ensuring conservation and promoting the objective of optimum utilization of such stocks throughout the region, both within and beyond the areas under national jurisdiction.

2. Conservation and management measures established for the high seas and those adopted for areas under national jurisdiction shall be compatible in order to ensure conservation and management of the straddling fish stocks and highly migratory fish stocks in their entirety. To this end, coastal States and States fishing on the high seas have a duty to cooperate for the purpose of achieving compatible measures in respect of such stocks. In determining compatible conservation and management measures, States shall:

(a) take into account the conservation and management measures adopted and applied in accordance with article 61 of the Convention in respect of the same stocks by coastal States within areas under national jurisdiction and ensure that measures established in respect of such stocks for the high seas do not undermine the effectiveness of such measures;

(b) take into account previously agreed measures established and applied for the high seas in accordance with the Convention in respect of the same stocks by relevant coastal States and States fishing on the high seas;

(c) take into account previously agreed measures established and applied in accordance with the Convention in respect of the same stocks by a subregional or regional fisheries management organization or arrangement;

(d) take into account the biological unity and other biological characteristics of the stocks and the relationships between the distribution of the stocks, the fisheries and the geographical particularities of the region concerned, including the extent to which the stocks occur and are fished in areas under national jurisdiction;

(e) take into account the respective dependence of the coastal States and the States fishing on the high seas on the stocks concerned; and

(f) ensure that such measures do not result in harmful impact on the living marine resources as a whole.

3. In giving effect to their duty to co-operate, States shall make every effort to agree on compatible conservation and management measures within a reasonable period of time.

4. If no agreement can be reached within a reasonable period of time, any of the States concerned may invoke the procedures for the settlement of disputes provided for in Part VIII.

5. Pending agreement on compatible conservation and management measures, the States concerned, in a spirit of understanding and cooperation, shall make every effort to enter into provisional arrangements of a practical nature. In the event that they are unable to agree on such arrangements, any of the States concerned may, for the purpose of obtaining provisional measures, submit the dispute to a court or tribunal in accordance with the procedures for the settlement of disputes provided for in Part VIII.

6. Provisional arrangements or measures entered into or prescribed pursuant to paragraph 5 shall take into account the provisions of this Part, shall have due regard to the rights and obligations of all States concerned, shall not jeopardize or hamper the reaching of final agreement on compatible conservation and management measures and shall be without prejudice to the final outcome of any dispute settlement procedure.

7. Coastal States shall regularly inform States fishing on the high seas in the subregion or region, either directly or through appropriate subregional or regional fisheries management organizations or arrangements, or through other appropriate means, of the measures they have adopted for straddling fish stocks and highly migratory fish stocks within areas under their national jurisdiction.

8. States fishing on the high seas shall regularly inform other interested States, either directly or through appropriate subregional or regional fisheries management organizations or arrangements, or through other appropriate means, of the measures they have adopted for regulating the activities of vessels flying their flag which fish for such stocks on the high seas.

Annex I: Standard Requirements for the Collection and Sharing of Data; Annex II: Guidelines for the Application of Precautionary Reference Points in Conservation and Management of Straddling Fish Stocks and Highly Migratory Fish Stocks [not reproduced]

International Convention for the Regulation of Whaling

Adopted on 2 December 1946 at Washington. Entered into force on 10 November 1948. Source: 161 *UNTS* 72 (the text reproduced is amended by the Protocol of 19 November 1956). Number of parties: 52. Further information: International Whaling Commission, Cambridge, UK, http://www.iwcoffice.org

The Governments whose duly authorised representatives have subscribed hereto,

Recognizing the interest of the nations of the world in safeguarding for future generations the great natural resources represented by the whale stocks;

Considering that the history of whaling has seen over-fishing of one area after another and of one species of whale after another to such a degree that it is essential to protect all species of whales from further over-fishing;

Recognizing that the whale stocks are susceptible of natural increases if whaling is properly regulated, and that increases in the size of whale stocks will permit increases in the number of whales which may be captured without endangering these natural resources;

Recognizing that it is in the common interest to achieve the optimum level of whale stocks as rapidly as possible without causing widespread economic and nutritional distress;

Recognizing that in the course of achieving these objectives, whaling operations should be confined to those species best able to sustain exploitation in order to give an interval for recovery to certain species of whales now depleted in numbers;

Desiring to establish a system of international regulation for the whale fisheries to ensure proper and effective conservation and development of whale stocks on the basis of the principles embodied in the provisions of the International Agreement for the Regulation of Whaling, signed in London on 8th June, 1937, and the protocols to that Agreement signed in London on 24th June, 1938, and 26th November, 1945; and

Having decided to conclude a convention to provide for the proper conservation of whale stocks and thus make possible the orderly development of the whaling industry;

Have agreed as follows:

Article I

1. This Convention includes the Schedule attached thereto which forms an integral part thereof. All references to 'Convention' shall be understood as including the said Schedule either in its present terms or as amended in accordance with the provisions of Article V.

2. This Convention applies to factory ships, land stations, and whale catchers under the jurisdiction of the Contracting Governments, and to all waters in which whaling is prosecuted by such factory ships, land stations, and whale catchers.

Article II

As used in this Convention:

1. 'factory ship' means a ship in which or on which whales are treated either wholly or in part;

2. 'land station' means a factory on the land at which whales are treated whether wholly or in part;

3. 'whale catcher' means a helicopter, or other aircraft, or a ship, used for the purpose of hunting, taking, killing, towing, holding on to, or scouting for whales;

4. 'Contracting Government' means any Government which has deposited an instrument of ratification or has given notice of adherence to this Convention.

Article III

1. The Contracting Governments agree to establish an International Whaling Commission, hereinafter referred to as the Commission, to be composed of one member from each Contracting Government. Each member shall have one vote and may be accompanied by one or more experts and advisers.

2. The Commission shall elect from its own members a Chairman and Vice-Chairman and shall determine its own Rules of Procedure. Decisions of the Commission shall be taken by a simple majority of those members voting except that a three-fourths majority of those members voting shall be required for action in pursuance of Article V. The Rules of Procedure may provide for decisions otherwise than at meetings of the Commission.

3. The Commission may appoint its own Secretary and staff.

4. The Commission may set up, from among its own members and experts or advisers, such committees as it considers desirable to perform such functions as it may authorize.

5. The expenses of each member of the Commission and of his experts and advisers shall be determined and paid by his own Government.

6. Recognizing that specialized agencies related to the United Nations will be concerned with the conservation and development of whale fisheries and the products arising therefrom and desiring to avoid duplication of functions, the Contracting Governments will consult among themselves within two years after the coming into force of this Convention to decide whether the Commission shall be brought within the framework of a specialized agency related to the United Nations.

7. In the meantime the Government of the United Kingdom of Great Britain and Northern Ireland shall arrange, in consultation with the other Contracting Governments, to convene the first meeting of the Commission, and shall initiate the consultation referred to in paragraph 6 above.

8. Subsequent meetings of the Commission shall be convened as the Commission may determine.

Article IV

1. The Commission may either in collaboration with or through independent agencies of the Contracting Governments or other public or private agencies, establishments, or organizations, or independently

(a) encourage, recommend, oı if necessary, organize studies and investigations relating to whales and whaling;

(b) collect and analyze statistical information concerning the current condition and trend of the whale stocks and the effects of whaling activities thereon;

(c) study, appraise, and disseminate information concerning methods of maintaining and increasing the populations of whale stocks.

2. The Commission shall arrange for the publication of reports of its activities, and it may publish independently or in collaboration with the International Bureau for Whaling Statistics at Sandefjord in Norway and other organizations and agencies such reports as it deems appropriate, as well as statistical, scientific, and other pertinent information relating to whales and whaling.

Article V

1. The Commission may amend from time to time the provisions of the Schedule by adopting regulations with respect to the conservation and utilization of whale resources, fixing (a) protected and unprotected species; (b) open and closed seasons; (c) open and closed waters, including the designation of sanctuary areas; (d) size limits for each species; (e) time, methods, and intensity of whaling (including the maximum catch of whales to be taken in any one season); (f) types and specifications of gear and apparatus and appliances which may be used; (g) methods of measurement; (h) catch returns and other statistical and biological records; and (i) methods of inspection.

2. These amendments of the Schedule (a) shall be such as are necessary to carry out the objectives and purposes of this Convention and to provide for the conservation, development, and optimum utilization of the whale resources; (b) shall be based on scientific findings; (c) shall not involve restrictions on the number or nationality of factory ships or land stations, nor allocate specific quotas to any factory or ship or land station or to any group of factory ships or land stations; and (d) shall take into consideration the interests of the consumers of whale products and the whaling industry.

3. Each of such amendments shall become effective with respect to the Contracting Governments ninety days following notification of the amendment by the Commission to each of the Contracting Governments, except that (a) if any Government presents to the Commission objection to any amendment prior to the expiration of this ninety-day period, the amendment shall not become effective with respect to any of the Governments for an additional ninety days; (b) thereupon, any other Contracting Government may present objection to the amendment at any time

prior to the expiration of the additional ninety-day period, or before the expiration of thirty days from the date of receipt of the last objection received during such additional ninety-day period, whichever date shall be the later; and (c) thereafter, the amendment shall become effective with respect to all Contracting Governments which have not presented objection but shall not become effective with respect to any Government which has so objected until such date as the objection is withdrawn. The Commission shall notify each Contracting Government immediately upon receipt of each objection and withdrawal and each Contracting Government shall acknowledge receipt of all notifications of amendments, objections, and withdrawals.

4. No amendments shall become effective before 1st July, 1949.

Article VI

The Commission may from time to time make recommendations to any or all Contracting Governments on any matters which relate to whales or whaling and to the objectives and purposes of this Convention.

Article VII

The Contracting Government shall ensure prompt transmission to the International Bureau for Whaling Statistics at Sandefjord in Norway, or to such other body as the Commission may designate, of notifications and statistical and other information required by this Convention in such form and manner as may be prescribed by the Commission.

Article VIII

1. Notwithstanding anything contained in this Convention, any Contracting Government may grant to any of its nationals a special permit authorizing that national to kill, take and treat whales for purposes of scientific research subject to such restrictions as to number and subject to such other conditions as the Contracting Government thinks fit, and the killing, taking, and treating of whales in accordance with the provisions of this Article shall be exempt from the operation of this Convention. Each Contracting Government shall report at once to the Commission all such authorizations which it has granted. Each Contracting Government may at any time revoke any such special permit which it has granted.

2. Any whales taken under these special permits shall so far as practicable be processed and the proceeds shall be dealt with in accordance with directions issued by the Government by which the permit was granted.

3. Each Contracting Government shall transmit to such body as may be designated by the Commission, in so far as practicable, and at intervals of not more than one year, scientific information available to that Government with respect to whales and whaling, including the results of research conducted pursuant to paragraph 1 of this Article and to Article IV.

4. Recognizing that continuous collection and analysis of biological data in connection with the operations of factory ships and land stations are indispensable

to sound and constructive management of the whale fisheries, the Contracting Governments will take all practicable measures to obtain such data.

Article IX

1. Each Contracting Government shall take appropriate measures to ensure the application of the provisions of this Convention and the punishment of infractions against the said provisions in operations carried out by persons or by vessels under its jurisdiction.

2. No bonus or other remuneration calculated with relation to the results of their work shall be paid to the gunners and crews of whale catchers in respect of any whales the taking of which is forbidden by this Convention.

3. Prosecution for infractions against or contraventions of this Convention shall be instituted by the Government having jurisdiction over the offence.

4. Each Contracting Government shall transmit to the Commission full details of each infraction of the provisions of this Convention by persons or vessels under the jurisdiction of that Government as reported by its inspectors. This information shall include a statement of measures taken for dealing with the infraction and of penalties imposed.

Article X

1. This Convention shall be ratified and the instruments of ratifications shall be deposited with the Government of the United States of America.

2. Any Government which has not signed this Convention may adhere thereto after it enters into force by a notification in writing to the Government of the United States of America.

3. The Government of the United States of America shall inform all other signatory Governments and all adhering Governments of all ratifications deposited and adherences received.

4. This Convention shall, when instruments of ratification have been deposited by at least six signatory Governments, which shall include the Governments of the Netherlands, Norway, the Union of Soviet Socialist Republics, the United Kingdom of Great Britain and Northern Ireland, and the United States of America, enter into force with respect to those Governments and shall enter into force with respect to each Government which subsequently ratifies or adheres on the date of the deposit of its instrument of ratification or the receipt of its notification of adherence.

5. The provisions of the Schedule shall not apply prior to 1st July, 1948. Amendments to the Schedule adopted pursuant to Article V shall not apply prior to 1st July, 1949.

Article XI

Any Contracting Government may withdraw from this Convention on 30th June, of any year by giving notice on or before 1st January, of the same year to the depository Government, which upon receipt of such a notice shall at once communicate it to the other Contracting Governments. Any other Contracting Government may, in like manner, within one month of the receipt of a copy of such a notice from the depository Government, give notice of withdrawal, so that the Convention shall cease to be in force on 30th June, of the same year with respect to the Government giving such notice of withdrawal.

The Convention shall bear the date on which it is opened for signature and shall remain open for signature for a period of fourteen days thereafter.

In witness whereof the undersigned, being duly authorized, have signed this Convention.

Done in Washington this second day of December, 1946, in the English language, the original of which shall be deposited in the archives of the Government of the United States of America. The Government of the United States of America shall transmit certified copies thereof to all the other signatory and adhering Governments.

Schedule [not reproduced]

International watercourses

Convention on the Law of the Non-navigational Uses of International Watercourses

Adopted on 21 May 1997 at New York. Not in force. Source: Doc. A/51/869. Further information: UN, New York, USA, http://www.un.org/law/ilc/texts/nnavfra.htm

The Parties to the present Convention,

Conscious of the importance of international watercourses and the non-navigational uses thereof in many regions of the world,

Having in mind Article 13, paragraph 1 (a), of the Charter of the United Nations, which provides that the General Assembly shall initiate studies and make recommendations for the purpose of encouraging the progressive development of international law and its codification,

Considering that successful codification and progressive development of rules of international law regarding non-navigational uses of international watercourses would assist in promoting and implementing the purposes and principles set forth in Articles 1 and 2 of the Charter of the United Nations,

Taking into account the problems affecting many international watercourses resulting from, among other things, increasing demands and pollution,

Expressing the conviction that a framework convention will ensure the utilization, development, conservation, management and protection of international watercourses and the promotion of the optimal and sustainable utilization thereof for present and future generations,

Affirming the importance of international cooperation and good-neighbourliness in this field,

Aware of the special situation and needs of developing countries, Recalling the principles and recommendations adopted by the United Nations Conference on Environment and Development of 1992 in the Rio Declaration and Agenda 21,

Recalling also the existing bilateral and multilateral agreements regarding the non-navigational uses of international watercourses,

Mindful of the valuable contribution of international organizations, both governmental and non-governmental, to the codification and progressive development of international law in this field,

Appreciative of the work carried out by the International Law Commission on the law of the non-navigational uses of international watercourses,

Bearing in mind United Nations General Assembly resolution 49/52 of 9 December 1994,

Have agreed as follows:

Part I: Introduction

Article 1: Scope of the present Convention

1. The present Convention applies to uses of international watercourses and of their waters for purposes other than navigation and to measures of protection, preservation and management related to the uses of those watercourses and their waters.

2. The uses of international watercourses for navigation is not within the scope of the present Convention except insofar as other uses affect navigation or are affected by navigation.

Article 2: Use of terms

For the purposes of the present Convention:

(a) 'Watercourse' means a system of surface waters and ground waters constituting by virtue of their physical relationship a unitary whole and normally flowing into a common terminus;

(b) 'International watercourse' means a watercourse, parts of which are situated in different States;

(c) 'Watercourse State' means a State Party to the present Convention in whose territory part of an international watercourse is situated, or a Party that is a regional economic integration organization, in the territory of one or more of whose Member States part of an international watercourse is situated;

(d) 'Regional economic integration organization' means an organization constituted by sovereign States of a given region, to which its member States have transferred competence in respect of matters governed by this Convention and which has been duly authorized in accordance with its internal procedures, to sign, ratify, accept, approve or accede to it.

Article 3: Watercourse agreements

1. In the absence of an agreement to the contrary, nothing in the present Convention shall affect the rights or obligations of a watercourse State arising from agreements in force for it on the date on which it became a party to the present Convention.

2. Notwithstanding the provisions of paragraph 1, parties to agreements referred to in paragraph 1 may, where necessary, consider harmonizing such agreements with the basic principles of the present Convention.

3. Watercourse States may enter into one or more agreements, hereinafter referred to as 'watercourse agreements', which apply and adjust the provisions of the present Convention to the characteristics and uses of a particular international watercourse or part thereof.

4. Where a watercourse agreement is concluded between two or more watercourse States, it shall define the waters to which it applies. Such an agreement may be entered into with respect to an entire international watercourse or any part thereof or a particular project, programme or use except insofar as the agreement adversely affects, to a significant extent, the use by one or more other watercourse States of the waters of the watercourse, without their express consent.

5. Where a watercourse State considers that adjustment and application of the provisions of the present Convention is required because of the characteristics and uses of a particular international watercourse, watercourse States shall consult with a view to negotiating in good faith for the purpose of concluding a watercourse agreement or agreements.

6. Where some but not all watercourse States to a particular international watercourse are parties to an agreement, nothing in such agreement shall affect the rights or obligations under the present Convention of watercourse States that are not parties to such an agreement.

Article 4: Parties to watercourse agreements

1. Every watercourse State is entitled to participate in the negotiation of and to become a party to any watercourse agreement that applies to the entire international watercourse, as well as to participate in any relevant consultations.

2. A watercourse State whose use of an international watercourse may be affected to a significant extent by the implementation of a proposed watercourse agreement that applies only to a part of the watercourse or to a particular project, programme or use is entitled to participate in consultations on such an agreement and, where

appropriate, in the negotiation thereof in good faith with a view to becoming a party thereto, to the extent that its use is thereby affected.

Part II: General principles

Article 5: Equitable and reasonable utilization and participation

1. Watercourse States shall in their respective territories utilize an international watercourse in an equitable and reasonable manner. In particular, an international watercourse shall be used and developed by watercourse States with a view to attaining optimal and sustainable utilization thereof and benefits therefrom, taking into account the interests of the watercourse States concerned, consistent with adequate protection of the watercourse.

2. Watercourse States shall participate in the use, development and protection of an international watercourse in an equitable and reasonable manner. Such participation includes both the right to utilize the watercourse and the duty to cooperate in the protection and development thereof, as provided in the present Convention.

Article 6: Factors relevant to equitable and reasonable utilization

1. Utilization of an international watercourse in an equitable and reasonable manner within the meaning of article 5 requires taking into account all relevant factors and circumstances, including:

(a) Geographic, hydrographic, hydrological, climatic, ecological and other factors of a natural character;

(b) The social and economic needs of the watercourse States concerned;

(c) The population dependent on the watercourse in each watercourse State;

(d) The effects of the use or uses of the watercourses in one watercourse State on other watercourse States;

(e) Existing and potential uses of the watercourse;

(f) Conservation, protection, development and economy of use of the water resources of the watercourse and the costs of measures taken to that effect;

(g) The availability of alternatives, of comparable value, to a particular planned or existing use.

2. In the application of article 5 or paragraph 1 of this article, watercourse States concerned shall, when the need arises, enter into consultations in a spirit of cooperation.

3. The weight to be given to each factor is to be determined by its importance in comparison with that of other relevant factors. In determining what is a reasonable and equitable use, all relevant factors are to be considered together and a conclusion reached on the basis of the whole.

Article 7: Obligation not to cause significant harm

1. Watercourse States shall, in utilizing an international watercourse in their territories, take all appropriate measures to prevent the causing of significant harm to other watercourse States.

2. Where significant harm nevertheless is caused to another watercourse State, the States whose use causes such harm shall, in the absence of agreement to such use, take all appropriate measures, having due regard for the provisions of articles 5 and 6, in consultation with the affected State, to eliminate or mitigate such harm and, where appropriate, to discuss the question of compensation.

Article 8: General obligation to cooperate

1. Watercourse States shall cooperate on the basis of sovereign equality, territorial integrity, mutual benefit and good faith in order to attain optimal utilization and adequate protection of an international watercourse.

2. In determining the manner of such cooperation, watercourse States may consider the establishment of joint mechanisms or commissions, as deemed necessary by them, to facilitate cooperation on relevant measures and procedures in the light of experience gained through cooperation in existing joint mechanisms and commissions in various regions.

Article 9: Regular exchange of data and information

1. Pursuant to article 8, watercourse States shall on a regular basis exchange readily available data and information on the condition of the watercourse, in particular that of a hydrological, meteorological, hydrogeological and ecological nature and related to the water quality as well as related forecasts.

2. If a watercourse State is requested by another watercourse State to provide data or information that is not readily available, it shall employ its best efforts to comply with the request but may condition its compliance upon payment by the requesting State of the reasonable costs of collecting and, where appropriate, processing such data or information.

3. Watercourse States shall employ their best efforts to collect and, where appropriate, to process data and information in a manner which facilitates its utilization by the other watercourse States to which it is communicated.

Article 10: Relationship between different kinds of uses

1. In the absence of agreement or custom to the contrary, no use of an international watercourse enjoys inherent priority over other uses.

2. In the event of a conflict between uses of an international watercourse, it shall be resolved with reference to articles 5 to 7, with special regard being given to the requirements of vital human needs.

Part III: Planned measures

Article 11: Information concerning planned measures

Watercourse States shall exchange information and consult each other and, if necessary, negotiate on the possible effects of planned measures on the condition of an international watercourse.

Article 12: Notification concerning planned measures with possible adverse effects

Before a watercourse State implements or permits the implementation of planned measures which may have a significant adverse effect upon other watercourse States, it shall provide those States with timely notification thereof. Such notification shall be accompanied by available technical data and information, including the results of any environmental impact assessment, in order to enable the notified States to evaluate the possible effects of the planned measures.

Article 13: Period for reply to notification

Unless otherwise agreed:

(a) A watercourse State providing a notification under article 12 shall allow the notified States a period of six months within which to study and evaluate the possible effects of the planned measures and to communicate the findings to it;

(b) This period shall, at the request of a notified State for which the evaluation of the planned measures poses special difficulty, be extended for a period of six months.

Article 14: Obligations of the notifying State during the period for reply

During the period referred to in article 13, the notifying State:

(a) Shall cooperate with the notified States by providing them, on request, with any additional data and information that is available and necessary for an accurate evaluation; and

(b) Shall not implement or permit the implementation of the planned measures without the consent of the notified States.

Article 15: Reply to notification

The notified States shall communicate their findings to the notifying State as early as possible within the period applicable pursuant to article 13. If a notified State finds that implementation of the planned measures would be inconsistent with the provisions of articles 5 or 7, it shall attach to its finding a documented explanation setting forth the reasons for the finding.

Article 16: Absence of reply to notification

1. If, within the period applicable pursuant to article 13, the notifying State receives no communication under article 15, it may, subject to its obligations under articles 5 and 7, proceed with the implementation of the planned measures, in accordance with the notification and any other data and information provided to the notified States.

2. Any claim to compensation by a notified State which has failed to reply within the period applicable pursuant to article 13 may be offset by the costs incurred by the notifying State for action undertaken after the expiration of the time for a reply which would not have been undertaken if the notified State had objected within that period.

Article 17: Consultations and negotiations concerning planned measures

1. If a communication is made under article 15 that implementation of the planned measures would be inconsistent with the provisions of articles 5 or 7, the notifying State and the State making the communication shall enter into consultations and, if necessary, negotiations with a view to arriving at an equitable resolution of the situation.

2. The consultations and negotiations shall be conducted on the basis that each State must in good faith pay reasonable regard to the rights and legitimate interests of the other State.

3. During the course of the consultations and negotiations, the notifying State shall, if so requested by the notified State at the time it makes the communication, refrain from implementing or permitting the implementation of the planned measures for a period of six months unless otherwise agreed.

Article 18: Procedures in the absence of notification

1. If a watercourse State has reasonable grounds to believe that another watercourse State is planning measures that may have a significant adverse effect upon it, the former State may request the latter to apply the provisions of article 12. The request shall be accompanied by a documented explanation setting forth its grounds.

2. In the event that the State planning the measures nevertheless finds that it is not under an obligation to provide a notification under article 12, it shall so inform the other State, providing a documented explanation setting forth the reasons for such finding. If this finding does not satisfy the other State, the two States shall, at the request of that other State, promptly enter into consultations and negotiations in the manner indicated in paragraphs 1 and 2 of article 17.

3. During the course of the consultations and negotiations, the State planning the measures shall, if so requested by the other State at the time it requests the initiation of consultations and negotiations, refrain from implementing or permitting the implementation of those measures for a period of six months unless otherwise agreed.

Article 19: Urgent implementation of planned measures

1. In the event that the implementation of planned measures is of the utmost urgency in order to protect public health, public safety or other equally important interests, the State planning the measures may, subject to articles 5 and 7, immediately proceed to implementation, notwithstanding the provisions of article 14 and paragraph 3 of article 17.

2. In such case, a formal declaration of the urgency of the measures shall be communicated without delay to the other watercourse States referred to in article 12 together with the relevant data and information.

3. The State planning the measures shall, at the request of any of the States referred to in paragraph 2, promptly enter into consultations and negotiations with it in the manner indicated in paragraphs 1 and 2 of article 17.

Part IV: Protection, preservation and management

Article 20: Protection and preservation of ecosystems

Watercourse States shall, individually and, where appropriate, jointly, protect and preserve the ecosystems of international watercourses.

Article 21: Prevention, reduction and control of pollution

1. For the purpose of this article, 'pollution of an international watercourse' means any detrimental alteration in the composition or quality of the waters of an international watercourse which results directly or indirectly from human conduct.

2. Watercourse States shall, individually and, where appropriate, jointly, prevent, reduce and control the pollution of an international watercourse that may cause significant harm to other watercourse States or to their environment, including harm to human health or safety, to the use of the waters for any beneficial purpose or to the living resources of the watercourse. Watercourse States shall take steps to harmonize their policies in this connection.

3. Watercourse States shall, at the request of any of them, consult with a view to arriving at mutually agreeable measures and methods to prevent, reduce and control pollution of an international watercourse, such as:

(a) Setting joint water quality objectives and criteria;
(b) Establishing techniques and practices to address pollution from point and non-point sources;
(c) Establishing lists of substances the introduction of which into the waters of an international watercourse is to be prohibited, limited, investigated or monitored.

Article 22: Introduction of alien or new species

Watercourse States shall take all measures necessary to prevent the introduction of species, alien or new, into an international watercourse which may have effects detrimental to the ecosystem of the watercourse resulting in significant harm to other watercourse States.

Article 23: Protection and preservation of the marine environment

Watercourse States shall, individually and, where appropriate, in cooperation with other States, take all measures with respect to an international watercourse that are necessary to protect and preserve the marine environment, including estuaries, taking into account generally accepted international rules and standards.

Article 24: Management

1. Watercourse States shall, at the request of any of them, enter into consultations concerning the management of an international watercourse, which may include the establishment of a joint management mechanism.

2. For the purposes of this article, 'management' refers, in particular, to:

(a) Planning the sustainable development of an international watercourse and providing for the implementation of any plans adopted; and
(b) Otherwise promoting the rational and optimal utilization, protection and control of the watercourse.

Article 25: Regulation

1. Watercourse States shall cooperate, where appropriate, to respond to needs or opportunities for regulation of the flow of the waters of an international watercourse.

2. Unless otherwise agreed, watercourse States shall participate on an equitable basis in the construction and maintenance or defrayal of the costs of such regulation works as they may have agreed to undertake.

3. For the purposes of this article, 'regulation' means the use of hydraulic works or any other continuing measure to alter, vary or otherwise control the flow of the waters of an international watercourse.

Article 26: Installations

1. Watercourse States shall, within their respective territories, employ their best efforts to maintain and protect installations, facilities and other works related to an international watercourse.

2. Watercourse States shall, at the request of any of them which has reasonable grounds to believe that it may suffer significant adverse effects, enter into consultations with regard to:
(a) The safe operation and maintenance of installations, facilities or other works related to an international watercourse; and
(b) The protection of installations, facilities or other works from wilful or negligent acts or the forces of nature.

Part V: Harmful conditions and emergency situations

Article 27: Prevention and mitigation of harmful conditions

Watercourse States shall, individually and, where appropriate, jointly, take all appropriate measures to prevent or mitigate conditions related to an international watercourse that may be harmful to other watercourse States, whether resulting from natural causes or human conduct, such as flood or ice conditions, water-borne diseases, siltation, erosion, salt-water intrusion, drought or desertification.

Article 28: Emergency situations

1. For the purposes of this article, 'emergency' means a situation that causes, or poses an imminent threat of causing, serious harm to watercourse States or other States and that results suddenly from natural causes, such as floods, the breaking up of ice, landslides or earthquakes, or from human conduct, such as industrial accidents.

2. A watercourse State shall, without delay and by the most expeditious means available, notify other potentially affected States and competent international organizations of any emergency originating within its territory.

3. A watercourse State within whose territory an emergency originates shall, in cooperation with potentially affected States and, where appropriate, competent international organizations, immediately take all practicable measures necessitated by the circumstances to prevent, mitigate and eliminate harmful effects of the emergency.

4. When necessary, watercourse States shall jointly develop contingency plans for responding to emergencies, in cooperation, where appropriate, with other potentially affected States and competent international organizations.

Part VI: Miscellaneous provisions

Article 29: International watercourses and installations in time of armed conflict

International watercourses and related installations, facilities and other works shall enjoy the protection accorded by the principles and rules of international law applicable in international and non-international armed conflict and shall not be used in violation of those principles and rules.

Article 30: Indirect procedures

In cases where there are serious obstacles to direct contacts between watercourse States, the States concerned shall fulfil their obligations of cooperation provided for in the present Convention, including exchange of data and information, notification, communication, consultations and negotiations, through any indirect procedure accepted by them.

Article 31: Data and information vital to national defence or security

Nothing in the present Convention obliges a watercourse State to provide data or information vital to its national defence or security. Nevertheless, that State shall cooperate in good faith with the other watercourse States with a view to providing as much information as possible under the circumstances.

Article 32: Non-discrimination

Unless the watercourse States concerned have agreed otherwise for the protection of the interests of persons, natural or juridical, who have suffered or are under a serious threat of suffering significant transboundary harm as a result of activities related to an international watercourse, a watercourse State shall not discriminate on the basis of nationality or residence or place where the injury occurred, in granting to such persons, in accordance with its legal system, access to judicial or other procedures, or a right to claim compensation or other relief in respect of significant harm caused by such activities carried on in its territory.

Article 33: Settlement of disputes

1. In the event of a dispute between two or more Parties concerning the interpretation or application of the present Convention, the Parties concerned shall,

in the absence of an applicable agreement between them, seek a settlement of the dispute by peaceful means in accordance with the following provisions.

2. If the Parties concerned cannot reach agreement by negotiation requested by one of them, they may jointly seek the good offices of, or request mediation or conciliation by, a third party, or make use, as appropriate, of any joint watercourse institutions that may have been established by them or agree to submit the dispute to arbitration or to the International Court of Justice.

3. Subject to the operation of paragraph 10, if after six months from the time of the request for negotiations referred to in paragraph 2, the Parties concerned have not been able to settle their dispute through negotiation or any other means referred to in paragraph 2, the dispute shall be submitted, at the request of any of the parties to the dispute, to impartial fact-finding in accordance with paragraphs 4 to 9, unless the Parties otherwise agree.

4. A Fact-finding Commission shall be established, composed of one member nominated by each Party concerned and in addition a member not having the nationality of any of the Parties concerned chosen by the nominated members who shall serve as Chairman.

5. If the members nominated by the Parties are unable to agree on a Chairman within three months of the request for the establishment of the Commission, any Party concerned may request the Secretary-General of the United Nations to appoint the Chairman who shall not have the nationality of any of the parties to the dispute or of any riparian State of the watercourse concerned. If one of the Parties fails to nominate a member within three months of the initial request pursuant to paragraph 3, any other Party concerned may request the Secretary-General of the United Nations to appoint a person who shall not have the nationality of any of the parties to the dispute or of any riparian State of the watercourse concerned. The person so appointed shall constitute a single-member Commission.

6. The Commission shall determine its own procedure.

7. The Parties concerned have the obligation to provide the Commission with such information as it may require and, on request, to permit the Commission to have access to their respective territory and to inspect any facilities, plant, equipment, construction or natural feature relevant for the purpose of its inquiry.

8. The Commission shall adopt its report by a majority vote, unless it is a single-member Commission, and shall submit that report to the Parties concerned setting forth its findings and the reasons therefor and such recommendations as it deems appropriate for an equitable solution of the dispute, which the Parties concerned shall consider in good faith.

9. The expenses of the Commission shall be borne equally by the Parties concerned.

10. When ratifying, accepting, approving or acceding to the present Convention, or at any time thereafter, a Party which is not a regional economic integration

organization may declare in a written instrument submitted to the Depositary that, in respect of any dispute not resolved in accordance with paragraph 2, it recognizes as compulsory ipso facto and without special agreement in relation to any Party accepting the same obligation:

(a) Submission of the dispute to the International Court of Justice; and/or

(b) Arbitration by an arbitral tribunal established and operating, unless the parties to the dispute otherwise agreed, in accordance with the procedure laid down in the annex to the present Convention.

A Party which is a regional economic integration organization may make a declaration with like effect in relation to arbitration in accordance with subparagraph (b).

Part VII: Final clauses

Article 34: Signature

The present Convention shall be open for signature by all States and by regional economic integration organizations from 21 May 1997 until 20 May 2000 at United Nations Headquarters in New York.

Article 35: Ratification, acceptance, approval or accession

1. The present Convention is subject to ratification, acceptance, approval or accession by States and by regional economic integration organizations. The instruments of ratification, acceptance, approval or accession shall be deposited with the Secretary-General of the United Nations.

2. Any regional economic integration organization which becomes a Party to this Convention without any of its member States being a Party shall be bound by all the obligations under the Convention. In the case of such organizations, one or more of whose member States is a Party to this Convention, the organization and its member States shall decide on their respective responsibilities for the performance of their obligations under the Convention. In such cases, the organization and the member States shall not be entitled to exercise rights under the Convention concurrently.

3. In their instruments of ratification, acceptance, approval or accession, the regional economic integration organizations shall declare the extent of their competence with respect to the matters governed by the Convention. These organizations shall also inform the Secretary-General of the United Nations of any substantial modification in the extent of their competence.

Article 36: Entry into force

1. The present Convention shall enter into force on the ninetieth day following the date of deposit of the thirty-fifth instrument of ratification, acceptance, approval or accession with the Secretary-General of the United Nations.

2. For each State or regional economic integration organization that ratifies, accepts or approves the Convention or accedes thereto after the deposit of the

thirty-fifth instrument of ratification, acceptance, approval or accession, the Convention shall enter into force on the ninetieth day after the deposit by such State or regional economic integration organization of its instrument of ratification, acceptance, approval or accession.

3. For the purposes of paragraphs 1 and 2, any instrument deposited by a regional economic integration organization shall not be counted as additional to those deposited by States.

Article 37: Authentic texts

The original of the present Convention, of which the Arabic, Chinese, English, French, Russian and Spanish texts are equally authentic, shall be deposited with the Secretary-General of the United Nations.

Annex: Arbitration [not reproduced]

Chapter 9

Trade, Finance and Intellectual Property

Introduction

This chapter focuses on the links between environmental conservation on the one hand and trade, finance and intellectual property on the other. The first section reproduces a selection of documents concerning trade and the environment. It attempts to highlight some of the provisions and instruments which are particularly relevant from the point of view of the trade-environment interface. The section includes some provisions of the 1947 GATT that are often invoked in dispute settlement proceedings involving environmental issues.[1] It also includes the 1994 Decision on Trade and Environment which provides the basis for the work of the WTO Committee on Trade and Environment, the only body within the WTO which specifically considers the nexus between trade and environmental matters. This section also reproduces part of the regional 1993 NAAEC because it goes much further than existing WTO documents in its treatment of the relationship between trade and the environment.

The second section reproduces the main instrument concerning environmental finance, the 1994 instrument establishing the GEF. The GEF is the only financial mechanism specifically devoted to addressing global environmental problems. It fulfils this function by providing finance to developing countries primarily to help them implement their obligations under specific conventions dealing with global environmental problems. This section also includes extracts from one specific aid treaty between the EU and ACP countries to illustrate the place that environmental considerations take in recent aid related treaties. Other international documents of interest include World Bank policies related to environmental management. These policies, while of great practical importance, do not find their place in this compilation of basic instruments since they only apply within the context of the World Bank.[2]

The last section focuses on intellectual property, another field which is unrelated to environmental protection but which needs to be considered here

---

1 Excerpts of the Understanding on Rules and Procedures Governing the Settlement of Disputes are reproduced at p. 597.

2 Bank policies are embodied in Operational Policies (OPs), Bank Procedures (BPs), and Good Practices (GPs), available at http://www.worldbank.org. OPs and BPs contain strict, mandatory rules for Bank staff, while GPs set out advisory guidance.

because the implementation of intellectual property laws has direct and indirect impacts on environmental management. This section includes extracts from two of the main treaties in this field. Firstly, it reproduces the general provisions of the 1994 TRIPS Agreement as well as the section on patent rights. This serves to illustrate the basic structure of the Agreement and the limited extent to which environmental considerations are integrated. It also reproduces part of the 1961/1991 UPOV Convention, a treaty which provides a form of intellectual property protection, plant breeders' rights, as an incentive for the development of the commercial seed sector. As illustrated by the PGRFA Treaty reproduced at page 208, there are strong links between environmental management and agriculture. The legal incentives given to the seed industry also have a significant impact on environmental management and warrant specific consideration even if the main intent of plant breeders' rights is unrelated to environmental management.

Selected readings

Trade

Blakeney, M. and MacMillan, F., *The WTO and the Environment* (London: Sweet and Maxwell, 2001).

Gaines, S.E., 'Triangulating Sustainable Development: International Trade, Environmental Protection, and Development', 32 *Envtl L. Reporter* 10318 (2002).

Steinberg R.H. (ed.), *The Greening of Trade Law - International Trade Organizations and Environmental Issues* (Lanham: Rowman and Littlefield, 2002).

Winter, G., 'The GATT and Environmental Protection - Problems of Construction', 15 *JEL* 113 (2003).

Finance

Bierman, F., 'Financing Environmental Policies in the South - Experiences from the Multilateral Ozone Fund', 9 *Int'l Envtl Affairs* 179 (1997).

Boisson de Chazournes, L., 'The Global Environment Facility as a Pioneering Institution - Lessons Learned and Looking Ahead' (Washington, DC: GEF, GEF Working Paper N° 19, 2003).

Plesmann, W. and Goller, B., 'Financial Mechanisms', *in* Morrison, F.L. and Wolfrum, R. (eds.), *International, Regional and National Environmental Law* (The Hague: Kluwer Law International, 2000), p. 887.

Sand, P.H., 'Trusts for the Earth: New International Financial Mechanisms for Sustainable Development', *in* Lang, W. (ed.), *Sustainable Development and International Law* (London: Graham and Trotman, 1995), p. 167.

Intellectual property rights

Cullet, P. and Raja, J., 'Intellectual Property Rights and Biodiversity Management: The Case of India', 4 *Global Envtl Politics* 97 (2004).

Drahos, P. and Mayne, R. (eds.), *Global Intellectual Property Rights - Knowledge, Access and Development* (Basingstoke: Palgrave Macmillan, 2002).

McManis, Ch. R., 'The Interface Between International Intellectual Property and Environmental Protection: Biodiversity and Biotechnology', 76 *Washington University L. Quarterly* 255 (1998).

Walden, I., 'Preserving Biodiversity: The Role of Property Rights', *in* Swanson, T. (ed.), *Intellectual Property Rights and Biodiversity Conservation* (Cambridge: Cambridge University Press, 1995), p. 176.

Trade

General Agreement on Tariffs and Trade 1947/1994 [excerpts]

Adopted on 31 October 1947 at Geneva. Entered into force on 1 January 1948. Source: 55 *UNTS* 187. Number of parties: 147. Further information: WTO, Geneva, Switzerland, http://www.wto.org

Part I

Article I: General most-favoured-nation treatment

1. With respect to customs duties and charges of any kind imposed on or in connection with importation or exportation or imposed on the international transfer of payments for imports or exports, and with respect to the method of levying such duties and charges, and with respect to all rules and formalities in connection with importation and exportation, and with respect to all matters referred to in paragraphs 2 and 4 of Article III, any advantage, favour, privilege or immunity granted by any contracting party to any product originating in or destined for any other country shall be accorded immediately and unconditionally to the like product originating in or destined for the territories of all other contracting parties.

Part II

Article III: National treatment on internal taxation and regulation

1. The contracting parties recognize that internal taxes and other internal charges, and laws, regulations and requirements affecting the internal sale, offering for sale, purchase, transportation, distribution or use of products, and internal quantitative regulations requiring the mixture, processing or use of products in specified

amounts or proportions, should not be applied to imported or domestic products so as to afford protection to domestic production.

2. The products of the territory of any contracting party imported into the territory of any other contracting party shall not be subject, directly or indirectly, to internal taxes or other internal charges of any kind in excess of those applied, directly or indirectly, to like domestic products. Moreover, no contracting party shall otherwise apply internal taxes or other internal charges to imported or domestic products in a manner contrary to the principles set forth in paragraph 1.

3. With respect to any existing internal tax which is inconsistent with the provisions of paragraph 2, but which is specifically authorized under a trade agreement, in force on April 10, 1947, in which the import duty on the taxed product is bound against increase, the contracting party imposing the tax shall be free to postpone the application of the provisions of paragraph 2 to such tax until such time as it can obtain release from the obligations of such trade agreement in order to permit the increase of such duty to the extent necessary to compensate for the elimination of the protective element of the tax.

4. The products of the territory of any contracting party imported into the territory of any other contracting party shall be accorded treatment no less favourable than that accorded to like products of national origin in respect of all laws, regulations and requirements affecting their internal sale, offering for sale, purchase, transportation, distribution or use. The provisions of this paragraph shall not prevent the application of differential internal transportation charges which are based exclusively on the economic operation of the means of transport and not on the nationality of the product.

Article XI: General elimination of quantitative restrictions

1. No prohibitions or restrictions other than duties, taxes or other charges, whether made effective through quotas, import or export licences or other measures, shall be instituted or maintained by any contracting party on the importation of any product of the territory of any other contracting party or on the exportation or sale for export of any product destined for the territory of any other contracting party.

2. The provisions of paragraph 1 of this Article shall not extend to the following:

(a) Export prohibitions or restrictions temporarily applied to prevent or relieve critical shortages of foodstuffs or other products essential to the exporting contracting party;

(b) Import and export prohibitions or restrictions necessary to the application of standards or regulations for the classification, grading or marketing of commodities in international trade;

(c) Import restrictions on any agricultural or fisheries product, imported in any form, necessary to the enforcement of governmental measures which operate:

i) to restrict the quantities of the like domestic product permitted to be marketed or produced, or, if there is no substantial domestic production of the like product, of a domestic product for which the imported product can be directly substituted; or

ii) to remove a temporary surplus of the like domestic product, or, if there is no substantial domestic production of the like product, of a domestic product for which the imported product can be directly substituted, by making the surplus available to certain groups of domestic consumers free of charge or at prices below the current market level; or

iii) to restrict the quantities permitted to be produced of any animal product the production of which is directly dependent, wholly or mainly, on the imported commodity, if the domestic production of that commodity is relatively negligible.

Any contracting party applying restrictions on the importation of any product pursuant to sub-paragraph (*c*) of this paragraph shall give public notice of the total quantity or value of the product permitted to be imported during a specified future period and of any change in such quantity or value. Moreover, any restrictions applied under (i) above shall not be such as will reduce the total of imports relative to the total of domestic production, as compared with the proportion which might reasonably be expected to rule between the two in the absence of restrictions. In determining this proportion, the contracting party shall pay due regard to the proportion prevailing during a previous representative period and to any special factors which may have affected or may be affecting the trade in the product concerned.

Article XX: General exceptions

Subject to the requirement that such measures are not applied in a manner which would constitute a means of arbitrary or unjustifiable discrimination between countries where the same conditions prevail, or a disguised restriction on international trade, nothing in this Agreement shall be construed to prevent the adoption or enforcement by any contracting party of measures:

(a) necessary to protect public morals;

(b) necessary to protect human, animal or plant life or health;

(f) imposed for the protection of national treasures of artistic, historic or archaeological value;

(g) relating to the conservation of exhaustible natural resources if such measures are made effective in conjunction with restrictions on domestic production or consumption;

World Trade Organization - Trade and Environment

Decision of 14 April 1994. Source: Doc. MTN.TNC/MIN(94)/1/Rev.1. Further information: Committee on Trade and Environment, WTO, Geneva, Switzerland, http://www.wto.org/english/tratop_e/envir_e/envir_e.htm

Ministers,

Meeting on the occasion of signing the Final Act Embodying the Results of the Uruguay Round of Multilateral Trade Negotiations at Marrakesh on 15 April 1994,

Recalling the preamble of the Agreement establishing the World Trade Organization (WTO), which states that members' 'relations in the field of trade and economic endeavour should be conducted with a view to raising standards of living, ensuring full employment and a large and steadily growing volume of real income and effective demand, and expanding the production of and trade in goods and services, while allowing for the optimal use of the world's resources in accordance with the objective of sustainable development, seeking both to protect and preserve the environment and to enhance the means for doing so in a manner consistent with their respective needs and concerns at different levels of economic development,'

Noting:

- the Rio Declaration on Environment and Development, Agenda 21, and its follow-up in GATT, as reflected in the statement of the Chairman of the Council of Representatives to the CONTRACTING PARTIES at their 48th Session in December 1992, as well as the work of the Group on Environmental Measures and International Trade, the Committee on Trade and Development, and the Council of Representatives;

- the work programme envisaged in the Decision on Trade in Services and the Environment; and

- the relevant provisions of the Agreement on Trade-Related Aspects of Intellectual Property Rights,

Considering that there should not be, nor need be, any policy contradiction between upholding and safeguarding an open, non-discriminatory and equitable multilateral trading system on the one hand, and acting for the protection of the environment, and the promotion of sustainable development on the other,

Desiring to coordinate the policies in the field of trade and environment, and this without exceeding the competence of the multilateral trading system, which is limited to trade policies and those trade-related aspects of environmental policies which may result in significant trade effects for its members,

Decide:

- to direct the first meeting of the General Council of the WTO to establish a Committee on Trade and Environment open to all members of the WTO to report to the first biennial meeting of the Ministerial Conference after the entry into force of the WTO when the work and terms of reference of the Committee will be reviewed, in the light of recommendations of the Committee,
- that the TNC Decision of 15 December 1993 which reads, in part, as follows:

  'a) to identify the relationship between trade measures and environmental measures, in order to promote sustainable development;

  b) to make appropriate recommendations on whether any modifications of the provisions of the multilateral trading system are required, compatible with the open, equitable and non-discriminatory nature of the system, as regards, in particular:

  - the need for rules to enhance positive interaction between trade and environmental measures, for the promotion of sustainable development, with special consideration to the needs of developing countries, in particular those of the least developed among them; and
  - the avoidance of protectionist trade measures, and the adherence to effective multilateral disciplines to ensure responsiveness of the multilateral trading system to environmental objectives set forth in Agenda 21 and the Rio Declaration, in particular Principle 12; and
  - surveillance of trade measures used for environmental purposes, of trade-related aspects of environmental measures which have significant trade effects, and of effective implementation of the multilateral disciplines governing those measures;'

  constitutes, along with the preambular language above, the terms of reference of the Committee on Trade and Environment,
- that, within these terms of reference, and with the aim of making international trade and environmental policies mutually supportive, the Committee will initially address the following matters, in relation to which any relevant issue may be raised:
  - the relationship between the provisions of the multilateral trading system and trade measures for environmental purposes, including those pursuant to multilateral environmental agreements;
  - the relationship between environmental policies relevant to trade and environmental measures with significant trade effects and the provisions of the multilateral trading system;
  - the relationship between the provisions of the multilateral trading system and:

(a) charges and taxes for environmental purposes;

(b) requirements for environmental purposes relating to products, including standards and technical regulations, packaging, labelling and recycling;

- the provisions of the multilateral trading system with respect to the transparency of trade measures used for environmental purposes and environmental measures and requirements which have significant trade effects;
- the relationship between the dispute settlement mechanisms in the multilateral trading system and those found in multilateral environmental agreements;
- the effect of environmental measures on market access, especially in relation to developing countries, in particular to the least developed among them, and environmental benefits of removing trade restrictions and distortions;
- the issue of exports of domestically prohibited goods;

- that the Committee on Trade and Environment will consider the work programme envisaged in the Decision on Trade in Services and the Environment and the relevant provisions of the Agreement on Trade-Related Aspects of Intellectual Property Rights as an integral part of its work, within the above terms of reference,
- that, pending the first meeting of the General Council of the WTO, the work of the Committee on Trade and Environment should be carried out by a Sub-Committee of the Preparatory Committee of the World Trade Organization (PCWTO), open to all members of the PCWTO,
- to invite the Sub-Committee of the Preparatory Committee, and the Committee on Trade and Environment when it is established, to provide input to the relevant bodies in respect of appropriate arrangements for relations with intergovernmental and non-governmental organizations referred to in Article V of the WTO.

World Trade Organization - Ministerial Declaration 2001 [excerpts]

Adopted on 14 November 2001 at Doha. Source: Doc. WT/MIN(01)/DEC/1. Further information: WTO, Geneva, Switzerland, http://www.wto.org

Trade and Environment

31. With a view to enhancing the mutual supportiveness of trade and environment, we agree to negotiations, without prejudging their outcome, on:

i) the relationship between existing WTO rules and specific trade obligations set out in multilateral environmental agreements (MEAs). The negotiations shall be limited in scope to the applicability of such existing WTO rules as among parties to the MEA in question. The negotiations shall not prejudice the WTO rights of any Member that is not a party to the MEA in question;
ii) procedures for regular information exchange between MEA Secretariats and the relevant WTO committees, and the criteria for the granting of observer status;
iii) the reduction or, as appropriate, elimination of tariff and non-tariff barriers to environmental goods and services.

We note that fisheries subsidies form part of the negotiations provided for in paragraph 28.

32. We instruct the Committee on Trade and Environment, in pursuing work on all items on its agenda within its current terms of reference, to give particular attention to:

i) the effect of environmental measures on market access, especially in relation to developing countries, in particular the least-developed among them, and those situations in which the elimination or reduction of trade restrictions and distortions would benefit trade, the environment and development;
ii) the relevant provisions of the Agreement on Trade-Related Aspects of Intellectual Property Rights; and
iii) labelling requirements for environmental purposes.

Work on these issues should include the identification of any need to clarify relevant WTO rules. The Committee shall report to the Fifth Session of the Ministerial Conference, and make recommendations, where appropriate, with respect to future action, including the desirability of negotiations. The outcome of this work as well as the negotiations carried out under paragraph 31(i) and (ii) shall be compatible with the open and non-discriminatory nature of the multilateral trading system, shall not add to or diminish the rights and obligations of Members under existing WTO agreements, in particular the Agreement on the Application of Sanitary and Phytosanitary Measures, nor alter the balance of these rights and obligations, and will take into account the needs of developing and least-developed countries.

33. We recognize the importance of technical assistance and capacity building in the field of trade and environment to developing countries, in particular the least-developed among them. We also encourage that expertise and experience be shared with Members wishing to perform environmental reviews at the national level. A report shall be prepared on these activities for the Fifth Session.

North American Agreement on Environmental Cooperation, Part 1: Objectives and Part 2: Obligations[3]

Adopted on 14 September 1993 at Mexico/Ottawa/Washington, DC. Entered into force on 1 January 1994. Number of parties: 3. Further information: CEC, Montreal, Canada, http://www.cec.org

Preamble

The Government of Canada, the Government of the United Mexican States and the Government of the United States of America:

Convinced of the importance of the conservation, protection and enhancement of the environment in their territories and the essential role of cooperation in these areas in achieving sustainable development for the well-being of present and future generations;

Reaffirming the sovereign right of States to exploit their own resources pursuant to their own environmental and development policies and their responsibility to ensure that activities within their jurisdiction or control do not cause damage to the environment of other States or of areas beyond the limits of national jurisdiction;

Recognizing the interrelationship of their environments;

Acknowledging the growing economic and social links between them, including the North American Free Trade Agreement (NAFTA);

Reconfirming the importance of the environmental goals and objectives of the NAFTA, including enhanced levels of environmental protection;

Emphasizing the importance of public participation in conserving, protecting and enhancing the environment;

Noting the existence of differences in their respective natural endowments, climatic and geographical conditions, and economic, technological and infrastructural capabilities;

Reaffirming the *Stockholm Declaration on the Human Environment* of 1972 and the *Rio Declaration on Environment and Development* of 1992;

Recalling their tradition of environmental cooperation and expressing their desire to support and build on international environmental agreements and existing policies and laws, in order to promote cooperation between them; and

---

3 The part of NAAEC concerning the CEC is reproduced below at p. 606.

Convinced of the benefits to be derived from a framework, including a Commission, to facilitate effective cooperation on the conservation, protection and enhancement of the environment in their territories;

Have agreed as follows:

Part One: Objectives

Article 1: Objectives

The objectives of this Agreement are to:

(a) foster the protection and improvement of the environment in the territories of the Parties for the well-being of present and future generations;

(b) promote sustainable development based on cooperation and mutually supportive environmental and economic policies;

(c) increase cooperation between the Parties to better conserve, protect, and enhance the environment, including wild flora and fauna;

(d) support the environmental goals and objectives of the NAFTA;

(e) avoid creating trade distortions or new trade barriers;

(f) strengthen cooperation on the development and improvement of environmental laws, regulations, procedures, policies and practices;

(g) enhance compliance with, and enforcement of, environmental laws and regulations;

(h) promote transparency and public participation in the development of environmental laws, regulations and policies;

(i) promote economically efficient and effective environmental measures; and

(j) promote pollution prevention policies and practices.

Part Two: Obligations

Article 2: General commitments

1. Each Party shall, with respect to its territory:
(a) periodically prepare and make publicly available reports on the state of the environment;
(b) develop and review environmental emergency preparedness measures;
(c) promote education in environmental matters, including environmental law;
(d) further scientific research and technology development in respect of environmental matters;
(e) assess, as appropriate, environmental impacts; and
(f) promote the use of economic instruments for the efficient achievement of environmental goals.

2. Each Party shall consider implementing in its law any recommendation developed by the Council under Article 10(5)(b).

3. Each Party shall consider prohibiting the export to the territories of the other Parties of a pesticide or toxic substance whose use is prohibited within the Party's territory. When a Party adopts a measure prohibiting or severely restricting the use of a pesticide or toxic substance in its territory, it shall notify the other Parties of the measure, either directly or through an appropriate international organization.

Article 3: Levels of protection

Recognizing the right of each Party to establish its own levels of domestic environmental protection and environmental development policies and priorities, and to adopt or modify accordingly its environmental laws and regulations, each Party shall ensure that its laws and regulations provide for high levels of environmental protection and shall strive to continue to improve those laws and regulations.

Article 4: Publication

1. Each Party shall ensure that its laws, regulations, procedures and administrative rulings of general application respecting any matter covered by this Agreement are promptly published or otherwise made available in such a manner as to enable interested persons and Parties to become acquainted with them.

2. To the extent possible, each Party shall:
(a) publish in advance any such measure that it proposes to adopt; and
(b) provide interested persons and Parties a reasonable opportunity to comment on such proposed measures.

Article 5: Government enforcement action

1. With the aim of achieving high levels of environmental protection and compliance with its environmental laws and regulations, each Party shall effectively enforce its environmental laws and regulations through appropriate governmental action, subject to Article 37, such as:
(a) appointing and training inspectors;
(b) monitoring compliance and investigating suspected violations, including through on-site inspections;
(c) seeking assurances of voluntary compliance and compliance agreements;
(d) publicly releasing non-compliance information;
(e) issuing bulletins or other periodic statements on enforcement procedures;
(f) promoting environmental audits;
(g) requiring record keeping and reporting;
(h) providing or encouraging mediation and arbitration services;
(i) using licenses, permits or authorizations;
(j) initiating, in a timely manner, judicial, quasi-judicial or administrative proceedings to seek appropriate sanctions or remedies for violations of its environmental laws and regulations;

(k) providing for search, seizure or detention; or
(l) issuing administrative orders, including orders of a preventative, curative or emergency nature.

2. Each party shall ensure that judicial, quasi-judicial or administrative enforcement proceedings are available under its law to sanction or remedy violations of its environmental laws and regulations.

3. Sanctions and remedies provided for a violation of a Party's environmental laws and regulations shall, as appropriate:
(a) take into consideration the nature and gravity of the violation, any economic benefit derived from the violation by the violator, the economic condition of the violator, and other relevant factors; and
(b) include compliance agreements, fines, imprisonment, injunctions, the closure of facilities, and the cost of containing or cleaning up pollution.

Article 6: Private access to remedies

1. Each Party shall ensure that interested persons may request the Party's competent authorities to investigate alleged violations of its environmental laws and regulations and shall give such requests due consideration in accordance with law.

2. Each Party shall ensure that persons with a legally recognized interest under its law in a particular matter have appropriate access to administrative, quasi-judicial or judicial proceedings for the enforcement of the Party's environmental laws and regulations.

3. Private access to remedies shall include rights, in accordance with the Party's law, such as:
(a) to sue another person under that Party's jurisdiction for damages;
(b) to seek sanctions or remedies such as monetary penalties, emergency closures or orders to mitigate the consequences of violations of its environmental laws and regulations;
(c) to request the competent authorities to take appropriate action to enforce that Party's environmental laws and regulations in order to protect the environment or to avoid environmental harm; or
(d) to seek injunctions where a person suffers, or may suffer, loss, damage or injury as a result of conduct by another person under that Party's jurisdiction contrary to that Party's environmental laws and regulations or from tortious conduct.

Article 7: Procedural guarantees

1. Each Party shall ensure that its administrative, quasi-judicial and judicial proceedings referred to in Articles 5(2) and 6(2) are fair, open and equitable, and to this end shall provide that such proceedings:
(a) comply with due process of law;

(b) are open to the public, except where the administration of justice otherwise requires;
(c) entitle the parties to the proceedings to support or defend their respective positions and to present information or evidence; and
(d) are not unnecessarily complicated and do not entail unreasonable charges or time limits or unwarranted delays.

2. Each Party shall provide that final decisions on the merits of the case in such proceedings are:
(a) in writing and preferably state the reasons on which the decisions are based;
(b) made available without undue delay to the parties to the proceedings and, consistent with its law, to the public; and
(c) based on information or evidence in respect of which the parties were offered the opportunity to be heard.

3. Each Party shall provide, as appropriate, that parties to such proceedings have the right, in accordance with its law, to seek review and, where warranted, correction of final decisions issued in such proceedings.

4. Each Party shall ensure that tribunals that conduct or review such proceedings are impartial and independent and do not have any substantial interest in the outcome of the matter.

Finance

Instrument for the Establishment of the Restructured Global Environment Facility

Adopted on 16 March 1994 at Geneva. Entered into force on 7 July 1994 (the text reproduced incorporates the amendments adopted at the Second Global Environment Facility Assembly in 2002). Number of parties: 176. Further information: GEF Secretariat, Washington, DC, USA, http://www.gefweb.org

Preamble

Whereas:

(a) The Global Environment Facility (GEF or the Facility) was established in the International Bank for Reconstruction and Development (IBRD or World Bank) as a pilot program in order to assist in the protection of the global environment and promote thereby environmentally sound and sustainable economic development, by resolution of the Executive Directors of the World Bank and related interagency arrangements between the United Nations Development Programme (UNDP), the United Nations Environment Programme (UNEP), and the World Bank;

(b) In April 1992, Participants in the GEF agreed that its structure and modalities should be modified. Agenda 21 (the action plan of the 1992 United Nations Conference on Environment and Development), the United Nations Framework Convention on Climate Change and the Convention on Biological Diversity subsequently called for the restructuring of the Facility;

(c) Representatives of the States participating at present in the Facility and of other States wishing to participate in it have requested that the Facility be restructured in order to take account of these developments, to establish the GEF as one of the principal mechanisms for global environment funding, to ensure a governance that is transparent and democratic in nature, to promote universality in its participation and to provide for full cooperation in its implementation among UNDP, UNEP and the World Bank (together referred to hereinafter as the Implementing Agencies), and to benefit from the evaluation of experience with the operation of the Facility since its establishment;

(d) It is necessary to replenish the resources for these purposes under a restructured Facility which includes a new GEF Trust Fund on the basis of this Instrument;

(e) It is desirable to terminate the existing Global Environment Trust Fund (GET) and to transfer any funds, receipts, assets and liabilities held in it upon termination to the new GEF Trust Fund;

(f) The Implementing Agencies have reached a common understanding of principles for cooperation as set forth in the present Instrument, subject to approval of their participation by their respective governing bodies;
It is resolved as follows:

I. Basic provisions

Restructuring and purpose of GEF

1. The restructured GEF shall be established in accordance with the present Instrument. This Instrument, having been accepted by representatives of the States participating in the GEF at their meeting in Geneva, Switzerland, from March 14 to 16, 1994, shall be adopted by the Implementing Agencies in accordance with their respective rules and procedural requirements.

2. The GEF shall operate, on the basis of collaboration and partnership among the Implementing Agencies, as a mechanism for international cooperation for the purpose of providing new and additional grant and concessional funding to meet the agreed incremental costs of measures to achieve agreed global environmental benefits in the following focal areas:
(a) climate change,
(b) biological diversity,
(c) international waters,

(d) ozone layer depletion,
(e) land degradation, primarily desertification and deforestation, and
(f) persistent organic pollutants.

3. The agreed incremental costs of activities to achieve global environmental benefits concerning chemicals management as they relate to the above focal areas shall be eligible for funding. The agreed incremental costs of other relevant activities under Agenda 21 that may be agreed by the Council shall also be eligible for funding insofar as they achieve global environmental benefits by protecting the global environment in the focal areas.

4. The GEF shall ensure the cost-effectiveness of its activities in addressing the targeted global environmental issues, shall fund programs and projects which are country-driven and based on national priorities designed to support sustainable development and shall maintain sufficient flexibility to respond to changing circumstances in order to achieve its purposes.

5. The GEF operational policies shall be determined by the Council in accordance with paragraph 20(f) and with respect to GEF-financed projects shall provide for full disclosure of all non-confidential information, and consultation with, and participation as appropriate of, major groups and local communities throughout the project cycle.

6. In partial fulfillment of its purposes, the GEF shall, on an interim basis, operate the financial mechanism for the implementation of the United Nations Framework Convention on Climate Change and shall be, on an interim basis, the institutional structure which carries out the operation of the financial mechanism for the implementation of the Convention on Biological Diversity, in accordance with such cooperative arrangements or agreements as may be made pursuant to paragraphs 27 and 31. The GEF shall be available to continue to serve for the purposes of the financial mechanisms for the implementation of those conventions if it is requested to do so by their Conferences of the Parties. The GEF shall also be available to serve as an entity entrusted with the operation of the financial mechanism of the Stockholm Convention on Persistent Organic Pollutants. In such respects, the GEF shall function under the guidance of, and be accountable to, the Conferences of the Parties which shall decide on policies, program priorities and eligibility criteria for the purposes of the conventions. The GEF shall also be available to meet the agreed full costs of activities under Article 12, paragraph 1, of the United Nations Framework Convention on Climate Change.

Participation

7. Any State member of the United Nations or of any of its specialized agencies may become a Participant in the GEF by depositing with the Secretariat an instrument of participation substantially in the form set out in Annex A. In the case of a State contributing to the GEF Trust Fund, an instrument of commitment shall be deemed to serve as an instrument of participation. Any Participant may

withdraw from the GEF by depositing with the Secretariat an instrument of termination of participation substantially in the form set out in Annex A.

Establishment of GEF Trust Fund

8. The new GEF Trust Fund shall be established, and the World Bank shall be invited to serve as the Trustee of the Fund. The GEF Trust Fund shall consist of the contributions received in accordance with the present Instrument, the balance of funds transferred from the GET pursuant to paragraph 32, and any other assets and receipts of the Fund. In serving as the Trustee of the Fund, the World Bank shall serve in a fiduciary and administrative capacity, and shall be bound by its Articles of Agreement, By-Laws, rules and decisions, as specified in Annex B.

Eligibility

9. GEF funding shall be made available for activities within the focal areas defined in paragraphs 2 and 3 of this Instrument in accordance with the following eligibility criteria:

(a) GEF grants that are made available within the framework of the financial mechanisms of the conventions referred to in paragraph 6 shall be in conformity with the eligibility criteria decided by the Conference of the Parties of each convention, as provided under the arrangements or agreements referred to in paragraph 27.

(b) All other GEF grants shall be made available to eligible recipient countries and, where appropriate, for other activities promoting the purposes of the Facility in accordance with this paragraph and any additional eligibility criteria determined by the Council. A country shall be an eligible recipient of GEF grants if it is eligible to borrow from the World Bank (IBRD and/or IDA) or if it is an eligible recipient of UNDP technical assistance through its country Indicative Planning Figure (IPF). GEF grants for activities within a focal area addressed by a convention referred to in paragraph 6 but outside the framework of the financial mechanism of the convention, shall only be made available to eligible recipient countries that are party to the convention concerned.

(c) GEF concessional financing in a form other than grants that is made available within the framework of the financial mechanism of the conventions referred to in paragraph 6 shall be in conformity with eligibility criteria decided by the Conference of the Parties of each convention, as provided under the arrangements or agreements referred to in paragraph 27. GEF concessional financing in a form other than grants may also be made available outside those frameworks on terms to be determined by the Council.

II. Contributions and other financial provisions for replenishment

10. Contributions to the GEF Trust Fund for the first replenishment period shall be made to the Trustee by Contributing Participants in accordance with the financial provisions for replenishment as specified in Annex C. The Trustee's responsibility for mobilization of resources pursuant to paragraph 20(e) of this Instrument and

paragraph 4(a) of Annex B shall be initiated for subsequent replenishments at the request of the Council.

III. Governance and structure

11. The GEF shall have an Assembly, a Council and a Secretariat. In accordance with paragraph 24, a Scientific and Technical Advisory Panel (STAP) shall provide appropriate advice.

12. The Implementing Agencies shall establish a process for their collaboration in accordance with an interagency agreement to be concluded on the basis of the principles set forth in Annex D.

Assembly

13. The Assembly shall consist of Representatives of all Participants. The Assembly shall meet once every three years. Each Participant may appoint one Representative and one Alternate to the Assembly in such manner as it may determine. Each Representative and each Alternate shall serve until replaced. The Assembly shall elect its Chairperson from among the Representatives.

14. The Assembly shall:

(a) review the general policies of the Facility;
(b) review and evaluate the operation of the Facility on the basis of reports submitted by the Council;
(c) keep under review the membership of the Facility; and
(d) consider, for approval by consensus, amendments to the present Instrument on the basis of recommendations by the Council.

Council

15. The Council shall be responsible for developing, adopting and evaluating the operational policies and programs for GEF-financed activities, in conformity with the present Instrument and fully taking into account reviews carried out by the Assembly. Where the GEF serves for the purposes of the financial mechanisms of the conventions referred to in paragraph 6, the Council shall act in conformity with the policies, program priorities and eligibility criteria decided by the Conference of the Parties for the purposes of the convention concerned.

16. The Council shall consist of 32 Members, representing constituency groupings formulated and distributed taking into account the need for balanced and equitable representation of all Participants and giving due weight to the funding efforts of all donors. There shall be 16 Members from developing countries, 14 Members from developed countries and 2 Members from the countries of central and eastern Europe and the former Soviet Union, in accordance with Annex E. There shall be an equal number of Alternate Members. The Member and Alternate representing a constituency shall be appointed by the Participants in each constituency. Unless the constituency decides otherwise, each Member of the Council and each Alternate shall serve for three years or until a new Member is appointed by the constituency,

whichever comes first. A Member or Alternate may be reappointed by the constituency. Members and Alternates shall serve without compensation. The Alternate Member shall have full power to act for the absent Member.

17. The Council shall meet semi-annually or as frequently as necessary at the seat of the Secretariat to enable it to discharge its responsibilities. Two-thirds of the Members of the Council shall constitute a quorum.

18. At each meeting, the Council shall elect a Chairperson from among its Members for the duration of that meeting. The elected Chairperson shall conduct deliberations of the Council at that meeting on issues related to Council responsibilities listed in paragraphs 20(b), (g), (i), (j) and (k). The position of elected Chairperson shall alternate from one meeting to another between recipient and non-recipient Council Members. The Chief Executive Officer of the Facility (CEO) shall conduct deliberations of the Council on issues related to Council responsibilities listed in paragraphs 20(c), (e), (f) and (h). The elected Chairperson and the CEO shall jointly conduct deliberations of the Council on issues related to paragraph 20(a).

19. Costs of Council meetings, including travel and subsistence of Council Members from developing countries, in particular the Least Developed Countries, shall be disbursed from the administrative budget of the Secretariat as necessary.

20. The Council shall:

(a) keep under review the operation of the Facility with respect to its purposes, scope and objectives;

(b) ensure that GEF policies, programs, operational strategies and projects are monitored and evaluated on a regular basis;

(c) review and approve the work program referred to in paragraph 29, monitor and evaluate progress in the implementation of the work program and provide related guidance to the Secretariat, the Implementing Agencies and the other bodies referred to in paragraph 28, recognizing that the Implementing Agencies will retain responsibility for the further preparation of individual projects approved in the work program;

(d) arrange for Council Members to receive final project documents and within four weeks transmit to the CEO any concerns they may have prior to the CEO endorsing a project document for final approval by the Implementing Agency;

(e) direct the utilization of GEF funds, review the availability of resources from the GEF Trust Fund and cooperate with the Trustee to mobilize financial resources;

(f) approve and periodically review operational modalities for the Facility, including operational strategies and directives for project selection, means to facilitate arrangements for project preparation and execution by organizations and entities referred to in paragraph 28, additional eligibility and other financing criteria in accordance with paragraphs 9(b) and 9(c) respectively, procedural steps to be included in the project cycle, and the mandate, composition and role of STAP;

(g) act as the focal point for the purpose of relations with the Conferences of the Parties to the conventions referred to in paragraph 6, including consideration, approval and review of the arrangements or agreements with such Conferences, receipt of guidance and recommendations from them and compliance with requirements under these arrangements or agreements for reporting to them;
(h) in accordance with paragraphs 26 and 27, ensure that GEF-financed activities relating to the conventions referred to in paragraph 6 conform with the policies, program priorities and eligibility criteria decided by the Conference of the Parties for the purposes of the convention concerned;
(i) appoint the CEO in accordance with paragraph 21, oversee the work of the Secretariat, and assign specific tasks and responsibilities to the Secretariat;
(j) review and approve the administrative budget of the GEF and arrange for periodic financial and performance audits of the Secretariat and the Implementing Agencies with regard to activities undertaken for the Facility;
(k) in accordance with paragraph 31, approve an annual report and keep the UN Commission on Sustainable Development apprised of its activities; and
(l) exercise such other operational functions as may be appropriate to fulfill the purposes of the Facility.

Secretariat

21. The GEF Secretariat shall service and report to the Assembly and the Council. The Secretariat, which shall be headed by the CEO/Chairperson of the Facility, shall be supported administratively by the World Bank and shall operate in a functionally independent and effective manner. The CEO shall be appointed to serve for three years on a full time basis by the Council on the joint recommendation of the Implementing Agencies. Such recommendation shall be made after consultation with the Council. The CEO may be reappointed by the Council. The CEO may be removed by the Council only for cause. The staff of the Secretariat shall include staff members seconded from the Implementing Agencies as well as individuals hired competitively on an as needed basis by one of the Implementing Agencies. The CEO shall be responsible for the organization, appointment and dismissal of Secretariat staff. The CEO shall be accountable for the performance of the Secretariat functions to the Council. The Secretariat shall, on behalf of the Council, exercise the following functions:
(a) implement effectively the decisions of the Assembly and the Council;
(b) coordinate the formulation and oversee the implementation of program activities pursuant to the joint work program, ensuring liaison with other bodies as required, particularly in the context of the cooperative arrangements or agreements referred to in paragraph 27;
(c) in consultation with the Implementing Agencies, ensure the implementation of the operational policies adopted by the Council through the preparation of common guidelines on the project cycle. Such guidelines shall address project identification and development, including the proper and adequate review of project and work program proposals, consultation with and participation of

local communities and other interested parties, monitoring of project implementation and evaluation of project results;

(d) review and report to the Council on the adequacy of arrangements made by the Implementing Agencies in accordance with the guidelines referred to in paragraph (c) above, and if warranted, recommend to the Council and the Implementing Agencies additional arrangements for project preparation and execution under paragraphs 20(f) and 28;

(e) chair interagency group meetings to ensure the effective execution of the Council's decisions and to facilitate coordination and collaboration among the Implementing Agencies;

(f) coordinate with the Secretariats of other relevant international bodies, in particular the Secretariats of the conventions referred to in paragraph 6, the Secretariats of the Montreal Protocol on Substances that Deplete the Ozone Layer and its Multilateral Fund and the United Nations Convention to Combat Desertification in Countries Experiencing Serious Drought and/or Desertification, Particularly in Africa;

(g) report to the Assembly, the Council and other institutions as directed by the Council;

(h) provide the Trustee with all relevant information to enable it to carry out its responsibilities; and

(i) perform any other functions assigned to the Secretariat by the Council.

Implementing Agencies

22. The Implementing Agencies of the GEF shall be UNDP, UNEP, and the World Bank. The Implementing Agencies shall be accountable to the Council for their GEF-financed activities, including the preparation and cost-effectiveness of GEF projects, and for the implementation of the operational policies, strategies and decisions of the Council within their respective areas of competence and in accordance with an interagency agreement to be concluded on the basis of the principles of cooperation set forth in Annex D to the present Instrument. The Implementing Agencies shall cooperate with the Participants, the Secretariat, parties receiving assistance under the GEF, and other interested parties, including local communities and non-governmental organizations, to promote the purposes of the Facility.

23. The CEO shall periodically convene meetings with the heads of the Implementing Agencies to promote interagency collaboration and communication, and to review operational policy issues regarding the implementation of GEF-financed activities. The CEO shall transmit their conclusions and recommendations to the Council for its consideration.

Scientific and Technical Advisory Panel (STAP)

24. UNEP shall establish, in consultation with UNDP and the World Bank and on the basis of guidelines and criteria established by the Council, the Scientific and Technical Advisory Panel (STAP) as an advisory body to the Facility. UNEP shall

provide the STAP's Secretariat and shall operate as the liaison between the Facility and the STAP.

IV. Principles of decision-making

25. (a) Procedure

The Assembly and the Council shall each adopt by consensus regulations as may be necessary or appropriate to perform their respective functions transparently; in particular, they shall determine any aspect of their respective procedures, including the admission of observers and, in the case of the Council, provision for executive sessions.

(b) Consensus

Decisions of the Assembly and the Council shall be taken by consensus. In the case of the Council if, in the consideration of any matter of substance, all practicable efforts by the Council and its Chairperson have been made and no consensus appears attainable, any member of the Council may require a formal vote.

(c) Formal Vote

i) Unless otherwise provided in this Instrument, decisions requiring a formal vote by the Council shall be taken by a double weighted majority, that is, an affirmative vote representing both a 60 percent majority of the total number of Participants and a 60 percent majority of the total contributions.

ii) Each Member of the Council shall cast the votes of the Participant or Participants he/she represents. A Member of the Council appointed by a group of Participants may cast separately the votes of each Participant in the constituency he/she represents.

iii) For the purpose of voting power, total contributions shall consist of the actual cumulative contributions made to the GEF Trust Fund as specified in Annex C (Attachment 1) and in subsequent replenishments of the GEF Trust Fund, contributions made to the GET, and the grant equivalent of co-financing and parallel financing made under the GEF pilot program, or agreed with the Trustee, until the effective date of the GEF Trust Fund. Until the effective date of the GEF Trust Fund, advance contributions made under paragraph 7(c) of Annex C shall be deemed to be contributions to the GET.

V. Relationship and cooperation with conventions

26. The Council shall ensure the effective operation of the GEF as a source of funding activities under the conventions referred to in paragraph 6. The use of the GEF resources for purposes of such conventions shall be in conformity with the policies, program priorities and eligibility criteria decided by the Conference of the Parties of each of those conventions.

27. The Council shall consider and approve cooperative arrangements or agreements with the Conferences of the Parties to the conventions referred to in paragraph 6, including reciprocal arrangements for representation in meetings.

Such arrangements or agreements shall be in conformity with the relevant provisions of the convention concerned regarding its financial mechanism and shall include procedures for determining jointly the aggregate GEF funding requirements for the purpose of the convention. With regard to each convention referred to in paragraph 6, until the first meeting of its Conference of the Parties, the Council shall consult the convention's interim body.

VI. Cooperation with other bodies

28. The Secretariat and the Implementing Agencies under the guidance of the Council shall cooperate with other international organizations to promote achievement of the purposes of the GEF. The Implementing Agencies may make arrangements for GEF project preparation and execution by multilateral development banks, specialized agencies and programs of the United Nations, other international organizations, bilateral development agencies, national institutions, non-governmental organizations, private sector entities and academic institutions, taking into account their comparative advantages in efficient and cost-effective project execution. Such arrangements shall be made in accordance with national priorities. Pursuant to paragraph 20(f), the Council may request the Secretariat to make similar arrangements in accordance with national priorities. In the event of disagreements among the Implementing Agencies or between an Implementing Agency and any entity concerning project preparation or execution, an Implementing Agency or any entity referred to in this paragraph may request the Secretariat to seek to resolve such disagreements.

VII. Operational modalities

29. The Secretariat shall coordinate the preparation of and determine the content of a joint work program for the GEF among the Implementing Agencies, including an indication of the financial resources required for the program, for approval by the Council. The work program shall be prepared in accordance with paragraph 4 and in cooperation with eligible recipients and any executing agency referred to in paragraph 28.

30. GEF projects shall be subject to endorsement by the CEO before final project approval. If at least four Council Members request that a project be reviewed at a Council meeting because in their view the project is not consistent with the Instrument or GEF policies and procedures, the CEO shall submit the project document to the next Council meeting, and shall only endorse the project for final approval by the Implementing Agency if the Council finds that the project is consistent with the Instrument and GEF policies and procedures.

VIII. Reporting

31. The Council shall approve an annual report on the activities of the GEF. The report shall be prepared by the Secretariat and circulated to all Participants. It shall contain information on the activities carried out under the GEF, including a list of project ideas submitted for consideration and a review of the project activities

funded by the Facility and their outcomes. The report shall contain all the information necessary to meet the principles of accountability and transparency that shall characterize the Facility as well as the requirements arising from the reporting arrangements agreed with each Conference of the Parties to the conventions referred to in paragraph 6. The report shall be conveyed to each of these Conferences of the Parties, the United Nations Commission on Sustainable Development and any other international organization deemed appropriate by the Council.

IX. Transitional and final provisions

Termination of the GET

32. The World Bank shall be invited to terminate the existing Global Environment Trust Fund (GET) on the effective date of the establishment of the new GEF Trust Fund, and any funds, receipts, assets and liabilities held in the GET upon termination, including the administration of any cofinancing by the Trustee in accordance with the provisions of Resolution No. 91-5 of the Executive Directors of the World Bank, shall be transferred to the new GEF Trust Fund. Pending the termination of the GET under this provision, projects financed from the GET resources shall continue to be processed and approved subject to the rules and procedures applicable to the GET.

Interim period

33. The Council may, pursuant to the provisions of this Instrument, be convened during the period from the adoption of this Instrument and its annexes by the Implementing Agencies until the effective date of the establishment of the new GEF Trust Fund (a) to appoint, by consensus, the CEO in order to enable him/her to assume the work of the Secretariat, and (b) to prepare the Council's rules of procedure and the operational modalities for the Facility. The first meeting of the Council shall be organized by the secretariat of the GEF pilot program. Administrative expenses during this interim period shall be covered by the existing GET.

Amendment and termination

34. Amendment or termination of the present Instrument may be approved by consensus by the Assembly upon the recommendation of the Council, after taking into account the views of the Implementing Agencies and the Trustee, and shall become effective after adoption by the Implementing Agencies and the Trustee in accordance with their respective rules and procedural requirements. This paragraph shall apply to the amendment of any annex to this Instrument unless the annex concerned provides otherwise.

35. The Trustee may at any time terminate its role as trustee in accordance with paragraph 14 of Annex B, and an Implementing Agency may at any time terminate its role as implementing agency, after consultation with the other Implementing Agencies and after giving the Council six months notice in writing.

Annex A: Notification of participation/termination of participation; Annex B: Role and fiduciary responsibilities of the Trustee of the GEF Trust Fund; Annex C: GEF Trust Fund - Financial provisions for replenishment; Annex D: Principles of cooperation among the Implementing Agencies; Annex E: Constituencies of the GEF Council [not reproduced]

Partnership Agreement between the members of the African, Caribbean and Pacific Group of States of the one part, and the European Community and its Member States, of the other part [excerpts]

Adopted on 23 June 2000 at Cotonou. Entered into force on 1 April 2003. Source: *Official Journal of the European Communities* L317/3, 15 December 2000. Number of parties: 91 and the European Communities. Further information: European Commission, DG Development, Brussels, Belgium, http://europa.eu.int/comm/development/index_en.htm

Article 1: Objectives of the partnership

The Community and its Member States, of the one part, and the ACP States, of the other part, hereinafter referred to as the 'Parties' hereby conclude this Agreement in order to promote and expedite the economic, cultural and social development of the ACP States, with a view to contributing to peace and security and to promoting a stable and democratic political environment.

The partnership shall be centred on the objective of reducing and eventually eradicating poverty consistent with the objectives of sustainable development and the gradual integration of the ACP countries into the world economy.

These objectives and the Parties' international commitments shall inform all development strategies and shall be tackled through an integrated approach taking account at the same time of the political, economic, social, cultural and environmental aspects of development. The partnership shall provide a coherent support framework for the development strategies adopted by each ACP State.

Sustained economic growth, developing the private sector, increasing employment and improving access to productive resources shall all be part of this framework. Support shall be given to the respect of the rights of the individual and meeting basic needs, the promotion of social development and the conditions for an equitable distribution of the fruits of growth. Regional and sub-regional integration processes which foster the integration of the ACP countries into the world economy in terms of trade and private investment shall be encouraged and supported. Building the capacity of the actors in development and improving the institutional framework necessary for social cohesion, for the functioning of a democratic society and market economy, and for the emergence of an active and organised civil society shall be integral to the approach. Systematic account shall be taken of the situation of women and gender issues in all areas - political, economic and social. The principles of sustainable management of natural resources and the environment shall be applied and integrated at every level of the partnership.

Article 20: The approach

1. The objectives of ACP-EC development cooperation shall be pursued through integrated strategies that incorporate economic, social, cultural, environmental and institutional elements that must be locally owned. Cooperation shall thus provide a coherent enabling framework of support to the ACP's own development strategies, ensuring complementarity and interaction between the various elements. In this context and within the framework of development policies and reforms pursued by the ACP States, ACP-EC cooperation strategies shall aim at:

a. achieving rapid and sustained job-creating economic growth, developing the private sector, increasing employment, improving access to productive economic activities and resource, and fostering regional cooperation and integration;
b. promoting human and social development helping to ensure that the fruits of growth are widely and equitably shared and promoting gender equality;
c. promoting cultural values of communities and specific interactions with economic, political and social elements;
d. promoting institutional reforms and development, strengthening the institutions necessary for the consolidation of democracy, good governance and for efficient and competitive market economies; and building capacity for development and partnership; and
e. promoting environmental sustainability, regeneration and best practices, and the preservation of natural resource base.

2. Systematic account shall be taken in mainstreaming into all areas of cooperation the following thematic or cross-cutting themes: gender issues, environmental issues and institutional development and capacity building. These areas shall also be eligible for Community support.

[Paragraph 3 not reproduced]

Article 32: Environment and natural resources

1. Cooperation on environmental protection and sustainable utilisation and management of natural resources shall aim at:

(a) mainstreaming environmental sustainability into all aspects of development cooperation and support programmes and projects implemented by the various actors;
(b) building and/or strengthening the scientific and technical human and institutional capacity for environmental management for all environmental stakeholders;

(c) supporting specific measures and schemes aimed at addressing critical sustainable management issues and also relating to current and future regional and international commitments concerning mineral and natural resources such as:

i) tropical forests, water resources, coastal, marine and fisheries resources, wildlife, soils, biodiversity;

ii) protection of fragile ecosystems (e.g. coral reef);

iii) renewable energy sources notably solar energy and energy efficiency;

iv) sustainable rural and urban development;

v) desertification, drought and deforestation;

vi) developing innovative solutions to urban environmental problems; and

vii) promotion of sustainable tourism.

(d) Taking into account issues relating to the transport and disposal of hazardous waste.

2. Cooperation shall also take account of:

(a) the vulnerability of small island ACP countries, especially to the threat posed by climate change;

(b) the worsening drought and desertification problems especially of least developed and land-locked countries; and

(c) institutional development and capacity building.

Article 49: Trade and environment

1. The Parties reaffirm their commitment to promoting the development of international trade in such a way as to ensure sustainable and sound management of the environment, in accordance with the international conventions and undertakings in this area and with due regard to their respective level of development. They agree that the special needs and requirements of ACP States should be taken into account in the design and implementation of environment measures.

2. Bearing in mind the Rio Principles and with a view to reinforcing the mutual supportiveness of trade and environment, the Parties agree to enhance their cooperation in this field. Cooperation shall in particular aim at the establishment of coherent national, regional and international policies, reinforcement of quality controls of goods and services related to the environment, the improvement of environment-friendly production methods in relevant sectors.

Intellectual property rights

Agreement on Trade-Related Aspects of Intellectual Property Rights

Adopted on 15 April 1994 at Marrakesh. Entered into force on 1 January 1995 for developed countries, 1 January 2000 for developing countries and 1 January 2006 for least developed countries. Source: 1867 *UNTS* 3 (the text reproduced does not incorporate the footnotes). Number of parties: 146. Further information: WTO, Geneva, Switzerland, http://www.wto.org

[Preamble not reproduced]

Article 1: Nature and scope of obligations

1. Members shall give effect to the provisions of this Agreement. Members may, but shall not be obliged to, implement in their law more extensive protection than is required by this Agreement, provided that such protection does not contravene the provisions of this Agreement. Members shall be free to determine the appropriate method of implementing the provisions of this Agreement within their own legal system and practice.

2. For the purposes of this Agreement, the term 'intellectual property' refers to all categories of intellectual property that are the subject of Sections 1 through 7 of Part II.

3. Members shall accord the treatment provided for in this Agreement to the nationals of other Members. In respect of the relevant intellectual property right, the nationals of other Members shall be understood as those natural or legal persons that would meet the criteria for eligibility for protection provided for in the Paris Convention (1967), the Berne Convention (1971), the Rome Convention and the Treaty on Intellectual Property in Respect of Integrated Circuits, were all Members of the WTO members of those conventions. Any Member availing itself of the possibilities provided in paragraph 3 of Article 5 or paragraph 2 of Article 6 of the Rome Convention shall make a notification as foreseen in those provisions to the Council for Trade-Related Aspects of Intellectual Property Rights (the 'Council for TRIPS').

Article 2: Intellectual property conventions

1. In respect of Parts II, III and IV of this Agreement, Members shall comply with Articles 1 through 12, and Article 19, of the Paris Convention (1967).

2. Nothing in Parts I to IV of this Agreement shall derogate from existing obligations that Members may have to each other under the Paris Convention, the Berne Convention, the Rome Convention and the Treaty on Intellectual Property in Respect of Integrated Circuits.

Article 3: National treatment

1. Each Member shall accord to the nationals of other Members treatment no less favourable than that it accords to its own nationals with regard to the protection of intellectual property, subject to the exceptions already provided in, respectively, the Paris Convention (1967), the Berne Convention (1971), the Rome Convention or the Treaty on Intellectual Property in Respect of Integrated Circuits. In respect of performers, producers of phonograms and broadcasting organizations, this obligation only applies in respect of the rights provided under this Agreement. Any Member availing itself of the possibilities provided in Article 6 of the Berne Convention (1971) or paragraph 1(b) of Article 16 of the Rome Convention shall make a notification as foreseen in those provisions to the Council for TRIPS.

2. Members may avail themselves of the exceptions permitted under paragraph 1 in relation to judicial and administrative procedures, including the designation of an address for service or the appointment of an agent within the jurisdiction of a Member, only where such exceptions are necessary to secure compliance with laws and regulations which are not inconsistent with the provisions of this Agreement and where such practices are not applied in a manner which would constitute a disguised restriction on trade.

Article 4: Most-favoured-nation treatment

With regard to the protection of intellectual property, any advantage, favour, privilege or immunity granted by a Member to the nationals of any other country shall be accorded immediately and unconditionally to the nationals of all other Members. Exempted from this obligation are any advantage, favour, privilege or immunity accorded by a Member:

(a) deriving from international agreements on judicial assistance or law enforcement of a general nature and not particularly confined to the protection of intellectual property;

(b) granted in accordance with the provisions of the Berne Convention (1971) or the Rome Convention authorizing that the treatment accorded be a function not of national treatment but of the treatment accorded in another country;

(c) in respect of the rights of performers, producers of phonograms and broadcasting organizations not provided under this Agreement;

(d) deriving from international agreements related to the protection of intellectual property which entered into force prior to the entry into force of the WTO Agreement, provided that such agreements are notified to the Council for TRIPS and do not constitute an arbitrary or unjustifiable discrimination against nationals of other Members.

Article 5: Multilateral agreements on acquisition or maintenance of protection

The obligations under Articles 3 and 4 do not apply to procedures provided in multilateral agreements concluded under the auspices of WIPO relating to the acquisition or maintenance of intellectual property rights.

Article 6: Exhaustion

For the purposes of dispute settlement under this Agreement, subject to the provisions of Articles 3 and 4 nothing in this Agreement shall be used to address the issue of the exhaustion of intellectual property rights.

Article 7: Objectives

The protection and enforcement of intellectual property rights should contribute to the promotion of technological innovation and to the transfer and dissemination of technology, to the mutual advantage of producers and users of technological knowledge and in a manner conducive to social and economic welfare, and to a balance of rights and obligations.

Article 8: Principles

1. Members may, in formulating or amending their laws and regulations, adopt measures necessary to protect public health and nutrition, and to promote the public interest in sectors of vital importance to their socio-economic and technological development, provided that such measures are consistent with the provisions of this Agreement.

2. Appropriate measures, provided that they are consistent with the provisions of this Agreement, may be needed to prevent the abuse of intellectual property rights by right holders or the resort to practices which unreasonably restrain trade or adversely affect the international transfer of technology.

[Articles 9-26 not reproduced]

Section 5: Patents

Article 27: Patentable subject matter

1. Subject to the provisions of paragraphs 2 and 3, patents shall be available for any inventions, whether products or processes, in all fields of technology, provided that they are new, involve an inventive step and are capable of industrial application. Subject to paragraph 4 of Article 65, paragraph 8 of Article 70 and paragraph 3 of this Article, patents shall be available and patent rights enjoyable without discrimination as to the place of invention, the field of technology and whether products are imported or locally produced.

2. Members may exclude from patentability inventions, the prevention within their territory of the commercial exploitation of which is necessary to protect *ordre public* or morality, including to protect human, animal or plant life or health or to avoid serious prejudice to the environment, provided that such exclusion is not made merely because the exploitation is prohibited by their law.

3. Members may also exclude from patentability:

(a) diagnostic, therapeutic and surgical methods for the treatment of humans or animals;

(b) plants and animals other than micro-organisms, and essentially biological processes for the production of plants or animals other than non-biological and microbiological processes. However, Members shall provide for the protection of plant varieties either by patents or by an effective *sui generis* system or by any combination thereof. The provisions of this subparagraph shall be reviewed four years after the date of entry into force of the WTO Agreement.

Article 28: Rights conferred

1. A patent shall confer on its owner the following exclusive rights:

(a) where the subject matter of a patent is a product, to prevent third parties not having the owner's consent from the acts of: making, using, offering for sale, selling, or importing for these purposes that product;

(b) where the subject matter of a patent is a process, to prevent third parties not having the owner's consent from the act of using the process, and from the acts of: using, offering for sale, selling, or importing for these purposes at least the product obtained directly by that process.

2. Patent owners shall also have the right to assign, or transfer by succession, the patent and to conclude licensing contracts.

Article 29: Conditions on patent applicants

1. Members shall require that an applicant for a patent shall disclose the invention in a manner sufficiently clear and complete for the invention to be carried out by a person skilled in the art and may require the applicant to indicate the best mode for carrying out the invention known to the inventor at the filing date or, where priority is claimed, at the priority date of the application.

2. Members may require an applicant for a patent to provide information concerning the applicant's corresponding foreign applications and grants.

Article 30: Exceptions to rights conferred

Members may provide limited exceptions to the exclusive rights conferred by a patent, provided that such exceptions do not unreasonably conflict with a normal exploitation of the patent and do not unreasonably prejudice the legitimate interests of the patent owner, taking account of the legitimate interests of third parties.

Article 31: Other use without authorization of the right holder

Where the law of a Member allows for other use of the subject matter of a patent without the authorization of the right holder, including use by the government or third parties authorized by the government, the following provisions shall be respected:

(a) authorization of such use shall be considered on its individual merits;

(b) such use may only be permitted if, prior to such use, the proposed user has made efforts to obtain authorization from the right holder on reasonable commercial terms and conditions and that such efforts have not been successful within a reasonable period of time. This requirement may be waived by a Member in the case of a national emergency or other circumstances of extreme urgency or in cases of public non-commercial use. In situations of national emergency or other circumstances of extreme urgency, the right holder shall, nevertheless, be notified as soon as reasonably practicable. In the case of public non-commercial use, where the government or contractor, without making a patent search, knows or has demonstrable grounds to know that a valid patent is or will be used by or for the government, the right holder shall be informed promptly;

(c) the scope and duration of such use shall be limited to the purpose for which it was authorized, and in the case of semi-conductor technology shall only be for public non-commercial use or to remedy a practice determined after judicial or administrative process to be anti-competitive;

(d) such use shall be non-exclusive;

(e) such use shall be non-assignable, except with that part of the enterprise or goodwill which enjoys such use;

(f) any such use shall be authorized predominantly for the supply of the domestic market of the Member authorizing such use;

(g) authorization for such use shall be liable, subject to adequate protection of the legitimate interests of the persons so authorized, to be terminated if and when the circumstances which led to it cease to exist and are unlikely to recur. The competent authority shall have the authority to review, upon motivated request, the continued existence of these circumstances;

(h) the right holder shall be paid adequate remuneration in the circumstances of each case, taking into account the economic value of the authorization;

(i) the legal validity of any decision relating to the authorization of such use shall be subject to judicial review or other independent review by a distinct higher authority in that Member;

(j) any decision relating to the remuneration provided in respect of such use shall be subject to judicial review or other independent review by a distinct higher authority in that Member;

(k) Members are not obliged to apply the conditions set forth in subparagraphs (b) and (f) where such use is permitted to remedy a practice determined after judicial or administrative process to be anti-competitive. The need to correct anti-competitive practices may be taken into account in determining the amount of remuneration in such cases. Competent authorities shall have the authority to refuse termination of authorization if and when the conditions which led to such authorization are likely to recur;

(l) where such use is authorized to permit the exploitation of a patent ('the second patent') which cannot be exploited without infringing another patent ('the first patent'), the following additional conditions shall apply:

i) the invention claimed in the second patent shall involve an important technical advance of considerable economic significance in relation to the invention claimed in the first patent;
ii) the owner of the first patent shall be entitled to a cross-licence on reasonable terms to use the invention claimed in the second patent; and
iii) the use authorized in respect of the first patent shall be non-assignable except with the assignment of the second patent.

Article 32: Revocation/forfeiture

An opportunity for judicial review of any decision to revoke or forfeit a patent shall be available.

Article 33: Term of protection

The term of protection available shall not end before the expiration of a period of twenty years counted from the filing date.

Article 34: Process patents: burden of proof

1. For the purposes of civil proceedings in respect of the infringement of the rights of the owner referred to in paragraph 1(b) of Article 28, if the subject matter of a patent is a process for obtaining a product, the judicial authorities shall have the authority to order the defendant to prove that the process to obtain an identical product is different from the patented process. Therefore, Members shall provide, in at least one of the following circumstances, that any identical product when produced without the consent of the patent owner shall, in the absence of proof to the contrary, be deemed to have been obtained by the patented process:

(a) if the product obtained by the patented process is new;
(b) if there is a substantial likelihood that the identical product was made by the process and the owner of the patent has been unable through reasonable efforts to determine the process actually used.

2. Any Member shall be free to provide that the burden of proof indicated in paragraph 1 shall be on the alleged infringer only if the condition referred to in subparagraph (a) is fulfilled or only if the condition referred to in subparagraph (b) is fulfilled.

3. In the adduction of proof to the contrary, the legitimate interests of defendants in protecting their manufacturing and business secrets shall be taken into account.

[Articles 35-73 not reproduced]

International Convention for the Protection of New Varieties of Plants

Adopted on 2 December 1961 at Paris. Entered into force on 10 August 1968. Source: 1861 *UNTS* 281 (the text reproduced incorporates the amendments adopted at Geneva on 19 March 1991). Number of parties: 54. Further information: UPOV, Geneva, Switzerland, http://www.upov.int

[Preamble not reproduced]

Chapter I: Definitions

Article 1: Definitions

For the purposes of this Act:

i) 'this Convention' means the present (1991) Act of the International Convention for the Protection of New Varieties of Plants;

ii) 'Act of 1961/1972' means the International Convention for the Protection of New Varieties of Plants of December 2, 1961, as amended by the Additional Act of November 10, 1972;

iii) 'Act of 1978' means the Act of October 23, 1978, of the International Convention for the Protection of New Varieties of Plants;

iv) 'breeder' means
- the person who bred, or discovered and developed, a variety,
- the person who is the employer of the aforementioned person or who has commissioned the latter's work, where the laws of the relevant Contracting Party so provide, or
- the successor in title of the first or second aforementioned person, as the case may be;

v) 'breeder's right' means the right of the breeder provided for in this Convention;

vi) 'variety' means a plant grouping within a single botanical taxon of the lowest known rank, which grouping, irrespective of whether the conditions for the grant of a breeder's right are fully met, can be
- defined by the expression of the characteristics resulting from a given genotype or combination of genotypes,
- distinguished from any other plant grouping by the expression of at least one of the said characteristics and
- considered as a unit with regard to its suitability for being propagated unchanged;

vii) 'Contracting Party' means a State or an intergovernmental organization party to this Convention;

viii) 'territory,' in relation to a Contracting Party, means, where the Contracting Party is a State, the territory of that State and, where the Contracting Party is an intergovernmental organization, the territory in which the constituting treaty of that intergovernmental organization applies;

ix) 'authority' means the authority referred to in Article 30(1)(ii);

x) 'Union' means the Union for the Protection of New Varieties of Plants founded by the Act of 1961 and further mentioned in the Act of 1972, the Act of 1978 and in this Convention;

xi) 'member of the Union' means a State party to the Act of 1961/1972 or the Act of 1978, or a Contracting Party.

Chapter II: General obligations of the Contracting Parties

Article 2: Basic obligation of the Contracting Parties

Each Contracting Party shall grant and protect breeders' rights.

Article 3: Genera and species to be protected

(1) [States already members of the Union] Each Contracting Party which is bound by the Act of 1961/1972 or the Act of 1978 shall apply the provisions of this Convention,

i) at the date on which it becomes bound by this Convention, to all plant genera and species to which it applies, on the said date, the provisions of the Act of 1961/1972 or the Act of 1978 and,
ii) at the latest by the expiration of a period of five years after the said date, to all plant genera and species.

(2) [New members of the Union] Each Contracting Party which is not bound by the Act of 1961/1972 or the Act of 1978 shall apply the provisions of this Convention,

i) at the date on which it becomes bound by this Convention, to at least 15 plant genera or species and,
ii) at the latest by the expiration of a period of 10 years from the said date, to all plant genera and species.

Article 4: National treatment

(1) [Treatment] Without prejudice to the rights specified in this Convention, nationals of a Contracting Party as well as natural persons resident and legal entities having their registered offices within the territory of a Contracting Party shall, insofar as the grant and protection of breeders' rights are concerned, enjoy within the territory of each other Contracting Party the same treatment as is accorded or may hereafter be accorded by the laws of each such other Contracting Party to its own nationals, provided that the said nationals, natural persons or legal entities comply with the conditions and formalities imposed on the nationals of the said other Contracting Party.

(2) ['Nationals'] For the purposes of the preceding paragraph, 'nationals' means, where the Contracting Party is a State, the nationals of that State and, where the Contracting Party is an intergovernmental organization, the nationals of the States which are members of that organization.

Chapter III: Conditions for the grant of the breeder's right

Article 5: Conditions of protection

(1) [Criteria to be satisfied] The breeder's right shall be granted where the variety is
i) new,
ii) distinct,
iii) uniform and
iv) stable.

(2) [Other conditions] The grant of the breeder's right shall not be subject to any further or different conditions, provided that the variety is designated by a denomination in accordance with the provisions of Article 20, that the applicant complies with the formalities provided for by the law of the Contracting Party with whose authority the application has been filed and that he pays the required fees.

Article 6: Novelty

(1) [Criteria] the variety shall be deemed to be new if, at the date of filing of the application for a breeder's right, propagating or harvested material of the variety has not been sold or otherwise disposed of to others, by or with the consent of the breeder, for purposes of exploitation of the variety
i) in the territory of the Contracting Party in which the application has been filed earlier than one year before that date and
ii) in a territory other than that of the Contracting Party in which the application has been filed earlier than four years or, in the case of trees or of vines, earlier than six years before the said date.

(2) [Varieties of recent creation] Where a Contracting Party applies this Convention to a plant genus or species to which it did not previously apply this Convention or an earlier Act, it may consider a variety of recent creation existing at the date of such extension of protection to satisfy the condition of novelty defined in paragraph (1) even where the sale or disposal to others described in that paragraph took place earlier than the time limits defined in that paragraph.

(3) ['Territory' in certain cases] For the purposes of paragraph (1), all the Contracting Parties which are member States of one and the same intergovernmental organization may act jointly, where the regulations of that organization so require, to assimilate acts done on the territories of the States members of that organization to acts done on their own territories and, should they do so, shall notify the Secretary-General accordingly.

Article 7: Distinctness

The variety shall be deemed to be distinct if it is clearly distinguishable from any other variety whose existence is a matter of common knowledge at the time of the filing of the application. In particular, the filing of an application for the granting of a breeder's right or for the entering of another variety in an official register of varieties, in any country, shall be deemed to render that other variety a matter of common knowledge from the date of the application, provided that the application leads to the granting of a breeder's right or to the entering of the said other variety in the official register of varieties, as the case may be.

Article 8: Uniformity

The variety shall be deemed to be uniform if, subject to the variation that may be expected from the particular features of its propagation, it is sufficiently uniform in its relevant characteristics.

Article 9: Stability

The variety shall be deemed to be stable if its relevant characteristics remain unchanged after repeated propagation or, in the case of a particular cycle of propagation, at the end of each such cycle.

[Articles 10-13 not reproduced]

Chapter V: The rights of the breeder

Article 14: Scope of the breeder's right

(1) [Acts in respect of the propagating material]

(a) Subject to Articles 15 and 16, the following acts in respect of the propagating material of the protected variety shall require the authorization of the breeder:
- i) production or reproduction (multiplication),
- ii) conditioning for the purpose of propagation,
- iii) offering for sale,
- iv) selling or other marketing,
- v) exporting,
- vi) importing,
- vii) stocking for any of the purposes mentioned in (i) to (vi), above.

(b) The breeder may make his authorization subject to conditions and limitations.

(2) [Acts in respect of the harvested material] Subject to Articles 15 and 16, the acts referred to in items (i) to (vii) of paragraph (1)(a) in respect of harvested material, including entire plants and parts of plants, obtained through the unauthorized use of propagating material of the protected variety shall require the authorization of the breeder, unless the breeder has had reasonable opportunity to exercise his right in relation to the said propagating material.

(3) [Acts in respect of certain products] Each Contracting Party may provide that, subject to Articles 15 and 16, the acts referred to in items (i) to (vii) of paragraph

(1)(a) in respect of products made directly from harvested material of the protected variety falling within the provisions of paragraph (2) through the unauthorized use of the said harvested material shall require the authorization of the breeder, unless the breeder has had reasonable opportunity to exercise his right in relation to the said harvested material.

(4) [Possible additional acts] Each Contracting Party may provide that, subject to Articles 15 and 16, acts other than those referred to in items (i) to (vii) of paragraph (1)(a) shall also require the authorization of the breeder.

(5) [Essentially derived and certain other varieties]
(a) The provisions of paragraphs (1) to (4) shall also apply in relation to
  i) varieties which are essentially derived from the protected variety, where the protected variety is not itself an essentially derived variety,
  ii) varieties which are not clearly distinguishable in accordance with Article 7 from the protected variety and
  iii) varieties whose production requires the repeated use of the protected variety.
(b) For the purposes of subparagraph (a)(i), a variety shall be deemed to be essentially derived from another variety ('the initial variety') when
  i) it is predominantly derived from the initial variety, or from a variety that is itself predominantly derived from the initial variety, while retaining the expression of the essential characteristics that result from the genotype or combination of genotypes of the initial variety,
  ii) it is clearly distinguishable from the initial variety and
  iii) except for the differences which result from the act of derivation, it conforms to the initial variety in the expression of the essential characteristics that result from the genotype or combination of genotypes of the initial variety.
(c) Essentially derived varieties may be obtained for example by the selection of a natural or induced mutant, or of a somaclonal variant, the selection of a variant individual from plants of the initial variety, backcrossing, or transformation by genetic engineering.

Article 15: Exceptions to the breeder's right

(1) [Compulsory exceptions] The breeder's right shall not extend to
i) acts done privately and for non-commercial purposes,
ii) acts done for experimental purposes and
iii) acts done for the purpose of breeding other varieties, and, except where the provisions of Article 14(5) apply, acts referred to in Article 14(1) to (4) in respect of such other varieties.

(2) [Optional exception] Notwithstanding Article 14, each Contracting Party may, within reasonable limits and subject to the safeguarding of the legitimate interests of the breeder, restrict the breeder's right in relation to any variety in order to permit farmers to use for propagating purposes, on their own holdings, the product

of the harvest which they have obtained by planting, on their own holdings, the protected variety or a variety covered by Article 14(5)(a)(i) or (ii).

Article 16: Exhaustion of the breeder's right

(1) [Exhaustion of right] The breeder's right shall not extend to acts concerning any material of the protected variety, or of a variety covered by the provisions of Article 14(5), which has been sold or otherwise marketed by the breeder or with his consent in the territory of the Contracting Party concerned, or any material derived from the said material, unless such acts

i) involve further propagation of the variety in question or
ii) involve an export of material of the variety, which enables the propagation of the variety, into a country which does not protect varieties of the plant genus or species to which the variety belongs, except where the exported material is for final consumption purposes.

(2) [Meaning of 'material'] For the purposes of paragraph (1), 'material' means, in relation to a variety,

i) propagating material of any kind,
ii) harvested material, including entire plants and parts of plants, and
iii) any product made directly from the harvested material.

(3) ['Territory' in certain cases] For the purposes of paragraph (1), all the Contracting Parties which are member States of one and the same intergovernmental organization may act jointly, where the regulations of that organization so require, to assimilate acts done on the territories of the States members of that organization to acts done on their own territories and, should they do so, shall notify the Secretary-General accordingly.

Article 17: Restrictions on the exercise of the breeder's right

(1) [Public interest] Except where expressly provided in this Convention, no Contracting Party may restrict the free exercise of a breeder's right for reasons other than of public interest.

(2) [Equitable remuneration] When any such restriction has the effect of authorizing a third party to perform any act for which the breeder's authorization is required, the Contracting Party concerned shall take all measures necessary to ensure that the breeder receives equitable remuneration.

Article 18: Measures regulating commerce

The breeder's right shall be independent of any measure taken by a Contracting Party to regulate within its territory the production, certification and marketing of material of varieties or the importing or exporting of such material. In any case, such measures shall not affect the application of the provisions of this Convention.

Article 19: Duration of the breeder's right

(1) [Period of protection] The breeder's right shall be granted for a fixed period.

(2) [Minimum period] The said period shall not be shorter than 20 years from the date of the grant of the breeder's right. For trees and vines, the said period shall not be shorter than 25 years from the said date.

[Articles 20-42 not reproduced]

Chapter 10

Liability and Redress

Introduction

The present chapter reproduces instruments providing general or specific liability and redress regimes for environmental harm. The rapid development of liability and redress is one of the significant developments in international environmental law in recent years and is linked to the realisation that after a period of rapid adoption of a number of substantive treaties, there is a need to consolidate the legal framework already adopted by ensuring that existing standards are effectively implemented. The adoption of liability and redress regimes remains relatively contentious as illustrated by the fact that ratification of adopted treaties is sometimes very slow.[1]

This chapter first reproduces the only existing convention which seeks to provide a general framework for civil liability related to activities causing damage to the environment. The 1993 Lugano Convention, though a regional treaty of the Council of Europe, constitutes an interesting attempt at addressing the question of environmental liability in general. Other treaties reproduced are sectoral international treaties which provide liability and redress regimes in the context of a specific activity or treaty. This chapter includes for illustrative purposes a liability treaty concerning oil pollution damage at sea, a treaty concerning civil liability for nuclear damage and the 1999 Protocol on liability to the Basel Convention. Among the other treaties which are not reproduced here, the recently adopted 2003 UNECE liability protocol is noteworthy.[2]

This chapter does not include the international law documents concerning state responsibility because there has been comparatively very little interest in developing state responsibility rules concerning environmental damage. Readers may wish to refer to two different instruments in this field. Firstly, general rules concerning state responsibility have been adopted by the International Law

---

1 This is in particular the case of the Lugano Convention which is still expecting its first ratification more than ten years after its adoption.

2 *See* Protocol on Civil Liability and Compensation for Damage Caused by the Transboundary Effects of Industrial Accidents on Transboundary Waters to the 1992 Convention on the Protection and use of Transboundary Watercourses and International Lakes and to the 1992 Convention on the Transboundary Effects of Industrial Accidents, Kiev, 21 May 2003, available at http://www.unece.org/env/civil-liability/documents/protocol_e.pdf

Commission.[3] These rules are not environment-specific but provide the general principles concerning state responsibility. Secondly, there exists one interesting treaty providing for strict liability of states for damage caused by their space objects.[4]

Selected readings

Bowman, M. and Boyle, A. (eds.), *Environmental Damage in International and Comparative Law - Problems of Definition and Valuation* (Oxford: Oxford University Press, 2002).

Fitzmaurice, M., 'Liability for Environmental Damage Caused to the Global Commons', 5 *RECIEL* 305 (1996).

Lee, M., 'Civil Liability of the Nuclear Industry', 12 *JEL* 317 (2000).

Mackenzie, R. and Khalastchi, R., 'Liability and Compensation for Environmental Damage in the Context of the Work of the United Nations Compensation Commission', 5 *RECIEL* 281 (1996).

Liability and redress

Convention on Civil Liability for Damage Resulting from Activities Dangerous to the Environment

Adopted on 21 June 1993 at Lugano. Not in force (no ratifications). Source: *European Treaty Series* - No. 150. Further information: Council of Europe, Strasbourg, France, http://conventions.coe.int

The member States of the Council of Europe, the other States and the European Economic Community signatory hereto,

Considering that the aim of the Council of Europe is to achieve a greater unity between its members;

---

3 International Law Commission, Draft Articles on the Responsibility of States for Internationally Wrongful Acts, Report on the work of its fifty-third session, Doc. A/56/10, p. 43 (2001).

4 Convention on International Liability for Damage Caused by Space Objects, London, 29 March 1972, 961 *UNTS* 187, available at http://www.oosa.unvienna.org/SpaceLaw/liabilitytxt.htm

Noting that one of the objectives of the Council of Europe is to contribute to the quality of life of human beings, in particular by promoting a natural, healthy and agreeable environment;

Considering the wish of the Council of Europe to co-operate with other States in the field of nature conservation and protection of the environment;

Realising that man, the environment and property are exposed to specific dangers caused by certain activities;

Considering that emissions released in one country may cause damage in another country and that, therefore, the problems of adequate compensation for such damage are also of an international nature;

Having regard to the desirability of providing for strict liability in this field taking into account the 'Polluter Pays' Principle;

Mindful of the work which has already been carried out at an international level, in particular to prevent damage and to deal with damage caused by nuclear substances and the carriage of dangerous goods;

Having noted Principle 13 of the 1992 Rio Declaration on Environment and Development, according to which 'States shall develop national law regarding liability and compensation for the victims of pollution and other environmental damage; they shall also co-operate in an expeditious and more determined manner to develop further international law regarding liability and compensation for adverse effects of environmental damage caused by activities within their jurisdiction or control to areas beyond their jurisdiction';

Recognising the need to adopt further measures to deal with grave and imminent threats of damage from dangerous activities and to facilitate the burden of proof for persons requesting compensation for such damage,

Have agreed as follows:

Chapter I: General provisions

Article 1: Object and purpose

This Convention aims at ensuring adequate compensation for damage resulting from activities dangerous to the environment and also provides for means of prevention and reinstatement.

Article 2: Definitions

For the purpose of this Convention:

1 'Dangerous activity' means one or more of the following activities provided that it is performed professionally, including activities conducted by public authorities:

a the production, handling, storage, use or discharge of one or more dangerous substances or any operation of a similar nature dealing with such substances;

b the production, culturing, handling, storage, use, destruction, disposal, release or any other operation dealing with one or more:
  - genetically modified organisms which as a result of the properties of the organism, the genetic modification and the conditions under which the operation is exercised, pose a significant risk for man, the environment or property;
  - micro-organisms which as a result of their properties and the conditions under which the operation is exercised pose a significant risk for man, the environment or property, such as those micro-organisms which are pathogenic or which produce toxins;

c the operation of an installation or site for the incineration, treatment, handling or recycling of waste, such as those installations or sites specified in Annex II, provided that the quantities involved pose a significant risk for man, the environment or property;

d the operation of a site for the permanent deposit of waste.

2 'Dangerous substance' means:

a substances or preparations which have properties which constitute a significant risk for man, the environment or property. A substance or preparation which is explosive, oxidizing, extremely flammable, highly flammable, flammable, very toxic, toxic, harmful, corrosive, irritant, sensitizing, carcinogenic, mutagenic, toxic for reproduction or dangerous for the environment within the meaning of Annex I, Part A to this Convention shall in any event be deemed to constitute such a risk;

b substances specified in Annex I, Part B to this Convention. Without prejudice to the application of sub-paragraph a above, Annex I, Part B may restrict the specification of dangerous substances to certain quantities or concentrations, certain risks or certain situations.

3 'Genetically modified organism' means any organism in which the genetic material has been altered in a way which does not occur naturally by mating and/or natural recombination.

However, the following genetically modified organisms are not covered by the Convention:

- organisms obtained by mutagenesis on condition that the genetic modification does not involve the use of genetically modified organisms as recipient organisms; and
- plants obtained by cell fusion (including protoplast fusion) if the resulting plant can also be produced by traditional breeding methods and on condition that the genetic modification does not involve the use of genetically modified organisms as parental organisms.

'Organism' refers to any biological entity capable of replication or of transferring genetic material.

4 'Micro-organism' means any microbiological entity, cellular or non-cellular, capable of replication or of transferring genetic material.

5 'Operator' means the person who exercises the control of a dangerous activity.

6 'Person' means any individual or partnership or any body governed by public or private law, whether corporate or not, including a State or any of its constituent subdivisions.

7 'Damage' means:

a loss of life or personal injury;

b loss of or damage to property other than to the installation itself or property held under the control of the operator, at the site of the dangerous activity;

c loss or damage by impairment of the environment in so far as this is not considered to be damage within the meaning of sub-paragraphs a or b above provided that compensation for impairment of the environment, other than for loss of profit from such impairment, shall be limited to the costs of measures of reinstatement actually undertaken or to be undertaken;

d the costs of preventive measures and any loss or damage caused by preventive measures,

to the extent that the loss or damage referred to in sub-paragraphs a to c of this paragraph arises out of or results from the hazardous properties of the dangerous substances, genetically modified organisms or micro-organisms or arises or results from waste.

8 'Measures of reinstatement' means any reasonable measures aiming to reinstate or restore damaged or destroyed components of the environment, or to introduce, where reasonable, the equivalent of these components into the environment. Internal law may indicate who will be entitled to take such measures.

9 'Preventive measures' means any reasonable measures taken by any person, after an incident has occurred to prevent or minimise loss or damage as referred to in paragraph 7, sub-paragraphs a to c of this article.

10 'Environment' includes:

- natural resources both abiotic and biotic, such as air, water, soil, fauna and flora and the interaction between the same factors;
- property which forms part of the cultural heritage; and
- the characteristic aspects of the landscape.

11 'Incident' means any sudden occurrence or continuous occurrence or any series of occurrences having the same origin, which causes damage or creates a grave and imminent threat of causing damage.

Article 3: Geographical scope

Without prejudice to the provisions of Chapter III, this Convention shall apply:

a when the incident occurs in the territory of a Party, as determined in accordance with Article 34, regardless of where the damage is suffered;

b when the incident occurs outside the territory referred to in sub-paragraph a above and the conflict of laws rules lead to the application of the law in force for the territory referred to in sub-paragraph a above.

Article 4: Exceptions

1 This Convention shall not apply to damage arising from carriage; carriage includes the period from the beginning of the process of loading until the end of the process of unloading. However, the Convention shall apply to carriage by pipeline, as well as to carriage performed entirely in an installation or on a site unaccessible to the public where it is accessory to other activities and is an integral part thereof.

2 This Convention shall not apply to damage caused by a nuclear substance:

a arising from a nuclear incident the liability of which is regulated either by the Paris Convention of 29 July 1960 on third party liability in the field of nuclear energy, and its Additional Protocol of 28 January 1964, or the Vienna Convention of 21 May 1963 on civil liability for nuclear damage; or

b if liability for such damage is regulated by a specific internal law, provided that such law is as favourable, with regard to compensation for damage, as any of the instruments referred to under sub-paragraph a above.

3 This Convention shall not apply to the extent that it is incompatible with the rules of the applicable law relating to workmen's compensation or social security schemes.

Chapter II: Liability

Article 5: Transitional provisions

1 The provisions of this chapter shall apply to incidents occurring after the entry into force of the Convention in respect of a Party. When the incident consists of a continuous occurrence or a series of occurrences having the same origin and part of these occurrences took place before the entry into force of this Convention, this chapter shall only apply to damage caused by occurrences or part of a continuous occurrence taking place after the entry into force.

2 In respect of damage caused by waste deposited at a site for the permanent deposit of waste the provisions of this chapter shall apply to damage which becomes known after the entry into force of the Convention in respect of the Party on the territory of which the site is situated. However this chapter shall not apply if:

a the site was closed in accordance with the provisions of internal law before the entry into force of the Convention;

b the operator proves, in the case where the operation of the site continues after that entry into force of the Convention, that the damage was caused solely by waste deposited there before that entry into force.

Article 6: Liability in respect of substances, organisms and certain waste installations or sites

1 The operator in respect of a dangerous activity mentioned under Article 2, paragraph 1, sub-paragraphs a to c shall be liable for the damage caused by the activity as a result of incidents at the time or during the period when he was exercising the control of that activity.

2 If an incident consists of a continuous occurrence, all operators successively exercising the control of the dangerous activity during that occurrence shall be jointly and severally liable. However, the operator who proves that the occurrence during the period when he was exercising the control of the dangerous activity caused only a part of the damage shall be liable for that part of the damage only.

3 If an incident consists of a series of occurrences having the same origin, the operators at the time of any such occurrence shall be jointly and severally liable. However, the operator who proves that the occurrence at the time when he was exercising the control of the dangerous activity caused only a part of the damage shall be liable for that part of the damage only.

4 If the damage resulting from a dangerous activity becomes known after all such dangerous activity in the installation or on the site has ceased, the last operator of this activity shall be liable for that damage unless he or the person who suffered damage proves that all or part of the damage resulted from an incident which occurred at a time before he became the operator. If it is so proved, the provisions of paragraphs 1 to 3 of this article shall apply.

5 Nothing in this Convention shall prejudice any right of recourse of the operator against any third party.

Article 7: Liability in respect of sites for the permanent deposit of waste

1 The operator of a site for the permanent deposit of waste at the time when damage caused by waste deposited at that site becomes known, shall be liable for this damage. Should the damage caused by waste deposited before the closure of such a site become known after that closure, the last operator shall be liable.

2 Liability under this article shall apply to the exclusion of any liability of the operator under Article 6, irrespective of the nature of the waste.

3 Liability under this article shall apply to the exclusion of any liability of the operator under Article 6 if the same operator conducts another dangerous activity on the site for the permanent deposit of waste.

However, if this operator or the person who has suffered damage proves that only a part of the damage was caused by the activity concerning the permanent deposit of waste, this article shall only apply to that part of the damage.

4 Nothing in this Convention shall prejudice any right of recourse of the operator against any third party.

Article 8: Exemptions

The operator shall not be liable under this Convention for damage which he proves:

a was caused by an act of war, hostilities, civil war, insurrection or a natural phenomenon of an exceptional, inevitable and irresistible character;

b was caused by an act done with the intent to cause damage by a third party, despite safety measures appropriate to the type of dangerous activity in question;

c resulted necessarily from compliance with a specific order or compulsory measure of a public authority;

d was caused by pollution at tolerable levels under local relevant circumstances; or

e was caused by a dangerous activity taken lawfully in the interests of the person who suffered the damage, whereby it was reasonable towards this person to expose him to the risks of the dangerous activity.

Article 9: Fault of the person who suffered the damage

If the person who suffered the damage or a person for whom he is responsible under internal law, has, by his own fault, contributed to the damage, the compensation may be reduced or disallowed having regard to all the circumstances.

Article 10: Causality

When considering evidence of the causal link between the incident and the damage or, in the context of a dangerous activity as defined in Article 2, paragraph 1, sub-paragraph d, between the activity and the damage, the court shall take due account of the increased danger of causing such damage inherent in the dangerous activity.

Article 11: Plurality of installations or sites

When damage results from incidents which have occurred in several installations or on several sites where dangerous activities are conducted or from dangerous activities under Article 2, paragraph 1, sub-paragraph d, the operators of the installations or sites concerned shall be jointly and severally liable for all such damage. However, the operator who proves that only part of the damage was caused by an incident in the installation or on the site where he conducts the dangerous activity or by a dangerous activity under Article 2, paragraph 1, sub-paragraph d, shall be liable for that part of the damage only.

Article 12: Compulsory financial security scheme

Each Party shall ensure that where appropriate, taking due account of the risks of the activity, operators conducting a dangerous activity on its territory be required to participate in a financial security scheme or to have and maintain a financial guarantee up to a certain limit, of such type and terms as specified by internal law, to cover the liability under this Convention.

Chapter III: Access to information

Article 13: Definition of public authorities

For the purpose of this chapter 'public authorities' means any public administration of a Party at national, regional or local level with responsibilities, and possessing information relating to the environment, with the exception of bodies acting in a judicial or legislative capacity.

Article 14: Access to information held by public authorities

1 Any person shall, at his request and without his having to prove an interest, have access to information relating to the environment held by public authorities.

The Parties shall define the practical arrangements under which such information is effectively made available.

2 The right of access may be restricted under internal law where it affects:
- the confidentiality of the proceedings of public authorities, international relations and national defence;
- public security;
- matters which are or have been sub judice, or under enquiry (including disciplinary enquiries), or which are the subject of preliminary investigation proceedings;
- commercial and industrial confidentiality, including intellectual property;
- the confidentiality of personal data and/or files;
- material supplied by a third party without that party being under a legal obligation to do so; or
- material, the disclosure of which would make it more likely that the environment to which that material related would be damaged.

Information held by public authorities shall be supplied in part where it is possible to separate out information on items concerning the interests referred to above.

3 A request for information may be refused where it would involve the supply of unfinished documents or data or internal communications, or where the request is manifestly unreasonable or formulated in too general a manner.

4 A public authority shall respond to a person requesting information as soon as possible and at the latest within two months. The reasons for a refusal to provide the information requested must be given.

5 A person who considers that his request for information has been unreasonably refused or ignored, or has been inadequately answered by a public authority, may seek a judicial or administrative review of the decision, in accordance with the relevant internal legal system.

6 The Parties may make a charge for supplying the information, but such a charge may not exceed a reasonable cost.

Article 15: Access to information held by bodies with public responsibilities for the environment

On the same terms and conditions as those set out in Article 14 any person shall have access to information relating to the environment held by bodies with public responsibilities for the environment and under the control of a public authority. Access shall be given via the competent public administration or directly by the bodies themselves.

Article 16: Access to specific information held by operators

1 The person who suffered the damage may, at any time, request the court to order an operator to provide him with specific information, in so far as this is necessary to establish the existence of a claim for compensation under this Convention.

2 Where, under this Convention, a claim for compensation is made to an operator, whether or not in the framework of judicial proceedings, this operator may request the court to order another operator to provide him with specific information, in so far as this is necessary to establish the extent of his possible obligation to compensate the person who has suffered the damage, or of his own right to compensation from the other operator.

3 The operator shall be required to provide information under paragraphs 1 and 2 of this article concerning the elements which are available to him and dealing essentially with the particulars of the equipment, the machinery used, the kind and concentration of the dangerous substances or waste as well as the nature of genetically modified organisms or micro-organisms.

4 These measures shall not affect measures of investigation which may legally be ordered under internal law.

5 The court may refuse a request which places a disproportionate burden on the operator, taking into account all the interests involved.

6 In addition to the restrictions under Article 14, paragraph 2 of this Convention, which shall apply *mutatis mutandis*, the operator may refuse to provide information where such information would incriminate him.

7 Any reasonable charge shall be paid by the person requesting the information. The operator may require an appropriate guarantee for such payment. However a court, when allowing a claim for compensation, may establish that this charge shall be borne by the operator, except to the extent that the request resulted in unnecessary costs.

Chapter IV: Actions for compensation and other claims

Article 17: Limitation periods

1 Actions for compensation under this Convention shall be subject to a limitation period of three years from the date on which the claimant knew or ought reasonably

to have known of the damage and of the identity of the operator. The laws of the Parties regulating suspension or interruption of limitation periods shall apply to the limitation period prescribed in this paragraph.

2 However, in no case shall actions be brought after thirty years from the date of the incident which caused the damage. Where the incident consists of a continuous occurrence the thirty years' period shall run from the end of that occurrence. Where the incident consists of a series of occurrences having the same origin the thirty years' period shall run from the date of the last of such occurrences. In respect of a site for the permanent deposit of waste the thirty years' period shall at the latest run from the date on which the site was closed in accordance with the provisions of internal law.

Article 18: Requests by organisations

1 Any association or foundation which according to its statutes aims at the protection of the environment and which complies with any further conditions of internal law of the Party where the request is submitted may, at any time, request:

a the prohibition of a dangerous activity which is unlawful and poses a grave threat of damage to the environment;
b that the operator be ordered to take measures to prevent an incident or damage;
c that the operator be ordered to take measures, after an incident, to prevent damage; or
d that the operator be ordered to take measures of reinstatement.

2 Internal law may stipulate cases where the request is inadmissible.

3 Internal law may specify the body, whether administrative or judicial, before which the request referred to in paragraph 1 above should be made. In all cases provision shall be made for a right of review.

4 Before deciding upon a request mentioned under paragraph 1 above the requested body may, in view of the general interests involved, hear the competent public authorities.

5 When the internal law of a Party requires that the association or foundation has its registered seat or the effective centre of its activities in its territory, the Party may declare at any time, by means of a notification addressed to the Secretary General of the Council of Europe, that, on the basis of reciprocity, an association or foundation having its seat or centre of activities in the territory of another Party and complying in that other Party with the other conditions mentioned in paragraph 1 above shall have the right to submit requests in accordance with paragraphs 1 to 3 above. The declaration will become effective on the first day of the month following the expiration of a period of three months after the date of its reception by the Secretary General.

Article 19: Jurisdiction

1 Actions for compensation under this Convention may only be brought within a Party at the court of the place:
a where the damage was suffered;
b where the dangerous activity was conducted; or
c where the defendant has his habitual residence.

2 Requests for access to specific information held by operators under Article 16, paragraphs 1 and 2 may only be submitted within a Party at the court of the place:
a where the dangerous activity is conducted; or
b where the operator who may be required to provide the information has his habitual residence.

3 Requests by organisations under Article 18, paragraph 1, sub-paragraph a may only be submitted within a Party at the court or, if internal law so provides, at a competent administrative authority of the place where the dangerous activity is or will be conducted.

4 Requests by organisations under Article 18, paragraph 1, sub-paragraphs b, c and d may only be submitted within a Party at the court or, if internal law so provides, at a competent administrative authority:
a of the place where the dangerous activity is or will be conducted; or
b of the place where the measures are to be taken.

Article 20: Notification

The court shall stay the proceedings so long as it is not shown that the defendant has been able to receive the document instituting the proceedings or an equivalent document in sufficient time to enable him to arrange for his defence, or that all necessary steps have been taken to this end.

Article 21: *Lis pendens*

1 Where proceedings involving the same cause of action and between the same parties are brought in the courts of different Parties, any court other than the court first seised shall of its own motion stay its proceedings until such time as the jurisdiction of the court first seised is established.

2 Where the jurisdiction of the court first seised is established, any court other than the court first seised shall decline jurisdiction in favour of that court.

Article 22: Related actions

1 Where related actions are brought in the courts of different Parties, any court other than the court first seised may, while the actions are pending at first instance, stay its proceedings.

2 A court other than the court first seised may also, on the application of one of the parties, decline jurisdiction if the law of that court permits the consolidation of related actions and the court first seised has jurisdiction over both actions.

3 For the purposes of this article, actions are deemed to be related where they are so closely connected that it is expedient to hear and determine them together to avoid the risk of irreconcilable judgments resulting from separate proceedings.

Article 23: Recognition and enforcement

1 Any decision given by a court with jurisdiction in accordance with Article 19 above where it is no longer subject to ordinary forms of review, shall be recognised in any Party, unless:

a such recognition is contrary to public policy in the Party in which recognition is sought;

b it was given in default of appearance and the defendant was not duly served with the document which instituted the proceedings or with an equivalent document in sufficient time to enable him to arrange for his defence;

c the decision is irreconcilable with a decision given in a dispute between the same parties in the Party in which recognition is sought; or

d the decision is irreconcilable with an earlier decision given in another State involving the same cause of action and between the same parties, provided that this latter decision fulfils the conditions necessary for its recognition in the Party addressed.

2 A decision recognised under paragraph 1 above which is enforceable in the Party of origin shall be enforceable in each Party as soon as the formalities required by that Party have been completed. The formalities shall not permit the merits of the case to be re-opened.

Article 24: Other treaties relating to jurisdiction, recognition and enforcement

Whenever two or more Parties are bound by a treaty establishing rules of jurisdiction or providing for recognition and enforcement in a Party of decisions given in another Party, the provisions of that treaty shall replace the corresponding provisions of Articles 19 to 23.

Chapter V: Relation between this Convention and other provisions

Article 25: Relation between this Convention and other provisions

1 Nothing in this Convention shall be construed as limiting or derogating from any of the rights of the persons who have suffered the damage or as limiting the provisions concerning the protection or reinstatement of the environment which may be provided under the laws of any Party or under any other treaty to which it is a Party.

2 In their mutual relations, Parties which are members of the European Economic Community shall apply Community rules and shall therefore not apply the rules arising from this Convention except in so far as there is no Community rule governing the particular subject concerned.

[Articles 26-31 not reproduced]

Chapter VIII: Final clauses

Article 32: Signature, ratification and entry into force

1 This Convention shall be open for signature by the member States of the Council of Europe, the non-member States which have participated in its elaboration and by the European Economic Community.

2 This Convention is subject to ratification, acceptance or approval. Instruments of ratification, acceptance or approval shall be deposited with the Secretary General of the Council of Europe.

3 This Convention shall enter into force on the first day of the month following the expiration of a period of three months after the date on which three States, including at least two member States of the Council of Europe, have expressed their consent to be bound by the Convention in accordance with the provisions of paragraph 2 of the present article.

4 In respect of any Signatory which subsequently expresses its consent to be bound by it, the Convention shall enter into force on the first day of the month following the expiration of a period of three months after the date of the deposit of its instrument of ratification, acceptance or approval.

[Articles 33-34 not reproduced]

Article 35: Reservations

1 Any Signatory may declare, at the time of signature or when depositing its instrument of ratification, acceptance or approval, that it reserves the right:

a to apply Article 3, sub-paragraph a, to damage suffered in the territory of the States which are not Parties to this Convention only on the basis of reciprocity;

b to provide in its internal law that, without prejudice to Article 8, the operator shall not be liable if he proves that in the case of damage caused by a dangerous activity mentioned under Article 2, paragraph 1, sub-paragraphs a and b, the state of scientific and technical knowledge at the time of the incident was not such as to enable the existence of the dangerous properties of the substance or the significant risk involved in the operation dealing with the organism to be discovered;

c not to apply Article 18.

Any other State may formulate the same reservations when depositing its instrument of accession.

2 Any Signatory or any other State which makes use of a reservation shall notify the Secretary General of the Council of Europe of the relevant contents of its internal law.

3 Any Party which extends the application of this Convention to a territory mentioned in the declaration referred to in Article 34, paragraph 2, may, in respect

of the territory concerned, make a reservation in accordance with the provisions of the preceding paragraphs.

4 No reservation shall be made to the provisions of this Convention, except those mentioned in this article.

5 Any Party which has made one of the reservations mentioned in this article may withdraw it by means of a declaration addressed to the Secretary General of the Council of Europe. The withdrawal shall become effective on the first day of the month following the expiration of a period of one month after the date of its receipt by the Secretary General.

[Articles 36-37 not reproduced]

Annex I: Dangerous substances; Annex II: Installations or sites for the incineration, treatment, handling or recycling of waste [not reproduced]

International Convention on Civil Liability for Oil Pollution Damage, 1992

Adopted on 27 November 1992 at London. Entered into force on 30 May 1996. Source: 1956 *UNTS* 255 and 973 *UNTS* 3 (the text reproduced includes the amendment adopted on 18 October 2000). Number of parties: 44. Further information: International Oil Pollution Compensation Funds, London, UK, http://www.iopcfund.org

The States Parties to the present Convention,

Conscious of the dangers of pollution posed by the worldwide maritime carriage of oil in bulk,

Convinced of the need to ensure that adequate compensation is available to persons who suffer damage caused by pollution resulting from the escape or discharge of oil from ships,

Desiring to adopt uniform international rules and procedures for determining questions of liability and providing adequate compensation in such cases,

Have agreed as follows:

Article I

For the purposes of this Convention:

1. 'Ship' means any sea-going vessel and seaborne craft of any type whatsoever constructed or adapted for the carriage of oil in bulk as cargo, provided that a ship capable of carrying oil and other cargoes shall be regarded as a ship only when it is actually carrying oil in bulk as cargo and during any voyage following such

carriage unless it is proved that it has no residues of such carriage of oil in bulk aboard.

2. 'Person' means any individual or partnership or any public or private body, whether corporate or not, including a State or any of its constituent subdivisions.

3. 'Owner' means the person or persons registered as the owner of the ship or, in the absence of registration, the person or persons owning the ship. However in the case of a ship owned by a State and operated by a company which in that State is registered as the ship's operator, 'owner' shall mean such company.

4. 'State of the ship's registry' means in relation to registered ships the State of registration of the ship, and in relation to unregistered ships the State whose flag the ship is flying.

5. 'Oil' means any persistent hydrocarbon mineral oil such as crude oil, fuel oil, heavy diesel oil and lubricating oil, whether carried on board a ship as cargo or in the bunkers of such a ship.

6. 'Pollution damage' means:

a) loss or damage caused outside the ship by contamination resulting from the escape or discharge of oil from the ship, wherever such escape or discharge may occur, provided that compensation for impairment of the environment other than loss of profit from such impairment shall be limited to costs of reasonable measures of reinstatement actually undertaken or to be undertaken;
b) the costs of preventive measures and further loss or damage caused by preventive measures.

7. 'Preventive measures' means any reasonable measures taken by any person after an incident has occurred to prevent or minimize pollution damage.

8. 'Incident' means any occurrence, or series of occurrences having the same origin, which causes pollution damage or creates a grave and imminent threat of causing such damage.

9. 'Organization' means the International Maritime Organization.

10. '1969 Liability Convention' means the International Convention on Civil Liability for Oil Pollution Damage, 1969. For States Parties to the Protocol of 1976 to that Convention, the term shall be deemed to include the 1969 Liability Convention as amended by that Protocol.

Article II

This Convention shall apply exclusively:

a) to pollution damage caused:

i) in the territory, including the territorial sea, of a Contracting State, and
ii) in the exclusive economic zone of a Contracting State, established in accordance with international law, or, if a Contracting State has not established

such a zone, in an area beyond and adjacent to the territorial sea of that State determined by that State in accordance with international law and extending not more than 200 nautical miles from the baselines from which the breadth of its territorial sea is measured;

b) to preventive measures, wherever taken, to prevent or minimize such damage.

Article III

1. Except as provided in paragraphs 2 and 3 of this Article, the owner of a ship at the time of an incident, or, where the incident consists of a series of occurrences, at the time of the first such occurrence, shall be liable for any pollution damage caused by the ship as a result of the incident.

2. No liability for pollution damage shall attach to the owner if he proves that the damage:

a) resulted from an act of war, hostilities, civil war, insurrection or a natural phenomenon of an exceptional, inevitable and irresistible character, or
b) was wholly caused by an act or omission done with intent to cause damage by a third party, or
c) was wholly caused by the negligence or other wrongful act of any Government or other authority responsible for the maintenance of lights or other navigational aids in the exercise of that function.

3. If the owner proves that the pollution damage resulted wholly or partially either from an act or omission done with intent to cause damage by the person who suffered the damage or from the negligence of that person, the owner may be exonerated wholly or partially from his liability to such person.

4. No claim for compensation for pollution damage may be made against the owner otherwise than in accordance with this Convention. Subject to paragraph 5 of this Article, no claim for compensation for pollution damage under this Convention or otherwise may be made against:

(a) the servants or agents of the owner or the members of the crew;
(b) the pilot or any other person who, without being a member of the crew, performs services for the ship;
(c) any charterer (howsoever described, including a bareboat charterer), manager or operator of the ship;
(d) any person performing salvage operations with the consent of the owner or on the instructions of a competent public authority;
(e) any person taking preventive measures;
(f) all servants or agents of persons mentioned in subparagraphs (c), (d) and (e);

unless the damage resulted from their personal act or omission, committed with the intent to cause such damage, or recklessly and with knowledge that such damage would probably result.

5. Nothing in this Convention shall prejudice any right of recourse of the owner against third parties.

Article IV

When an incident involving two or more ships occurs and pollution damage results therefrom, the owners of all the ships concerned, unless exonerated under Article Ill, shall be jointly and severally liable for all such damage which is not reasonably separable.

Article V

1. The owner of a ship shall be entitled to limit his liability under this Convention in respect of any one incident to an aggregate amount calculated as follows:
(a) 4,510,000 units of account for a ship not exceeding 5,000 units of tonnage;
(b) for a ship with a tonnage in excess thereof, for each additional unit of tonnage, 631 units of account in addition to the amount mentioned in sub-paragraph (a);

provided, however, that this aggregate amount shall not in any event exceed 89,770,000 units of account.

2. The owner shall not be entitled to limit his liability under this Convention if it is proved that the pollution damage resulted from his personal act or omission, committed with the intent to cause such damage, or recklessly and with knowledge that such damage would probably result.

3. For the purpose of availing himself of the benefit of limitation provided for in paragraph 1 of this Article the owner shall constitute a fund for the total sum representing the limit of his liability with the Court or other competent authority of anyone of the Contracting States in which action is brought under Article IX or, if no action is brought, with any Court or other competent authority in anyone of the Contracting States in which an action can be brought under Article IX. The fund can be constituted either by depositing the sum or by producing a bank guarantee or other guarantee, acceptable under the legislation of the Contracting State where the fund is constituted, and considered to be adequate by the Court or other competent authority.

4. The fund shall be distributed among the claimants in proportion to the amounts of their established claims.

5. If before the fund is distributed the owner or any of his servants or agents or any person providing him insurance or other financial security has as a result of the incident in question, paid compensation for pollution damage, such person shall, up to the amount he has paid, acquire by subrogation the rights which the person so compensated would have enjoyed under this Convention.

6. The right of subrogation provided for in paragraph 5 of this Article may also be exercised by a person other than those mentioned therein in respect of any amount of compensation for pollution damage which he may have paid but only to the extent that such subrogation is permitted under the applicable national law.

7. Where the owner or any other person establishes that he may be compelled to pay at a later date in whole or in part any such amount of compensation, with regard to which such person would have enjoyed a right of subrogation under paragraphs 5 or 6 of this Article, had the compensation been paid before the fund was distributed, the Court or other competent authority of the State where the fund has been constituted may order that a sufficient sum shall be provisionally set aside to enable such person at such later date to enforce his claim against the fund.

8. Claims in respect of expenses reasonably incurred or sacrifices reasonably made by the owner voluntarily to prevent or minimize pollution damage shall rank equally with other claims against the fund.

9. (a) The 'unit of account' referred to in paragraph 1 of this Article is the Special Drawing Right as defined by the International Monetary Fund. The amounts mentioned in paragraph 1 shall be converted into national currency on the basis of the value of that currency by reference to the Special Drawing Right on the date of the constitution of the fund referred to in paragraph 3. The value of the national currency, in terms of the Special Drawing Right, of a Contracting State which is a member of the International Monetary Fund shall be calculated in accordance with the method of valuation applied by the International Monetary Fund in effect on the date in question for its operations and transactions. The value of the national currency, in terms of the Special Drawing Right, of a Contracting State which is not a member of the International Monetary Fund shall be calculated in a manner determined by that State.

(b) Nevertheless, a Contracting State which is not a member of the International Monetary Fund and whose law does not permit the application of the provisions of paragraph 9(a) may, at the time of ratification, acceptance, approval of or accession to this Convention or at any time thereafter, declare that the unit of account referred to in paragraph 9(a) shall be equal to 15 gold francs. The gold franc referred to in this paragraph corresponds to sixty-five and a half milligrammes of gold of millesimal fineness nine hundred. The conversion of the gold franc into the national currency shall be made according to the law of the State concerned.

(c) The calculation mentioned in the last sentence of paragraph 9(a) and the conversion mentioned in paragraph 9(b) shall be made in such manner as to express in the national currency of the Contracting State as far as possible the same real value for the amounts in paragraph 1 as would result from the application of the first three sentences of paragraph 9(a). Contracting States shall communicate to the depositary the manner of calculation pursuant to paragraph 9(a), or the result of the conversion in paragraph 9(b) as the case may be, when depositing an instrument of ratification, acceptance, approval of or accession to this Convention and whenever there is a change in either.

10. For the purpose of this Article the ship's tonnage shall be the gross tonnage calculated in accordance with the tonnage measurement regulations contained in Annex I of the International Convention on Tonnage Measurement of Ships, 1969.

11. The insurer or other person providing financial security shall be entitled to constitute a fund in accordance with this Article on the same conditions and having the same effect as if it were constituted by the owner. Such a fund may be constituted even if, under the provisions of paragraph 2, the owner is not entitled to limit his liability, but its constitution shall in that case not prejudice the rights of any claimant against the owner.

Article VI

1. Where the owner, after an incident, has constituted a fund in accordance with Article V, and is entitled to limit his liability,

(a) no person having a claim for pollution damage arising out of that incident shall be entitled to exercise any right against any other assets of the owner in respect of such claim;
(b) the Court or other competent authority of any Contracting State shall order the release of any ship or other property belonging to the owner which has been arrested in respect of a claim for pollution damage arising out of that incident, and shall similarly release any bail or other security furnished to avoid such arrest.

2. The foregoing shall, however, only apply if the claimant has access to the Court administering the fund and the fund is actually available in respect of his claim.

Article VII

1. The owner of a ship registered in a Contracting State and carrying more than 2,000 tons of oil in bulk as cargo shall be required to maintain insurance or other financial security, such as the guarantee of a bank or a certificate delivered by an international compensation fund, in the sums fixed by applying the limits of liability prescribed in Article V, paragraph 1 to cover his liability for pollution damage under this Convention.

2. A certificate attesting that insurance or other financial security is in force in accordance with the provisions of this Convention shall be issued to each ship after the appropriate authority of a Contracting State has determined that the requirements of paragraph 1 have been complied with. With respect to a ship registered in a Contracting State such certificate shall be issued or certified by the appropriate authority of the State of the ship's registry; with respect to a ship not registered in a Contracting State it may be issued or certified by the appropriate authority of any Contracting State. This certificate shall be in the form of the annexed model and shall contain the following particulars:

(a) name of ship and port of registration;
(b) name and principal place of business of owner;
(c) type of security;
(d) name and principal place of business of insurer or other person giving security and, where appropriate, place of business where the insurance or security is established;

(e) period of validity of certificate which shall not be longer than the period of validity of the insurance or other security.

3. The certificate shall be in the official language or languages of the issuing State. If the language used is neither English nor French, the text shall include a translation into one of these languages.

4. The certificate shall be carried on board the ship and a copy shall be deposited with the authorities who keep the record of the ship's registry or, if the ship is not registered in a Contracting State, with the authorities of the State issuing or certifying the certificate.

5. An insurance or other financial security shall not satisfy the requirements of this Article if it can cease, for reasons other than the expiry of the period of validity of the insurance or security specified in the certificate under paragraph 2 of this Article, before three months have elapsed from the date on which notice of its termination is given to the authorities referred to in paragraph 4 of this Article, unless the certificate has been surrendered to these authorities or a new certificate has been issued within the said period. The foregoing provisions shall similarly apply to any modification which results in the insurance or security no longer satisfying the requirements of this Article.

6. The State of registry shall, subject to the provisions of this Article, determine the conditions of issue and validity of the certificate.

7. Certificates issued or certified under the authority of a Contracting State in accordance with paragraph 2 shall be accepted by other Contracting States for the purposes of this Convention and shall be regarded by other Contracting States as having the same force as certificates issued or certified by them even if issued or certified in respect of a ship not registered in a Contracting State. A Contracting State may at any time request consultation with the issuing or certifying State should it believe that the insurer or guarantor named in the certificate is not financially capable of meeting the obligations imposed by this Convention.

8. Any claim for compensation for pollution damage may be brought directly against the insurer or other person providing financial security for the owner's liability for pollution damage. In such case the defendant may, even if the owner is not entitled to limit his liability according to Article V, paragraph 2, avail himself of the limits of liability prescribed in Article V, paragraph 1. He may further avail himself of the defences (other than the bankruptcy or winding up of the owner) which the owner himself would have been entitled to invoke. Furthermore, the defendant may avail himself of the defence that the pollution damage resulted from the wilful misconduct of the owner himself, but the defendant shall not avail himself of any other defence which he might have been entitled to invoke in proceedings brought by the owner against him. The defendant shall in any event have the right to require the owner to be joined in the proceedings.

9. Any sums provided by insurance or by other financial security maintained in accordance with paragraph 1 of this Article shall be available exclusively for the satisfaction of claims under this Convention.

10. A Contracting State shall not permit a ship under its flag to which this Article applies to trade unless a certificate has been issued under paragraph 2 or 12 of this Article.

11. Subject to the provisions of this Article, each Contracting State shall ensure, under its national legislation, that insurance or other security to the extent specified in paragraph 1 of this Article is in force in respect of any ship, wherever registered, entering or leaving a port in its territory, or arriving at or leaving an off-shore terminal in its territorial sea, if the ship actually carries more than 2,000 tons of oil in bulk as cargo.

12. If insurance or other financial security is not maintained in respect of a ship owned by a Contracting State, the provisions of this Article relating thereto shall not be applicable to such ship, but the ship shall carry a certificate issued by the appropriate authorities of the State of the ship's registry stating that the ship is owned by that State and that the ship's liability is covered within the limits prescribed by Article V, paragraph 1. Such a certificate shall follow as closely as practicable the model prescribed by paragraph 2 of this Article.

Article VIII

Rights of compensation under this Convention shall be extinguished unless an action is brought thereunder within three years from the date when the damage occurred. However, in no case shall an action be brought after six years from the date of the incident which caused the damage. Where this incident consists of a series of occurrences, the six years' period shall run from the date of the first such occurrence.

Article IX

1. Where an incident has caused pollution damage in the territory, including the territorial sea or an area referred to in Article II, of one or more Contracting States or preventive measures have been taken to prevent or minimize pollution damage in such territory including the territorial sea or area, actions for compensation may only be brought in the Courts of any such Contracting State or States. Reasonable notice of any such action shall be given to the defendant.

2. Each Contracting State shall ensure that its Courts possess the necessary jurisdiction to entertain such actions for compensation.

3. After the fund has been constituted in accordance with Article V the Courts of the State in which the fund is constituted shall be exclusively competent to determine all matters relating to the apportionment and distribution of the fund.

Article X

1. Any judgment given by a Court with jurisdiction in accordance with Article IX which is enforceable in the State of origin where it is no longer subject to ordinary forms of review, shall be recognized in any Contracting State, except:

(a) where the judgment was obtained by fraud; or

(b) where the defendant was not given reasonable notice and a fair opportunity to present his case.

2. A judgment recognized under paragraph 1 of this Article shall be enforceable in each Contracting State as soon as the formalities required in that State have been complied with. The formalities shall not permit the merits of the case to be re-opened.

Article XI

1. The provisions of this Convention shall not apply to warships or other ships owned or operated by a State and used, for the time being, only on government non-commercial service.

2. With respect to ships owned by a Contracting State and used for commercial purposes, each State shall be subject to suit in the jurisdictions set forth in Article IX and shall waive all defences based on its status as a sovereign State.

Article XII

This Convention shall supersede any International Conventions in force or open for signature, ratification or accession at the date on which the Convention is opened for signature, but only to the extent that such Conventions would be in conflict with it; however, nothing in this Article shall affect the obligations of Contracting States to non-Contracting States arising under such International Conventions.

Convention on Civil Liability for Nuclear Damage

Adopted on 21 May 1963 at Vienna. Entered into force on 12 November 1977. Source: Doc. INFCIRC/500 (the text reproduced is the consolidated text Convention as amended by the Protocol of 12 September 1997 which entered into force on 4 October 2003). Number of parties: 32, Protocol: 5. Further information: IAEA, Vienna, Austria, http://www.iaea.org

The Contracting Parties,

Having recognized the desirability of establishing some minimum standards to provide financial protection against damage resulting from certain peaceful uses of nuclear energy,

Believing that a convention on civil liability for nuclear damage would also contribute to the development of friendly relations among nations, irrespective of their differing constitutional and social systems,

Have decided to conclude a convention for such purposes, and thereto have agreed as follows -

Article I

1. For the purposes of this Convention -

a. 'Person' means any individual, partnership, any private or public body whether corporate or not, any international organization enjoying legal personality under the law of the Installation State, and any State or any of its constituent sub-divisions.

b. 'National of a Contracting Party' includes a Contracting Party or any of its constituent sub-divisions, a partnership, or any private or public body whether corporate or not established within the territory of a Contracting Party.

c. 'Operator', in relation to a nuclear installation, means the person designated or recognized by the Installation State as the operator of that installation.

d. 'Installation State', in relation to a nuclear installation, means the Contracting Party within whose territory that installation is situated or, if it is not situated within the territory of any State, the Contracting Party by which or under the authority of which the nuclear installation is operated.

e. 'Law of the competent court' means the law of the court having jurisdiction under this Convention, including any rules of such law relating to conflict of laws.

f. 'Nuclear fuel' means any material which is capable of producing energy by a self-sustaining chain process of nuclear fission.

g. 'Radioactive products or waste' means any radioactive material produced in, or any material made radioactive by exposure to the radiation incidental to, the production or utilization of nuclear fuel, but does not include radioisotopes which have reached the final stage of fabrication so as to be usable for any scientific, medical, agricultural, commercial or industrial purpose.

h. 'Nuclear material' means -

   i. nuclear fuel, other than natural uranium and depleted uranium, capable of producing energy by a self-sustaining chain process of nuclear fission outside a nuclear reactor, either alone or in combination with some other material; and

   ii. radioactive products or waste.

i. 'Nuclear reactor' means any structure containing nuclear fuel in such an arrangement that a self-sustaining chain process of nuclear fission can occur therein without an additional source of neutrons.

j. 'Nuclear installation' means -

   i. any nuclear reactor other than one with which a means of sea or air transport is equipped for use as a source of power, whether for propulsion thereof or for any other purpose;

ii. any factory using nuclear fuel for the production of nuclear material, or any factory for the processing of nuclear material, including any factory for the re-processing of irradiated nuclear fuel;
iii. any facility where nuclear material is stored, other than storage incidental to the carriage of such material; and
iv. such other installations in which there are nuclear fuel or radioactive products or waste as the Board of Governors of the International Atomic Energy Agency shall from time to time determine;

provided that the Installation State may determine that several nuclear installations of one operator which are located at the same site shall be considered as a single nuclear installation.

k. 'Nuclear damage' means -

i. loss of life, any personal injury;
ii. loss of or damage to property;

and each of the following to the extent determined by the law of the competent court -

iii. economic loss arising from loss or damage referred to in sub-paragraph (i) or (ii), insofar as not included in those sub-paragraphs, if incurred by a person entitled to claim in respect of such loss or damage;
iv. the costs of measures of reinstatement of impaired environment, unless such impairment is insignificant, if such measures are actually taken or to be taken, and insofar as not included in sub-paragraph (ii);
v. loss of income deriving from an economic interest in any use or enjoyment of the environment, incurred as a result of a significant impairment of that environment, and insofar as not included in sub-paragraph (ii);
vi. the costs of preventive measures, and further loss or damage caused by such measures;
vii. any other economic loss, other than any caused by the impairment of the environment, if permitted by the general law on civil liability of the competent court,

in the case of sub-paragraphs (i) to (v) and (vii) above, to the extent that the loss or damage arises out of or results from ionizing radiation emitted by any source of radiation inside a nuclear installation, or emitted from nuclear fuel or radioactive products or waste in, or of nuclear material coming from, originating in, or sent to, a nuclear installation, whether so arising from the radioactive properties of such matter, or from a combination of radioactive properties with toxic, explosive or other hazardous properties of such matter.

l. 'Nuclear incident' means any occurrence or series of occurrences having the same origin which causes nuclear damage or, but only with respect to preventive measures, creates a grave and imminent threat of causing such damage.

m. 'Measures of reinstatement' means any reasonable measures which have been approved by the competent authorities of the State where the measures were taken, and which aim to reinstate or restore damaged or destroyed components of the environment, or to introduce, where reasonable, the equivalent of these components into the environment. The law of the State where the damage is suffered shall determine who is entitled to take such measures.

n. 'Preventive measures' means any reasonable measures taken by any person after a nuclear incident has occurred to prevent or minimize damage referred to in sub-paragraphs (k)(i) to (v) or (vii), subject to any approval of the competent authorities required by the law of the State where the measures were taken.
o. 'Reasonable measures' means measures which are found under the law of the competent court to be appropriate and proportionate having regard to all the circumstances, for example -
   i. the nature and extent of the damage incurred or, in the case of preventive measures, the nature and extent of the risk of such damage;
   ii. the extent to which, at the time they are taken, such measures are likely to be effective; and
   iii. relevant scientific and technical expertise.
p. 'Special Drawing Right', hereinafter referred to as SDR, means the unit of account defined by the International Monetary Fund and used by it for its own operations and transactions.

2. An Installation State may, if the small extent of the risks involved so warrants, exclude any nuclear installation or small quantities of nuclear material from the application of this Convention, provided that -
a. with respect to nuclear installations, criteria for such exclusion have been established by the Board of Governors of the International Atomic Energy Agency and any exclusion by an Installation State satisfies such criteria; and
b. with respect to small quantities of nuclear material, maximum limits for the exclusion of such quantities have been established by the Board of Governors of the International Atomic Energy Agency and any exclusion by an Installation State is within such established limits.

The criteria for the exclusion of nuclear installations and the maximum limits for the exclusion of small quantities of nuclear material shall be reviewed periodically by the Board of Governors.

Article I A

1. This Convention shall apply to nuclear damage wherever suffered.

2. However, the legislation of the Installation State may exclude from the application of this Convention damage suffered -
a. in the territory of a non-Contracting State; or
b. in any maritime zones established by a non-Contracting State in accordance with the international law of the sea.

3. An exclusion pursuant to paragraph 2 of this Article may apply only in respect of a non-Contracting State which at the time of the incident -

a. has a nuclear installation in its territory or in any maritime zones established by it in accordance with the international law of the sea; and
b. does not afford equivalent reciprocal benefits.

4. Any exclusion pursuant to paragraph 2 of this Article shall not affect the rights referred to in sub-paragraph (a) of paragraph 2 of Article IX and any exclusion pursuant to paragraph 2(b) of this Article shall not extend to damage on board or to a ship or an aircraft.

Article I B

This Convention shall not apply to nuclear installations used for non-peaceful purposes.

Article II

1. The operator of a nuclear installation shall be liable for nuclear damage upon proof that such damage has been caused by a nuclear incident -

a. in his nuclear installation; or
b. involving nuclear material coming from or originating in his nuclear installation, and occurring -
    i. before liability with regard to nuclear incidents involving the nuclear material has been assumed, pursuant to the express terms of a contract in writing, by the operator of another nuclear installation;
    ii. in the absence of such express terms, before the operator of another nuclear installation has taken charge of the nuclear material; or
    iii. where the nuclear material is intended to be used in a nuclear reactor with which a means of transport is equipped for use as a source of power, whether for propulsion thereof or for any other purpose, before the person duly authorized to operate such reactor has taken charge of the nuclear material; but
    iv. where the nuclear material has been sent to a person within the territory of a non-Contracting State, before it has been unloaded from the means of transport by which it has arrived in the territory of that non-Contracting State;
c. involving nuclear material sent to his nuclear installation, and occurring -
    i. after liability with regard to nuclear incidents involving the nuclear material has been assumed by him, pursuant to the express terms of a contract in writing, from the operator of another nuclear installation;
    ii. in the absence of such express terms, after he has taken charge of the nuclear material; or
    iii. after he has taken charge of the nuclear material from a person operating a nuclear reactor with which a means of transport is equipped for use as a source of power, whether for propulsion thereof or for any other purpose; but
    iv. where the nuclear material has, with the written consent of the operator, been sent from a person within the territory of a non-Contracting State, only

after it has been loaded on the means of transport by which it is to be carried from the territory of that State;

provided that, if nuclear damage is caused by a nuclear incident occurring in a nuclear installation and involving nuclear material stored therein incidentally to the carriage of such material, the provisions of sub-paragraph (a) of this paragraph shall not apply where another operator or person is solely liable pursuant to the provisions of sub-paragraph (b) or (c) of this paragraph.

2. The Installation State may provide by legislation that, in accordance with such terms as may be specified therein, a carrier of nuclear material or a person handling radioactive waste may, at his request and with the consent of the operator concerned, be designated or recognized as operator in the place of that operator in respect of such nuclear material or radioactive waste respectively. In this case such carrier or such person shall be considered, for all the purposes of this Convention, as an operator of a nuclear installation situated within the territory of that State.

3. a. Where nuclear damage engages the liability of more than one operator, the operators involved shall, in so far as the damage attributable to each operator is not reasonably separable, be jointly and severally liable. The Installation State may limit the amount of public funds made available per incident to the difference, if any, between the amounts hereby established and the amount established pursuant to paragraph 1 of Article V.

b. Where a nuclear incident occurs in the course of carriage of nuclear material, either in one and the same means of transport, or, in the case of storage incidental to the carriage, in one and the same nuclear installation, and causes nuclear damage which engages the liability of more than one operator, the total liability shall not exceed the highest amount applicable with respect to any one of them pursuant to Article V.

c. In neither of the cases referred to in sub-paragraphs (a) and (b) of this paragraph shall the liability of any one operator exceed the amount applicable with respect to him pursuant to Article V.

4. Subject to the provisions of paragraph 3 of this Article, where several nuclear installations of one and the same operator are involved in one nuclear incident, such operator shall be liable in respect of each nuclear installation involved up to the amount applicable with respect to him pursuant to Article V. The Installation State may limit the amount of public funds made available as provided for in sub-paragraph (a) of paragraph 3 of this Article.

5. Except as otherwise provided in this Convention, no person other than the operator shall be liable for nuclear damage. This, however, shall not affect the application of any international convention in the field of transport in force or open for signature, ratification or accession at the date on which this Convention is opened for signature.

6. No person shall be liable for any loss or damage which is not nuclear damage pursuant to sub-paragraph (k) of paragraph 1 of Article I but which could have been determined as such pursuant to the provisions of that sub-paragraph.

7. Direct action shall lie against the person furnishing financial security pursuant to Article VII, if the law of the competent court so provides.

Article III

The operator liable in accordance with this Convention shall provide the carrier with a certificate issued by or on behalf of the insurer or other financial guarantor furnishing the financial security required pursuant to Article VII. However, the Installation State may exclude this obligation in relation to carriage which takes place wholly within its own territory. The certificate shall state the name and address of that operator and the amount, type and duration of the security, and these statements may not be disputed by the person by whom or on whose behalf the certificate was issued. The certificate shall also indicate the nuclear material in respect of which the security applies and shall include a statement by the competent public authority of the Installation State that the person named is an operator within the meaning of this Convention.

Article IV

1. The liability of the operator for nuclear damage under this Convention shall be absolute.

2. If the operator proves that the nuclear damage resulted wholly or partly either from the gross negligence of the person suffering the damage or from an act or omission of such person done with intent to cause damage, the competent court may, if its law so provides, relieve the operator wholly or partly from his obligation to pay compensation in respect of the damage suffered by such person.

3. No liability under this Convention shall attach to an operator if he proves that the nuclear damage is directly due to an act of armed conflict, hostilities, civil war or insurrection.

4. Whenever both nuclear damage and damage other than nuclear damage have been caused by a nuclear incident or jointly by a nuclear incident and one or more other occurrences, such other damage shall, to the extent that it is not reasonably separable from the nuclear damage, be deemed, for the purposes of this Convention, to be nuclear damage caused by that nuclear incident. Where, however, damage is caused jointly by a nuclear incident covered by this Convention and by an emission of ionizing radiation not covered by it, nothing in this Convention shall limit or otherwise affect the liability, either as regards any person suffering nuclear damage or by way of recourse or contribution, of any person who may be held liable in connection with that emission of ionizing radiation.

5. The operator shall not be liable under this Convention for nuclear damage -

a. to the nuclear installation itself or any other nuclear installation, including a nuclear installation under construction, on the site where that installation is located; and
b. to any property on that same site which is used or to be used in connection with any such installation.

6. Compensation for damage caused to the means of transport upon which the nuclear material is involved was at the time of the nuclear incident shall not have the effect of reducing the liability of the operator in respect of other damage to an amount less than either 150 million SDRs, or any higher amount established by the legislation of a Contracting Party, or an amount established pursuant to sub-paragraph (c) of paragraph 1 of Article V.

7. Nothing in this Convention shall affect the liability of any individual for nuclear damage for which the operator, by virtue of paragraph 3 or 5 of this Article, is not liable under this Convention and which that individual caused by an act or omission done with intent to cause damage.

Article V

1. The liability of the operator may be limited by the Installation State for any one nuclear incident, either -
a. to not less than 300 million SDRs; or
b. to not less than 150 million SDRs provided that in excess of that amount and up to at least 300 million SDRs public funds shall be made available by that State to compensate nuclear damage; or
c. for a maximum of 15 years from the date of entry into force of this Protocol, to a transitional amount of not less than 100 million SDRs in respect of a nuclear incident occurring within that period. An amount lower than 100 million SDRs may be established, provided that public funds shall be made available by that State to compensate nuclear damage between that lesser amount and 100 million SDRs.

2. Notwithstanding paragraph 1 of this Article, the Installation State, having regard to the nature of the nuclear installation or the nuclear substances involved and to the likely consequences of an incident originating therefrom, may establish a lower amount of liability of the operator, provided that in no event shall any amount so established be less than 5 million SDRs, and provided that the Installation State ensures that public funds shall be made available up to the amount established pursuant to paragraph 1.

3. The amounts established by the Installations State of the liable operator in accordance with paragraphs 1 and 2 of this Article and paragraph 6 of Article IV shall apply wherever the nuclear incident occurs.

Article V A

1. Interest and costs awarded by a court in actions for compensation of nuclear damage shall be payable in addition to the amounts referred to in Article V.

2. The amounts mentioned in Article V and paragraph 6 of Article IV may be converted into national currency in round figures.

Article V B

Each Contracting Party shall ensure that persons suffering damage may enforce their rights to compensation without having to bring separate proceedings according to the origin of the funds provided for such compensation.

Article V C

1. If the courts having jurisdiction are those of a Contracting Party other than the Installation State, the public funds required under sub-paragraphs (b) and (c) of paragraph 1 of Article V and under paragraph 1 of Article VII, as well as interest and costs awarded by a court, may be made available by the first-named Contracting Party. The Installation State shall reimburse to the other Contracting Party any such sums paid. These two Contracting Parties shall agree on the procedure for reimbursement.

2. If the courts having jurisdiction are those of a Contracting Party other than the Installation State, the Contracting Party whose courts have jurisdiction shall take all measures necessary to enable the Installation State to intervene in proceedings and to participate in any settlement concerning compensation.

Article V D

1. A meeting of the Contracting Parties shall be convened by the Director General of the International Atomic Energy Agency to amend the limits of liability referred to in Article V if one-third of the Contracting Parties express a desire to that effect.

2. Amendments shall be adopted by a two-thirds majority of the Contracting Parties present and voting, provided that at least one-half of the Contracting Parties shall be present at the time of the voting.

3. When acting on a proposal to amend the limits, the meeting of the Contracting Parties shall take into account, *inter alia*, the risk of damage resulting from a nuclear incident, changes in the monetary values, and the capacity of the insurance market.

4. a. Any amendment adopted in accordance with paragraph 2 of this Article shall be notified by the Director General of the IAEA to all Contracting Parties for acceptance. The amendment shall be considered accepted at the end of a period of 18 months after it has been notified provided that at least one-third of the Contracting Parties at the time of the adoption of the amendment by the meeting have communicated to the Director General of the IAEA that they accept the amendment. An amendment accepted in accordance with this paragraph shall

enter into force 12 months after its acceptance for those Contracting Parties which have accepted it.

b. If, within a period of 18 months from the date of notification for acceptance, an amendment has not been accepted in accordance with sub-paragraph (a), the amendment shall be considered rejected.

5. For each Contracting Party accepting an amendment after it has been accepted but not entered into force or after its entry into force in accordance with paragraph 4 of this Article, the amendment shall enter into force 12 months after its acceptance by that Contracting Party.

6. A State which becomes a Party to this Convention after the entry into force of an amendment in accordance with paragraph 4 of this Article shall, failing an expression of a different intention by that State

a. be considered as a Party to this Convention as so amended; and

b. be considered as a Party to the unamended Convention in relation to any State Party not bound by the amendment.

Article VI

1. a. Rights of compensation under this Convention shall be extinguished if an action is not brought within -

   i. with respect to loss of life and personal injury, thirty years from the date of the nuclear incident;

   ii. with respect to other damage, ten years from the date of the nuclear incident.

b. If, however, under the law of the Installation State, the liability of the operator is covered by insurance or other financial security including State funds for a longer period, the law of the competent court may provide that rights of compensation against the operator shall only be extinguished after such a longer period which shall not exceed the period for which his liability is so covered under the law of the Installation State.

c. Actions for compensation with respect to loss of life and personal injury or, pursuant to an extension under sub-paragraph (b) of this paragraph with respect to other damage, which are brought after a period of ten years from the date of the nuclear incident shall in no case affect the rights of compensation under this Convention of any person who has brought an action against the operator before the expiry of that period.

2. Deleted.

3. Rights of compensation under the Convention shall be subject to prescription or extinction, as provided by the law of the competent court, if an action is not brought within three years from the date on which the person suffering damage had knowledge or ought reasonably to have had knowledge of the damage and of the operator liable for the damage, provided that the periods established pursuant to sub-paragraphs (a) and (b) of paragraph 1 of this Article shall not be exceeded.

4. Unless the law of the competent court otherwise provides, any person who claims to have suffered nuclear damage and who has brought an action for compensation within the period applicable pursuant to this Article may amend his claim to take into account any aggravation of the damage, even after the expiry of that period, provided that final judgement has not been entered.

5. Where jurisdiction is to be determined pursuant to sub-paragraph (b) of paragraph 3 of Article XI and a request has been made within the period applicable pursuant to this Article to any one of the Contracting Parties empowered so to determine, but the time remaining after such determination is less than six months, the period within which an action may be brought shall be six months, reckoned from the date of such determination.

Article VII

1. a. The operator shall be required to maintain insurance or other financial security covering his liability for nuclear damage in such amount, of such type and in such terms as the Installation State shall specify. The Installation State shall ensure the payment of claims for compensation for nuclear damage which have been established against the operator by providing the necessary funds to the extent that the yield of insurance or other financial security is inadequate to satisfy such claims, but not in excess of the limit, if any, established pursuant to Article V. Where the liability of the operator is unlimited, the Installation State may establish a limit of the financial security of the operator liable, provided that such limit is not lower than 300 million SDRs. The Installation State shall ensure the payment of claims for compensation for nuclear damage which have been established against the operator to the extent that the yield of the financial security is inadequate to satisfy such claims, but not in excess of the amount of the financial security to be provided under this paragraph.

b. Notwithstanding sub-paragraph (a) of this paragraph, where the liability of the operator is unlimited, the Installation State, having regard to the nature of the nuclear installation or the nuclear substances involved and to the likely consequences of an incident originating therefrom, may establish a lower amount of financial security of the operator, provided that in no event shall any amount so established be less than 5 million SDRs, and provided that the Installation State ensures the payment of claims for compensation for nuclear damage which have been established against the operator by providing necessary funds to the extent that the yield of insurance or other financial security is inadequate to satisfy such claims, and up to the limit provided pursuant to sub-paragraph (a) of this paragraph.

2. Nothing in paragraph 1 of this Article shall require a Contracting Party or any of its constituent sub-divisions, such as States or Republics, to maintain insurance or other financial security to cover their liability as operators.

3. The funds provided by insurance, by other financial security or by the Installation State pursuant to paragraph 1 of this Article or sub-paragraphs (b) and

(c) of paragraph 1 of Article V shall be exclusively available for compensation due under this Convention.

4. No insurer or other financial guarantor shall suspend or cancel the insurance or other financial security provided pursuant to paragraph 1 of this Article without giving notice in writing of at least two months to the competent public authority or, in so far as such insurance or other financial security relates to the carriage of nuclear material, during the period of the carriage in question.

Article VIII

1. Subject to the provisions of this Convention, the nature, form and extent of the compensation, as well as the equitable distribution thereof, shall be governed by the law of the competent court.

2. Subject to application of the rule of sub-paragraph (c) of paragraph 1 of Article VI, where in respect of claims brought against the operator the damage to be compensated under this Convention exceeds, or is likely to exceed, the maximum amount made available pursuant to paragraph 1 of Article V, priority in the distribution of the compensation shall be given to claims in respect of loss of life or personal injury.

Article IX

1. Where provisions of national or public health insurance, social insurance, social security, workmen's compensation or occupational disease compensation systems include compensation for nuclear damage, rights of beneficiaries of such systems to obtain compensation under this Convention and rights of recourse by virtue of such systems against the operator liable shall be determined, subject to the provisions of this Convention, by the law of the Contracting Party in which such systems have been established, or by the regulations of the intergovernmental organization which has established such systems.

2. a. If a person who is a national of a Contracting Party, other than the operator, has paid compensation for nuclear damage under an international convention or under the law of a non-Contracting State, such person shall, up to the amount which he has paid, acquire by subrogation the rights under this Convention of the person so compensated. No rights shall be so acquired by any person to the extent that the operator has a right of recourse against such person under this Convention.

b. Nothing in this Convention shall preclude an operator who has paid compensation for nuclear damage out of funds other than those provided pursuant to paragraph 1 of Article VII from recovering from the person providing financial security pursuant to that paragraph or from the Installation State, up to the amount he has paid, the sum which the person so compensated would have obtained under this Convention.

Article X

The operator shall have a right of recourse only -

a. if this is expressly provided for by a contract in writing; or

b. if the nuclear incident results from an act or omission done with intent to cause damage, against the individual who has acted or omitted to act with such intent.

The right of recourse provided for under this Article may also be extended to benefit the Installation State insofar as it has provided public funds pursuant to this Convention.

Article XI

1. Except as otherwise provided in this Article, jurisdiction over actions under Article II shall lie only with the courts of the Contracting Party within whose territory the nuclear incident occurred.

1bis. Where a nuclear incident occurs within the area of the exclusive economic zone of a Contracting Party or, if such a zone has not been established, in an area not exceeding the limits of an exclusive economic zone, were one to be established, jurisdiction over actions concerning nuclear damage from that nuclear incident shall, for the purposes of this Convention, lie only with the courts of that Party. The preceding sentence shall apply if that Contracting Party has notified the Depositary of such area prior to the nuclear incident. Nothing in this paragraph shall be interpreted as permitting the exercise of jurisdiction in a manner which is contrary to the international law of the sea, including the United Nations Convention on the Law of the Sea.

2. Where a nuclear incident does not occur within the territory of any Contracting Party, or within an area notified pursuant to paragraph 1bis, or where the place of the nuclear incident cannot be determined with certainty, jurisdiction over such actions shall lie with the courts of the Installation State of the operator liable.

3. Where under paragraph 1, 1bis or 2 of this Article, jurisdiction would lie with the courts of more than one Contracting Party, jurisdiction shall lie -

a. if the nuclear incident occurred partly outside the territory of any Contracting Party, and partly within the territory of a single Contracting Party, with the courts of the latter; and

b. in any other case, with the courts of that Contracting Party which is determined by agreement between the Contracting Parties whose courts would be competent under paragraph 1, 1bis or 2 of this Article.

4. The Contracting Party whose courts have jurisdiction shall ensure that only one of its courts shall have jurisdiction in relation to any one nuclear incident.

Article XI A

The Contracting Party whose courts have jurisdiction shall ensure that in relation to actions for compensation of nuclear damage -

a. any State may bring an action on behalf of persons who have suffered nuclear damage, who are nationals of that State or have their domicile or residence in its territory, and who have consented thereto; and

b. any person may bring an action to enforce rights under this Convention acquired by subrogation or assignment.

Article XII

1. A judgment that is no longer subject to ordinary forms of review entered by a court of a Contracting Party having jurisdiction shall be recognized, except -

a. where the judgment was obtained by fraud;
b. where the party against whom the judgment was pronounced was not given a fair opportunity to present his case; or
c. where the judgment is contrary to the public policy of the Contracting Party within the territory of which recognition is sought, or is not in accord with fundamental standards of justice.

2. A judgment which is recognized under paragraph 1 of this Article shall, upon being presented for enforcement in accordance with the formalities required by the law of the Contracting Party where enforcement is sought, be enforceable as if it were a judgment of a court of that Contracting Party. The merits of a claim on which the judgment has been given shall not be subject to further proceedings.

Article XIII

1. This Convention and the national law applicable thereunder shall be applied without any discrimination based upon nationality, domicile or residence.

2. Notwithstanding paragraph 1 of this Article, insofar as compensation for nuclear damage is in excess of 150 million SDRs, the legislation of the Installation State may derogate from the provisions of this Convention with respect to nuclear damage suffered in the territory, or in any maritime zone established in accordance with the international law of the sea, of another State which at the time of the incident, has a nuclear installation in such territory, to the extend that it does not afford reciprocal benefits of an equivalent amount.

Article XIV

Except in respect of measures of execution, jurisdictional immunities under rules of national or international law shall not be invoked in actions under this Convention before the courts competent pursuant to Article XI.

Article XV

The Contracting Parties shall take appropriate measures to ensure that compensation for nuclear damage, interest and costs awarded by a court in connection therewith, insurance and reinsurance premiums and funds provided by insurance, reinsurance or other financial security, or funds provided by the Installation State, pursuant to this Convention, shall be freely transferable into the currency of the Contracting Party within whose territory the damage is suffered, and of the Contracting Party within whose territory the claimant is habitually resident, and, as regards insurance or reinsurance premiums and payments, into the currencies specified in the insurance or reinsurance contract.

Article XVI

No person shall be entitled to recover compensation under this Convention to the extent that he has recovered compensation in respect of the same nuclear damage under another international convention on civil liability in the field of nuclear energy.

Article XVII

This Convention shall not, as between the parties to them, affect the application of any international agreements or international conventions on civil liability in the field of nuclear energy in force, or open for signature, ratification or accession at the date on which this Convention is opened for signature.

Article XVIII

This Convention shall not affect the rights and obligations of a Contracting Party under the general rules of public international law.

Article XIX

1. Any Contracting Party entering into an agreement pursuant to subparagraph (b) of paragraph 3 of Article XI shall furnish without delay to the Director General of the International Atomic Energy Agency for information and dissemination to the other Contracting Parties a copy of such agreement.

2. The Contracting Parties shall furnish to the Director General for information and dissemination to the other Contracting Parties copies of their respective laws and regulations relating to matters covered by this Convention.

Article XX

Deleted.

Article XX A

1. In the event of a dispute between Contracting Parties concerning the interpretation or application of this Convention, the parties to the dispute shall consult with a view to the settlement of the dispute by negotiation or by any other peaceful means of settling disputes acceptable to them.

2. If a dispute of this character referred to in paragraph 1 of this Article cannot be settled within six months from the request for consultation pursuant to paragraph 1 of this Article, it shall, at the request of any party to such dispute, be submitted to arbitration or referred to the International Court of Justice for decision. Where a dispute is submitted to arbitration, if, within six months from the date of the request, the parties to the dispute are unable to agree on the organization of the

arbitration, a party may request the President of the International Court of Justice or the Secretary-General of the United Nations to appoint one or more arbitrators. In cases of conflicting requests by the parties to the dispute, the request to the Secretary-General of the United Nations shall have priority.

3. When ratifying, accepting, approving or acceding to this Convention, a State may declare that it does not consider itself bound by either or both of the dispute settlement procedures provided for in paragraph 2 of this Article. The other Contracting Parties shall not be bound by a dispute settlement procedure provided for in paragraph 2 of this Article with respect to a Contracting Party for which such a declaration is in force.

4. A Contracting Party which has made a declaration in accordance with paragraph 3 of this Article may at any time withdraw it by notification to the depositary.

Article XXI

Deleted.

Article XXII

Deleted.

Article XXIII

Deleted.

Article XXIV

Deleted.

Article XXV

Deleted.

Article XXVI

A conference shall be convened by the Director General of the International Atomic Energy Agency at any time after the expiry of a period of five years from the date of the entry into force of this Convention in order to consider the revision thereof, if one-third of the Contracting Parties express a desire to that effect.

Article XXVII

Deleted.

Article XXVIII

This Convention shall be registered by the Director General of the International Atomic Energy Agency in accordance with Article 102 of the Charter of the United Nations.

Article XXIX

Deleted.

Protocol on Liability and Compensation for Damage resulting from Transboundary Movements of Hazardous Wastes and their Disposal[5]

Adopted on 10 December 1999 at Basel. Not in force (1 ratification). Source: Report of the Fifth Meeting of the Conference of the Parties to the Basel Convention, UNEP/CHW.5/29 (Annex III) (1999). Further information: Basel Convention Secretariat, Geneva, Switzerland, http://www.basel.int

The Parties to the Protocol,

Having taken into account the relevant provisions of Principle 13 of the 1992 Rio Declaration on Environment and Development, according to which States shall develop international and national legal instruments regarding liability and compensation for the victims of pollution and other environmental damage,

Being Parties to the Basel Convention on the Control of Transboundary Movements of Hazardous Wastes and their Disposal,

Mindful of their obligations under the Convention,

Aware of the risk of damage to human health, property and the environment caused by hazardous wastes and other wastes and the transboundary movement and disposal thereof,

Concerned about the problem of illegal transboundary traffic in hazardous wastes and other wastes,

Committed to Article 12 of the Convention, and emphasizing the need to set out appropriate rules and procedures in the field of liability and compensation for damage resulting from the transboundary movement and disposal of hazardous wastes and other wastes,

Convinced of the need to provide for third party liability and environmental liability in order to ensure that adequate and prompt compensation is available for damage resulting from the transboundary movement and disposal of hazardous wastes and other wastes,

Have agreed as follows:

Article 1: Objective

The objective of the Protocol is to provide for a comprehensive regime for liability and for adequate and prompt compensation for damage resulting from the transboundary movement of hazardous wastes and other wastes and their disposal including illegal traffic in those wastes.

---

[5] The Basel Convention is reproduced at p. 331.

Article 2: Definitions

1. The definitions of terms contained in the Convention apply to the Protocol, unless expressly provided otherwise in the Protocol.

2. For the purposes of the Protocol:

(a) 'The Convention' means the Basel Convention on the Control of Transboundary Movements of Hazardous Wastes and their Disposal;

(b) 'Hazardous wastes and other wastes' means hazardous wastes and other wastes within the meaning of Article 1 of the Convention;

(c) 'Damage' means:

i) Loss of life or personal injury;

ii) Loss of or damage to property other than property held by the person liable in accordance with the present Protocol;

iii) Loss of income directly deriving from an economic interest in any use of the environment, incurred as a result of impairment of the environment, taking into account savings and costs;

iv) The costs of measures of reinstatement of the impaired environment, limited to the costs of measures actually taken or to be undertaken; and

v) The costs of preventive measures, including any loss or damage caused by such measures, to the extent that the damage arises out of or results from hazardous properties of the wastes involved in the transboundary movement and disposal of hazardous wastes and other wastes subject to the Convention;

(d) 'Measures of reinstatement' means any reasonable measures aiming to assess, reinstate or restore damaged or destroyed components of the environment. Domestic law may indicate who will be entitled to take such measures;

(e) 'Preventive measures' means any reasonable measures taken by any person in response to an incident, to prevent, minimize, or mitigate loss or damage, or to effect environmental clean-up;

(f) 'Contracting Party' means a Party to the Protocol;

(g) 'Protocol' means the present Protocol;

(h) 'Incident' means any occurrence, or series of occurrences having the same origin that causes damage or creates a grave and imminent threat of causing damage;

(i) 'Regional economic integration organization' means an organization constituted by sovereign States to which its member States have transferred competence in respect of matters governed by the Protocol and which has been duly authorized, in accordance with its internal procedures, to sign, ratify, accept, approve, formally confirm or accede to it;

(j) 'Unit of account' means the Special Drawing Right as defined by the International Monetary Fund.

Article 3: Scope of application

1. The Protocol shall apply to damage due to an incident occurring during a transboundary movement of hazardous wastes and other wastes and their disposal, including illegal traffic, from the point where the wastes are loaded on the means of transport in an area under the national jurisdiction of a State of export. Any Contracting Party may by way of notification to the Depositary exclude the application of the Protocol, in respect of all transboundary movements for which it is the State of export, for such incidents which occur in an area under its national jurisdiction, as regards damage in its area of national jurisdiction. The Secretariat shall inform all Contracting Parties of notifications received in accordance with this Article.

2. The Protocol shall apply:

(a) In relation to movements destined for one of the operations specified in Annex IV to the Convention other than D13, D14, D15, R12 or R13, until the time at which the notification of completion of disposal pursuant to Article 6, paragraph 9, of the Convention has occurred, or, where such notification has not been made, completion of disposal has occurred; and

(b) In relation to movements destined for the operations specified in D13, D14, D15, R12 or R13 of Annex IV to the Convention, until completion of the subsequent disposal operation specified in D1 to D12 and R1 to R11 of Annex IV to the Convention.

3. (a) The Protocol shall apply only to damage suffered in an area under the national jurisdiction of a Contracting Party arising from an incident as referred to in paragraph 1;

(b) When the State of import, but not the State of export, is a Contracting Party, the Protocol shall apply only with respect to damage arising from an incident as referred to in paragraph 1 which takes place after the moment at which the disposer has taken possession of the hazardous wastes and other wastes. When the State of export, but not the State of import, is a Contracting Party, the Protocol shall apply only with respect to damage arising from an incident as referred to in paragraph 1 which takes place prior to the moment at which the disposer takes possession of the hazardous wastes and other wastes. When neither the State of export nor the State of import is a Contracting Party, the Protocol shall not apply;

(c) Notwithstanding subparagraph (a), the Protocol shall also apply to the damages specified in Article 2, subparagraphs 2 (c) (i), (ii) and (v), of the Protocol occurring in areas beyond any national jurisdiction;

(d) Notwithstanding subparagraph (a), the Protocol shall, in relation to rights under the Protocol, also apply to damages suffered in an area under the national jurisdiction of a State of transit which is not a Contracting Party provided that such State appears in Annex A and has acceded to a multilateral or regional agreement concerning transboundary movements of hazardous waste which is in force. Subparagraph (b) will apply *mutatis mutandis*.

4. Notwithstanding paragraph 1, in case of re-importation under Article 8 or Article 9, subparagraph 2 (a), and Article 9, paragraph 4, of the Convention, the provisions of the Protocol shall apply until the hazardous wastes and other wastes reach the original State of export.

5. Nothing in the Protocol shall affect in any way the sovereignty of States over their territorial seas and their jurisdiction and the right in their respective exclusive economic zones and continental shelves in accordance with international law.

6. Notwithstanding paragraph 1 and subject to paragraph 2 of this Article:

(a) The Protocol shall not apply to damage that has arisen from a transboundary movement of hazardous wastes and other wastes that has commenced before the entry into force of the Protocol for the Contracting Party concerned;

(b) The Protocol shall apply to damage resulting from an incident occurring during a transboundary movement of wastes falling under Article 1, subparagraph 1 (b), of the Convention only if those wastes have been notified in accordance with Article 3 of the Convention by the State of export or import, or both, and the damage arises in an area under the national jurisdiction of a State, including a State of transit, that has defined or considers those wastes as hazardous provided that the requirements of Article 3 of the Convention have been met. In this case strict liability shall be channelled in accordance with Article 4 of the Protocol.

7. (a) The Protocol shall not apply to damage due to an incident occurring during a transboundary movement of hazardous wastes and other wastes and their disposal pursuant to a bilateral, multilateral or regional agreement or arrangement concluded and notified in accordance with Article 11 of the Convention if:

i) The damage occurred in an area under the national jurisdiction of any of the Parties to the agreement or arrangement;

ii) There exists a liability and compensation regime, which is in force and is applicable to the damage resulting from such a transboundary movement or disposal provided it fully meets, or exceeds the objective of the Protocol by providing a high level of protection to persons who have suffered damage;

iii) The Party to the Article 11 agreement or arrangement in which the damage has occurred has previously notified the Depositary of the non-application of the Protocol to any damage occurring in an area under its national jurisdiction due to an incident resulting from movements or disposals referred to in this subparagraph; and

iv) The Parties to the Article 11 agreement or arrangement have not declared that the Protocol shall be applicable;

(b) In order to promote transparency, a Contracting Party that has notified the Depositary of the non-application of the Protocol shall notify the Secretariat of the applicable liability and compensation regime referred to in subparagraph (a) (ii) and include a description of the regime. The Secretariat shall submit to the

Meeting of the Parties, on a regular basis, summary reports on the notifications received;

(c) After a notification pursuant to subparagraph (a) (iii) is made, actions for compensation for damage to which subparagraph (a) (i) applies may not be made under the Protocol.

8. The exclusion set out in paragraph 7 of this Article shall neither affect any of the rights or obligations under the Protocol of a Contracting Party which is not party to the agreement or arrangement mentioned above, nor shall it affect rights of States of transit which are not Contracting Parties.

9. Article 3, paragraph 2, shall not affect the application of Article 16 to all Contracting Parties.

Article 4: Strict liability

1. The person who notifies in accordance with Article 6 of the Convention, shall be liable for damage until the disposer has taken possession of the hazardous wastes and other wastes. Thereafter the disposer shall be liable for damage. If the State of export is the notifier or if no notification has taken place, the exporter shall be liable for damage until the disposer has taken possession of the hazardous wastes and other wastes. With respect to Article 3, subparagraph 6 (b), of the Protocol, Article 6, paragraph 5, of the Convention shall apply *mutatis mutandis*. Thereafter the disposer shall be liable for damage.

2. Without prejudice to paragraph 1, with respect to wastes under Article 1, subparagraph 1 (b), of the Convention that have been notified as hazardous by the State of import in accordance with Article 3 of the Convention but not by the State of export, the importer shall be liable until the disposer has taken possession of the wastes, if the State of import is the notifier or if no notification has taken place. Thereafter the disposer shall be liable for damage.

3. Should the hazardous wastes and other wastes be re-imported in accordance with Article 8 of the Convention, the person who notified shall be liable for damage from the time the hazardous wastes leave the disposal site, until the wastes are taken into possession by the exporter, if applicable, or by the alternate disposer.

4. Should the hazardous wastes and other wastes be re-imported under Article 9, subparagraph 2 (a), or Article 9, paragraph 4, of the Convention, subject to Article 3 of the Protocol, the person who re-imports shall be held liable for damage until the wastes are taken into possession by the exporter if applicable, or by the alternate disposer.

5. No liability in accordance with this Article shall attach to the person referred to in paragraphs 1 and 2 of this Article, if that person proves that the damage was:

(a) The result of an act of armed conflict, hostilities, civil war or insurrection;

(b) The result of a natural phenomenon of exceptional, inevitable, unforeseeable and irresistible character;

(c) Wholly the result of compliance with a compulsory measure of a public authority of the State where the damage occurred; or
(d) Wholly the result of the wrongful intentional conduct of a third party, including the person who suffered the damage.

6. If two or more persons are liable according to this Article, the claimant shall have the right to seek full compensation for the damage from any or all of the persons liable.

Article 5: Fault-based liability

Without prejudice to Article 4, any person shall be liable for damage caused or contributed to by his lack of compliance with the provisions implementing the Convention or by his wrongful intentional, reckless or negligent acts or omissions. This Article shall not affect the domestic law of the Contracting Parties governing liability of servants and agents.

Article 6: Preventive measures

1. Subject to any requirement of domestic law any person in operational control of hazardous wastes and other wastes at the time of an incident shall take all reasonable measures to mitigate damage arising therefrom.

2. Notwithstanding any other provision in the Protocol, any person in possession and/or control of hazardous wastes and other wastes for the sole purpose of taking preventive measures, provided that this person acted reasonably and in accordance with any domestic law regarding preventive measures, is not thereby subject to liability under the Protocol.

Article 7: Combined cause of the damage

1. Where damage is caused by wastes covered by the Protocol and wastes not covered by the Protocol, a person otherwise liable shall only be liable according to the Protocol in proportion to the contribution made by the wastes covered by the Protocol to the damage.

2. The proportion of the contribution to the damage of the wastes referred to in paragraph 1 shall be determined with regard to the volume and properties of the wastes involved, and the type of damage occurring.

3. In respect of damage where it is not possible to distinguish between the contribution made by wastes covered by the Protocol and wastes not covered by the Protocol, all damage shall be considered to be covered by the Protocol.

Article 8: Right of recourse

1. Any person liable under the Protocol shall be entitled to a right of recourse in accordance with the rules of procedure of the competent court:
(a) Against any other person also liable under the Protocol; and
(b) As expressly provided for in contractual arrangements.

2. Nothing in the Protocol shall prejudice any rights of recourse to which the person liable might be entitled pursuant to the law of the competent court.

Article 9: Contributory fault

Compensation may be reduced or disallowed if the person who suffered the damage, or a person for whom he is responsible under the domestic law, by his own fault, has caused or contributed to the damage having regard to all circumstances.

Article 10: Implementation

1. The Contracting Parties shall adopt the legislative, regulatory and administrative measures necessary to implement the Protocol.

2. In order to promote transparency, Contracting Parties shall inform the Secretariat of measures to implement the Protocol, including any limits of liability established pursuant to paragraph 1 of Annex B.

3. The provisions of the Protocol shall be applied without discrimination based on nationality, domicile or residence.

Article 11: Conflicts with other liability and compensation agreements

Whenever the provisions of the Protocol and the provisions of a bilateral, multilateral or regional agreement apply to liability and compensation for damage caused by an incident arising during the same portion of a transboundary movement, the Protocol shall not apply provided the other agreement is in force for the Party or Parties concerned and had been opened for signature when the Protocol was opened for signature, even if the agreement was amended afterwards.

Article 12: Financial limits

1. Financial limits for the liability under Article 4 of the Protocol are specified in Annex B to the Protocol. Such limits shall not include any interest or costs awarded by the competent court.

2. There shall be no financial limit on liability under Article 5.

Article 13: Time limit of liability

1. Claims for compensation under the Protocol shall not be admissible unless they are brought within ten years from the date of the incident.

2. Claims for compensation under the Protocol shall not be admissible unless they are brought within five years from the date the claimant knew or ought reasonably to have known of the damage provided that the time limits established pursuant to paragraph 1 of this Article are not exceeded.

3. Where the incident consists of a series of occurrences having the same origin, time limits established pursuant to this Article shall run from the date of the last of such occurrences. Where the incident consists of a continuous occurrence, such time limits shall run from the end of that continuous occurrence.

Article 14: Insurance and other financial guarantees

1. The persons liable under Article 4 shall establish and maintain during the period of the time limit of liability, insurance, bonds or other financial guarantees covering their liability under Article 4 of the Protocol for amounts not less than the minimum limits specified in paragraph 2 of Annex B. States may fulfil their obligation under this paragraph by a declaration of self-insurance. Nothing in this paragraph shall prevent the use of deductibles or co-payments as between the insurer and the insured, but the failure of the insured to pay any deductible or co-payment shall not be a defence against the person who has suffered the damage.

2. With regard to the liability of the notifier, or exporter under Article 4, paragraph 1, or of the importer under Article 4, paragraph 2, insurance, bonds or other financial guarantees referred to in paragraph 1 of this Article shall only be drawn upon in order to provide compensation for damage covered by Article 2 of the Protocol.

3. A document reflecting the coverage of the liability of the notifier or exporter under Article 4, paragraph 1, or of the importer under Article 4, paragraph 2, of the Protocol shall accompany the notification referred to in Article 6 of the Convention. Proof of coverage of the liability of the disposer shall be delivered to the competent authorities of the State of import.

4. Any claim under the Protocol may be asserted directly against any person providing insurance, bonds or other financial guarantees. The insurer or the person providing the financial guarantee shall have the right to require the person liable under Article 4 to be joined in the proceedings. Insurers and persons providing financial guarantees may invoke the defences which the person liable under Article 4 would be entitled to invoke.

5. Notwithstanding paragraph 4, a Contracting Party shall, by notification to the Depositary at the time of signature, ratification, or approval of, or accession to the Protocol, indicate if it does not provide for a right to bring a direct action pursuant to paragraph 4. The Secretariat shall maintain a record of the Contracting Parties who have given notification pursuant to this paragraph.

Article 15: Financial mechanism

1. Where compensation under the Protocol does not cover the costs of damage, additional and supplementary measures aimed at ensuring adequate and prompt compensation may be taken using existing mechanisms.

2. The Meeting of the Parties shall keep under review the need for and possibility of improving existing mechanisms or establishing a new mechanism.

Article 16: State responsibility

The Protocol shall not affect the rights and obligations of the Contracting Parties under the rules of general international law with respect to State responsibility.

Procedures

Article 17: Competent courts

1. Claims for compensation under the Protocol may be brought in the courts of a Contracting Party only where either:
(a) The damage was suffered; or
(b) The incident occurred; or
(c) The defendant has his habitual residence, or has his principal place of business.

2. Each Contracting Party shall ensure that its courts possess the necessary competence to entertain such claims for compensation.

Article 18: Related actions

1. Where related actions are brought in the courts of different Parties, any court other than the court first seized may, while the actions are pending at first instance, stay its proceedings.

2. A court may, on the application of one of the Parties, decline jurisdiction if the law of that court permits the consolidation of related actions and another court has jurisdiction over both actions.

3. For the purpose of this Article, actions are deemed to be related where they are so closely connected that it is expedient to hear and determine them together to avoid the risk of irreconcilable judgements resulting from separate proceedings.

Article 19: Applicable law

All matters of substance or procedure regarding claims before the competent court which are not specifically regulated in the Protocol shall be governed by the law of that court including any rules of such law relating to conflict of laws.

Article 20: Relation between the Protocol and the law of the competent court

1. Subject to paragraph 2, nothing in the Protocol shall be construed as limiting or derogating from any rights of persons who have suffered damage, or as limiting the protection or reinstatement of the environment which may be provided under domestic law.

2. No claims for compensation for damage based on the strict liability of the notifier or the exporter liable under Article 4, paragraph 1, or the importer liable under Article 4, paragraph 2, of the Protocol, shall be made otherwise than in accordance with the Protocol.

Article 21: Mutual recognition and enforcement of judgements

1. Any judgement of a court having jurisdiction in accordance with Article 17 of the Protocol, which is enforceable in the State of origin and is no longer subject to ordinary forms of review, shall be recognized in any Contracting Party as soon as the formalities required in that Party have been completed, except:
(a) Where the judgement was obtained by fraud;

(b) Where the defendant was not given reasonable notice and a fair opportunity to present his case;
(c) Where the judgement is irreconcilable with an earlier judgement validly pronounced in another Contracting Party with regard to the same cause of action and the same parties; or
(d) Where the judgement is contrary to the public policy of the Contracting Party in which its recognition is sought.

2. A judgement recognized under paragraph 1 of this Article shall be enforceable in each Contracting Party as soon as the formalities required in that Party have been completed. The formalities shall not permit the merits of the case to be re-opened.

3. The provisions of paragraphs 1 and 2 of this Article shall not apply between Contracting Parties that are Parties to an agreement or arrangement in force on mutual recognition and enforcement of judgements under which the judgement would be recognizable and enforceable.

Article 22: Relationship of the Protocol with the Basel Convention

Except as otherwise provided in the Protocol, the provisions of the Convention relating to its Protocols shall apply to the Protocol.

Article 23: Amendment of Annex B

1. At its sixth meeting, the Conference of the Parties to the Basel Convention may amend paragraph 2 of Annex B following the procedure set out in Article 18 of the Basel Convention.

2. Such an amendment may be made before the Protocol enters into force.

Final clauses

Article 24: Meeting of the Parties

1. A Meeting of the Parties is hereby established. The Secretariat shall convene the first Meeting of the Parties in conjunction with the first meeting of the Conference of the Parties to the Convention after entry into force of the Protocol.

2. Subsequent ordinary Meetings of the Parties shall be held in conjunction with meetings of the Conference of the Parties to the Convention unless the Meeting of the Parties decides otherwise. Extraordinary Meetings of the Parties shall be held at such other times as may be deemed necessary by a Meeting of the Parties, or at the written request of any Contracting Party, provided that within six months of such a request being communicated to them by the Secretariat, it is supported by at least one third of the Contracting Parties.

3. The Contracting Parties, at their first meeting, shall adopt by consensus rules of procedure for their meetings as well as financial rules.

4. The functions of the Meeting of the Parties shall be:
(a) To review the implementation of and compliance with the Protocol;

(b) To provide for reporting and establish guidelines and procedures for such reporting where necessary;
(c) To consider and adopt, where necessary, proposals for amendment of the Protocol or any annexes and for any new annexes; and
(d) To consider and undertake any additional action that may be required for the purposes of the Protocol.

Article 25: Secretariat

1. For the purposes of the Protocol, the Secretariat shall:
(a) Arrange for and service Meetings of the Parties as provided for in Article 24;
(b) Prepare reports, including financial data, on its activities carried out in implementation of its functions under the Protocol and present them to the Meeting of the Parties;
(c) Ensure the necessary coordination with relevant international bodies, and in particular enter into such administrative and contractual arrangements as may be required for the effective discharge of its functions;
(d) Compile information concerning the national laws and administrative provisions of Contracting Parties implementing the Protocol;
(e) Cooperate with Contracting Parties and with relevant and competent international organisations and agencies in the provision of experts and equipment for the purpose of rapid assistance to States in the event of an emergency situation;
(f) Encourage non-Parties to attend the Meetings of the Parties as observers and to act in accordance with the provisions of the Protocol; and
(g) Perform such other functions for the achievement of the purposes of this Protocol as may be assigned to it by the Meetings of the Parties.

2. The secretariat functions shall be carried out by the Secretariat of the Basel Convention.

Article 26: Signature

The Protocol shall be open for signature by States and by regional economic integration organizations Parties to the Basel Convention in Berne at the Federal Department of Foreign Affairs of Switzerland from 6 to 17 March 2000 and at United Nations Headquarters in New York from 1 April 2000 to 10 December 2000.

Article 27: Ratification, acceptance, formal confirmation or approval

1. The Protocol shall be subject to ratification, acceptance or approval by States and to formal confirmation or approval by regional economic integration organizations. Instruments of ratification, acceptance, formal confirmation, or approval shall be deposited with the Depositary.

2. Any organization referred to in paragraph 1 of this Article which becomes a Contracting Party without any of its member States being a Contracting Party shall

be bound by all the obligations under the Protocol. In the case of such organizations, one or more of whose member States is a Contracting Party, the organization and its member States shall decide on their respective responsibilities for the performance of their obligations under the Protocol. In such cases, the organization and the member States shall not be entitled to exercise rights under the Protocol concurrently.

3. In their instruments of formal confirmation or approval, the organizations referred to in paragraph 1 of this Article shall declare the extent of their competence with respect to the matters governed by the Protocol. These organizations shall also inform the Depositary, who will inform the Contracting Parties, of any substantial modification in the extent of their competence.

Article 28: Accession

1. The Protocol shall be open for accession by any States and by any regional economic integration organization Party to the Basel Convention which has not signed the Protocol. The instruments of accession shall be deposited with the Depositary.

2. In their instruments of accession, the organizations referred to in paragraph 1 of this Article shall declare the extent of their competence with respect to the matters governed by the Protocol. These organizations shall also inform the Depositary of any substantial modification in the extent of their competence.

3. The provisions of Article 27, paragraph 2, shall apply to regional economic integration organizations which accede to the Protocol.

Article 29: Entry into force

1. The Protocol shall enter into force on the ninetieth day after the date of deposit of the twentieth instrument of ratification, acceptance, formal confirmation, approval or accession.

2. For each State or regional economic integration organization which ratifies, accepts, approves or formally confirms the Protocol or accedes thereto after the date of the deposit of the twentieth instrument of ratification, acceptance, approval, formal confirmation or accession, it shall enter into force on the ninetieth day after the date of deposit by such State or regional economic integration organization of its instrument of ratification, acceptance, approval, formal confirmation or accession.

3. For the purpose of paragraphs 1 and 2 of this Article, any instrument deposited by a regional economic integration organization shall not be counted as additional to those deposited by member States of such organization.

Article 30: Reservations and declarations

1. No reservation or exception may be made to the Protocol. For the purposes of the Protocol, notifications according to Article 3, paragraph 1, Article 3, paragraph 6, or Article 14, paragraph 5, shall not be regarded as reservations or exceptions.

2. Paragraph 1 of this Article does not preclude a State or a regional economic integration organization, when signing, ratifying, accepting, approving, formally confirming or acceding to the Protocol, from making declarations or statements, however phrased or named, with a view, *inter alia*, to the harmonization of its laws and regulations with the provisions of the Protocol, provided that such declarations or statements do not purport to exclude or to modify the legal effects of the provisions of the Protocol in their application to that State or that organization.

[Articles 31-33 not reproduced]

Annex A: List of States of transit as referred to in Article 3, Subparagraph 3 (D);
Annex B: Financial limits [not reproduced]

Chapter 11

Dispute Settlement and Compliance

Introduction

This chapter addresses the question of dispute settlement and compliance in international environmental law by reproducing a selection of instruments providing different fora to address violations of environmental obligations. There is no specialized international environmental court, although the international court of general jurisdiction, the ICJ, has had the opportunity to consider cases with environmental implications under its Statute.[1] Conversely, specialized dispute settlement bodies established in the fields of law of the sea and international trade law have generated an important case-law on disputes involving environmental aspects. Reproduced in the first section of this chapter, Part XV of the 1982 UNCLOS submits disputes arising under the Convention with respect to the marine environment and marine living resources to compulsory third-party dispute settlement. It provides several options for states parties to settle disputes, including conciliation, arbitration[2] and recourse to the ICJ and ITLOS.[3] In the field of trade

---

1 Statute of the International Court of Justice, 26 June 1945, 1976 *UN Ybk* 1052. ICJ cases with environmental aspects include, *e.g.*, Nuclear Tests (Australia v. France and New Zealand v. France), Judgement, *ICJ Reports* 253 and 457 (1974); Certain Phosphate Lands in Nauru (Nauru v. Australia), Preliminary Objections, Judgement, *ICJ Reports* 240 (1992); Legality of the Threat or Use of Nuclear Weapons, Advisory Opinion, *ICJ Reports* 226 (1996); Gabčikovo-Nagymaros Project (Hungary/Slovakia), Judgement, *ICJ Reports* 7 (1997); and Fisheries Jurisdiction (Spain v. Canada), Judgement, *ICJ Reports* 432 (1998). In 1993, the ICJ established a specialized chamber for environmental cases under Article 26(1) of its Statute. No cases have to this date been brought to the environmental chamber.

2 *See, e.g.*, Arbitral Tribunal Constituted Under Article VII of the United Nations Convention on the Law of the Sea (UNCLOS): Southern Bluefin Tuna Case (Australia and New Zealand v. Japan), Award on Jurisdiction and Admissibility, 4 August 2000, 39 *ILM* 1359 (2000).

3 ITLOS is a specialized court with the jurisdiction to hear cases not only relating to disputes arising under the UNCLOS, but all disputes concerning the law of the sea, the protection of the marine environment and the conservation of marine living resources. *See* UNCLOS, Annex VI: Statute of the International Tribunal for the Law of the Sea, available at http://www.itlos.org. For relevant cases, readers can refer to, *e.g.*, Southern Bluefin Tuna Case (Australia and New Zealand v. Japan), Order of 27 August 1999, Request for Provisional Measures, 38 *ILM* 1624 (1999); and The Mox

law, the WTO Dispute Settlement Understanding (DSU) establishes a system of compulsory binding adjudication of disputes arising under WTO agreements, whose significance derives from the fact that it has allowed the review of cases concerning the compatibility of environmental measures with trade obligations.[4] From a regional perspective, the procedure set up under the NAAEC is an example of complaint-based monitoring allowing NGOs or private parties to file petitions with the CEC alleging that a state party is failing effectively to enforce its environmental laws.

As illustrated in the third section, cooperative solutions to non-compliance have been favoured in the specific framework of multilateral environmental agreements, particularly in the form of non-compliance procedures (NCPs). NCPs aim to secure compliance by parties with the terms of the treaty whilst providing a non-judicial and non-adversarial framework to address cases of non-compliance.[5] The Montreal Protocol was the first multilateral environmental agreement to establish an institutionalized NCP to address cases of non-compliance under the Protocol. Bodies established under other environmental treaties have followed suit, most notably the Kyoto Protocol and the Basel Convention. The singularity of the NCP instituted by the parties to the Århus Convention, a regional instrument, rests both in the composition of its Compliance Committee, whose members are nominated not only by parties but also by NGOs, and in the possibility for the Committee to receive communications from the public.

This chapter finally provides an insight into the mechanisms that have been developed within certain multilateral development banks allowing private parties to bring complaints against the organisations for their non-compliance with internal environmental regulations during the course of development lending operations. It

---

Plant Case (Ireland v. United Kingdom), Order of 3 December 2001, Request for Provisional Measures, 41 *ILM* 405 (2002).

4 For GATT Panel decisions with environmental implications, *see*, *e.g.*, Report on United States Restrictions on Imports of Tuna, 16 August 1991, 30 *ILM* 1594 (1991); and Report on United States Restrictions on Imports of Tuna, June 1994, 33 *ILM* 839 (1994). Relevant WTO cases include United States - Standards for Reformulated and Conventional Gasoline, 20 May 1996, 35 *ILM* 603 (1996); European Communities - Measures Affecting Meat and Meat Products (Hormones), 16 January 1998, WT/DS26/AB/R, WT/DS48/AB/R; United States - Import Prohibitions of Certain Shrimp and Shrimp Products, 12 October 1998, WT/DS58/AB/R, 38 *ILM* 118 (1999); Australia - Measures Affecting Importation of Salmon, 20 October 1998, WT/DS18/AB/R; Japan - Measures Affecting Agricultural Products, 22 February 1999, WT/DS76/AB/R; and European Communities - Measures Affecting Asbestos and Asbestos-Containing Projects, 18 September 2000, WT/DS135/R and 12 March 2001, WT/DS135/AB/R, 40 *ILM* 1193 (2001).

5 For examples of provisions in other multilateral environmental agreements requiring the establishment of a NCP, *see* Article 34 of the Cartagena Protocol (reproduced at p. 188); Article 17 of the Rotterdam Convention (reproduced at p. 352); and Article 17 of the Stockholm Convention (reproduced at p. 368).

reproduces the 1993 Resolution establishing the World Bank[6] Inspection Panel, the earliest of such mechanisms, which is competent to review, and if appropriate, investigate, requests brought by private parties.[7]

Selected readings

Law of the sea

Boyle, A.E., 'Dispute Settlement and the Law of the Sea Convention: Problems of Fragmentation and Jurisdiction', 46 *ICLQ* 37 (1997).

Colson, D.A. and Hoyle, P., 'Satisfying the Procedural Prerequisites to the Compulsory Dispute Settlement Mechanisms of the 1982 Law of the Sea Convention: Did the *Southern Bluefin Tuna* Tribunal Get It Right?', 34 *Ocean Development & Int'l L.* 59 (2003).

Röben, V., 'The *Southern Bluefin Tuna* Cases: Re-Regionalization of the Settlement of Law of the Sea Disputes?', 62 *ZaöRV* 61 (2002).

Treves, T., 'Dispute-Settlement Clauses in the Law of the Sea Convention and their Impact on the Protection of the Marine Environment: Some Observations', 8 *RECIEL* 6 (1999).

Trade

Brown Weiss, E. and Johnson, J.H. (eds.), *Reconciling Environment and Trade Compliance* (Ardsley, NY: Transnational Publishers, 2001).

Cameron, J. and Gray, K.R., 'Principles of International Law in the WTO Dispute Settlement Body', 50 *ICLQ* 248 (2001).

de Mestral, A., 'The NAFTA Commission on Environmental Cooperation - Voice for the North American Environment?', *in* Kiss, A., Shelton, D. and Ishibashi, K. (eds.), *Economic Globalization and Compliance with International Environmental Agreements* (The Hague: Kluwer Law International, 2003), p. 283.

Fitzmaurice, M., 'Public Participation in the North American Agreement on Environmental Cooperation', 52 *ICLQ* 333 (2003).

Palmeter, D. and Mavroidis, P.C., *Dispute Settlement in the World Trade Organization: Practice and Procedure* (Cambridge: Cambridge University Press, 2nd edn. 2004).

---

6 The term 'World Bank' refers here to the International Bank for Reconstruction and Development (IBRD) and the International Development Association (IDA).

7 The International Finance Corporation (IFC) and the Multilateral Investment Guarantee Agency (MIGA) have established the Compliance Advisor/Ombudsman (CAO). Regional banks that have set up inspection procedures include the Inter-American Development Bank, the Asian Development Bank and the European Bank for Reconstruction and Development.

Multilateral environmental agreements

Fitzmaurice, M.A. and Redgwell, C., 'Environmental Non-Compliance Procedures and International Law', 31 *Netherlands Ybk Int'l L.* 35 (2000).

Koskenniemi, M., 'Breach of Treaty or Non-Compliance? Reflections on the Enforcement of the Montreal Protocol', 3 *YbIEL* 123 (1992).

Montini, M., 'Improving Compliance with Multilateral Environmental Agreements through Positive Measures: The Case of the Kyoto Protocol on Climate Change', *in* Kiss, A., Shelton, D. and Ishibashi, K. (eds.), *Economic Globalization and Compliance with International Environmental Agreements* (The Hague: Kluwer Law International, 2003), p. 157.

Shibata, A., 'The Basel Compliance Mechanism', 12 *RECIEL* 183 (2003).

Wang, X. and Wiser, G., 'The Implementation and Compliance Regimes under the Climate Change Convention and its Kyoto Protocol', 11 *RECIEL* 181 (2002).

World Bank

Alfredsson, G. and Ring, R. (eds.), *The Inspection Panel of the World Bank: A Different Complaints Procedure* (The Hague: Martinus Nijhoff Publishers, 2001).

Gowlland Gualtieri, A., 'The Environmental Accountability of the World Bank to Non-State Actors: Insights from the Inspection Panel', 72 *BYIL* 213 (2001).

Rigo Sureda, A., 'Process Integrity and Institutional Independence in International Organizations: The Inspection Panel and the Sanctions Committee of the World Bank', *in* Boisson de Chazournes, L., Romano, C. and Mackenzie, R., *International Organizations and International Dispute Settlement: Trends and Prospects* (Ardsley, NY: Transnational Publishers, 2002), p. 165.

Shihata, I.F.I., *The World Bank Inspection Panel: In Practice* (Oxford: Oxford University Press, 2nd edn. 2000).

Law of the sea

United Nations Convention on the Law of the Sea, Part XV: Settlement of Disputes[8]

Adopted on 10 December 1982 at Montego Bay. Entered into force on 16 November 1994. Source: 1833 *UNTS* 3. Number of parties: 145. Further information: Division for Ocean Affairs and the Law of the Sea, UN, New York, USA, http://www.un.org/Depts/los/index.htm

---

8 This compilation also reproduces Parts XII, p. 425, V, p. 457, VII, p. 466, and XI p. 468, of the UNCLOS.

Section 1: General provisions

Article 279: Obligation to settle disputes by peaceful means

States Parties shall settle any dispute between them concerning the interpretation or application of this Convention by peaceful means in accordance with Article 2, paragraph 3, of the Charter of the United Nations and, to this end, shall seek a solution by the means indicated in Article 33, paragraph 1, of the Charter.

Article 280: Settlement of disputes by any peaceful means chosen by the parties

Nothing in this Part impairs the right of any States Parties to agree at any time to settle a dispute between them concerning the interpretation or application of this Convention by any peaceful means of their own choice.

Article 281: Procedure where no settlement has been reached by the parties

1. If the States Parties which are parties to a dispute concerning the interpretation or application of this Convention have agreed to seek settlement of the dispute by a peaceful means of their own choice, the procedures provided for in this Part apply only where no settlement has been reached by recourse to such means and the agreement between the parties does not exclude any further procedure.

2. If the parties have also agreed on a time-limit, paragraph 1 applies only upon the expiration of that time-limit.

Article 282: Obligations under general, regional or bilateral agreements

If the States Parties which are parties to a dispute concerning the interpretation or application of this Convention have agreed, through a general, regional or bilateral agreement or otherwise, that such dispute shall, at the request of any party to the dispute, be submitted to a procedure that entails a binding decision, that procedure shall apply in lieu of the procedures provided for in this Part, unless the parties to the dispute otherwise agree.

Article 283: Obligation to exchange views

1. When a dispute arises between States Parties concerning the interpretation or application of this Convention, the parties to the dispute shall proceed expeditiously to an exchange of views regarding its settlement by negotiation or other peaceful means.

2. The parties shall also proceed expeditiously to an exchange of views where a procedure for the settlement of such a dispute has been terminated without a settlement or where a settlement has been reached and the circumstances require consultation regarding the manner of implementing the settlement.

Article 284: Conciliation

1. A State Party which is a party to a dispute concerning the interpretation or application of this Convention may invite the other party or parties to submit the dispute to conciliation in accordance with the procedure under Annex V, section 1, or another conciliation procedure.

2. If the invitation is accepted and if the parties agree upon the conciliation procedure to be applied, any party may submit the dispute to that procedure.

3. If the invitation is not accepted or the parties do not agree upon the procedure, the conciliation proceedings shall be deemed to be terminated.

4. Unless the parties otherwise agree, when a dispute has been submitted to conciliation, the proceedings may be terminated only in accordance with the agreed conciliation procedure.

Article 285: Application of this section to disputes submitted pursuant to Part XI

This section applies to any dispute which pursuant to Part XI, section 5, is to be settled in accordance with procedures provided for in this Part. If an entity other than a State Party is a party to such a dispute, this section applies *mutatis mutandis*.

Section 2: Compulsory procedures entailing binding decisions

Article 286: Application of procedures under this section

Subject to section 3, any dispute concerning the interpretation or application of this Convention shall, where no settlement has been reached by recourse to section 1, be submitted at the request of any party to the dispute to the court or tribunal having jurisdiction under this section.

Article 287: Choice of procedure

1. When signing, ratifying or acceding to this Convention or at any time thereafter, a State shall be free to choose, by means of a written declaration, one or more of the following means for the settlement of disputes concerning the interpretation or application of this Convention:

(a) the International Tribunal for the Law of the Sea established in accordance with Annex VI;
(b) the International Court of Justice;
(c) an arbitral tribunal constituted in accordance with Annex VII;
(d) a special arbitral tribunal constituted in accordance with Annex VIII for one or more of the categories of disputes specified therein.

2. A declaration made under paragraph 1 shall not affect or be affected by the obligation of a State Party to accept the jurisdiction of the Sea-Bed Disputes Chamber of the International Tribunal for the Law of the Sea to the extent and in the manner provided for in Part XI, section 5.

3. A State Party, which is a party to a dispute not covered by a declaration in force, shall be deemed to have accepted arbitration in accordance with Annex VII.

4. If the parties to a dispute have accepted the same procedure for the settlement of the dispute, it may be submitted only to that procedure, unless the parties otherwise agree.

5. If the parties to a dispute have not accepted the same procedure for the settlement of the dispute, it may be submitted only to arbitration in accordance with Annex VII, unless the parties otherwise agree.

6. A declaration made under paragraph 1 shall remain in force until three months after notice of revocation has been deposited with the Secretary-General of the United Nations.

7. A new declaration, a notice of revocation or the expiry of a declaration does not in any way affect proceedings pending before a court or tribunal having jurisdiction under this article, unless the parties otherwise agree.

8. Declarations and notices referred to in this article shall be deposited with the Secretary-General of the United Nations, who shall transmit copies thereof to the States Parties.

Article 288: Jurisdiction

1. A court or tribunal referred to in article 287 shall have jurisdiction over any dispute concerning the interpretation or application of this Convention which is submitted to it in accordance with this Part.

2. A court or tribunal referred to in article 287 shall also have jurisdiction over any dispute concerning the interpretation or application of an international agreement related to the purposes of this Convention, which is submitted to it in accordance with the agreement.

3. The Sea-Bed Disputes Chamber of the International Tribunal for the Law of the Sea established in accordance with Annex VI, and any other chamber or arbitral tribunal referred to in Part XI, section 5, shall have jurisdiction in any matter which is submitted to it in accordance therewith.

4. In the event of a dispute as to whether a court or tribunal has jurisdiction, the matter shall be settled by decision of that court or tribunal.

Article 289: Experts

In any dispute involving scientific or technical matters, a court or tribunal exercising jurisdiction under this section may, at the request of a party or *proprio motu*, select in consultation with the parties no fewer than two scientific or technical experts chosen preferably from the relevant list prepared in accordance with Annex VIII, article 2, to sit with the court or tribunal but without the right to vote.

Article 290: Provisional measures

1. If a dispute has been duly submitted to a court or tribunal which considers that *prima facie* it has jurisdiction under this Part or Part XI, section 5, the court or tribunal may prescribe any provisional measures which it considers appropriate under the circumstances to preserve the respective rights of the parties to the dispute or to prevent serious harm to the marine environment, pending the final decision.

2. Provisional measures may be modified or revoked as soon as the circumstances justifying them have changed or ceased to exist.

3. Provisional measures may be prescribed, modified or revoked under this article only at the request of a party to the dispute and after the parties have been given an opportunity to be heard.

4. The court or tribunal shall forthwith give notice to the parties to the dispute, and to such other States Parties as it considers appropriate, of the prescription, modification or revocation of provisional measures.

5. Pending the constitution of an arbitral tribunal to which a dispute is being submitted under this section, any court or tribunal agreed upon by the parties or, failing such agreement within two weeks from the date of the request for provisional measures, the International Tribunal for the Law of the Sea or, with respect to activities in the Area,[9] the Sea-Bed Disputes Chamber, may prescribe, modify or revoke provisional measures in accordance with this article if it considers that *prima facie* the tribunal which is to be constituted would have jurisdiction and that the urgency of the situation so requires. Once constituted, the tribunal to which the dispute has been submitted may modify, revoke or affirm those provisional measures, acting in conformity with paragraphs 1 to 4.

6. The parties to the dispute shall comply promptly with any provisional measures prescribed under this article.

Article 291: Access

1. All the dispute settlement procedures specified in this Part shall be open to States Parties.

2. The dispute settlement procedures specified in this Part shall be open to entities other than States Parties only as specifically provided for in this Convention.

Article 292: Prompt release of vessels and crews

1. Where the authorities of a State Party have detained a vessel flying the flag of another State Party and it is alleged that the detaining State has not complied with the provisions of this Convention for the prompt release of the vessel or its crew upon the posting of a reasonable bond or other financial security, the question of release from detention may be submitted to any court or tribunal agreed upon by the parties or, failing such agreement within 10 days from the time of detention, to a court or tribunal accepted by the detaining State under article 287 or to the International Tribunal for the Law of the Sea, unless the parties otherwise agree.

2. The application for release may be made only by or on behalf of the flag State of the vessel.

---

9 *Editors' note*: As per Article 1.1(1) of the UNCLOS, 'Area' means 'the seabed and ocean floor and subsoil thereof, beyond the limits of national jurisdiction', and, according to Article 1.1(3), 'activities in the Area' means 'all activities of exploration for, and exploitation of, the resources of the Area'.

3. The court or tribunal shall deal without delay with the application for release and shall deal only with the question of release, without prejudice to the merits of any case before the appropriate domestic forum against the vessel, its owner or its crew. The authorities of the detaining State remain competent to release the vessel or its crew at any time.

4. Upon the posting of the bond or other financial security determined by the court or tribunal, the authorities of the detaining State shall comply promptly with the decision of the court or tribunal concerning the release of the vessel or its crew.

Article 293: Applicable law

1. A court or tribunal having jurisdiction under this section shall apply this Convention and other rules of international law not incompatible with this Convention.

2. Paragraph 1 does not prejudice the power of the court or tribunal having jurisdiction under this section to decide a case *ex aequo et bono*, if the parties so agree.

Article 294: Preliminary proceedings

1. A court or tribunal provided for in article 287 to which an application is made in respect of a dispute referred to in article 297 shall determine at the request of a party, or may determine *proprio motu*, whether the claim constitutes an abuse of legal process or whether *prima facie* it is well founded. If the court or tribunal determines that the claim constitutes an abuse of legal process or is *prima facie* unfounded, it shall take no further action in the case.

2. Upon receipt of the application, the court or tribunal shall immediately notify the other party or parties of the application, and shall fix a reasonable time-limit within which they may request it to make a determination in accordance with paragraph 1.

3. Nothing in this article affects the right of any party to a dispute to make preliminary objections in accordance with the applicable rules of procedure.

Article 295: Exhaustion of local remedies

Any dispute between States Parties concerning the interpretation or application of this Convention may be submitted to the procedures provided for in this section only after local remedies have been exhausted where this is required by international law.

Article 296: Finality and binding force of decisions

1. Any decision rendered by a court or tribunal having jurisdiction under this section shall be final and shall be complied with by all the parties to the dispute.

2. Any such decision shall have no binding force except between the parties and in respect of that particular dispute.

Section 3: Limitations and exceptions to applicability of section 2

Article 297: Limitations on applicability of section 2

1. Disputes concerning the interpretation or application of this Convention with regard to the exercise by a coastal State of its sovereign rights or jurisdiction provided for in this Convention shall be subject to the procedures provided for in section 2 in the following cases:

(a) when it is alleged that a coastal State has acted in contravention of the provisions of this Convention in regard to the freedoms and rights of navigation, overflight or the laying of submarine cables and pipelines, or in regard to other internationally lawful uses of the sea specified in article 58;

(b) when it is alleged that a State in exercising the aforementioned freedoms, rights or uses has acted in contravention of this Convention or of laws or regulations adopted by the coastal State in conformity with this Convention and other rules of international law not incompatible with this Convention; or

(c) when it is alleged that a coastal State has acted in contravention of specified international rules and standards for the protection and preservation of the marine environment which are applicable to the coastal State and which have been established by this Convention or through a competent international organization or diplomatic conference in accordance with this Convention.

2. (a) Disputes concerning the interpretation or application of the provisions of this Convention with regard to marine scientific research shall be settled in accordance with section 2, except that the coastal State shall not be obliged to accept the submission to such settlement of any dispute arising out of:

i) the exercise by the coastal State of a right or discretion in accordance with article 246; or

ii) a decision by the coastal State to order suspension or cessation of a research project in accordance with article 253.

(b) A dispute arising from an allegation by the researching State that with respect to a specific project the coastal State is not exercising its rights under articles 246 and 253 in a manner compatible with this Convention shall be submitted, at the request of either party, to conciliation under Annex V, section 2, provided that the conciliation commission shall not call in question the exercise by the coastal State of its discretion to designate specific areas as referred to in article 246, paragraph 6, or of its discretion to withhold consent in accordance with article 246, paragraph 5.

3. (a) Disputes concerning the interpretation or application of the provisions of this Convention with regard to fisheries shall be settled in accordance with section 2, except that the coastal State shall not be obliged to accept the submission to such settlement of any dispute relating to its sovereign rights with respect to the living resources in the exclusive economic zone or their exercise, including its discretionary powers for determining the allowable catch, its harvesting capacity, the allocation of surpluses to other States and the terms and conditions established in its conservation and management laws and regulations.

(b) Where no settlement has been reached by recourse to section 1 of this Part, a dispute shall be submitted to conciliation under Annex V, section 2, at the request of any party to the dispute, when it is alleged that:

i) a coastal State has manifestly failed to comply with its obligations to ensure through proper conservation and management measures that the maintenance of the living resources in the exclusive economic zone is not seriously endangered;

ii) a coastal State has arbitrarily refused to determine, at the request of another State, the allowable catch and its capacity to harvest living resources with respect to stocks which that other State is interested in fishing; or

iii) a coastal State has arbitrarily refused to allocate to any State, under articles 62, 69 and 70 and under the terms and conditions established by the coastal State consistent with this Convention, the whole or part of the surplus it has declared to exist.

(c) In no case shall the conciliation commission substitute its discretion for that of the coastal State.

(d) The report of the conciliation commission shall be communicated to the appropriate international organizations.

(e) In negotiating agreements pursuant to articles 69 and 70, States Parties, unless they otherwise agree, shall include a clause on measures which they shall take in order to minimize the possibility of a disagreement concerning the interpretation or application of the agreement, and on how they should proceed if a disagreement nevertheless arises.

[Articles 298-299 not reproduced]

Trade

World Trade Organization - Understanding on Rules and Procedures Governing the Settlement of Disputes[10]

Adopted on 15 April 1994 at Marrakesh. Entered into force on 1 January 1995. Source: 1867 *UNTS* 3. Number of parties: 147. Further information: WTO, Geneva, Switzerland, http://www.wto.org/english/tratop_e/dispu_e/dispu_e.htm

Members hereby *agree* as follows:

---

[10] This compilation also reproduces the GATT, at p. 497, the 1994 Decision on Trade and Environment, at p. 500 and the Doha Ministerial Declaration, at p. 502.

Article 1: Coverage and application

1. The rules and procedures of this Understanding shall apply to disputes brought pursuant to the consultation and dispute settlement provisions of the agreements listed in Appendix 1 to this Understanding (referred to in this Understanding as the 'covered agreements'). The rules and procedures of this Understanding shall also apply to consultations and the settlement of disputes between Members concerning their rights and obligations under the provisions of the Agreement Establishing the World Trade Organization (referred to in this Understanding as the 'WTO Agreement') and of this Understanding taken in isolation or in combination with any other covered agreement.

2. The rules and procedures of this Understanding shall apply subject to such special or additional rules and procedures on dispute settlement contained in the covered agreements as are identified in Appendix 2 to this Understanding. To the extent that there is a difference between the rules and procedures of this Understanding and the special or additional rules and procedures set forth in Appendix 2, the special or additional rules and procedures in Appendix 2 shall prevail. In disputes involving rules and procedures under more than one covered agreement, if there is a conflict between special or additional rules and procedures of such agreements under review, and where the parties to the dispute cannot agree on rules and procedures within 20 days of the establishment of the panel, the Chairman of the Dispute Settlement Body provided for in paragraph 1 of Article 2 (referred to in this Understanding as the 'DSB'), in consultation with the parties to the dispute, shall determine the rules and procedures to be followed within 10 days after a request by either Member. The Chairman shall be guided by the principle that special or additional rules and procedures should be used where possible, and the rules and procedures set out in this Understanding should be used to the extent necessary to avoid conflict.

Article 2: Administration

1. The Dispute Settlement Body is hereby established to administer these rules and procedures and, except as otherwise provided in a covered agreement, the consultation and dispute settlement provisions of the covered agreements. Accordingly, the DSB shall have the authority to establish panels, adopt panel and Appellate Body reports, maintain surveillance of implementation of rulings and recommendations, and authorize suspension of concessions and other obligations under the covered agreements. With respect to disputes arising under a covered agreement which is a Plurilateral Trade Agreement, the term 'Member' as used herein shall refer only to those Members that are parties to the relevant Plurilateral Trade Agreement. Where the DSB administers the dispute settlement provisions of a Plurilateral Trade Agreement, only those Members that are parties to that Agreement may participate in decisions or actions taken by the DSB with respect to that dispute.

2. The DSB shall inform the relevant WTO Councils and Committees of any developments in disputes related to provisions of the respective covered agreements.

3. The DSB shall meet as often as necessary to carry out its functions within the time-frames provided in this Understanding.

4. Where the rules and procedures of this Understanding provide for the DSB to take a decision, it shall do so by consensus.*

Article 3: General provisions

1. Members affirm their adherence to the principles for the management of disputes heretofore applied under Articles XXII and XXIII of GATT 1947, and the rules and procedures as further elaborated and modified herein.

2. The dispute settlement system of the WTO is a central element in providing security and predictability to the multilateral trading system. The Members recognize that it serves to preserve the rights and obligations of Members under the covered agreements, and to clarify the existing provisions of those agreements in accordance with customary rules of interpretation of public international law. Recommendations and rulings of the DSB cannot add to or diminish the rights and obligations provided in the covered agreements.

3. The prompt settlement of situations in which a Member considers that any benefits accruing to it directly or indirectly under the covered agreements are being impaired by measures taken by another Member is essential to the effective functioning of the WTO and the maintenance of a proper balance between the rights and obligations of Members.

4. Recommendations or rulings made by the DSB shall be aimed at achieving a satisfactory settlement of the matter in accordance with the rights and obligations under this Understanding and under the covered agreements.

5. All solutions to matters formally raised under the consultation and dispute settlement provisions of the covered agreements, including arbitration awards, shall be consistent with those agreements and shall not nullify or impair benefits accruing to any Member under those agreements, nor impede the attainment of any objective of those agreements.

6. Mutually agreed solutions to matters formally raised under the consultation and dispute settlement provisions of the covered agreements shall be notified to the DSB and the relevant Councils and Committees, where any Member may raise any point relating thereto.

7. Before bringing a case, a Member shall exercise its judgement as to whether action under these procedures would be fruitful. The aim of the dispute settlement

---

* The DSB shall be deemed to have decided by consensus on a matter submitted for its consideration, if no Member, present at the meeting of the DSB when the decision is taken, formally objects to the proposed decision.

mechanism is to secure a positive solution to a dispute. A solution mutually acceptable to the parties to a dispute and consistent with the covered agreements is clearly to be preferred. In the absence of a mutually agreed solution, the first objective of the dispute settlement mechanism is usually to secure the withdrawal of the measures concerned if these are found to be inconsistent with the provisions of any of the covered agreements. The provision of compensation should be resorted to only if the immediate withdrawal of the measure is impracticable and as a temporary measure pending the withdrawal of the measure which is inconsistent with a covered agreement. The last resort which this Understanding provides to the Member invoking the dispute settlement procedures is the possibility of suspending the application of concessions or other obligations under the covered agreements on a discriminatory basis vis-à-vis the other Member, subject to authorization by the DSB of such measures.

[Paragraphs 8-12 not reproduced]

Article 4: Consultations

1. Members affirm their resolve to strengthen and improve the effectiveness of the consultation procedures employed by Members.

2. Each Member undertakes to accord sympathetic consideration to and afford adequate opportunity for consultation regarding any representations made by another Member concerning measures affecting the operation of any covered agreement taken within the territory of the former.*

[Paragraphs 3-11 not reproduced]

Article 5: Good offices, conciliation and mediation

1. Good offices, conciliation and mediation are procedures that are undertaken voluntarily if the parties to the dispute so agree.

2. Proceedings involving good offices, conciliation and mediation, and in particular positions taken by the parties to the dispute during these proceedings, shall be confidential, and without prejudice to the rights of either party in any further proceedings under these procedures.

3. Good offices, conciliation or mediation may be requested at any time by any party to a dispute. They may begin at any time and be terminated at any time. Once procedures for good offices, conciliation or mediation are terminated, a complaining party may then proceed with a request for the establishment of a panel.

[Paragraphs 4-6 not reproduced]

---

* Where the provisions of any other covered agreement concerning measures taken by regional or local governments or authorities within the territory of a Member contain provisions different from the provisions of this paragraph, the provisions of such other covered agreement shall prevail.

Article 6: Establishment of panels

1. If the complaining party so requests, a panel shall be established at the latest at the DSB meeting following that at which the request first appears as an item on the DSB's agenda, unless at that meeting the DSB decides by consensus not to establish a panel.*

2. The request for the establishment of a panel shall be made in writing. It shall indicate whether consultations were held, identify the specific measures at issue and provide a brief summary of the legal basis of the complaint sufficient to present the problem clearly. In case the applicant requests the establishment of a panel with other than standard terms of reference, the written request shall include the proposed text of special terms of reference.

Article 7: Terms of reference of panels

1. Panels shall have the following terms of reference unless the parties to the dispute agree otherwise within 20 days from the establishment of the panel:

'To examine, in the light of the relevant provisions in (name of the covered agreement(s) cited by the parties to the dispute), the matter referred to the DSB by (name of party) in document ... and to make such findings as will assist the DSB in making the recommendations or in giving the rulings provided for in that/those agreement(s).'

2. Panels shall address the relevant provisions in any covered agreement or agreements cited by the parties to the dispute.

3. In establishing a panel, the DSB may authorize its Chairman to draw up the terms of reference of the panel in consultation with the parties to the dispute, subject to the provisions of paragraph 1. The terms of reference thus drawn up shall be circulated to all Members. If other than standard terms of reference are agreed upon, any Member may raise any point relating thereto in the DSB.

[Articles 8-10 not reproduced]

Article 11: Function of panels

The function of panels is to assist the DSB in discharging its responsibilities under this Understanding and the covered agreements. Accordingly, a panel should make an objective assessment of the matter before it, including an objective assessment of the facts of the case and the applicability of and conformity with the relevant covered agreements, and make such other findings as will assist the DSB in making the recommendations or in giving the rulings provided for in the covered agreements. Panels should consult regularly with the parties to the dispute and give them adequate opportunity to develop a mutually satisfactory solution.

---

* If the complaining party so requests, a meeting of the DSB shall be convened for this purpose within 15 days of the request, provided that at least 10 days' advance notice of the meeting is given.

[Articles 12-15 not reproduced]

Article 16: Adoption of panel reports

1. In order to provide sufficient time for the Members to consider panel reports, the reports shall not be considered for adoption by the DSB until 20 days after the date they have been circulated to the Members.

2. Members having objections to a panel report shall give written reasons to explain their objections for circulation at least 10 days prior to the DSB meeting at which the panel report will be considered.

3. The parties to a dispute shall have the right to participate fully in the consideration of the panel report by the DSB, and their views shall be fully recorded.

4. Within 60 days after the date of circulation of a panel report to the Members, the report shall be adopted at a DSB meeting* unless a party to the dispute formally notifies the DSB of its decision to appeal or the DSB decides by consensus not to adopt the report. If a party has notified its decision to appeal, the report by the panel shall not be considered for adoption by the DSB until after completion of the appeal. This adoption procedure is without prejudice to the right of Members to express their views on a panel report.

Article 17: Appellate review

Standing Appellate Body

1. A standing Appellate Body shall be established by the DSB. The Appellate Body shall hear appeals from panel cases. It shall be composed of seven persons, three of whom shall serve on any one case. Persons serving on the Appellate Body shall serve in rotation. Such rotation shall be determined in the working procedures of the Appellate Body.

2. The DSB shall appoint persons to serve on the Appellate Body for a four-year term, and each person may be reappointed once. However, the terms of three of the seven persons appointed immediately after the entry into force of the WTO Agreement shall expire at the end of two years, to be determined by lot. Vacancies shall be filled as they arise. A person appointed to replace a person whose term of office has not expired shall hold office for the remainder of the predecessor's term.

3. The Appellate Body shall comprise persons of recognized authority, with demonstrated expertise in law, international trade and the subject matter of the covered agreements generally. They shall be unaffiliated with any government. The Appellate Body membership shall be broadly representative of membership in the WTO. All persons serving on the Appellate Body shall be available at all times and on short notice, and shall stay abreast of dispute settlement activities and other

---

* If a meeting of the DSB is not scheduled within this period at a time that enables the requirements of paragraphs 1 and 4 of Article 16 to be met, a meeting of the DSB shall be held for this purpose.

relevant activities of the WTO. They shall not participate in the consideration of any disputes that would create a direct or indirect conflict of interest.

4. Only parties to the dispute, not third parties, may appeal a panel report. Third parties which have notified the DSB of a substantial interest in the matter pursuant to paragraph 2 of Article 10 may make written submissions to, and be given an opportunity to be heard by, the Appellate Body.

[Paragraphs 5-8 not reproduced]

Procedures for appellate review

9. Working procedures shall be drawn up by the Appellate Body in consultation with the Chairman of the DSB and the Director-General, and communicated to the Members for their information.

10. The proceedings of the Appellate Body shall be confidential. The reports of the Appellate Body shall be drafted without the presence of the parties to the dispute and in the light of the information provided and the statements made.

11. Opinions expressed in the Appellate Body report by individuals serving on the Appellate Body shall be anonymous.

12. The Appellate Body shall address each of the issues raised in accordance with paragraph 6 during the appellate proceeding.

13. The Appellate Body may uphold, modify or reverse the legal findings and conclusions of the panel.

Adoption of Appellate Body reports

14. An Appellate Body report shall be adopted by the DSB and unconditionally accepted by the parties to the dispute unless the DSB decides by consensus not to adopt the Appellate Body report within 30 days following its circulation to the Members.* This adoption procedure is without prejudice to the right of Members to express their views on an Appellate Body report.

Article 18: Communications with the Panel or Appellate Body

1. There shall be no *ex parte* communications with the panel or Appellate Body concerning matters under consideration by the panel or Appellate Body.

2. Written submissions to the panel or the Appellate Body shall be treated as confidential, but shall be made available to the parties to the dispute. Nothing in this Understanding shall preclude a party to a dispute from disclosing statements of its own positions to the public. Members shall treat as confidential information submitted by another Member to the panel or the Appellate Body which that Member has designated as confidential. A party to a dispute shall also, upon request of a Member, provide a non-confidential summary of the information contained in its written submissions that could be disclosed to the public.

---

* If a meeting of the DSB is not scheduled during this period, such a meeting of the DSB shall be held for this purpose.

Article 19: Panel and Appellate Body recommendations

1. Where a panel or the Appellate Body concludes that a measure is inconsistent with a covered agreement, it shall recommend that the Member concerned* bring the measure into conformity with that agreement.** In addition to its recommendations, the panel or Appellate Body may suggest ways in which the Member concerned could implement the recommendations.

2. In accordance with paragraph 2 of Article 3, in their findings and recommendations, the panel and Appellate Body cannot add to or diminish the rights and obligations provided in the covered agreements.

Article 20: Time-frame for DSB decisions

Unless otherwise agreed to by the parties to the dispute, the period from the date of establishment of the panel by the DSB until the date the DSB considers the panel or appellate report for adoption shall as a general rule not exceed nine months where the panel report is not appealed or 12 months where the report is appealed. Where either the panel or the Appellate Body has acted, pursuant to paragraph 9 of Article 12 or paragraph 5 of Article 17, to extend the time for providing its report, the additional time taken shall be added to the above periods.

Article 21: Surveillance of implementation of recommendations and rulings

1. Prompt compliance with recommendations or rulings of the DSB is essential in order to ensure effective resolution of disputes to the benefit of all Members.

2. Particular attention should be paid to matters affecting the interests of developing country Members with respect to measures which have been subject to dispute settlement.

[Paragraphs 3-8 not reproduced]

Article 22: Compensation and the suspension of concessions

1. Compensation and the suspension of concessions or other obligations are temporary measures available in the event that the recommendations and rulings are not implemented within a reasonable period of time. However, neither compensation nor the suspension of concessions or other obligations is preferred to full implementation of a recommendation to bring a measure into conformity with the covered agreements. Compensation is voluntary and, if granted, shall be consistent with the covered agreements.

2. If the Member concerned fails to bring the measure found to be inconsistent with a covered agreement into compliance therewith or otherwise comply with the recommendations and rulings within the reasonable period of time determined pursuant to paragraph 3 of Article 21, such Member shall, if so requested, and no

---

* The 'Member concerned' is the party to the dispute to which the panel or Appellate Body recommendations are directed.

** With respect to recommendations in cases not involving a violation of GATT 1994 or any other covered agreement, see Article 26.

later than the expiry of the reasonable period of time, enter into negotiations with any party having invoked the dispute settlement procedures, with a view to developing mutually acceptable compensation. If no satisfactory compensation has been agreed within 20 days after the date of expiry of the reasonable period of time, any party having invoked the dispute settlement procedures may request authorization from the DSB to suspend the application to the Member concerned of concessions or other obligations under the covered agreements.

[Paragraphs 3-9 not reproduced]

Article 23: Strengthening of the multilateral system

1. When Members seek the redress of a violation of obligations or other nullification or impairment of benefits under the covered agreements or an impediment to the attainment of any objective of the covered agreements, they shall have recourse to, and abide by, the rules and procedures of this Understanding.

2. In such cases, Members shall:

(a) not make a determination to the effect that a violation has occurred, that benefits have been nullified or impaired or that the attainment of any objective of the covered agreements has been impeded, except through recourse to dispute settlement in accordance with the rules and procedures of this Understanding, and shall make any such determination consistent with the findings contained in the panel or Appellate Body report adopted by the DSB or an arbitration award rendered under this Understanding;

(b) follow the procedures set forth in Article 21 to determine the reasonable period of time for the Member concerned to implement the recommendations and rulings; and

(c) follow the procedures set forth in Article 22 to determine the level of suspension of concessions or other obligations and obtain DSB authorization in accordance with those procedures before suspending concessions or other obligations under the covered agreements in response to the failure of the Member concerned to implement the recommendations and rulings within that reasonable period of time.

[Article 24 not reproduced]

Article 25: Arbitration

1. Expeditious arbitration within the WTO as an alternative means of dispute settlement can facilitate the solution of certain disputes that concern issues that are clearly defined by both parties.

2. Except as otherwise provided in this Understanding, resort to arbitration shall be subject to mutual agreement of the parties which shall agree on the procedures to be followed. Agreements to resort to arbitration shall be notified to all Members sufficiently in advance of the actual commencement of the arbitration process.

3. Other Members may become party to an arbitration proceeding only upon the agreement of the parties which have agreed to have recourse to arbitration. The

parties to the proceeding shall agree to abide by the arbitration award. Arbitration awards shall be notified to the DSB and the Council or Committee of any relevant agreement where any Member may raise any point relating thereto.

[Articles 26-27 not reproduced]

Appendix 1: Agreements covered by the Understanding; Appendix 2: Special or additional rules and procedures contained in the covered agreements; Appendix 3: Working procedures; Appendix 4: Expert review groups [not reproduced]

North American Agreement on Environmental Cooperation, Part 3: Commission for Environmental Cooperation[11]

Adopted on 14 September 1993 at Mexico/Ottawa/Washington. Entered into force on 1 January 1994. Number of parties: 3. Further information: CEC, Montreal, Canada, http://www.cec.org

Article 8: The Commission

1. The Parties hereby establish the Commission for Environmental Cooperation.

2. The Commission shall comprise a Council, a Secretariat and a Joint Public Advisory Committee.

Article 14: Submissions on enforcement matters

1. The Secretariat may consider a submission from any non-governmental organization or person asserting that a Party is failing to effectively enforce its environmental law, if the Secretariat finds that the submission:

(a) is in writing in a language designated by that Party in a notification to the Secretariat;
(b) clearly identifies the person or organization making the submission;
(c) provides sufficient information to allow the Secretariat to review the submission, including any documentary evidence on which the submission may be based;
(d) appears to be aimed at promoting enforcement rather than at harassing industry;
(e) indicates that the matter has been communicated in writing to the relevant authorities of the Party and indicates the Party's response, if any; and
(f) is filed by a person or organization residing or established in the territory of a Party.

2. Where the Secretariat determines that a submission meets the criteria set out in paragraph 1, the Secretariat shall determine whether the submission merits

[11] Parts I and II of NAAEC are reproduced at p. 504.

requesting a response from the Party. In deciding whether to request a response, the Secretariat shall be guided by whether:

(a) the submission alleges harm to the person or organization making the submission;
(b) the submission, alone or in combination with other submissions, raises matters whose further study in this process would advance the goals of this Agreement;
(c) private remedies available under the Party's law have been pursued; and
(d) the submission is drawn exclusively from mass media reports.

Where the Secretariat makes such a request, it shall forward to the Party a copy of the submission and any supporting information provided with the submission.

3. The Party shall advise the Secretariat within 30 days or, in exceptional circumstances and on notification to the Secretariat, within 60 days of delivery of the request:

(a) whether the matter is the subject of a pending judicial or administrative proceeding, in which case the Secretariat shall proceed no further; and
(b) of any other information that the Party wishes to submit, such as
    i) whether the matter was previously the subject of a judicial or administrative proceeding, and
    ii) whether private remedies in connection with the matter are available to the person or organization making the submission and whether they have been pursued.

Article 15: Factual record

1. If the Secretariat considers that the submission, in the light of any response provided by the Party, warrants developing a factual record, the Secretariat shall so inform the Council and provide its reasons.

2. The Secretariat shall prepare a factual record if the Council, by a two-thirds vote, instructs it to do so.

3. The preparation of a factual record by the Secretariat pursuant to this Article shall be without prejudice to any further steps that may be taken with respect to any submission.

4. In preparing a factual record, the Secretariat shall consider any information furnished by a Party and may consider any relevant technical, scientific or other information:

(a) that is publicly available;
(b) submitted by interested non-governmental organizations or persons;
(c) submitted by the Joint Public Advisory Committee; or
(d) developed by the Secretariat or by independent experts.

5. The Secretariat shall submit a draft factual record to the Council. Any Party may provide comments on the accuracy of the draft within 45 days thereafter.

6. The Secretariat shall incorporate, as appropriate, any such comments in the final factual record and submit it to the Council.

7. The Council may, by a two-thirds vote, make the final factual record publicly available, normally within 60 days following its submission.

Multilateral environmental agreements

Non-Compliance Procedure of the Montreal Protocol on Substances that Deplete the Ozone Layer[12]

Source: Decision II/5, Second Meeting of the Parties, 27-29 June 1990, Doc. UNEP/OzL.Pro.2/3; Decision IV/5 and Annexes IV-V, Fourth Meeting of the Parties, 23-25 November 1992, Doc. UNEP/OzL.Pro.4/15 (the text reproduced incorporates the amendments adopted in 1998 by Decision X/10). Further information: Ozone Secretariat, Nairobi, Kenya, http://www.unep.org/ozone

The following procedure has been formulated pursuant to Article 8 of the Montreal Protocol. It shall apply without prejudice to the operation of the settlement of disputes procedure laid down in Article 11 of the Vienna Convention.

1. If one or more Parties have reservations regarding another Party's implementation of its obligations under the Protocol, those concerns may be addressed in writing to the Secretariat. Such a submission shall be supported by corroborating information.

2. The Secretariat shall, within two weeks of its receiving a submission, send a copy of that submission to the Party whose implementation of a particular provision of the Protocol is at issue. Any reply and information in support thereof are to be submitted to the Secretariat and to the Parties involved within three months of the date of the dispatch or such longer period as the circumstances of any particular case may require. If the Secretariat has not received a reply from the Party three months after sending it the original submission, the Secretariat shall send a reminder to the Party that it has yet to provide its reply. The Secretariat shall, as soon as the reply and information from the Party are available, but not later than six months after receiving the submission, transmit the submission, the reply and the information, if any, provided by the Parties to the Implementation Committee referred to in paragraph 5, which shall consider the matter as soon as practicable.

3. Where the Secretariat, during the course of preparing its report, becomes aware of possible non-compliance by any Party with its obligations under the Protocol, it may request the Party concerned to furnish necessary information about the matter. If there is no response from the Party concerned within three months or such longer

12 The Montreal Protocol is reproduced at p. 99.

period as the circumstances of the matter may require or the matter is not resolved through administrative action or through diplomatic contacts, the Secretariat shall include the matter in its report to the Meeting of the Parties pursuant to Article 12 (c) of the Protocol and inform the Implementation Committee, which shall consider the matter as soon as practicable.

4. Where a Party concludes that, despite having made its best, bona fide efforts, it is unable to comply fully with its obligations under the Protocol, it may address to the Secretariat a submission in writing, explaining, in particular, the specific circumstances that it considers to be the cause of its noncompliance. The Secretariat shall transmit such submission to the Implementation Committee which shall consider it as soon as practicable.

5. An Implementation Committee is hereby established. It shall consist of 10 Parties elected by the Meeting of the Parties for two years, based on equitable geographical distribution. Each Party so elected to the Committee shall be requested to notify the Secretariat, within two months of its election, of who is to represent it and shall endeavour to ensure that such representation remains throughout the entire term of office. Outgoing Parties may be re-elected for one immediate consecutive term. A Party that has completed a second consecutive two-year term as a Committee member shall be eligible for election again only after an absence of one year from the Committee. The Committee shall elect its own President and Vice-President. Each shall serve for one year at a time. The Vice-President shall, in addition, serve as the rapporteur of the Committee.

6. The Implementation Committee shall, unless it decides otherwise, meet twice a year. The Secretariat shall arrange for and service its meetings.

7. The functions of the Implementation Committee shall be:

(a) To receive, consider and report on any submission in accordance with paragraphs 1, 2 and 4;

(b) To receive, consider and report on any information or observations forwarded by the Secretariat in connection with the preparation of the reports referred to in Article 12 (c) of the Protocol and on any other information received and forwarded by the Secretariat concerning compliance with the provisions of the Protocol;

(c) To request, where it considers necessary, through the Secretariat, further information on matters under its consideration;

(d) To identify the facts and possible causes relating to individual cases of non-compliance referred to the Committee, as best it can, and make appropriate recommendations to the Meeting of the Parties;

(e) To undertake, upon the invitation of the Party concerned, information-gathering in the territory of that Party for fulfilling the functions of the Committee;

(f) To maintain, in particular for the purposes of drawing up its recommendations, an exchange of information with the Executive Committee of the Multilateral Fund related to the provision of financial and technical cooperation, including the transfer of technologies to Parties operating under Article 5, paragraph 1, of the Protocol.

8. The Implementation Committee shall consider the submissions, information and observations referred to in paragraph 7 with a view to securing an amicable solution of the matter on the basis of respect for the provisions of the Protocol.

9. The Implementation Committee shall report to the Meeting of the Parties, including any recommendations it considers appropriate. The report shall be made available to the Parties not later than six weeks before their meeting. After receiving a report by the Committee the Parties may, taking into consideration the circumstances of the matter, decide upon and call for steps to bring about full compliance with the Protocol, including measures to assist the Parties' compliance with the Protocol, and to further the Protocol's objectives.

10. Where a Party that is not a member of the Implementation Committee is identified in a submission under paragraph 1, or itself makes such a submission, it shall be entitled to participate in the consideration by the Committee of that submission.

11. No Party, whether or not a member of the Implementation Committee, involved in a matter under consideration by the Implementation Committee, shall take part in the elaboration and adoption of recommendations on that matter to be included in the report of the Committee.

12. The Parties involved in a matter referred to in paragraphs 1, 3 or 4 shall inform, through the Secretariat, the Meeting of the Parties of the results of proceedings taken under Article 11 of the Convention regarding possible non-compliance, about implementation of those results and about implementation of any decision of the Parties pursuant to paragraph 9.

13. The Meeting of the Parties may, pending completion of proceedings initiated under Article 11 of the Convention, issue an interim call and/or recommendations.

14. The Meeting of the Parties may request the Implementation Committee to make recommendations to assist the Meeting's consideration of matters of possible non-compliance.

15. The members of the Implementation Committee and any Party involved in its deliberations shall protect the confidentiality of information they receive in confidence.

16. The report, which shall not contain any information received in confidence, shall be made available to any person upon request. All information exchanged by or with the Committee that is related to any recommendation by the Committee to the Meeting of the Parties shall be made available by the Secretariat to any Party upon its request; that Party shall ensure the confidentiality of the information it has received in confidence.

Indicative list of measures that might be taken by a Meeting of the Parties in respect of non-compliance with the Protocol

A. Appropriate assistance, including assistance for the collection and reporting of data, technical assistance, technology transfer and financial assistance, information transfer and training.

B. Issuing cautions.

C. Suspension, in accordance with the applicable rules of international law concerning the suspension of the operation of a treaty, of specific rights and privileges under the Protocol, whether or not subject to time limits, including those concerned with industrial rationalization, production, consumption, trade, transfer of technology, financial mechanism and institutional arrangements.

Procedures and Mechanisms Relating to Compliance under the Kyoto Protocol to the United Nations Framework Convention on Climate Change[13]

Source: Decision 24/CP.7 (Annex), Seventh Conference of the Parties, 29 October-10 November 2001, Doc. FCCC/CP/2001/13/Add.3. Further information: UNFCCC Secretariat, Bonn, Germany, http://www.unfccc.int

In pursuit of the ultimate objective of the United Nations Framework Convention on Climate Change, hereinafter referred to as 'the Convention', as stated in its Article 2,

Recalling the provisions of the United Nations Framework Convention on Climate Change, and the Kyoto Protocol to the Convention, herein after referred to as 'the Protocol',

Being guided by Article 3 of the Convention,

Pursuant to the mandate adopted in decision 8/CP.4 by the Conference of the Parties at its fourth session,

The following procedures and mechanisms *have been adopted*:

I. Objective

The objective of these procedures and mechanisms is to facilitate, promote and enforce compliance with the commitments under the Protocol.

II. Compliance Committee

1. A compliance committee, hereinafter referred to as 'the Committee', is hereby established.

---

13 The Kyoto Protocol is reproduced at p. 145.

2. The Committee shall function through a plenary, a bureau and two branches, namely, the facilitative branch and the enforcement branch.

3. The Committee shall consist of twenty members elected by the Conference of the Parties serving as the meeting of the Parties to the Protocol, ten of whom are to be elected to serve in the facilitative branch and ten to be elected to serve in the enforcement branch.

4. Each branch shall elect, from among its members and for a term of two years, a chairperson and a vice-chairperson, one of whom shall be from a Party included in Annex I and one from a Party not included in Annex I. These persons shall constitute the bureau of the Committee. The chairing of each branch shall rotate between Parties included in Annex I and Parties not included in Annex I in such a manner that at any time one chairperson shall be from among the Parties included in Annex I and the other chairperson shall be from among the Parties not included in Annex I.

5. For each member of the Committee, the Conference of the Parties serving as the meeting of the Parties to the Protocol shall elect an alternate member.

6. Members of the Committee and their alternates shall serve in their individual capacities. They shall have recognized competence relating to climate change and in relevant fields such as the scientific, technical, socio-economic or legal fields.

7. The facilitative branch and the enforcement branch shall interact and cooperate in their functioning and, as necessary, on a case-by-case basis, the bureau of the Committee may designate one or more members of one branch to contribute to the work of the other branch on a non-voting basis.

8. The adoption of decisions by the Committee shall require a quorum of at least three fourths of the members to be present.

9. The Committee shall make every effort to reach agreement on any decisions by consensus. If all efforts at reaching consensus have been exhausted, the decisions shall as a last resort be adopted by a majority of at least three fourths of the members present and voting. In addition, the adoption of decisions by the enforcement branch shall require a majority of members from Parties included in Annex I present and voting, as well as a majority of members from Parties not included in Annex I present and voting. 'Members present and voting' means members present and casting an affirmative or a negative vote.

10. The Committee shall, unless it decides otherwise, meet at least twice each year, taking into account the desirability of holding such meetings in conjunction with the meetings of the subsidiary bodies under the Convention.

11. The Committee shall take into account any degree of flexibility allowed by the Conference of the Parties serving as the meeting of the Parties to the Protocol, pursuant to Article 3, paragraph 6, of the Protocol and taking into account Article 4, paragraph 6, of the Convention, to the Parties included in Annex I undergoing the process of transition to a market economy.

III. Plenary of the Committee

1. The plenary shall consist of the members of the facilitative branch and the enforcement branch. The chairpersons of the two branches shall be the co-chairpersons of the plenary.

2. The functions of the plenary shall be:

(a) To report on the activities of the Committee, including a list of decisions taken by the branches, to each ordinary session of the Conference of the Parties serving as the meeting of the Parties to the Protocol;

(b) To apply the general policy guidance referred to in section XII (c) below, received from the Conference of the Parties serving as the meeting of the Parties to the Protocol;

(c) To submit proposals on administrative and budgetary matters to the Conference of the Parties serving as the meeting of the Parties to the Protocol for the effective functioning of the Committee;

(d) To develop any further rules of procedure that may be needed, including rules on confidentiality, conflict of interest, submission of information by intergovernmental and nongovernmental organizations, and translation, for adoption by the Conference of the Parties serving as the meeting of the Parties to the Protocol by consensus; and

(e) To perform such other functions as may be requested by the Conference of the Parties serving as the meeting of the Parties to the Protocol for the effective functioning of the Committee.

IV. Facilitative branch

1. The facilitative branch shall be composed of:

(a) One member from each of the five regional groups of the United Nations and one member from the small island developing States, taking into account the interest groups as reflected by the current practice in the Bureau of the Conference of the Parties;

(b) Two members from Parties included in Annex I; and

(c) Two members from Parties not included in Annex I.

2. The Conference of the Parties serving as the meeting of the Parties to the Protocol shall elect five members for a term of two years and five members for a term of four years. Each time thereafter, the Conference of the Parties serving as the meeting of the Parties to the Protocol shall elect five new members for a term of four years. Members shall not serve for more than two consecutive terms.

3. In electing the members of the facilitative branch, the Conference of the Parties serving as the meeting of the Parties to the Protocol shall seek to reflect competences in a balanced manner in the fields referred to in section II, paragraph 6, above.

4. The facilitative branch shall be responsible for providing advice and facilitation to Parties in implementing the Protocol, and for promoting compliance by Parties with their commitments under the Protocol, taking into account the principle of

common but differentiated responsibilities and respective capabilities as contained in Article 3, paragraph 1, of the Convention. It shall also take into account the circumstances pertaining to the questions before it.

5. Within its overall mandate, as specified in paragraph 4 above, and falling outside the mandate of the enforcement branch, as specified in section V, paragraph 4, below, the facilitative branch shall be responsible for addressing questions of implementation:

(a) Relating to Article 3, paragraph 14, of the Protocol, including questions of implementation arising from the consideration of information on how a Party included in Annex I is striving to implement Article 3, paragraph 14, of the Protocol; and
(b) With respect to the provision of information on the use by a Party included in Annex I of Articles 6, 12 and 17 of the Protocol as supplemental to its domestic action, taking into account any reporting under Article 3, paragraph 2, of the Protocol.

6. With the aim of promoting compliance and providing for early warning of potential noncompliance, the facilitative branch shall be further responsible for providing advice and facilitation for compliance with:

(a) Commitments under Article 3, paragraph 1, of the Protocol, prior to the beginning of the relevant commitment period and during that commitment period;
(b) Commitments under Article 5, paragraphs 1 and 2, of the Protocol, prior to the beginning of the first commitment period; and
(c) Commitments under Article 7, paragraphs 1 and 4, of the Protocol prior to the beginning of the first commitment period.

7. The facilitative branch shall be responsible for applying the consequences set out in section XIV below.

V. Enforcement branch

1. The enforcement branch shall be composed of:

(a) One member from each of the five regional groups of the United Nations and one member from the small island developing States, taking into account the interest groups as reflected by the current practice in the Bureau of the Conference of the Parties;
(b) Two members from Parties included in Annex I; and
(c) Two members from Parties not included in Annex I.

2. The Conference of the Parties serving as the meeting of the Parties to the Protocol shall elect five members for a term of two years and five members for a term of four years. Each time thereafter, the Conference of the Parties serving as the meeting of the Parties to the Protocol shall elect five new members for a term of four years. Members shall not serve for more than two consecutive terms.

3. In electing the members of the enforcement branch, the Conference of the Parties serving as the meeting of the Parties to the Protocol shall be satisfied that the members have legal experience.

4. The enforcement branch shall be responsible for determining whether a Party included in Annex I is not in compliance with:

(a) Its quantified emission limitation or reduction commitment under Article 3, paragraph 1, of the Protocol;

(b) The methodological and reporting requirements under Article 5, paragraphs 1 and 2, and Article 7, paragraphs 1 and 4, of the Protocol; and

(c) The eligibility requirements under Articles 6, 12 and 17 of the Protocol.

5. The enforcement branch shall also determine whether to apply:

(a) Adjustments to inventories under Article 5, paragraph 2, of the Protocol, in the event of a disagreement between an expert review team under Article 8 of the Protocol and the Party involved; and

(b) A correction to the compilation and accounting database for the accounting of assigned amounts under Article 7, paragraph 4, of the Protocol, in the event of a disagreement between an expert review team under Article 8 of the Protocol and the Party involved concerning the validity of a transaction or such Party's failure to take corrective action.

6. The enforcement branch shall be responsible for applying the consequences set out in section XV below for the cases of non-compliance mentioned in paragraph 4 above. The consequences of non-compliance with Article 3, paragraph 1, of the Protocol to be applied by the enforcement branch shall be aimed at the restoration of compliance to ensure environmental integrity, and shall provide for an incentive to comply.

VI. Submissions

1. The Committee shall receive, through the secretariat, questions of implementation indicated in reports of expert review teams under Article 8 of the Protocol, together with any written comments by the Party which is subject to the report, or questions of implementation submitted by:

(a) Any Party with respect to itself; or

(b) Any Party with respect to another Party, supported by corroborating information.

2. The secretariat shall forthwith make available to the Party in respect of which the question of implementation is raised, hereinafter referred to as 'the Party concerned', any question of implementation submitted under paragraph 1 above.

3. In addition to the reports referred to in paragraph 1 above, the Committee shall also receive, through the secretariat, other final reports of expert review teams.

VII. Allocation and preliminary examination

1. The bureau of the Committee shall allocate questions of implementation to the appropriate branch in accordance with the mandates of each branch set out in section IV, paragraphs 4-7, and Section V, paragraphs 4-6.

2. The relevant branch shall undertake a preliminary examination of questions of implementation to ensure that, except in the case of a question raised by a Party with respect to itself, the question before it:
(a) Is supported by sufficient information;
(b) Is not *de minimis* or ill-founded; and
(c) Is based on the requirements of the Protocol.

3. The preliminary examination of questions of implementation shall be completed within three weeks from the date of receipt of these questions by the relevant branch.

4. After the preliminary examination of questions of implementation, the Party concerned shall, through the secretariat, be notified in writing of the decision and, in the event of a decision to proceed, be provided with a statement identifying the question of implementation, the information on which the question is based and the branch that will consider the question.

5. In the event of the review of eligibility requirements for a Party included in Annex I under Articles 6, 12 and 17 of the Protocol, the enforcement branch shall also, through the secretariat, notify forthwith the Party concerned, in writing, of the decision not to proceed with questions of implementation relating to eligibility requirements under those articles.

6. Any decision not to proceed shall be made available by the secretariat to other Parties and to the public.

7. The Party concerned shall be given an opportunity to comment in writing on all information relevant to the question of implementation and the decision to proceed.

VIII. General procedures

1. Following the preliminary examination of questions of implementation, the procedures set out in this section shall apply to the Committee, except where otherwise provided in these procedures and mechanisms.

2. The Party concerned shall be entitled to designate one or more persons to represent it during the consideration of the question of implementation by the relevant branch. This Party shall not be present during the elaboration and adoption of a decision of the branch.

3. Each branch shall base its deliberations on any relevant information provided by:
(a) Reports of the expert review teams under Article 8 of the Protocol;
(b) The Party concerned;
(c) The Party that has submitted a question of implementation with respect to another Party;

(d) Reports of the Conference of the Parties, the Conference of the Parties serving as the meeting of the Parties to the Protocol, and the subsidiary bodies under the Convention and the Protocol; and

(e) The other branch.

4. Competent intergovernmental and non-governmental organizations may submit relevant factual and technical information to the relevant branch.

5. Each branch may seek expert advice.

6. Any information considered by the relevant branch shall be made available to the Party concerned. The branch shall indicate to the Party concerned which parts of this information it has considered. The Party concerned shall be given an opportunity to comment in writing on such information. Subject to any rules relating to confidentiality, the information considered by the branch shall also be made available to the public, unless the branch decides, of its own accord or at the request of the Party concerned, that information provided by the Party concerned shall not be made available to the public until its decision has become final.

7. Decisions shall include conclusions and reasons. The relevant branch shall forthwith, through the secretariat, notify the Party concerned in writing of its decision, including conclusions and reasons therefor. The secretariat shall make final decisions available to other Parties and to the public.

8. The Party concerned shall be given an opportunity to comment in writing on any decision of the relevant branch.

9. If the Party concerned so requests, any question of implementation submitted under section VI, paragraph 1; any notification under section VII, paragraph 4; any information under paragraph 3 above; and any decision of the relevant branch, including conclusions and reasons therefor, shall be translated into one of the six official languages of the United Nations.

IX. Procedures for the enforcement branch

1. Within ten weeks from the date of receipt of the notification under section VII, paragraph 4, the Party concerned may make a written submission to the enforcement branch, including rebuttal of information submitted to the branch.

2. If so requested in writing by the Party concerned within ten weeks from the date of receipt of the notification under section VII, paragraph 4, the enforcement branch shall hold a hearing at which the Party concerned shall have the opportunity to present its views. The hearing shall take place within four weeks from the date of receipt of the request or of the written submission under paragraph 1 above, whichever is the later. The Party concerned may present expert testimony or opinion at the hearing. Such a hearing shall be held in public, unless the enforcement branch decides, of its own accord or at the request of the Party concerned, that part or all of the hearing shall take place in private.

3. The enforcement branch may put questions to and seek clarification from the Party concerned, either in the course of such a hearing or at any time in writing, and the Party concerned shall provide a response within six weeks thereafter.

4. Within four weeks from the date of receipt of the written submission of the Party concerned under paragraph 1 above, or within four weeks from the date of any hearing pursuant to paragraph 2 above, or within fourteen weeks from the notification under section VII, paragraph 4, if the Party has not provided a written submission, whichever is the latest, the enforcement branch shall:

(a) Adopt a preliminary finding that the Party concerned is not in compliance with commitments under one or more of the articles of the Protocol referred to in section V, paragraph 4; or

(b) Otherwise determine not to proceed further with the question.

5. The preliminary finding, or the decision not to proceed, shall include conclusions and reasons therefor.

6. The enforcement branch shall forthwith, through the secretariat, notify the Party concerned in writing of its preliminary finding or decision not to proceed. The secretariat shall make the decision not to proceed available to the other Parties and to the public.

7. Within ten weeks from the date of receipt of the notification of the preliminary finding, the Party concerned may provide a further written submission to the enforcement branch. If the Party concerned does not do so within that period of time, the enforcement branch shall forthwith adopt a final decision confirming its preliminary finding.

8. If the Party concerned provides a further written submission, the enforcement branch shall, within four weeks from the date it received the further submission, consider it and adopt a final decision, indicating whether the preliminary finding, as a whole or any part of it to be specified, is confirmed.

9. The final decision shall include conclusions and reasons therefor.

10. The enforcement branch shall forthwith, through the secretariat, notify the Party concerned in writing of its final decision. The secretariat shall make the final decision available to the other Parties and to the public.

11. The enforcement branch, when the circumstances of an individual case so warrant, may extend any time frames provided for in this section.

12. Where appropriate, the enforcement branch may, at any time, refer a question of implementation to the facilitative branch for consideration.

X. Expedited procedures for the enforcement branch

1. Where a question of implementation relates to eligibility requirements under Articles 6, 12 and 17 of the Protocol, sections VII to IX shall apply, except that:

(a) The preliminary examination referred to in section VII, paragraph 2, shall be completed within two weeks from the date of receipt of the question of implementation by the enforcement branch;

(b) The Party concerned may make a written submission within four weeks from the date of receipt of the notification under section VII, paragraph 4;

(c) If so requested in writing by the Party concerned within two weeks from the date of receipt of the notification under section VII, paragraph 4, the enforcement branch shall hold a hearing as referred to in section IX, paragraph 2, that shall take place within two weeks from the date of receipt of the request or of the written submission under subparagraph (b) above, whichever is the later;

(d) The enforcement branch shall adopt its preliminary finding or a decision not to proceed within six weeks of the notification under section VII, paragraph 4, or within two weeks of a hearing under section IX, paragraph 2, whichever is the shorter;

(e) The Party concerned may make a further written submission within four weeks from the date of receipt of the notification referred to in section IX, paragraph 6;

(f) The enforcement branch shall adopt its final decision within two weeks from the date of receipt of any further written submission referred to in section IX, paragraph 7; and

(g) The periods of time stipulated in section IX shall apply only if, in the opinion of the enforcement branch, they do not interfere with the adoption of decisions in accordance with subparagraphs (d) and (f) above.

2. Where the eligibility of a Party included in Annex I under Articles 6, 12 and 17 of the Protocol has been suspended under section XV, paragraph 4, the Party concerned may submit a request to reinstate its eligibility, either through an expert review team or directly to the enforcement branch. If the enforcement branch receives a report from the expert review team indicating that there is no longer a question of implementation with respect to the eligibility of the Party concerned, it shall reinstate that Party's eligibility, unless the enforcement branch considers that there continues to be such a question of implementation, in which case the procedure referred to in paragraph 1 above shall apply. In response to a request submitted to it directly by the Party concerned, the enforcement branch shall decide as soon as possible, either that there no longer continues to be a question of implementation with respect to that Party's eligibility in which case it shall reinstate that Party's eligibility, or that the procedure referred to in paragraph 1 above shall apply.

3. Where the eligibility of a Party to make transfers under Article 17 of the Protocol has been suspended under section XV, paragraph 5 (c), the Party may request the enforcement branch to reinstate that eligibility. On the basis of the compliance action plan submitted by the Party in accordance with section XV, paragraph 6, and any progress reports submitted by the Party including information on its emissions trends, the enforcement branch shall reinstate that eligibility, unless it determines that the Party has not demonstrated that it will meet its quantified emission limitation or reduction commitment in the commitment period

subsequent to the one for which the Party was determined to be in non-compliance, hereinafter referred to as 'the subsequent commitment period'. The enforcement branch shall apply the procedure referred to in paragraph 1 above, adapted insofar as necessary for the purposes of the procedure in the present paragraph.

4. Where the eligibility of a Party to make transfers under Article 17 of the Protocol has been suspended under section XV, paragraph 5 (c), the enforcement branch shall reinstate that eligibility forthwith if the Party demonstrates that it has met its quantified emission limitation or reduction commitment in the subsequent commitment period, either through the report of the expert review team under Article 8 of the Protocol for the final year of the subsequent commitment period or through a decision of the enforcement branch.

5. In the event of a disagreement whether to apply adjustments to inventories under Article 5, paragraph 2, of the Protocol, or whether to apply a correction to the compilation and accounting database for the accounting of assigned amounts under Article 7, paragraph 4, of the Protocol, the enforcement branch shall decide on the matter within twelve weeks of being informed in writing of such disagreement. In doing so, the enforcement branch may seek expert advice.

XI. Appeals

1. The Party in respect of which a final decision has been taken may appeal to the Conference of the Parties serving as the meeting of the Parties to the Protocol against a decision of the enforcement branch relating to Article 3, paragraph 1, of the Protocol if that Party believes it has been denied due process.

2. The appeal shall be lodged with the secretariat within 45 days after the Party has been informed of the decision of the enforcement branch. The Conference of the Parties serving as the meeting of the Parties to the Protocol shall consider the appeal at its first session after the lodging of the appeal.

3. The Conference of the Parties serving as the meeting of the Parties to the Protocol may agree by a three-fourths majority vote of the Parties present and voting at the meeting to override the decision of the enforcement branch, in which event the Conference of the Parties serving as the meeting of the Parties to the Protocol shall refer the matter of the appeal back to the enforcement branch.

4. The decision of the enforcement branch shall stand pending the decision on appeal. It shall become definitive if, after 45 days, no appeal has been made against it.

XII. Relationship with the Conference of the Parties serving as the meeting of the Parties to the Protocol

The Conference of the Parties serving as the meeting of the Parties to the Protocol shall:

(a) In considering the reports of the expert review teams in accordance with Article 8, paragraphs 5 and 6 of the Protocol, identify any general problems that should be addressed in the general policy guidance referred to in subparagraph (c) below;

(b) Consider the reports of the plenary on the progress of its work;

(c) Provide general policy guidance, including on any issues regarding implementation that may have implications for the work of the subsidiary bodies under the Protocol;

(d) Adopt decisions on proposals on administrative and budgetary matters; and

(e) Consider and decide appeals in accordance with section XI.

XIII. Additional period for fulfilling commitments

For the purpose of fulfilling commitments under Article 3, paragraph 1, of the Protocol, a Party may, until the hundredth day after the date set by the Conference of the Parties serving as the meeting of the Parties to the Protocol for the completion of the expert review process under Article 8 of the Protocol for the last year of the commitment period, continue to acquire, and other Parties may transfer to such Party, emission reduction units, certified emission reductions, assigned amount units and removal units under Articles 6, 12 and 17 of the Protocol, from the preceding commitment period, provided the eligibility of any such Party has not been suspended in accordance with section XV, paragraph 4.

XIV. Consequences applied by the facilitative branch

The facilitative branch, taking into account the principle of common but differentiated responsibilities and respective capabilities, shall decide on the application of one or more of the following consequences:

(a) Provision of advice and facilitation of assistance to individual Parties regarding the implementation of the Protocol;

(b) Facilitation of financial and technical assistance to any Party concerned, including technology transfer and capacity building from sources other than those established under the Convention and the Protocol for the developing countries;

(c) Facilitation of financial and technical assistance, including technology transfer and capacity building, taking into account Article 4, paragraphs 3, 4 and 5, of the Convention;

and

(d) Formulation of recommendations to the Party concerned, taking into account Article 4, paragraph 7, of the Convention.

XV. Consequences applied by the enforcement branch

1. Where the enforcement branch has determined that a Party is not in compliance with Article 5, paragraph 1 or paragraph 2, or Article 7, paragraph 1 or paragraph 4, of the Protocol, it shall apply the following consequences, taking into account the cause, type, degree and frequency of the non-compliance of that Party:

(a) Declaration of non-compliance; and

(b) Development of a plan in accordance with paragraphs 2 and 3 below.

2. The Party not in compliance under paragraph 1 above, shall, within three months after the determination of non-compliance, or such longer period that the enforcement branch considers appropriate, submit to the enforcement branch for review and assessment a plan that includes:

(a) An analysis of the causes of non-compliance of the Party;

(b) Measures that the Party intends to implement in order to remedy the noncompliance;

and

(c) A timetable for implementing such measures within a time frame not exceeding twelve months which enables the assessment of progress in the implementation.

3. The Party not in compliance under paragraph 1 above shall submit to the enforcement branch progress reports on the implementation of the plan on a regular basis.

4. Where the enforcement branch has determined that a Party included in Annex I does not meet one or more of the eligibility requirements under Articles 6, 12 and 17 of the Protocol, it shall suspend the eligibility of that Party in accordance with relevant provisions under those articles. At the request of the Party concerned, eligibility may be reinstated in accordance with the procedure in section X, paragraph 2.

5. Where the enforcement branch has determined that the emissions of a Party have exceeded its assigned amount, calculated pursuant to its quantified emission limitation or reduction commitment inscribed in Annex B to the Protocol and in accordance with the provisions of Article 3 of the Protocol as well as the modalities for the accounting of assigned amounts under Article 7, paragraph 4, of the Protocol, taking into account emission reduction units, certified emission reductions, assigned amount units and removal units the Party has acquired in accordance with section XIII, it shall declare that that Party is not in compliance with its commitments under Article 3, paragraph 1, of the Protocol, and shall apply the following consequences:

(a) Deduction from the Party's assigned amount for the second commitment period of a number of tonnes equal to 1.3 times the amount in tonnes of excess emissions;

(b) Development of a compliance action plan in accordance with paragraphs 6 and 7 below; and

(c) Suspension of the eligibility to make transfers under Article 17 of the Protocol until the Party is reinstated in accordance with section X, paragraph 3 or paragraph 4.

6. The Party not in compliance under paragraph 5 above shall, within three months after the determination of non-compliance or, where the circumstances of an individual case so warrant, such longer period that the enforcement branch considers appropriate, submit to the enforcement branch for review and assessment a compliance action plan that includes:

(a) An analysis of the causes of the non-compliance of the Party;

(b) Action that the Party intends to implement in order to meet its quantified emission limitation or reduction commitment in the subsequent commitment period, giving priority to domestic policies and measures; and

(c) A timetable for implementing such action, which enables the assessment of annual progress in the implementation, within a time frame that does not exceed three years or up to the end of the subsequent commitment period, whichever occurs sooner. At the request of the Party, the enforcement branch may, where the circumstances of an individual case so warrant, extend the time for implementing such action for a period which shall not exceed the maximum period of three years mentioned above.

7. The Party not in compliance under paragraph 5 above shall submit to the enforcement branch a progress report on the implementation of the compliance action plan on an annual basis.

8. For subsequent commitment periods, the rate referred to in paragraph 5 (a) above shall be determined by an amendment.

XVI. Relationship with Articles 16 and 19 of the Protocol

The procedures and mechanisms relating to compliance shall operate without prejudice to Articles 16 and 19 of the Protocol.

XVII. Secretariat

The secretariat referred to in Article 14 of the Protocol shall serve as the secretariat of the Committee.

Review of Compliance of the Århus Convention on Access to Information, Public Participation in Decision-making and Access to Justice in Environmental Matters[14]

Source: Decision I/7 (Annex), First Meeting of the Parties, 21-23 October 2002, Doc. ECE/MP.PP/2/Add.8. Further information: Århus Convention Secretariat (UNECE), Geneva, Switzerland, http://www.unece.org/env/pp

Structure and functions of the Compliance Committee and procedures for the review of compliance

I. Structure

1. The Committee shall consist of eight members, who shall serve in their personal capacity.

2. The Committee shall be composed of nationals of the Parties and Signatories to the Convention who shall be persons of high moral character and recognized

14 The Århus Convention is reproduced at p. 46.

competence in the fields to which the Convention relates, including persons having legal experience.

3. The Committee may not include more than one national of the same State.

4. Candidates meeting the requirements of paragraph 2 shall be nominated by Parties, Signatories and non-governmental organizations falling within the scope of article 10, paragraph 5, of the Convention and promoting environmental protection, for election pursuant to paragraph 7.

5. Unless the Meeting of the Parties, in a particular instance, decides otherwise, the procedure for the nomination of candidates for the Committee shall be the following:

(a) Nominations shall be sent to the secretariat in at least one of the official languages of the Convention not later than 12 weeks before the opening of the meeting of the Parties during which the election is to take place;

(b) Each nomination shall be accompanied by a curriculum vitae (CV) of the candidate not exceeding 600 words and may include supporting material;

(c) The secretariat shall distribute the nominations and the CVs, together with any supporting material, in accordance with rule 10 of the Rules of Procedure.

6. Committee members shall be elected on the basis of nominations in accordance with paragraphs 4 and 5. The Meeting of the Parties shall give due consideration to all nominations.

[Paragraphs 7-11 not reproduced]

II. Meetings

12. The Committee shall, unless it decides otherwise, meet at least once a year. The secretariat shall arrange for and service the meetings of the Committee.

III. Functions of the Committee

13. The Committee shall:

(a) Consider any submission, referral or communication made in accordance with paragraphs 15 to 24 below;

(b) Prepare, at the request of the Meeting of the Parties, a report on compliance with or implementation of the provisions of the Convention; and

(c) Monitor, assess and facilitate the implementation of and compliance with the reporting requirements under article 10, paragraph 2, of the Convention;

and act pursuant to paragraphs 36 and 37.

14. The Committee may examine compliance issues and make recommendations if and as appropriate.

IV. Submissions by Parties

15. A submission may be brought before the Committee by one or more Parties that have reservations about another Party's compliance with its obligations under the Convention. Such a submission shall be addressed in writing to the secretariat and supported by corroborating information. The secretariat shall, within two weeks of

receiving a submission, send a copy of it to the Party whose compliance is at issue. Any reply and supporting information shall be submitted to the secretariat and to the Parties involved within three months or such longer period as the circumstances of a particular case may require but in no case later than six months. The secretariat shall transmit the submission and the reply, as well as all corroborating and supporting information, to the Committee, which shall consider the matter as soon as practicable.

16. A submission may be brought before the Committee by a Party that concludes that, despite its best endeavours, it is or will be unable to comply fully with its obligations under the Convention. Such a submission shall be addressed in writing to the secretariat and explain, in particular, the specific circumstances that the Party considers to be the cause of its non-compliance. The secretariat shall transmit the submission to the Committee, which shall consider the matter as soon as practicable.

V. Referrals by the Secretariat

17. Where the secretariat, in particular upon considering the reports submitted in accordance with the Convention's reporting requirements, becomes aware of possible non-compliance by a Party with its obligations under the Convention, it may request the Party concerned to furnish necessary information about the matter. If there is no response or the matter is not resolved within three months, or such longer period as the circumstances of the matter may require but in no case later than six months, the secretariat shall bring the matter to the attention of the Committee, which shall consider the matter as soon as practicable.

VI. Communications from the public

18. On the expiry of twelve months from either the date of adoption of this decision or from the date of the entry into force of the Convention with respect to a Party, whichever is the later, communications may be brought before the Committee by one or more members of the public concerning that Party's compliance with the Convention, unless that Party has notified the Depositary in writing by the end of the applicable period that it is unable to accept, for a period of not more than four years, the consideration of such communications by the Committee. The Depositary shall without delay notify all Parties of any such notification received. During the four-year period mentioned above, the Party may revoke its notification thereby accepting that, from that date, communications may be brought before the Committee by one or more members of the public concerning that Party's compliance with the Convention.

19. The communications referred to in paragraph 18 shall be addressed to the Committee through the secretariat in writing and may be in electronic form. The communications shall be supported by corroborating information.

20. The Committee shall consider any such communication unless it determines that the communication is:

(a) Anonymous;
(b) An abuse of the right to make such communications;
(c) Manifestly unreasonable;
(d) Incompatible with the provisions of this decision or with the Convention.

21. The Committee should at all relevant stages take into account any available domestic remedy unless the application of the remedy is unreasonably prolonged or obviously does not provide an effective and sufficient means of redress.

22. Subject to the provisions of paragraph 20, the Committee shall as soon as possible bring any communications submitted to it under paragraph 18 to the attention of the Party alleged to be in non-compliance.

23. A Party shall, as soon as possible but not later than five months after any communication is brought to its attention by the Committee, submit to the Committee written explanations or statements clarifying the matter and describing any response that it may have made.

24. The Committee shall, as soon as practicable, further consider communications submitted to it pursuant to this chapter and take into account all relevant written information made available to it, and may hold hearings.

[Article VII not reproduced]

VIII. Confidentiality

26. Save as otherwise provided for in this chapter, no information held by the Committee shall be kept confidential.

27. The Committee and any person involved in its work shall ensure the confidentiality of any information that falls within the scope of the exceptions provided for in article 4, paragraphs 3 (c) and 4, of the Convention and that has been provided in confidence.

28. The Committee and any person involved in its work shall ensure the confidentiality of information that has been provided to it in confidence by a Party when making a submission in respect of its own compliance in accordance with paragraph 16 above.

29. Information submitted to the Committee, including all information relating to the identity of the member of the public submitting the information, shall be kept confidential if submitted by a person who asks that it be kept confidential because of a concern that he or she may be penalized, persecuted or harassed.

30. If necessary to ensure the confidentiality of information in any of the above cases, the Committee shall hold closed meetings.

31. Committee reports shall not contain any information that the Committee must keep confidential under paragraphs 27 to 29 above. Information that the Committee must keep confidential under paragraph 29 shall not be made available to any Party. All other information that the Committee receives in confidence and that is related to any recommendations by the Committee to the Meeting of the Parties

shall be made available to any Party upon its request; that Party shall ensure the confidentiality of the information that it has received in confidence.

IX. Entitlement to participate

32. A Party in respect of which a submission, referral or communication is made or which makes a submission, as well as the member of the public making a communication, shall be entitled to participate in the discussions of the Committee with respect to that submission, referral or communication.

33. The Party and the member of the public shall not take part in the preparation and adoption of any findings, any measures or any recommendations of the Committee.

34. The Committee shall send a copy of its draft findings, draft measures and any draft recommendations to the Parties concerned and the member of the public who submitted the communication if applicable, and shall take into account any comments made by them in the finalization of those findings, measures and recommendations.

[Article X not reproduced]

XI. Consideration by the Compliance Committee

36. Pending consideration by the Meeting of the Parties, with a view to addressing compliance issues without delay, the Compliance Committee may:

(a) In consultation with the Party concerned, take the measures listed in paragraph 37 (a);

(b) Subject to agreement with the Party concerned, take the measures listed in paragraph 37 (b), (c) and (d).

XII. Consideration by the Meeting of the Parties

37. The Meeting of the Parties may, upon consideration of a report and any recommendations of the Committee, decide upon appropriate measures to bring about full compliance with the Convention. The Meeting of the Parties may, depending on the particular question before it and taking into account the cause, degree and frequency of the non-compliance, decide upon one or more of the following measures:

(a) Provide advice and facilitate assistance to individual Parties regarding the implementation of the Convention;

(b) Make recommendations to the Party concerned;

(c) Request the Party concerned to submit a strategy, including a time schedule, to the Compliance Committee regarding the achievement of compliance with the Convention and to report on the implementation of this strategy;

(d) In cases of communications from the public, make recommendations to the Party concerned on specific measures to address the matter raised by the member of the public;

(e) Issue declarations of non-compliance;

(f) Issue cautions;

(g) Suspend, in accordance with the applicable rules of international law concerning the suspension of the operation of a treaty, the special rights and privileges accorded to the Party concerned under the Convention;
(h) Take such other non-confrontational, non-judicial and consultative measures as may be appropriate.

[Articles XIII-XIV not reproduced]

Mechanism for Promoting Implementation and Compliance of the Basel Convention on the Control of Transboundary Movements of Hazardous Wastes and their Disposal[15]

Source: Decision VI/12 (Appendix), Sixth Conference of the Parties, 9-13 December 2002, Doc. UNEP/CHW.6/40. Further information: Basel Convention Secretariat, Geneva, Switzerland, http://www.basel.int/

Terms of reference

Objectives

1. The objective of the mechanism is to assist Parties to comply with their obligations under the Convention and to facilitate, promote, monitor and aim to secure the implementation of and compliance with the obligations under the Convention.

Nature of the mechanism

2. The mechanism shall be non-confrontational, transparent, cost-effective and preventive in nature, simple, flexible, non-binding and oriented in the direction of helping parties to implement the provisions of the Basel Convention. It will pay particular attention to the special needs of developing countries and countries with economies in transition, and is intended to promote cooperation between all Parties. The mechanism should complement work performed by other Convention bodies and by the Basel Convention Regional Centres.

Composition and tenure

3. A Committee for administrating this mechanism ('the Committee') is hereby established. It shall consist of 15 Members nominated by the Parties, serving in accordance with paragraph 4, and based on equitable geographical representation of the five regional groups of the United Nations, elected by the Conference of the Parties.

---

15 The Basel Convention is reproduced at p. 331.

4. If a Member of the Committee resigns or is otherwise unable to complete his or her term of office or to perform his or her functions, the Party who nominated that member shall nominate an alternate to serve for the remainder of the mandate.

5. Members of the Committee will serve objectively and in the best interest of the Convention. They shall have expertise relating to the subject matter of the Convention in areas including scientific, technical, socio-economic and/or legal fields.

6. At the meeting at which the decision establishing the mechanism is adopted, the Conference of the Parties shall elect five members, one from each region, for one term, and ten members, two from each region, for two terms. The Conference of the Parties shall, at each ordinary meeting thereafter, elect for two full terms new members to replace those members whose period of office has expired, or is about to expire. Members shall not serve for more than two consecutive terms. For the purposes of the present terms of reference 'term' means the period that begins at the end of one ordinary meeting of the Conference of the Parties and ends at the end of the next ordinary meeting of the Parties.

7. The Committee shall elect its officers - a Chair, three Vice-chairs and a Rapporteur - based on equitable geographical representation of the five regional groups of the United Nations.

8. The Committee shall meet at least once between each regular meeting of the Conference of the Parties, and in conjunction with meetings of other Convention bodies. The secretariat shall arrange for and service the meetings of the Committee.

Procedures for specific submissions

9. Submissions may be made to the Committee by:

(a) A Party that concludes that, despite its best efforts, it is or will be unable to fully implement or comply with its obligations under the Convention;

(b) A Party that has concerns or is affected by a failure to comply with and/or implement the Convention's obligations by another Party with whom it is directly involved under the Convention. A Party intending to make a submission under this subparagraph shall inform the Party whose compliance is in question, and both Parties should then try to resolve the matter through consultations;

(c) The secretariat, if, while acting pursuant to its functions under articles 13 and 16, it becomes aware of possible difficulties of any Party in complying with its reporting obligations under article 13, paragraph 3 of the Convention, provided that the matter has not been resolved within three months by consultation with the Party concerned.

10. Any submission, except one made under paragraph 9 (c), shall be addressed in writing to the secretariat, and shall set out:

(a) The matter of concern;

(b) The relevant provisions of the Convention; and

(c) Where paragraph 9 (b) applies, information substantiating the submission.

11. Where a submission is made under paragraph 9 (a), the secretariat shall forward the submission, within two weeks of its receiving the submission, to the Committee for consideration at its next meeting.

12. The Party whose compliance is in question may present responses and/or comments at every step of the proceedings described in this decision.

13. In cases of a submission other than by a Party with respect to its own compliance, the secretariat shall send, within two weeks of its receiving the submission, a copy to the Party whose compliance with the Convention is in question and to the Committee for consideration at its next meeting.

14. Without prejudice to paragraph 12, additional information provided in response by the Party whose compliance is in question should be forwarded to the secretariat within three months of the date of the receipt of the submission by the Party in question, unless the circumstances of a particular case require an extended period of time. Such information will be immediately transmitted to the members of the Committee for consideration at its next meeting. Where a submission has been made pursuant to paragraph 9 (b), the information shall also be forwarded by the secretariat to the Party that made the submission.

15. Where a Party is identified in a submission or itself makes a submission, it shall be invited to participate in the consideration of the submission by the Committee. Such a Party, however, shall not take part in the elaboration and adoption of the conclusions or recommendations by the Committee. Conclusions and recommendations shall be shared with the Party concerned for consideration and an opportunity to comment. Any such comments shall be forwarded with the report of the Committee to the Conference of the Parties.

16. Meetings dealing with specific submissions relating to the compliance of an individual Party shall not be open to other Parties or the public, unless the Committee and the Party whose compliance is in question agree otherwise.

17. Under the compliance mechanism, a Party may also consider and use relevant and appropriate information provided by civil society on compliance difficulties.

18. The Committee may decide not to proceed with a submission which it considers is:

(a) *de minimis*; or

(b) manifestly ill-founded

Facilitation procedure

19. The Committee shall consider any submission made to it in accordance with paragraph 10 with a view to determining the facts and root causes of the matter of concern and, assist in its resolution. As part of this process, the Committee may provide a Party, after coordination with that Party, with advice, non-binding recommendations and information relating to, inter alia;

(a) Establishing and/or strengthening its domestic/regional regulatory regimes;

(b) Facilitation of assistance in particular to developing countries and countries with economies in transition, including on how to access financial and technical support, including technology transfer and capacity-building;
(c) Elaborating, as appropriate and with the cooperation of the Party or Parties faced with the compliance problems, voluntary compliance action plans, and review their implementation. A voluntary compliance action plan may include benchmarks, objectives and indicators of the plan, as well as an indicative timeline for its implementation;
(d) Any follow-up arrangements for progress reporting to the Committee, including through the national reporting procedure under article 13.

Advice, non-binding recommendations and information other than those listed in subparagraphs (a) to (d) above should be provided in agreement with that Party.

Recommendation to the Conference of the Parties on additional measures

20. If, after undertaking the facilitation procedure in paragraph 19 above and taking into account the cause, type, degree and frequency of compliance difficulties, as well as the capacity of the Party whose compliance is in question, the Committee considers it necessary in the light of paragraphs 1 and 2 to pursue further measures to address a Party's compliance difficulties, it may recommend to the Conference of the Parties that it consider:
(a) Further support under the Convention for the Party concerned, including prioritization of technical assistance and capacity-building and access to financial resources; or
(b) Issuing a cautionary statement and providing advice regarding future compliance in order to help Parties to implement the provisions of the Basel Convention and to promote cooperation between all Parties.

Any such action shall be consistent with article 15 of the Convention.

General review

21. The Committee shall, as directed by the Conference of Parties, review general issues of compliance and implementation under the Convention relating to, inter alia:
(a) Ensuring the environmentally sound management and disposal of hazardous and other wastes;
(b) Training customs and other personnel;
(c) Accessing technical and financial support, particularly for developing countries, including technology transfer and capacity-building;
(d) Establishing and developing means of detecting and eradicating illegal traffic, including investigating, sampling and testing;
(e) Monitoring, assessing and facilitating reporting under article 13 of the Convention; and
(f) The implementation of, and compliance with, specified obligations under the Convention.

Consultation and information

22. In carrying out its functions, the Committee may, inter alia:

(a) Request further information from all Parties, through the secretariat, on general issues of compliance and implementation under its consideration;

(b) Consult with other bodies of the Convention;

(c) Request further information from any sources and draw upon outside expertise, as it considers necessary and appropriate, either with the consent of the Party concerned or as directed by the Conference of the Parties;

(d) Undertake, with the agreement of a Party(ies), information gathering in its or their territory for the purpose of fulfilling the functions of the Committee;

(e) Consult with the secretariat and draw upon its experience and knowledge base compiled under article 16 of the Convention and request through the secretariat information, where appropriate in the form of a report, on matters under the Committee's consideration; and

(f) Review the national reports of Parties provided under article 13 of the Convention.

Reporting

23. The Committee shall report to each ordinary meeting of the Conference of the Parties on the work it has carried out to fulfil its functions under paragraphs 19 and 20 for the information and/or the consideration of the Conference of the Parties.

24. The Committee shall also report to each ordinary meeting of the Conference of the Parties on any conclusions and/or recommendations it has developed under paragraph 21 and on its suggestions for any future work that may be required on general issues of compliance and implementation, for the consideration and approval of the Conference of the Parties.

Decision-making

25. The Committee shall make every effort to reach agreement on all matters of substance by consensus. Where this is not possible, the report and recommendations shall reflect the views of all the Committee members. If all efforts to reach consensus have been exhausted and no agreement has been reached, any decision shall, as a last resort, be taken by a two-third majority of the members present and voting or by eight members, whichever is the greater. Ten members of the Committee shall constitute a quorum.

Confidentiality

26. The Committee, any Party or others involved in its deliberations shall protect the confidentiality of information received in confidence.

Relationship with provisions of the Convention

27. The present mechanism shall be without prejudice to the provisions of article 20 on settlement of disputes.

28. In performing its functions under paragraphs 19, 20 and 21, the Committee shall take into account any specific procedures provided for under the Convention concerning failures to meet Convention obligations.

World Bank

The World Bank Inspection Panel[16]

Adopted on 22 September 1993. Source: World Bank Board of Executive Directors, Resolution No. IBRD 93-10 and No. IDA 93-6. Further information: World Bank, Washington DC, USA, http://www.worldbank.org/inspectionpanel

The Executive Directors:
Hereby resolve:

1. There is established an independent Inspection Panel (hereinafter called the Panel), which shall have the powers and shall function as stated in this resolution.

Composition of the Panel

2. The Panel shall consist of three members of different nationalities from Bank member countries. The President, after consultation with the Executive Directors, shall nominate the members of the Panel to be appointed by the Executive Directors.

3. The first members of the Panel shall be appointed as follows: one for three years, one for four years and one for five years. Each vacancy thereafter shall be filled for a period of five years, provided that no member may serve for more than one term. The term of appointment of each member of the Panel shall be subject to the continuity of the inspection function established by this Resolution.

4. Members of the Panel shall be selected on the basis of their ability to deal thoroughly and fairly with the requests brought to them, their integrity and their independence from the Bank's Management, and their exposure to developmental issues and to living conditions in developing countries. Knowledge and experience of the Bank's operations will also be desirable.

5. Executive Directors, Alternates, Advisors and staff members of the Bank Group may not serve on the Panel until two years have elapsed since the end of their

---

16 The two sets of Clarifications reproduced at p. 637 and 639 below were adopted by the World Bank's Board of Executive Directors in 1996 and 1999 to provide interpretations of notions found in the text of the Inspection Panel Resolution and general practices developed under it.

service in the Bank Group. For purposes of this Resolution, the term 'staff' shall mean all persons holding Bank Group appointments as defined in Staff Rule 4.01 including persons holding consultant and local consultant appointments.

6. A Panel member shall be disqualified from participation in the hearing and investigation of any request related to a matter in which he/she has a personal interest or had significant involvement in any capacity.

7. The Panel member initially appointed for five years shall be the first Chairperson of the Panel, and shall hold such office for one year. Thereafter, the members of the Panel shall elect a Chairperson for a period of one year.

8. Members of the Panel may be removed from office only by decision of the Executive Directors, for cause.

9. With the exception of the Chairperson who shall work on a full-time basis at Bank headquarters, members of the Panel shall be expected to work on a full-time basis only when their workload justifies such an arrangement, as will be decided by the Executive Directors on the recommendation of the Panel.

10. In the performance of their functions, members of the Panel shall be officials of the Bank enjoying the privileges and immunities accorded to Bank officials, and shall be subject to the requirements of the Bank's Articles of Agreement concerning their exclusive loyalty to the Bank and to the obligations of subparagraphs (c) and (d) of paragraph 3.1 and paragraph 3.2 of the Principles of Staff Employment concerning their conduct as officials of the Bank. Once they begin to work on a full-time basis, they shall receive remuneration at a level to be determined by the Executive Directors upon a recommendation of the President, plus normal benefits available to Bank fixed-term staff. Prior to that time, they shall be remunerated on a per diem basis and shall be reimbursed for their expenses on the same basis as the members of the Bank's Administrative Tribunal. Members of the Panel may not be employed by the Bank Group, following the end of their service on the Panel.

11. The President, after consultation with the Executive Directors, shall assign a staff member to the Panel as Executive Secretary, who need not act on a full-time basis until the workload so justifies. The Panel shall be given such budgetary resources as shall be sufficient to carry out its activities.

Powers of the Panel

12. The Panel shall receive requests for inspection presented to it by an affected party in the territory of the borrower which is not a single individual (i.e., a community of persons such as an organization, association, society or other grouping of individuals), or by the local representative of such party or by another representative in the exceptional cases where the party submitting the request contends that appropriate representation is not locally available and the Executive Directors so agree at the time they consider the request for inspection. Any such representative shall present to the Panel written evidence that he is acting as agent of the party on behalf of which the request is made. The affected party must

demonstrate that its rights or interests have been or are likely to be directly affected by an action or omission of the Bank as a result of a failure of the Bank to follow its operational policies and procedures with respect to the design, appraisal and/or implementation of a project financed by the Bank (including situations where the Bank is alleged to have failed in its follow-up on the borrower's obligations under loan agreements with respect to such policies and procedures) provided in all cases that such failure has had, or threatens to have, a material adverse effect. In view of the institutional responsibilities of Executive Directors in the observance by the Bank of its operational policies and procedures, an Executive Director may in special cases of serious alleged violations of such policies and procedures ask the Panel for an investigation, subject to the requirements of paragraphs 13 and 14 below. The Executive Directors, acting as a Board, may at any time instruct the Panel to conduct an investigation. For purposes of this Resolution, 'operational policies and procedures' consist of the Bank's Operational Policies, Bank Procedures and Operational Directives, and similar documents issued before these series were started, and does not include Guidelines and Best Practices and similar documents or statements.

13. The Panel shall satisfy itself before a request for inspection is heard that the subject matter of the request has been dealt with by the Management of the Bank and Management has failed to demonstrate that it has followed, or is taking adequate steps to follow the Bank's policies and procedures. The Panel shall also satisfy itself that the alleged violation of the Bank's policies and procedures is of a serious character.

14. In considering requests under paragraph 12 above, the following requests shall not be heard by the Panel:

(a) Complaints with respect to actions which are the responsibility of other parties, such as a borrower, or potential borrower, and which do not involve any action or omission on the part of the Bank.

(b) Complaints against procurement decisions by Bank borrowers from suppliers of goods and services financed or expected to be financed by the Bank under a loan agreement, or from losing tenderers for the supply of any such goods and services, which will continue to be addressed by staff under existing procedures.

(c) Requests filed after the Closing Date of the loan financing the project with respect to which the request is filed or after the loan financing the project has been substantially disbursed. This will be deemed to be the case when at least ninety five percent of the loan proceeds have been disbursed.

(d) Requests related to a particular matter or matters over which the Panel has already made its recommendation upon having received a prior request, unless justified by new evidence or circumstances not known at the time of the prior request.

15. The Panel shall seek the advice of the Bank's Legal Department on matters related to the Bank's rights and obligations with respect to the request under consideration.

Procedures

16. Requests for inspection shall be in writing and shall state all relevant facts, including, in the case of a request by an affected party, the harm suffered by or threatened to such party or parties by the alleged action or omission of the Bank. All requests shall explain the steps already taken to deal with the issue, as well as the nature of the alleged actions or omissions and shall specify the actions taken to bring the issue to the attention of Management, and Management's response to such action.

17. The Chairperson of the Panel shall inform the Executive Directors and the President of the Bank promptly upon receiving a request for inspection.

18. Within 21 days of being notified of a request for inspection, the Management of the Bank shall provide the Panel with evidence that it has complied, or intends to comply with the Bank's relevant policies and procedures.

19. Within 21 days of receiving the response of the Management as provided in the preceding paragraph, the Panel shall determine whether the request meets the eligibility criteria set out in paragraphs 12 to 14 above and shall make a recommendation to the Executive Directors as to whether the matter should be investigated. The recommendation of the Panel shall be circulated to the Executive Directors for decision within the normal distribution period. In case the request was initiated by an affected party, such party shall be informed of the decision of the Executive Directors within two weeks of the date of such decision.

20. If a decision is made by the Executive Directors to investigate the request, the Chairperson of the Panel shall designate one or more of the Panel's members (Inspectors) who shall have primary responsibility for conducting the inspection. The Inspector(s) shall report his/her (their) findings to the Panel within a period to be determined by the Panel taking into account the nature of each request.

21. In the discharge of their functions, the members of the Panel shall have access to all staff who may contribute information and to all pertinent Bank records and shall consult as needed with the Director General, Operations Evaluation Department and the Internal Auditor. The borrower and the Executive Director representing the borrowing (or guaranteeing) country shall be consulted on the subject matter both before the Panel's recommendation on whether to proceed with the investigation and during the investigation. Inspection in the territory of such country shall be carried out with its prior consent.

22. The Panel shall submit its report to the Executive Directors and the President. The report of the Panel shall consider all relevant facts, and shall conclude with the Panel's findings on whether the Bank has complied with all relevant Bank policies and procedures.

23. Within six weeks from receiving the Panel's findings, Management will submit to the Executive Directors for their consideration a report indicating its recommendations in response to such findings. The findings of the Panel and the actions completed during project preparation also will be discussed in the Staff

Appraisal Report when the project is submitted to the Executive Directors for financing. In all cases of a request made by an affected party, the Bank shall, within two weeks of the Executive Directors' consideration of the matter, inform such party of the results of the investigation and the action taken in its respect, if any.

Decisions of the Panel

24. All decisions of the Panel on procedural matters, its recommendations to the Executive Directors on whether to proceed with the investigation of a request, and its reports pursuant to paragraph 22, shall be reached by consensus and, in the absence of a consensus, the majority and minority views shall be stated.

Reports

25. After the Executive Directors have considered a request for an inspection as set out in paragraph 19, the Bank shall make such request publicly available together with the recommendation of the Panel on whether to proceed with the inspection and the decision of the Executive Directors in this respect. The Bank shall make publicly available the report submitted by the Panel pursuant to paragraph 22 and the Bank's response thereon within two weeks after consideration by the Executive Directors of the report.

26. In addition to the material referred to in paragraph 25, the Panel shall furnish an annual report to the President and the Executive Directors concerning its activities. The annual report shall be published by the Bank.

Review

27. The Executive Directors shall review the experience of the inspection function established by this Resolution after two years from the date of the appointment of the first members of the Panel.

Application to IDA projects

28. In this resolution, references to the Bank and to loans include references to the Association and to development credits.

Review of the Resolution Establishing the Inspection Panel: Clarifications of Certain Aspects of the Resolution

Adopted by the World Bank's Board of Executive Directors on 17 October 1996.

The Resolution establishing the Inspection Panel calls for a review after two years from the date of appointment of the first panel members. On October 17, 1996, the Executive Directors of the Bank and IDA completed the review process (except for the question of inspection of World Bank Group private sector projects) by considering and endorsing the clarifications recommended by Management on the basis of the discussions of the Executive Directors' Committee on Development

Effectiveness (CODE). The Inspection Panel and Management are requested by the Executive Directors to observe the clarifications in their application of the Resolution. The clarifications are set out below.

The Panel's function

Since the Resolution limits the first phase of the inspection process to ascertaining the eligibility of the request, this phase should normally be completed within the 21 days stated in the Resolution. However, in cases where the Inspection Panel believes that it would be appropriate to undertake a 'preliminary assessment' of the damages alleged by the requester (in particular when such preliminary assessment could lead to a resolution of the matter without the need for a full investigation), the Panel may undertake the preliminary assessment and indicate to the Board the date on which it would present its findings and recommendations as to the need, if any, for a full investigation. If such a date is expected by the Panel to exceed eight weeks from the date of receipt of Management's comments, the Panel should seek Board approval for the extension, possibly on a 'no-objection' basis. What is needed at this preliminary stage is not to establish that a serious violation of the Bank's policy has actually resulted in damages suffered by the affected party, but rather to establish whether the complaint is prima facie justified and warrants a full investigation because it is eligible under the Resolution.

Panel investigations will continue to result in 'findings' and the Board will continue to act on investigations on the basis of recommendations of Management with respect to such remedial action as may be needed.

Eligibility and access

It is understood that the 'affected party' which the Resolution describes as 'a community of persons such as an organization, association, society or other grouping of individuals' includes any two or more persons who share some common interests or concerns.

The word 'project' as used in the Resolution has the same meaning as it generally has in the Bank's practice, and includes projects under consideration by Bank management as well as projects already approved by the Executive Directors.

The Panel's mandate does not extend to reviewing the consistency of the Bank's practice with any of its policies and procedures, but, as stated in the Resolution, is limited to cases of alleged failure by the Bank to follow its operational policies and procedures with respect to the design, appraisal and/or implementation of projects, including cases of alleged failure by the bank to follow-up on the borrowers' obligations under loan agreements, with respect to such policies and procedures.

No procurement action is subject to inspection by the Panel, whether taken by the Bank or by a borrower. A separate mechanism is available for addressing procurement-related complaints.

Outreach

Management will make its response to requests for inspection available to the public within three days after the Board has decided on whether to authorize the inspection. Management will also make available to the public opinions of the General Counsel related to Inspection Panel matters promptly after the Executive Directors have dealt with the issues involved, unless the Board decides otherwise in a specific case.

Management will make significant efforts to make the Inspection Panel better known in borrowing countries, but will not provide technical assistance or funding to potential requesters.

Composition of the Panel

No change in the composition of the Panel is being made at this time.

Role of the Board

The Board will continue to have authority to (i) interpret the Resolution; and (ii) authorize inspections. In applying the Resolution to specific cases, the Panel will apply it as it understands it, subject to the Board's review. As stated in the Resolution, '[t]he Panel shall seek the advice of the Bank's Legal Department on matters related to the Bank's rights and obligations with respect to the request under consideration.'

Conclusions of the Board's Second Review of the Inspection Panel

Adopted by the World Bank's Board of Executive Directors on 20 April 1999.

The Executive Directors approved today, April 20, 1999, with immediate effect, the report of the Working Group on the Second Review of the Inspection Panel, as revised in light of the extensive consultations that took place after the report was first circulated.

The report confirms the soundness of the Resolution establishing the Inspection Panel (IBRD Resolution No. 93-10, IDA Resolution No. 93-6 of September 22, 1993, hereinafter 'the Resolution') and provides clarifications for its application. These clarifications supplement the clarifications issued by the Board on October 17, 1996 and prevail over them in case of conflict. The report's recommendations approved by the Board are as follows:

- The Board reaffirms the Resolution, the importance of the Panel's function, its independence and integrity.
- Management will follow the Resolution. It will not communicate with the Board on matters associated with the request for inspection, except as provided for in the Resolution. It will thus direct its response to the request, including

any steps it intends to take to address its failures, if any, to the Panel. Management will report to the Board any recommendations it may have, after the Panel completes its inspection and submits its findings, as envisaged in paragraph 23 of the Resolution.

- In its initial response to the request for inspection, Management will provide evidence that
  - it has complied with the relevant Bank operational policies and procedures; or that
  - there are serious failures attributable exclusively to its own actions or omissions in complying, but that it intends to comply with the relevant policies and procedures; or that
  - the serious failures that may exist are exclusively attributable to the borrower or to other factors external to the Bank; or that
  - the serious failures that may exist are attributable both to the Bank's non-compliance with the relevant operational policies and procedures and to the borrower or other external factors.

The Inspection Panel may independently agree or disagree, totally or partially, with Management's position and will proceed accordingly.

- When Management responds, admitting serious failures that are attributable exclusively or partly to the Bank, it will provide evidence that it has complied or intends to comply with the relevant operating policies and procedures. This response will contain only those actions that the Bank has implemented or can implement by itself.
- The Inspection Panel will satisfy itself as to whether the Bank's compliance or evidence of intention to comply is adequate, and reflect this assessment in its reporting to the Board.
- The Panel will determine the eligibility of a request for inspection independently of any views that may be expressed by Management. With respect to matters relating to the Bank's rights and obligations with respect to the request under consideration, the Panel will seek the advice of the Bank's Legal Department as required by the Resolution.
- For its recommendation on whether an investigation should be carried out, the Panel will satisfy itself that all the eligibility criteria provided for in the Resolution have been met. It will base its recommendation on the information presented in the request, in the Management response, and on other documentary evidence. The Panel may decide to visit the project country if it believes that this is necessary to establish the eligibility of the request. In respect of such field visits, the Panel will not report on the Bank's failure to comply with its policies and procedures or its resulting material adverse effect; any definitive assessment of a serious failure of the Bank that has caused material adverse effect will be done after the Panel has completed its investigation.

- The original time limit, set forth in the Resolution for both Management's response to the request and the Panel's recommendation, will be strictly observed except for reasons of force majeure, i.e. reasons that are clearly beyond Management's or the Panel's control, respectively, as may be approved by the Board on a no objection basis.
- If the Panel so recommends, the Board will authorize an investigation without making a judgement on the merits of the claimants' request, and without discussion except with respect to the following technical eligibility criteria:
  - The affected party consists of any two or more persons with common interests or concerns and who are in the borrower's territory (Resolution para.12).
  - The request does assert in substance that a serious violation by the Bank of its operational policies and procedures has or is likely to have a material adverse effect on the requester (Resolution paras. 12 and 14a).
  - The request does assert that its subject matter has been brought to Management's attention and that, in the requester's view, Management has failed to respond adequately demonstrating that it has followed or is taking steps to follow the Bank's policies and procedures (Resolution para. 13).
  - The matter is not related to procurement (Resolution para. 14b).
  - The related loan has not been closed or substantially disbursed (Resolution para. 14c).
  - The Panel has not previously made a recommendation on the subject matter or, if it has, that the request does assert that there is new evidence or circumstances not known at the time of the prior request (Resolution para. 14d).
- Issues of interpretation of the Resolution will be cleared with the Board.
- The 'preliminary assessment' concept, as described in the October 1996 Clarification, is no longer needed. The paragraph entitled 'The Panel's Function' in the October 1996 'Clarifications' is thus deleted.
- The profile of Panel activities, in-country, during the course of an investigation, should be kept as low as possible in keeping with its role as a fact-finding body on behalf of the Board. The Panel's methods of investigation should not create the impression that it is investigating the borrower's performance. However, the Board, acknowledging the important role of the Panel in contacting the requesters and in fact-finding on behalf of the Board, welcomes the Panel's efforts to gather information through consultations with affected people. Given the need to conduct such work in an independent and low-profile manner, the Panel - and Management - should decline media contacts while an investigation is pending or underway. Under those circumstances in which, in the judgement of the Panel or Management, it is necessary to respond to the media, comments should be limited to the process.

They will make it clear that the Panel's role is to investigate the Bank and not the borrower.

- As required by the Resolution, the Panel's report to the Board will focus on whether there is a serious Bank failure to observe its operational policies and procedures with respect to project design, appraisal and/or implementation. The report will include all relevant facts that are needed to understand fully the context and basis for the panel's findings and conclusions. The Panel will discuss in its written report only those material adverse effects, alleged in the request, that have totally or partially resulted from serious Bank failure of compliance with its policies and procedures. If the request alleges a material adverse effect and the Panel finds that it is not totally or partially caused by Bank failure, the Panel's report will so state without entering into analysis of the material adverse effect itself or its causes.
- For assessing material adverse effect, the without-project situation should be used as the base case for comparison, taking into account what baseline information may be available. Non-accomplishments and unfulfilled expectations that do not generate a material deterioration compared to the without-project situation will not be considered as a material adverse effect for this purpose. As the assessment of material adverse effect in the context of the complex reality of a specific project can be difficult, the Panel will have to exercise carefully its judgement on these matters, and be guided by Bank policies and procedures where relevant.
- A distinction has to be made between Management's report to the Board (Resolution para. 23), which addresses Bank failure and possible Bank remedial efforts and 'action plans,' agreed between the borrower and the Bank, in consultation with the requesters, that seek to improve project implementation. The latter 'action plans' are outside the purview of the Resolution, its 1996 clarification, and these clarifications. In the event of agreement by the Bank and borrower on an action plan for the project, Management will communicate to the Panel the nature and outcomes of consultations with affected parties on the action plan. Such an action plan, if warranted, will normally be considered by the Board in conjunction with the Management's report, submitted under Resolution para. 23.
- The Panel may submit to the Executive Directors for their consideration a report on their view of the adequacy of consultations with affected parties in the preparation of the action plans. The Board should not ask the Panel for its view on other aspects of the action plans nor would it ask the Panel to monitor the implementation of the action plans. The Panel's view on consultation with affected parties will be based on the information available to it by all means, but additional country visits will take place only by government invitation.

- The Board underlines the need for Management to make significant efforts to make the Inspection Panel better known in borrowing countries, as specified in the 1996 'Clarifications.'
- The Board emphasizes the importance of prompt disclosure of information to claimants and the public, as stipulated in the Resolution (paras. 23 and 25) and in its 1996 Clarifications. The Board requires that such information be provided by Management to claimants in their language, to the extent possible.
- The Board recognizes that enhancing the effectiveness of the Inspection Panel process through the above clarifications assumes adherence to them by all parties in good faith. It also assumes the borrowers' consent for field visits envisaged in the Resolution. If these assumptions prove to be incorrect, the Board will revisit the above conclusions.

